Double Duty

Double Duty

Dual Dynamics
Within the Chemically
Dependent Home

Claudia Black

BALLANTINE BOOKS
NEW YORK

Grateful acknowledgment is made to the following for permission to reprint previously published material:

ADULT CHILDREN OF ALCOHOLICS: "The Original Laundry List." Reprinted by permission of Tony A., co-author of *The ACOA Experience*.

AL-ANON FAMILY GROUP HEADQUARTERS, INC.: "Al-Anon: Is It For You?" Copyright© 1980 by Al-Anon Family Group Headquarters, Inc. Reprinted by permission of Al-Anon Family Group Headquarters, Inc.; The Twelve Steps and Traditions of Al-Anon are adapted by permission of AA World Services, Inc. and reprinted by permission of Al-Anon Family Group Headquarters, Inc.

ALCOHOLICS ANONYMOUS WORLD SERVICES, INC.: The Twelve Steps and Traditions of Alcoholics Anonymous are reprinted by permission of Alcoholics World Services, Inc. Permission to reprint and adapt The Twelve Steps and Traditions does not mean that AA has reviewed or approved the contents of this publication, nor that AA agrees with the views expressed herein. AA is a program of recovery from alcoholism. Use of The Twelve Steps and Traditions in connection with programs which are patterned after AA but which address other problems does not imply otherwise.

CO-DEPENDENTS ANONYMOUS, INC,: "Compliance and Control Patterns. Reprinted from the pamphlet "What is Codependency?" with permission of Co-Dependency Anonymous, Inc., Phoenix, AZ. Copyright © 1988.

THE FRESS PRESS: Figure entitled "Alcohol Addiction" from *Alcohol Problems and Alcoholism* by James E. Royce. Copyright© 1981 by The Free Press. Reprinted with permission of The Free Press, a division of Macmillan, Inc.

HEALTH COMMUNICATIONS, INC.: "Are You Addicted to Work?" reprinted from Work *Addiction: Hidden Legacies of Adult Children* by Bryan E. Robinson. Copyright © 1989 by Health Communications, Inc. Reprinted by permission of the publishers, Health Communications, Inc., Deerfield Beach, Florida, and the author.

NATIONAL COUNCIL ON ALCOHOLISM AND DRUG DEPENDENCE, INC.: "What Are the Signs of Alcoholism?" reprinted by permission of the National Council on Alcoholism and Drug Dependence, Inc. Preprinted copies are available from NCAAD, 12 West 21st Street, New York, NY 10010

ST. MARTIN'S PRESS, INC. AND SUSAN SCHULMAN LITERARY AGENCY, INC.: "Relationship Addicion" from *Women Who Love Too Much* by Robin Norwood. Copyright © 1985 by Robin Norwood. First published in hardcover by Jeremy P. Tarcher, Inc., Los Angeles. Reprinted by permission of St. Martin's Press, Inc. and Susan Schulman Literacy Agency, Inc.

SEXAHOLICS ANONYMOUS: "Sexual Addiction" from Sexaholics Anonymous. Copyright © 1989 by SA Literature. Reprinted by permission.

SIMON & SCHUSTER, INC.: "Are You a Food Addict?" "Are You Addicted to Prescription Drugs?" from *The Recovery Sourcebook* by Barbara Yoder. Copyright © by Wink Books. Reprinted by permission of Simon & Schuster, Inc.

WORLD SERVICE OFFICE, INC.: "Am I an Addict?" Reprinted by permission of World Service Office, Inc., Van Nuys, CA.

Library of Congress Cataloging-in-Publication Data
Black, Claudia.
   Double duty: dual dynamics within the chemically dependent home /
Claudia Black.—1st ed.
     p. cm.
   ISBN 0-345-36152-0
   1. Adult children of alcoholics—United States.
   2. Children of alcoholics—United States.
   3. Problem families—United States.
  I. Title.
  HV5132.B53 1990
  362.29'23—dc20   90-34167
                             CIP

First Edition: October 1990

10 9 8 7 6 5 4 3 2 1

In memory of my brother, Doug,
the inspiration for *Double Duty*

Contents

Acknowledgments

I would like to express my gratitude and say thank you, first and foremost, to all the contributors who participated in this project. While only forty-one life stories appear in the final book, I am also greatly indebted to many other contributors who offered stories that were not included. Each of your individual contributions helped me to better understand the particular Double Duty/Dual Identity issues presented here.

I would also like to thank my friends and colleagues who gave me such thoughtful feedback on chapters: Dr. Leslie Drozd, who reviewed nearly all the chapters; Victoria Danzig, M.S.W.; Don Steckdaub, M.A.; Doug Braun, M.F.C.; Jill Borman; Jael Greenleaf; Ed Ellis, Ph.D.; Dana Finnegan; Emily McNally; Mel Pohl, M.D.; Skip Sauvain, M.A.; Wynn Block, M.A.; Mark McQuire, M.S.W.; Anna Sorrell; Donna Pablo; Lottie Jones; Emma Redmond; Wayne Smith; Jefferson Breen, Ed.D.; Betty La Porte; Sam Ryan; Jo Ann Kaufman; Pam McClung James; Maria Elvira; and Conrado Gerardo and Ron Brown.

Mary McClellan, of San Francisco, was a dream—without her it would have been very difficult to sort through 100 heart-rending stories. She worked with me closely to help present our contributors' deeply personal writings in a consistent format.

Jack Fahey, my husband, business partner, and prime supporter, has one more time walked with me every inch of the way, reading and re-reading every version of every chapter. Thank you, Jack, for believing in me and my work so strongly.

Anne Marsin typed and retyped this manuscript before and after the editors had gotten to it. She's still having dreams of *Double Duty* never ending. It isn't enough to just say thanks here. Anne also spent countless hours talking to those who participated in this book, typing and revising their stories, managing Federal Express, and playing musical telephones. Through it all, Anne, you were sensitive, conscientious, and a good friend.

Barbara Shor, a heartfelt thanks for your final hand polishing of my prose and for always maintaining my intention and my tone.

Cheryl Woodruff, my editor—what does one say? It has been a great experience. Writing on such a serious subject has been a deeply personal and challenging experience for both of us from beginning to end, and you have always been sensitive and caring. A multitude of thanks—for believing in me and in the importance of this work. Now, as this book leaves our hands and moves out into the world, we can both take pleasure in the results of our hard work.

Lastly, I want to thank the many dear friends in my life. This book has taken longer than any of us could have imagined and, for all of us, many things occurred in these past four years. I know you are there for me. Thank you.

Preface

Dear Reader:

After each book I have written I am never certain where my professional work and personal growth will take me next. When *It Will Never Happen to Me* was published in 1981, it represented an exploration in uncharted territory—it contributed to the start of something new—the Adult Children of Alcoholics movement.

While there has been a proliferation of books about Young and Adult Children of Alcoholics since that time, it is important to recognize that the Adult Children of Alcoholics movement is still very young. We are only beginning to understand the complexity of the actual trauma within the dysfunctional family systems that so many Adult Children have experienced, and the various ways this has compromised their adulthood.

Over the years thousands of Adult Children have begun their process of self-healing. There have been many wonderful miracles. Yet, as I've watched people moving through their recovery, I've also seen many individuals hit a baffling, impenetrable wall that halted their progress. There seemed to be a missing link or another piece to the puzzle.

A very big piece of what I believe causes such blockage is the experience of double duty. This book is my effort to piece together the puzzle of the impact of multiple trauma-producing dynamics in the lives of Adult Children. It is through exploring these issues that we will be able to recognize and confront these challenging dynamics and move on to lasting recovery.

One of the key premises of the ACOA recovery process is putting the past behind us. That only occurs when the truth of one's experience is acknowledged. Up to this time in the evolution of the ACOA movement, the stories told—and as a result the issues addressed—have tended to be very generalized. This stage of emphasizing the experiences all ACOAs have in common has been incredibly valuable. However, now that many Adult Children have spent several years in recovery from their ACOA issues, I believe it is time to explore how Adult Children differ from each other. And that difference is what *Double Duty* is all about.

During the past decade I've taught workshops and conducted professional training sessions from Seattle to Kansas City and Boston to Rio de Janeiro, Tokyo, and Garmish, West Germany. One recurring theme has struck a deep chord in me—the problems people have encountered because of what I've come to call "Double Duty/Dual Identity" issues. These are the intensified life experiences of ACOAs who not only have had to contend with the trauma of family alcoholism, but who have also had to defend against an additional powerful dynamic that profoundly affected their lives. The additional struggle might be with incest or physical disability, being gay or lesbian or a person of color. I met Adult Children who'd been physically abused; ACOAs who'd been sexually abused; ACOAs who had eating disorders; ACOAs who were also chemically dependent; ACOAs who'd been raised as the only child in the family nightmare.

The questions such individuals posed in my workshops/trainings all coalesced in the same psychological pool: "How do I address my ACOA issues in light of my eating disorder?" "How long should I be sober before I address my Adult Child issues?" "How do I factor in the impact of my physical disability as I address my ACOA issues?" "How does my sexual orientation affect my Adult Child issues?" "I'm an ACOA and a minority—sometimes I feel different and alone 'in these rooms.' " And the question so many are asking: "Why am I having such a hard time in therapy?"

All of these individuals were experiencing the same things—when they looked in the mirror they saw their identities expressed in two or more ways. Instead of being able to identify themselves in an either/or fashion as an ACOA or as a physically disabled person, they recognized themselves as both. And in that recognition—in that process of looking in the mirror and unearthing their own histories—they began to recognize that what was reflected back to them was not one, but two equally powerful dynamics. These had created profoundly disruptive internal messages that they knew had to be recognized and healed before they could make peace with themselves.

I believe that no human being deserves the shame that is often created by these Double Duty/Dual Identity situations. No one deserves to live with the depth of fear, loneliness, deprivation, and isolation found in the lives of the people throughout this book. I believe that we all deserve to have choices in our lives. In *Double Duty* my intention has been to offer validation to the unique life experiences of these Adult Children and, equally important, to offer an explanation for that "wall" so many ACOAs run into during their recovery process.

It is my hope that the life stories in this book will help all Adult Children come to believe that, no matter how traumatic their past experiences, recovery is possible.

This book has given me the opportunity to work with over seventy-five survivors of Double Duty/Dual Identity issues. Over the four years it has taken me to bring this project to fruition, I have come to understand that when you volunteer to participate in a work of this magnitude, you never know quite what you're getting into until it's over.

The contributors to *Double Duty* knew they would be sharing their life stories. They trusted in me and my work. But more than anything, they hoped that their life experiences would make a difference for other re-covering Adult Children. After years of working with these individuals, I have no doubt about the indisputable value of their contributions. By openly exploring their Double Duty/Dual Identity issues, they have displayed not only rare courage and generosity—they have also reached deeply into themselves and discovered yet another level of their own recovery.

It takes a great deal of inner strength to tell others these kinds of stories and to share so openly. The contributors said things they had never previously spoken, written, or shared in any manner. In opening their souls at such a deep level, they ran the gamut of emotions. They cried; they laughed; they became angry; they grew sad. But as they revealed their vulnerability, they also trusted in the process of their re-covery.

At the beginning of our work together nearly all the contributors were strangers to me—though not in spirit. Most of them volunteered their stories for the book at workshops or conferences. While a few people were initially interviewed in depth, others put their stories on paper or tape and waited to see what I would do with their material. They heard their stories read over the telephone and later saw them in the context of a chapter. And now they offer them to you.

I was deeply moved by the contributors sharing with me so intimately. I wanted to protect them all from their pain. I wanted to cry for them, scream for them. I can remember that some of the life stories I received in the mail were packaged with a note that read, "Handle with Care."

This wise caution is valuable counsel for all who will read this book. Handle yourself—and the lives of those who are sharing with us—with great care and compassion. These Adult Children are revealing some of their most painful memories of events they experienced at ages five, seven, twelve—memories filled with profound feelings of fear, loneliness, and shame that they have carried from childhood into adulthood.

While I was writing *Double Duty,* the Adult Children in these pages were continuing to live their lives. Partnerships were created, marriages celebrated, babies were born, parents died, college graduations occurred, people moved in and out of many aspects of their lives. The contributors were living their recoveries.

While I was writing, I found that, in spite of the fact that I didn't have personal experience of some issues, as an Adult Child I was nonetheless deeply touched by and identified with aspects of every chapter. I came to believe that very few of us have escaped the experience of Double Duty/Dual Identity in our lives. The challenges reflected in many of these stories are often far more common than one might initially imagine. All of us face some of the Double Duty/Dual Identity challenges. We experience the isolation of the ACOA/only child, the feelings of discrimination and prejudice of the person of color or the gay or lesbian, the hopelessness of the ACOA who is chemically dependent or has an eating disorder, the fear and shame of the ACOA who has been physically or sexually abused. Our experiences differ only by degree. *Double Duty* cannot fail to offer those individuals with an open mind and a compassionate heart a deeper understanding of themselves and their families, friends, and colleagues.

There has been a tendency by some to be critical of Adult Children for not moving forward more quickly in recovery. My hope is that *Double Duty* will offer validation to those who have not been able to move on because they first needed a clearer perspective from which to examine their lives. I hope that this book will promote both an expanded sense of self for Double Duty/Dual Identity survivors and a greater understanding of the genuine complexity of the Double Duty/Dual Identity issues by families, friends, and therapists.

I have deep respect for all Adult Children who have been willing to walk from denial into truth and to face the emotional pain that comes with acknowledging the past and its present consequences. Recognizing Double Duty/Dual Identity issues has only strengthened my resolve to speak out more fiercely on behalf of all Children of Alcoholics, both young and adult. For every Adult Child in recovery today there still remains a young child living unprotected in a chemically dependent home who needs us to advocate for them and to provide services for them.

I hope that *Double Duty* will be another step in the process of recovery for all of us. I am honored by the trust that so many of you have placed in me.

I am with you in spirit.

Claudia Black
October 1990

Double
Duty

1

The Challenge of
Double Duty/Dual Identity

Out of the seven of us kids, three are alcoholic, two are married to
alcoholics, and the other two are just all screwed up.

—Adult Child

Adult Children of Alcoholics (ACA or ACOA) is a term that describes an adult person who was raised in a family affected by
parental chemical dependency and co-dependence.

The wording is not meant to imply that this adult-age person behaves
as a child. It means that within this person there is an inner spirit—an
inner child—who has been hurt and who now needs to be recognized,
validated, and healed. Inside this Adult Child is an adult-age person who
is as emotionally vulnerable as a nine-year-old or a twelve-year-old. I
picture the Adult Child as a nine-year-old with thirty-five years of pain or
a twelve-year-old with forty-five years of pain.

The phrase *Adult Children* acknowledges that within each of these
adult-age individuals there is a child who has difficulty experiencing a
healthy life until he (or she) is able to speak the truth about his childhood
and free himself from the bondage of his past. Until this recognition and
healing of the past occurs, Adult Children are destined to continue reliving
old scripts.

The ACOA movement has allowed thousands of people to recover
from the pain of their childhoods. It has given them hope and a sense of

direction. It has offered them choices about how they will continue to live their lives from now on.

I first used the term *Adult Children of Alcoholics* (*ACA* or *ACOA*) in 1977, in the initial phases of the development of the concept. Since then the phrase and its acronym have moved through a variety of changes.

Today, when people speak of ACOAs, they're usually referring to Adult Children who were raised in chemically dependent families. Until recently, "alcoholism" is the term that has been most widely used in the field of substance abuse to describe chemically dependent families. However, over the past decade, "chemical dependency" has become a much more commonly used phrase because it covers both alcohol and other drug dependencies. To be even more inclusive, some professionals use the phrase *Adult Children of Addicted Families.*

More and more people are identifying with Adult Children characteristics—whether or not they were raised in alcoholic families. And because so many are also finding answers in the process of recovery used by ACOAs, this concept has expanded even further until it has become "Adult Children of Dysfunctional Families."

How to Recognize the Adult Child

- We become isolated and afraid of other people, especially authority figures.
- We are frightened by anger and any personal criticism.
- We judge ourselves harshly and have low self-esteem.
- We don't act—we react.
- We are dependent personalities who are terrified of abandonment.
- We will do anything to hold on to a relationship. This is the way we avoid feeling the pain of our parents not having been there for us emotionally.
- We become alcoholics, marry them, or do both. Or we find another compulsive personality, such as a workaholic or an overeater, with whom we continue to play out our fear of abandonment.
- We have become addicted to excitement from years of living in the midst of a traumatic and often dangerous family soap opera.
- We live life from the viewpoint of victims or rescuers and are attracted to victims or rescuers in our love, friendship, and career relationships.
- We confuse love with pity and tend to love people whom we can pity and rescue.

- We felt responsible for the problems of our unstable families, and as a result we do not feel entitled to live independent lives now.
- We get guilt feelings if we stand up for ourselves instead of giving in to others.
- We became approval seekers and lost our own identities in the process.
- We have an overdeveloped sense of responsibility toward others, but we rarely consider our responsibility to ourselves.
- We had to deny our feelings in our traumatic childhoods. This estranged us from all our feelings, and we lost our ability to recognize and express them.

This collection of statements is often referred to as the "Laundry List for Adult Children." It exists in many forms and is widely used in Adult Child self-help groups. See appendix 15, page 568, for another variation.

Troubled Families

If you identify with many of the issues presented in the laundry list, it is likely that you were raised in a chemically dependent or otherwise dysfunctional family. What is true for Adult Children from addicted families is also true for people from other kinds of troubled families. These family systems are usually affected by denial, rigidity, isolation, and shame. Sometimes Adult Children can identify the primary source of the dysfunction in the family, sometimes not. It isn't as important to know exactly what caused the dysfunction as it is to recognize the messages internalized during your childhood that you are still reenacting today.

The common denominator for those who identify with Adult Child characteristics is a pervading sense of loss. These are people who as children were raised in families where they experienced loss on a chronic basis. That loss may have been due to physical abandonment, emotional abandonment, or both.

Children from alcoholic and other troubled families could also be referred to as "Children of Denial" or "Children of Trauma." As young people they learned to continually deny, minimize, rationalize, and discount their feelings and their experiences. Some learned to lie blatantly to protect themselves or their family image. Others learned simply not to speak up—so the truth was never told.

Living with such chronic loss—at a time in their young lives when they

were developing their identity and sense of self-worth—was very traumatic. Too often people forget that we are referring to children of three,
seven, eleven, fifteen years of age. The trauma in their lives has been
easy to discount because those around them discounted it and also because COAs demonstrate such phenomenal survivorship skills.

For decades the treatment focus of the chemically dependent family
was the alcoholic; it was not until the problems of the emotionally dependent spouse or partner of the alcoholic were recognized that the term
co-alcoholic was coined. Co-alcoholic implied that the partner was also
significantly affected by the disease on psychological, mental, social, and
even physical levels as a result of being in a close relationship with a
chemically dependent person. Because of this, it was believed that these
individuals also needed and deserved treatment and a recovery process
of their own. The term ''co-dependent'' soon replaced ''co-alcoholic''
because alcoholics were increasingly being referred to as ''chemically
dependent.''

Today, co-dependency no longer reflects only those traits exhibited by
the spouse or partner of an alcoholic. It also refers to people whose
behavior is characterized by the numbing of feelings, by denial, low self-
worth, and compulsive behavior. It manifests itself in relationships when
you give another person power over your self-esteem. The ACOA movement was the precursor of the co-dependency movement.

At a recent national conference on co-dependency, a group of 1,800
educators agreed upon a definition of the term. Co-dependency was seen
as ''a pattern of painful dependency on compulsive behaviors and on approval from others in an attempt to find safety, self-worth, and identity.''
However, although the great majority of Adult Children manifest co-
dependency traits, not all co-dependents are ACOAs.

Double Duty is a book for anyone who identifies with being an Adult
Child, no matter what the cause of trauma in the family.

The Healthy Family

Some people question whether or not any of us comes from a healthy
family. Cartoonist Jennifer Berman brilliantly captures this sentiment in
her cartoon that shows a nearly empty auditorium with a large sign in the
back reading, ''ADULT CHILDREN OF NORMAL PARENTS ANNUAL
CONVENTION.''

Although it is true that anyone reading the laundry list could identify
with some of the statements on it, only those who have been raised with

chronic loss are able to identify with most of them. Such individuals actively need to address what their past means—and how it continues to affect them—in order to create greater choice and balance in their present lives.

Still, it is my belief that there are indeed healthy family systems. In fact, it is often recovering Adult Children who are creating those healthy systems today.

All of us can benefit by looking at the behavioral patterns we encountered in our birth families so that we can take responsibility for reshaping our lives differently as adults. One of the greatest gifts of the Adult Children's movement is the energy directed toward understanding and creating the dynamics of a healthy family.

Since many Adult Children often lack an understanding of what is normal or healthy in family life, the following lists may be helpful.

IN A NURTURING FAMILY . . .

- People feel free to talk about inner feelings.
- All feelings are okay.
- The person is more important than performance.
- All subjects are open to discussion.
- Individual differences are accepted.
- Each person is responsible for his/her own actions.
- Respectful criticism is offered along with appropriate consequences for actions.
- There are few "shoulds."
- There are clear, flexible rules.
- The atmosphere is relaxed.
- There is joy.
- Family members face up to and work through stress.
- People have energy.
- People feel loving.
- Growth is celebrated.
- People have high self-worth.
- There is a strong parental coalition.

IN A DYSFUNCTIONAL FAMILY . . .

- People compulsively protect inner feelings.
- Only "certain" feelings are okay.
- Performance is more important than the person.

- There are many taboo subjects, lots of secrets.
- Everyone must conform to the strongest person's ideas and values.
- There is a great deal of control and criticism.
- There is punishment, shaming.
- There are lots of "shoulds."
- The rules are unclear, inconsistent, and rigid.
- The atmosphere is tense.
- There is much anger and fear.
- Stress is avoided and denied.
- People feel tired, hurt, and disappointed.
- Growth is discouraged.
- People have low self-worth.
- Coalitions form across generations.[1]

Alcoholism as a Disease

Some people in recovery have come to an understanding of the disease process of chemical dependency. Yet this concept is confusing to those who may recognize that their parent was dependent on alcohol or other drugs but still perceive that parent as being willful or bad. What parents do as a result of their chemical dependency may be bad, but it is because of the disease process that they have lost the opportunity for choice. I don't know what those parents would have been like had they not been chemically dependent. But I do know that they would have had a greater range of choices about how they handled their parenting and how they expressed those choices.

Alcoholism has been a part of human history since the beginning of recorded time. But to the astonishment of many, it has been barely twenty-five years since it was formally recognized as a disease. Many professionals think of 1956 as the date of recognition for the disease concept, for it was in that year that the American Medical Association (AMA) first endorsed the admission of alcoholics to general hospitals. It was a major step toward formal recognition of alcoholism as a disease, but that did not occur officially until November 26, 1966, when the house of delegates of the AMA, meeting in Houston, Texas, adopted the following resolution:

Whereas, the American Medical Association of 1966 recognized that alcoholism is a disease that merits the serious concern of all members of health professions; and whereas, alcoholism is recognized as a se-

rious major health problem throughout the land; therefore be it RE-
SOLVED, that the American Medical Association identifies alcoholism
as a complex disease and as such recognizes that the medical compo-
nents are medicine's responsibility. Such recognition is not intended
to relieve the alcoholic of moral or legal responsibility, as provided by
law, for any acts committed when inebriated; nor does this recognition
preclude civil arrest and imprisonment, as provided by the law, for
antisocial acts committed when inebriated.

The *Random House Dictionary* defines disease as "a disordered or
incorrectly functioning . . . system of the body resulting from the effect
of genetic or developmental errors, . . . poisons, . . . [or] toxicity."

Clearly, alcohol and other drugs are poisons to the body. Although not
everyone who drinks experiences delirious effects, 8 to 12 percent of our
adult population become dependent psychologically and often physically.

Yet alcoholism is no more a single disease entity than cancer. Many
people are confused about alcoholism because there is not one specific
pattern of behavior typical to the alcoholic. Alcoholics often differ in their
styles of drinking, and the consequences of their drinking vary widely.
Some alcoholics drink daily; others drink in episodic patterns; some stay
dry for long intervals between binges. Some drink enormous quantities
of alcohol; others do not. Some alcoholics drink only beer; some drink
only wine; others choose distilled liquor. Many consume a wide variety
of alcoholic beverages and possibly other drugs as well. Today, many
alcoholics are dual-addicted—that is, they are addicted to alcohol and another drug, such as marijuana, cocaine, or a prescription pill.

Although alcoholism appears very early in the lives of some people,
for others it takes years to develop. Some claim to have started drinking
alcoholically from their first drink. Many others report drinking for years
before crossing over the "invisible line" that separates social drinking
from alcoholic drinking.

While there are exceptions and variations to the rule, most alcoholics
experience a progression in their disease. The following "dip chart,"
originally published in 1974 by British physician M.M. Glatt, describes
the progression of both the active disease and recovery.

As you read the life stories in the chapters that follow, you will see
children responding to parents who are in different stages of the disease.
Typically, alcoholism is not even identifiable until someone is in at least
middle-stage chemical dependency. This means that children live with the
insidious effects of the disease long before it is recognized as a real problem. When alcohol or other drug usage does become more recognizable

Alcohol Addiction: The Progression of the Disease

EARLY STAGE

OCCASIONAL RELIEF DRINKING

CONSTANT RELIEF DRINKING COMMENCES

INCREASE IN ALCOHOL TOLERANCE

SNEAKING DRINKS

ONSET OF MEMORY BLACKOUTS (IN SOME PERSONS)

URGENCY OF FIRST DRINKS

AVOID REFERENCE TO DRINKING

INCREASING DEPENDENCE ON ALCOHOL

CONCERN/COMPLAINTS BY FAMILY

FEELINGS OF GUILT

PREOCCUPATION WITH ALCOHOL

MEMORY BLACKOUTS INCREASE OR BEGIN

DECREASE OF ABILITY TO STOP DRINKING WHEN OTHERS DO

LOSS OF CONTROL

MIDDLE STAGE

GRANDIOSE AND AGGRESSIVE BEHAVIOR OR EXTRAVAGANCE

ALIBIS FOR DRINKING

FAMILY MORE WORRIED, ANGRY

PERSISTENT REMORSE

GOES ON WAGON

CHANGE OF PATTERN

EFFORTS TO CONTROL FAIL REPEATEDLY

TELEPHONITIS

TRIES GEOGRAPHICAL ESCAPE

HIDES BOTTLES

PROMISES OR RESOLUTIONS FAIL

LOSS OF OTHER INTERESTS

FURTHER INCREASE IN MEMORY BLACKOUTS

FAMILY AND FRIENDS AVOIDED

UNREASONABLE RESENTMENTS

DENIAL

WORK AND MONEY TROUBLES

TREMORS AND EARLY MORNING DRINKS

NEGLECT OF FOOD

LATE STAGE

PROTECTS SUPPLY

PHYSICAL DETORIORATION

DECREASE IN ALCOHOL TOLERANCE

IMPAIRED THINKING

ONSET OF LENGTHY INTOXICATIONS

DRINKING WITH INFERIORS

INDEFINABLE FEARS

OBSESSION WITH DRINKING

UNABLE TO INITIATE ACTION

VAGUE SPIRITUAL DESIRES

ALL ALIBIS EXHAUSTED

ETHICAL DETERIORATION

COMPLETE DEFEAT ADMITTED

OBSESSIVE DRINKING CONTINUES IN VICIOUS CIRCLES

Source: James Royce, *Alcohol Problems and Alcoholism* (New York: Macmillan/Free Press, 1981).

THE ROAD TO RECOVERY

ENLIGHTENED AND INTERESTING WAY
OF LIFE OPENS UP WITH ROAD
AHEAD TO HIGHER LEVELS THAN
EVER BEFORE

FULL APPRECIATION OF
SPIRITUAL VALUES

GROUP THERAPY AND MUTUAL HELP CONTINUE

CONTENTMENT IN SOBRIETY

FIRST STEPS TOWARD
ECONOMIC STABILITY

CONFIDENCE OF EMPLOYERS

INCREASE OF EMOTIONAL CONTROL

APPRECIATION OF REAL VALUES

FACTS FACED WITH COURAGE

REBIRTH OF IDEALS

NEW CIRCLE OF STABLE FRIENDS

NEW INTERESTS DEVELOP

ADJUSTMENTS TO FAMILY NEEDS

FAMILY AND FRIENDS APPRECIATE EFFORTS

REHABILITATION

DESIRE TO ESCAPE GOES

REALISTIC THINKING

RETURN OF SELF-ESTEEM

REGULAR NOURISHMENT TAKEN

DIMINISHING FEARS OF THE
UNKNOWN FUTURE

APPRECIATION OF POSSIBILITIES
OF NEW WAY OF LIFE

CARE OF PERSONAL APPEARANCE

ONSET OF NEW HOPE

START OF GROUP THERAPY

PHYSICAL OVERHAUL BY DOCTOR

GUILT REDUCTION

RIGHT THINKING BEGINS

SPIRITUAL NEEDS
EXAMINED

MEETS HAPPY SOBER ALCOHOLICS

STOPS TAKING
ALCOHOL

TOLD ADDICITON CAN BE ARRESTED

LEARNS ALCOHOLISM IS AN ILLNESS

HONEST DESIRE FOR HELP

Modified from M. M. Glatt

as a key contributor to the problem, denial, misinformation, and stigma have already spread throughout the family system. Family members have learned their adaptive roles and are trying to survive. At this point, many children still don't recognize their parents' chemical dependency in spite of its blatancy because they have learned the rules of all dysfunctional families: 1) Don't talk; 2) Don't feel; 3) Don't trust; 4) Don't think; 5) Don't ask questions. There is also another problem—very often many family members don't understand alcoholism well enough to recognize it when it smacks them in the face.

Not every alcoholic will experience all of the symptoms shown on the chart, nor do the symptoms have to occur in the exact order presented. In addition, the disease's rate of progression varies. Alcoholism tends to be more rapid for some individuals in some races, which is probably the result of a physiological predisposition. Generally, the progression of the disease is faster for women and young alcoholics than for men. Some alcoholics take thirty or forty years to reach the "chronic" late stage. Others remain in the middle stage indefinitely. However, my clinical experience has demonstrated that Children of Alcoholics who have problems with alcohol move through the progression much more quickly than those with alcohol problems which are not biologically related.

Children within the family may be affected differently. One reason for the variance is birth order. As each child is born, he or she enters the family life story at a different point in the progression of the disease. Should they enter the family prior to the onset of chemical dependency or in the earlier stages of the disease, they are more likely to have had attention focused on them as individual children rather than merely as objects, and they would have experienced greater stability and predictable adult behavior in their earlier years. This frequently creates a greater internal sense of security than that experienced by siblings who enter the family drama at a later point.

But we must recognize that children are not affected only by the chemically dependent parent. They are equally affected by the entire family system, which includes the nonchemically dependent parent (if there is one). Most typically, as the chemically dependent partner moves through the disease progression, the nonaddicted spouse will become more and more preoccupied with the partner's drinking and what that person is thinking and doing. The spouse often begins to display "enabling" behavior to the alcoholic by learning to deny what is going on. Also, the spouse keeps trying to control the alcoholic's behavior, often without understanding what is actually happening.

As the disease progresses, the co-dependent mate becomes angry and depressed and often seeks forms of escape to handle his or her own escalating confusion, guilt, and helplessness. It is no surprise that the children often get left behind in the shuffle and end up living without the focus and attention they need. Their lives are distorted by the unrealistic expectations, unpredictability, rigid (or total lack of) discipline, chaos, tense silence, and abuse from both the alcoholic and the co-dependent parent.

Effects of Family Roles

Children in chemically dependent families do whatever they can to withstand the losses they are experiencing in the family environment. Surprisingly, most children from troubled families have the ability to "look good" to outsiders despite what may be happening in the home. Unfortunately, for the most part looking good is based on survivorship and denial. Children accommodate themselves to whatever environment they are being raised in. They keep trying to bring consistency, structure, and safety into a household that is unpredictable, chaotic, and frightening. To do this they adopt certain roles, or a mixture of these roles, in the family. My research indicates that 60 percent of COAs identify themselves as the *overly responsible* (hero) child; 63 percent identify themselves as the family *placater*; 40 percent identify with being the *adjuster* (lost child); and 20 percent identify with being the *acting-out* child (scapegoat).[2] As the statistics indicate, most people identify with more than one role or recognize that at certain times their roles switch. Many people from other types of troubled families identify with those roles as well.

THE RESPONSIBLE CHILD

This is the child who takes responsibility for whatever is tangible in the environment—people, places, and things. This is the child who sets the table, puts dinner on the table, and sees to it that the children are all sitting down with the right expressions on their faces before the alcoholic parent gets to the table. This is the child known as the "little adult," or the "household top sergeant."

Responsible children become their own parent, a parent to their siblings, and a parent to the parents. It is extremely difficult for these children to be perceived as being in any emotional trouble because, externally, they look very good. They often become the face for the chemically dependent home. Their appearance says to themselves and to the community that everything is just fine here, things are under control.

CORE EMOTIONS:
Fear
Loneliness
Hurt
Powerlessness
Anger
Sadness
Embarrassment

STRENGTHS:
Organized
Goal-oriented
Self-disciplined
Leadership ability
Willingness to take charge
Decisive

DEFICITS:
Difficulty with listening
Difficulty with following
Difficulty with negotiating
Difficulty with asking for help, input, or advice
Difficulty playing
Perfectionist behavior

EMOTIONALLY:
Serious
Rigidly removed from feelings
Perceives experiencing feelings as a loss of control

THE ADJUSTER

This is the child who doesn't want to be emotionally or socially invested in what is occurring in the family. These children shrug their shoulders and say, "It doesn't bother me. I don't care."

Adjusters spend their time trying to be less visible and, as a result, don't draw much attention to themselves—negative or positive. An adjuster is often referred to as the "lost child." These children also don't have the ability to cry out for help or to say there is something wrong in their lives. They take the stance of, "I can handle it. I'm tough. I can adjust. If I am not invested, then I am not going to get hurt. Just don't think about it. "

STRENGTHS:
Flexibility
Ability to adjust
Easygoing attitude and personality
Not willing to be preoccupied with negativity

DEFICITS:
Inability to lead
Inability to initiate
Fearful of making decisions
Inability to see options
Reacts without thinking

EMOTIONALLY:
Aloof
Withdrawn, or can be pleasant as a defense mechanism

THE PLACATER

This is the "household social worker," the child who takes responsibility for the emotional well-being of all the family members. This child takes on the task of reducing and minimizing the expressed and sometimes unexpressed fears, sadness, anger, and embarrassment of the whole family. Placaters are warm, caring, empathetic young people. Again, they are expert at not drawing attention to themselves as children in need.

STRENGTHS:
Warm
Caring
Empathetic
Good listener
Nice smile
Ability to give
Sensitive to others

DEFICITS:
Difficulty with receiving
Inability to focus on self
Incredible guilt for self-focus
Highly tolerant of inappropriate behavior
Highly fearful of mistakes

EMOTIONALLY:
Extremely warm and interested in others
Closed to their own feelings of inadequacy, fear, and sadness

THE ACTING-OUT CHILD

This is the one who is willing to scream to the world that there is something wrong here. Unfortunately, even when this child does so, the alcoholism may still not get identified or addressed. This child challenges authority more blatantly than the others and, as a result, is more likely to be in trouble in school and in the community. In reality, acting-out children tend to suffer less from denial than the others in the chemically dependent family. They are closer to knowing the truth and are acting out the dysfunction of the family.

STRENGTHS:
Good leadership ability, recognizing they just lead in the wrong
    direction
Less denial, closer to the truth
Less apt to subscribe to the "Don't talk" rule
Creative

DEFICITS:
Hurtful expression of anger
Greater lack of social skills
Intrusive with others
Greater difficulty entering the mainstream of life due to tendency
    to challenge authority and unwillingness to follow directions

EMOTIONALLY:
Angry
Most fearful of their sadness and their fears

Acting-out children, more than the other role players, are more likely to enter into an addictive process at a younger age. If their addiction is chemical dependency, they will progress through the stages of their drug/alcohol dependency at a younger age. Consequently they may also die earlier from those dependencies—or get well sooner.

Whether these role players are drawing positive or negative attention to themselves, or being invisible, all of these ACOAs are learning such rules as:

Don't talk honestly.
Don't express your feelings.
Your feelings don't count.
You are not important.
You can't trust anybody.
No one will be there for you.
Your perceptions aren't accurate.
There is no time to play.
Other people's needs are more important than your own.

These roles typify the experiences of children who have lived with great loneliness, fear, sadness, disappointment, anger, guilt, and shame. They are COAs who have lived and struggled with powerlessness. The roles they have adopted are the ways they learned to mask their chronic losses and their different methods of coping with their feelings.

The Adult Child and Progression

It is important to understand that what has been seeded in a dysfunctional childhood takes a grave toll in dramatic ways in adulthood. And it is in adulthood that these problems finally begin to surface. There are many symptoms:

- Depression
- Inability to develop or maintain a healthy relationship
- Remaining victimized within a destructive relationship
- Poor parenting skills
- Inability to actualize one's potential or talent, inability to experience accomplishments in spite of proven abilities
- Compulsive behaviors
- Addictions

The problems of Adult Children are rarely identified until the individuals are at least in their late twenties or early thirties. When seventeen-, eighteen-, and nineteen-year-old Adult Children begin to leave their families of origin, there is usually no time for quiet self-reflection. At this point many ACOAs hold on to their survivorship skills for dear life and, as many put it, "move on," not thinking, not feeling, not talking about their growing-up years. Yet they usually continue to stay emotionally enmeshed with their families.

It is not until ACOAs begin to experience more of a normal daily routine in their lives that these issues become increasingly visible to themselves and possibly others. As with alcoholism, Adult Child issues escalate over time. But these problems don't tend to hit like a dramatic bolt of lightning. Adult Children are often deep in the throes of a troubling situation before they recognize that there is a problem.

Not recognizing a problem until it reaches the crisis stage is one of the core issues of ACOAs. This is because they have spent years learning to dismiss relevant cues and signals in order to survive. Such a capacity for denial can create an endless loop in which ACOAs are forever reacting to problems.

Another Adult Child issue that interferes with the process of seeking help is that, as young people, they learned that it was not safe or okay to ask for help. They came to believe that no one would be there for them if they did.

When we add up these three dynamics—that problems enter and escalate in our lives slowly; that we don't recognize a problem until it has reached the crisis stage; and that we don't trust the process of asking for help—we can begin to understand why it may have taken us such a long time to be able to address these issues.

Another significant factor in recovery for Adult Children is that, until the ACOA movement began, information about these problems and their solutions wasn't available. Our understanding of these dynamics did not begin until the late 1970s, and recovery resources have only been widely available since the mid-1980s.

It is very common for ACOAs to berate themselves for being so "old" before they began to recognize that they were Adult Children and see how it has affected their lives. Please remember that it doesn't matter how old you are when you begin your recovery. What matters is that you are here now and ready to begin this work. Recovery is possible for anyone at any age. To date, my oldest Adult Child was eighty-six, and most recently I met a woman who had just begun her Adult Child recovery at an enthusiastic seventy-five.

Beyond Survivorship

Denial has been a powerful part of every ACOA's life. If you've allowed yourself even a few thoughts about your dysfunctional or troubled family, you might at first have seen only your strengths. Adult Children are incredible survivors! As a youngster some of the strengths you learned were:

> To take charge, to lead
> To make adult decisions
> To be self-reliant
> To be autonomous
> To solve problems creatively
> To be a hard worker
> To be loyal
> To develop empathic skills
> To develop your talents in art, writing, music, and so on, to provide a
>   safe escape
> To respond effectively in a crisis.

The list could go on and on.

We certainly deserve to feel good about our strengths however they were developed. Yet by ignoring what it was we didn't learn, our lives remain very limited. It is by acknowledging what didn't get learned in our childhood, as well as discovering what we learned that is no longer useful, that Adult Children can establish a direction for recovery.

Adult Children need to explore their past, and in doing so, they need to identify the helpful and the hurtful aspects of their growing-up years. The skills that were helpful in the past, and that remain helpful today, can certainly support you in your recovery. However, that which is hurtful must be stopped and new behavior learned in its place.

For example, learning self-reliance may have been most helpful as a child. However, as an adult you may be self-reliant to the point where you totally exclude others, which leaves you feeling lonely and isolated. Moving out of the perception that only extremes are valid will allow you to maintain a healthy self-reliance while simultaneously learning how to become interdependent with others. Recovery means that you will now have the opportunity to make conscious decisions in your life.

People in recovery are highly critical of what they refer to as their co-dependent behavior when they were children and adolescents. We must remember that these were survival skills. I don't think it was possible for us to behave any differently under the circumstances at that time in our lives. Don't be critical of your survivor self. Be accepting of your courage and vulnerability under difficult circumstances. The key to healthy living in adulthood is to recognize when we are maintaining survival skills that no longer work for us. We need to let go of old behavior that interferes with enjoying the type of life we would like to live now. Remember, childhood survivor skills carried into adulthood can continue to maintain a co-dependent life-style.

Many Adult Children are hesitant about beginning their recovery because they don't want to blame their parents for what they see as their own adult problems. *Recovery is not a blaming process.* Rather, it is a process of examining and speaking your truths. It is the process of breaking your denial, of acknowledging and taking ownership of your feelings and your life. In doing so, you may need to acknowledge pain from childhood and to be specific about where that pain came from. However, the goal is not to blame, but to be able to break the rules that have kept you in denial and disengaged from your self. Adult Children are fiercely loyal and are often frightened of betraying their families. But if there is any betrayal here, it is of the chemical addiction and co-dependency. You aren't betraying those parts of your mother and father that loved you. I believe our parents truly want us to be healthy and happy, but often their afflictions have gotten in the way. The only true act of betrayal is when we betray ourselves by not speaking our own truth.

Resources for Recovery

Some people began working on their ACOA issues before the concept of Adult Children came into being. Special focus groups for the Adult Child did not begin to develop until the late 1970s. Until that time, when people did seek help, many could not identify themselves as "Adult Children." Although some individuals were able to resolve issues related to their childhood without this label, most people ignored the primary issues.

In 1976 and 1977, when I began my work with Adult Children in southern California, Stephanie Brown was also addressing the issues at the Stanford Alcohol Clinic; and Sharon Wegscheider-Cruse, then in Minneapolis, was spreading the word about family alcoholism. In the late seventies in New York City a small group of Twelve Step Al-Anon members met at the Smithers Institute to form a new group called Hope for Adult Children of Alcoholics. This first formal meeting was also held under the auspices of Al-Anon.

At that time one of the members of this group, Tony A., developed the original "laundry list" of Adult Child symptoms (see appendix, page 568). This list has become a mainstay for ACOA self-help groups throughout the country. Over the next few years there was some confusion about nonapproved literature at meetings and whether or not Adult Children needed to organize separate Al-Anon meetings for themselves. As a result of such concerns, there are a few hundred Al-Anon-affiliated Adult Child groups nationwide, while several hundred other Twelve Step groups for Adult Children exist that are not affiliated with Al-Anon.

TWELVE STEP GROUPS

You will see that many of the people in this book have sought recovery through the use of various Twelve Step programs, such as ACA Al-Anon, ACA/ACOA, non–Al-Anon ACA/ACOA, traditional Al-Anon, Overeaters Anonymous (OA), Incest Survivors Anonymous (ISA), Cocaine Anonymous (CA), Narcotics Anonymous (NA), and others. These groups were spawned as an outgrowth of the oldest, largest ongoing self-help Twelve Step program in the world—Alcoholics Anonymous (AA). The groups that have followed in the path of AA, which began in 1935, have developed a spiritual self-help program based on AA's Twelve Steps and Twelve Traditions. See the appendix, page 555.

The self-help groups familiar to most Adult Children of Alcoholics are AA, ACA/ACOA Anonymous, ACA Al-Anon, Al-Anon, Co-Dependents Anonymous (CODA), and Incest Survivors Anonymous (ISA). These particular groups are organized around Twelve Step meetings. They usually last an hour to an hour and a half (depending on the region of the country). They adhere to the leaderless group model and follow a similar format, with a different person directing the meetings each time. The group usually begins with a reading of the laundry list and the Twelve Steps, and this is followed by a qualifying discussion or a discussion of a selected topic chosen from the program literature.

In these meetings people speak from their own experiences. They talk about whatever is on their minds as it relates to addiction and recovery or to unhealthy behavior they have identified in themselves and are beginning to change. There is no cross talk—which means that no one is allowed to give advice or direct another person's process. No one is required to share. There are no dues or fees.

Twelve Step and other self-help groups offer people an opportunity to realize that their experiences and feelings are not unique, but that in fact their problems are very similar to those each group member has experienced at some time.

Another unifying aspect of recovery support groups is that they practice the rule of anonymity. Who you are by name is not what is important, and as a rule, last names are not used. As well, the information shared in the meeting is not to be disclosed outside the room. In this way no matter what your financial or social status, you are considered equal to all human beings who suffer from the same issues as yourself. Each participant is helped through the support and understanding of the group.

ACOA groups offer a simple program with guidelines for understanding your situation and suggested steps to help you develop and sustain the new strengths and capabilities needed to counteract the old internalized messages of your dysfunctional past. These groups also provide opportunities for social interaction and feedback from recovering peers.

Some Adult Children have also found resources through self-help groups that are not Twelve Step–oriented. Often such alternatives may simply be a group of Adult Children who choose to get together and develop their own support network.

THERAPY AS A RESOURCE

My theory is that ACOAs who are addressing Double Duty/Dual Identity issues—where difficulty in trusting others is often primary—are most likely to feel safer in the one-to-one therapy process before they feel ready for a group. Many Double Duty/Dual Identity people may need individual therapy before they can effectively use group therapy, or they may find that using both simultaneously proves to be the most beneficial.

Many Adult Children like and benefit from the group model but prefer it to be led by a counselor, educator, or therapist. Educators and clinicians have readily responded to information and a model of treatment that is proving to be particularly helpful to Adult Children. Adult Children often begin their work with an educational, time-limited support group with a small number of other Adult Children led by a therapist. Such groups are usually highly structured in terms of their content and will be limited to a certain number of meetings. People often move into long-term group therapy after participating in such educational groups or individual therapy.

Each of us is an individual, and each of us is in a different place in our recovery. While some Adult Children choose to work on their issues in a more isolated fashion through reading, others are using support groups offered by their churches. Most people use a combination of resources, including different self-help groups, reading, pastoral and psychological counseling, and individual and group therapy. Above all, what is important is to choose a path of recovery that is right for you, that is safe, and that offers you exactly what you want.

It is also my hope that the counselors and therapists reading this book will recognize that, because different ACOAs experience the same issues with differing intensities, it is important to develop a greater respect for individual pacing in the therapeutic process. We may not necessarily be able to use the same treatment plan for each Adult Child. We need to start where the client is.

The Growth of the ACOA Movement

ACOA is a very young movement—one that developed from the grass-roots level. However, it commanded a great deal of media attention. In a very short period of time—approximately ten years—thousands of Adult Children self-help groups have been created, and hundreds of books are now available on the subject. Many therapists are now targeting their practices to serve this special client population. Elementary schools and high schools are developing support groups for young COAs. National advocacy groups such as the National Association for Children of Alcoholics are developing and offering resources. The concept of co-dependency, although not limited to ACOAs, has also emerged as an accepted phenomenon, and it too has created its own proliferation of books, organizations, and attention.

Conferences for ACOAs are now being routinely held in every city in the nation, and these command large audiences. Entertainers and famous athletes are speaking out about their personal experiences as ACOAs. Publishers in other countries are rapidly translating books on these topics so that recovery support will soon be available worldwide—from Japan to India, and from Germany to Uruguay.

Of course, as with any movement that seizes the imagination of so many, the ACOA movement has generated enough energy to create a strong counterreaction. There are individuals who genuinely believe that it is only a fad. There are individuals who say the ACOA movement is self-serving for a small group of professionals, or that it is the "yuppie disease," meaning that it isn't relevant to a mainstream population and therefore has no value. Some say it is composed of adults who want to blame others and not take responsibility for their own lives. The objections go on and on.

The loudest critics appear to be those who are often the most unin-formed or misinformed. These individuals revel in taking a single word of knowledge and transforming it into a volume of misinformation. They are often very frightened and quite possibly in denial themselves. Often they are individuals who have not been willing to open up to their own vulner-abilities.

Yet, as in any movement, there are aspects that can be hurtful. There may be people who take advantage of the movement or who take advan-tage of Adult Children by attempting to simplify serious issues that need to be addressed in great depth. But throwing the baby out with the bath-water serves no purpose. Valid criticism does not invalidate the impor-tance and the value of this movement.

There are people who have spent years in therapy who are still unable to address their core issues because their family-of-origin issues were discounted or ignored. There are thousands of people within our com-munities who are the "walking wounded" because their ACOA issues have not been recognized or addressed. Their pain, which has both a legitimate basis and the potential for resolution, was not allowed to emerge. These people were encouraged to discount their feelings and keep them hidden.

That denial does not have to continue. Today there are hundreds of thousands of people from all walks of life—from prisons and psychiatric facilities to schoolrooms and corporate boardrooms—who are benefiting from what we have learned about Adult Children and the process of re-covery. Today, Adult Children can heal, learn to make choices, and ac-cept responsibility for how they live their lives.

The ACOA movement developed because so many Adult Children have begun to recognize what they have in common with each other. For the first time in their lives they no longer feel alone and isolated. They no longer feel as if there is something inherently wrong with who they are. They understand that there are reasons for how they have lived their lives. Guilt, shame, loneliness, and fear have been lessened. Hope and joy have become a genuine part of lives once dominated by pain.

Adult Children are learning basic skills, such as identifying and ex-pressing feelings, problem-solving, establishing boundaries, setting lim-its. They are learning to trust and find healthy ways to include others in their lives. As a result of this collective effort, resources such as self-help groups specifically oriented toward Adult Children and private ther-apy groups for Adult Children are now available nationwide.

Double Duty/Dual Identity

I have observed many Adult Children belittling and criticizing themselves for not moving through recovery as easily or as speedily as others they know. I have found that when ACOAs are unable to work through the process with as much ease or speed as they would like, it is often because of their need to identify and address multiple issues in recovery. People who have multiple issues often have an additional need to protect themselves, and this may be why they do not connect with self-help groups or the group therapy process as quickly as others.

This book describes in detail the process the child experiences in an alcoholic family. It also examines the special problems of multiple issues—which I call "Double Duty/Dual Identity" (DD/DI)—that these Adult Children face, and the step-by-step process of their recovery. We can no longer continue to apply generic recovery programs to all ACOAs. While general recovery information is most often what one needs to focus on in early recovery, in time an individual's unique life situation has to be and deserves to be addressed. By refusing to look at the specifics of an individual's experiences we can inadvertently trivialize the purpose of the entire movement.

The concept of Double Duty is not meant to encourage people to use their differentness to keep others away or to resist new opportunities. I believe we must first see our commonalities, and humble and comfort ourselves in the realization that we are not unique. Although we suffered separately, we have not suffered alone. Only after we have acknowledged this common ground should we take the time to explore what may have been unique to our experiences.

There are many reasons for differences among Adult Children. Birth order affects children differently, sex role expectations affect children differently. Who the chemically dependent parent is, and the dynamics of how co-dependency shows itself, create differences among ACOAs. While many areas merit exploration, I have chosen nine that warrant deeper examination for the Adult Child in the recovery process. It is my hope that the areas explored in *Double Duty* will offer a conceptual model upon which others may build.

Double Duty exists when a child has one major trauma-inducing dynamic in the family and there exists an additional dynamic that reinforces the consequences through added trauma or complexity. Sometimes the additional dynamic may be physical abuse; other times it might be a life circumstance such as being an only child. (Being an only child in and of itself doesn't have to lead to trauma; in fact, it can have many advantages.

But in the context of an alcoholic or troubled family, being an only child is a major disadvantage.)

I envision the Double Duty COA as a small child, hunched over, dragging unwieldy boxes and overflowing bags of trauma, when suddenly a dump truck comes roaring up and adds another load of pain.

For instance, if there is a terminally ill sibling in a child's family, growing up can be quite traumatic. But it does not have to create lifelong trauma if there is a healthy family system to help the surviving child respond to the situation. However, put the same set of circumstances in an alcoholic or otherwise troubled family, and the child involved will suffer many long-lasting effects from both issues. This is what I mean by a Double Duty situation.

In order to endure such trauma and added complexity—simply in order to survive—this child has to toughen up much more than other children. In adulthood, such survivors are likely to have their defenses rigidly in place and their emotions very hardened.

By contrast, Dual Identity is a special form of Double Duty in which one has at least two equally commanding aspects to one's identity—such as being a COA and a person of color, or being a COA and gay or lesbian. It is like looking into a two-sided mirror and seeing one image of yourself on one side and an equally real but different image on the other side. Although the images are different, they are invisibly enmeshed. This leaves Adult Children even more confused about who they are and what is most important in their lives.

For an Adult Child to experience a full recovery it is important to recognize that, as an ACOA, there may be other, equally significant aspects of your identity that need to be recognized and addressed—beyond those of having been raised in a chemically dependent family.

Double Duty/Dual Identity are examples of the synergistic effect of multiple-core issues that many Adult Children experience. The added dynamics of Double Duty/Dual Identity often force children to protect themselves even further. As a result, issues such as not trusting, not feeling, fear of losing control, and an overwhelming sense of shame are experienced even more deeply. It then becomes much more difficult for the afflicted ACOA to ask for help or to feel any hope. Very often the feeling of being overwhelmed by emotion or of having frozen emotions greatly impedes the ability to connect with a recovery process.

There are many people who know they are Adult Children, who know resources are available, who may even truly want to change their lives— yet always find that something seems to get in the way when they try to connect with a helping resource or try to stay involved once they've found that resource. There are others who are so powerfully defended against their pain that their level of denial is too strong for them even to recognize that their lives could be better. Still others become stuck in the process of recovery and "spin their wheels." These are often the DD/DI people.

While there are many life experiences that might merit the Double Duty or Dual Identity label, the following are examples of the ones I have chosen to examine in this particular book. I have by no means meant to discount other Double Duty/Dual Identity situations. In fact, it is my hope that the life stories included in this volume will offer validation not only to those who recognize aspects of themselves in the lives presented here, but to those who experience Double Duty/Dual Identity situations that we have not addressed.

ONLY CHILDREN

Being an only child does not have to have dysfunctional consequences. However, only children who have been raised in chemically dependent families do experience Double Duty. They have a greater need to defend themselves in an alcoholic or otherwise troubled family because they do not have the psychological or physical buffer that siblings can and do provide. It is true that COAs with siblings can become very isolated from each other within an alcoholic family, but without that buffer an only child's need to be defended escalates to survival level. This child lives with more chronic loneliness than do most other Children of Alcoholics. Surrogate families and imaginary friends are more a part of their daily lives. Their sense of isolation creates a deeper level of shame. They become more self-reliant and controlling because they live more emotionally and socially isolated lives.

CHILDREN WITH TWO CHEMICALLY DEPENDENT PARENTS

As difficult as it is for the COA with one alcoholic parent and a co-dependent parent, children with two chemically dependent parents experience even greater trauma. Both parents become equally inaccessible, and the children have an even stronger need to protect themselves. They are also more apt to experience violence and neglect. As a result, they are much more focused on day-to-day survivorship—isolated self-sufficiency becomes part of their response to the dilemma.

CHILDREN WHO SUFFER FROM PHYSICAL AND SEXUAL ABUSE

Having one's physical being attacked, whether through hitting or slapping, or verbal or sexual abuse, is terribly traumatizing and creates many long-term problems. When chemical dependency is added to that family system, the trauma is exacerbated. The effects multiply rapidly and constitute a Double Duty phenomenon.

Although there are many similarities between physical abuse and childhood sexual abuse, I believe that each warrants its own chapter because there are also important differences. In both situations a child is being treated as an object rather than as a person. When the offender is using force, whether the weapon is a hand, a belt, or a sexual organ, the act is one of domination. Both forms of violence are perpetrated by those who are supposed to be caretakers of children, yet both behaviors clearly show disregard and disrespect for the child. In both physical and sexual abuse, the children are powerless and shamed.

Incest is more covert than physical abuse. It often remains hidden from other family members, conducted behind closed doors. Physical abuse is much more likely to be witnessed by others. There is a further difficulty in that society has always sanctioned physical punishment for children, and this complicates the issue of parental rights versus children's rights.

On the one hand, children who are abused are much more likely to believe that they have done something wrong and that they are rightfully being punished. They develop the belief that they deserve what they get in life. The child who is physically abused is responding to a blatantly hostile, angry person.

On the other hand, there has always been a social taboo against incest—although it has occurred for centuries. The message is that any type of sexual behavior with a child is illegal and immoral. To make matters worse, incest is often perpetrated by a family member under the guise of a loving relative who nevertheless insists on compliance with his or her demands.

Sexual abuse is the one topic in this book that has been written about extensively. Many fine books have been published on the dynamics of sexual abuse and healing for adult survivors. However, this chapter is also a reminder that often one is not only an incest survivor, but also an Adult Child of a chemically dependent family. For the recovery process to be effective, these dynamics must be recognized and addressed in their duality.

Dual Identity: A Special Case of Double Duty

The following are aspects of one's identity that, when coupled with being raised in a chemically dependent family, create the Dual Identity effect. Dual Identity is a special case of Double Duty.

PEOPLE OF COLOR

Children who live in a world in which adverse circumstances exist based on the color of their skin and ethnicity are constantly confronted with circumstances that they had no hand in creating. All children deserve to feel good about themselves. To prepare them to deal with discrimination and racism, they will need special support and guidance. They will need to learn how to protect themselves.

But when such children are raised in chemically dependent families, healthy survival skills and a positive attitude toward their cultural heritage are not likely to be taught. The sense of feeling different and isolated that all COAs experience is especially exaggerated for the minority COA. Such Dual Identity survivors suffer from very low self-esteem. They believe there is something deficient in them, that they are not good enough. This is not only Dual Identity, it also qualifies as Double Duty. The internalized self-hate created by generations of oppression and societal racism creates an even greater shame base for the Adult Child of color. Denial and secrets are more tightly held to protect and maintain some sense of cultural pride and identity.

GAYS AND LESBIANS

Being a gay or lesbian Adult Child also reflects a Dual Identity and Double Duty combination. Because homosexuality is less visible than skin color, its secrets are doubly reinforced: compounded shame and guilt exacerbate the already existing sense of being out of the norm. For these Dual Identity survivors, loneliness and isolation become a way of life. Without recovery and acceptance of self, to "come out" as an Adult Child or being gay or lesbian is a natural step toward examining the other significant identity issues.

THE PHYSICALLY DISABLED

When people who have physical disabilities are raised in nontroubled families, they can usually cope with their handicap. In fact, they often find a greater strength within themselves as a result of living with their disability. This full expression of the self is often the fruit of the support offered by a healthy family.

However, when such children are raised in a chemically dependent family, they do not get the support they need to cope with their physical disability. And this creates a Double Duty situation. These children are left to their own resources, which are physically limited, to make sense of the world. But they must also respond to the chemically dependent family at the same time. When physically disabled people approach their Adult Child issues in recovery, they must identify and come to an understanding of the role their physical disability has played in forming their identity.

The complexity of this Dual Identity situation is apparent when one sees how the denial around one aspect of identity reinforces the denial that surrounds the other. Physically disabled ACOAs must consider the impact of guilt and shame on their sense of differentness—then they must sort out how control and powerlessness are often confused owing to the coupling of the physical disability with the rampant disease of family chemical dependency.

The last two Dual Identities we discuss in the book concern food addictions and chemical addictions. These differ from the other Dual Identities in that they are direct consequences of living with substance abuse. They represent the two most predominant addictions for Adult Children. It is important for all Adult Children in recovery from substance addictions to examine carefully the interplay between both identities.

FOOD ADDICTIONS

The majority of people with food addictions begin that pattern of compromise in childhood. Food offers solace and comfort. It becomes a friend to an already lonely child. Eating, purging, or starving may be a way to exhibit some control in a life that is out of control. But it may also offer a punishment for feelings of inadequacy. In addition, eating can represent one's defiance of powerlessness. The COA's relationship with food often becomes disturbed and takes on meaning beyond the sustenance it is meant to provide.

CHEMICAL ADDICTIONS

Alcohol and other drugs are an excellent way for people to anesthetize a life of pain, to medicate, and to feel a greater sense of power to compensate for powerlessness. Alcohol/drugs may offer ACOAs a way to feel "a part of" rather than always feeling "apart from." Adult Children are already predisposed physiologically to the addictive nature of chemicals; add to this the aspect of psychological reinforcement, and it is easier to understand how so many Adult Children of Alcoholics become chemically dependent themselves.

Identifying with One Another

Most of us can identify with a number of Double Duty/Dual Identity issues indirectly if not directly. In many cases, denial keeps a number of us from identifying our additional issues.

For example, many ACOAs grew up believing they had only one chemically dependent parent. Then, at a point well into recovery, when they were able to be more truthful with themselves, or were given additional information, they finally realized that both parents were chemically dependent. Physical and sexual abuses are frequently not recognized until well into the recovery process, due to both a lack of understanding of what constitutes abuse and because of the fear and shame that is often experienced when people break through longstanding denial.

ACOAs with physical disabilities tend to ignore that aspect of their lives because the family alcoholism overrode everything else. While that can have its advantages, for a full recovery, both identities need to be dealt with.

Sometimes gays or lesbians believe that they have dysfunctional relationships because they are homosexual, when in fact it is their Adult Child issues that so deeply affect who they are and how they relate in a relationship.

Other points of identification may emerge for ACOAs when they begin to identify with the Life Stories and their previously repressed feelings. For example, some may find themselves identifying with aspects of being an only child where there is a large age span between siblings. Then again, although we may not have any physical disabilities, it is possible that we have experienced a serious illness at some point in our lives that limited our physical abilities and well-being. And while we may not have been sexually or physically abused, it is not possible to be raised in a chemically dependent home and not be emotionally abused. Even if our families were not chemically dependent, most of us have experienced and have had to respond to intrusiveness and a lack of boundaries. However, once many people move through denial and a lack of knowledge, they begin to recognize forms of physical and sexual abuse that they did not identify until recovery.

Although a smaller percentage of Adult Children have two chemically dependent parents, it is common that at some point in our lives we will experience the extreme stress of living in a closed environment where others define our reality or identity. Even if we are not members of a racial minority, we have most likely had the experience of being the minority among a majority of others whose values, culture, and history are different from our own.

Those raised in rural communities may identify with the aspect of community alcoholism that is portrayed more in the Native American stories. Although many of us may not have a chemical or food addiction, it is possible that at some point we will find ourselves losing control around the consumption of a physical substance. In today's world the tendency toward extremes and excessiveness is more and more a part of the human experience.

Adult Children have demonstrated a lot of courage and strength in their lives. By speaking of their lives and recovery, others raised in chemically dependent families may have an opportunity to deal with their silence, too. It is my hope that by portraying a more specific picture of the lives of many Adult Children *Double Duty* will offer a greater validation and understanding of these life experiences. More importantly, I hope it will offer both inspiration and a path for recovery.

Notes

1. Found through ACOA Self-Help Literature. Original source unknown.
2. C. Black, S. Bucky, S. Padilla, "The Interpersonal and Emotional Consequences of Being an Adult Child of an Alcoholic," *Journal of International Addictions* 21 (May 1986); 213-32.

Life
Stories

How to Use This Book

In each chapter of *Double Duty*, I have illustrated the issues of a particular Double Duty group through the truth of their life stories. In each chapter three to six people have been chosen to deliver the message. The participants are in many different phases of recovery and have used different resources in the recovery process. Many contributors could easily have fit in more than one chapter because their stories combine several double duties or identities. The decision to place individuals in their particular chapters was based in large part on the most significant dynamic in their experience or recovery.

For the purposes of anonymity, all names have been changed. Portions of stories have been altered to provide even further anonymity. Any resemblance to your life, or to the life of someone you know, is coincidental and most likely due to the myriad commonalities in alcoholic and troubled families.

Each chapter opens with information relevant to the specific additional dynamic experienced by the Double Duty/Dual Identity group. This introductory information is discussed in the context of the life stories that follow. Then we meet the contributors, who talk about their experiences of growing up in families affected by chemical dependency. These stories are followed by extensive commentary on the larger dynamics at play.

We follow up the childhood stories with additional information from our contributors about the consequences of childhood experiences on their adult lives, how they found their way into recovery, their current status, and their hopes for the future. The concluding section of each chapter, "Recovery Considerations," is designed specifically for each Double Duty issue presented.

In many of these stories you might find yourself wishing for additional information or wondering what happened next. Please recognize that the gaps that appear in the stories may reflect gaps in the memories of the contributors themselves. Some contributors chose not to share aspects of their lives to protect anonymity and to maintain personal boundaries. Moreover, the purpose of this book is to explore Double Duty/Dual Identity issues. In order to maintain this focus, it was not possible to offer a more extensive description of each contributor's life.

As you read about Dual Identities it might occur to you that not all gays and lesbians are from these types of families; or that not all members of minorities experience such abuse. On more than one occasion I took myself to task about the possibility of unintentionally reinforcing negative stereotypes. Each time I reminded myself that *Double Duty* is first and foremost about people who were raised in alcoholic or otherwise dysfunctional families.

The children of these families were not scarred by being born as people of color or by being gay or lesbian. Their primary wound was inflicted in their alcoholic or otherwise dysfunctional families. The impact of dual dynamics is what creates such dysfunctional consequences for these children. It has not been my intention to stereotype certain groups. Rather, I wished to give validation to the extraordinary conditions these Adult Children had to endure under the influence of familial- and community-reinforced alcoholism.

It is very easy to identify with many of the Double Duty/Dual Identity variables in this book. My advice is to try not to become overwhelmed or preoccupied with the number of additional dynamics that have operated in your life. It is much more important to focus on acknowledging that there are legitimate reasons why you experience your life as you do. Coming from a Double Duty or Dual Identity background is one of those reasons. Always remember: You are not crazy. You are not at fault. Owning this will move you through recovery with a greater acceptance of yourself—one that will ultimately support a deeper level of healing.

Obviously *Double Duty* is a very serious book, and I pray that it is an equally sensitive book. As you read, think ahead to how you can best take care of yourself if you find you are feeling vulnerable, angry, or sad.

Who knows you are reading this book? Do you have someone trustworthy to talk with if the going gets rough? I believe it is very important to share your feelings with another Adult Child or a counselor or therapist at this time. You will undoubtedly be experiencing feelings and memories of experiences that you never realized had significance from your past, and the intensity of these emotions must not be denied.

Keeping a Journal. As you become immersed in the life stories of the contributors, you may find that keeping a journal can be extremely helpful in your own recovery work. You may want to underline or highlight the statements or themes in *Double Duty* that you find especially meaningful and relevant to your own life. Then use your journal to record your own personal history, memories, flashes of insight, and questions for further thought that emerge as a result of reading that particular passage in the book.

You may want to begin the journal work each time by first writing down the date. This will help you keep track of your own inner journey by following the trail of insights as they occur one by one. Next, you might transcribe the passage in the book (noting the page number) that is triggering your response.

Then, just let your process flow as it will. Simply write down whatever thought first pops into your head, and the next thought, and the next. Try not to be critical of what you're writing or how you're writing it— that makes no difference. What is important is what you are saying to yourself.

Just let the flow continue until you have nothing more to say at that point. Then, either continue reading the book or, if you find yourself fatigued, just stop for the day. Return to the reading and journaling process whenever it feels right to you. If you find passages in the book too painful to read, try not to be frightened by your feelings. Simply remind yourself that it is critical that you be truly aware of how personal the story you are reading has become for you.

You might want to wait a few days to read what you've written in your journal. You may find yourself surprised by what you've written and the depth of your own wisdom. New insights may be triggered by rereading your journal from time to time as you're working through *Double Duty*. You might also find it helpful to share some of your journal entries with your therapist. But keeping a journal is like having a private rendezvous with yourself—you may not wish to share it with anyone, and you don't have to.

Final Considerations. *Double Duty* was never meant to be read quickly— certainly not in one sitting. Read it slowly. And read it with the support of people who love you and who understand the nature of the issues you may be struggling with.

It is my wish that readers who identify themselves as Double Duty/ Dual Identity will find validation for their experiences in this book. Your first instinct may be to go straight to what you feel is your particular chapter in *Double Duty*. This is fine. But do also try to read the other chapters as well, even if you feel the subject matter does not concern you personally. Hopefully, by reading all these life stories you will feel more connected to other Adult Childern in the recovery process. You may also discover an identification with multiple issues. May we all develop a greater patience and love for those who struggle with Double Duty issues.

Now let me introduce you to the lives of Adult Children affected by Double Duty and/or Dual Identity.

2

Only Children

Being an only child for me was not a blessing.
                                                —Adult Child

People have argued for many years about the advantages and disadvantages of being an only child. First, there's the idealized notion
of being the only child:

> I never minded being an only child. There are some tremendous ad-
> vantages. I was the center of attention; nobody got in my way; a lot
> of love was lavished on me.

> If you want to achieve, create, have interesting experiences, reach
> your potential, then you should be an only child. Being an only child
> gives you a greater chance of moving toward your potential.

Then there's the negative stereotype of only children as selfish, willful
tyrants who always get their way:

> Only children never learned to share. They always think they should
> get everything. It is "Give me, give me, give me."

Although those are common stereotypes of only children, they're
mostly anecdotal stories. There is little research about being an only

child. Yet I am comfortable offering the following information from my clinical experiences and reading.

- Only children spend a lot of time alone. The consequences of this range from being shy and lonely to being confident self-starters.
- Only children are often more confident and act like "little adults." In fact, they tend to be more comfortable around adults than with their peers because they spend the greatest amount of their time with adults.
- On the one hand, parents put all of their expectations into their one child, and the child strives to meet those expectations. Such children often become self-critical perfectionists—and they can be quite harsh with themselves.
- On the other hand, only children are also used to being the sole recipients of their parents' attention. They aren't accustomed to sharing attention and praise, and they can be uncomfortable if they're not in the "starring role."
- Although some only children don't seem to mind not having siblings, others see only the disadvantages. In fact, when only children complain about not having siblings, one has the feeling that they're criticizing their parents. If parents are offering lots of goodies to a child, he or she is not so likely to want to share. But if the only child is getting nothing but bad stuff, quite understandably there's a desire for siblings to shoulder some of the burdens.[1]
- Compared with children who have siblings, only children are more likely to create a fantasy life to fill the void of being alone. And they often talk about their fantasy friends and imaginary playmates.
- Only children also find it more difficult to physically separate from their parents in their early adult years. They tend to stay in the home longer or to live in close physical proximity when they do move out.
- Limited research shows that only children are overrepresented among alcoholics and substance abusers.

There are advantages and disadvantages to being an only child in a healthy family. However, when the only child is raised in a dysfunctional family, such as one affected by chemical dependency or physical or sexual abuse, then there are only disadvantages.

Only Child/Adult Child

Children from chemically dependent families also find that they may spend a lot of time alone. They certainly become "little adults" before their time. They too have difficulty accepting themselves when they make mistakes, and they are constantly striving for perfection. Although an only child may be the sole recipient of attention, and the COA may get little attention, both feel as if they didn't get enough from their parents. COAs learn self-reliance, as do most only children, but they learn it through fear and need. While only children are physically separate from other children, COAs also experience an inner sense of separateness; they tend to feel different from others even though they may have siblings.

Any advantage in being an only child disappears when one is an only child in an alcoholic family. In fact, the disadvantages become profound. Only children in chemically dependent families experience even greater isolation and loneliness, for they are either the total focus of their parents' attention—or suffer from the total lack of it.

Without the psychological and physical buffer that siblings can provide, only children in alcoholic families don't have access to the validation, support, or help with problem-solving typical in other families. Yet they are faced with many more problems. They are the lone recipients of the cumulative family losses. They experience the pain of family dependency—fear, denial, confusion, and shame. To survive, they must fight even harder to learn survival skills.

At one time or another the only child usually plays each of the roles common to children in alcoholic families: the responsible one, the placater, the adjuster, the scapegoat. As a result, only children must also deal with the consequences of each of these roles. They often have greater fears of abandonment and more difficulty in trusting other people. They generally mistrust their feelings and find it hard to establish relationships.

Because they experienced so little opportunity for validation, they find it difficult to trust their own perceptions. They become so accustomed to being alone that it's nearly impossible to reach out in a time of need. As one only child said: "I had no one to talk to, to ask questions of. And today I don't ask questions. It doesn't dawn on me to look to others. I forget—I literally forget—to speak my thoughts."

One of the advantages only children have over other Children of Alcoholics is that they're often more capable of coping with being alone. They're also more likely to initiate actions and to act independently of others. These qualities are often very helpful in the survival process of growing up in an alcoholic home, and they can be useful in the recovery process as well. Yet the very attributes that help the only child survive childhood can also create a prison from which there seems no escape.

Life Stories: Growing-Up Years

The following life stories are told by only children raised in chemically dependent families. Because of the chemical dependency, the histories of these children often differ from the typical only child with two parents. Two of the stories reflect the problems of living with a single parent from a young age. Darrell Sifford, author of *The Only Child,* reports that mothers of only children have a divorce rate twice as high as women with two to four children. This means it is more common for only children to be raised by a single parent. Two people in this chapter have not one but two chemically dependent parents. One of them had to deal not only with the dysfunctional relationship between his parents, but with his mother's long-term lover as well.

Many people have asked, "What's so bad about being an only child? How can that compare with having two alcoholic parents or being abused?" Through the life stories of these only children, we come to understand something about the additional difficulty of being an only child in a chemically dependent home. They experience the abandonment, abuse, neglect, and inappropriate expectations common in such families all by themselves, in isolation. That is their additional trauma.

At times the pain of this Double Duty goes unrecognized because they're so emotionally defended. Unshared pain often makes only children more controlled, more emotionally detached, than other COAs. On the surface this makes it harder to empathize with them—until we see the loneliness, confusion, and hurt of their lives.

Due to a greater lack of family support, and lack of a number of family members to connect with, it is easier for this Adult Child to get lost in the shuffle and not hear or be encouraged to become involved in ACA recovery. The only child's high tolerance for aloneness, ability to be in control, to be more self-reliant, sabotages recovery.

Although the five only children below discuss many issues, they explore in depth the roles of loneliness, isolation, surrogate families, self-reliance and control, survival roles, and, later in this chapter, recovery considerations.

RON
Age: 39
Mother: Co-dependent
Father: Alcoholic, out of home
Birth Order: Only child, single
    parent
Raised: Small southern city
Socioeconomic Status: Working
    class

Ron's mother was only fifteen when he was born, and he was barely six when his alcoholic father left the family. Ron's mother went to work to support the two of them. At the age of eight Ron took on the role of the "man in the family" by getting his first job.

Ron's memories of his father are few but vivid. His father had a violent temper when he drank, often embarrassing Ron in front of neighbors and friends. His father's behavior was also completely unpredictable: he would be the understanding father one minute and the violent disciplinarian the next.

RON: *"My father was very inconsistent. One time my cousins and I were playing with matches, and we accidentally set a fire in a field behind my uncle's greenhouse. The fire resulted in some serious damage. I was afraid my father was going to kill me! Instead, he talked to me about the value of telling the truth. I'd owned up to what I'd done and just got a lecture. Another time, though, I came home twenty minutes late and my father whipped me with a belt. I never knew what to expect from him from one time to the next."*

Ron remembers he would lie in bed at night with the covers pulled over his head, praying for the yelling to stop.

"My father was very violent when he drank. I remember one time, when I was about five years old, I was playing with some older kids. One of the kids accidentally hit me, giving me a bloody nose. My father got so angry, he created a horrendous scene. The police had to be called. I thought he was going to kill this kid. That's the kind of drinker he was."

Ron's early developmental years were influenced by a teenaged mother and a young alcoholic father. Although Ron did not see his father again

after the age of six, young children are psychologically most impression-
able during the first six years of their lives.

Ron experienced abandonment when his father left; and he also experienced abandonment because his mother acted more like his peer than
his parent. In his very early years, while his father was still at home, Ron
felt like a Ping-Pong ball bouncing back and forth between his father's
unpredictability and his mother's passivity. At a very early age he learned
to trust no one other than himself.

"I became Mr. Self-Reliance and Mr. Autonomy by the age of eight."

Ron was very proud of his ability to deal with things. Yet although other
children envied his independence, Ron had the sense that no one wanted to
know where he was or what he was doing. He was also aware that his mother
couldn't be there for him. There was no one else around to share the burden
with, no one to validate his perception of what was going on.

*"My mother seldom wanted to know where I was going, who I was with,
what I was doing. She never asked any questions about my friends or
school. It was as if she treated me like an adult who would always do the
responsible thing. My friends envied me for my freedom, but I felt as if
nobody cared about me."*

Ron took on the role of ringleader in playing with other children. He
spent most of his time with kids who were younger than he was, especially those who needed someone to lead them or protect them. He also
had a few male friends who were quite a bit older than he was.

*"I think at the time I was searching for some positive male role models
because I didn't have any around the house."*

In school Ron sought out things he could do by himself, on his own.
He avoided any kind of competition that required team effort or relying
upon other people.

*"When I was in high school I always shied away from team sports. I
would only compete as an individual in athletics or games. I have never
been a part of a group effort. I always took up things that I could do
alone. That way, if I succeeded it was me, and if I failed it was me. I
didn't have to worry about satisfying the team, pulling my weight with
the team, being looked down upon because I couldn't cut it for the team.
I would win or lose on my own."*

Ron's self-esteem was very low, and he continually questioned why
anyone would like him.

"Why would anyone want to be in a relationship with me? All through high school I'd dated one girl because it was safe—it was mostly a sexual relationship. I chose someone who didn't ask for much, who wasn't sought after by others, and who tolerated my independence. Then, at seventeen, I got involved with a thirty-four-year-old woman—she was three years older than my mother. I felt really validated by this relationship. Now I knew I could be attractive to others. I'd been so lacking in confidence, so insecure. For me, this relationship was a badge of honor."

Being involved with a woman his mother's age might also have reflected Ron's greater acceptance of himself as a peer to his mother and people her age than his actual peers. Yet he found a validation that at that time was important to him. It is possible the relationship with this woman provided some maternal nurturing he desperately needed. This is not a pattern he continued.

Ron then graduated from high school and enrolled in a junior college. Fiercely self-reliant as always, he worked his way through school. But, by the same token, he had no sense of connection with others and no sense of purpose. Ultimately this led to aimlessness and poor grades, which lost him his military deferment. But, making sure he stayed in charge of his life, Ron joined the Navy before he could be drafted.

MOLLY
Age: 48
Mother: Alcoholic
Father: Alcoholic
Birth order: Only child
Raised: Northwest
Socioeconomic Status: Working
    class

Molly spent most of her childhood being shunted from one family to another. Although both her mother and father were alcoholics, it was her father's alcoholism that was central to her growing-up years. She perceived her mother as the stable parent, with her father creating the arguments that her mother had to respond to. It was not until adulthood that she was able to see that her mother was an alcoholic as well.

Molly remembers that, as a small child, she would cower in bed, frightened, while her parents threw furniture and screamed at each other.

MOLLY: "I felt trapped, helpless, and frightened. I remember one time I was standing in the kitchen while my mother and father were yelling and screaming at each other. I was only about four years old—much too young to understand what they were fighting about. My dad picked up a butcher knife and threw it at my mother. My mother started screaming that if it had been higher, she would have been killed. I was so scared and confused."

Molly's father abandoned her when she was very young, and her mother went to work as a waitress to support the two of them. Molly was frequently sent to live with various baby-sitters and relatives; often these were people she didn't know. Many of the homes in which she stayed while she was growing up were also alcoholic.

Until the age of nine, Molly's growing-up years were as troubled by the chronic disruption of where she was living as by the family alcoholism. The neglect that Molly experienced from her parents was made even worse by the unrealistic rules that she had to follow in all of her temporary homes. There, she was never allowed to be a child, never allowed to play. And she was usually kept isolated from any other children.

"None of my physical and emotional needs were ever met. Meals were always at the same time. My bedtime and bathtime were always the same. I was never allowed to get dirty. I was never hugged or touched. I had no one."

Children respond positively to warm, caring, respectful touch. Although some COAs experienced positive touch in spite of the chaos in their families, many were physically abused, and others report never being touched. To be held, patted, hugged, is a way of offering a child attention, support, and validation.

Hungry for some outward sign of affection, Molly was a likely victim for sexual abuse. Offenders often pick desperately lonely children. During one of her weekend visits to her mother when Molly was eight years old, one of her mother's boyfriends sexually abused her.

"Mom's boyfriend was very nice to me. He had a toy train that I loved to play with. I would go to his apartment after school and play with the train set. But then he began to fondle me sexually. I have no idea how long this went on. I was a lonely, emotionally starved little girl.

"I became frightened, though, and told my mother about it. She pro-

tected me and made sure that I never saw this man again. However, what left the greatest impression on me is what she said. Before I went to sleep that night, she told me, 'Pray to God so He will forgive you.' After that I always felt 'bad'—as if I had done something wrong; as if it were my fault.''

Because of the chaos in alcoholic families, children rarely get the supervision—and therefore the protection—they need from potential sexual offenders. For the only child, the chances of being sexually molested are even greater, for they experience greater loneliness than children with brothers or sisters. The ploy molesters often use is, "You are my friend." At first these advances make the child feel valued, important, and special.

Children need and deserve to feel this way about themselves. But when they receive this message through inappropriate sexual behavior, the child is terribly confused. It is very difficult to know whether such behavior is wrong or to experience it as hurtful. Offenders rely on that.

Fortunately, Molly quickly became frightened and had the ability to speak up. While her mother implied that Molly had done something wrong and needed forgiveness from God, she nonetheless managed to protect Molly from future contact with this man.

When Molly was nine she went to live with her mother's sister and her husband, who had no children. Molly lived with them as an "only child" until she graduated from high school.

"I didn't cry when I left my mother. My aunt and uncle lived on a farm, and my life was completely changed. My uncle was an alcoholic. I remember he would go to town and get so drunk that he could hardly drive home. If he didn't get back in time to do the chores, my aunt and I would do them alone. I remember finding liquor bottles hidden in the hay in the barns.

"But basically my life there was pretty happy. I had much more freedom, and I was able to have friends. I became very active in school, singing, cheerleading, performing in speech class, and anything else in which I could get involved. I was obsessed with experiencing lots of different things, making up for lost time.''

As Molly went from one alcoholic home to another, she came to tolerate and expect alcoholism. In her aunt and uncle's home she was able to find a semblance of happiness, which for her simply meant the absence of overt trauma.

The problem with such an upbringing is that Molly, and others like her, learn to develop low expectations for themselves and with others. This sets up children for ongoing victimization.

JUDY
Age: 46
Mother: Adult Child
Father: Alcoholic
Birth Order: Only child
Raised: Midwest
Socioeconomic Status: Middle class

Judy grew up on a small midwestern farm, living with her father, who was a farmer and an alcoholic, and her mother, who taught school and was herself an Adult Child.

Judy describes her father as an alcoholic who never drank in public. His drinking was very secretive. She and her mother were the only ones who knew about it, and as she said, they became part of the conspiracy.

JUDY: "I can remember one time being with my father when he bought three cases of beer at the grocery store. The checkout clerk commented, 'Boy, you must be having some kind of party!' My father was very embarrassed, so we started going to a different grocery store every week. He didn't want people to know that he drank three cases of beer a week by himself."

For Judy's father to feel enough embarrassment in that situation to change stores implies that he probably felt shame—he felt exposed, fearful that someone would see him as a "lush." His need to drink—alone and isolated—also reflects shame. It is not surprising that as a child, Judy would take on some of her father's shame and sense of unworthiness.

"At the end of the week, when the beer was gone, my father would become unbearable. He would be verbally abusive, caustic, belittling, loud, dominating, opinionated, and mean. In desperation, I used to think, Please give him a beer!"

Judy remembers her mother as being a "very unhappy person." She was disorganized and easily frustrated, giving up on activities, duties, or chores she had started. This behavior would make her an easy target for Judy's father's anger and criticism. Judy became her mother's protector.

She would try to protect her mother by cleaning the house, preparing the meals, and even helping to correct students' papers. Judy became the family mediator and placater. She was the one who quieted her father, supported her mother, and tried to bring peace to the family.

Judy managed to escape the family nightmare at school. She was an average student, and she never got into trouble. And she was popular, enjoying the company of many friends. Yet because her parents left her alone most of the time, what Judy remembers most is feeling terribly alone, with no one to talk to. She assumed all children lived as she lived. Like many children growing up in dysfunctional families, she didn't trust anyone to believe her. Young as she was, like many COAs, she was already "feeling alone in a crowd."

Judy describes how she would make a sculpture of her family.

"I would have my parents facing each other, about five inches apart, with fists clenched and raised, ready to hit each other. My mother is locked into my father's gaze. I would be grabbing my mother's arm, desperately trying to get her attention. But she's immovable, never glancing my way.

"I'd try to break in between them, but it's as though there's a glass case around them. I can't break in. So I leave them standing there, and I move about twenty feet away to join a special boy and three or four girls. That's where I stay. That's how I would have sculpted them when I was ten years old, and that's how I would sculpt them today, thirty years later."

Judy married within a year of graduating from high school.

LAURENCE
Age: 51
Mother: Co-dependent
Father: Alcoholic
Birth Order: Only child
Raised: New England
Socioeconomic Status: Lower
    working class

Laurence, age fifty-one, was raised in a small New England city. His earliest memories are of his alcoholic father being physically violent or "helplessly funny and silly" when he was drunk. He recalls many instances of his mother "awakening" him in the middle of the night.

LAURENCE: "She and Dad would have slugged and screamed it out. With bags packed, Mother and I would descend the five stories of our apartment building staircase. I would be feigning sleep in order not to upset my mother.

"My recall of my father during the first five or six years of my life is that he viewed me as an impediment. He saw me as a threat, somebody who took my mother's attention away from him. 'Keep that brat quiet,' is one of the consistent screams I heard from him."

As his childhood unfolded, Laurence became more and more attached to his mother.

"As she withdrew more and more from my father, she made me the centerpiece of her life. Mother lavished me with material goods during my childhood and constantly exhorted me to achieve and accomplish. But she also exerted a lot of control over me. I always felt I had to be perfect in virtually everything I did or else, because Mother was always warning me, 'You'll end up being just like your father!' "

Laurence had an added dynamic that put great pressure on him. His mother had had what he described as a "sugar daddy" from the time Laurence was five until he was in high school. Since Laurence's mother did not have enough money to support herself and her son because of her husband's financial irresponsibility, she told Laurence that she had to hang on to this other relationship in order to survive.

Laurence was terribly confused by the triangle he found himself in. He had mixed emotions toward his alcoholic father. Although he felt fear and anxiety most of the time, he also remembers a two- to three-year period when his father stopped drinking and family life was comfortable. Yet his mother still maintained her "outside" relationship.

"This was a disturbing time for me because it was such a secret. Actually I liked this other man. We developed a close relationship. But I was overwhelmed with feelings of betrayal, confusion, and anxiety. I was distant with my father, but I always felt that we could have had a closer relationship if my mother hadn't constantly tried to poison my mind against him."

Laurence's mother used him as her confidant, her peer. He was the sole recipient of his mother's unrealistic expectations and inappropriate behavior. As his mother's ally, Laurence was caught in a triangle in which he could not be close to his father without betraying his mother. Being an only child, he carried the total burden of the family secrets and in this case the burden of "betrayal." As a child, the secret that Laurence held reinforced his sense of being the betrayer of his father by having to hold on to the hidden information.

Like many only children, Laurence found friendship and escape in books. He said that he started going to the library by himself in the third grade. Books became his companions, as did the radio.

"I would just sit and listen to the radio all by myself. Then again, there weren't a lot of people around to listen with me."

Laurence grew up in a lower-working-class neighborhood, and most of his play time was on the streets with other kids. He found himself drawn to the older boys, looking for models. Because he was big in size and more adult in attitude, they allowed him to hang around. By high school Laurence had found his hook, his place to feel good. He took to sports with fanaticism—he was an excellent athlete and was attracted to the attention he received from the coaches.

"Sports saved me. It gave me a way to feel good about myself. It was also something that was mine—it had nothing to do with my mother or father. I allowed sports to take all of my after-school time."

Athletics and other after-school activities are often the only socially acceptable ways COAs find relief from the emotional pain of their lives. Unless the sport is an isolated one, this allows them to interact with their peers and thus enhances their sense of belonging. Many of these children, such as Laurence and Ron, speak of the validation they received from the attention offered them by athletic coaches. It gave them a safe setting in which to spend their time. It also gave them a legitimate reason to be away from home.

Growing up with no brothers or sisters means the only child misses out on the daily experiences of social interaction with peers. Many parents try to compensate for this by encouraging their only children to find other social outlets. But such encouragement is not as likely in alcoholic families. As a result, these only children are much more likely to be insecure and suffer from low self-esteem. They are often very frightened and emotionally isolated.

When only children of alcoholic parents do venture into friendships, it is common for them to seek out only one or two friends at a time. Since their concepts of exchange and sharing are rarely adequately developed, experiencing more than one or two relationships at a time is usually overwhelming.

Another complication in the COAs' development of friendships is the issue of dating. The idea of dating is often intriguing and frightening for adolescents in general. But for COAs it is more conflictual. The inability to play, be spontaneous, share feelings, and set limits, plus the need for approval and the fear of rejection are just a few issues complicating an already awkward experience. In addition, many COAs are conflicted with guilt when they share affection and loyalty with those outside the family. Yet for some, dating may be perceived as the "way out" of the family, which makes it intriguing and desirable. The conflict or the perception of rescue is often even greater for the only child.

Laurence had his first dating experience as a senior in high school.

"I'd been dating this one girl for a few months in my senior year when one night my father came rolling into the apartment, and I knew something significant had occurred. I could feel it. My mother was the one to tell me. We were a lower-working-class family, and my girlfriend's dad owned the local brewery. They had money.

My father knew who her father was, and he'd gone to see him, loaded to the gills, demanding a job!

"For me it was the worst thing ever. The shame was overwhelming. Life was difficult enough within the home, and suddenly the secret was out. Then my girlfriend's father called and told me not to worry about what had happened, and that he wouldn't say anything to his daughter. But the shame was still with me. And now I had another secret to keep."

Laurence lived at home with his parents until he was twenty-nine. He completed five years of college, commuting from his parents' home.

"I was real out of touch with myself. My mother indicated that I was welcome to stay at home while I went to college, and I'd never learned to question my mother. I did leave for a year at age twenty-five or twenty-six when I was accepted into a special year-long program in another state. But I then returned to my parents' home and took a job close by, although I had other opportunities in other cities. At twenty-nine I finally moved out when I got married."

Because they have so little sense of self separate from their parents, many children from alcoholic families will stay in the home long past what is perceived as the emancipation years—even in the most traumatic situations. In Laurence's case, he was so emotionally enmeshed with his family's dysfunctional dynamic that he could not separate from his parents.

Even if they separate physically from their parents, Adult Children re-create the dynamics of the family with new characters. Laurence did just that. At twenty-nine he married another Adult Child, although this would not be acknowledged or addressed for many years to come.

DEBBIE
Age: 36
Mother: Chemically Dependent
Father: Chemically Dependent
Birth Order: Only child
Raised: Midwest
Socioeconomic Status: Upper
    middle class

Debbie was raised by two alcoholic parents who were both attractive and social—outsiders perceived them as the "perfect little family." Debbie's parents were financially comfortable thanks to her mother's family inheritance and her father's success in residential real estate. Yet, being raised in material comfort only increased Debbie's sense of craziness because the money made it easier for her parents to hide the effects of the family alcoholism.

DEBBIE: "I was to be the beautiful child who would fulfill all of my parents' dreams of what a beautiful child should be. My father had begun to exhibit alcoholic behavior by the time he was in his mid-twenties, but he controlled it enough to become very successful in his career."

Debbie's parents socialized at the country club, where they would both get very drunk. When they got home they would get into violent arguments.

"I would be terrified. The voices were loud, and sometimes my mother would throw things. I pretended I heard nothing. I would lie in bed terrified that something awful would happen. Sometimes the police would come, sometimes the neighbors. When it got really bad, my mother would come, pull me out of bed, and tell me to pack. I would obey, and we would leave. This became a routine.
"I would write a good-bye letter to my father, telling him what a great dad he had been. He would then hold out the letter to my mother, screaming that he would use this in court against her. Then she would be furious at me for 'betraying' her. I could never win. I was always in

the middle. No matter what happened, it was my fault. I was always apologizing—but I never knew what for.''

Debbie was caught in the middle of no-win situation. She couldn't please both of her parents—one was always angry or disappointed with her. There was simply no way to be the "perfect child" for this seemingly "perfect couple."

"For as long as I can remember I've been angry and sad that I had no brothers or sisters. I've always felt very different from other people. I think I first began grieving over this loss of connectedness when I was four, and it never really stopped—although I accept it today."

Because of their obsessive worry that something bad might happen to their "only" child, parents of only children often make their offspring targets of their controlling fears. When alcoholism is added to this imbalance, it feeds this obsessive preoccupation.

"I prayed that my parents would leave me alone for just one minute. My problem was really my mother—because my father was too busy with his career. He would have also been more lenient with me, but my mother watched every move I made, read my diary, listened in on my phone conversations, followed me in the car on my dates, called me home from parties on a whim, and made my life miserable."

When she was twelve, Debbie began to act out.

"I started hanging out with a pretty wild group of kids. Actually, I think they were pretty normal, just kids growing up and being rebellious. I learned how to be popular at school by hanging out with these kids, and I started flunking courses, sneaking out, and lying. I was always on restriction. I couldn't see certain people. I couldn't go anywhere after school. I couldn't watch TV—all for my own good. My home became a prison with these two crazy people!"

For Debbie, as with many only children in alcoholic families, friends were her only refuge. Her friends became her family; they gave her the only sense of belonging she ever had.

"Finally, at fourteen, I was sent to a private girls' school in an effort to get me away from these 'bad influences.' I was forced to take piano, tennis, and dance lessons, none of which I wanted. All the while I was told that I was a spoiled brat for not appreciating these wonderful things. As angry as I was, I also felt guilty and depressed. I was very aware that

I was their only hope for all their missed dreams, and that I had to live up to all their expectations.''

Unfortunately, this parental attitude of high expectations for an only child is both unfair and common. And for only children in alcoholic families these expectations are even more unrealistic, as they are generally grandiose, always negating the legitimate needs of the child.

The four years Debbie spent at the private girls' school was what she remembers as the most repressive, controlled time in her life. She was an object to be manipulated by her parents.

Special Issues for the Only Child ACOA

LONELINESS

All children in alcoholic families experience loneliness. This is a feeling of emptiness mixed with great sadness.

Without siblings to share the experience and to validate the child's perception of what is happening, the only child in an alcoholic family is truly left alone. Although being alone or physically separated from others doesn't always result in loneliness—in a dysfunctional family it does. Even when only children have access to others, the atmosphere of denial and shame in their family keeps them from being able to share their pain.

RON: ''One of the feelings I have had pretty consistently when I think about my childhood is this total aloneness—this lonesome, against-all-odds kind of feeling. I had no one to respond to me, no one to validate that I was even there. I was totally alone with all that was happening.

''I feel that if I'd had brothers and sisters, I wouldn't have felt so alone. I would have had people to talk with and to share with as a child. Even if this had been limited, they'd have still been there. Grief loves company. We'd have been together through that.''

Only children aren't trying to say that others deserve to have the pain, too. They are saying that they need to be comforted. They feel that if they could have shared their pain, they would have found comfort and validation.

MOLLY: ''Like other Children of Alcoholics, I learned, 'Don't feel, don't trust, don't talk.' But not having brothers or sisters, who was I going to talk with? Who was I going to care about? Who was I supposed to trust? As a small child, I not only felt alone—I was alone. That was my reality.

I had no idea what a relationship should be like, because I didn't have brothers or sisters to learn from. I think being an only child made it harder for me to feel, to trust, and to talk to others because no one was ever there."

To the outside world, Debbie's was the family of lavish parties, exotic trips, and country club appearances. However, at home the scene was one of angry fights followed by bitter silences. The contrast with how her family was seen publicly made her loneliness that much more unbearable.

DEBBIE: *"Some nights we would all sit at the dinner table in total silence, no one looking up from his or her plate, no one making a move. The silence was deafening. This is when I was very aware that there were no other children here. I was trapped in this silence and in this house by myself. And I couldn't talk to anyone about it. To make things even worse, my parents looked wonderful—we were the perfect family—no one would have believed what went on here."*

JUDY: *"The most significant emotion I remember having growing up was loneliness. I didn't feel there was anyone I could talk to about my father's drinking. I knew that it was not a topic that was to be taken out of the family. But every time I attempted to discuss it with my mother, I wouldn't get anywhere either. She used to tell me that my father didn't drink that much, or that he worked hard and had a right to a few drinks after work. I often wondered, would I have felt so lonely if I'd had brothers and sisters? I also wonder if my sense of identity would have been stronger if I'd had siblings who looked like me or could discuss my personal life with me."*

Laurence doesn't remember feeling lonely because he was so merged with his mother. He had no sense of himself as separate from her. He felt what she felt—what she wanted him to feel. This is referred to as "enmeshed boundaries." Laurence's life reflects the "all or nothing" phenomenon characterized by chemically dependent families. You either feel very lonely and are isolated or, as in Laurence's case, there is no emotional or physical separation.

LAURENCE: *"I was never alone. I was so focused on my mother, I couldn't feel for myself. I do recall saying that I was glad to be an only child, and I'm certain that this idea was reinforced by my mother. After all, I was the sole recipient of all these toys, clothes, and material possessions. Yet, occasionally, my mother would remark that she might adopt another child. In my placating way, I would respond positively to this idea, but inwardly I resented and feared another sibling. I was certain that what little love my mother was able to give emotionally, as contrasted with materially, would be taken away from me. Then the ultimate threat of physical and emotional abandonment would come true."*

Laurence vividly describes his horror and fear of abandonment and loss whenever his mother was away from him. He perceived her to be his only protector, that without her he was alone in the world.

"I can remember my mother going out one evening a week from the time I was five or six until early adolescence. Usually I was left in the care of a baby-sitter since my father was either at work, womanizing, or on a binge. My memory of these evenings is one of sheer terror since my whole life—my survival—depended on my mother. I can remember trying to get to sleep before she came home to avoid the horror of abandonment and loss I feared if she didn't come home. My mother also made me so dependent on her, with her frequent hints that she might have to place me in another family because of financial pressures, that I obsessed about her abandoning me all during the times she was away from me."

Although siblings might not have provided the comfort and validation only children feel they need, there is a deep desire among only children in alcoholic families to have experienced such a possibility. The desire for a normal, nurturing, peaceful family environment is compounded by the desire for companionship. The fantasy of the comforting sibling creates a sense of what might have been.

JUDY: *"I remember feeling the most lonely when I tried to be a mediator during the fights between my mother and my father—when I physically tried to stop their fighting. But they never paid any attention to me. They never heard me. I always gave up and went to my room, where I covered my head with a pillow to drown out the noise. I was so scared and alone. It was those times that I desperately wished I had a brother or sister to help me."*

FANTASY

Imaginary playmates often supply the companionship missing for only children in alcoholic families. The only child needs to create a confidant, someone with whom to share the secret.

DEBBIE: *"When I was in school, I lied to my teachers and a few other people that my best friend, Linda, was really, in fact, my sister. I re-*

member very clearly one day in the first grade being asked to point out my sister. I did. I think the teacher just tried to understand.''

Without the validation of siblings and friends, only children also have trouble separating fantasy from reality. These children often develop an extensive fantasy life as a means of survival.

DEBBIE: *"All through my childhood I developed an elaborate fantasy life as a survival technique. When you sit alone in your room night after night, with no connection with the outside and no one to talk to, you develop wild and extensive fantasies. As a child, I talked to my animals. I had names for all of them, and they all had different voices. As a teenager and later, I fantasized about what it would be like when I got away. Most often this would be by some tragic event in which my parents would either die or feel very guilty, or by some man rescuing me from this mess, or by my merely disappearing."*

MOLLY: *"I always played alone. I remember I read a lot, usually fairy tales. I liked the ones that ended 'and they all lived happily ever after.' I had many imaginary people around me. My dolls became my playmates, and I would talk to them. We would play 'waitress.' I guess it gave me some kind of connection with my mother because she was a waitress."*

Molly's belief that playing waitress offered her a connection with her mother is probably quite accurate. But it is also likely that playing waitress gave her control over people.

LAURENCE: *"My fantasy life was stimulated tremendously by my mother, who always told me that I was the best. Of course, I did not hear this as a possibility, but as an imperative. Her meaning was clear: If you're going to continue to make up for your drunken father, you had better be the best, or you will be a failure in my eyes.*

"I assumed that if I failed, I'd lose my mother's love. Therefore my fantasy world went beyond the normal sphere. I particularly enjoyed reading about distant places, and I could see myself living in some utopia.

"Toy soldiers also became an obsession for me in my fantasy world. I had dozens of them and would create battle scenes in which the enemy would be totally wiped out, but only a few of the good guys would be wounded. I would then establish a hospital in which I would restore them to health through my ministerings. As I look back now, I can interpret my fantasy world as one in which, through the medium of toy soldiers, I could stamp out evil, injustice, and badness as I experienced it in my

*alcoholic family, and then heal the good soldiers, who probably repre-
sented me and made my existence worthwhile after all.''*

Imaginary playmates and friends often provide solace and comfort to
only children. They become surrogate siblings. But in the alcoholic family
such relationships can become an escape. The only child in the alcoholic
family uses them as a way to separate from the daily confusion and pain
and pervasive sense of loss. Although this is a legitimate survival technique, it can also serve to reinforce the sense of isolation and prevent
the child from reaching out to other people.

Only children often become comfortable in their aloneness; they learn
how to occupy their time without a sense of loss. But to do this they've
also learned to separate from their feelings.

SURROGATE FAMILIES

The sense of abandonment felt by most children in alcoholic homes is
particularly strong for only children. As a result, many naturally look to
other people to fill the vacancies left by the parents' physical and/or
emotional abandonment. Grandparents, aunts and uncles, teachers, and
the parents of friends often fill these needs, or friends are "adopted" as
surrogate family.

*DEBBIE: "I was always drawn to families that were very large and had
animals and noise and freedom. I felt that I was in heaven when I was in
those homes, and I tried to spend as much time there as I could. I loved
being around a lot of people, and yet this made me aware of how different
and alone I was."*

*JUDY: "I always had a special boyfriend and three to five girlfriends. They
became my 'family.' They were the ones I bonded with."*

Surrogate families are often chosen by the child to provide what parents can't. For many children in alcoholic families, surrogate family members provide the nurturing, predictability, and stability that the parents
fail to provide. They can give the child a sense of specialness that is
particularly important to someone who is growing up feeling ignored and
abandoned.

However, some children find themselves being raised by strangers or
by people with whom they feel no connection. As a result of parental
neglect, Molly was moved around from family to family. In most of these
homes she only experienced more neglect and trauma. Rather than pro-

viding the parenting she needed, most of her surrogate families merely reinforced her image of the dysfunctional family as the norm.

Laurence was often left with one of his mother's close friends for several days at a time.

LAURENCE: "I experienced it as weeks, though. My mother would tell me she had to go to the hospital and assure me that she would be okay and that she would bring me lots of toys. But she would always add that in the event that something happened to her, I would be fine since her friend would take care of me. I would be terror-stricken emotionally at the possibility of ultimate abandonment. My mother had become my whole world. I was always the 'good' child, because I kept these feelings locked inside. Looking back now, I realize that my mother really went off on trips with her sugar daddy.

"The other dimension of this surrogate family existence was that the woman that I had to stay with—and her family—were cold, distant, intim- idating, and physically and emotionally abusive. As a child, the thought of being left permanently with this monster in the event of the loss of my mother was gut-wrenching."

ISOLATION

The loneliness and isolation COAs experience are usually intertwined. Loneliness comes from within. It is more internal, a feeling of emptiness mixed with great sadness. Isolation is more external, like an invisible but ever-present wall. When we feel lonely, we feel disconnected from the inside. When we feel isolated, we feel disconnected from everything out- side of us.

Isolation often permeates the life of the only child in an alcoholic family. While most only children feel a heightened sense of loneliness, adding chemical dependency to their environment creates isolation. It is a prison from which the child cannot escape.

The isolation is a result of many factors:

- The denial that prevents the child from sharing his or her pain.
- The lack of peers to validate the child's feelings.
- The fantasy world that doesn't mesh with the reality of the home.
- The focus of the alcoholic and co-dependent upon each other to the exclusion of the child.

Only children in alcoholic families experience being isolated from the parents within the home every bit as much as they feel isolated from those outside the home.

Ron and Laurence eventually discovered that their isolation from others became a comforting defense mechanism. Ron describes his isolation as creating a "plastic shield" between himself and the world.

RON: "I could see everyone and even talk and physically touch them, but the plastic shield was always there to protect me. It's like I could never really get involved or touch anyone else. But the benefit was that they couldn't get to me, either.

"I remember one place we lived there would be hurricanes. I looked forward to the nasty weather because I knew people would leave me alone. I wouldn't have to worry about anybody calling and asking me to do something or to help out or to be somewhere. No one would drop by. I could really be alone. I took the greatest amount of comfort in being by myself."

Laurence's shame was so great that he found great comfort in his isolation. He not only tended to stay more isolated from his peers through solitary activities such as reading, he also found the need to seek isolation within the home.

LAURENCE: "I spent a lot of hours in my growing-up years hiding. I would set up a card table in a far corner of our apartment, drop a large blanket over it, and hide underneath. It was so safe there. I also remember playing hide-and-seek with other kids—I loved not being found."

Because of the shame children in alcoholic families feel about their home life, they often remain isolated from their peers. Although some only children are able to pursue friends to take the place of their lost family, most are unable or afraid to talk honestly about what is going on at home. Because they don't want their friends to witness the humiliating and/or embarrassing behavior of their alcoholic parents, they cannot share the normal give and take of childhood friendships.

JUDY: "I remember feeling very different from the other kids I ran around with because I never talked about my family. Especially after the weekend, other kids would talk about their family outings and I would just stay quiet and listen.

"I had very few friends that I allowed to come to my home because I never knew the kind of shape my father would be in at any given moment.

My best friend, Amy, would occasionally come over to pick me up, and she'd come in just when my father would be drunk. After we'd leave, she'd be so kind. She wouldn't say anything about what she'd just experienced. I never invited other kids to spent the night with me, though I would often spend the night with other kids."

Molly's sense of isolation was made worse by the strict rules she had to obey.

MOLLY: *"I was not allowed to cross the street to play with the other children in the neighborhood. When I started school, I was not allowed to play on the outdoor equipment. I used to stand and watch the other kids play on the swings, the teeter-totter, and the slide. One time, I did play on the swings, and some older kids bumped me off and I scraped my knee. I was afraid to go home. When I did, I was spanked with a belt. That was the last time I played on the swings or went near the other children."*

The only child's profound sense of isolation can lead to a feeling of being invisible, nonexistent. Unfortunately for most children, chronic invisibility is the same as shame—they believe that they don't matter.

RON: *"I felt detached somehow, as if I were observing myself go through my childhood rather than really living it and being involved in it. My greatest sadness and anger had to do with this sense that my childhood didn't exist. I was never told I was loved. I was never told I was hated. I just seemed to be some kind of tenant who helped out and did some chores. It was as if I was never part of the lives of those around me."*

MOLLY: *"My dad was never around; neither was my mother. I remember feeling nothingness, like I didn't exist. I had no one to talk to, and no one was ever there for me. I lived in a vacuum."*

JUDY: *"I learned I was the only resource I had to depend on in the whole world. If I couldn't solve my problems and everyone else's—my dad's, especially—there was no way out and I wouldn't exist anymore."*

Although the "conspiracy of silence" is common to most alcoholic families, the silence is especially hard on only children. Even though siblings in alcoholic homes are often unable to verbalize their feelings to each other, there is still some comfort in not being alone. The only child receives no validation and is particularly vulnerable to the "crazy making" effects of denial and to the "no one else must know" syndrome.

DEBBIE: "I could not trust my own perceptions or intuition because my parents kept telling me that the things I saw, heard, and felt were not real, or they were wrong, or they weren't the way I interpreted them."

These are all children who will spend more time alone than others because they are only children. But with the chemical dependency in their lives, that aloneness is clouded with shame. This creates an ongoing sense of separateness, making it more difficult for them to feel a part of, a connectedness with, others.

SELF-RELIANCE

The isolation many only children experience is compounded because they have had to become self-reliant—giving out the message that they are content and/or capable of handling whatever comes their way.

Like most children in alcoholic families, only children learn not to trust or depend upon other people for comfort, guidance, and support. Ultimately, they come to rely solely upon themselves. Only children have an advantage in developing this independence because they are used to being alone and more practiced at creating survival skills within their own private worlds. Yet this same ability often works against them in adolescence and adulthood because it undermines the development of healthy relationships.

MOLLY: "Growing up the way I did made me not trust or depend on anyone for support. I had to depend on myself and no one else. By the time I was six I was going to the dentist by myself, I even bought my own shoes. I was put in a position where I had to do things without ever being taught how to do them. There was no guidance. There was no preparation. I was scared to death to go to a store by myself and buy my own shoes when I was so little. I was terrified to take myself to the dentist. But I was told to do it—so I did! I didn't even have a sense of achievement because I was always operating from a basis of fear.

"I assumed I was a nuisance and a bother to others, so I tried not to ask anyone for anything. I knew no one cared about my feelings, so self-reliance became a way of life. As an adult, this self-reliance has created problems for me. At times I can be so autonomous, so separate from others, that there's no space for sharing, for connecting. And most of the time I don't even know I've been missing anything."

Self-reliance is an admirable trait, but Molly learned it from a basis of fear and as a consequence of abandonment. Her self-reliance becomes survivorship; it will be where she finds some level of protection for herself. As Molly talks about the feelings that underlie her need to be self-reliant, Debbie and Ron will show how they've already "assumed the position" of taking care of themselves and do not have any expectations of their parent(s)."

DEBBIE: "I knew how to exist alone. I was incredibly self-sufficient. I never thought of leaning on anyone or asking for anything. As a matter of fact, the only time I felt fear was when I had to ask for something or rely on someone else."

RON: "My mother often worked the early shift, so I got up by myself in the morning and made my own lunch for school. I can remember sharing with people how proud I was that at six and seven I could be home alone and not need a baby-sitter. I was helping the family save money by being very adult and responsible.

"I got my first job when I was eight. It gave me a sense of validation to be able to use the money I earned to help pay some of the bills. I thought that was just great. In some ways, I began to fill the role of the husband. I was a breadwinner, a provider. I was also usually the one who picked up and cleaned the house. I would do other chores, such as woodworking, painting, hammering, or mending a loose leg on a chair. It made me feel a little superior to my friends that I was able to do so many 'adult' tasks, that I was so responsible.

"Yet having to rely on yourself keeps you from reaching out. It just snowballs. Because you've always been alone, you take pride in being able to do everything yourself. As that feeling grows, it reinforces itself. The more alone and self-reliant I became, the deeper I got into it, the more stuck I became."

In Laurence's case his mother actually interfered with the development of his self-reliance.

LAURENCE: "Because of my mother's dysfunctional bond with me, my self-reliance was limited. Although my mother verbalized the virtues of self-reliance to me, I can recall the confusion I always felt when I would behave self-reliantly and she would respond by subtly discouraging me. I might complete a task well in my judgment, but there was always a flaw of some sort in her judgment. It would tap my insecurity. I see this now as her not allowing me to become too self-reliant, otherwise she might lose her control of me."

Laurence's life was very possibly more affected by his mother's controlling behavior and need of him than by his father's lack of involvement in his life. Her emotional needs were often met by Laurence's psychological attachment to her. In addition, his mother did not have to confront her denial of her husband's alcoholism as long as she had surrogate husbands in both her son and her lover.

By fulfilling his mother's needs, Laurence felt a sense of belonging that is a crucial developmental step for children. Also, by meeting her needs he felt less likely to be abandoned by her. Unfortunately, any sense of belonging he developed only served to facilitate the enmeshment with his mother, which would, in time, interfere with another crucial developmental step—individuating and separating.

CONTROL

COAs seek to control whatever they can in their lives in order to feel safer and to overcome an incredible sense of powerlessness. They demonstrate external control by manipulating people and things, and internal control by withholding feelings and diminishing their needs. Although the issue of control is important for all Children of Alcoholics, in the case of only children it can be even more critical. This is because only children are left to provide all their own defenses, while children with siblings may find outside protection. Being protected by others reduces the need to defend oneself.

JUDY: "I realized at a very young age that I could never say or do anything that would influence or control my father's anger. However, I did have complete control over my world, myself, my thinking, and my routine. I could take care of myself. I could do everything by myself."

Control for Molly and Laurence, as for so many Children of Alcoholics, was manifested internally through control of their feelings.

MOLLY: "As a child, I felt powerless. I didn't see any choices. So I learned to control my feelings, never showing my vulnerability. I didn't know how to show my feelings even if I wanted to. I tried to look and act perfect."

LAURENCE: "It became a part of my behavioral repertoire to control my feelings by learning to read the emotional cues of both my father and mother. I learned early that it was inappropriate to express anger or to cry. I would 'assume the position'—producing a calm or smiling countenance. But I recall moments when I'd hide from the eyes and ears of my mother and sob. I did it less and less as I grew older because of my sense of futility in not having someone to share my pain with."

Self-reliance and control can be wonderful traits. Unfortunately, for the only child, these are usually survival skills learned through immediate need and based in fear. Emotionally the child detaches from the fear, but the memory remains, quickly triggering an Adult Child's sense of vulnerability. In order to protect themselves, they seek control. But, over time, this controlled self-reliance creates a smaller and smaller world for the Adult Child—a world by themselves.

SURVIVAL ROLES

One of the most difficult aspects of being an only child in an alcoholic family is the need to play multiple roles just to survive. In families where there are siblings, the children usually divide up the roles of placater, scapegoat, adjuster, and responsible one.

Only children often find themselves in the position of trying to be everything to everybody at once. In some homes the parents view their one child as the "only hope"—the focus of all their dreams. This child is often seen as "the best child" or, alternately, "the spoiled brat." When the child doesn't behave perfectly, he or she becomes the recipient of all the parents' anger and disappointment.

Only children often find themselves switching from one role to the next, trying to assess what's needed at the time. For some, the roles may change from day to day; for others, the roles may not switch for years.

DEBBIE: *"By the time I was eleven I had begun to confront my parents and tried to act as a mediator in their fights. I became the caretaker, the people pleaser, the scapegoat, the placater. I had to take on all these roles because there was only one of me. I'd switch into whatever role I thought would solve the situation. I became everything to everyone. I was the perfect child. I made A's, I was pretty, popular, I ordered groceries, did the dishes, made both my parents laugh. It made me feel as though I were in control of everything in my house. I was needed! Still, I was never sure when I came home from school whether I'd be the adored child or the selfish brat who thought only of herself."*

Judy identifies with being both the placater and the responsible child in her early years. However, by the time she was ten she had become angry. Yet instead of acknowledging the anger, she moved into the adjusting role.

JUDY: "In response to my mother, I became the responsible child. My mother always seemed to be disorganized. She would become frustrated easily and give up on activities, duties, or chores. This made her an easy target for Dad's caustic remarks. I would clean the house and prepare meals. I would help Mom organize the teaching schedules for her class and help her correct piles of papers. I also had complete control over my own life: my studies, my daily schedule, and the organization of my room.

"In general, from the time I was three until I was ten I was the placater. I tried to make my mother happy, to make her stop crying after fights with my father. I tried to be a mediator during their fights, physically trying to stop their fighting. But they never paid any attention to me; they never heard me.

"The last time I played this role, I was ten. It was after a terrible fight between my parents. Dad went down to the basement to get a beer. My mother was crying on a chair. I was kneeling beside her, trying to comfort her. I told her that she should divorce my dad. We could go away and make it on our own. My mother pushed me away. I got up and went to my room. From that moment on I divorced myself emotionally from both my parents. No longer would I try to help them. I would just take care of myself and live my own life. They would have to handle their own problems."

Judy had already learned to detach emotionally from her father.

"I had realized at a very young age that I could never say or do anything that would influence my father's behavior or control his anger. This made me try to adjust, to blend in or mold myself to whatever situation I was in rather than go through the frustration, disappointment, and anger I felt at not being able to change the situation or another person's attitude."

Adjusting—having no emotional investment in anything—would become Judy's way of not getting hurt.

Children try to be what their parents want them to be—good and not a problem. Only children often try to take care of the adults' problems, striving to be responsible. But as the only child in the family, the only one trying to influence the parent, they quickly learn the need to accommodate. This often means switching to being the placater.

Being all alone in an alcoholic family can be such an energy drain that many only children find they have to adopt an attitude of adjusting or detaching in order to get some time out. Some finally give up and become openly angry. Yet the childhood ability to play all the roles in order to survive becomes a deficit in adulthood. Because Adult Children are so at ease in their chameleonlike stance, they have access to a whole range of defenses in which they can find some sense of comfort. This makes it more difficult for them to feel the consequences of any one role.

MOLLY: *"I played all the roles at various times. But because my home situation was so unpredictable and changeable when I was young, I saw myself mainly as the adjuster. I tried to adapt to whatever situation I found myself in.*

"As a teenager I acted out somewhat, but I always had a sense of responsibility to others, and I cared what they thought of me. I was very vulnerable to other people's expectations—it never occurred to me that they could be unrealistic. I just thought I was incapable. So I looked for reinforcement in being a good student, where I was always complimented for my maturity."

Laurence played a combination of therapist and responsible child.

LAURENCE: *"By the time I was five I had learned how to take care of others. My parents have repeatedly told me the story of what happened when I was in the hospital at age five for a tonsillectomy. While waiting in the 'preop' room, another five-year-old girl began to cry in anticipation of her surgery. I went to her and very expertly calmed and soothed her fear. In retrospect, I only did what I'd been trained for. That's what I did at home with my mother. I had to mask all of my own feelings in order to bring happiness to everyone else.*

"Since I was also my mother's projected ideal male image, I remained in the role of the responsible one all of my formative years. The message I received from my mother was 'Be the best,' 'Excel,' 'Don't let anybody beat you.' While these exhortations were not necessarily bad in themselves, there was always that unspoken threat . . . 'or else you'll end up just like your father.'

"I developed a perfectionist mind-set—anything short of being number one meant failure. I particularly excelled in academics and athletics. However, the price I paid was never feeling I had the choice of being irresponsible. On top of this, any feeling of accomplishment was usually short-lived. The joy of the achievement lacked intrinsic motivation for me."

The dynamics of switching roles from "parent to child" to "child to parent" is initially confusing for Children of Alcoholics. Children need and want protection, guidance, and support from their parents. But because of the chemical dependency in the family, many COAs experience their parents as failing to meet their basic needs. Further complicating this sense of loss is their feeling that they are expected to offer support, guidance, and possibly protection to the parent(s). In time this reversal of roles becomes accepted. Commonly, this behavior is adopted by either the oldest child or the only child in a chemically dependent family.

RON: "I can remember the sharing. It was never in the context of a mother-son kind of sharing, though. It was as if she shared with me the way she would have with one of her friends or somebody she worked with. And, in fact, there were lots of times I felt like one of her buddies. I have no idea what feeling like a son is supposed to be like. Just none. Even today, I kind of guess at it."

As a result of the stress of role switching, only children become quite adept at detaching from their emotions in order to cope with the survival need of the moment. They become "human chameleons." Although they take pride in this adaptability, they also lose any sense of who they are and what they really want to be.

Life Stories: Adulthood and Recovery

RON
Age: 39
Partner Status: Second marriage,
   two children
Occupation: Educator,
   psychotherapist
Recovery Process: Al-Anon, ACOA,
   therapy

Today, Ron has a son and a daughter of his own. His first marriage was brief and ended in divorce. He has been happily married to his second wife for ten years and is successful professionally. He has been actively working on his Adult Child issues for six years.

When Ron graduated from high school at seventeen, he immediately enrolled in a junior college and began working his way through school. But he felt very little direction and got poor grades. This occurred during the Vietnam War, and because of his poor grades he lost his 2-F draft deferment. He immediately joined the Navy, where he served three tours in Vietnam in four years.

RON: "The service was like a parent to me—the parent I'd never had. It gave me do's and don'ts; it gave me boundaries and parameters. I loved it. It gave me structure, direction, and a purpose at a time when I was totally without any sense of what I wanted or needed."

It is easy to see that many Adult Children would gravitate to the military and find the rewards that Ron did. His Adult Child issues of wanting to feel connected were being met for the first time in his life. But at the same time the Adult Child dynamic of needing excitement, which often keeps people from experiencing their feelings, was also being satisfied.

"The flight deck of an aircraft carrier was full of excitement and activity. It was my element. I was fuel petty officer—a dangerous and important job that had to be done right because I was responsible for other people's lives. The three guys before me didn't last in this position more than two months each. I stayed for three tours. I was always doing four and five things at a time. I had to perform!

"I saw this time as a great adventure. I had the chance to do things. I met people. And I traveled on my various leaves. I didn't come home once.

"When I finally came home from the military, I used my GI loan to finish my college education. By then I was much more disciplined and had a lot more direction in my life. Yet I was still aloof and distant from people. I was very self-conscious. I felt a lot of anxiety when I had to approach people."

Ron completed a college degree in special education and began working as a technician in a mental health facility. It was here that he first began to have insights about himself.

"My life was a mess. I was very lonely, frightened. I controlled everything. I felt so empty, and I didn't know why. I had always looked outside myself for the answers to the problems in my life. I had no idea that I might be a part of the problem, or that I might possibly find the answers within me."

This is the time that Ron first heard about Adult Child issues.

"When I discovered ACOA, I had an immediate and positive response. The Adult Child notion gave my life perspective. I had thought there were few words to describe what I felt, but the process tapped into my loneliness, and I immediately reached out to learn more. In doing so, for the first time I began to feel comfort in not being alone. Over the next several

years I sought answers and solutions through Al-Anon, ACOA, and therapy.

"I can remember, in therapy, when I first really got in touch with my sense of isolation. In my first marriage, if I came home and found the door locked and I didn't have my key, I would feel this incredible rush of anger and rage. It just came up from my gut. I had this sense that someone was on the inside who wouldn't let me in. I would get the same feeling when I was driving and people would crowd me on the road, trying to cut me off.

"It's like the person isn't going to let you in even though you have a right to be there. It reminded me of the way I was treated as a child. But now I was saying, 'I have a real need to exist, to occupy my own space. Don't lock me out. Don't tell me I can't come in. Don't take up my space. I have a right to be here.' "

Ron's anger was a reflection of his growing self-esteem. He was seeking to claim himself and his space in this world. He wanted to participate in life and would no longer settle for being invisible and alone. As scary as anger is to Adult Children, it is often the key that unlocks the door to their rigidity and control. In Ron's case it will also lead to greater awareness of his fears and sadness. As Ron becomes increasingly in touch with his vulnerability, he will be able to hold on to the strengths of his survivorship but find even more skills that offer him greater freedom and choice.

As a part of his recovery process, Ron began to experiment with opening up to others. He had trusted himself, and now he was willing to venture out and see if he could trust in others. This is a very scary step. Some people's fear is so great, they choose to stay within the plastic shield.

"One of the things I really wanted to change was not having many close friends. And I've been able to do that. Today, I have lots of good friends. I used to go out of my way to be alone, such as driving by myself to parties. This gave me the option to leave whenever I wanted and to be alone on the ride there and back. The thought of being in the car with all those people, with no opportunity to be by myself, made me feel trapped. Being alone was my safe place, my refuge, and I guarded it.

"I'm still overly self-reliant. I have a hard time trusting the people I work with to get things done the way I'd like them to be done. But I'm continuing to work on that."

Ron also began to take a look at the guilt and anger he felt as a child. He experienced a lot of "false guilt"—feeling responsible for other people's behavior and feelings. He had loaded himself down with adult expectations when he was only a child. Recovery is about developing empathy for oneself as a child. It's about not being critical of having been Mr. Self-Reliant and Mr. Autonomy. It's about learning to love and honor yourself for the courageous and intelligent way you protected your own vulnerability.

"I've had to realize I was not to blame. I see now that I did the best I could with what I had then. The more things I look at now in the light of reality, the more perspective I have on them. I don't deny the pain and the hurt any longer, nor do I see them as my fault. Now I can go back and find some things to hold on to, to anchor myself, to see that I did have a childhood. Maybe it wasn't all I would have liked it to be, but it doesn't plague me the way it used to."

It's very easy for Adult Children to be critical of themselves. This is because they internalized adult expectations at a young age and there were few people who offered them any positive feedback; thus it becomes easier to understand why it's so hard for ACOAs to be self-validating or self-approving. Through the support and direction of other people in recovery, Ron is now able to see who he is and to enjoy being who he is.

"Being ignored played havoc with my self-esteem and self-worth. For years I kept trying to project the ideal image that I thought was expected of me. But thanks to Al-Anon and ACOA I can now look at myself as a container, a reservoir, of things to feel good about—things that are truly me, that represent my values and my beliefs, my likes and my dislikes.

"It has taken many years for me to be able to recognize who I really am. But at last I feel free of the terrible weight of having to live for someone else, of feeling that I have to be in control—not only of myself, but of everyone around me. One of the beautiful things about becoming more aware of myself and of my needs is that when I do realize a goal or achieve an objective, there's no sense of 'I should' or 'somebody told me to' anymore. I have a real feeling of happiness and joy about that.

"Today, as a result of therapy and Twelve Step programs, I find it easier to talk about myself and to trust other people. I have filled in some of the memory gaps. I can even remember some of the positive things about my life and not just the negative ones. I no longer have that gnawing hole, that emptiness in my gut, when I think back on my childhood."

MOLLY
Age: 48
Partner Status: Married, three
   children
Occupation: School counselor
Recovery Process: Therapy,
   Overeaters Anonymous

Molly married soon after graduating from high school. Her husband had already exhibited alcoholic behavior in high school, and eventually his drinking would create problems in the relationship.

After twenty-five years of a difficult marriage, she filed for divorce. That move propelled her husband into seeking help, and today their marriage continues. Over the past nine years Molly and her family have experienced recovery.

Molly said she knew her husband had a drinking problem when she married him. But she'd told herself, as so many Adult Children do, "He isn't as bad as Dad." Then she rationalized how he was different from her father. In her case, her husband was a good provider, and he didn't beat her. But to so willingly go into a marriage with someone with a drinking problem speaks volumes about the low self-worth and lack of higher expectations that are the legacy of being raised in an alcoholic family.

The main thing that young people like Molly do not know is the progressiveness of alcoholism. Her husband could easily have become an abuser and a poor provider. And if that had happened, it's very likely Molly would still have remained in the marriage, overwhelmed by her sense of powerlessness and poor self-worth.

MOLLY: *"After I had my family, I started going to college, majoring in education and social work. I then went on to receive a graduate degree in counseling. I know now that I was attempting to find some answers for my life."*

Molly said that she was in her marriage fifteen years before she began to confront her husband about his drinking. She knew he was an alcoholic and told him so. This phase continued for over ten years. Molly says she knew she stayed in the marriage because of her insecurities and fears.

Looking back now, she also believes that going to school was her way of learning to provide for herself so that she could leave her marriage.

When Molly became a school counselor, she began feeling better about herself. Because of a growing sense that she deserved more, she decided to seek counseling for herself.

"After I'd been in counseling for several months, I realized that I couldn't take the pain of the marriage any longer. Things had gotten somewhat better because I'd been reading everything I could get my hands on about alcoholism and had attempted to get help. But my own emotional needs were still not being met. We separated for three months, during which period my husband stopped drinking and sought professional help himself. When we got back together, we began to do a great deal of talking.

"With my husband's sobriety, and the counseling that we received, we began anew. I continued to read a lot about alcoholic families and addiction issues; I was professionally involved in working with younger kids about these issues. While life got much better, I was being confronted with the reality that I still had to face my own addiction."

Adult Children of Alcoholics are prime candidates for addictions themselves. They are at higher risk of becoming chemically dependent than any other identifiable group of people. If the addiction is not alcohol or other drugs, it is most likely food. When one lives with a practicing alcoholic, it is very easy to become focused on the alcoholic and the resulting problems and to ignore your own addictive tendencies or behaviors. Once recovery became a part of Molly's family life, her defense began eroding and her own addiction became more and more apparent.

"Food was my addiction. I'd been dieting on and off my entire life. I fluctuated in and out of obesity. Up to this point I'd been focusing too much on everyone else, but now I only had myself to deal with. Then I went to my first Overeaters Anonymous (OA) group and knew I'd come home."

Today, Molly has been in OA for two and a half years, abstinent for one and a half years.

"I've changed a lot. When I finally faced my compulsive overeating, my need for control, which had continued to be a problem for me as an adult, went out the window. Now I'm learning to let things go, to be more accepting of myself and of others. I'm more honest now, less fearful.

"Food addiction is a disease of isolation—one that I learned well as a child. I would eat in secret, believing that others did not know. Food was a comfort— it comforted my fears, my loneliness—any and all of my feelings. Isolating myself had always been the way I dealt with things as a child, and until I found Overeaters Anonymous, it had continued to be my way of life.

"If I'd had a brother or sister, I don't think my sense of isolation would have been so profound. There would have been someone there physically who would have experienced similar things. I don't mean to say that having a brother or sister would have prevented my food addiction, but I do believe that my profound sense of loneliness, and the isolation that only children experience, set me up for the dynamics of food addiction.

"Today, in recovery, I can still feel isolated at times. When I do, I ask myself what it is that I'm feeling. I know that I need to get out of isolation and be more honest with myself and others in order to stay in recovery. This is an ongoing struggle. My tendency is to withdraw. For the first twenty years of my life, isolation meant safety. In recovery, I have learned to have close friends with whom I can talk and share my feelings. For me, being an only child was not a blessing."

Molly's mother recently died of alcoholism.

"I'd always thought it was just my father who was the alcoholic. I didn't want to believe it of my mother, too. But now I had to face it. I attempted to talk with Mom about her alcoholism and about her relationship with her abusive husband. I told her that I loved her and that I didn't want her to die. She refused to listen to me and continued to drink and to take the abuse from her husband. The 'Serenity Prayer' gave me a great deal of help in getting through this. I really needed it.

"When she died, it affected me tremendously. In some ways I was crying for the little girl I had been and all that I had lost. For some time afterward I kept asking myself if I'd done everything I could for Mom."

Although Molly's mother was not active in raising Molly after age nine, Molly continued to feel responsible for her mother's well-being. This is a great testimony to the love and loyalty children feel toward their parents. Like many only children, Molly didn't feel safe to grieve for herself until after her mother had died. If one has recovery tools at hand, the death of a parent can often be the catalyst for one's own grief work. When the parent is no longer living, the focus is more apt to return to oneself. Molly doesn't have to feel the conflict of being the kind, caring daughter who is in a process of identifying her own pain. She is free to turn her focus to herself.

Dependency issues continue to be a strong part of Molly's family dynamics. Her oldest son is a compulsive gambler who recently completed treatment for gambling and alcoholism. The family has also confronted the middle son about his drinking. Whether or not he has a problem is yet to be identified. The youngest son has been actively addressing his dependency issues. He has found answers through therapy, Al-Anon, and ACOA meetings.

Today, Molly stays close to her friends and her Overeaters Anonymous program. She says she's feeling great about her recovery.

JUDY
Age: 46
Partner Status: Married, two
    children
Occupation: Homemaker
Recovery Process: Therapy

Judy is now forty-six and has earned a master's degree in nursing. She has been married nearly twenty-five years and has two daughters.

Married at nineteen, Judy moved with her husband to a university town, where he did graduate work and she continued her undergraduate education. There, her most predominant Adult Child issue quickly manifested itself—anxiety attacks.

JUDY: "After I married I still didn't feel bonded to any special man. I couldn't bond with my husband. I still felt all alone and scared. I began having anxiety attacks in my classes. And then I became afraid of leaving our apartment."

When Judy sought medical help for her anxiety, the doctor told her that she could end up with a form of hysteria if she didn't go home and make her husband the center of her life. She then sought psychiatric help. The psychiatrist told her there was nothing wrong with her. He said she should "go home and keep busy."

Unfortunately, this advice simply fueled Judy's Adult Child dynamics of negating herself and denying her feelings. She was much more likely to end up a "hysteric" by going home and keeping busy. She needed someone to address the reasons for her anxiety. However, following the physician's advice, Judy decided to focus her attention on being a good wife and mother. When her first daughter was a year old, Judy developed a neurological problem, initially diagnosed as multiple sclerosis.

"I was devastated! I immediately became pregnant again, so that my daughter wouldn't have to be an only child. I knew she would need a brother or sister to help her take care of me. I went through a rough postpartum depression, but I didn't seek outside help. I was terrified of losing control, so I followed the psychiatrist's advice and kept as busy as I could. I became an attentive wife and mother. I joined church activities. I started back to college to earn a degree."

The fact that Judy's first response to multiple sclerosis was to worry about her daughter being an only child is a testament to how strong her pain had been as an only child. Her fear of asking for help, of needing to be in control, was so powerful that it took greater priority than the disease.

Although in time the symptoms of multiple sclerosis disappeared, Judy's anxiety continued. Unfortunately all she knew how to do was to keep busy. Judy did what many Adult Children do—she got a degree in a field that allowed her to learn about herself. The process of getting her degree in social work gave her the confidence and esteem she needed to seek help for herself. After receiving her bachelor's degree, she sought help in dealing with her fears. By then Judy was in her late thirties.

"I still wasn't able to feel connected with other people. I was fearful of everything and everyone. I was having trouble remembering, and was afraid of becoming an amnesiac. I felt I was losing control. I can remember looking in the mirror and seeing that the person in the mirror did not look like the person I knew I was. The person in the mirror was not the same person inside of me. I truly thought I was going crazy.

"At this point I decided to get some counseling. It was the greatest gift I ever gave myself! My counselor listened to me, she focused on me, she clarified and explained my fears. She helped me identify who I was and showed me my strengths and my weaknesses. She told me that I wasn't crazy. She gave me permission to stop trying to prove to myself that I was normal."

Judy's words—"I truly thought I was going crazy"—are the very ones many Adult Children use to describe the events that precipitate their going into therapy. What actually happens is just what Judy describes— losing control. What had worked for her in her growing-up years stopped working in her adulthood, and she had no sense of who she was or what she wanted.

The ability to project one image to the world while experiencing yourself as an entirely different person is very common to Adult Children. Judy finally hit the point where she wasn't able to run from that reality, and keeping busy didn't work any longer.

"That was seven years ago. Now I'm doing great with my own identity. I worked as a social worker for two years before returning to graduate school to earn my master's degree in nursing. I decided not to work this year since my youngest daughter is a senior in high school and it's my last chance to be a full-time mother. Next fall, with both daughters in college, I'm looking forward to starting the second half of my life—especially now that I finally have an understanding of who I am."

LAURENCE
Age: 51
Partner Status: Second marriage,
   two children
Occupation: Educator
Recovery Process: Therapy

Laurence is now fifty-one and has two young daughters with his second wife of nine years. After ten years, what he described as a "jet set" marriage to a professional dancer and beauty queen came to an end. Although many people viewed this as a "superstar" arrangement between two professionally successful people, Laurence says the final years lacked stability, trust, and fidelity. Both Laurence and his wife were Adult Children without the skills to address what that meant in their lives. They both hung on to the fact that "they looked so good." This brought them a great deal of social reinforcement.

Although Laurence had been in therapy during the final years of his first marriage, he believed that the therapies he received, although valuable, never got to the core of his Adult Child issues. As a result of his immersion in the ACOA movement, both personally and professionally, Laurence believes that he has made major strides in his recovery.

LAURENCE: "During my first marriage, I can recall the overwhelming fear and anxiety I would experience in the late evenings waiting for my wife to come home from work. It was as if I were reexperiencing the isolation and abandonment I felt from my mother when I was younger. The bitter irony of my first marriage occurred when I discovered that my wife was involved in an affair with another man. As I look back now, my first marriage was similar in certain respects to my parents' marriage. My wife's behavior particularly paralleled my mother's in the way they denied their affairs.

"I can remember spending long contemplative hours struggling to find the 'road' I needed to pursue in order to 'recover.' Ironically, I found that even without resorting to my father's alcoholism, I repeated some of his history by becoming involved in what I would call 'retaliatory' affairs. But they only made me feel more hollow and empty.

"After a stormy, litigious divorce, I met the woman who would become my second wife. But I still found myself in denial of my ACOA dynamics. Denial for me meant repeating my old pattern of running around to various parts of the globe and being the ultrasuccessful person my co-dependent mother had developed."

In the intense enmeshment Laurence had developed with his mother as a child, he had come to believe that the only chance he had for acceptance consisted of being "ultra-successful" in all aspects of life. But what success did not include for Laurence was a loving family relationship.

"As a result of my election by my co-dependent mother to the position of idealized male, the full range of my human potential had been constricted. Part of the script I inherited from my mother was: 'You'll never meet another woman who will love you as much as I do.' The other message was that 'kids are a pain.' Needless to say, these messages could certainly thwart a commitment to a love relationship and obstruct the development of a family!"

Part of recovery is identifying specific hurtful messages from your parents that you may have internalized. Laurence had to replace his mother's messages with supportive ones that he found valuable. He had to define his own belief system so that, for the first time in his life, he could create a path of his own choosing.

Identifying and defining your own belief system is a part of separating from your parents. It's normal. It's healthy. When it isn't done as a child, it can still be done in adulthood. In order for Laurence to do that, he also found it important to discipline his mother's motivations in imparting such hurtful messages.

"As I have come to understand my mother's dysfunctional behavior and the alcoholic system she experienced from her own childhood on, I have been able to let go of my own reactions—most of the time—and to understand emotionally the tragedy of my mother's life. As a result, I'm now free to focus on my own life. I've been able to risk the tremendous vulnerability I needed in order to trust my relationship with my second wife, and to take the big step of having children."

With the decision to have children, Laurence faced the problem many Adult Children have when they become parents.

"I've had to guess at normal parenting behavior toward my own children. I've had to overcome my own tendencies to superimpose what I learned from my own childhood, which was rigidly controlled and directed by my mother. However, I find that as I learn to talk more openly about my childhood issues, to trust and to feel my emotions more, I am able to be more gentle, relaxed, and nondemanding in the expression of my love for my daughters. I have no doubt, however, that my children are being nurtured in an emotional climate that is significantly different from the one I experienced."

Laurence found it important to confront his parents about their dysfunctional dynamics both as parents and as a couple. Not only did he find that it helped him to lessen his denial, but it also was another step in reframing his relationship with them. Now he is re-creating new boundaries.

"Although this action on my part did not change their behavior, it loosened my denial of their relationship in that I talked about it with my therapists and my close friends. In conjunction with this, I was able to demonstrate a greater range and depth of feeling. I could now experience joy and sorrow, anger and acceptance, and begin to believe that it was okay to feel these polarities.

"As a result of my assertiveness with my parents, I've found that I'm now able to understand and to forgive them. Although I still have some tendencies to want to rescue them, I find that this behavior is minimal. The feeling of loss I now experience for them as parents is a more normal emotion, one that is richer and more honest than my previous denial or numbing.

"The final aspect of my recovery as an adult lies in my friendships with males. I think that as a result of the absence of my alcoholic father, I was attracted to men whose friendship was conditional. Drinking had to be the centerpiece of most of these social relationships.

"Although several of them did contain some important aspects of what I view as a good friendship, it was always unpredictable whether my 'friends' would be there for me in the difficult times. If the alcohol and drinking weren't taking center stage, then there would be other reasons for distance or detachment in the friendship. In short, it was a repetitive compulsion for me to be attracted to male friends who were alcoholic or heavy drinkers, and who served as extensions of my father, and for whom I unconsciously felt responsible.

"As I look back now, I can recall an almost chronic discomfort at being in their company. They would either behave in a crazy fashion while drinking, or, if there was no drinking, there would often be angry outbursts that the situation did not call for. At best, there were frequent moody episodes. I want to make it clear that I am not blaming these individuals. Rather I look at my attraction to these unhealthy relationships as my responsibility, and as a challenge for my recovery."

What Laurence describes with his male relationships is a dynamic that many people only look at with respect to their partners. However, it is important to develop friendships with people of the same sex and the opposite sex with whom we will not become sexual. We need to look at our friendships as closely as we look at our partner relationships.

Recovery includes learning how to have realistic expectations in friendships, how to give and receive, to share—and for the only child this is a significant aspect of moving out of isolation and loneliness. Friendships offer Adult Children validation, support, and a way of being connected with and belonging in the universe.

DEBBIE
Age: 36
Partner Status: Single
Occupation: Airlines reservations
    agent
Recovery Process: ACOA, CODA,
    therapy

After she left home at age eighteen, Debbie completed two years of college. Although she had yearned to be clear of her parents' control, she was aimless and confused when she finally began to separate. Unclear about what to do with her life, she began to work at various jobs. After experiencing many dysfunctional relationships, she moved in with a man who was an alcoholic. The relationship nearly destroyed her mental and physical health, and she eventually had to move back in with her parents.

DEBBIE: "Living at home again with my parents was the worst thing I could have done. Their drinking had become so bad, and they were so abusive to me and to each other, that I finally had to admit myself to a psychiatric ward so I wouldn't die. During all this I continued to feel very alone. There was no one to reach out to, and my parents just kept reinforcing the idea that I was crazy. I had to rely totally on myself and on God."

In an attempt to escape from the family madness, Debbie married a good friend. Her husband did give her some of the support she needed, encouraging her to go back to school. She eventually graduated cum laude from college and began working for an airline. Although this husband appeared to offer Debbie the support and emotional stability she yearned for, she didn't find feelings she thought she was supposed to have. Feeling more confident of herself, she left the friend she'd married.

Debbie's experience is not uncommon. She had very poor modeling for a healthy marriage; she didn't know herself enough to know what she valued, liked, needed, or felt—outside of safety. He offered her safety. With safety she became more confident, but like many Adult Children she didn't know how to exist outside of chaos and excitement; she would become bored. She wanted something different, or more.

"I did finally leave my husband, but I immediately became involved with another man who was into smoking pot. He and I smoked pot daily for three years. We finally broke up when I quit doing drugs. Then, after another unsuccessful relationship with another addictive person, I entered therapy."

Debbie clearly sought refuge in relationships of excitement and chaos. She didn't know how to be in a relationship without such intensity. She hadn't yet learned her own worth, nor did she have the skills to protect that worth. Yet she would periodically find enough value in herself to seek help—the psychiatric center, the good friend, school, and, in time, therapy. This last move led her to Adult Child self-help meetings.

"In ACOA, for the first time in my life, things began to make sense. I now understood why my life had been this way and, most important, I could forgive myself for all the insanity. Truly, I did not know any other *way of living. In forgiving myself, I have also given myself permission to take responsibility for my life. To let go of the blame and to go on from here.*

"Awareness has been the real key. When we have to tell our own story over and over, we can no longer deny that these things happened— or that they will continue to happen unless we ourselves change. ACOA is special for me because it means I finally have a family of brothers and sisters who love me exactly where I am today. I'm still very independent and self-sufficient, but I'm learning to lean on my friends in ACOA."

In recovery, Debbie found it important to abstain from sexual relationships. In doing so she took the time to develop friendships with both males and females.

Debbie attended Adult Child meetings regularly the first three years and in the last year has gone to both ACOA and Co-Dependents Anonymous (CODA) meetings. She asks questions, she seeks feedback. She maintains contact with her friends through the telephone. This is crucial for an only child who felt so alone during her growing-up years. She is also able to recognize her strengths.

"I feel that my independence has been an asset for me in my job—it gives me confidence in myself. While I believe I'm working below my potential, I also know that will change. I live comfortably, I own my own home and car, I exercise and eat well, I take care of myself, and I have plenty of friends. Life is a lot more consistent today. I try not to create crises or drama. I live one day at a time."

Recovery Considerations

There are many considerations that only children and those helping them need to keep in mind. The following discussion of core issues is not meant as criticism, but rather as words of caution and guidance.

ISOLATION

Vulnerability is a major aspect of early recovery. Although it is typical of all Adult Children to fall back on their old defenses when they feel vulnerable, only children are usually so adept at being alone and relying on themselves that they quickly shut others out when they're feeling vulnerable.

The problem is that, very often, only children have learned to tolerate aloneness to the point of hurtful isolation. Therefore it's very important for people such as Ron, Molly, Judy, Laurence, and Debbie to become skilled at recognizing how they have used that defense in the past and sharing that insight with others. As you work on knowing what you're really feeling, it will become easier to recognize that you sought out aloneness because of fear, anger, or hurt. This frees you to attend to the feelings directly, rather than resorting to isolation and numbing.

Recovery means owning the loneliness that was part of the aloneness, along with the sadness, fears, and anger that are also part of the loneliness. Owning the loneliness that is attached to having been so alone amidst chaos, hurt, and fear will help motivate the Adult Child to move beyond the isolation. It is often only after we identify our feelings that we can attend to them and have our needs met.

INVOLVING OTHERS

In recovery, only children actively need to work at including other people in their daily lives. You may be tired of being so alone and welcome the involvement with others. Yet only children often don't have the social skills to get the most out of the interactions. You may be less skilled at asking questions of others. Because you may not know what is normal or typical in friendships, you may also be unrealistic in your expectations. Don't assume that you know what others are thinking, what they know, or what they may want. Check out your perceptions with others. It's okay to ask questions.

Only children also tend to latch on to one person at time—be it a friend or a lover. But when you do, you may overwhelm that person in your unconscious desire for them to be what your parents or your nonexistent siblings were never able to be. The healthiest thing is not to limit one's friendships and support network to one particular person. You deserve many people in your life.

GROUP PARTICIPATION

So much of what has made the Adult Child phenomenon a major move-ment is the validation Adult Children find in talking to each other. Hearing what other Adult Children say about their lives helps you to feel less isolated from others, less unique. Once you come to understand you're not at fault, you're well on the way to self-acceptance.

One of the greatest gifts of meeting other recovering Adult Children, and other only children as well, is the validation it bestows upon your feelings and experiences. Creating a family for the first time with other Adult Children can bring you a great sense of meaning, of self-worth. Often it's when you have the opportunity to hear the experience of other only children that you truly begin to feel a part of—no longer alone.

It is unrealistic to expect only children to be comfortable in large groups—unless they use them to get lost. Yet you can only benefit by meeting so many other Adult Children in a group setting. If the size of a self-help group is too overwhelming, find a smaller group, or begin recovery with a private therapist. Nevertheless, somewhere—and the sooner the better—a group experience will be very valuable in re-covery.

Opening yourself to the opportunity for validation can bring you a sense of connectedness with others and strengthen your ability to trust your perceptions. Yet validation is not always recognizable to Adult Children. Because you're so accustomed to operating on your own, you may not recognize it or accept it. At such times simply stop. Listen. Stay with it. In time you will come to accept it.

Another wonderful by-product of experiencing the group process is that it teaches you cooperation and sharing. It gives you the opportunity to ask questions, to learn from others, and to receive feedback. Only children don't have the experience of teamwork. These group experi-ences may be the first model you have for learning cooperation, for striv-ing toward similar goals with other people.

PATIENCE

Because of their severe lack of support, validation, and help with problem-solving, only children in addictive families may need to adhere to their defenses more rigidly than ACOAs with siblings. This often—

means that initially in recovery you may hang on to your layers of denial longer, and it may take you longer to trust in the support of others. That is understandable. Try not to judge your recovery by someone else's recovery. Take little steps. Take all the time you need. Once you learn that the process works, it becomes easier to give up the old defense system.

FANTASY

It is often likely that a child who had a strong fantasy life will, as an adult, live a life of unfulfilled expectations. You need to surround yourself with people who are willing to offer feedback when they believe you're being unrealistic. As you learn to be more and more honest with yourself, there will be less need for fantasy. That does not mean you have to give up the fun aspect of fantasy—it can easily be incorporated into play and dreams. What is important is finding an inner balance.

SURVIVAL ROLES/IDENTITY

Because only children have learned to adopt a combination of survival roles, they often become adept at fitting into any situation. That flexibility can be a strength. And in recovery you may keep the strength that came with each role.

However, the roles that helped you survive as a child were a reaction to living in a sick system. They were not an identity. Recovery means you are building an identity based on learning what you want, what you desire, what you need. As you give up placating, adjusting, being responsible, or acting out as a means of protection, you will find yourself becoming freer and freer.

Remember, as an only child you have many strengths. As painful as life has been, now is the time to take pride in your ability to survive. You did this all by yourself. There were no others to offer you validation and support. You were left to operate in a vacuum most of the time. You were often the focus of all your parents' unrealistic expectations. Yet you were creative and imaginative. You learned how to develop your own sense of safety, even though you had few resources. You learned to use great initiative. You learned adaptability. Although those childhood strengths can become problematic in adulthood, the point is, they

were significant acts of a lone child who developed self-care. These childhood traits indicate internal strengths that are within you today.

*In recovery I have created a family of choice. It has given me many
brothers and sisters. I never have to be alone again.*
                                                        —*Only Child, Adult Child*

Notes

1. D. Sifford, *The Only Child* (New York: G. P. Putnam 1989).

3

Two Chemically Dependent Parents

It was natural to see both of my parents with a drink in hand and another waiting. As long as they had a drink nothing mattered, including me.

—Adult Child

In 20 percent of chemically dependent families, both parents are addicted to alcohol or other drugs, and there is no nonalcoholic parent to offset the influence. In this particular case, both of the parents are drugged and not able to think clearly. Both parents live in overwhelming denial and are often delusional. This means that over five million children in the United States are being raised by two people who have a need to drink and/or use drugs that is a primary dependency. In time that dependency will supersede all other priorities—including the healthy parenting of children.

Living with chemical dependency often takes place without the child recognizing that dependency in either parent or perhaps recognizing it only in one parent. Looking back, many Adult Children realize that they identified as alcoholic the parent who was further along in the progression of the dependency. It often comes as a shock years later, after the progression is more identifiable, to recognize the other parent's chemical dependency. Sometimes one of the two chemically dependent parents is addicted to prescription pills and the addiction is not as recognizable. It's always easier to recognize chemical dependency when the primary chemical is alcohol or a street drug.

With two chemically dependent parents, the children's needs are even less likely to be addressed. Emotional neglect, child abuse, and a poorer quality of child care are more pronounced.[1] And the children are more likely to experience foster care or surrogate families. As a result, these children develop a less integrated and less stable sense of self.[2,3,4] They grow up with a greater sense of abandonment, which leads to an even more powerful drive to become self-sufficient and overly responsible at a very early age. This self-sufficiency is derived from an even stronger base than that of the commonly recognized "responsible child."

The purpose of being the responsible child in a family with one chemically dependent parent is to bring greater stability and predictability to one's life. This is done by manipulating whatever is tangible in one's environment—people, places, and things. It is reflected in a child's taking charge and making decisions for himself and others.

However, although people with two chemically dependent parents may identify with this, there is less focus on taking charge, making decisions, and manipulating others. Rather, there is a stronger need to protect their emotional well-being and to dodge the blatant trauma. Survivorship means simply getting through the moment at hand. In this case, self-sufficiency is based on fear without the ability to trust in others. This results in a greater need to defend oneself emotionally against an overwhelming sense of powerlessness.

Adult Children with two chemically dependent parents frequently have more difficulty in the recovery process because of the devastating trauma of growing up in a home where alcoholism is "normal." They walk through life always guessing at what "normal" really is, not knowing what is appropriate or inappropriate. Having learned to tolerate the abnormal, the denial of their own drinking or chemical abuse is severe because, although their alcohol usage may be extremely high, they construe their drinking to be normal. They have very little sense of a healthy life and emotionally rewarding relationships.

My clinical experience has shown that, as a group, people with two chemically dependent parents don't have the ability to "look good"—to be as functional in their daily lives as other COAs. Their adult years are much more apt to be affected by addictions, compulsions, depression, and rage.

Research indicates that where both parents are alcoholic, the alcoholism developed at earlier ages for both. This increases the probability that Children of Alcoholics will also be exposed to parental alcoholism at earlier ages than when only one parent is alcoholic.[5] The younger children are at the onset of their parents' alcoholism, the more deeply they're affected.

Additional research suggests that Adult Children of two alcoholic parents are more likely to begin drinking at an earlier age and that they are more susceptible to alcoholism at an earlier age.[6]

Life Stories: Growing-Up Years

The following life stories of Adult Children who were raised with two (or more) chemically dependent parents reflect the extreme, yet unfortunately far too frequent, aspects of alcoholism. Physical violence pervades these families. At twelve one child loses her mother to cirrhosis. Another watches from behind the curtain as her mother "cooks her drugs."

It's almost a given that the person with two chemically dependent parents is not just in a "double duty" situation, but in fact has multiple duties—for example, having two chemically dependent parents plus physical abuse. Two addicted parents also creates a greater threat of death in the immediate family. These children are so focused on day-to-day survival, they have little opportunity to try to show the world that they are okay. Although they too find solace in school and sports, alcohol and drugs are an easier answer for them. We will explore the dynamics of abandonment, neglect, abuse, self-sufficiency, and recovery considerations.

KELLY
Age: 44
Mother: Chemically Dependent
Father and Stepfather: Alcoholic
Birth Order: Oldest of five children
Raised: Southern California
Socioeconomic Status: Middle Class

Kelly's parents married during World War II, when her mother was only sixteen years old. Kelly's father was in the army and was shipped overseas almost immediately. Kelly's mother went to live with her husband's parents. One day, on the way to the market, Kelly's mother was attacked by several men and beaten severely. While she was recovering, she was in so much pain that the doctor prescribed morphine, and she quickly became addicted.

Kelly was born when her mother was twenty and her father had returned from the war. Her mother was still doing drugs, and her parents fought constantly.

KELLY: "My mother was still very much like a child. She was very lazy. She didn't act like the home was hers, but as if she were a child living there. My father was a very picky, sarcastic person. Needless to say, they didn't get along. My aunt and my grandmother would take care of me when my mother wasn't feeling well. My father spent most of his time away from home, playing around.

"From the time I was born until I was two and a half, I was passed back and forth from one set of grandparents to the other to be taken care of. Then my parents divorced. My father got married and moved to Austria to live for a couple of years.

"Then my mother met and married my stepfather, who was in the Air Force. She remained on drugs. As far back as I can remember, there was always this terrible smell each day in our house. My mother was always cooking this awful-smelling stuff. Now I know that the smell was related to her preparing her drugs. Back then all I knew was I'd better not question my mother about it. My mom didn't pay much attention to me anyway, and I was afraid to question her about anything."

Kelly was five when her brother was born, and she became his sole caretaker. The children were constantly left alone, even at night.

"Sometimes my mother would go out to get drugs. Other times my grandmother told me the dealer would come right to the house because my mother was in such bad shape she couldn't even get up. My grandmother found this out only after my mother was arrested.

"One night some men came to our house. They were police detectives and had been watching my mother. They arrested her for illegal use and possession. That night the police took us children away. I went to live with my great-grandmother, and my brother went to live with someone on his father's side of the family.

"When my mother came home, we moved to another house. My sister was born when I was six. Now I had two babies to take care of."

Kelly's automatic reaction that she was responsible for the two babies is typical. She does not expect or perceive that her mother will act like a parent. Since the children were left alone so frequently, it was only natural for her as the oldest to assume "parental" responsibility. This role adaptation usually creates a lot of boundary confusion and guilt for the COA in adulthood.

In time, another move occurred. The family went to live with Kelly's stepfather's parents.

"We lived in their basement, which was like a little apartment. My step-father's mother hated my mother, and she hated me. When my mother and stepfather would go out, his mother would lock me out of the house so she could have her real grandchildren all to herself. I think I even had to stay downstairs when the rest of them were upstairs. I was always alone down there or locked out and across the street in the park.

"We finally moved into another house in a nice neighborhood with lots of kids. Things seemed to be pretty normal for a while, but that terrible smell was still there. My mother was not so out of it at first, and my stepfather was around more. But this didn't last long."

In a divorced family where the children remain with the substance-abusing parent, it is very common for the parent's future partners to be chemical users as well. Chemical dependency attracts chemical dependency. Because of his own dependency, Kelly's stepfather basically ignored her. Given the circumstances, this may have been the healthiest response that Kelly could receive. When the Korean War started, Kelly's stepfather was sent overseas.

"When he left, hell started for us at home. My mother really went over the edge. I would catch her shooting stuff in her legs, and her thighs had huge black-and-blue marks on them. She would do crazy things, like put white stuff on her face and wear a sheet. Then she'd turn out all the lights and chase us all over the house. She scared me so much. She spent her days sleeping and her nights drinking and shooting up. She was in and out of hospitals all the time. We kids were sent from one relative to another."

Because Kelly was moving so much of the time, she was also developing a tolerance for lack of security. She had already taken on the role of parent for two babies, and her mother was clearly frightening to her. But it would soon get worse.

Given these circumstances, it's easy to see how COAs develop a tolerance for hurtful, inappropriate behavior. It's also easy to understand why some people say, "But it wasn't that bad." They know that the bad can become worse. Children grab on to whatever security and safety they can.

When Kelly's stepfather came home from the war, it became apparent that he, too, had a serious drinking problem.

"Not only was my mother taking drugs, but she was drinking with him all the time. The house was always a mess, and the kids were always dirty and in trouble. To top it off, my mother got pregnant again. While my mother was in the hospital having the baby, my stepfather stayed home to take care of us. He was drunk most of the time or out of the house. We were left alone at night. When he came home, he would be drunk. Sometimes he would tell me to come sleep with him, but I was old enough to know that I shouldn't do that. Most of the time he'd fall asleep and leave me alone. When he was sober, he was always talking about getting us a new mother."

Soon after she had the baby, Kelly's mother was hospitalized for six months. Kelly's grandmother hired a housekeeper who cleaned the house and provided clean clothes and food for the children. But when Kelly's mother returned, the drugs, drinking, and abuse continued.

When Kelly was nine her mother became pregnant again (that child was born in prison). Kelly's great-grandmother arranged to have Kelly sent to live with her father's parents. Kelly said her paternal grandparents were warm, kind, and financially well off. They became her protectors. She believes she was favored because she was the son's grandchild.

"I had to be tricked to go with my grandparents. I was told that I was just going for a visit. I was very worried about my family. The first year was very difficult. How could the kids get along without me? I spent that summer in deep depression. I guess I really knew that I wasn't going back. But I'd been the kids' parent. They needed me.

"Life with my grandparents was pleasant, only I missed everyone, even all the problems. It was strange to go from being the caretaker of three kids in a bizarre family to a Disneyland-like family. It was as if I had blanked out all the bad stuff.

"Then the phone calls started. My mother would be drugged and drunk, and she'd call me up and beg me to come home, saying she couldn't handle things without me, and that the other kids missed me so much. I began to dread it whenever the phone rang. It got to the point where I could no longer talk with her when she called. By now the kids had all been placed in a Veterans of Foreign Wars home. The last three years I just quit thinking about my brothers and sister. I just quit thinking of them."

Kelly had lived a life filled with tragedy and abandonment, all by the age of nine. Denial had become her primary defense for survival. Fortunate to have a loving extended family available, Kelly was grateful to them for having given her the only love she'd ever known. But, at the same time, she was overwhelmed with guilt and confusion.

When Kelly was thirteen, her father came back from Austria and stayed with his parents and Kelly for a while. By now he'd been married four times. Later he moved to another town and married a seventeen-year-old girl. Kelly's grandfather died that summer, and she and her grandmother moved to be near her father.

After two years her father's marriage failed, and he asked Kelly to come live with him to take care of him. At fifteen she moved in and took over all the household responsibilities. She wanted to move in with her father, having idolized him in his absence. She perceived him as carefree and fun. It wasn't until later that she realized he was simply immature.

"I didn't idolize him because I expected him to provide stability. By that time I didn't know what stability was, and I didn't expect it."

Clearly, Kelly's development was being deeply affected by this constant moving to and from various family members. The fact that she felt loved by her grandparents was her lifeline. However, as a form of protection, Kelly detached from thinking about the past or the future. She learned to survive on a day-to-day basis. Flexibility and compliance were her strong suits.

"When my father retired from the military, he began developing this anxiety that he was having a heart attack. He wouldn't give up drinking and partying, but he was sure he was going to die any day. Many of my nights were spent sitting by his bed to make sure he didn't die. He wouldn't believe any of the doctors when they told him he was fine."

This is another example of Kelly's perception of herself as having to caretake.

"I took care of my dad because of my strong sense of responsibility. He was there, and therefore I had to be responsible."

Kelly believed that other people's expectations of her were not to be questioned. Compliance was the rule. Doing what others expected had become the key to her survival; she'd never found it safe to question others. She had learned to do what they wanted when they wanted. To do that, she'd had to minimize her own feelings and needs.

"As a teenager, I was probably quieter and more fearful of getting into trouble than most of my friends. I just didn't want to rock the boat. I

read a great deal. When my friends would ask me to do something, I almost always made up excuses not to go. I felt I needed to stay home and take care of my dad.''

Kelly's father's drinking grew progressively worse. He began dating a friend of Kelly's who was only twenty. They would drink together and fight, then Kelly's father would take it out on her. He'd tell her she couldn't do anything right and load her down with more and more chores, insisting that everything had to be perfect.

After she graduated from high school, Kelly finally had enough of her father's bullying, and she moved back in with her grandmother. Her only contact with her mother for eight years had been on the phone.

''I tried not to think about my mother. It was a relief when she wasn't in my life. My mother called me only when she was overdosed on something. Her calls were depressing and upsetting. I worried about her, but I was also very frightened of her.

''She'd tell me how much she loved me and that she wanted me to come and take care of her and the kids. But I knew I couldn't help her. She had become such a frightening entity to me. My life pivoted around her. She had all of this unspoken power.

''My grandparents, aunts and uncles, and dad just pretended my mother didn't exist. Yet at any moment she could and would come into my life, and suddenly there was chaos and crisis.''

The power Kelly's mother projected to Kelly was the power of chemical dependency in all addicted families. The chemically dependent person is the pivotal person in the family. Everybody has automatic knee-jerk responses and reactions to the moods and behavior of that person. Even when Kelly wasn't living at home, her mother still held the greatest power over her life.

Kelly was also describing a situation true for many COAs. There was no opportunity for her to feel intimacy with members of her family. Her mother only created trauma. Kelly does not remember any endearing times or receiving any sense of love from her mother. Although Kelly cared for her siblings, she was so busy being shunted from one family to the next that she didn't have the opportunity to feel connected with them outside of duty or obligation as the oldest sister.

Her attachment to her father was more out of gratitude to her father's parents. When he periodically invited Kelly into his life, she was expected to be his caretaker. In recovery, it was helpful for Kelly to learn to express gratitude without having to compromise herself.

When one has had little or no opportunity as a child to develop closeness with immediate family members, there is little in adulthood to base
a relationship on outside of duty, obligation, or family loyalty.

Adult Children often feel guilty about not loving their parents or siblings. But when so little love is offered from parents, and so little opportunity is available for sharing and playing with brothers and sisters, there
is no basis from which love can be developed. That is nothing to feel
guilty about.

One can still have a respectful relationship while working on developing
a more intimate one. But it needs to be based on respect—not guilt, fear,
duty, or other people's demands. While Kelly was emotionally distant
from her immediate family members, her grandparents made her feel
loved, and she reciprocated that love.

During her senior year in high school, Kelly met a young man named
Bill. They would marry the following year.

JEFF
Age: 33
Mother: Alcoholic
Father: Alcoholic
Birth Order: Youngest of four
    children
Raised: New England
Socioeconomic Status: Lower
    working class

The youngest of four children, Jeff was born near a small New England
mill town. His parents came from poor families, and he remembers there
were always financial problems. When they were young the kids lived on
a farm, but by the time he was school age, the family had moved into
town. Jeff's father was a hell raiser, and his drunken exploits were well
known in their town. He worked as a traveling salesman, and his mother
worked in the mill.

Jeff grew up in an environment of violence. Both parents were loud
and boisterous in their alcoholism. While his father was physically violent,
his mother was a mix of being verbally abusive and oblivious to the
children. Most of his memories are of fighting between his father and his
brothers or between his father and himself.

JEFF: "My father's way of punishing us was to lock up all of the kids in the closet. If we cried, he would take his belt and whip us after supper, and then he and Mom would leave. They always came home drunk and fighting."

Jeff remembers being scared more than anything else during his childhood. He saw both of his parents as frightening at all times. He doesn't remember feeling any love from either of them, although at times he recalls his mother being nice to him. He remembers her asking how school was going. But then it was as if she hadn't asked because she never listened to his response.

School meant time out from the horrors of home life. It was safer to be at school than at home.

"It was safe because people left me alone. I didn't have lots of friends, but I didn't want lots of friends. I had two guys I palled around with in grade school. I think they came from homes like mine. We hung around the playgrounds a lot and didn't spend time at any of our homes.

"When I had to be at home, I watched television if I could. I was pretty quiet. If someone wanted to change the channel on me, I let them. I liked to draw a lot, so I did that. I never showed my drawings to anyone, though. I thought they'd make fun of me.

"People in my family were always arguing. One brother liked to pick on me by calling me names. We weren't close, yet there was a sort of closeness in knowing that what was happening to us wasn't fair or right. We didn't talk about it, though—just sort of knew it."

Jeff's growing-up years depict a young boy who survived by being as quiet and inconspicuous as possible. He learned to not want, to detach himself from caring—all attempts to protect himself.

BETH

Age: 26
Mother: Alcoholic
Father: Alcoholic
Birth Order: Youngest of five
    children
Raised: Southeast
Socioeconomic Status: Middle class

Beth was the youngest of five children, all born within an eight-year span. Both her parents worked. Beth's father was in sales, and her mother worked in payroll for a major corporation. The family income was always steady, as both parents managed to hold on to their jobs for many years. But the five children were never left with baby-sitters. The older children took care of the younger ones.

BETH: *"Mom and Dad would begin to drink promptly upon arriving home—five-thirty, six P.M. Mom would drink while cooking. With the exception of Sundays, she would only cook dinner for Dad, she didn't cook for us. We could eat what was left over. We fed ourselves. I had lots of macaroni dinners out of boxes and frozen TV dinners. They drank through their meal and just kept on drinking until they either went to bed or fell asleep on the couch.*

"Most of the time I just stayed out of their way. Sometimes I would go into the television room where they were, but they'd just ignore me. It was as if you weren't there. I can remember trying to tell them things, just little things, and they wouldn't even hear you. It was like being invisible.

"Sometimes my dad might stop to play catch with me in the front yard for a few minutes when he'd come home from work. But once he went into the house—into the room where he and Mom drank—he became inaccessible. I can remember my mom would be nice to us if we were out of the house doing something like grocery shopping. But then once she was home and in that room, it was as if she could care less about us."

Like many children in alcoholic homes, Beth thought everyone lived as she did. Since both parents were preoccupied with drinking, she didn't have one to offset the other. Neither had she yet identified drinking as the source of the problem: it was simply a part of the norm that she was raised with. An abnormal experience became the "norm" in her family. With this neglect, the children tried to take care of themselves. They were forced to become self-sufficient.

If the children did anything to displease their parents, the parents smacked them.

"You never really knew what provoked them, but they were quick to raise their voices or hit you. I might be watching TV and suddenly Mom would pick a fight with me out of nowhere and hit me. Or you could be doing something that you'd done lots of times without their ever saying anything—like going out to play without telling them—and suddenly this time they noticed and you got hit for it. If you didn't do the dishes right, you could get hit. It never made sense. It just seemed to be related to their mood at the time. It was as if they just wanted to show you they were in charge. My parents only seemed to notice you if you were doing something wrong. They seemed to think that was what parents were supposed to do."

Children learn quickly that if they're only noticed when they're doing something wrong—then that is the way to get attention. Children prefer negative attention over no attention.

Another consequence of getting attention only when you're misbehaving is that you have to guess about whether or not you're doing things correctly when you're trying to behave. People don't acknowledge the good or the positive. This results in a lot of insecurity. For some children it reinforces any tendencies toward simply giving up and no longer trying to do things well or behave appropriately.

Beth was a lively, spirited youngster. She struggled to be a child when it wasn't okay to be one. The tendency to fight for what is properly one's own—being a child—is more likely to occur when older siblings make it possible for the younger children to act their age. Yet the older siblings are still children themselves. They all suffer from the neglect of their parents.

Though Beth's siblings may have tried to give her the maternal and/ or paternal attention she needed, they were still just children themselves.

"I can remember being such a brat just to get noticed. I was forever calling attention to myself by punching, yelling, throwing things. I would bite. I was forever the one who got into trouble. And I was always the one blamed for any problems, whether or not I was the cause, because I was the one most likely to be seen as the instigator."

All during her childhood Beth had very few friends. This didn't change until her high school years, and then those friends were drug abusers like herself. Beth is typical of many COAs in that the isolation and distance she experienced outside of the home was also felt inside.

"I've always felt alone. It made me want more and more attention. But the more I wanted it, the more it seemed my sisters and brothers ran from me. They would play these games of hide-and-seek—and I would hide and they'd run away. They made up stories to get rid of me. I was always being shut out of their rooms."

Feeling "picked on" by older siblings is not unusual for most children. But since Beth experienced her siblings as her only source of affection, the loss of their attention created an even greater void in her life than it would have had her parents been accessible.

Beth not only felt abandoned by her parents' noninvolvement in her life, but she felt alone all of her childhood.

"There I was with four siblings, with my sister Judy as my caretaker. But I forever felt alone. Being the youngest, it seemed as though none of them wanted me around. They would often deliberately leave me. When I wasn't looking, they would disappear—off to the streets or the playground."

Even at such a young age Beth was already experiencing that no matter how much attention she received, it was not going to be sufficient. This, coupled with the fact that she was not receiving the attention she needed, meant that feeling abandoned was perfectly valid.

Beth was easily scapegoated within her family. As a result, she learned to be an adjuster as well and experienced herself as invisible. The fact that she felt she'd lost her parents to their chemical dependency was made all the worse by being lost in a sea of brothers and sisters. Being a part of a large family exacerbated her feelings of invisibility.

"In junior high, I even lost my first name. Everybody started to call me by my last name. I was just one of a group of five children. I hated that. No one noticed me for being me."

Beth clearly felt that she, rather than her parents' chemical dependency, was thought to be the "family problem."

"I was often referred to as 'the brat' and told to keep my mouth shut. It was so confusing for me."

Despite the fact that Beth had two chemically dependent parents, they managed to "look good," so the abuse and neglect were not visible to outsiders. But Beth felt the abuse. She felt severe neglect. And she received no validation for her perceptions. Beth's acting-out behavior was a child's attempt to draw attention to the very thing that was so destructive to her, yet so hidden from view. Beth's confusion stemmed from struggling to trust her own valid perceptions when everyone else wanted to deny the reality.

While Beth perceives herself as having been a brat, she also identifies with being an adjusting child. She learned to adjust, to go along with the rules.

"The rules were: Don't question. Don't ask if you can get away with it. When you wanted attention and didn't get it, that was just the way it was. If they said you were going somewhere and you didn't, you had to accept it. If they said go pick a bag of weeds for no good reason, you went and picked the bag of weeds. If they hit you, you did nothing, and you felt nothing."

Beth was ambivalent about school. Part of her liked being there, and another part of her disliked it. Being a spirited child, she often found herself the teacher's pet.

"I liked that because the teachers would depend on me and have confidence in me. They would ask me to do things. I got good grades in spite of being absent a lot. Yet I also disliked school from my very first day. My first day of kindergarten, all the moms took their kids and stayed the whole day. I was the only one whose dad took her. He stayed twenty minutes and left. I clearly remember not liking school from that moment on."

Beth learned at a young age to defend against hurt. But school seemed to be the place where her pain was closest to the surface. She had wanted her mother there the first day of school. This is one of her most distinct childhood memories. She was aware of being different and on some level understood that there was something wrong. Unfortunately, when this is felt by a child as young as Beth, that "something wrong" usually implies there is something wrong with her. She was going to take her anger out on school.

As early as second grade, Beth began a history of truancy from school. She developed pneumonia and was out of school for two weeks. From then on she found herself staying home from school as frequently as two or three times a month.

"No one seemed to notice or care whether or not I was at school or at home. My parents didn't say much. They let me stay home, and they went off to work."

One of the areas where Beth excelled and strove to be noticed was athletics. In junior high she became active in various sports and did well.

"From two forty-five to five-fifteen every day, I played every sport there was. My parents could have come to the games on Saturdays, but they never did. I received lots of sports awards. But my parents wouldn't even come to the awards dinners. They said they were too tired or used other excuses. One of my brothers or sisters always went with me to the dinners.

"In high school, I gave up sports. I was sick of having my parents not notice me or my accomplishments. In my sophomore year, I got so depressed that I refused to go to school for three months. I actually got away with it. Finally I was sent to a psychologist. In order to stay out of school, the principal said I needed to see a psychologist. I felt I was winning. My parents were beginning to notice me.

"In the beginning my parents would drop me off for my appointments and leave, so I didn't go in. To make sure I went in they had to walk me to the door. But they didn't come to the sessions. So I wouldn't say anything in my sessions other than, 'I'm not the problem—they're the problem. I'm not the problem, they're the problem!' Then I would sit there. I knew their drinking was the cause of everything because by the time I was twelve I refused to keep pouring them their drinks. I wanted them to quit drinking, and I wanted them to come to my school events. I wanted some attention!

"I saw the psychologist four times. School ended without my going back to see him or back to class. The next September I was to go to a different school, so I went. I went back to school in the fall and became involved in sports again. My whole family came to my first game. But eventually they stopped coming, so I dropped sports once again."

Beth's plea for attention could not have been more blatant. It is not normal for a child to be truant from school for three months. It is not normal for a school psychologist to insist on seeing the child before the parents respond to the situation—unless there is severe dysfunction in a family. The inability for anyone to respond appropriately was profound in Beth's family.

In her desperation, Beth found that alcohol and marijuana provided solace.

"By ninth grade, I'd started to drink and to smoke marijuana. I was getting loaded before school. My school locker was like a liquor cabinet. I was also the one who forged other kids' notes from parents. I'd drink throughout the school day and party on weekends. I was still well liked because I was the class clown and made people laugh. I was also a good athlete. No matter how much I got in trouble, it was ignored."

Beth's story is an example of severe emotional neglect and abuse. Although it's more covert abuse than blatant physical violence, it can hardly be described as subtle.

In spite of the fact that Beth was behaving in a self-sabotaging manner during her high school days, she managed to graduate from high school, quickly got a full-time secretarial job, and was married by age twenty.

JAMES
Age: 36
Mother: Chemically Dependent
Father: Alcoholic
Birth Order: Youngest of two boys
Raised: Midwest
Socioeconomic Status: Middle class

James's father worked in the automobile industry, rarely missing work even though he was actively chemically dependent. James's mother worked to put his father through college and then quit working when James was born and remained a housewife.

James said that both of his parents had been drinking ever since he can remember.

JAMES: "I used to think it was natural and normal to see them with beer in their hands all the time. I didn't realize that alcohol played such an important part in their lives until I was in my twenties. I just thought we did things like bowling or picnics because they liked to, not because alcohol was easily accessible. Another thing that confused the situation was that my mother's father was an alcoholic, but the family talked about it openly. He literally could not stop drinking once he started. So with that stereotype, I didn't recognize my parents' alcoholism."

James describes the family setting as one of fear.

"The closer it came for Dad to get home from work, the more the tension grew. Mom would usually take a couple of phenobarbitals to 'ready' herself. We would turn off the music or the television, and we would wait. Mom would have his drink ready as he walked in the door. Dad would drink it down, change clothes, have another, or two, eat dinner, have another, and then, if we were lucky, fall asleep.

"Mom's usage would begin in the afternoon, though. She'd combine tranquilizers with her drinks to 'steady her nerves.'

"Dad wasn't particularly violent. He was just sarcastic, negative, critical, and very unpredictable. Usually after Mom had a few drinks after dinner, she would start on him to wake up and go to bed. They would fight and carry on until she either went to bed without him, leaving him passed out on the couch, or he'd get up and stumble to bed. Sometimes she would provoke him to the point where he'd lash out and hit her—but that was infrequent."

James is like many COAs who have two chemically dependent parents. He reacts more to the parent whose drinking is more blatant or whose behavior is more abusive. In his case that was his dad. The family life appeared to revolve around his father, whereas in Jan's case, which we'll discuss next, the disruption revolved around her mother. Jan's father's progression was slower than her mother's, and he was much more functional in his chemical dependency. In James's situation, his mother and father may have been close in the progression of their disease, but between his dad's more critical personality and his mother's dependency upon prescription pills, the mother's addiction is more subtle. James's mother sets herself up as victim and martyr, needing pills to cope with her husband—all the while continuing to feed her own addiction.

The "Don't talk" rule was learned quickly in James's family. It was accepted as a way of life.

"My brother and I never talked about what was going on at home much. We've both had a hard time trusting and believing that others would be there for us.

"By the time I was in high school my father had disowned my brother for going to a Christian college. Dad thought he was a religious nut because he wanted to be in a caring and Christian environment at college. I kept changing sides, understanding my brother's needs but also angry at him because he got to get out of the house. My loyalties were confused. I heard my father's comments on a daily basis about my brother. Even after deciding to help him financially, Dad was unbearable. I knew that if he spoke of my brother that way, he had to have similar thoughts

about me. I decided then never to ask him for anything. I never wanted him to feel that way about me."

James sought escape and relief by becoming involved in school activities.

"I was very involved in school. I was a good student and liked by my teachers. I was a good athlete and usually one of the best players. I was a particularly good tennis player, very competitive. I was befriended by two coaches, which also made me feel special. It didn't make me feel more special than the other guys, but it did make me feel that I had some value to someone since I didn't feel that way at home.

"Neither of my parents came to school open houses or those special nights where parents were invited at the beginning of the school year, let alone to my ball games or tennis matches. I can actually remember thinking how weird it was to have other kids' parents there at school, meddling and intruding in what I thought was the kids' business."

The indifference James endured from his parents—particularly with respect to his sports activities—forced him to reframe his perception of what normal parent/child interactions might be. This is why he saw other kids' parents as meddling. In order for children in these situations to hang on to any sense of their worth, they must have low or even no expectations of their parents.

"By late high school my older brother was encouraging me to get out of the house as much as I could. He had great friends and saw that I was clearly making poor choices. I was growing pot in the backyard, enjoying drug-using friends, and life was pretty miserable. But I didn't know anything else."

James talks about school and athletics positively. Yet although many COAs are able to perform well in school and to be leaders in school activities, the added trauma of having two alcoholic parents, compared with only one alcoholic parent, interferes with these children's ability to maintain a source of satisfaction or esteem through school. Both James and Beth clearly demonstrate this by turning away from the positive attention they received in school to alcohol and drugs and, in Beth's case, truancy.

JAN
Age: 33
Mother: Alcoholic
Father: Alcoholic
Birth Order: Only child
Raised: Midwest
Socioeconomic Status: Upper
    middle class

Jan grew up in a large midwestern city, the only child in a home with two alcoholic parents. Her father was a physician, and although her mother had teaching credentials, she had never worked.

Jan remembers feeling safe and clearly remembers acts of affection between her parents until she was in her second year of school. Jan said school was always very difficult for her. The kids teased her, and she cried a lot. The teachers were always reprimanding her for disrupting class with her incessant need to talk to her neighbors in the classroom.

By this point Jan's mother was getting drunk on holidays and weekends. Jan remembers cold dinners and everyone trying to act normal.

JAN: *"Mom would pass out on her chair or bed. Dad and I would eat silently. Then he and I would go for a walk and he'd tell me mom was sick and didn't mean to do the things she did. He promised it would get better. We had a lot of those walks. I cried at first, but I stopped once I began to realize things were going to continue the way they were."*

Jan, like many Children of Alcoholics, suffered from broken promises.

"I was having lots of problems making and keeping friends in school and in our neighborhood. When Mom was drinking, she was incoherent; and when she was sober, she would embarrass me. She would call the other kids' mothers and harass them to make their kids stop picking on me. But this only encouraged them to do it more. My dad told me he'd had similar problems when he was little. He told me I marched to a different drummer and someday the other kids would all follow my lead. He also encouraged me to fight back when the boys teased or hit me at school. I did—and I got sent to the principal's office a lot.

"Upper grade school was like one dark, pain-filled tunnel in my mind.

Mom got worse. Now she was drinking every day and every night. She was never sober and wouldn't eat. She was too drunk to leave the house, so a local liquor store made daily deliveries. She was drinking a fifth of gin straight by ten-thirty A.M. every day. Both Dad and I took to watering down her bottles.

"By late elementary school, Dad was away in the evenings, supposedly working, and I was left at home alone with Mom at night. The good nights were when she'd stay passed out all night. Most often, though, she'd wake up in a rage, screaming and swearing at Dad and me for hiding her booze. I was terrified night after night, wishing there was a lock on my bedroom door.

"I don't know if Dad became alcoholic then or if he'd always been. I think I chose to ignore some of the crazy things he did because I was dependent on him for my survival. At least he was sane and would take me to school and fix dinner for me. I fixed my own breakfast and lunch."

Jan's father was in the earlier stages of his disease compared with her mother. He was still able to provide some of the basic parenting that Jan needed in her very early years. But, eventually, the progression of his disease got so bad that he could no longer be there for her.

"By junior high, things had gone from bad to worse. I rode my bike home crying most days. I was overwhelmed. Life was bleak at best, terrifying at worst—to be trudged through, with my head down, ready to jump in case someone came after me.

"Three things kept me sane: my love of horses, my talent for writing, and food. I had loved horses and read horse stories since I could read. My room was plastered with pictures and drawings of horses, and I dreamed of owning my own horse. My sixth-grade teacher recognized I had a talent for writing and encouraged me."

Like many COAs, Jan actively sought out refuge and found safety in animals. Nearly any Child of an Alcoholic who had animals will speak of the significant role a dog, cat, rabbit, or, in this case, horse, was able to play. Although Jan did not actually have a horse, her ability to fantasize about, write, and draw them gave her an escape that brought her comfort. The type of animal one finds comfort in at times may be an indicator of a particular need. Horses offer a symbolic opportunity to ride away from all of one's problems. Animals don't abandon you. Animals don't let you down. Animals offer unconditional love.

Jan is also like many others in choosing the solitary refuge of writing. For her, writing was a wonderful way to get her feelings out, to have dreams, to feel connected with something other than the pain in her life. It was also a way to draw positive attention to herself.

Children choose a variety of escapes. With COAs these escapes are often socially acceptable, such as school activities, participation with animals, writing, or reading. This is a reflection of their need for safety. These escapes provide time-out periods from other people and from having to react to trauma. Being involved with school activities or, as in Jan's case, with writing is, simultaneously, an escape and a way to get positive attention.

"By the fourth grade, though, I was preoccupied with food. I told myself in a proud way that I was addicted to Coca-Cola, just like Mom was addicted to booze. I was right."

Like many other children in pain, at an early age Jan turned to a substance for solace—food by her grade school years and alcohol by her latter teenage years.

When Jan was twelve her parents divorced, and she went to live with her father. When she was thirteen her mother died, alone in an apartment, of cirrhosis of the liver and starvation. Jan says she missed a week of school on account of the death.

"Then things got back to 'normal.' Dad worked, came home long enough to cook dinner, and then went back to work or out drinking. I told him he was an alcoholic, and he told me I was distraught over Mom's death and couldn't perceive reality."

An important adult in Jan's life denies her perception, denies her reality. This makes it very difficult for Jan to trust others and to trust herself.

It was not possible for Jan to grieve over her mother's death. She had never learned how to feel safe with her feelings. She didn't have people in her life who were able to offer her support, guidance, and a safe setting in which to be a thirteen-year-old girl whose mother had just died. As she said, she missed a week of school and "then things went back to normal."

Going back to normal meant going back to living in a vacuum—an emptiness. Jan was a young girl left to raise herself. This was nothing new for her. In essence she'd been doing that when both of her parents were alive and present. Jan had needed to detach herself emotionally from her surroundings. It's possible she didn't experience a sense of loss. For Jan, and for most COAs, the experience of loss and grief becomes a delayed response, one to be dealt with in adulthood.

For the next four years Jan was in an all-girls' college prep school and doing well academically. Coming "home" to visit meant sleeping overnight on a couch at her father's girlfriends' apartments. She saw less and less of her father.

Although Jan's relationship with her father was emotionally distant, when they were together he made her his confidante. However, her father made all the decisions regarding her schooling, and twice in the next few years he would suddenly pull her out and send her to a "better school" for her own good. She was compliant and did what her father dictated. But the toll of being so discounted throughout her life began showing up in her promiscuous behavior and drinking.

Special Issues for the ACOA with Two Chemically Dependent Parents

ABANDONMENT AND NEGLECT

Children in alcoholic homes experience a strong sense of abandonment, of having no one available to them. Abandonment can be either physical or emotional.

Physical abandonment means that one's physical needs are not consistently attended to. Examples are when a child repetitively misses meals, is left alone for hours or days, or is without adequate supervision. Children need appropriate clothing, physical warmth, food, and housing. They need protection from those who would hurt them physically and emotionally.

Emotional abandonment occurs when a child's emotional needs are not consistently attended to—when the primary caretaker(s) is not available emotionally. Although physical survival needs may be met, there is little or no nurturing, hugging, or emotional intimacy between the parent and the child.

Children need to be told that they are loved, they need caretakers who spend time playing and talking with them. They need parents to have age-appropriate expectations. The underlying messages for both emotional and physical abandonment are the same: "You are not of value." "You are not wanted." "You are in the way."

When both parents are chemically dependent, the child experiences even greater abandonment because neither parent is physically or emotionally available. These children are left to fend for themselves and often suffer from severe neglect. They may have to fix their own meals and take care of their own physical needs. They have no one to monitor their progress in school, to offer direction or guidance. The older children have to take care of the younger children, assuming a burden of responsibility far beyond their years. Although these older siblings are often praised for their maturity, the situation is still one of children raising children. There are no healthy adult resources available.

Beth's sense of abandonment and neglect grew out of her parents' complete indifference to her existence.

BETH: *"When my parents were gone, they would never leave us with a sitter. The oldest sister or brother, whoever was there, would look after me. One time, my parents went away for the weekend and left my sixteen-year-old sister in charge. But my sister went out and got in trouble with the police. When the police called my parents, they didn't even come home right away."*

Beth felt as if her parents were never there for her. Her relationship with her parents made it hard for her to establish relationships with other adults.

"I was mostly afraid of my friends' parents. I didn't know how to act in front of them. That worried me. But there was one friend I liked to stay overnight with. Her father would come in and give us each a good-night kiss. That was one of the reasons I liked going there—I wanted my kiss good night.

"There were good things in my childhood, too. But they mostly involved people other than my family, such as going camping with friends or playing with a friend's toy. My fun experiences were with other families. My parents didn't care where we were going or when we were coming back."

One of the ways that parents show they care about their children is by knowing where their children are and by setting limits. That did not occur for Beth. Not only did she feel neglected by her parents, but she felt the pain of being abandoned by her sisters and brothers as well.

"I didn't know how to get anyone to pay attention to me. My brothers and sisters were forever shutting their doors to keep me out, telling me to go away. No matter what I did it was wrong."

Beth felt very alone in her life. She'd been abandoned by her parents, and she couldn't get her parental needs met by siblings. She had few friends in school. Alcohol and drugs were to become a way out. Yet her "little child" found escape in cartoons.

"I was still watching TV cartoons all the way through high school. Cartoons were a safe escape for me."

Beth experienced grave neglect of her basic physical needs.

"We never had the basics. We never had enough underwear, socks, pajamas. We never had slippers or robes. There was this major sense of being without. No one told us how to keep clean, or how often. No one told us what to wear.

"One time the school called my parents to have them pick my sister up and bathe her. Another time one of my sisters became embarrassed when a friend realized she didn't change her underwear. At age sixteen, my sister told all of us we were to change our underwear. But we didn't even have enough for all of us to change!

"We tried so hard. We did our own laundry and didn't know how. When it came time to shop for school clothes, my mom would give us a little bit of money, and we'd ride our bikes to the store and shop by ourselves. But then we didn't have anyplace to put things so they'd stay nice. We didn't have any space that was our own. I had nothing that I felt was truly mine. It could be borrowed, stolen, or wrecked at any time."

The family's dysfunction was so extreme that not only was Beth lost and confused about basic hygiene, none of her siblings were aware of the most basic standards of cleanliness.

Beth is an example of a child clearly suffering from abandonment and neglect and blatantly screaming for help. She had three-month absences from school. By the ninth grade she was drinking and using daily. However, she was also drawing positive attention to herself through her excellence in sports. Yet she was still ignored by her parents, and potentially helping adults did not recognize or address the needs of a child in crisis.

Jeff consciously came to tolerate neglect.

JEFF: *"I really didn't question all the drinking because I had to spend so much time responding to the abuse. The neglect was okay—at least then they weren't deliberately hurting you. We had food in the house, but it was on a 'first come, first served' basis. That meant I often went hungry because there was never enough food for us. We'd just grab from the stove and take it anywhere in the house. We didn't really eat together. We fixed a lot of our own meals. But sometimes if our parents were really angry with us, or were really drunk, we didn't eat at all.*

Jeff had come to tolerate being ignored as well. In his life, it was safer than being noticed.

"I can remember a teacher in junior high school paying attention to me. It made me nervous. I couldn't figure out why. Had I done something wrong? I finally realized he just liked me, but I was always nervous around him, always thinking that I was going to get into trouble."

Jan clearly speaks to abandonment when she describes staying at home at night with her mother, who would pass out and wake up only long enough to fly into rages. Her mother was not there to attend to any of her needs. She was not there to offer Jan physical protection, emotional or social support, or to attend to Jan's academic needs. Jan was there to attend to her mother's needs. This dynamic taught Jan that she was only valued by others when she attended to them and was willing to negate her own needs.

Clearly, Jan's father offered more support than her mother. Jan lived with him after the divorce. He provided dinner for her. This may seem like very little, considering the circumstances. Nonetheless, he might just as easily have left Jan with her mother.

While Jan's father maintained some fragments of the parenting role, attending to her physical and educational needs, he was not able to provide her with the proper living arrangements or the parenting model she needed. As his drinking escalated into his priority and preoccupation, he became physically unavailable to Jan, leaving her alone with her drunken mother nearly every evening of her early growing-up years. That is neglect.

Yet when one alcoholic parent is more functional than the other, and gives the child more than the other parent (in Jan's case her father was her lifeline, although a weak one), it is difficult for the child with two alcoholic parents to recognize the alcoholism of the more functional parent.

The neglect and sense of loss that children with two chemically dependent parents suffer is often made worse by chronic moving. The family environment is already disruptive and unpredictable because of the parents' dependence on drugs and alcohol. When the parents are unable to provide a consistent and stable home environment, the child's need for stability is exacerbated. Chronic moving forces children to abandon the familiar for the unknown, destroying any sense of security they may have had.

In Kelly's childhood she was constantly being abandoned, both physically and emotionally. Her mother's chemical addiction left Kelly completely on her own. She was shuttled back and forth from one relative's home to the next. When Kelly was only a toddler, her parents divorced. Her father then moved out of the country, abandoning her to an unpredictable and unsafe environment.

Kelly spent her childhood moving from her mother's house to her father's and also being shuttled between her maternal and paternal grandparents. Even if surrogate parents do provide a happier and saner environment, it doesn't compensate children for feelings of abandonment by their birth parents.

When Kelly did live with her mother, the woman was unable to provide the basics of healthy parenting. As the oldest child, Kelly was left to be the sole caretaker of the younger children. She fixed meals, cleaned the house, and saw that they were taken care of. When her mother remarried another alcoholic, the two would go drinking at night, leaving the children alone.

KELLY: "I'd leave in the morning to go to school and come home to a rancid-smelling house. My mother would be asleep, and the kids would be dirty and hungry. I'd wake her up and then take the kids out to play. When we'd come back, my mother would be making something for dinner, but only because my stepfather would be coming home and he'd want something to eat."

James describes neglect in his family when he talks about how his parents ignored childhood illnesses. He said his brother was often seriously ill as a child, often with infections that were the result of previous illnesses being ignored.

JAMES: "They were so preoccupied with their drinking that they were too busy to take either of us to a doctor until it was an emergency. It often became an emergency for my brother. He ended up with rheumatic fever, high blood pressure, and having a kidney removed, all before he was eighteen."

Neglect is a form of abuse. There is a tendency for Adult Children to negate and deny the hurt so often by saying, "But it wasn't that bad—it could have been worse," as a defense against the pain. Yes, it's possible it could have been worse, but that does not take away the loss and trauma.

VIOLENCE

In addition to feeling abandoned and neglected, children with two chemically dependent parents are also more likely to suffer physical violence.

When both parents are drunk, there is more potential for violence within the home. The parents fight with each other, and they may fight physically with the children, who may in turn fight among themselves. The violence adds to the chaos of the home, creating fear and anger within the children. The home becomes a ''war zone'' in which the combatants may lash out at any time.

It has long been understood that children who witness violence become as traumatized as, or even more so than, those who are the direct recipients of violence. Kelly was not beaten as a child, but her brother was. The violence was just as devastating to her because of her profound sense of helplessness.

KELLY: *"They beat my oldest brother all the time. He didn't breathe right, and he was a living reminder of something bad to both my mother and stepfather. They used belts on him until he had welts. Once they started, they were crazed. Many times I had to drag my mother away from him. My sister and littlest brother were also mistreated, but not that badly.*

"My parents never touched me. I was the light of our whole family life. I think they knew that because of my relationship with my grandparents there would be hell to pay if anything ever happened to me."

The unpredictability of the two chemically dependent parents sets up an atmosphere of terror. The children live in fear of the violence, never knowing when it is going to explode again.

BETH: *"If we got out of line, Mom would pull us by the hair, pull our pants down, and hit us. She would hit anywhere she could get you. I was also afraid of my dad hitting us. I used to spy on my father and avoid going into any room he happened to be in. My older brothers and sisters were hit more than I was. I remember one of my older brothers saying to my father, 'Hit me. I'm bigger.'*

"I was terrified whenever my father would yell at me. He would yell and point his finger in my face. As a child, I had a frequently recurring dream that a giant was chasing me. I would be so scared that I would run to my parents. But they always gave me to the giant.

"We never had our own space, never had our own rooms. Our rooms were pigpens. Your own space was never clearly defined. So someone was always invading someone else's territory—and fighting would ensue. We slapped, slugged, and punched. We pulled hair. We would bite each other. My one sister had a scar for years from my biting her. If anybody ever tried to separate me from a fight, my brother or sister were always

given the benefit of the doubt. I was perceived as the 'troublemaker.' I once gave my sister a fat lip, and my parents didn't even respond to it. They completely ignored it.''

Abuse often takes the form of verbal criticism. Parents tease their children in a manner that rapidly escalates into abusive criticism. This becomes a permanent reference for how children perceive themselves. They learn: "No matter what I do, it's never good enough."

"My parents would become rude and hostile. My father would tease me and make inappropriate sexual remarks like 'Did you get laid today?' Or he'd call me a 'bitch.' I was always really embarrassed and hurt. Why were they doing this? Then I'd feel angry, but that didn't do any good, so I'd just try to forget it.''

For children such as Beth, being angry is healthy. Because of her anger, she was not as quick as others to move into helplessness. Many children have their spirits broken at such a young age that helplessness plagues them all through their lives. Staying aware of the anger fights the helplessness. Yet Beth was still a child, and it was difficult to maintain pure anger. It became mixed with powerlessness and fear.

When Kelly was a teenager, her father's drinking became worse, and he became more and more critical.

KELLY: *"He was becoming especially hard to handle. I walked on eggs all the time. One day he started yelling at me because he didn't think his underwear was white enough. On a scale of one to ten, my self-confidence was a one.*

"When I was learning how to drive, perfection was the name of the game. If I did something wrong while I was driving, my father would backhand me in the mouth. Needless to say, it wasn't easy to drive with tears, frustration, and anger. I had four learner's permits by the time I was eighteen. I was almost twenty-two before I had enough courage to get my license, and I was twenty-seven before I could drive on the freeway.''

Jeff and Jan describe what are thought of as more devastating forms of physical abuse.

JEFF: *"When Saturday came around, our home would turn into a nightmare. My parents went out on Saturday nights, and they would get totally drunk. As soon as they got home they would begin to fight. My father would beat on my mother without mercy. Her groans and her begging him to stop would be unbearable. My sisters and brother and I would yell down the stairs, pleading with them to stop. My parents would then use our pleading as a way to divide our allegiance between each other. We would feel even more isolated then. The yelling and abuse would go on for hours.*

"We always dreaded Sunday morning. We never knew what Mother would look like. Would she be alive? What would the apartment look like? It was always a miserable mess. But when things got really bad, we would have to call my aunt, who was a nurse, to come and 'doctor' Mother so she would be presentable for work. I couldn't understand why my aunt never said a word about the violence taking place in our house. Once the immediate crisis was over, it was as if nothing had ever happened."

Very often the "Don't talk" rule extends outside of the immediate family as well. It is absolutely crazy making for children when others know of the abuse and do so little to intervene. This feeds the helplessness, powerlessness, and rage of the child.

Jan vividly remembers hearing her parents' physical fights and her mom's inadvertent self-abuse. She says she would often be awakened from a sound sleep by her mother screaming at her father.

JAN: "They would scuffle, and I would hear drunken footfalls and the sounds of bodies bumping into walls. She would scratch and scream at him. He would slap her. I could hear punching. Then, in time, her screams got weaker, they became pleadings, and eventually stopped.

"The next day, Dad would always tell me nothing happened. He hadn't beaten Mom. He would tell me I imagined the whole thing. Everything was fine. But I would find the nightgown she had been wearing ripped apart and stuffed away, and other clues to what had really gone on. Yet I'd still doubt my own perceptions of reality when my father told me I was wrong. Every time these things would happen, he'd tell me the same thing."

Being told your perceptions are wrong when the proof that you're right is clearly available adds to the craziness of a child's life. Jan was confused by what her father told her; after all, he was a person who loved her. He was a physician, so he should be smart. He was older, therefore he was supposed to be smarter. Eventually Jan learned to keep her thoughts to herself. In time, she tried not to even hear any of her own thoughts about a situation. That is difficult when the violence is so blatant, but it's necessary when you're a child trying to survive.

"We became late night pajama regulars at the local hospital's emergency ward. For instance, one night Mom dropped a gin bottle on her foot and

sliced one of her tendons. Another time she was washing dishes drunk, broke a glass, and sliced a tendon in her arm. Another night she threw a salt shaker at Dad, got him in the forehead, and he needed stitches.

"Once when I was alone with Mom, she fell through the window and was lying there in blood and broken glass, half on the patio, half in the family room. I phoned Dad and he yelled at me to pull her in from the window so she wouldn't fall farther and slice herself in half.

"I got down on my hands and knees in the broken glass. I stuck myself through the hole she'd fallen through and moved enough glass away from her so I could pull her inside without cutting her up too badly. Then I cleaned her off and waited for Dad."

So often outsiders who hear such stories ask, "What happened then?" Nothing happens then. Nothing. Life goes on, and the kids are supposed to ignore it. But something does occur—the spirit is deadened. Children learn to repress their fears, sadness, anger, and humiliation. Yet somewhere in their bodies the depth of those experiences and feelings remain, typically dictating how they will perceive and respond to themselves and others. They walk through life conditioned by years of helplessness and powerlessness, their hopes deadened.

While the others in this chapter experienced physical abuse and neglect, James experienced a more subtle form of sexual abuse.

JAMES: *"Somewhere down the line I became my mother's confidant. She would talk to me about her problems with my dad. I was the listening post she'd lean on when she had any sense about her and was legitimately worried. She didn't have any friends. She'd even talk to me about her sex life. I believed that my mother needed me to take care of her emotionally. I felt like her parent. I did resent her putting her own needs first, but I wasn't able to talk to her. When she'd talk sexually, I never knew what to say. I don't think she realized I was just a kid."*

In her alcoholism, it's probable that James's mother could no longer distinguish appropriate parent/child boundaries. She may have talked with James explicitly about her sexual behavior without once considering the ramifications and the effects that kind of discussion would have on her son.

Such behavior is abusive in a child's development. Yet offenders, whether overt or covert, never consider the effects on the victim. James said that he never thought his mother was trying to embarrass him or to approach him physically. He truly accepted that she had taken him on as her friend and confidant and had forgotten that he was a teenage child, let alone her son.

But James's innocence was robbed. His childhood and adolescence were violated. He was left with information and feelings that were difficult for him to sort out.

James also drank a lot with his mother.

"We would go to lunch and be best friends."

This was an emotionally incestuous relationship. Children need their parents to maintain a parent-to-child relationship, not a peer relationship. Having lunch with your children and enjoying them as they develop into adults is normal and healthy. But it is abusive to use them as personal friends and to discuss intimate areas of your life with them. That only serves to confuse, intimidate, and create embarrassment or shame in children.

Abuse and neglect create feelings of hopelessness in children. They grow up with little or no sense of self-esteem, never having felt safe, nurtured, or loved. The burden of responsibility that they carry gives them a feeling that they will never be able to live up to what is expected of them, never be able to do all that needs to be done. They are easily overwhelmed by feelings of inadequacy and powerlessness. This sets up an even stronger possibility that the child will seek to numb the pain through alcohol and other drugs. It also makes recovery a very slow and difficult process.

SELF-SUFFICIENCY

With no one to take care of them, COAs with two chemically dependent parents develop an incredible drive to be self-sufficient. If neither parent is able to provide for the child, the need becomes one of actual physical survival. Although the child may take on different roles in terms of the family dynamics, such as adjuster or scapegoat, the need to take care of one's self is critical.

BETH: *"Every one of our friends thought that we had the best parents because we could do anything we wanted. We didn't have to ask for anything. We were very self-sufficient. My parents never taught us how to dress, never taught us how to bathe. We did our own laundry. As soon as you were big enough to reach over a washing machine, you began to do your own laundry. The house was a pigpen. There was no etiquette, no sense of what was proper and what wasn't."*

Beth's process can be described as "learning self-sufficiency in an insufficient way." Like many young COAs, she had to make assumptions about how to do things without feedback and/or problem-solving assistance from adults. Beth learned by guessing or from other children who had to learn from their own experiences. Most COAs develop skills based on an emotional foundation of insecurity.

"If we were sick, we just took care of ourselves. Sometimes we'd ask an older brother or sister to take care of us. My parents would even yell at us when we were sick and tell us to call the doctor ourselves. We'd make our own appointments and then ride our bicycles to the doctor or to the dentist.

"When I was in second grade, I got very sick and missed two weeks of school. Every night for two weeks my ten-year-old sister would set her alarm for midnight to give me my medicine. She also brought me my homework, did it with me, and took it back to school."

Since her mother and father were unable to care for her, Kelly not only had to be self-sufficient, she had to take on the responsibility of the younger children in the home as well.

KELLY: "I was five when my brother was born. He became my sole responsibility. I was his mother. Then my sister was born when I was six. I did literally everything in the house. I cleaned, cooked, washed, took care of the kids, took care of my mother, and waited hand and foot on my stepfather.

"After I moved in with my father, my life didn't change much. I went to school, did all the cooking, cleaning, washing, and ironing. Plus I had to keep my grades up to the level he expected. I was his housekeeper, baby-sitter, nursemaid, and whatever else he needed."

Jeff says that all four of his brothers were pretty self-sufficient.

JEFF: "We got up and put our clothes on, fed ourselves, and went to school. I got a job working in a stockroom as soon as I could. It gave me money of my own to buy clothes and go to the movies and some school events. I wanted to be around other kids, but I was always on the fringes. Yet I'd still go to things."

Jeff did what many COAs do, he diminished his needs.

"I needed very little. What I did need I could manage to get. I would quietly go about taking care of myself.

"I didn't think of it as guilt at the time, but now I know I had a lot of

guilt in my childhood years. I felt as if I were responsible for all the bad feelings. Every time my parents looked at me, it seemed they didn't like something I'd done or how I looked. I felt so bad about myself. My way of coping was by trying to separate myself from others, which probably has a lot to do with my still being so quiet around others. I have this fear that I'll always do the wrong thing. The irony is, I don't do anything, wrong or right.''

It's easy to understand why Jeff needed to diminish his needs in order to protect himself. But in the long run he will grow up not being able to identify his needs and not getting them met. This leads to a lot of depression.

James is a person who became self-sufficient without feeling he also had to be overly responsible. Many Children of Alcoholics who become self-sufficient also become primary caretakers for siblings and parents. They become the "responsible child" I've written about in my previous books.

However, the self-sufficient child may or may not take on that level of responsibility. Often, children who have two chemically dependent parents only take responsibility for themselves. This is because the chaos and unpredictability of the parents sabotages the child's attempts to control others or the environment.

James's self-sufficiency became his way of life. He quickly and quietly learned to accept that others weren't going to take care of him. Unfortunately, because self-sufficiency was one of the few areas in which he could develop self-worth, he often finds that he chastises himself when he can't do things by himself.

JAMES: "When my brother was sick it was an important time for me because I needed to take on additional responsibilities. I can remember one of these crises when I was eleven. I distinctly felt a sense of pride in being able to deny my own needs and be strong because my parents didn't need my adding any additional stress in their lives. So I was never sick, or at least I never told them when I was. I stayed away as much as possible, and when I was home I was very quiet. Yet I had a lot of guilt with this around my brother. I felt guilty because he was always sick, and I was always healthy.''

While Jan's self-sufficiency helped her to survive, it also kept her in isolation. She dressed herself, kept her clothes clean, made her breakfast and lunch. She entertained herself and found escape in her love of horses and in writing. As it is for so many others, she felt there was no choice.

JAN: "I felt as if I was living in hell every day and that there was no escape. There were no adults who wanted to listen or were in a position to help. My mom's family blamed Dad and myself for Mom's drinking, and Dad's side of the family lived four hundred miles away.

"At school I became an achieving student, but I didn't trust any of the adults there. I don't think any of them even noticed that anything was wrong. Interestingly, looking back at the private school I was in, the people there were busy solving their internal political problems and keeping the wealthy parishioners happy. It would have been a shameful disgrace for them to acknowledge that one of the children in their expensive school was living in an alcoholic home. I believe this is true because I did talk about what was going on at home to teachers and to other kids, but nobody ever tried to help. Of course, Dad had the 'Don't talk' rule going anyway, so I was risking punishment from him each time I told someone what was going on."

After her mother died, Jan's high school years meant continuing to raise herself and not drawing any attention to herself as a child in need. When she lost her mother to a very stigmatizing illness—cirrhosis of the liver—she simply "missed a week of school and things got back to normal." "Normal" meant Jan got ignored, and her grief had to go on hold for many years—until she was an adult.

After her recovery from chemical dependency and bulimia, Jan finally began a process where it became emotionally safe for her to grieve. First she needed to grieve for the loss of the relationship with her mother when she was living. Then she had to face the loss of her mother through death.

Life Stories: Adulthood and Recovery

KELLY
Age: 44
Partner Status: Married, one
    daughter
Occupation: Floral Designer
Recovery Process: On her own

Kelly met Bill while she was in high school. He was a handsome, quiet man who loved her but was startled by her family situation. They married within a year of her graduation from high school. This was earlier than they might otherwise have married, but they did it to get Kelly out of her chaotic and unreasonable family situation. She had a baby the following year and was establishing a good relationship with her husband.

However, when Kelly was twenty her mother managed to get her phone number and called. Kelly hadn't seen her mother for ten years, but once again her mother wanted something from her—she wanted her to take care of her oldest brother, who was in very bad shape.

KELLY: *"My mother wanted us to straighten out my brother's life. I hadn't seen him for ten years, either, and when he arrived he was a mental mess. He'd lived with pain, suffering, and beatings; and he didn't even have me to help him through. We did what we could, but he will never really be all right. I always felt responsible, and therefore I was always trying to help.*

"Then my mother decided to come for a visit. I was panicked. It brought everything back—nightmares, insecurity. I was so worried. When she came, all was well for a couple of weeks. Then one morning I walked into the kitchen and found her stoned. My worst fears had come true. It started us on another roller coaster—drug overdoses, heavy drinking, three suicide attempts. We had to make my grandparents come and get her. She and my brother got an apartment close by. It took a year for them to move away. One year of hell. There was no peace for any of us.

"My older brothers and sisters had been sent to a VFW home. Why couldn't I have taken care of all of them? I lived with such terrible guilt all the time. My aunt helped me get my feelings under control. She helped me to see that my first responsibility was to my husband and baby. I had to make sure that nothing like this would ever happen to me or to my family.

"Something my aunt told me has always stuck with me: 'There but for the grace of God go I.' I have always lived with the guilt that I couldn't help the ones I loved. But I knew I had to do all I could to make sure that I didn't fall into the same trap. I knew God was protecting me, but I also knew I had to help, too. So I don't drink, except on rare occasions, and then I just have fun-type drinks. I don't take drugs. They scare me to death."

With the love and support of her husband and daughter, Kelly began to feel happier and more emotionally secure. Her parents were both trying to put demands on her, but she was beginning to focus on her own needs and those of her own family.

"The guilt feelings were lessening, and I was beginning to feel almost normal."

When Kelly wasn't interacting with her mother, father, and siblings, she felt fine. Although she continued to live her life on a more or less day-to-day basis, as she had learned as a child, now she had a partner whom she could trust, someone who brought stability and security to her life. She has not sought therapy or an active recovery program, but she has surrounded herself with kind, caring, and appropriate people. By putting herself in a nontoxic environment, she began to experience a thawing-out process. Kelly has now learned to depend on others, to become more aware of her feelings, to set limits for herself, and to define healthy values for relationships and for the parenting of her child.

"Eventually I was able to go back to visit my family. I was scared because I felt that somehow they could make me stay there. My husband and daughter were my life rafts. We stayed with my grandmother. I always feel safe with her, even when my mom is there.

"It took me another ten years to go back after that. Then, out of love for my grandmother, we've gone every year for the past four."

Five years ago Kelly's father became seriously ill. She and her husband spent the next three months visiting him almost every day.

"He was so helpless. I couldn't help wanting to make his last days the best I could. I did it for him because I couldn't stand for him to feel so alone. But I did it for me mostly, because I hate guilt so much. I couldn't stand the thought of not doing what I knew I should do and then feeling guilty. So I'm glad I did all I could for him, and I'm glad I did it for me. I'm sad he died so young. He was only sixty-four—but he had abused himself terribly.

"My mother died last year. I went back for the funeral. I was frightened to see people from my past. I felt scared of my emotions—of either not having any or having too many. I saw my baby brother, whom I hadn't seen in thirty-two years. It was good to see him, but I'm afraid I'll probably never see him again. I was so fearful of too much emotion that I hardly felt any.

"Everything I did, I did for my grandmother and for me. I felt sad for my mother. She was just sixty-one years old when she died. She had a terrible life. But mostly I felt relief when she died. She was out of her misery and could no longer cause so much misery for the rest of us."

Kelly is now forty-four. She has a happy and healthy relationship with her husband and her daughter, but she still deals with many of the effects of her traumatic childhood. She is working on coming to terms with her feelings about what her parents put her through.

It was Kelly's twenty-two-year-old daughter who recently introduced her mother to ACOA readings. Knowing of her mother's history, the daughter knew it would provide Kelly with solace and validation.

"Since my parents are gone now, I feel as if all the bad stuff happened to someone else. I feel such relief. I don't have to worry about them anymore. It has become safe to work on my Adult Child issues. I see some things I'd like to change. I have very little confidence. I'd like to be more confident, to take risks, to be less wishy-washy, to try new things. My greatest regret is a lack of career due to fear. Yet I don't know if I would want to be someone else. I think I'm stuck with me. But a lot of me and my life I like.

"I am lucky to have such a wonderful husband and daughter. Bill has always been so patient and understanding and supportive. I could not have survived without him.

"My daughter is the joy of my life. She represents everything I would have liked for myself. I have tried not to let my problems interfere with her growing up normally. I have tried to make my daughter's life totally different. I've stayed away from addictive-type things.

"Except for my grandmother, I've kept my family out of our life. I want my daughter to know how I lived, but I don't want her to live it, too. I think my family has had an effect on her, though. She seems to be more tolerant, patient, and giving than most girls her age. I hope she gets healthy rewards for those virtues. In her case, I think of them as virtues. In my case, I consider them part of the bad things in my life because they weren't given in love but out of fear and guilt."

Today Kelly is still in conflict over guilt versus responsibility, and she can find feelings to be frightening. But she has very quietly developed an inner core of strength. She has a clear sense of fairness and of right and wrong. She has chosen a quiet but equally caring, kind, and responsible partner. They are enjoying their life as a team.

Kelly's healing has occurred without a focused recovery program. Her extended family provided her with values and an inner strength that helped her to understand she deserved nice, healthy people in her life. Kelly has attracted that. She has created a small world for herself where she is safe, protected, and happy.

JEFF
Age: 33
Partner Status: Single
Occupation: Architect
Recovery Process: Support group,
    therapy

At age thirty-three, in addition to struggling with his Adult Child issues, Jeff has also had to come to grips with his sexual orientation.

Jeff graduated from high school without any fanfare—pretty much unnoticed by others. He worked his way through college and today is satisfied with his work as an architect. His being an architect very possibly has been derived from hours of finding solace and comfort in drawing in childhood. He described being alone and drawing as his safe place.

College in and of itself was a safe place for Jeff. He didn't have to listen to violence. No one knew who his parents were, and again he felt safe at school. Now that he was free to be his own person he trusted an inner strength, and knowing that he was gay, he joined a gay therapy group to address his ACOA fears.

JEFF: "I am gay and have no doubts about that. But, at the same time, I had such a fear of men that I was confused. When I had heard of this group on campus, I became a part of it. Here I was, a gay man and fearful of men. I had a terrible time with men who even hinted at being out of control. Men who raised their voices made me feel very uncomfortable. Anything that hints of violence makes me sick to my stomach, the way I felt as a child every Saturday night. People described me as very sensitive, caring, loving, nice—you name it. The last thing I wanted to do was raise the wrath of another individual. I was so fearful of getting someone upset. I hated any confrontation, perceived or real."

Jeff's fear of other people's anger is very natural, considering the violence with which he was raised. For him, anger equaled violence. However, in recovery Adult Children learn that that does not have to be true. In Jeff's family it is likely that fear, hurt, frustration, embarrassment, and shame were all being meshed with anger. And anger was an out-of-control feeling for Jeff's father. For Jeff, anger meant being hit, being locked in a closet. As an adult, Jeff couldn't separate his father's behavior from other people's potential emotional responses.

"It was in the gay therapy group that I heard about Adult Child self-help groups. I went to meetings, but I would get so scared I couldn't keep going. Yet I had done well in therapy, so about two years after I graduated and was settled in my work, I decided to try Adult Child therapy."

Many Adult Children become frightened in their first few self-help groups. Jeff knew he was scared. Some people rationalize later what they don't like about the meetings. Others mask their fear with anger. For Jeff, the promise of what the self-help group might offer was stronger than his fear. He had enough recovery to be able to recognize his feelings, and he wasn't critical of himself. In the end he chose what he found to be a setting that was less frightening, so he continued to address his Adult Child issues. He decided to go into individual therapy to focus on Adult Child issues, and over time he made the transition to Adult Child group therapy.

Although Jeff focused indirectly on many Adult Child issues in his gay therapy group, he realized he needed a resource where the total focus was on ACOA issues. For many Adult Children, particularly Double Duty/ Dual Identity, a group process is too scary initially. Yet in time Jeff sought it out as a replacement for individual therapy. The validation he received simply being with other Adult Children, realizing that he no longer had to live in isolation, was tremendous. His fears and shame lessened as he no longer experienced himself as unique. He was listened to. He was valued.

"After six months of individual therapy I joined a group, and I'm still in it. I've worked a lot on what happens to me in relationships. I usually spend most of my time trying to show people how good I can be. I've felt that if I give them enough love, they might love me back equally. Clearly, I've had a lot of Adult Child issues to deal with. But today I attract healthy people into my life. I don't have such a need to show them I'm worthwhile. Now I feel worthwhile. Today my partner of one year is honest, caring, and not a drunk!

"I spent so much of my childhood afraid. That's been the area that therapy has helped me the most. I'm not nearly so afraid of what people think of me or of what they might do that would be hurtful.

"Another area concerns my having spent so much of my childhood being quiet, following the 'Don't talk' rule. While I still tend to be on the quiet side, I'm comfortable around other people now and become engaged in conversation with ease.

"Now that two of my brothers are in a recovery process, too, I actually have somewhat of a relationship with them.

"I never kept up a relationship with my parents after I left home. I'd occasionally stop by the first few years, but it didn't seem to matter to anyone, so I decided, What's the use? I don't feel bad about this—there's just never been any love from my parents. Today, my dad has died from his alcoholism, and my mother is remarried. I've heard that she and her new husband abuse each other as well. Maybe if she gets well and wants a relationship, we could become closer, but until then I am quietly rebuilding my life."

BETH
Age: 26
Partner Status: Single, divorced,
    one child
Occupation: Legal assistant
Recovery Process: Therapy, ACOA

After Beth graduated from high school she took a secretarial position. She was making good money for someone her age, and she felt very self-sufficient. She had her own car and was supporting herself. Then she began doing cocaine. She moved in with a man whom she had been dating. He had no idea she was doing cocaine. Her drug taking was completely secretive.

Shortly after they were living together she had a traumatic experience on cocaine. This scared her enough to give up drugs permanently.

Beth became pregnant and then married at age twenty. But her marriage would suffer from her lack of experience in healthy relationships as well as her husband's dysfunctional upbringing.

BETH: *"I knew nothing about relationships. I didn't know what was appropriate to give in a relationship, so I just gave, gave, gave. I had only learned to do what I was told. I didn't know what my needs were. I didn't know how to ask for what I wanted. I had learned no one really cared or was interested. My needs had never been met. I was unhappy, but I didn't know why. Then we had a baby, and our problems just got worse. We were soon divorced. I went on to have two more significant, but unhealthy, relationships."*

Beth is now twenty-six and is working on her Adult Child issues in therapy.

"My active recovery in therapy has only recently begun. It took me a long time to even begin to talk honestly. I can see how many people would prefer never to look at these things. But once I begin to talk about one thing, something else starts to pour out. It's like someone cut me open—more keeps pouring out! I am in the middle of the pain. I trust it does get better, but it is very painful. I cannot believe that there is so much to address."

Just like Jeff, Beth is very afraid of other people's anger.

"I used to have such a hard time with anger. I was afraid of it because of how my dad was when he was angry. I've also had a lot of fear, but I wasn't able to tell anyone about it. I was afraid to show affection because I didn't know how someone would respond. I was afraid I wouldn't get any back. Now I'm learning to express my anger and fear without worrying about being rejected or abandoned. I know my feelings today and am no longer self-destructive with them."

Beth has only been out of her parents' home a few years, yet she is already in the position of parenting a child. That is a daily struggle when you're still in the process of reparenting yourself. Yet because so many COAs aren't in a position to address these issues until their adulthood, many Adult Children find themselves working on their own childhood issues at the same time that they're attempting to create a healthy childhood for their own children.

"I still have trouble seeing myself as responsible at times, although I am very responsible with my daughter. She's very special to me. I want to give her what I didn't receive as a child and at the same time recognize what her individual needs are. I can still be irresponsible about doing things for myself. I put off little things that need to be done—I put them off, or I'm unprepared. At times the responsibility of being a mother overwhelms me. I would like to be taken care of sometimes, but I have a difficult time letting someone take care of me and love me."

Beth's pattern was to rush into relationships with men who would take care of her. In return, she became whatever they wanted her to be. But she had no sense of what she wanted from them, other than not being rejected. In recovery, it will be important for Beth to develop friendships with both men and women.

"Today I am not in a significant relationship, and I rarely date. I have a greater sense of my own needs. I have a greater sense of appropriate expectations. I communicate more directly. I'm not as worried about being rejected."

Beth is building her self-confidence and a strong sense of herself. Her feelings of safety and security are no longer contingent on somebody else providing them.

"I've learned that I'm a nice person, and I'm becoming happy with who I am. If someone doesn't like who I am, I'm beginning to see it as their loss. I'm becoming friends with who I am today."

Beth's spiritedness has resulted in a quick sense of humor. She speaks laughingly about having two of everything.

"I still spend a lot of time compensating for material deprivation as a child. I have lots of underwear, socks, bras, panties.

"I'm very conscious of having physical space that is mine. It has been important to make sure that my daughter has clothes that allow her to look good. We always looked like slobs as children, my parents didn't care. I care. I also have tons of personal-hygiene items in my bathroom. I could open a drugstore! I realize this is a reaction to being without for so long. But although it is an Adult Child phenomenon, I don't find it particularly hurtful in my life today."

One can't address everything at once in recovery. Beth is wisely choosing to focus on the areas of her life that are more crucial at the moment. In time she may not find it necessary to have two of everything. In the meantime, she's enjoying the security this gives her as she addresses other issues.

Beth doesn't remember having more than a few friends in her high school years. She says she would have no one to seek out at a high school reunion.

It is difficult for COAs to develop friendships. They can't invite friends to their home for fear of embarrassment. They have shameful secrets to hide, so they can't be honest. Their family life is so overwhelming and demanding that it interferes with spontaneous sharing in daily contact during childhood years. Developing friends, becoming intimate with friends, are significant steps for many Adult Children.

"I choose healthy friends, and I'm a good friend to them. I'm a better listener than I used to be. The Twelve Step Adult Child meetings have been very helpful in teaching me how to listen. When you go to meetings,

you have to learn to listen. In my family, everyone always butted in. Having no cross-talk is wonderful for me. It makes you think more about what you say to people. I used to be so quick to say cruel or sarcastic things. Now I'm beginning to learn that this is inappropriate behavior, and I'm trying to change it.''

Beth is one of the youngest people in this book. There aren't as many young persons in their early or mid-twenties who are willing to take the time to explore this aspect of their lives. Very often, the closer in age people are to the time they left their parents' home, the more difficult it is for them to break their denial and recognize that, in spite of their survivorship skills, there have been negative consequences. In addition, this is often still a time of seeking greater emotional separation from family, which reinforces the desire not to even think about the growing-up years.

For Beth, the consequences came quickly—divorce and a cocaine problem. Yet many Adult Children would have ignored those and kept on adding to the list. But Beth was never able to deny her feelings. Because of this, and because a friend told her about Adult Children, she was able to begin recovery young.

JAMES
Age: 36
Partner Status: Single
Occupation: Self-employed
    businessperson
Recovery Process: ACOA, AL-ANON

James's early adult years were spent succeeding academically in college. But his feelings of inadequacy and incompetence kept him in school. It was a safe setting for him. His childhood self-sufficiency proved useful in helping him provide for himself, but the jobs were well below his abilities.

James's early postcollege years were filled with aimlessness.

JAMES: ''I didn't know what I was doing with my life, but that didn't bother me for a long time. I did a lot of drinking and using. Life seemed to be one big party. I didn't have any real goals. I didn't care about much, and nobody seemed to care about me.''

James said he would have intimate relationships off and on, but it wasn't until his mid-thirties that he began to feel he had much to offer in a relationship.

"There have always been women around, but I've never offered them any stability, or even an ability to care. I learned to be strong and not show my vulnerability. Any sign of weakness caused me great anxiety. I became very inflexible—I did things the way I wanted them done. I didn't really need anyone and could take care of myself—so I thought."

Like many COAs, James says he learned to be aloof. But this tendency to stay distanced from people was exacerbated by having had two chemically dependent parents. He'd had to develop an "I don't care" attitude to protect himself from being hurt.

"I didn't want to let someone in and then have to live with the fear that they might not be there for me when I needed them. Because my parents drank a lot yet did not appear drunk, it was their subtle unavailability that made me think I wasn't important. That I had nothing to contribute. That I had to handle things on my own."

Having two chemically dependent parents makes it difficult to get any idea of what appropriate behavior might be with respect to others. It also makes it difficult to develop healthy expectations of what is appropriate in given situations.

Although James abused alcohol and drugs, he was fortunate—he didn't become dependent. As aimless as his life was, he did recognize that his life was going nowhere and that his drinking life-style was contributing to that.

"I knew I deserved more. Finally, a friend told me of a good experience she'd had in counseling; and then my brother told me that he'd talked to someone in the counseling department at his school. That was the beginning. That's when I began to understand that I could make some changes in my life. If my brother could talk to someone outside the family, if he could break the 'Don't talk' rule, then so could I."

James stopped using drugs when he was twenty-eight. He then went back to college, received a master's degree in business, and began a career. At the age of thirty-one he decided to quit drinking.

After two years of feeling greater accomplishment in his work, James became aware that he was depressed, and for a second time he sought counseling. This was when he heard of the Adult Child self-help groups. He has been a member of those groups for four years now.

"I have taken that rigidity of mine and applied it to making a commitment to myself. I go to groups weekly, both Adult Child and at times traditional Al-Anon. I have worked the Twelve Step program and participated in Twelve-Step study groups. As a result, I've learned a lot about myself, and I now have choices about how I live my life.

"Work is good. I like it. But what is really different today is that I can count on others to be there for me. I choose healthy friends, mostly men. I still use sports as an outlet, but I try not to be compulsive. I've had two brief but important relationships with women in the past four years. With each one I grew. With each I received. I'm not so worried now about whether or not I'll be able to have a long-term relationship some-day. I don't worry about the future as much as I used to. I really do practice taking care of today.

"I've learned to ask, to trust, to show vulnerability. I find this really exciting. I don't feel so different from other people any longer. I talk about feelings, stresses, mistakes, and even needs."

James's excitement is deserved. COAs with two dependent parents were raised with broken promises, with twice the unpredictability and twice the unavailability. In this case neither parent could relate to the child with honesty; they were drug-affected. Trust isn't automatic, it's learned and earned.

Today James and other ACOAs are learning the joy of trust.

James has learned that it is possible to have a caring relationship with his parents. He has lowered his expectations and made them more real-istic. He also limits the amount of time in which he talks or visits with his parents. In doing this, he is no longer operating in the "all or nothing" style characteristic of his earlier years. Now he is able to accept the love his parents offer without the pain that was associated with his "wanting more but never getting it." He can now give his love more freely.

"My relationship with my parents is limited today. But I'm much more realistic about them. I'd like things to be better between us, but I can only do my part, not theirs. They both still drink a lot and don't under-stand my not drinking. Today I can see their alcoholism clearly. As a child I was too young to recognize the disease. I will continue to stay involved in their lives to some extent—as long as it isn't harmful to me and my commitment to my own personal growth."

James's relationship with his brother is also limited today. They sur-vived their childhood together, and James was encouraged by his brother to get out of the home to protect himself. His brother was also a positive role model for good friends and good decisions. But as is often true, in adulthood the brother hung on to his survival skills with rigidity as his fears slowly crept to the surface, creating a very controlling, narrow-minded, joyless person. Possibly James's recovery will someday offer his brother the path that he tried to offer James as a teenager.

"I'm now learning to trust myself and my feelings. This is just as important as learning to trust others."

JAN
Age: 33
Partner Status: Single
Occupation: Self-employed graphics
   designer
Recovery Process: Therapy, AA,
   Metaphysics

Jan's adulthood has been overshadowed by her alcohol and drug addiction. She was able to finish a four-year degree in college. College was a safe place for her. It provided structure, and she found rules and a purpose there.

College is a safe haven for many COAs. Like the military, college often provides structure and purpose. For some people it also offers a "place of belonging."

On the other hand, some Adult Children find college and the military to be negative experiences. In college they may feel very little structure and in the military too much authoritarianism. When they've experienced so little authority in their lives, this may be a difficult adjustment. One's response depends on one's background. Clearly, Jan felt college was the most secure place she'd ever found.

It was when she left college that her disease progressed from bad to worse.

JAN: *"In the early eighties my disease consisted of heavy drinking, cocaine use, and a series of one-night stands. I loved the rush alcohol and drugs gave me. I loved the excitement. I had always been too tall, too ugly, and too fat. But with alcohol and drugs, people saw me as sexy.*

"Drinking also gave me a way to be friends with my dad. We'd sit in bars for hours and he'd talk to me. I could finally get his attention. Drink-

ing was also a way for me to be bad—I used alcohol and drugs to be bad.
I now see this as self-destructive anger. I was too afraid of my anger to
lash out, so I turned it inward.

"Drinking helped me to forget my mom. I swore I wouldn't become
her. I had hated my mom for years. I hated taking care of her. I hated
putting her to bed. I hated never knowing what to expect when I got
home—and it was always bad. I hated her for never letting me sleep. I
hated her for my always being tired. Drinking was a way for me to forget
my mother."

Alcohol was medication for Jan. It was an anesthetic for her pain. Yet
as much as she never wanted to be like her mother, alcohol and drugs
became Jan's answer to pain—as it most likely had been for her mother
and very possibly her father. As much as Jan was like her parents in her
chemical dependency, she differed from them by seeking help for her
addictions.

"In desperation, I went into therapy in 1983. By that time I was a raging
bulimic as well as an alcoholic. The therapy helped me stop throwing up.
But my drinking and drug use progressed for two more years. By then I
saw suicide as my only option. I was having chronic anxiety attacks in
which I would become physically immobilized.

"Therapy felt safe. I could talk. The therapist helped me with day-to-
day living things. She was practical with me, and I needed it because I
was becoming so nonfunctional. It was slow. But there was hope. I didn't
realize it then, but she bought me time, she gave me a way to keep
living. Yet I was still using a lot and drinking, and I was still suicidal."

Jan was cross-addicted to alcohol and other drugs, plus she had a food
addiction. Multiple addictions are more common in Adult Children from
families with two chemically dependent parents than they are in the general COA population. Given these multiple addictions, plus the anxiety
attacks and suicidal tendencies, Jan's therapist was very astute in offering
her day-to-day survivorship skills until she had the inner strength to face
her addictions directly.

"My therapist finally told me I had to quit drinking and using. I went to
my first Alcoholics Anonymous meeting and knew I had come home. I
felt different from the people there, but spiritually I felt safe. I knew I
didn't have to take my life or drink again. I saw drugs, alcohol, and suicide
all in one package. I knew I had to give up both alcohol and drugs. Since
the day I joined AA, my life has been one long miracle—even the bad
times."

Jan needed to get clean and sober before she was able to address her Adult Child issues.

"My first identity is with my alcoholism. If I'm sober, I won't have the other problems. Although these began before my drinking and using, drinking is the quickest route to suicide for me. I needed to get sober first to be able to address the other issues both emotionally and spiritually. I spent my first year in AA getting sober. Although I'd quit throwing up, I spent a lot of my second year of sobriety working on my bulimia. This meant also working on my Adult Child issues.

"I couldn't trust my own perceptions or intuition because my parents kept telling me that the things I saw, heard, and felt were not real, or were wrong, or weren't the way I interpreted them. I also learned to tolerate a high level of inappropriate behavior from men. I allowed them to violate my boundaries again and again because I was looking for empathy from them by sleeping with them. The empathy was not forthcoming. I learned that strong, successful, masculine men can also be violent and dangerous. Very early in my sobriety, I worked on trusting my perceptions and setting boundaries."

Healthy boundaries and limit setting is confusing for all Adult Children. But it's even more so with the chaos that children with two dependent parents have been raised with. Jan never had the opportunity to be a child. She was often the parent to her mother and was certainly her own parent. In her teenage years she became her father's confidante. She was not raised with a healthy perspective on who was responsible for what. Roles were switched, turned upside down. Expectations were inappropriate. This crucial issue had to be addressed early in Jan's recovery, as her lack of boundaries was blatantly self-destructive.

"I could not trust others because I'd never been able to rely on anyone. But to stay sober, to stay alive, I had to deal with that immediately. I finally realized I was drowning, and I reached out to a sponsor. Since then I have been learning about trust. Growing up, I had learned I couldn't share who I really was or what my needs were with another person, because if I did, that person would abandon me. Today this is all very different for me. I know that not everyone will abandon me—particularly when they aren't practicing alcoholics."

Jan is learning to set boundaries, to discriminate. She is learning to trust herself as well as others. Although this is hard work, it is also an exciting part of the miracle of recovery.

"All of my life I had learned to keep up a successful appearance at all costs, even when I felt I was dying. To survive, I had to give that up.

"I had learned I was the only resource I had in the whole world to depend on, and if I couldn't solve my problems, there was no way out— I shouldn't exist anymore. Now I'm learning to have friends, and I choose healthy friends. I needed to begin by choosing women friends. Some of these women are nurturing, motherly types, which has been very helpful. With men I take it slow. But my fears are lessening, and I know there are men capable of being nonabusive."

Jan's Adult Child issues are exacerbated not only because she has two chemically dependent parents, but because she is also an only child. Being an only child reinforces both her self-reliance and separateness from others.

Every person raised in a physically abusive family has to address the fear of anger. Anyone who has lived with as much violence as Jan and the others in this chapter needs to address those experiences specifically. Jan needs to develop an empathy for the vulnerability of the child who had to witness and respond to the abuse. There will be fear, sadness, rage, powerlessness. These feelings need to be purged. Jan's bulimic purging may have been symbolic. She will need to learn slowly how to let those feelings out. As she builds inner strength and new skills through her self-help groups, she will discover that she has the strength and the support to walk through the pain and put it behind her.

"I learned never to be emotional, never to show my anger. Anger meant hitting or being hit. Today I have models who are healthy, and I'm watching others to see how they handle their anger.

"I learned to punish myself constantly with alcohol, drugs, hurtful relationships, or purging. I no longer do that. I can still punish myself with critical self-talk, but over the last three years this has been lessening.

"Today I am finding recovery in Alcoholics Anonymous and in metaphysical teachings. I have read literature and attended some Adult Child seminars. I have found there is a way out of the pain, the hell, the desperation. I can now feel my inner strength and compassion. I know I am a capable person. I can take responsibility for my life. I wasn't able to do that as a child, but now I can.

"Today I have found acceptance for myself and my parents. I have a distant relationship with my father, but I am reserving a space to let him in when I feel it is safe. I set limits, but I do love him."

Recovery Considerations

Many variables affect a child's growing-up years, but a childhood spent with two chemically dependent parents is one of the most disruptive situations anyone can experience. For some of the people in this chapter there are additional double duties: Jan is an only child with an eating disorder; Jeff is gay.

Some people feel pride about their survivorship and insist, "It wasn't that bad," or, "I'm okay in spite of . . ." Or they can give in and say, "All right, it was terrible. So what am I supposed to do about it now?"

Each and every person raised in this kind of environment is a survivor. It's helpful to identify your strengths and to feel good about them. But remember, survivorship is based on a powerful reaction to negativity, to loss, to abandonment. Until the past can be fully acknowledged, until you can speak the emotional truth about your experiences, you'll keep on living with the consequences—chronic fear, inability to connect with others, need for approval, depression, alcohol or drug abuse, food addiction. The following points are critical for the person with two chemically dependent parents. When you pay attention to them, you know you're addressing the core issues.

IDENTIFYING AND EXPRESSING FEELINGS

Adult Children in general have great difficulty identifying and expressing their feelings. But with two alcoholic parents, the need to defend is much greater because children are left to respond to an insidious illness with very few opportunities to experience healthy parenting or guidance. As a result, these Adult Children are even more removed from their feelings because at a very early age they've had to create a protective wall between themselves and all the pain, confusion, and chaos of their lives.

The ACOAs with two chemically dependent parents are also more likely to feel emotionally drained. With two alcoholic parents you have given so much, and you have endured so much emotionally during childhood and adolescence, that you may find it difficult to care about anything. This is described as "emotional fatigue" or "numbness." This is also what Adult Children are referring to when they say they feel "so old." Their inner resources are depleted. When Adult Children say they feel numb, they are. They're numb from having to hold in so many feelings for so long; numb from having to build and maintain that protective wall around their inner child.

Often Adult Children want to feel but don't know how. On top of this, there's a sense of being overwhelmed, confused, even terrified, when you begin to express your feelings. The more feelings you've kept in, the greater the likelihood of your identifying with other ACOAs when they say they feel like they're going to "lose it." Usually they are referring to "losing control."

Controlling one's feelings to the point of not showing them is a normal response to a childhood in which displaying your feelings often resulted in pain. So when feelings begin to emerge, many Adult Children are terrified of "losing it." This sense of losing control can be so frightening, you think you're going crazy. What often happens is that an Adult Child can move into an even more controlling stance to stop being overwhelmed with feelings, with anxiety, panic, or terror. It is very important for Adult Children with two alcoholic parents to understand that they may act in a more controlling manner than others because they had even less opportunity to trust in others and thus have a greater need for safety.

Controlling behavior can be manifested both internally and externally. You control internally by withholding feelings and ignoring your needs. Externally, control is maintained by manipulating people, places, and things because you are so detached and frightened of feelings. Controlling behavior puts distance between you and others.

As scary as it may be, in recovery you need to begin to let go of the control over some of your feelings. It's not a case of "all or nothing." You don't have to show all of your feelings to everybody. Find a supportive place where other people are comfortable with feelings, and then slowly begin to talk about yourself. You might want to begin simply by listening to others talk about their feelings; that in itself is often a new and valuable experience. But don't keep sitting there in fear. Call on the courage of your survivorship and begin to share some of your feelings with others.

Being raised in a family with two alcoholic parents means living in a state of chronic trauma. It's incredible that one has managed to survive so well! Because recovery can be so emotional, Adult Children with two alcoholic parents need to allow themselves the opportunity for a more structured environment in which to feel greater safety as they begin to explore their childhood.

If a group process is too frightening, begin your recovery with one-on-one counseling. You can gradually move into a group format when it feels safer.

GIVING UP CONTROL

Giving up control can be threatening and very difficult when control has been a haven in a storm. Yet nothing bad has to happen when you begin to give up control. You have choices about how much control you give up and with whom you share your vulnerability. Don't equate control with power. As you begin to give up some control, you will in fact become more empowered. This is difficult to understand at first, because initially all we can experience is our vulnerability.

When you begin to let go of control, you will feel the sadness, fear, and anger that accompanied the abandonment, neglect, and chronic abuse you experienced in your childhood. During this process, some Adult Children quickly feel a sense of relief when they begin to let go. Others feel as if their feelings are so thick, they're trudging through mud. Some people build up such resistance to knowing their feelings, it's as if they're poking at the farthest edges of their feelings with a long stick. Others feel like volcanoes erupting with feelings they can't even name yet. Don't be critical of yourself. Just keep the process going, knowing that however it happens for you is the right way.

There is one cardinal rule: *Do not do this work alone!*

In this process you will confront how alone and abandoned you have been in your life. But as you move through the process, you will also begin to recognize the people who have been there for you. If you allow others to be a part of this process of letting go, you will also see that you don't have to continue to be alone in your life.

TRUSTING OTHERS

As part of the fierce self-sufficiency and survivorship traits these Adult Children have developed, they learned to trust only themselves. Although you may not want to give up the strength inherent in being self-reliant, you will want to develop a balance between independence and interdependence. Other people can be trustworthy. Once we begin to trust others, we no longer have to carry the burdens of the world on our own shoulders.

The balance comes in learning how to involve others in your life. If you have become rigidly autonomous, be open to asking for help. Chances are you're probably so skilled at coping that it doesn't dawn on you that you could possibly need help. As an experiment—even if you don't think you need help—try asking someone for their input or assistance. It can be an enjoyable experience. Life is a lot more fun when others are involved, and their input and support can open up surprising new opportunities and options.

RELATIONSHIPS

Fear of abandonment keeps people from getting too close in personal relationships—or else they go in and out of them or stay in hurtful relationships. Some people get out before they get hurt; others get into hurtful relationships and stay in them, sacrificing their integrity just so they won't be abandoned.

Trusting others is very difficult for adults who learned that autonomy was necessary for survival. To trust, you need someone who is trustworthy. Adult Children need to be discriminating about whom they trust. This is an area in which it takes time to develop real skills. You will need to examine carefully your choice of partners and friends. If your choice of partners is poor, and you are presently single, stop getting into sexual relationships until you have the experience of choosing healthier friends. Work on recognizing how you really feel. It's not possible to experience happiness, love, grief, or passion if you cannot feel. Adult Children need to learn to trust their perceptions, to identify their needs, to develop boundaries. You need to have respect for yourself to create greater respect from others.

The more you know and respect yourself, the more likely you are to invite healthier people into your life. You will be able to choose whom you spend your time with and how. Do not take an "all or nothing" approach about trusting others. Learn to trust yourself with your own feelings first. Then begin to share your feelings with others by degrees. Remember, trust in relationships is established over time. It is not a given.

NEEDS

Because COAs with two chemically dependent parents tend to be ignored more than most, they are very skilled at diminishing their needs. They often say, "I don't need anything!" Translated, this means, "If I don't need anything, I won't get hurt."

Learn to be open to having needs. Very quietly take in these messages: "It's okay to have needs." "My needs can be met." "People do care about my needs." "I deserve to have my needs met."

Before most Adult Children feel comfortable about recognizing and acting on their needs, they first have to acknowledge the childhood needs that were not met. You will have to respond directly—to the pain, the anger, the fear, the sadness—to everything associated with not having your needs met. For those who have been doubly abandoned, the thought of "needing another" can create an almost violent response. Just remember, as you walk through the pain that comes with recognizing unmet needs, you will become more open about personal and interpersonal needs.

When you decide to explore your childhood needs, choose a safe environment, one with support and a structure that you trust. This process can be paced so that it is safe. In it, you will develop a greater clarity about yourself and your needs. You will also find relief and greater positive energy. You will come to recognize your special inner strengths.

ANGER

Due to the double-barreled losses in a family with two chemically dependent parents, the Adult Child is more apt to experience anger as an "all or nothing" phenomenon. Because anger has seldom been a safe emotion, this child succumbs to a state of powerlessness or becomes rigidly self-sufficient. Some find themselves flipping back and forth between the two.

For the more frightened, powerless Adult Child—terrifying and impossible as it sounds—there are valid reasons to be angry. Anger does not have to hurt. Anger can empower. Being angry does not make you a bad person; it can make you more honest. You can learn appropriate ways to express anger, but first you have to risk discovering that you have things to be legitimately angry about.

Anger needs to be addressed whether you identify with powerlessness and fear or with rigid self-sufficiency. Either way, you still have a great deal to be angry about. But by the time you get to be an Adult Child, anger has often become a defense. The first thing you need to do is take time to look at how anger has protected you. Also recognize that, in doing this, you will be addressing other aspects of yourself—your fears, sadness, loneliness, embarrassment.

BREAKING THE "DON'T TALK" RULE—LOYALTY ISSUES

Although Adult Children with two chemically dependent parents have often experienced abandonment, they nonetheless frequently feel a great sense of disloyalty once they begin to acknowledge the losses of their childhood years. Their need for approval and acceptance is so great that they will accept whatever attention they can get—negative or positive—in a family that is chaotic, painful, and neglectful of children's needs.

Don't be confused by this conflict. When some Adult Children begin recovery, they are afraid of losing the most fragile thread of a relationship. But others will ask, "Isn't no relationship better than a hurtful relationship?" This question can be argued in both directions. What the Adult Child needs to know is that relationships are not an either-or proposition. Your recovery doesn't eradicate the possibility of a relationship with your parents. As you grow in recovery you will discover that you can still have a relationship, but it often means lowering expectations and defining boundaries more clearly.

In addition, how much you share verbally with your parents or friends about your recovery process is your individual decision. You are not betraying your parents when you do your recovery work. If there is any act of betrayal here, it lies with the disease of chemical dependency. However, to continue to discount yourself as an adult is to betray yourself. You deserve more.

If my parents ever get well, we may be able to be closer. But until then I'm rebuilding my own life.
                                    —Adult Child, two chemically dependent parents

Notes

1. C. Black, S. Bucky, S. Padilla, "The Interpersonal and Emotional Consequences of Being an Adult Child of an Alcoholic," *Journal of International Addictions* 21 (May 1986): 213–232.
2. L. Drozd, "A Sense of Self Model for Treatment of (Female) Children of Alcoholics," (Ph.D. diss., California School of Professional Psychology, San Diego, 1986).
3. R. S. Marlow, "Social-Psychological Differences Between Male and Female Adult Children of Alcoholics," (Ph.D. diss., Ohio State University, Columbus, Ohio, 1988).
4. M. Russell et al., "Family Studies in Alcoholism, Children of Alcoholics: A Review of the Literature" (New York: Children of Alcoholics Foundation, 1984).
5. D. W. Goodwin, "Alcoholism and Genetics" *Archives of General Psychiatry* 42 (1985): 171–174.
6. B. Volicer et al., "Variation in Length of Time to Development of Alcoholism by Family History of Problem Drinking," *Drug and Alcohol Dependence* 12(1) (1983): 69–83.

4

Physical Abuse

We never knew when or why he would blow up, or who would be the target of his anger.

—Adult Child

The Prevalence of Physical Abuse

Chemical dependency and family violence often coexist in a dysfunctional family. One does not necessarily cause the other, but the frequency with which they are found together is astounding.

In the literature on the subject, estimates range from 50 to 80 percent on the number of families experiencing physical abuse that are also affected by alcohol abuse. The National Committee for the Prevention of Child Abuse (1989) recently reported that parental alcohol and drug abuse is a significant factor in over 80 percent of reported physical abuse cases. They also strongly recommend that alcohol and drug abuse be dealt with first, because without sobriety the physical abuse cannot be realistically addressed. Research by Black, Bucky, and Padilla has found that, in alcoholic families, fathers were ten times more likely, mothers four times more likely, and siblings two times more likely to be physically abusive than family members in non–chemically dependent families.[1]

When abuse exists in a family where alcoholism is also present, the abusing parent is not necessarily the alcoholic parent. Unfortunately, when this is true the other parent is often helpless to protect the child because of the alcoholism. When the abusers are the alcoholics, abuse doesn't necessarily occur when they're drinking (or using). In fact, sometimes it is when the alcoholics are not under the influence that they may become abusive.

Alcohol is not the cause of abuse, but it is often a contributing factor. When a child has two chemically dependent parents, the likelihood of physical abuse becomes even greater. And once there is parental abuse, the likelihood of sibling abuse is also greater. Often the older abused child becomes the abuser of the younger children in the home.

Despite the "Don't talk" rule in families plagued with alcoholism, this situation usually manages to reveal itself to others outside the family. However, family violence is much more hidden from those not living in the home. While alcoholics may be slowly committing suicide through their dependency, they are also indirectly endangering others in the family. Physical safety, including the possibility of imminent death, is always at stake in a violent family.

Abuse, even without the added dynamics of alcoholism, is clearly traumatizing. Children who have been abused often end up as runaways on the streets, which adds the danger of being homeless to the emotional burden they're already carrying. These abused people continue to live the life of victims because of their sense of shame and powerlessness. They have no doubt about their inadequacy; after all, those who supposedly cared about them hit them—and no one said a word about it or did anything to help. Confused, frightened, and angry, they succumb to helplessness or seek power in rage.

The act of physical violence against a child has always, to some extent, been a controversial subject. Many parents rationalize that it is their right to discipline their children however they please. For generations the prevailing cultural ethic has given license to the abuse of children with the "spare the rod and spoil the child" philosophy. Given the checkered history of such practices, children who are abused are much more likely to believe that they have done something wrong and that they are rightfully being punished.

In an abusing home, this becomes internalized as shame. Children learn that they can never be right, that they are wrong, inadequate. They also spend so much time in fear of the violent parent, or in attempting to alleviate potential abuse, that their personal growth is stymied. What is just as confusing to the child as the abuse itself is the fact that they are not protected and that their abuse is often totally ignored.

This chapter is not about spanking a child as a form of discipline. Rather, it addresses the issue of perceiving children as objects or property instead of people, wherein parents assume the right to hit, slap, and endanger the physical and emotional well-being of a child. It speaks to those forms of discipline designed to attack a child's self-worth and esteem.

Children in alcoholic families have already learned to ignore their feelings, not to trust, to deny and not tell anyone what is going on, to feel guilty and responsible for what happens, to live with unpredictability, and to feel powerless. When these children are also physically abused, the lessons that they have learned are doubly binding and the consequences even more devastating.

Defining Abuse

Because people who have been raised in abusive families have a high tolerance for inappropriate behavior and violence, it is often helpful to describe physically abusive behavior.

Physical abuse is the pushing and shoving of another. It is slapping, hitting, and punching another. It is the slamming of a person against the wall, to the floor, against the car. It is the kicking of another. These actions are inappropriate and excessive even when parents believe it is discipline.

It is a given that children who live with physical abuse are also subjected to emotional and mental abuse. This kind of unacceptable behavior includes name calling, the witnessing of physical abuse of siblings or the other parent—which is often more damaging than receiving the abuse oneself—and living with the fear of impending violence and death. This could occur with terrifying car rides or when a drunken, raving parent storms through the house brandishing a gun or a knife. What actually goes on in the day-to-day existence of one who lives in the shadow of physical violence is often beyond the imagination of those who have never had such an experience.

When people live with alcoholism, they are in an abusive environment. Even if not physically abusive, it is certain to be an emotionally abusive environment. Emotional abuse can be many things—chronic unpredictability, punishing silences, name calling, and inappropriate expectations. It is emotional abandonment—the lack of nurturing support.

It's not possible to live in an alcoholic family and not experience emotional abuse. Essentially it is emotionally abusive for a child to live with chronic loss. It's much easier to perceive this as abuse when you remember that such children are experiencing these things just when they're beginning to develop a sense of self-worth and their own identities.

Neglect is another form of abuse common in alcoholic families. It is demonstrated with inadequate supervision, such as leaving young children in the care of other children nearly as young as themselves or leaving children with no supervision at all. This occurs most often within the home, but it is also neglect when children are left unsupervised in the car for hours, which usually occurs when parents are in bars. Many ACOAs also remember being left with adult friends of their parents when their parents were away. But the adults they would be left with were also practicing alcoholics, which again meant poor supervision.

Neglect is inadequate physical care, such as not providing meals or proper clothing and shelter. Such children often describe never knowing what time dinner is. As one ACOA said, "It could be anywhere from six P.M. to midnight—it would range from Chinese take-out food to hot dogs or ice cream." Often, children have clothes that are too small or inadequate for the weather, such as thin coats or simply sweaters to withstand rain and snow.

Some children become so used to the neglect that they don't even question it. Often it is only in recovery, as they listen and receive feedback from others, that they begin to realize the extent of the deprivation in their lives.

Every chapter in this book reflects the fact that abuse is common to chemically dependent families. However, abuse is such a serious subject that it warrants a separate exposé. This chapter will deal with abuse as a part of life in a dysfunctional family. It discusses how the children and adults are affected and, finally, how recovery is possible.

Life Stories: Growing-Up Years

Of the three life stories presented, the first—Tom's story—depicts the most blatant physical violence. Yet he found his fear of impending violence to be even more torturous than the actual physical violence he experienced. Meredith's story depicts a pattern of family violence that changes over time. For the girls in the family, the physical abuse stops at adolescence, but not for the boys. Monica's story presents the life of a COA who is not physically abused herself, but who must live with the chronic, often paralyzing fear of witnessing blatant physical abuse within her family. The toll of trying to stay balanced on the tightrope of constant emotional trauma leaves scars that, though invisible to the eye, are soul deep.

TOM
Age: 37
Mother: Co-dependent
Father: Alcoholic, abuser
Birth Order: Fifth of eight children
Raised: Utah
Socioeconomic Status: Poverty level

Tom says that when he was growing up he thought he came from a normal family. Only as a young adult, after recovery from his own alcoholism, did he realize that he came from a violent, dysfunctional family.

Adult Children often struggle with knowing what normalcy is. This becomes even more problematic if they were raised in violent families.

TOM: *"Normal families do not make their children drink urine if they play in the toilet. Normal families do not initiate sibling rivalry that in time turns to hate. Normal families do not form beating circles of all the children to discover which child did something wrong.*

"My earliest remembrance of abuse occurred when I was a preschooler. Dad did not feel the house was cleaned well enough when he arrived home one evening, and he smacked Mom so hard that she crashed into the couch. From that time on, I knew who was in charge of our house.

"The two sisters just older than me were not as smart as the oldest two children, so they got beatings for poor grades when report card time came around. Later, when all eight children were in school, these beatings became a regular six-week ritual; five of us received beatings for poor grades, including me for poor citizenship. I remember being beaten so hard that blood came out of the welts on my legs.

"When I was about ten, Dad would come home drunk regularly at about three in the morning and drag my brother out of bed. He would beat him with his fists to make my brother 'a man.' Then Dad would hold him up to the mirror and say, "Is this what a man looks like?" The tears and fears that filled my brother's eyes were my tears and fears. I always wondered when Dad would try to make me a man."

In time, Tom would also learn to fight the pain in his life with his fists. But before that he did what most COAs do—what most children do—he sought approval from his parents.

"When I was younger I used to try to help Dad around the house or when he worked on the car. But he had no patience with children, and he'd hit me unexpectedly whenever I didn't live up to his expectations. Something as simple as not being able to use a screwdriver would fill me with fear."

Children of Alcoholics often learn that no matter what they do, it's never good enough. This leaves them with feelings of deep inadequacy. But when those children are also in physically violent homes, the threat to their physical well-being becomes linked to their feelings of inadequacy when what they do is not sufficient for parental approval. This fills them with absolute terror.

In order to get approval, it is typical that Tom and his brothers followed in their father's footsteps and used violence as a way of demonstrating their worth and their "manhood." Violence is also their only model for acting out their feelings of powerlessness and rage.

"I was always trying to prove I was a man—usually with my fists. I broke my sister's jaw once in an argument and felt no remorse or guilt. I was taught not to feel. I was learning that it was not manly to feel. Dad pounded into his sons' heads that we had to be tough to be a man, and violence was the answer for every situation."

Although some people can speak with tenderness and love about growing up in a large family, that is not possible in an alcoholic and/or abusive home. The excessive number of children only adds additional stress, and the already sick parents cannot respond appropriately. In such homes children tend to be treated as a litter instead of as members of a family. Children who are emotionally deprived in this manner often lose any sense of being special or of having any personal value.

"With eight children in the house, things were often misplaced, broken, or stolen. To get to the root of the problem, Dad would line us up from the oldest down to the youngest and continue whipping us until someone (often innocent) would confess. Dad would have Mom shut the windows in the summer, so the neighbors couldn't hear us scream. The younger ones would begin screaming, 'No, Daddy, no!' even before it was their 'turn' to be 'it.' This happened on a continuous basis until the four older children moved out of the house."

Although Tom lived with severe chronic emotional and physical abuse, he says what most people in violent homes report—that the emotional abuse was the most difficult of all to deal with. Emotional abuse is the constant fear of impending physical abuse and never knowing when it will come next.

"Because he was an alcoholic, Dad was not consistent in his moods. We never knew when he would blow up, or for what, and who would be the target of his anger. He would suddenly threaten one of us for no reason at all. His favorite saying was, 'This is my house, and I'll do what I want.' The rest of us realized his house was not our home, but Dad's materialistic possession."

Family rituals are a vital aspect of healthier family systems. Unfortunately, not only are such rituals usually ignored in alcoholic and abusive homes, they are often directly violated. Rituals that are significant for children are bedtime and morning behaviors, mealtimes, and holiday functions. When these rituals are denigrated, humiliation and loneliness are at their greatest, and the loss is profound.

"Dad came home drunk on my thirteenth birthday, and my present was the traditional heavy-handed birthday spanking. He spanked me so hard that I cried. My punishment for that was to be sent to bed immediately without cake or ice cream. I learned to hate birthdays since they were always a letdown."

Tom's description of this episode being a "letdown" also represents the need children have to minimize the depth of the abandonment and pain they feel at such times. Tom could not afford to feel his pain and humiliation—he was fighting to survive.

As most kids will, Tom sought escape and affirmation in socially acceptable activities. But he finally succumbed to his powerlessness when his father blatantly interfered with his attempts to be normal.

"One of the few constructive activities that brought me pleasure was basketball—good grades were necessary to remain on the team. But Dad ruined my high school basketball-playing opportunity, which took away my desire to try anything. Dad insisted I stay home to help remodel the house during the basketball tryouts. I had to miss all the tryouts, which prevented me from being on the team. And I had no other incentive to do good work in school. By the time I was fifteen I was drinking on a daily basis. My grades dropped as my drinking increased."

Sometimes it's difficult for outsiders to believe that Tom's father was deliberately trying to sabotage his son by insisting that he remain home to help with the remodeling. But anyone raised in an alcoholic and actively abusive home knows without doubt that such parental behavior was a conscious attempt to reassert waning authority and to show the child who was in charge, who was still calling the shots.

MEREDITH
Age: 43
Mother: Chemically Dependent
Father: Abusive
Birth Order: Fourth of six children
Raised: Northeast
Socioeconomic Status: Middle class

Meredith grew up with a physically abusive father and a chemically dependent mother. Most of the violence in the family was directed at the children, although Meredith's father was sometimes abusive to his wife as well.

MEREDITH: *"One of my most vivid childhood memories happened when I was five years old. I had drawn on the wallpaper in our breakfast room because I thought it would look prettier if all of the farm scenes it showed were connected by a fence. I got to work right after breakfast, and I used my best crayons, carefully filling in the pretty fence. When my mother found me doing this, she flew into a rage. She sent me to my room for the rest of the day, warning me that my father would punish me when he came home.*

"For the rest of the day, I had no food, no bathroom break, no escape. I remember sitting, standing, walking around my room, trying to find a way to comfort myself, because I knew that my father's 'punishment' meant being whipped with his thick leather belt on my bottom and on the backs of my legs. I don't remember the beating—it's too painful to recall—but I do remember the anguish of waiting all day for this dreaded event.

"I tried to find a comfortable place in my room, but I couldn't. I tried to find something to preoccupy my mind, but I couldn't. There were no toys in my room, but I couldn't have played with them if there were. I don't think I cried. But I recall feeling so very scared, sad, and alone. I wished very hard for a miracle: Maybe Daddy won't be mad. Maybe he

won't spank me. Maybe Mom won't tell him. Maybe staying in my room will be enough of a punishment.

"As the day went on, my wishes gradually became more realistic: Maybe Daddy will hit me only once with his hand. Maybe he won't hit me so hard. Maybe he'll come home early and get it over with fast."

Meredith was learning to bargain at a young age. She was bargaining with herself to ascertain what constituted hurt and pain. She was distancing herself emotionally from the soon-to-come physical reality. But she also knew she was powerless in her bargaining. There would be no fairness, no flexibility, nothing to negotiate, no way to problem-solve with her dad. He wouldn't even listen to anything she might say. He would just act on Meredith's mother's feelings and desires. As Meredith got older she would have to make a choice: either resign herself to her fate and become a victim, or actively find a way to fight for herself.

"Finally, I found a little jewelry box on my dresser. It had a picture of Jesus and the Last Supper on it. I held on to it for the rest of the day, trying to pray for a miracle, hoping that Jesus or God would save me from my fate. Instead, my father came home, prolonged my agony as he and my mother had their cocktails and discussed their days. Then he came up to give me my 'punishment.' "

Like many COAs and children in violent families, Meredith resorted to prayer, hoping that an all-loving God would save her from this unfair punishment. Unfortunately most of the Merediths of this world come to believe that not even God will help them. This simply reinforces the feelings of abandonment and helplessness they already have. At a very young age they are left spiritually bankrupt.

When Meredith was four, the family moved out of the city to a small farm in western Massachusetts. Meredith's father maintained a business in the city and was frantically trying to develop his farm and maintain his business at the same time. While Meredith does not believe her father was alcoholic, she does believe he was a workaholic.

"My father saw this farm as the answer to his dreams. He had grown up in Chicago, and he wanted a place where his six children could grow up healthy and 'free.' None of us, including my mother, shared this dream of his. It was his obsession, his first priority, his addiction. It turned out to be much more work than he had anticipated, but like a true co-dependent, he kept working to control it, to make it fit his dreams."

Abusive and addicted parents are so delusional in their thinking that they come to believe they are acting in their children's best interests. This violent man moved to a farm so his children could grow up happy and free. But moving there only served to isolate and imprison them in a violent family system.

Meredith had a sense of losing her parents once they moved to the farm. Her father was obsessed, never available except when he was yelling or hitting the kids and ordering them to do their chores. Her mother, who was unhappy with the move, did whatever her husband told her, which consumed most of her time and energy.

"My father vented all his frustrations on us. Once we settled into life on the farm he became abusive, volatile, explosive—a very unpredictable stranger to me. My mother's response to the changes in my father's behavior was to try harder to please him, which was an impossible task. She hated the work, but because she was a co-dependent, and my father was her primary addiction, she did whatever he wanted her to do. She had little time or energy left to devote to her children. My youngest sister, who was a baby at this time, was neglected from infancy on."

Meredith's father was very large, with big hands and big feet. And he was a man out of control. Children are physically smaller and weaker and are easily intimidated when adults loom over them. But when the adult is physically abusive as well, the hands and feet become huge in the child's view.

"He also had a booming voice. To discipline us, he had only to raise his voice—that was frightening enough. Even in striking us, his large hand and strong arm would have been sufficient to make us obey him. But he was so full of rage that he always raised his voice and then lashed out. He never smacked us on the bottom; he always whacked us on the back or side of our heads. He would also kick us as we scurried to do whatever he'd asked us to do.

"These physical assaults not only hurt terribly, they were also humiliating. The worst part is that they so often came unexpectedly. Sometimes they were out of context or out of sync with the mood of the moment. They always came as a shock because we were so unprepared for them."

Meredith grew up being unprotected. Her mother seldom intervened, and her brothers and sisters, victims of the abuse themselves, never talked about what was going on other than to warn each other, "If you do that, Dad's going to get you." These children lived in terror and powerlessness. Everyone, including their mother, were all possessions of their father.

Meredith's father was excessively abusive to her oldest brother, who had been given the same first name as her father.

"It seemed as if this brother was beaten, hit, smacked, kicked, yelled at, or otherwise punished almost nightly. My father was merciless with him, expecting the world of him but giving him no credit, no praise. My father was outraged at what he saw as my brother's 'imperfections.'

"Years later, we discovered that my brother had a learning disability. It's painful to remember how relentless my father was with him about his poor academic achievements. My brother still suffers from terribly low self-esteem and self-loathing."

In abusive families one child is frequently singled out for abuse more than another. Who that particular child is may vary, but the fact that one child is scapegoated over others is quite common. The targeted children are often the ones whom the abusers unconsciously perceive as being most like themselves. The abusers see themselves in the child, and they become determined to punish and/or control that child. The fact that Meredith's father picked the son who was his namesake for nightly beatings is probably no coincidence. Meredith clearly remembers her father being unrelentingly unrealistic with her brother. He was not the son her father wanted. He could never perform well enough to receive any positive validation from her father.

Sometimes it may be the child who reminds the abuser most of his or her spouse who stirs this misplaced hostility. Sometimes the child is clearly the most passive child, and the abuser is trying to evoke a response. At other times the victim may be the most verbal and feisty child. Here, the abuser is trying to put the child in his or her place, to make the child subservient, obedient.

"I believe now that my father's rages, his physical abuses, were addictive for him. They must have given him some rush or some relief from his inner turmoil. His behavior was very characteristic of an alcoholic's, although I never saw him abuse alcohol. It was my mother who was chemically dependent. But my father's addiction was the beatings. I don't believe he ever regretted or felt ashamed of his abusive behavior. His rages just seemed to feed on themselves."

Meredith says her father would become outraged when any of the children were not doing something right.

"If we were supposed to herd the cattle and one of them got away, Dad would punish all of us. We would all wait in a line as Dad prepared his switches, and then each would be beaten in turn. We wouldn't dare run. We had no choice but to wait our turn. Running meant being caught and then being beaten until we bled."

This type of punishment is torturous. The scenario becomes a toxic stew of fear and anger all mixed up with the terrible waiting and the growing sense of helplessness. Round-robin beatings were recurring events in the lives of both Tom and Meredith. The anger of watching and the humiliation, coupled with the powerlessness to act, leaves a child traumatized, particularly when such events are a way of life for so many years.

Meredith's primary defense was to fantasize.

"I usually had a movie playing in my head. I was always the star, the heroine—beautiful, strong, powerful. Sometimes I would save others. I also had an imaginary friend who provided constant companionship and comfort. Fantasizing was my only protection from living continually in the pain."

Solitary activities are the most common forms for abused children because they are less risky than those that involve others. There, you run the risk of outsiders seeing your shame. Fantasy is even safer than reading or drawing because it's invisible and can't be taken away as easily. Also, because it's not as visible, it's less likely to be ridiculed.

When Meredith was twelve years old, her father stopped abusing her physically.

"He had done the same thing when my two older sisters reached that age. My father seemed uncomfortable with our adolescence. He pulled away from us and turned us over to our mother. But she was unprepared for the job and didn't want the responsibility of having to discipline us."

Clearly, Meredith's father was now beginning to view his girls as sexual beings. In light of his own deep internal confusion about this transition, he removed himself from his only way of relating to the girls—physical punishment.

The father's ability to stop physically abusing his daughters while still continuing the abuse of his sons is a very frightening turn of events. It means this man *can* discriminate between whom he will and will not abuse. He has the ability to control his abusive behavior, and yet he still continues to abuse.

When Meredith was thirteen she developed diabetes, as had her older brother three years before.

"When my mother saw me developing the same symptoms as my brother, she ignored them, hoping it would all just go away. She couldn't face the reality of having another diabetic in the family, so she denied that it existed. I became very sick, but it wasn't until my oldest sister came home from college and insisted that my mother take me to the doctor that I got any treatment."

Meredith's abusive, dysfunctional family did not have the ability to respond rationally to a crisis. They had lived disconnected from each other for years, so expecting a healthy response to a major medical problem was very unlikely.

The onset of the diabetes meant the onset of a series of battles over control between Meredith and her mother. Her mother strictly supervised Meredith's meals, making sure that Meredith didn't eat anything with sugar in it. Meredith responded by eating sugary foods whenever her mother's back was turned. It was at this point that Meredith developed a sugar addiction.

"My mother would catch me eating sugar or find food missing and ground me for it. She would also keep a close watch on how much I urinated in order to tell whether or not I was following my diet regimen. Sometimes I would lie awake at night, desperately needing to go to the bathroom but afraid my mother would hear me and ground me for eating too much sugar, so I wouldn't go."

Frequent urination and thirst are both symptoms of too much sugar in a diabetic's system. This gave her mother clear signs that Meredith was eating too much sugar.

"I bought into my mother's concerns about my body, and ever since that time I have felt 'too fat' no matter how thin I've been. I think there was an element of competition in it because my father seemed very attracted to and impressed by my body when I was an adolescent."

Here, one can see the developing pattern of an eating disorder. Meredith would eat excessively out of anger, in order to have some control over her life and her body. She would sneak food. All of this was a direct response to the inappropriateness of her mother and father's preoccupation with her body. It is also possible that she ate excessively to become physically unattractive to her father. Compulsive overeating is sometimes an attempt to keep people away. As a result, Meredith's perception of her body size became distorted.

When Meredith was sixteen her parents separated. One night she came home about fifteen minutes late, a common occurrence for her at that age, and her father locked her out of the house and wouldn't let her back in. Her mother finally stepped in, defying Meredith's dad. Meredith's father left the next day without saying a word. Because the "Don't talk" rule was intact, for years afterward Meredith believed that her dad left because she came home late.

Meredith's mother took Meredith and her two younger siblings to live with her in a small suburban community.

"As soon as we settled into our new house, my mother and I became peers. We smoked cigarettes and talked after school, and I did a lot to keep her entertained. I realize now that my mother had transferred her co-dependency from my father to me. I became the parent of my mother, brother, and sister that year."

It was at the end of her senior year in high school, just as she was preparing to go to college, that Meredith began to notice that her mother was taking enormous amounts of pills.

"One day I looked in her medicine cabinet, and I was shocked to see a row of pill bottles on the bottom shelf. At first I thought, She must be very sick. But then at some level I realized that she was really unhappy, and she was taking a lot of pills to medicate her feelings. I tried not to think about it and hoped it would go away."

Meredith's father's abusive behavior had been such a focal point for Meredith and her family that it had been easy not to recognize her mother's chemical dependency. It's always more difficult to recognize chemical dependency when the drug is a prescription pill because pills are so easily kept out of the sight of others. Symptoms such as mood changes, criticalness, and lack of attention were accepted behavior from Meredith's mother over the year. And Meredith herself had become a master at minimizing her needs and not feeling. Her father's violence toward the children was just part of daily life, as was her mother's passive acceptance of the violence.

MONICA
Age: 44
Mother: Alcoholic
Father: Alcoholic, abusive
Birth Order: Youngest of two
Raised: Southeast
Socioeconomic Status: Working
class

Monica's growing-up years were riddled with family violence. For her the trauma was in the helplessness, guilt, and terror she experienced as the witness to abuse.

MONICA: Nothing ever happened in my family that didn't center around beer, booze, wine, or whatever was available. I don't ever remember a family gathering that didn't have at least one disagreement. If it didn't end up with somebody not talking to someone else, it was unusual. And it never stopped at the gathering. My parents brought it home.

"I remember when I was seven years old having to hide my mother in my bedroom so Daddy wouldn't throw her out of the house or hit her again. I felt as if I raised my mother. She wasn't capable of doing for herself."

Although Monica doesn't remember being beaten by her father, she does remember being the reluctant witness to acts of violence against her mother and her brother, who was nine years older.

"My father would beat my mother, especially when he was drunk. Most of their fighting took place after they'd done a lot of drinking together. He would beat my brother at any time, though. My father was a real bastard, especially when I was young. One night, Mom and Dad were fighting, and I tried to referee. Dad threw me onto a chair. In his hand he had a glass milk bottle; he told me to shut up or I'd get the bottle right across my face. I tried speaking once, but I quickly shut up. I firmly believe he would have done it. That's the closest I came to getting hit.

"But my brother was nine years older than me, and he really got beaten all the time. I remember being told never to go near the barn when Tom was 'in trouble.' But being a kid and curious, I did one time—

and one time only. I listened outside the locked door and heard my father threatening my brother: 'If you don't stand there and take this, I'll tie you to the bedsprings and whip you.' I knew about the whip inside the barn, but until then I never dreamed that it was actually used."

Monica's father kept three leather straps, so that one was always within his grasp—one in the barn, another in the car, and the third in the house. This was another way he exerted his control and abuse.

"There was a leather strap that my father kept in a drawer in the back room. The strap had one end cut into strips to get a particularly nasty effect. I would lie for my mom and my brother just so the hitting wouldn't start."

Children who witness abuse sometimes recognize that they have power others don't. The fact that Monica was singled out not to be hit gave her a sense of power—she believed she could protect her mother and brother. Although at times she was able to do it, most of the time she failed. This led to devastating bouts of "survivor guilt," heavily mixed with sadness, fear, and helplessness.

Monica's mother drank heavily and was extremely unstable emotionally.

"My mother spent time in the state hospital for the mentally disturbed. The best thing they did for her was dry her out. It didn't last long, though, because after she got home her old habits took over. One time our neighbor complained to my brother that Mom had dammed up the creek behind our house trying to hide empty beer cans and booze bottles.

"I saw my mom go from being the life of the party and loved by everybody to a lonely, neurotic woman that everybody wished would go away. She never realized that booze was a depressant. She just drowned in self-pity."

Monica's mother varied her drinking spots. She would often drink with her sisters and mother. They would drink in one person's home one day and then another person's the next. Or she'd spend the day in bars. Sometimes she would take the kids with her, and they would sit all day eating potato chips and drinking sodas while their mother drank.

"We drank one Coke after another. Then we'd begin to ask when we'd be going home. She'd tell us, 'After the next drink.' Well, after several more drinks, we'd quit asking."

Wherever she did her drinking, the children were there, witnesses to her getting drunk and passing out.

Monica was quiet and withdrawn as a child and kept pretty much to herself. She would usually have one close friend, but she never asked her friends over to her house.

Although Monica's father also drank heavily while she was growing up, in her teenage years his drinking tapered off and so did his abusive behavior.

"By now my brother had moved out. I didn't question things much. I'd learned to tolerate whatever was going on. After all, I'd tolerated his abuse. I just accepted things the way they were. It was as if I knew a Dr. Jekyll and Mr. Hyde.

"All of those years I always thought I respected my dad, and that was why I basically stayed out of trouble. I now realize it was fear. It's ironic that, as frightening a man as he was, he showed more interest in me than my mother did."

Monica's acceptance of her father's violence clearly demonstrates that when children are raised in such an atmosphere, they easily come to believe that if they just behave right and stay out of the way, they'll not be hit. They believe the victim is the cause.

Monica was also learning not to feel, not to ask questions, and not to think. This helped her distance herself from the pain and confusion of the family.

As fearful as she was of her father, she was even less bonded to her mother. Children who live with two chronically ill parents have few choices in life. They will take any attention they can get and be grateful for it.

Monica remained a loner throughout her childhood and teenage years. However, when she was in her late teens, her house became a place for drinking parties for her friends. Her parents accepted it as normal, and Monica and her friends would sit in the backyard or in the living room drinking along with her parents.

When Monica was seventeen, she got pregnant. Her boyfriend was four years older than she and just getting out of the service.

"I was happy about being pregnant. It was a way for me to keep my boyfriend—and be on my own. It was a way of proving I was worth something."

Special Issues for the Physically Abused ACOA

DENIAL

Denial is a part of life in a chemically dependent family. You're taught to deny what's going on, not to trust your perceptions. The message you keep getting loud and clear is: "That didn't happen."

Children growing up in alcoholic families in which there is physical abuse have had to deny both the alcoholism and the abuse. The parents make excuses for it. The battered wife will say that she tripped and fell or walked into a door to explain away the bruises on her body. The abusive parent will deny that he or she "hit" the child, instead calling it "punishment" or a "spanking." The child is made to feel as if he or she deserved it somehow.

This is particularly devastating for the child who is already feeling responsible—as so many ACOAs do—for the parent's drinking. Denial of what's really going on in the home creates a severe distortion of perception. ACOAs don't see the world clearly. They continue to discount and minimize—and, for children from abusive homes, to tolerate—inappropriate behavior. Denial is often the reason so many ACOAs are well into their adulthood before they realize that they were physically abused as children.

Tom says the "Don't talk" rule permeated and ruled his family.

TOM: *"We were taught not to love, not to speak, and not to feel. There were all of these kids in the same house, and it was as if there was this conspiracy among us. We were each other's witnesses, but it was as if our eyes and ears were closed. That was our form of self-protection. We silently accepted our doom. My mother was a quiet, religious woman, who was our model. She was physically present when the abuse was going on, but she never spoke of it and somehow shut her ears to it."*

When what is being denied is so blatantly painful, a child usually has to develop a powerful system of defenses. Tom used alcohol as his defense.

"Drinking made it possible to forget the past. It took away my fears. It enabled me to feel I could be anybody and do anything."

Meredith was thirty-nine years old before she was able to admit that the physical abuse and violence she was subjected to as a child was actually abuse and not discipline. In fact, Meredith not only denied the abuse, she and her siblings "idolized" their father.

MEREDITH: *"He was the good citizen, active on community boards, perceived as a good businessman; so nice to others. If he was such a good person, then there had to be something wrong with us. We must have deserved what we got.*

"I really came to believe that if I talked, my turn was next. I adhered to the rules: 'Don't think, be obedient; be good.' It was fear that kept me from talking.

"The 'Don't talk' rule was certainly adhered to in my family. My brothers and sisters and I never talked about my father's behavior. Never. My mother's way of coping with everything was to ignore it, thinking it would then go away. She did this with my diabetes, and she did this with my father's violent rages. Of course, later on she would do this with her drinking and her pill usage."

Monica had the "Don't talk" rule brought home to her very distinctly when she was about eight or nine.

MONICA: *"My mom was sitting on the toilet, and my father suddenly hit her so hard that she was slammed onto the bathroom floor. I was told to go roller-skating to get me out of the house. I was so worried about what condition my mother would be in when I got home that I told an adult who was on duty at the park what had happened. When I got home, I mentioned that I'd told someone. I don't remember getting hit for it, but I do remember a lot of yelling going on because of what I'd done. I never talked about what went on at home after that.*

"Nothing was ever said about my father's abuse. My mom would make excuses, saying that she bumped into things or fell down. I remember one time my mom spent the night sleeping in the car to hide from my father after one of his beatings. When she woke up the next morning, she said that she had run into the coffee table and that's why she was so black and blue."

The confusion these children experience is overwhelming. Monica's father's abuse was very related to being in a drunken rage, and her mother and father continuously antagonized each other when both were drunk. Yet she could also see her mother's total inability to defend herself physically.

Meredith learned that a man has the right to hit whomever he wants and whenever he wants, and it is not to be questioned. Tom learned that you deserve to get hit for not being smart, for not looking right, for not being manly enough. All of them learned that no one would be there to protect them.

POWERLESSNESS

Children in alcoholic families are constantly faced with their own sense of powerlessness. While they may feel responsible for their parents' drinking, they also feel powerless to control it or their own lives.

Children who are physically abused feel exceptionally powerless. They not only can't stop the drinking, they can't stop the beatings. They are physically small and vulnerable, and their parents are larger and dominant. Even the most defiant child cannot withstand a parent's physical attack. And, in fact, any attempt to fight back generally increases the parent's rage and doubles the intensity of the abuse. The abusive parent is out of control, and the child is powerless to stop it.

One of the ways in which children compensate for their powerlessness is to find ways to feel powerful. For Tom that was his drinking.

TOM: *"When I drank I could be anyone and do anything. At this time I was dominated by my anger and resentment. When Dad would hit me, I would transfer my pain by fighting someone, anyone—I didn't even care if I won or lost. Fighting was a way of releasing negative feelings dammed up inside of me. Fighting gave me a way to feel that I had some power over my life. It was my life force. It was energy. Fighting compensated for the nothingness I felt so often."*

Tom had valid reasons to be enraged. However, rage is also a mask for shame, for feelings of inadequacy. Rage gives people a way to overcome incredible powerlessness. When Tom drank, it loosened his defenses enough so he could get in touch with his rage and tap into his sense of power. The attraction was compelling and addicting.

Being violent isn't everyone's solution. Other children need to physically separate themselves from it as much as possible.

MEREDITH: *"I remember once seeing my father kick my mother across the room so hard that she landed under a chair. I felt paralyzed with fear and too powerless and impotent to help her. I remember walking away from the scene very quickly because I couldn't tolerate watching the look of humiliation on my mother's face."*

When young children don't often have the opportunity to physically separate from their surroundings, they often resort to emotional and mental separation. Some resort to fantasy, but most often they compartmentalize their feelings, or become numb to the experience. For many, in time, this often results in loss of memory of their experiences.

Because other people seldom intervene on behalf of these children, they learn early on that no one will protect them. The complicity inherent in the denial that surrounds the abuse increases the child's sense of powerlessness and vulnerability.

MEREDITH: *"Once when my father's mother was visiting, I sat between her and my father at dinner. I rarely sat next to my father at the dinner table because it was dangerous to do so. But I had a false sense of security that night because my grandmother was the one person who could put my father in his place. I saw her as strong and powerful, and I thought her strength could protect me.*

"My grandmother and father had gotten into an argument that seemed to go on for ages. It was carried on with some humor, though, and everyone at the table was laughing. It seemed as if we were having fun. Buoyed by my grandmother's strength, I risked speaking up. I told my father and grandmother to shut up. Out of nowhere, my father smacked me on the head—hard. It stopped me short, but everyone else, including my father and grandmother, continued to laugh. She scolded him jokingly, but it was as if she thought it was all part of the fun. I felt totally alone and unprotected.

"This memory stands out because it taught me that no one could protect me from my father's abuse, that it was never safe, under any circumstances, to let my guard down. I had to protect myself as best I could because he was never to be trusted."

Later on, when Meredith became the caretaker for her mother, she watched helplessly as her mother sank into a pattern of complete self-destruction.

"My mother would wake me up by crawling into bed with me, begging me to hold her. My bed was against the wall, and I felt utterly trapped, suffocated, and engulfed by her depression and her dependency. There was no escape, no remedy, no way out. I hated the intrusion. I hated the burden. I hated my mother and her helplessness. But most of all, I hated my own powerlessness in being unable to help her."

Monica also grew up with a sense of her own powerlessness. Forced to be a silent witness, she felt as if there were nothing she could do to stop the abuse against her mother and her brother. She remembers that her mother would come into her room and hide under her bed to escape her father's wrath.

MONICA: *"There was no choice—I just accepted it. I felt powerless. The only thing I felt I had any control over was to be as good as I could be.*

I always felt that it was this that spared me from my father's beatings. As long as I behaved well, I was okay.''

Monica felt equally powerless to do anything about her mother's drinking.

"My mother was on a mission to destroy herself, and there was nothing I could do to stop it. Somehow I always knew that."

FEELINGS

Like other children in alcoholic families, abused children learn to "stuff" their feelings. If they feel pain, they are taught to hide it because if they express it, things may get worse. As a result, when anger begins to rise in them, they deny it or direct it against anyone but the abuser. They feel shame at their own powerlessness, shame at their own sense of being victims. And they also feel guilt, as if somehow they deserve the beating and the abuse. They believe that the reason they are beaten is because they aren't "good enough." They live lives permeated with fear.

The feeling that Tom remembers most as a child was fear.

TOM: "I was so afraid of my father. I never knew 'when' to expect. I knew what to expect, but not when. That is what I feared. The rest of the time I didn't feel. I tried not to think about what was happening in my life. But it was too much—I just couldn't keep it all in me. Drinking became a solace for my fear, my confusion, my hurt, my shame. Drinking also gave me access to my anger. I was so full of anger and rage."

MEREDITH: "So often there was ridicule, shame, and humiliation attached to my father's abusive behavior. Frequently he would hit, kick, or beat one of us and then laugh about what we had done to incur this punishment. It was very confusing and painful to hear him laugh at those times."

Meredith said there was also a lot of merciless teasing among her siblings, which allowed them to vent their frustration and pain. Although siblings may unite for support in violent alcoholic homes, it is more common for them to be emotionally and socially detached. They have had no modeling or support for sharing. They coexist, as if they lived in encapsulated bubbles all lined up in a row. They've seen and heard each other's experiences, but they have not spoken to or touched the others directly. Often when they do interact, they simply model the behavior they've experienced, by abusing each other verbally and physically. Although all have been victims of parental abuse and neglect, some become aggressors, and others become the quiet victims one more time.

Most of Meredith's feelings were internalized.

"I locked it all in as much as I could. But periodically it would come out. I got angry a lot, but never at my dad. For instance, one of my chores on the farm was to take water over the hills to the chickens. During the winter, I would slip on the ice; I could never get to the chicken coop with all the water in the buckets. I was enraged, but it would be with the chickens, never with my dad. I'd hit the chickens with sticks, I'd break the eggs. I was furious."

It is not uncommon for children from violent families to abuse animals. As victims, children act out their shame and rage on that which they see as more vulnerable and weaker, sometimes a smaller, younger sibling, but often an animal. Animals are prime victims—they can't talk back.

"Mostly I felt defenseless and hopeless about the abuse. At some level, I felt I deserved it. I was always frightened at the prospect of its next occurrence."

That sense of being responsible for one's own sadness is typical of a child from a chemically dependent family. The inability to identify what is making you sad, and the resulting self-blame, is all part of this insidious pattern of denial and low self-esteem. The parents have denied their responsibility for the child's misery, so the child looks to himself or herself in order to blame someone. "I must have done something—or not done something—and that's why I feel this way."

MONICA: *"I spent a lot of time alone, often sitting in my room crying. I'd sit on my bed and cry, with no idea why. I just felt as if I wasn't good enough."*

The guilt that Meredith grew up with—her sense that bad things happened to her because she deserved it, manifested itself in her feelings toward her diabetes. Having heard that diabetes can be triggered by contacting a childhood disease such as measles, Meredith concluded that she was responsible for contracting her diabetes.

MEREDITH: *"I blamed myself for contracting the diabetes because I'd rubbed my face against my sister's when she had the measles. I did it so that I'd get the measles, too, and not have to work on the farm for a few days. I was eleven then, and I did contract the measles. Two years later I was diabetic."*

This type of thinking is common among children, but it is particularly prevalent when they come from violent homes. With such a distorted picture about behavior and consequences, it is easy to see how Meredith came to believe that she created diabetes from her sister's measles.

This sense of guilt was compounded by the scare tactics Meredith's mother would use on her to try to control her eating habits.

"My mother used to threaten me with all the terrible things that would happen to me if I didn't 'take care of myself.' She would describe in morbid detail how I would 'die a slow death,' losing an arm or leg first, then my sight. She told me I'd be lucky to live to be forty. For years I felt so guilty about my sneaking sugar and not taking care of myself that I was convinced I would die before I turned forty. I kept waiting to 'pay the price' for my past transgressions."

Monica was equally unable to identify or deal with the confusing feelings she had growing up in an abusive, alcoholic home. She also had a lot of anger. But, like Meredith, she knew that it was never safe to direct that anger at the abuser.

MONICA: *"I was angry a lot as a child. I had a really bad temper, and I was always telling someone off—mostly my cousins. We didn't have much money, and I felt like an outcast in our family. Even around other people I felt alone. I dealt with those feelings of loneliness and inadequacy by getting angry."*

These children not only learn not to trust their feelings and perceptions about what is going on, they learn never to trust other people as well. Adults are unreliable and unpredictable. Even siblings are seldom allies because they're in the same boat—they're just trying to survive. The parent who is not actively abusing is very often a victim, too, and of little help. These children learn that they are on their own, that no one is going to be there for them, no one is going to protect them.

Life Stories: Adulthood and Recovery

TOM
Age: 37
Partner Status: Married, three
    children
Occupation: Construction worker
Recovery Process: AA, ACOA

Tom's young adulthood was typical of an angry alcoholic.

TOM: *"At age nineteen, the acting-out child in me was in full bloom. I started using any drugs I could get my hands on. I used them in extremes, just as I used alcohol in extremes. By age twenty I was shooting up heroin. My dad caught me and tried to handle the situation with his fists. I took a geographical cure from him and my addiction by moving away and finding a job. Unfortunately it was in purchasing and shipping drugs for a hospital pharmacy. Needless to say, this job didn't last long— I was lucky not to end up incarcerated for stealing."*

Seeking some direction in his life, Tom joined the Air Force at the age of twenty-two. He had great difficulty responding both to authority and to his peers. His chemical dependency was blatant enough for him to be put into a drug and alcohol rehabilitation program.

"I fought the program until they realized I was hurting other people and kicked me out. My denial, like my dad's, was very strong. His character defects and traits no longer followed me—they were deeply embedded in me. Dad was a great teacher, and I was his prize pupil. I picked up all of his self-centeredness, dishonesty, demandingness, impatience, false promises, inconsiderate and outright abusive behavior—plus all the guilt, remorse, and low self-esteem that goes with it. I had always sworn I'd never be like Dad—but ultimately I got there."

"It Will Never Happen to Me" is the theme song of Children of Alcoholics. On the one hand, Tom's becoming alcoholic could simply have been genetic. On the other hand, Tom had very valid reasons for needing to medicate himself, which is often what Adult Children do. He needed something to take away the pain and the confusion of his life. Alcohol

provided that for him. The model of his father's alcoholism certainly reinforced characteristics common to alcoholics: self-centeredness, dishonesty, and impatience.

Tom spent the next few years in a lot of difficulty. He spent time in
jail, facing sixteen different charges for writing hot checks. He had two
bad automobile wrecks that left others severely injured. He took six geographical cures and ran through twenty different jobs. During this time
he also married and began to have children.

At the age of thirty-four, having been court-ordered to attend Alcoholic
Anonymous meetings, Tom admitted himself to a drug and alcohol treatment center.

*"It was there that I began to face my addictions. It was there that I
began to listen to others. It was there that I became open to Alcoholics
Anonymous."*

Tom had bottomed out. It took absolute despair for him to begin to
hear other people. With hindsight, it's easy to say that Tom had to get
sober or die, as he'd clearly become physically dangerous to himself by
this time. But Tom's life could have gone in either direction. The nature
of the disease is such that many people are unable to see that their lives
have hit such depths. And even if they did, many are not able to allow
others to help them. Somewhere in Tom there was enough will to live—
and to live the life of peace and serenity that each of us deserves—for
him to choose the path of recovery.

Tom found, as so many others do, that Alcoholics Anonymous was his
first safe home. In these groups he found guidance and direction as well
as unconditional love. In AA he found models for giving and receiving.
And Tom was ready and willing.

*"Since then Alcoholics Anonymous has been my way of life. I go to
meetings regularly. I work the Twelve Steps of AA. I pray to my Higher
Power on a daily basis. It was in AA that I began to feel and share the
love that has always been in me. Today I can show my wife and children
my love. I can look in the mirror and see someone I love. I can talk. It
was in AA that I learned to cry. Today I'm able to cry without thinking
of myself as less of a man."*

*"I had also heard people talking about being Adult Children, and I knew
that a lot of what I needed to work on was related to my childhood. My
wife had never known about my childhood until after I sobered up. It was
in sobriety that I could break my denial, and that I was given the opportunity to begin to trust others."*

It was not possible for Tom to begin his Adult Child recovery until he was sober. And it would only be after he was feeling safe in AA, able to trust others and be more trusting of himself, that Adult Child recovery could begin. There's a lot of his past that Tom needs to put behind him, and he needed the additional program that ACOA could provide.

Tom began to read about Adult Children and also to participate in Adult Child self-help groups.

"These groups are relatively new to me. But I'm developing a greater acceptance of myself in Adult Child meetings. I'm also more understanding with myself and not so quick to blame others. The more I could accept myself, the more I could accept others. My wife and I argue less and less. I'm more loving. There's been a lot of pain in my marriage, and some of it I can't take away. I only hope that my recovery will offer a climate for my wife to do the healing she needs to do, too. One of the areas I'm most grateful for is that my children are still young—they need me, and I take being a parent seriously. I want to be there for them. I want my wife and me to be there for them together. But that will take a bit more time.

"Today I have hope where there was no hope."

MEREDITH
Age: 43
Partner Status: Divorced, one child
Occupation: Nurse
Recovery Process: Therapy,
    Overeaters Anonymous, ACOA

When Meredith returned from her first year at college for Christmas vacation, she found her mother in an extremely bad state.

MEREDITH: *"I realized then that my mother was really in trouble. She was barely functioning, and my brother and sister were taking care of themselves. My mother was depressed, flat, and energyless.*

"My next oldest sister also came home at that time and convinced my mother to see another psychiatrist. The one she had been seeing was merely prescribing medication, which my mother was abusing. Even though my father visited regularly, he did nothing to help. Neither did the new psychiatrist."

When Meredith returned home for the summer, she was faced with a very difficult choice.

"My older sister sat me down and informed me that I would have to take over. She was going to graduate school out of state. It was up to me to take care of my mother, my brother, and my sister. I would have to drop out of college if my mother didn't get any better.

"That summer was a nightmare. My mother, who was later diagnosed as manic-depressive, was not functioning at all. In her agitated depression, she would spend the entire day, every day, wringing her hands and pacing the floor. She would repeatedly ask me for help and then respond to nothing I said. She would try desperately to wait until five P.M. to have her first drink. Once the clock struck five, she would have three or four large glasses of Scotch in rapid succession. Then she would stop pacing and wringing her hands, sit down at the dinner table, and obsess over which of her many pills she had taken already and which ones she should take for the evening."

Meredith attempted to control her mother's pill intake, fearful that the combination of alcohol and pills would kill her, but her mother became resentful of the interference. At night Meredith would lie in bed, listening to her mother's breathing, wondering if she would ever wake up again.

"It wasn't until my mother started to drink beer at noon and she began to fall down and pass out in the middle of the afternoon that I finally called my father and asked for help. He seemed very irritated by my call, and I felt guilty for having to ask. I kept trying to justify my reasons for calling. He said he'd see what he could do.

"Later that day, he arrived and asked me to pack a bag for my mother, saying that he was going to take her to a psychiatric hospital. I felt incredibly sad and guilty about letting my mother down, as I watched her being led to the car. I felt guilty for my anger at her, and I felt responsible for her plight because I hadn't been able to help her."

When this happened Meredith was only nineteen years old and was attempting to handle a mentally disturbed and alcoholic mother single-handedly. Her father had abdicated his parenting role—there were no other adult figures in these children's lives.

Meredith had clearly learned that she was responsible for others' well-being and behavior. She was already learning that her self-esteem and self-worth were based on being successful at helping others. It is not coincidental to see children from troubled families enter the helping professions. One could easily guess that Meredith would end up being a nurse with the script she'd had of taking care of her mother. This is what gave her a sense of value, a sense of worth.

Meredith's mother returned from the hospital depressed and vacant. She'd been given shock treatments and couldn't remember anything. She continued to drink and abuse pills.

Yet Meredith managed to continue her college education because the other children took turns taking care of their mother. Meredith was already using diet pills and just trying to survive. The "Don't think" and "Don't feel" rules were in full operation. But as strong as these rules are, feelings don't go away—fear, anger, guilt, loneliness, all fester within.

Many college-bound Adult Children are so overwhelmed by the past that they succumb to feeling powerless to act on their own behalves. Out of a sense of duty and obligation they often negate themselves, giving up what could be extremely helpful to them to stay locked in the dysfunctional family system. Therefore, Meredith's ability to continue in college was very important.

Meredith's mother's abuse continued for another ten years.

"My mother was very self-destructive, often making suicide attempts—two of them were nearly fatal. My brother and sister each did their 'tour of duty,' taking care of her until they went away to college. My father was available only at crisis times, when my mother required hospitalization."

Finally, a doctor diagnosed Meredith's mother as manic-depressive and prescribed lithium, which worked almost immediately. Meredith's mother remained fairly stable on the lithium, although she continued to abuse alcohol.

"While I was in college, I would repeatedly get involved with men who were like my father—abusive with power. I got very depressed myself and became hooked on diet pills, which were a part of my ongoing battle with my weight. Finally, in my sophomore year, I swore off diet pills and had a terrible emotional crash. I also swore off men like my father. But then I proceeded to get involved with men who were like my mother— depressed and crazy.

"In my twenties I finally got into therapy. It was apparent to me that I was depressed, and with my sister's urging I went into therapy. The therapist encouraged me to get in touch with the anger I felt about my mother. But we didn't look at any childhood abuse or father issues, we stayed focused on my adult relationship with Mom."

Although Meredith's therapy was helpful, its effects were not comprehensive since too much of her life was ignored in the process.

Meredith proceeded with her life—going to school and finding her niche in nursing. While she was doing graduate work in nursing, there was a period in which she was making home visits to those reported to be abusing children. But even at this time her own denial of having been an abused child remained intact. She could feel compassion for the other children. She could see their plight. But she was still so emotionally removed from herself that even while working with abusive families, she had no awareness of her own abused child self.

The inner pain is so overwhelming for children raised in violent homes that it is rare for them not to succumb to addictive substances or compulsive behavior as a means of medicating or separating themselves from their lives. For Meredith, sugar was the answer, beginning in her teenage years. She was constantly medicating herself with sugar. Consciously she was in such a struggle with her powerlessness over food versus her desire to be in control that for several years she yo-yoed between dieting and overeating. As time passed, though, she discovered that her ability to be self-controlling—and to deny—was waning.

"I would have private temper tantrums. I'd throw things, slam doors, and swear a lot. I'd become enraged at the slightest frustration—getting stuck in traffic or losing my keys, and not being able to get the door open. All the things I'd locked in as a child were slowly slipping out."

In her late twenties, Meredith began group therapy.

"I got involved with group therapy because I was still choosing very hurtful men in my life. It was here I recognized my terror when men would get physically near me, and I would panic because I wouldn't know what they'd do next. It helped when I stopped picking men like my father. But switching to ones like my mother wasn't a great improvement."

Meredith was developing insight and wanted to live her life differently, but she hadn't yet learned the skills that could make that happen.

When she was thirty-three, Meredith met the man who was to become her husband. Once they were married, though, she realized that she had once again picked someone who was just like her father.

"My husband was an alcoholic, in his early stages. He was emotionally and sexually abusive. By the second year of our marriage, I asked him to go to a marriage counselor with me. He lasted four sessions and then quit. I remained in counseling, and two and half years after we were married, we were divorced."

Up to this time Meredith had been determined not to pass on the family legacy of alcoholism and abuse. She felt she had no models for healthy parenting, and her fear was so great that she did not want children. Yet in what was clearly an unhealthy marriage, Meredith became pregnant. She was thirty-four years old and diabetic, but as much as she was frightened by the prospect of parenting, she also felt this was her only chance.

"With recovery I see how my not wanting a child was based on my fears, not out of choice. Today I know I have a great deal to offer my child."

Shortly after leaving the marriage, Meredith began to attend Overeaters Anonymous meetings. In her therapy, as she became increasingly more honest with herself, she was able to see that her sugar addiction was not only self-destructive, but, with her diabetes, it was lethal.

"I realized that if I continued to destroy myself with my sugar abuse, I would be abandoning my daughter even more than I myself had been abandoned.

"At OA I immediately felt I had come home—to a safe home—for the first time in my life."

Many ACOAs have this sense of coming home when they enter self-help groups. That has a lot to do with the person's readiness for the group, but it also has to do with seeing the group as a safe place. It is a place where shame-based people know they will not feel judged, so they can be less judgmental of themselves. It is a place where people find not only unconditional acceptance, but consistency. It's a place where people can speak the truth. That's what it represented to Meredith. And once she stopped using sugar, she found that feelings and memories from her childhood began to emerge.

A friend then offered her a book on co-dependency. She saw herself immediately. This led her to attend two workshops on ACOA and co-dependency issues, and it was here that her denial of physical abuse was broken.

"I was stunned! But at last I understood that it was not discipline I had been subjected to—I had been abused! And so blatantly.

"As the memories came up, I felt it important to find a therapist who specialized in physical and sexual abuse. I don't have a clear recall of my childhood, but my dreams and certain images that arise suggest to me that, in addition to physical abuse, I was also the victim of incest. My

youngest sister recalls being both physically and sexually abused by my father.''

Sugar had been a way for Meredith to exert control over the powerlessness of her life. But sugar is also medication that soothes and anesthetizes. Without it, it is common for physical and sexual abuse victims to begin to recall many memories that have been suppressed.

Meredith has since actively continued her recovery in OA. She sought out an inpatient co-dependency treatment program and actively participates in week-long co-dependency workshops throughout the year.

She also continues to work on her Adult Child and abuse issues. She regularly attends OA meetings as well as a co-dependency self-help group.

"Because of my ACOA background and my history of being abused, it has been hard for me to let people in. I'm only just beginning to do that, but I am becoming more trusting. The hardest part is trusting them to stay there once I let them in. I'm still frightened to show how vulnerable I am, although I have been able to do that a little in the last few months with my women friends.

"I'm learning to say what I need to say in my relationships with people without attempting to control the outcome. I need to be able to let go. Whenever I do, it gives me a new sense of integrity that I never had before. I feel as if I'm finally taking care of my inner child in a way she's never been taken care of before, both at work and with friends and family.

"I've done a lot of rage work, and today I believe my rage has lifted. There are no more sudden, eruptive tantrums. Now I can distance myself and think things through before I react. I'm consistent, and I'm learning to protect myself in healthy ways. I am healing, and I know I'll be able to walk safely through the incest issues that are arising now, too.

"I'm learning to put myself out there in ways that are not abusive or destructive to me. I have healthy friends. All in all, I have a better sense of what it means to be a healthy person. I realize that I have power in my life.

"I'm learning how to set safe and healthy limits around my anger. What I'm most grateful for is the opportunity to be a healthy mother. Today I see options when I interact with my daughter. Each time I talk things through with her rather than exploding, I know I'm mending inside. I make mistakes, and I have the ability to recognize them. But I am able to say, 'I'm sorry.' I never heard those words as a child. The miracle of recovery is that I get a chance to heal my own wounds as I parent my daughter differently from the way I was parented.''

MONICA

Age: 44
Partner Status: Remarried, three
   children
Occupation: Medical records
   assistant
Recovery Process: Church

At seventeen Monica found herself married to a man who was both alcoholic and abusive. They were married for twelve years and had three children.

MONICA: *"Our marriage was one long roller-coaster ride. There were extreme highs and extreme lows. Our two oldest children suffered the consequences of having children for parents."*

They also felt the consequences of having two alcohol-abusing parents, as Monica joined her husband and began drinking heavily. Her oldest daughter took on the role of the responsible child.

"By the time my daughter was nine years old, she was taking care of the household so her father and I could party. My husband was never home. He'd never help with anything, even when I was sick. I never knew where he was."

In the later years of their marriage, Monica's husband began to be physically abusive to her, often beating her until her face was so swollen she couldn't wear her glasses. He also abused the children with severe slapping on the side of the head. Monica herself would often lose control in trying to discipline the kids, and she too became abusive. She and her children were victims of generationally abusive behavior. As a child, Monica witnessed abuse. Now, as a wife, she was the direct recipient of it, and she herself abused her own children.

"I was a strict disciplinarian, especially with the two oldest ones. I would spank them and then lose control. I always responded to whatever they did in a physical way. Afterward I'd be so appalled by what I'd done that I'd feel mortified with guilt. But I couldn't seem to stop myself, and the beatings continued.

"The kids were so bruised at times that I was once reported for child

abuse. *Ironically, the time I was reported, they had found a little girl severely bruised in my neighborhood who was my daughter's age and everyone assumed she was my daughter. The neighbors had been listening for years to terrible ranting and raving by me toward my kids, and my children had certainly been bruised by my hitting.*

"Boy, the things I said I'd never do to my kids because of what happened to me when I was growing up! Unfortunately, here I was repeating it all over again."

Monica continued her pattern of partying and heavy drinking.

"I was running, ignoring, abusing alcohol. By the time my husband and I had been married eleven years, the beatings I was getting from him had become life-threatening, and I knew I had to get out. I wasn't going to be like my mother, so I divorced my husband. My mother wouldn't talk to me for a year after that. She believed that since she had lived through it, I should, too."

Monica was only able to identify with her mother once the beatings were perceived as life-threatening. Her denial was so great that she could not see the similarities between her parents' married life and her own— her brother's beatings, her abusive drinking, her children being abused, or her husband beating her so severely that she couldn't wear glasses.

Life remained difficult for Monica after the divorce. She became involved with a man who looked like, acted like, drank like, and beat her like her first husband.

In time she became so despondent that she attempted suicide with pills and alcohol. Monica is alive today only because a neighbor found her inadvertently. However, she soon realized that she didn't want to continue her mother's suicidal patterns of behavior.

"As a child, I couldn't stand my mother. As an adult, I could feel compassion and pity for her. But one thing I knew, I never wanted to be like her. In a way, I give her credit for saving my life. After my suicide attempt, no matter how bad things got, I refused to give in to the pressure and be weak."

Within two years of being divorced, Monica's son went to live with his father, who had remarried.

"I didn't fight it, because I was so hurt. I was working two jobs and partying, so obviously I wasn't home too much. Even when I was, I was usually drunk or hung over and not very pleasant to be around.

"By the time my oldest daughter was fourteen, she began running

away from home. Finally, when she was seventeen, she left and said she wouldn't come back. I thought I'd tried everything with her. But I never once gave up my drinking, and I never once faced how much she was drinking and drugging herself. We'd had a special relationship when she was younger, but it all went down the tubes for many years after that.''

Monica's thinking was distorted, like that of any alcohol abuser. She believed she'd tried everything with her daughter, yet she'd never considered that it might be her drinking life-style that was influencing her children. That is the nature of an alcoholic. Finally Monica gave up alcohol and tried to put her life back together.

''My youngest child wasn't willing to sit in silence. She began to confront me. I owe my changing to her. I was so tired by then, I knew I had to do something. Unconsciously I began repeating my father's pattern. I quit my heavy drinking just as my youngest child entered her teens. I quit partying and dating. I stayed home with my daughter and learned to enjoy being home. One by one, my partying friends stopped coming by.

''I became involved in the church again. Church had been important as a child. I found a lot of love there, and a lot of support and friendship. I just kept putting one foot in front of the other. I chose good, healthy friendships and learned what it means to feel supported and accepted. I began to open up more, and this helped me put my life back together. The more I opened up, the more I was able to deal with what I'd locked away inside myself, and the more I was able to let go of the anger.

''The biggest area I've had to work on is my anger. I've had to learn to think things through, to be fair to others. I had used anger to keep people away, and I had to take a hard look at that. I also learned about 'tough love,' which helped me a lot in becoming a better parent to my daughters.''

After ten years of being single, and three years of healing through her church, Monica met a man whom she eventually married.

''I was emotionally strong at this point. I was healthy, and I wasn't about to spend my life with someone who wasn't. Rob is also very strong, but I married him because I chose to be with him, not because I needed him to take over my life.

''My youngest daughter gets all the benefits of growing up with an emotionally stable man, but she remembers a lot from the bad years. She won't discuss it, though. She does stay out of trouble, and she seems to enjoy friendships with a healthy group of kids.

''My son was basically raised by his stepmother. But he and I are working on building a strong relationship, and it keeps getting better and

better. There's still so much to work at in recovery, but I'm learning to accept responsibility for what I do and what I've done.''

The legacy of abuse and chemical dependency was still overshadowing Monica's family. Though she had begun to heal, two of her children were essentially out of the home when this healing began.

And the generational cycle of abuse continued. In time Monica's oldest daughter was reported to the Children's Protective Services for child abuse. Wanting to be of support to her daughter, and wanting to commit to stopping the cycle of abuse, Monica and all of her children went into therapy together. Experiencing recovery, Monica says, "We are all growing."

Recovery Considerations

Since abused children cannot protect themselves physically, they fight doubly hard to protect their emotional being. That means they are usually even more frightened of showing their feelings than other Adult Children. When children are physically attacked, they feel this as a violent statement about their lack of worth. Because abused children need to protect themselves so much more, the fear of trusting others becomes incredibly powerful.

In addition, the need to defend has been so strong, and the pain of recovery is so great, that abused Adult Children need to move at a slower, safer pace than other ACOAs. I strongly encourage abused Adult Children to be open to using helping professionals. Therapists can provide the additional safety that allows one to take risks and do the sharing that is necessary.

In my experience, when Adult Children feel safe enough, they are more than willing to share. When they get the opportunity to hear others talk about the physical violence they suffered—and they are with a person or a group that is safe—they will find a sense of relief and a level of acceptance they never experienced before.

FEELINGS

These are very important messages:

- Nothing bad need happen when you show your feelings.
- Feelings are perfectly human.
- You are not unique; there isn't a feeling you have had that many others haven't experienced.

- You are not weak.
- You are a human being who has experienced much pain.
- You are vulnerable.
- You can have many feelings at the same time.

As pain from the past is expressed and released, there will be more room in your life for joy and happiness.

People who have been physically violated need to spend time on the issues with anger. However, sometimes they discount this need and focus on their depth of sadness and hurt. This is understandable and also necessary, but in time anger will also have to be addressed.

Someone who has been physically abused has much to be sad and angry about. To be physically—or sexually—abused is a terrible violation of who you are as a person. It is a blatant act of betrayal by those who are supposed to love and care for you—a betrayal by the abuser and by your other parent, who didn't protect you.

In recovery, as you begin to feel safe, and as you begin to talk about your experiences, the validation that comes with just being listened to often brings up a welter of feelings. The feelings that come first are those that seem to be the safest. Begin with those, and other feelings will follow. There is no right way to "do feelings," so don't judge yourself by how much or how little you cry or by how loud your voice is compared with another's. If you are struggling with having any feelings, talk about the fear you feel. Recognize that the fears are often based on childhood realities—but today, that reality has changed. Only by recognizing fear can it be confronted.

Below we will discuss a number of highly charged feelings in some detail:

Anger. Because anger burns out of control in abusive families, becoming angry still represents being out of control to many Adult Children. However, the anger and rage you lived with as a child does not have to be the anger you experience today. Yesterday's anger was rage and shame, acted out on innocent victims. Today, anger can be a healthy emotion that offers clues to your real needs.

There are ways to express anger properly, ways that allow your voice to be heard. You do not need to repeat your family's pattern. If you have any fears of physically acting out your anger, it is vital for you to be in therapy. Having lived with the combination of terror and powerlessness, the Adult Child often finds it necessary to speak to that pain. This is usually an emotionally charged process that the ACOA needs to physically act out in a safe setting. Rage does not need to be turned inward or toward others. In therapeutic settings, through the use of battacas, or pillows, ACOAs can speak or yell their anger and physically release their pain. A therapist can provide a safe setting to work with your anger and make certain that you do not hurt yourself or anyone else.

Ultimately you will need to own your anger about the past. As you become adept at owning other feelings, your anger will begin to feel less frightening and more focused. When you unload your anger about the past, it becomes possible to not overreact or underreact to the things that make you angry in the present. It becomes possible to find ways to express your anger so that you will not feel out of control and so it will not interfere with or influence what is occurring in the present.

Love and Hate. Adult Children are often confused about love. And those who experienced abuse are even more confused about love and hate. COAs live in families where the abuser and/or chemically dependent person changes personalities—shifting unexpectedly back and forth between Dr. Jekyll and Mr. Hyde. This is very crazy making because it feels as though you're dealing with two different people. Children learn to relate very differently to each of the personalities as they present themselves.

A part of the craziness in living in an alcoholic family is living with the inconsistency of personalities and the change of personalities over time. It is possible to feel love about or toward a parent at specific times. Many children learned to love a parent in the earlier years as he or she was more available, attentive, and responsive to their needs. As abuse and chemical dependency progressed, they became frightened, angry, and confused and rightfully questioned the love they once felt. Some Adult Children think they are crazy for still loving someone who has been so hurtful to them, or they feel crazy for loving and hating the same person.

Many Adult Children easily identify with loving and hating at the same time. To feel both love and hate is a perfectly normal response to an abnormal situation. Yet the hate many people experience is also mixed with rage. Hate is a more dispassionate feeling than rage; it is about loathing another, despising another. Rage is about intense feelings of anger combined with fear and humiliation.

Once you become more comfortable with identifying a range of feelings, you are less apt to feel as frightened as you were when you bounced from one extreme to another. There are many words to describe the vast range and shades of feelings between love and hate. Lovingness can be found in affection, devotion, fondness, comfort, and warmth. Hatefulness can be expressed in offensiveness, obnoxiousness, malice, and hostility.

Remember, when raised in troubled families it is very common to have mixed or contradictory feelings. People can, and do, have many feelings at the same time. The more skilled you become at naming your feelings, the less overwhelmed you'll feel in the face of seeming contradictions.

Love for Parents. Adult Children in general, but certainly people who have lived with abuse—physical or sexual—question whether or not they love their parent(s) or why they still feel love for their parent(s). A child such as Tom, who lived with chronic violence, may not have received enough caring from his father to feel any love toward him. *Recovery does not mandate that you love your parents.*

Although many Adult Children do still feel love for their parents— sometimes life was so heinous that love is nonexistent. If you don't love your parent, does that necessarily mean you hate your parent? No. Not at all. Remember, it need not be an all-or-nothing situation. There are many shades of love and many shades of hate—and a broad spectrum of feelings in between. The absence of love does not mean that hate is all that's left.

As Tom tells his story, he's still feeling very detached from his father. He feels an absence of love and little else. This is because he's just beginning to thaw out emotionally. He knows that he is feeling sad, and he's able to own how much fear he has felt in his life. Once he becomes more comfortable with his newfound feelings, he will be ready to find out how he really feels about his father. When he does, he will discover that he feels anger and rage. As he walks through those feelings in recovery, he will come to a greater acceptance of himself and have more clarity about his true feelings toward both parents.

Meredith and Monica were able to feel safe enough to speak of their anger early in recovery. This was partly because they had felt some attachment toward the abuser and partly because they didn't feel as much fear and shame as Tom.

Loving Others. Adult Children fear that if they weren't loved as children, they won't be able to experience love as adults. This is not true. Because we did not receive love on a consistent basis as children, we struggle with the meaning of love and how it is displayed. In recovery, however, we discover that we are very capable of loving. And we learn that the love we have for a friend, a child, or a lover is a different kind of love from that which we have for a parent. The bonding process involved in being totally dependent on someone is different from what we experience when we voluntarily choose to be with another person. The love bond between parent and child is nature's way of assuring survival. Parents are expected to provide their children with shelter—the basic necessities of life. As children we were physically, emotionally, psychologically, and socially dependent on our parents for the first several years of our lives. Because of our dependence on their care, they held total power over us. They were the supreme judges of our worth and value. But we are no longer dependent. We are now able to pick and choose those we love and have relationships with.

I believe that within each adult person there lives a wondrous loving child—wanting to love and to be loved. Although that person may literally have been beaten, that loving child remains within each and every one of us, whether we are five, twenty-five, or eighty-five.

We must first learn self-respect and self-love before we are truly capable of loving another. COAs internalize their anger and become self-loathing. Adult Children need to let go of this self-hate before they can fully receive or give love.

Some people are more adept at serving others' needs than their own. Early recovery entails learning to extend that caring to oneself. Loving yourself will make you a loving person to others. In recovery, that starts with learning basic self-care habits—learning to eat and sleep correctly, for example. It may mean learning how to bathe properly, learning skin care, hair care, and proper dress. Later it may mean going to school so that you have more options in life.

Loving yourself means asking what you want to give to yourself. What do you want in terms of friends, activities, health, and possessions? As you begin attending to your needs, you will develop a respect for yourself that, in turn, will lead to your being more respectful of others.

Self-Hate. Adult Children must challenge the hurtful messages they heard and internalized when they were little. When they don't, they continue to operate from a basis of those old, destructive attitudes:

- You are bad.

- You are stupid.

- You can't do anything right.

- You are incompetent. You can't do anything right.

- You are worthless. You don't deserve.

- You are a loser. You will never amount to anything.

These attitudes are learned as much from other people's behavior as from their words. When children are hit they receive the message that they are not of value. When children live with the continual fear of being hit, the message is that they are powerless. Adult Children need to say *No* to these hurtful messages and then create new, self-empowering messages:

- *No*, I am not bad. I am good.

- *No*, I am not stupid. I am smart.

- *No*, I am not a loser. I will amount to something.

- *No*, I am not incompetent. I can do things correctly.

- *No*, I am not worthless. I have value. I do deserve.

By saying *No*, you are now free to find the *Yes*es in your life. *Yes*, I am smart. *Yes*, I will amount to something. *Yes*, I can do things correctly. *Yes*, I am worthy. *Yes*, I do deserve.

No and *Yes* are important words in recovery. *No* is a particularly important word for those who were blatantly victimized, because it was most likely the least safe word to use. You couldn't say *No*—in words or behavior—to the abuser without the threat of further—and worse—abuse.

We learned that other people could use the word *No* to hurt us, but we weren't allowed to use *No* to protect ourselves. The use of the word *No* needs to be reframed. *No* is now a word that you may use for your own protection and safety. Saying *No* allows you to set limits, to protect boundaries. Being able to say *No* also gives a greater meaning to *Yes*. When you are free to say *No*, it means you are able to say *Yes* from choice, not from fear or the need for approval.

But before you practice using *No* on others, you need to use it with your internal messages. This can be more difficult than it sounds. It means believing in yourself after years of being ignored, hit, and terrorized, with no one to believe in you. Today, as you come to believe in yourself, and as you begin to surround yourself with healthier people, you will find that others do believe in you.

The whole issue of love is so confusing when one has been raised with violence. We learn that the people who supposedly love us seemingly have the right to hurt us. As adults, establishing healthy love relationships means setting healthy boundaries. *No*s and *Yes*es help to establish those boundaries.

SIBLINGS

Brothers and sisters in chemically dependent families may feel a survivorship bond, but more than likely there will also be a considerable emotional—and often physical—distance between them. This is even more true for those children who suffered abuse because they spent so much more time simply trying to survive. This, in turn, interfered with the normal activities of childhood—playing and sharing. What these abused children truly have in common is terror. Although sexual abuse is more hidden, and done behind closed doors, physical abuse is evident to all the other family members. Yet together they often keep the secret hidden from those outside the family.

When adult siblings are together, they are forced to come face to face with the deepest pain in their lives. Unless you are in a recovery process, often the presence of a sibling only serves to remind you of something you are still trying to defend against.

When one or two siblings are singled out for more abuse than their brothers or sisters, it creates even greater distances between them. The severely abused child may have a greater sense of self-loathing, a greater sense of "I am bad," contrasted with the belief that the spared siblings are "good." Perhaps of even greater significance, the abused child knows that the other brothers and sisters have witnessed this shaming.

Another dynamic that creates distance between siblings is when the "spared" children feel shame for having been helpless witnesses. In their inability to help the beaten child, they experience an overwhelming sense of inadequacy and powerlessness. The resulting shame and guilt only makes it more difficult for siblings to reach out and support each other.

REPEATING THE CYCLE

It is highly likely that your family has been part of a chain of abuse. If your great-grandfather had red hair, your grandfather had red hair, and your father had red hair, there is a very strong probability that you have red hair and your children will, too. Abuse is similar; it too passes from generation to generation. Though not all alcoholics learn their drinking at their parents' knees, children frequently imitate the drinking styles of their parents. Similarly, not all family abusers learn their behavior in their parents' homes. But the overwhelming tendency is to punish as we were punished, to construct our marriages as our parents did, and to continue to tolerate the levels of abuse we learned in childhood.

Abuse and its consequences can continue on and on in an unbroken line. However, with recovery, the cycle can be stopped. Because those who were physically abused are likely to become abusers themselves— or victims of others' abuse—it is vital to begin recovery by addressing Adult Child issues. This is a major step toward putting the past cycle behind you. The next, and equally important step, is to develop specific boundaries that have to do with abuse to help assure your recovery and the safety of those you love.

You Will Not Hit Anyone.
Think ahead. Make a plan for what you will do should you feel or see the clues that you are losing control and that you may become abusive. Certain words, a tightening of the jaw, clenching of your fists, a rush of blood to the face, may all be specific clues that indicate you may be heading toward a loss of control. It is crucial to identify your early-warning signs because that is the time to react.

What kind of plan of action can you respond to immediately? Many such plans include removing yourself from any potential victims at once. You can go into a different room or go out for a walk—you might even spend the night away. Obviously circumstances vary about what is feasible.

Know whom you will call for support and guidance. Should you hit a person, immediately seek the assistance of a helping professional. There are also support groups, such as Parents Anonymous and Parents United, for abusive parents, should you find yourself in a potential or actual child abuse situation. See appendix, page 571.

Realize that your history is too traumatic for you too resolve these issues on your own.

Very often, Adult Children don't even know what "normal" is. This means that when you're raising your own children, it can be difficult to know what is age appropriate when your parents were unrealistic in their expectations of you. They may not have offered you any basic care, which means you have no proper models for the care of your own children.

If this is true for you, take classes and read books on parenting skills. Talk to parents who have children the age of yours. Ask them how they do things. Don't parent in isolation. Ask questions, observe healthy families. Be constantly aware that your children are not here to meet your needs or to reflect your worth or self-image. They are entirely separate entities, unique individuals who need and deserve unconditional love and a physically safe environment in which to grow.

Do not allow yourself to be in a relationship where you or your children are hit.

Before you can continue to live with this person, the perpetrator must receive professional help and begin recovery. Only after he or she has made a commitment to receiving help and has begun that process should you consider any reconciliation.

And you too must receive help. This is not the time to get bogged down in self-criticism. Don't ask yourself yet again, "How can I do this to my own children?" or tell yourself, "I must have deserved this." At this time these questions are useless. Because abuse is generational, it is very easy to repeat the patterns. You deserve much better than this. And you can have it. But you must do the work. The chain can be broken.

You need not live in fear. Through recovery, you can find new freedom and new happiness.

I wasn't bad. I never was, and I am not today.

—Battered Adult Child

Notes

1. C. Black, S. Bucky, S. Padilla, "The Interpersonal and Emotional Consequences of Being an Adult Child of an Alcoholic," *Journal of International Addictions* 21 (May 1986), 213–23.

5

Sexual Abuse

I learned to cry quietly, if at all. I would blank out or drift off as if I weren't there. I felt dead.

—Adult Child

The Prevalence of Incest

Incest is one of our most ancient social taboos. Today it is both illegal and considered abhorrent. Yet it is commonly practiced in this country. According to a *Los Angeles Times* survey, it is estimated that nearly 38 million adults were sexually abused as children. Twenty-two percent of those questioned—27 percent of the women and 16 percent of the men—said they had been sexually abused as children.[1]

A survey of 250,000 cases, referred to a Child Sexual Assault Treatment Program, indicates that one in every three women and one in every seven men have been sexually abused by the time they reach the age of eighteen.[2]

In one of the largest and most complex studies of this type, Diana Russell, a Harvard sociologist, interviewed more than nine hundred randomly chosen women about their childhood sexual experiences. She found that nearly four women in every ten had been sexually abused before the age of eighteen by an adult relative or acquaintance.[3]

187

While incest is a taboo, it is much more prevalent than people are willing to accept. The greater taboo seems to be talking about it. But because incest is so traumatizing, when it is shrouded in silence the trauma is exacerbated.

Although I am focusing on incest in this chapter, I have no intention of minimizing the results of other types of sexual abuse. The effect of any sort of sexual abuse is always serious. But keeping with the focus of this book, I will specifically address incest within chemically dependent families.

Chemical dependency and incest often coexist in the same family. Several small studies have documented that more than 50 percent of known incest victims have lived in homes where alcohol abuse was a major problem. In my own research, I've found that daughters of alcoholics were two times more likely to be incest victims than daughters from nonaddicted families, and 27 percent of the female Adult Children I surveyed reported incidents of incest.[4]

In a more recent study, Dan Sexton and Dr. Jon Conte of the University of Chicago found that among six hundred adult survivors of child sexual abuse, 60 percent were self-described Children of Alcoholics.[5]

This is not meant to imply that one causes the other. What it does suggest is that both frequently occur within the same family, and therefore the possibility that both issues may exist must be addressed and responded to. This is important, because the treatment of recovery from one issue does not automatically offer a full recovery for the other.

How Incest Is Manifested

Incest is one form of childhood sexual abuse. Incest occurs when a person related to a child or in a parental role—a parent, aunt, uncle, grandparent, sibling, cousin, also a stepparent or one who assumes parenting duties—acts with sexual overtones and/or imposes sexual acts on a child to meet his or her own sexual/emotional needs and/or to superimpose his or her authority. It is an act of violence and selfishness, and it is a violation of a position of trust, power, and protection. Perpetrators seldom commit childhood sexual abuse solely to satisfy their own sexual needs. They do it to exercise power over someone. Incest is an abhorrent crime perpetrated on defenseless children. And it thrives on silence.

Because incest survivors have lived in silence so long, it may be helpful to describe some of the behavior that is to be considered sexually abusive. The following is an abbreviated list from Suzanne Sgroi, *Handbook of Clinical Intervention in Child Sexual Abuse:*

- Genital exposure by the adult to the child.
- Observation of child (watching a child undress, bathe, or urinate).
- Kissing. The adult kisses the child in a lingering or intimate way.
- Fondling. The adult fondles the child's breast, abdomen, genital area, inner thighs, or buttocks. The child may similarly fondle the adult at his or her request.
- Masturbation. The adult masturbates while the child observes; the adult observes the child masturbating; mutual masturbation.
- Cunnilingus/fellatio—oral-genital contact.
- Finger or object penetration.
- Penis penetration. Penetration may be either of the anus rectal or the vaginal area—or both.[6]

Abusers use power, age, experience, and position to persuade, coax, bribe, and threaten their victims into doing things they are not old enough or emotionally mature enough to cope with or defend against. The perpetrator takes advantage of the child's emotional, social, or physical dependence on him/her. If the person who becomes sexual with the child is even just a few years older than the child, or holds a position of power or authority, it is considered to be sexual molestation; if the person is related to the child, it is incest. Both constitute sexual abuse.

Even if the victim doesn't try to stop it, *the child is not responsible for the sexual abuse.* Remember, a child who is the victim of incest usually has no place to escape to and is too frightened to tell. Children are too young and immature to make the kinds of decisions that are involved in this type of sexual behavior. It is the responsibility—and the fault—of the older, more powerful person.

It is common for victims to become confused about the abuse when they were not physically forced to comply. But incest is an insidious type of violence that often does not require physical force. However, that does not mean the children wanted it to happen.

Perpetrators often play on trust to coerce their victim into meeting their demands. It is well known that abusers often choose children starving for attention, warmth, and affection. Children from troubled families are prime victims because they are particularly desperate for any sign of attention and affection.

Even more stressful, the victims are often afraid the family will break up if they don't go along with what the perpetrator wants. The alcoholic family is already on such shaky ground that children are terrified of losing the little they still have. They feel that if the family were to break up, they would be responsible for it.

In addition, victims often fear they will not be believed if they tell. And that could well be true, for this is already a family where telling the truth is not supported. As if this weren't enough, the perpetrator often threatens to hurt the victim, another family member, or a pet if the child tells. For the child in an alcoholic home, this is just one more threatening consequence of asking for help or telling the truth.

Another form of incest is one that is less easy to identify—especially for Adult Children. This is covert, or emotional, incest. Although emotional incest may be less overt, it is extremely traumatizing. Children are seriously damaged by emotional incest such as

- When their parents talk about specific sexual acts.
- When there is chronic nudity or nudity at inappropriate times.
- When children are forced to hear or even watch adults having sex.
- When there is sexual name calling.
- When they live in constant fear of sexual abuse occurring in their lives.

Children from alcoholic families are even less able to defend themselves against their offenders. They have greater difficulty knowing what their feelings are. They have a greater fear in trusting their own perceptions and trusting others. They are more confused about what constitutes appropriate limits and boundaries. And their sense of shame is already much greater than that experienced by children from nonalcoholic families. These problems occur without sexual abuse. But when sexual abuse also becomes a part of their life experience, the effects are even more intense.

COAs have already had to deal with a wall of denial when they attempt to discern the truth about what is going on in their lives. They have had to deal with a sense of powerlessness over the alcoholism. And now this is all compounded by a sense of total powerlessness over their own bodies. They have learned that there is no safe place for them. They are locked in because there is no way for them to confront their offenders. Confrontation means shame, guilt, denial, abandonment, and the possibility of physical violence. They see no way to break out of the cycle of abuse.

Incest is an overwhelming, damaging, and humiliating assault on a child's mind, soul, and body. It is a major act of betrayal, for not only is the body violated, but the child's trust and love are violated as well. When sexual abuse takes place in an already dysfunctional alcoholic family, the likelihood of the abuse continuing is greater, which compounds the damage.

Abuse affects self-esteem, one's relationships with others, one's developing sexuality, the ability to trust others, and the ability to be successful. It also seriously endangers one's physical health. Children who have been sexually abused often learn to medicate their pain through the use of alcohol, other drugs, or food. It is not uncommon to see a person raised in an alcoholic family, and who has been sexually abused, become an overeater, bulimic, anorexic, or chemically dependent. Because abuse victims come to feel ashamed, guilty, powerless, depressed, afraid, and angry, they are often attracted to love partners who abuse them physically, verbally, and sexually.

Obviously this kind of emotional damage extracts a heavy toll. As the child matures, anger intensifies, depression deepens, thoughts about suicide become attempts, panic attacks and phobias become a part of life. Time alone does not heal these wounds. But as the following life stories demonstrate, recovery, and a different way of life, is possible no matter what has occurred in one's childhood.

Life Stories: Growing-Up Years

The following three stories concern Adult Children who were sexually abused as they were growing up.

Amy was sexually abused by her grandfather for seven years. But she was also the witness to drunken sexual displays by her parents all of her growing-up years. Cindy was sexually abused by her father, brother, and male acquaintances. Josh was sexually abused by his mother, physically abused by his father, and the witness of drunken nudity and drunken sexual displays between his parents.

The fact that Josh, Cindy, and Amy all became alcoholic does not mean that all incest victims become chemically dependent. Many do; but others do not. Remember, these are stories of ACOAs, people genetically and psychologically more likely to become alcoholic. When sexual violence is added to their lives, alcohol and other drugs become even more necessary to medicate the pain and fear.

AMY
Age: 48
Mother: Alcoholic
Father: Alcoholic
Abusers: Both parents, grandfather
Birth Order: Oldest of two
Raised: Rocky Mountain states
Socioeconomic Status: Working
    class

Amy's father had been drinking heavily ever since she could remember. Her mother's drinking didn't become as obvious until Amy was around eight or nine years old.

Amy grew up with extremely inappropriate sexual behavior modeled for her by her parents.

AMY: *"Can you imagine what it was like to have both your parents drunk, nude, and making love—with the lights on—on the living room couch, while you, an eight-year-old, and your four-year-old brother watch from the open stairway door, feeling guilty for watching, but watching with a kind of horrified fascination, unable not to watch?"*

This behavior on her parents' part was very common throughout Amy's childhood. Amy's reaction to this would be one of shame and anger, although she was unable to identify these feelings.

"One time after unwillingly watching my parents have sex, I grabbed a butcher knife and went out to the chicken house. I sat there crying and talking to the chickens. My father must have noticed I was gone, because he came out looking for me. When he found me, he asked me what I was doing with the knife. I told him I didn't know, so he took the knife away from me and told me to go to bed. I told him I didn't like hearing what he and Mom were doing.

"The next morning, he gathered the family together and told my brother and me that he and Mom had a right to do whatever they wanted. He was really, really angry. He said that we weren't to mention it again. And I never did."

The "Don't talk" rule became a law. Amy's feeling self was turning to stone.

Amy's sexual confusion was compounded even more because she was a victim of incest at the hands of her paternal grandfather. From the time she was four and a half until she was eleven, her grandfather molested her on a regular basis.

"When I was young, my grandparents lived near us. My grandfather would frequently come to the house and ask permission to take me fishing. That was where the molestation would take place, out on the lake in the boat. My grandfather would fondle me, and I was expected to touch him also. This went on steadily for three years.

"The only way I could cope with what I know I must have been feeling at the time was to separate myself, to distance myself, from what was happening. I did what I could not to think and feel about it. I put my attention everywhere else I could.

"We finally moved away from that part of the country, and we saw my grandparents less frequently, but he still continued to molest me whenever they came to visit."

Amy's confusion and fear about what happened was made worse by the fact that she felt she couldn't talk to anybody about it. When you can't talk about things you don't understand, you become even more confused and upset.

"I was fat as a child. And when the woman next door was pregnant, I noticed her stomach was large. By then we'd been away from my grandparents for a year, but I didn't know anything about intercourse and pregnancy. The thought occurred to me that maybe I was pregnant since my stomach was large like this woman's. I can remember the terror I felt. I was afraid to go outside. I was afraid to have anyone look at me. I was almost immobilized by the fear and terror. But every day that I lived through it, it seemed as if I got less and less afraid."

What probably happened is that every day Amy "lived through it," her feelings became more and more frozen. This is what made survival more of a possibility. When a child so clearly talks about being afraid of having anyone look at her, and being afraid of going outside, it is almost a given that in adulthood her fear of going outside where others will see her will become even more painfully frightening.

Amy was an unwilling witness to her parents' sexual encounters, the victim of molestation by her grandfather, and totally lacking in any sort of healthy sex education. This made her the perfect victim.

Amy's parents' alcohol abuse continued to get worse.

"My father was seldom home evenings—he spent his time at the taverns. Weekends, especially Sundays, were eggshell days. We had to tiptoe around so as not to disturb my father. We didn't say much. We didn't do much. I think my brother and I learned this from my mother. She was emotionally afraid of my father, although he wasn't physically abusive to her or to us.

"Some Sundays we'd go for family drives. We'd pack sandwiches and drive to the lake. Mom and Dad would always be drinking. It would get dark, and my brother and I would be ready to go home. But my parents would both be pretty drunk by then, and sometimes they'd have sex on the beach in the dark, while my brother and I sat there waiting to go home."

Friday and Saturday nights, her parents went to the taverns to drink.

"When we were younger, my parents would take my brother and me along. He and I would sit in the family room at the tavern, eating while my parents drank."

Eating had obviously become a way for Amy to assuage the feelings that could not be expressed verbally. By fifth grade she weighed 145 pounds; by seventh grade, although she was only five feet tall, she weighed 185 pounds. Food may have medicated her feelings, but it also demonstrated how out of control she felt about her body. Eating became a way of masking her shame and the upsetting and confusing sexual development of her body.

The family moved a lot as Amy was growing up. They would often move because her father would find fault with his job or the town and decide to look for something better somewhere else.

This constant moving meant that Amy had to keep changing schools. However, she was a good student, and school seemed to be a safe haven for her, despite the fact that she was teased about her weight by the other students.

"School was escape for me. I made good grades. I could do well in class. But socially I was a loner. I had only one friend at a time, usually someone who was a misfit like me."

In many ways being loners protects children who move a lot. If they don't bond to other children, they don't feel the pain of separating. Also, if they don't bond, their "secrets" are less likely to come out. Unfortunately this life-style directly interferes with being able to bond with potential friends and love interests later on in life.

The summer Amy was eleven, her grandparents came for a visit.

"There was a racetrack nearby, and my grandfather asked me to go for a drive with him to the racetrack. I knew instantly what he wanted. But I knew that somehow I needed to go—and that this had to stop.

"There was no one at the racetrack, of course. I was sitting in the backseat. My grandfather stopped the car, turned around, and put his hand on my leg. He asked me why I didn't come sit with him in the front seat. I told him no. He asked me again to come sit in the front seat, and suddenly the words just came out of my mouth.

"I told him that if he ever touched me again, I would kill him. I was only eleven years old, but I meant what I said. I would try to kill him if he ever touched me again because it had to stop; I just couldn't take it anymore.

"He said, 'You don't really mean that, do you?'

"And I looked straight at him and said, 'Yes, I do.' He told me not to be that way. But I didn't say another word—I just sat there and looked at him.

"I guess he realized I was serious, because he turned around in the front seat of the car. No other words were spoken. He just drove me home, and he never ever touched me again."

Amy had found the strength and courage to say no. Saying no was fighting for her life. That "No, or I will kill you" was the outpouring of all the anger she'd been building up about the unfairness of her life.

Nevertheless, although Amy was able to stop the cycle of abuse by confronting her grandfather and saying no, irreversible damage had already been done. The combination of suffering the covert emotional sexual abuse of her parents and the overt physical sexual abuse of her grandfather left her feeling ashamed, dirty, and sexually confused.

"It was at about this time that I discovered masturbation. I felt very guilty about it, but it was a form of escape for me. I spent a lot of time doing it whenever I was alone and whenever I could."

Obsessive masturbation is common to incest and molestation survivors. It may offer solace, and it may also be a way of playing out conflicted feelings regarding the abuse.

Amy had also developed a fear of men, something that was not helped by the amount of time she spent in taverns, watching her parents drink.

She found the loud, drunken men who hung out in those places very threatening. But she was powerless to do anything with those feelings.

"At this point, I had begun consciously to hate alcohol and the taverns. I just wanted to tear all the taverns down."

When she was fourteen the family moved to the country, and Amy began to attend high school.

"We were out in the country, and my brother and I would spend a lot of evenings alone. Dad would come home from work, get Mom, and they'd go to town and drink.

"Long before I was old enough to get my driver's license, I had become the reluctant chauffeur in the wee hours of Sunday morning, after my parents had been out drinking all day and most of the night. The car had an automatic shift, and I'd drive very, very slowly. My fingers and hands would hurt from gripping the steering wheel so hard. My brother and I would be in the front seat, careful never to look in the back because we never knew what state of undress my mother and father might be in. Sometimes we'd talk just to drown out the noises. Sometimes my parents would be mad at each other, and then it wouldn't be so bad."

Amy began having trouble in school around her sophomore year. She had been used to getting mostly A's. But now her grades dropped to B's and C's.

Up to this time, Amy had done a good job of compartmentalizing her life. How she presented herself in public was very different from how she felt in private. She appeared happy, confident, bright, and attractive to others but felt terrified, insecure, and ugly. She had learned well how to separate her feelings and attitudes to portray to the world she was okay and to convince herself she was okay. She was fighting to survive. COAs and children who live with physical and sexual abuse often become adept at compartmentalizing their feelings and perceptions of people.

The greater the trauma—and in this case there are dual dynamics of both alcoholism and incest—the less a child is capable of compartmentalizing for as long as he or she may be able to if only responding to one dynamic.

"It was very difficult to go to school and concentrate. It just seemed like there was a gray fog that slipped down around my mind, and I couldn't concentrate anymore.

"My father never went to any of my school functions, and the one time my mother agreed to go, she was stark raving sober. Her hands shook continuously, and she was so horribly tense and irritable that I was

*ashamed of her and embarrassed. And then I'd feel guilty for being
ashamed of her. I just felt that my mom wasn't like the other girls' moms,
and I wasn't like the other girls. I felt we weren't as good, and I felt
awful. I seldom went to school functions after that.''*

Amy spent her last years of high school managing the household. She
prepared whatever meals were to be cooked and did all the cleaning and
washing. The pressures on her were enormous.

*"I was thin then, and I looked very good on the outside. But on the
inside, I felt extremely crazy. There was nothing for me at that time to
medicate the pain and fear. It was a very painful time for me, and I began
to think about suicide.''*

During that time, in the middle of a fight with her mother and brother,
Amy's father walked out of the house for good. He refused to give the
family any support, and even though Amy's mother was working at a
local restaurant, Amy had to buy her own food out of money from a part-
time job.

That Christmas Amy's father showed up at the house. He and Amy's
mother had been out drinking the night before, and when Amy got up
Christmas morning, her father and mother were in the living room.

*"They told my brother and me that they were thinking about getting
back together, but that the decision was up to us. My father made it very
clear that he would come home only if my brother and I would approve
of it. I couldn't accept the responsibility for that decision. I told him that
anything he and Mom decided was all right with me, but that it was their
decision to make.*

*"My father left, my mother began crying, and I felt guilty. It was a
no-win situation. But I also knew that if my father came back, nothing
would change. It would be the same old arguments, but somehow my
brother and I would then be responsible.''*

As many COAs do, Amy had acquired wisdom beyond her years. She
could see the no-win situation she was in. She was skillful enough to try
not to get caught in the middle, but she was correct about not being able
to win. And, again, as many COAs do, in spite of all this wisdom, she
found pregnancy and an early marriage the answer to her problems. Amy
got pregnant just before she finished high school. She graduated in May
and married Allen in September.

*"I knew Allen drank a lot, but I thought that was normal for teenagers.
He had already had a serious car accident because he'd been out drinking*

and had smashed the car into a tree on the way home. It's amazing to me now that I never saw his drinking as alcoholism; I never saw what I was getting into. I thought I was getting out of something—that he would get me away from that alcoholic home. It seemed to me that he knew what he wanted, and he worked every day and didn't drink every day, so he seemed okay to me."

Although Allen's alcohol abuse was blatant, what Amy didn't realize was that she was comparing his drinking with the later-stage chemical dependency of her parents. She had spent a number of years minimizing and denying. She'd been taught not to question. And then there was the clincher—Allen was her ticket out of the family.

CINDY
Age: 28
Mother: Alcoholic
Father: Sexual abuser
Other Abusers: Brother, brother's
    friends, strangers
Birth Order: Fifth of eight children
Raised: Northwest
Socioeconomic Status: Working
    class

CINDY: *"I had been in recovery for my alcoholism for four years, and I was doing a Fifth Step exercise. I was asked, 'Were you ever sexually abused?' I immediately answered, 'Yes.' Then I heard what I'd said and went into shock.*

"I had never thought of myself as sexually abused. But then I began to remember specific instances, although the memories weren't clear and I kept doubting whether any of it had happened or if I was just imagining it. I just didn't want it to be true."

Like many molestation and incest victims, Cindy had deeply suppressed the memory of the abuse. Not until adulthood does it resurface. Addiction and compulsive behaviors often help to keep memories suppressed.

But Cindy had begun a recovery process from an addiction.

As survivors give up their old defenses, their memories become more accessible. For some the memories come in dreams, for others in flashbacks, and at times—as it did for Cindy—as a spontaneous admission of factual memory.

As Laura Davis and Ellen Bass point out in their book, *The Courage to Heal,* remembering is the first step in healing. To begin the process one first has to remember that abuse actually occurred. Second come the memories of specific events. The third step in remembering is recovering one's feelings at the time the abuse took place. At this point Cindy has begun her recovery from sexual abuse.

Cindy's memories of her childhood are of her mother's drinking and her father treating her as his "special little girl."

"When I was young, my father wasn't violent as far as touching me. I was more Daddy's little girl. I went with him everywhere, even when he was meeting one of his lady friends. My mother was the practicing alcoholic, and I was the youngest of three girls. It seemed as if my dad were trying to protect me more than the rest of my siblings. I felt really special, and he always told me I was really special to him."

This bonding was a major contributing factor in Cindy's denial that the parent she was most attached to had actively violated her. The conflict was so great that she'd had no other option but to repress the memories.

Cindy's memories of her mother revolve around alcohol.

"My mother was always busy drinking. She was drunk a lot. I remember she would hide the beer bottles in the cereal cabinet or below the sink. There was always lots of booze around. She was loud when she drank. She would fall down a lot on the floor or into the walls. I was always afraid of her. She looked so mean. If she got mad, she'd go for the belt.

"She did manage to take care of the household stuff. With ten in the family, it seemed as if she was always folding laundry. She was an excellent cook, and supper was always at six, when Dad came home."

Cindy's feelings for her mother were mostly based on how uncomfortable she felt around her.

"My mother always kept her distance from everyone. I don't remember her spending much time alone with just me or even playing with me. In fact, I don't ever remember her doing that.

"Mom got mad a lot, and I never knew what caused it. She would yell, stomp around, and slam doors and cabinets really loudly."

Cindy looked to her father for companionship and comfort. She needed attention and affection. All children do.

"The times my dad spent at home, I always tried to be with him. I don't think my mom liked that very much because I got most of his attention. I would go on errands with him, and he'd talk to me about the women he was seeing.

"One time, he took me to a small garage where he stored things. He had a mattress in there. He lay down on the mattress and told me I could sit down. I had no idea what was going on.

"Then a lady walked in. I'll never forget her. I couldn't stand her. She was mean, and she yelled at kids a lot. She kissed my dad and lay next to him and hugged him. My dad touched her all over, making lots of noises. I kept thinking, Why is my dad doing this with another woman?

"This happened a lot when I was very young, and eventually there were other women. On the way home from each of these encounters, Dad would tell me the story I was to tell Mom, because she'd always ask me lots of questions. It got to the point where I hated going with my dad on errands, so I'd hide when I knew he was going somewhere."

This emotional incest eventually turned into physical incest.

"The farthest back I can remember it happening was when I was eight or nine years old. I used to wet my bed a lot, so sometimes my sister would wake me up and take me to the bathroom so she could change my bed. I was always a heavy sleeper, so I never knew if I was dreaming or awake.

"Did I really see my dad stooped down next to me with his fingers inside me while I was on the toilet? It felt like it. And it seemed weird that when my dad realized my eyes were open, he pulled his hands away from me and stood up quick. But I doubted my perceptions: first because dads didn't do that to daughters, and second because nothing was ever said, so I figured I'd dreamed it. I know now that it wasn't a dream."

Cindy cared for her father more deeply than her mother. She was more comfortable with him than her mother.

This again creates confusion for the survivor as the memories begin to surface. When a child chooses to spend time with a perpetrator, it is not for sex. The child doesn't want sex. The child wants to believe the parent is loving and good. Attention, hearing compliments, being held, are natural needs of a child. Generally the child is unable to avoid the offender(s) not just because (s)he may be an immediate family member, but also because the child is usually dependent on that person for daily needs.

The sexual abuse that Cindy experienced from her father was also carried on by her older brother.

"My father wasn't home very much. He was always away, 'taking care of business,' so my older brother took over the father role. Unfortunately he did this in more ways than one. I always looked up to my brother. I was also very afraid of him. He was big and strong, and I'll never forget the look in his eyes when he was mad. Fear would shoot through me. I would freeze and then do whatever he told me to.

"One day, the house was pretty empty. I don't know where everyone was. My brother asked me to come into his bedroom, which wasn't uncommon; he spent a lot of time there. He was lying down on his bed, and he said he had something for me to do, but not to worry because all kids our age did this. I was ten then, and he was fourteen. He told me it would feel good.

"I remember being scared, but I didn't know what I was scared of. Then he pulled out his penis, and I thought my heart stopped. He told me to rub it and help him feel good. He said if I did that, then he would make me feel good, too.

"I didn't know what to do. The thought of telling someone never crossed my mind. So I did what he told me to do. Forty-five minutes later I walked out of the room and totally blocked out what had just happened. After that first time, this went on quite often—at least three or four times a week."

It is very common for a child who is sexually exploited to be abused by more than one offender. The offenders may or may not recognize this, but the victim certainly knows. Some Adult Children begin recognizing sexual abuse by one offender first, then realize it has also happened with others. They won't necessarily be able to identify all the offenders at once because of residual guilt, shame, and denial.

Sibling incest can be as traumatic as incest between a parent and a child. Clearly, Cindy saw her brother as a power figure, an authority to be feared. Terrified and confused, she did as she was told. With sibling incest the greater the age difference, the greater the betrayal of trust and the more violent the incest tends to be.

Adult survivors often minimize the incest by believing that all siblings are sexual with each other. "Playing doctor" represents normal sexual experimentation when the siblings are young, very close to the same age, have equal power with each other and in the family, where there is no coercion, and when the sexual play is the result of natural curiosity, exploration, and mutual sexual naiveté. None of that was true of Cindy's sexual abuse by her brother.

The patterns of sexual abuse continued on into Cindy's teens. By that point her brother began to give her drugs for having sex with him.

"My brother was really into drugs, and he drank a lot of beer. By the time I was in my early teens, he was giving me drugs and letting me party with him and his friends. At the time, I thought I was so lucky and special."

Cindy was getting her attention through sex, first from her father and then from her brother. But there were still times when she tried to stop her brother from abusing her.

"My parents worked at my grandparents' lumber supply store. We kids would go there on weekends to help out. There was a loft above the store, and I'd hide up there whenever someone yelled at me, or sometimes I would just go up there to play.

"But the loft was also the place where I'd have to meet my brother. Sometimes I'd get brave and say I didn't want to do it. But then he would give me that look that said, 'You'd better do it or else!' I also knew that if I had sex with him, I'd get some of whatever he was dealing at the time."

As much as Cindy wanted the abuse to stop, by now her pain was so great and her sense of powerlessness so deep that she felt alcohol and drugs were her only answer.

Cindy's parents divorced when Cindy was fifteen. After her father moved, Cindy didn't see him much. When she did see him he always responded to her in a sexual way.

"He would greet me with, 'How's my sexy girl?' or, 'Hey, babe, you're looking good!' while eyeing me up and down. I'd laugh it off sometimes. Other times I wondered why he talked to me that way."

Cindy's father had given her the message over and over again that women were good for only one thing.

"He would talk about girls and how they were no good, filthy, worthless. He was always saying, 'All women are good for is housework and fucking,' 'Women get what they ask for—they ask to be hurt,' 'It's a woman's fault when she gets raped,' 'The man is the master of the house,' 'Women should be grateful to their men no matter how they're treated,' 'Women are pigs, and they smell.' "

Cindy was doing a lot of drugs and drinking heavily on a daily basis by then. She also began to be promiscuous.

"I wanted so much for someone to like me, to love me. I started going out with guys when I was fourteen. Almost immediately, I was having sex with them. The first guy I had sex with was at a party. I always thought that there were two things I knew I could do well: one was to drink, and the other was to get a guy in bed. I thought these two things were points of pride."

Cindy dropped out of high school her junior year. She was most likely a young girl barely noticed at school and barely noticed when she was no longer in school. However, she looked old for her age and began hanging out at bars and having sex with strangers.

"There were bars where I could get in and drink for free. I'd leave with some guy I didn't even know. I remember many times waking up and not even knowing who I was with or where I was."

Sex was the only way Cindy knew how to get attention from men. She didn't know how to develop friendships with girls. And her behavior prevented many girls from seeking her friendship.

The men whom Cindy was having sex with were usually four to eight years older than she was. She would meet them at bars or at parties.

"I remember one incident when I was sixteen years old. I was seeing a twenty-four-year-old who lived with three or four other guys. He and I had gone to bed. Later that night, someone came into the bedroom, lay next to me, and asked if I'd been fucked yet. I said yes. Then he took his clothes off, grabbed me by the hair, and made me suck his penis. This went on for about an hour. I thought I was going to be sick. My whole body was trembling. I had tears in my eyes, but I was scared to say no. I was afraid that he would hurt me worse. When he finished with me, he just got up and left the room. All I could do was lie there, crying to myself. The next day, he just totally ignored me.

"These nights would happen to me a lot. They didn't seem as bad when I was drunk, though. I couldn't remember what had happened then."

Cindy's self-destructive behavior went beyond the sex, alcohol, and drugs. She had reached such a point of self-hate that she began to try to find other ways to hurt herself.

"I'd get high any way I could. Then I'd carve my skin with needles, pens, blades—anything sharp. I also ran away a lot. Once I almost drank myself to death with one-hundred-ninety-proof alcohol."

The physical pain that comes with self-mutilation may be a way of distracting oneself from the emotional pain. It may also have been an attempt on Cindy's part to draw attention to get help for herself. The sad thing is that no one paid any attention.

Cindy took to hitchhiking by herself.

"I was always picked up by guys, never women. There were times when carloads of guys would pick me up and not let me out until they all got what they wanted. Then they'd kick me out of the car and I'd put out my thumb again. Sometimes I'd get picked up by the same car two or three times in a row."

When she was seventeen Cindy became pregnant by an eighteen-year-old boy she met at a bar. He said he would marry her, but that it was now or never. Though she was skeptical of marriage, she took the now.

JOSH
Age: 31
Mother: Alcoholic, sexually abusive
Father: Alcoholic, physically
    violent, and abusive
Birth Order: Fourth of five boys
Raised: West Coast
Socioeconomic Status: Middle class

This story reflects the life in an alcoholic family that was affected by both physical and sexual abuse. Stories of sexual abuse most often reflect female abuse, especially female abuse by a male. This leaves male survivors feeling isolated—and male survivors molested by females even more isolated. Josh's story is about mother-son abuse. It is also my observation that male incest occurs more frequently in alcoholic families when both parents are alcoholic, as in Josh's situation.

Josh's father was a violent drunk who would abuse both his wife and his sons.

JOSH: "I remember hiding in the closet with my brother when my dad started beating up my mother. I was only five or six at the time. I re-

member asking my mother why she stayed with a man who beat her up. She would respond that she loved him, or say, 'He's your father. Don't talk about him that way.' ''

It was about this same time that the sexual abuse began. Josh's mother would get drunk and molest him. He was seven the first time it happened.

"I'd stay home with my mother on Friday and Saturday nights, listening to her tell stories of her childhood. She'd drink one drink after another, and begin talking about how women were different from men. Then she'd do a striptease and tell me to touch her. After that, she'd lead me to the bedroom, where the incest would take place. I was so confused. I felt lost. I had seen my mother and father have intercourse many times, but I'd never had her direct her sexuality at me. I was also terrified that if my dad found out, he would kill me.

"I can clearly remember the first time. I was so scared and so confused, it felt as if my whole nervous system was on fire. I started to cut out during the experience. There was this splitting, this separation, and I was no longer in my body. It was as if I went to a new dimension. And I remained there until it was over and I came out of a fog."

The splitting Josh refers to is a common way for children to deal with the experience of being abused. Most survivors experience it to some degree. They describe it as living in the mental level; being in one's thoughts; not being fully present; leaving one's body; a sensation of floating above oneself; or doing as Josh did, going somewhere he can't identify, a different dimension. Splitting is a very understandable defense. These children cannot run away physically, so they emotionally and/or mentally leave their bodies.

Josh's feelings about the sexual abuse were also compounded by his fear of his father's homicidal rages. Very often he would endanger the children's lives.

"Once when I was seven, my father went into one of his rages and ordered my older brother and me to go out and stand in the street so he could run us over with the car. He physically threw us into the street, got in the car, and started driving straight for us. Luckily, we jumped out of his way in time. He even stopped and tried to back up, but we ran and hid in the woods. I never knew what we did that was so bad."

The message is so innocently clear to Josh, or to any child whose life is threatened by a parent: they are so bad, they must be killed. The child believes the parent must be right; after all, they are adults, and they know everything.

Josh was sexually abused by his mother until he was nearly twelve. She used the ploy that she was teaching him how to be a good lover and how to make a woman feel good. The incest included fondling, oral sex, masturbation, and penetration on two occasions.

In addition to his mother's molestation, Josh was forced to witness his parents' sexual behavior.

"They would have intercourse in front of us children at all hours. One time we were all in the car and they actually stopped the car and had us get out, and they had intercourse along the side of the road."

Experiencing a parent's nudity is humiliating and a covert form of sexual abuse—sexual abuse without the touch.

"My dad was always naked. He would eat naked. It was never safe to bring someone home. I always had to check and see if he had his pants on. Then I would take my friends to my room because I didn't know what they would see outside of my room.

"My dad was obsessed with the size of the penises of all of us boys. He would always make crude comments about our sexual prowess. We never had any pajamas or robes until we were older, and then we bought them for ourselves."

Taunting sexual comments and focusing on penis size is also sexual abuse without touch. It is very destructive to a child's healthy sexual development and self-worth.

To add to the confusion and sense of insanity, Josh's father would always try to put on a good face in front of the neighbors.

"One time, my father was chasing me around the house next door, trying to catch me. He stopped in the midst of his pursuit to wave hello to the neighbors who were sitting on their porch at the time. Then he continued to chase me until I tried to run into our house. He caught my leg in the door and kept me pinned there while he kept smashing my leg with the door and screaming, 'I'm going to kill you!' The reason for this rage was that I had accidentally broken a light bulb in the garage."

It is so difficult to imagine children living like this. Their lives are terrifying and crazy making. Children like Josh cannot make sense out of why they're forced to live as they do, so they actively respond to their life in the best way they can. By the time Josh was in the second grade, he had begun running away from home on a periodic basis. If he couldn't find a friends' home to stay at, he would stay out late.

"I didn't think I'd be missed. I'd go to a friend's house; I hoped that maybe his family would want to keep me for a while. But his parents would always call my parents to let them know I was okay. But at least I'd get to spend the night at my friend's."

At some level, Josh knew he deserved better. At times he'd go shopping for new parents.

"I would go to the parents of my friends and literally interview them. I would ask them about their house rules. I would ask whether or not they spanked their children. I wanted to know about allowances."

Josh needed someone to help him, someone to do it for him. He couldn't extricate himself from this family all by himself. At this young age, if someone had tried, it might have been possible. But within a few years he was so hooked psychologically, he couldn't leave even when he was legally able to do so. Josh summarizes it well.

"We were just five little boys all trying to raise ourselves."

Josh began drinking by the time he was ten.

"I drank to cover up the fear that seemed to follow me around. I didn't drink a lot at that time, but somehow I felt as if all this craziness was my fault. The drinking helped me forget the fear and my sense of guilt."

When Josh was thirteen, he began to notice that his mother was very sick.

"She was turning yellow, and I kept telling everyone she was sick. They all told me I was seeing things. It wasn't until my grandmother came to visit that my mother was taken to the doctor. The doctor said she had cirrhosis of the liver and put her in the hospital."

The hospitalization did nothing to stop her drinking, though.

"When I would go to visit her, she would beg me to bring her beer. My dad told me to do it, so I did. She got worse and worse, and they even tried experimental surgery on her, but nothing worked. I remember my father walking into her room, drunk, and asking her where she wanted to be buried. I began to cry, and my father grabbed me and shook me, saying, 'There's no reason to cry. That's the way things are.' "

Josh's mother would spend two years in and out of hospitals.

"In my own mind, the first time my mother went into the hospital is when she died. After that time she was always changed. Looking back now, I believe she had become psychotic—probably an alcoholic psychosis."

It was at the time of his mother's first hospitalization that Josh began to use Valium.

"I began to take Valium to help me cope with the stress and violence in my life. By the time I was fourteen I was addicted to it. I managed to control my use during school hours, probably out of fear of getting caught. But I would abuse it at night and on weekends."

Josh also became sexually active at a very young age, which is often true of incest victims. By the third grade he would engage girls in petting and kissing. By the fourth grade he was having dates in which he was going to the movies with girls and engaging in sexual behavior more typical of an adolescent. He was never forceful with girls. After all, his mother had taught him about pleasing girls. She had also told him, "If you ever hit or hurt a woman, I will shoot you."

At fifteen Josh got a job at a gas station in order to support himself, going home only to sleep. However, his employers found out that he was underage, and he lost the job.

"By the time I was sixteen, I frequently suffered from depression and thoughts of suicide. I had a girlfriend at the time who acted like a mother for me. She helped me go on even though there were times when I didn't want to."

This girlfriend probably saved Josh's life. She became a tenuous lifeline for him. Most Adult Children can look back and identify one or two people who made enough of a difference to keep them from becoming overwhelmed by rage or depression or from taking the final step and committing suicide.

When Josh was seventeen, however, he did attempt suicide.

"I just couldn't handle the pain and grief any longer, so I tried to overdose on pills. Luckily a friend stopped by unexpectedly. He worked in a hospital emergency room, so he did all the right things to keep me alive. When I woke up twelve hours later in the hospital, my friend was sitting right there."

After Josh graduated from high school, he went on to nursing school. But he continued to live at home even though his parents' drinking, his father's rages, and his mother's insanity grew worse.

Despite how traumatic life has been for them, many COAs don't leave home once they're legally of age or out of school. Often they stay in the home because they have little money and because they lack the needed social and emotional support to leave. Many don't leave out of fear of what might happen if they did. They believe their physical presence protects others in the home. This was true for Josh.

"I stayed at home to protect my mother. I was there to help her. I needed to protect her, to fix things. If I didn't, I felt she would literally die."

Special Issues for the Sexually Abused ACOA

DON'T TALK

One of the most difficult issues facing children who have been sexually abused is the alcoholic family's "Don't talk" rule. The children have already learned this negative admonition regarding the alcoholism in the family.

"Don't talk" carries with it an inappropriate sense of loyalty. By talking, the child is somehow betraying the family's secret. If the child does talk, especially to another family member, the child usually comes up against a wall of denial: "That never happened." "Your father would never do that!" After hearing that over and over, telling others quickly ceases to be an option. Children intuitively believe that others do not want to know and/or would not believe them. As Cindy says:

"I was the one who was always wrong."

Incest victims and COAs succumb to a powerlessness, a learned helplessness. By not talking, they discover that things are more peaceful at home. In fact, talking often worsens the situation. To suffer the abuse is degrading, humiliating, violating. Not to be believed only intensifies the trauma.

This denial, plus being betrayed by someone you love, can be extremely debilitating for abused children since they are already confused about what has happened to them. In the case of incest, a trusted family member is the offender. And this person then tells them that they must never tell anyone, that they must keep the secret. There may be threats of family separation or even death if the truth is told. This closes off their hope of stopping the abuse—the intervention of another adult.

Amy learned the "Don't talk" rule in relation to her parents' alcoholism.

AMY: *"As the alcoholism progressed in my family, the family got more and more silent and the house got more and more silent. We withdrew from each other. It got to the point where we really didn't talk to each other about much of anything. We couldn't even talk about 'safe' things, such as a TV program. How could we ever talk about the things we knew weren't safe?"*

Because the pattern of denial and silence had already been established in her family, Amy naturally extended that to the fact that her grandfather was molesting her. She didn't believe that telling anyone what was going on was even an option. The situation was made all the worse by the fact that there was no clear model for her about what was and what was not acceptable behavior.

"I had no model for what was healthy and normal. I had never been taught that if someone treated you badly or did something to you that was wrong, you had a choice of telling that person no. I had no inner resources to rely on to tell me what was not acceptable. My reaction was to think there must be something wrong with me."

Amy was also monetarily rewarded for her silence. This isn't what kept her silent, but it made the situation even more complex.

Amy's grandfather paid for her silence by giving her money each time he had sex with her. He was essentially rewarding her for "not talking." She used the money to buy food to "stuff" her feelings. Keeping the secret adds to the hopeless cycle.

Amy's grandfather gave her money, and Cindy's brother gave her drugs. Both girls were being bought off to help keep the secret. When abused children keep the payoff, that adds to their later guilt of thinking they complied and it gets interpreted as their being at fault for the incest. It is significant to note that both of these girls quickly got rid of their payoff—used the drugs, bought food. In both cases the payoffs offered medication.

Somehow, though, Amy did find the resources within herself to confront her offender. Although she was unable to talk to anyone else about the abuse until she was in recovery, at least she was able to break the silence by saying no to her grandfather when she was eleven.

Cindy had learned the "Don't talk" rule from her mother before the incest began.

CINDY: "I was so afraid of my mom as a little kid. We could never do anything right. So I stayed outside and tried to not draw attention to myself. To be safe I would hide in closets and in the cabinets in the bathroom. I would also get behind drapes close to the heat register and lie still. At times Mom would lock us out, and I would huddle by the heat vent from the dryer to stay warm."

The "Don't talk" rule isn't just about secrets. Cindy was learning not to talk about anything—talk of any kind was not safe. When abuse became a part of her life, she was already programmed to be silent.

The "Don't talk" message in Cindy's family was reinforced by threats. Cindy's brother and father both had violent tempers that terrorized her into silence and compliance. What made things worse was that it never occurred to her to tell anyone. Besides, whom could she tell?

Her mother had already abandoned her through her use of alcohol. Cindy was totally unable to perceive people outside the family as potential sources of help. And even if she had, what would she tell? She had so deeply denied her father's abuse that it wasn't until recovery that she began to realize that what she had experienced was real, not made up.

The pattern of denial was also very strong in Josh's household. No one talked about what was going on, and every attempt on Josh's part to identify the problem was rebuffed.

JOSH: "I learned not to trust my perceptions of what was going on. And the message not to talk about them openly came through loud and clear. What I learned was a warped version of 'What you see and what you hear, when you leave, you leave it here.' I believed that if I told anybody what I felt, my mom would find out and then she wouldn't like me, or even worse, she would tell my father. I knew what he would do if he found out. By that time, I had seen enough black eyes and bruises to assume that would be the price to pay.

"I knew that, no matter what, I was never to tell anybody anything."

POWERLESSNESS

Adult Children have learned to feel powerless. They have no control over their parents' alcoholism. And they are powerless to stop it.

AMY: "I was watching my parents die a day at a time, but I was powerless to do anything about it. I also equated powerlessness with being good. I learned at both church and school that good children were obedient. Being good meant doing what you were told. Taking power was not a 'good' thing.''

Children are so hungry for love and approval that inappropriate attention can easily confuse them. This is why they're so easily victimized. The needier they are, the more vulnerable they are, the more easily they fall prey to abuse.

Amy felt that food was the one thing she had some control over. Each time she sneaked food or went out and bought herself some candy or a banana split, she was trying to regain some of the power and control she felt she had lost.

AMY: *''The money gave me a sense of control, a sense of power. By spending the money to buy food, which I was using to anesthetize my pain and anger, I felt I was gaining the power not to have my food controlled.''*

Cindy had learned at a young age that her body was not her own. She learned that her father and brother had power over her body, and that she had no control over what they did to her. The few times as a teenager that she tried to stand up to her brother, he would threaten her and once again she would become powerless.

Cindy's sense of powerlessness was carried over into her relationships with other men. They were able to abuse her body and treat her horribly, and she never had the sense that she had any power to stop it.

CINDY: *''When I was around guys I always felt 'less than.' My shame would overwhelm me: my head would drop down, my body would shrivel, and I couldn't stand up straight. They didn't even have to say anything, their presence was enough to bring on a shame attack.''*

Cindy came to believe that her only value was in being used sexually.

Josh grew up feeling powerless to stop his father's physical abuse of himself, his brothers, and his mother. The only way to deal with it was to run, either physically or emotionally.

JOSH: *''I can remember hearing my mother begging my father to stop hitting her. I felt so powerless, I wanted to die. One time my brother and I confronted him and told him, 'Don't you hit her again!' But he just beat her more when we weren't there.*

''I was also afraid that if I hit him, I wouldn't be able to stop. I was certain I would kill him. I was powerless to hit him because I believed my rage was so murderous.''

As a child Josh would run, duck, or hide to avoid the beatings. He also learned to stay away from home, to avoid both his father's beatings and his mother's sexual abuse.

"I would leave the house a lot. Sometimes I'd go sleep in the woods and let nature take care of me. I just wanted to go to the woods and lie down. I couldn't handle what was happening at home."

As he grew older, Josh used alcohol and drugs as a way of hiding. Drugs and booze helped him forget his lack of control over his life.

The powerlessness that children feel in the hands of their abusers is overwhelming. Children in alcoholic families know nothing about healthy boundaries. No one has ever told them that their bodies are their own, or that they have the power to say no. They feel that the abuse is something they have to endure, something they are powerless to stop. Because they are children, they lack both the physical and the psychological power to protect themselves.

When abuse continues into adolescence, and the teen finally has the physical power to fight or run, this learned helplessness often keeps the young person in the victim role.

FEAR, GUILT, AND SHAME

Adult Children have learned to "stuff" their feelings. They have learned that it's not okay to cry. It's not okay to get angry. It's not okay to ask for help when you're afraid. The feelings of fear, guilt, and shame that permeate the life of the abused child must be shut down, locked away, or channeled toward less threatening targets.

AMY: "My parents' alcoholism and the accompanying poverty set up an atmosphere of fear, shame, and guilt. There was so much pain that I was forever seeking ways to escape it. I found food, fantasy, reading, and television. I was always looking for someplace safe. But I never did feel safe. And I never felt good about myself or even adequate. No matter what my successes or achievements, I never felt adequate. I was never enough."

Amy felt anger both toward her parents for their drinking and inappropriate sexual behavior and toward her grandfather for molesting her. But she had no safe place to release that anger.

"Anger was just not expressed in my home—particularly when my father was home. Feelings were not acceptable. Nobody talked about feelings,

and that was the message I got about anger. Women and children were never to get angry at men. If you got angry at Dad, he might leave.

"The underlying feeling was that if he left, you would die. The internal message I got from the shame and guilt and fear I felt because of the molestation was that I didn't have the right to be angry about anything. I always envied my brother's ability to express anger. He was the acting-out child. I just kept my anger locked up inside me."

The fear Amy felt about her abuse manifested itself in other ways.

"For a while when I was nearly twelve I suffered from agoraphobia. I was afraid to go out on the streets alone, to go to the grocery store for my mother, or anywhere else. I had an overwhelming terror of all men. I was afraid to look at the men I passed on the streets. I was afraid that they were looking at me. It was very painful. Whenever I was out I would feel sick. Finally, because I had no choice about going to school and having to go out, I simply became more and more numb."

Agoraphobia, the fear of open spaces, is common to both COAs and incest survivors. Amy's agoraphobia was precipitated by feelings of fear, of not being safe. Her menstrual cycle had just begun, and her family had just moved physically nearer her grandfather. Her fear was immobilizing.

"Early on, I tried not to feel the pain, not to feel the fear, not to feel anything. The problem was that along with trying not to feel those negative, destructive feelings, I was also not allowing myself to feel the positive, joyful feelings and experiences that might have been there for me. I did not allow myself to reach out to others who might have been able to be there emotionally for me. I was trying to protect myself in order to survive. But in doing so, I missed a lot of the good things I might have had in my life. I lost my ability to identify my feelings, to express them. I had become emotionally numb."

Cindy also learned to freeze her feelings.

CINDY: *"I came into this world not feeling safe. The first feelings I can ever recall were fear and not being wanted. I always felt as if I had somehow ruined my mother's life. She would tell me that I was a troublemaker. The message I got was that I wasn't worth anything. If your mother doesn't want you, then you must not be wanted by anyone. I soon learned to freeze my feelings. They were too painful to deal with.*

"Every time my father would spew out his hatred of women, I felt as if it were directed right at me. I would feel small, no good, filthy, worthless. I hated him when he talked that way, and he did it all the time. I'd

get very angry, but I knew if I told him I was angry, he'd just yell louder—and he might even start hitting me. So I kept everything inside."

The fear that Cindy experienced with her father and her brother was later extended to other men.

"I still get scared thinking about how it felt to be forced to have sex. My body shakes, and my legs hurt. I close or cross my legs because I feel pressure in my vagina. I hate it. God, I hate it.

"There were times when I'd be tied up, gagged, or hit. I learned to cry quietly, if at all. I would blank out or drift off as if I weren't there. I felt dead."

Cindy believed she was responsible for the sexual abuse, that she was somehow to blame. And because she blamed herself, she felt guilty and ashamed.

"I couldn't tell anybody what had happened to me. I felt too dirty and ashamed to admit it. All I wanted was love from someone. When I was a little girl, I'd crawl up onto my father's lap or lie next to him on the floor, and he'd pay some attention to me. That's why the strange touches didn't seem so bad. At least he noticed me.

"When my parents divorced, even though I outwardly blamed my mother, I thought I was the cause of their breakup. But then my father hardly ever called me, and he stopped spending any time with me. I couldn't understand it. I thought I was special to him. He had always told me how much he loved me and that he would always be there and never leave me. I figured I must have done something wrong to make him abandon me."

Cindy's confusion is so painful. The one person she feels some closeness to is one of her primary abusers. He is the only one who has ever given her any sense of worth; yet not only does he violate her himself, he does nothing to protect her or to stop the abuse by her brother or the men she meets at bars. Her need for her father's love and approval comes from such a vast emptiness.

Cindy's shame was so great that she felt it was something wrong in her that made men have sex with her and then abandon her.

"I was so mixed up. I kept trying to figure out what I was doing wrong that made these guys use me and then go away. Why didn't they like me unless I slept with them? I couldn't figure it out. Why wouldn't anyone love me?"

Feelings were never safe for Cindy. She would live out a pattern of self-destruction and self-loathing.

Josh learned from an early age not to trust his feelings or perceptions.

JOSH: "I learned, growing up, that it's no good to cry. I wasn't to cry when my father tried to kill me or hurt me. I wasn't to cry when I felt sadness for my mother. The message was that my feelings were not okay, and that I was not okay."

The sexual abuse that Josh suffered as a young boy added to his sense of shame and low self-esteem. He felt responsible for what had happened to him.

"I needed love and attention from my mom, but then she'd go into this striptease and molest me. I wanted her to stop, but I didn't know how. I felt so powerless. But I'd always understood that men had more power than women—that was very clear to me from the way my father treated my mother. I'd learned very graphically by the time I was five that he was always on top and she was always on the bottom.

"I thought I should have known what to do, how to get myself out of this situation. I should have been a grown-up and done the right thing. I had this terrible sense of shame because I didn't know what to do. I didn't know how to extricate myself from the pain.

"There was so much pain. My body hurt physically from beatings and emotionally from the craziness of my life. I was so confused sexually. I felt cheap, dirty, and totally ashamed. I was afraid of both my mother and my father. I felt guilty, as if I deserved their abuse."

These feelings of shame and inadequacy often lead incest survivors to self-destruction or compulsive behavior, which is an attempt to mask the shame. Amy resorted first to food, and then to compulsive masturbation. Cindy used alcohol, drugs, promiscuity, and razor blades for self-mutilation. Josh used alcohol and Valium. He also experienced anorexia. Although this eating disorder is more common among women, it is also prevalent among incest victims.

"Those times when I felt the greatest powerlessness, when I felt least in control in my life, I would stop eating and work compulsively. I would find a hundred things to do in two hours and do them all. If that didn't work, I'd drive around, just to keep moving."

Life for these children is a constant internal struggle. Living in an alcoholic or sexually abusing home is traumatic in and of itself. But when both occur together, the child needs to construct even greater defenses. However, these defenses don't usually stay intact as long as those of other Adult Children. Their inner child and physical being are just too tired. The pain begins to show itself quickly.

Life Stories: Adulthood and Recovery

AMY
Age: 48
Partner Status: Married, three
    children
Occupation: Office manager,
    insurance firm
Recovery Process: Al-Anon, OA,
    ACOA, AA, nine years sober

Amy was pregnant when she got married, and her son was born just before Christmas. She was very sick after he was born, and she and the baby spent their first New Year's Eve alone.

AMY: *"My husband went out by himself and got drunk. I can remember my sadness and the sinking feeling I had at the time. It was like a blow. I felt dazed. But I internalized the feelings. It was something I'd just have to accept. That was the way it was, there was really no escape, and it probably wasn't going to get any better."*

Amy had had years of practice in "accepting the intolerable," but she had deluded herself into thinking that her escape into marriage would make her life different and better. Within six months of her marriage, when she was only eighteen, she knew on some level that life was going to remain the same. This time she had no fight left, and she responded by spiraling into greater powerlessness.

Amy soon began to suffer from various illnesses, such as bronchitis, strep throat, and colitis. These can all be symptoms of the "silently enraged." As an ACOA, incest victim, and the wife of an alcoholic, Amy had many things to be angry about, but no self-worth or skills to deal with that anger effectively.

"During the early years of our marriage, it seemed as though the pain was acute all the time. I suffered from severe depression. It was all I could do to cook the meals and get the laundry done. I was also doing a lot of eating. I had gained forty or fifty pounds when I was pregnant the first time, and I never took it off. I continued to eat just to keep going."

Amy became pregnant again the following year. Her mother had been evicted from her apartment and came to stay with Amy and her husband.

"She said she needed help and had no place else to go. She said she just couldn't go on, so my husband and I took her to the doctor and then committed her to the state mental hospital. Then my brother came to live with us. He was sleeping on the floor of the kitchen, but after two months my husband finally contacted my dad and said he had to take my brother to live with him."

After Amy's mother got out of the hospital, she came to stay with Amy again.

"She was with us only a week before she started going downtown during the day and coming home drunk. I was very angry with her and just wanted her to go away. I couldn't take it anymore. She finally got a job and moved out."

Two weeks before Amy's second son was born, her husband had to have emergency surgery. With the family pressures, her husband's and her own illnesses, and her constant state of depression, Amy began to drink to relieve the pain.

"In the beginning, I drank to escape. It was the very best escape I'd found so far. It was also the most powerful. I didn't have that knot in my gut anymore. Alcohol seemed to transform me. I could begin to express my feelings. But I was also very afraid of drinking because I'd seen what alcohol had done to my parents."

Despite what Amy had seen with her parents, her attraction to alcohol soon became greater than her fear. Without any recourse to internal resources and skills, alcohol and food were Amy's only answers to her pain.

Amy combined eating binges with her drinking.

"I still continued to eat a lot during that time, and my diet consisted mostly of refined sugars and starches. I was getting both my alcohol fix and my sugar fix. But then my eating and drinking binges started getting closer and closer together. I was completely losing control."

Amy's husband was also drinking a great deal.

"When we were first married, my husband was kind of attentive. He seemed to be interested in me and what was happening with me. But then it was as if he changed overnight. He suddenly ceased to be affectionate. The few times I tried to approach him emotionally, he rejected me, so I learned not to take that risk. Coming out of the alcoholic background of my family, it was like a door had closed. I felt that this was the way it was going to be for the rest of my life and that I just had to learn to live with it. I felt no particular sense of loss or grief—it was just a matter of 'Don't think about it and go on. Just make the best of it.' "

Amy's third child was a daughter. Six months later, when Amy was twenty-one, she attempted suicide with pills.

For the next twenty years Amy continued to abuse alcohol and food. She was in an emotionally distant relationship, and she was depressed and suicidal. Finally she ran out of ways to try to hide from her pain.

"By now my husband and I were having drinking wars. I was so tired. I felt as if I'd been fighting my entire life. I had a friend who had gone to Al-Anon, and I had seen the change in her. I decided to try Al-Anon myself—I was totally oblivious to the fact that I was alcoholic.

"However, I believe that, for me, it was important to go to Al-Anon first. What Al-Anon did for me was to help me begin to address some of my resentments about my parents' alcoholism. In the meetings, some of the pain began to dissipate—just enough to begin the healing process.

"I had been carrying this big bag of pain loaded with fear, guilt, and shame all of my life, and it was in Al-Anon that I began to lighten the load a little bit at a time, without adding to it. I began to have hope for the first time in my life—hope that maybe I didn't have to continue the way I was. Hope that maybe things could be better for me.

"Once that started happening, I finally had to face my own drinking. I no longer had any rational excuse to drink. Yet I'd still find myself getting drunk occasionally, and I absolutely could not understand that. Finally, I had to face the fact that I was an alcoholic, that I was addicted to alcohol.

"Even though I was afraid of everything and everybody, including myself, I somehow found the courage to go to AA. At the meetings, for the first time in my life, I had a sense of "This is what a real family feels like. This is what home feels like.' "

Even though Amy had good feelings about finding a home, she had trouble learning to trust other people enough to open up and share.

"I think it was the fear that I would have to live my life drinking that kept me coming back. I had no other place to go. I didn't know how to get rid of my resentments, my anger, my fear of not being able to stay sober.

"My first two and a half years in AA was a very confusing time for me. About all I could hold on to was the fellowship and the feelings I had while I was at the meetings. I seemed unable to carry the information I got at the meetings outside and apply it to my life. The Twelve Steps meant nothing; they just didn't compute.

"I just kept trying, kept reading, and kept making an attempt to pray every now and then. I was very angry with my husband because he refused to go to meetings with me. He told me I was definitely not an alcoholic and that he wasn't going to any meetings or marriage counselors. I was very hurt and angry about that. I was envious of the people in AA and Al-Anon who had spouses who were participating, so I stopped going to Al-Anon."

Amy had also been attending Overeaters Anonymous meetings, but at this point she stopped attending them, too, and began bingeing again.

"I was just returning to one of my addictions. I wasn't drinking, but I was using other chemicals—refined sugar and starch."

Finally her self-destructiveness culminated in leaving AA. As Amy gradually quit using her support systems, her anger with her husband began to surface.

"I felt haunted by my husband during that period, as though I didn't have a moment to myself, that I didn't belong to myself anymore. He was always invading my space, demanding my constant attention. Now, I can see clearly that he was abusing me emotionally.

"On the days when he was the most abusive, he wanted sex. But I was trying to sort through my own issues regarding my molestation. My husband made me feel as if something was wrong with me, that I must be frigid because I didn't want to go to bed with him. I just wanted to get away from him, to escape somehow. But the more I pulled away, the more determined he became. It became a power struggle, a war."

Amy now realizes that her husband felt threatened by her recovery; that he felt his own alcoholism was being attacked. His actions were motivated by fear. His obsession with sex was just another addiction for him and a way to be abusive toward her.

Amy was trying to deal with her husband, her worries about the family's financial stability, and the knowledge that her children were suffering from the battles that were going on in the family. Three months after her last AA meeting, Amy went on a three-day drunk that scared her into facing what was going on.

"I went back to AA with the knowledge that it was time to get honest. I finally surrendered. I believe that this is when my real recovery began.

I had to get in touch with my Higher Power, but it was very difficult for me. I was afraid of God. I felt that God was very punishing. I had to find the proper words to pray. But I could no longer live with a God that I was afraid of. I needed to have a God that I could pray to for anything in this world and truly believe that He would not give me anything that would harm me. I had a lot of old ideas about God that I needed to get rid of.

"The first thing I had to do was allow myself to feel the anger. It was very powerful for me to do that. It was also very healing. I had to realize that I was angry at whatever Higher Power that allowed me to be sexually abused by my grandfather. I could not believe that a loving God could have allowed that.

"I finally came to realize that it wasn't God's will that I should be molested—it was a misuse of my grandfather's free will. My grandfather was a very sick man—maybe he'd been powerless to do anything else.

"The bottom line was that God had nothing to do with it. God did not will it. God did not wish it. If my grandfather had been able to listen to his Higher Power while it was going on, I believe that he would have heard God saying to him, 'Please don't do this!' And I believe that my Higher Power cried during those times, probably weeping for both of us."

Although some alcoholics find it best to put off their Adult Child or incest work until they have been sober for some length of time, Amy needed to address her incest very quickly. Now that she was no longer abusing food and alcohol, all her rage had surfaced. It was imperative for her to face that rage in order to be able to integrate the principles and teachings of the AA program.

Amy first heard about the concept of Adult Children of Alcoholics at an AA meeting. After that, things began to click. She realized that she had to look at the whole picture of her family in order to make progress in her own recovery.

"To me, my alcoholism is all one piece. Growing up in an alcoholic home is not a separate issue from my drinking or eating. To me, alcoholism

involves all of oneself—physical, mental, emotional, and spiritual. And I'd already had the mental, emotional, and spiritual illness before I began drinking. All it took was the addition of the alcohol for the physical symptoms of that illness to manifest.

"The resentment and anger I had about my grandfather haunted me in recovery. I became very aware that I needed to get rid of that resentment, to come to terms with it and find some peace. I made an attempt to pray for my grandfather, even though he has been dead for years. But after trying for a long time, I just realized I couldn't do it. I had to be honest with God about that. I told God that I knew that my grandfather was one of His children, and that I knew in my heart that he was very sick. But I had to own my honest feelings. I hoped my grandfather burned in hell for what he'd done to me. Not just for the physical abuse, but for all the emotional pain, the losses that I suffered over the years because of him, my inability to get close to a man emotionally and sexually—all the destruction it caused in my life.

"I admitted to God that I could not forgive my grandfather, that I could not have any good feelings about him, that I truly hated him for what he'd done to me. I asked God to go in my place and do that which I could not do for myself—forgive my grandfather. I asked God to do that for me."

Many Adult Children and incest survivors want to forgive their abusers before they have fully owned the depth of their own experiences. I don't think it is possible to forgive if you haven't walked through your anger and rage first. It is possible to come to an intellectual understanding—but not to truly forgive.

When Amy realized that she couldn't forgive, but that her God was able to do what she could not, she found the freedom to let go of some of her anger and resentment. Eventually she found the strength to talk about the molestation at one of her meetings. The feedback she received, especially from some other members who were dealing with their own abuse issues, was very validating.

Many incest survivors need to participate in a same-sex group. An all-women's or all-men's group can offer great comfort and support. Ultimately, however, incest survivors will heal even more so when they allow themselves to participate in a group experience where the focus is on incest.

Amy had reasons to be angry at her parents for not protecting her from her grandfather and for their openly displayed sexual behavior. She found she needed to speak to that anger as well.

"I have written a lot of letters to my family that were not mailed. I read the letters out loud to other recovering Adult Children and then destroyed the letters.

"My next step was to work on anger toward myself. I needed to forgive myself for not telling anyone what was happening to me. I had to understand why and forgive myself for that."

Letter writing is a technique many Adult Children have found helpful in their healing process. They write a letter to a particular person. It is a letter not to be mailed, shown, or read to the person it's directed toward (unless it's a letter to oneself). But it is a letter that the Adult Child will very likely read out loud to a therapist or other recovering person. The focus of the letters may vary, but in general the letters to a family member(s) express experiences, feelings, and needs that were neglected—so much of what has never been safe to acknowledge. It's an emotionally cathartic healing process that offers the Adult Child greater clarity about feelings and needs of the past and present.

Intertwined with the issue of anger, Amy is facing the role of abandonment in her life.

"Sometimes it seems as if I was abandoned emotionally. But other times it feels as if I was never claimed in the first place. It's as if the adults around me were unable to acknowledge me. It always felt as if something had been taken away, as if my parents had walked away from me or left me alone.

"Looking back on it, I realize that because I couldn't express the pain, the shame, and the anger that I felt when I was a child, I had abandoned myself. I'd had no other choice. In order to survive, I had to walk away. I had to abandon that child, abandon those feelings as best I could.

"Part of the struggle in my recovery is to reverse that process. Now I need to reclaim the child I walked away from so long ago. There's so much healing in that. Sometimes I feel so sad for that little girl. And sometimes I'm just amazed that I managed to survive it all, and that I'm doing as well as I am.

"I have also come to realize that what my grandfather did to me was not about sex; it was about power. It's an abuse issue that has more to do with self-esteem. I realize I have no reason to feel guilty about what happened. I know now that my body belongs to me and to God. Who I allow to touch me, who I allow to get close to me, is between God and me. It's my choice. And no one else's. There is a great deal of freedom in that. In recognizing that I do have choices, I've come a long way."

CINDY
Age: 28
Partner Status: Married, two sons
Occupation: Computer programmer
Recovery Process: AA, six years
    sober; Adult Child therapy

Cindy was eighteen when she had her first child. Fifteen months later she had her second child. She says that her attitude was that it didn't matter if she got pregnant, while at the same time she believed magically that it wouldn't happen. And when it did happen she was totally unprepared.

CINDY: *"I spent a lot of time at home with my first child. My husband worked during the day and spent the nights until closing time in bars. By the time my second baby arrived, I was going out more. I left my kids with my sisters or my mother-in-law. I can clearly remember holding my second baby when he was an infant and my husband, Tom, and I playing Pass Out, drinking gallons of booze.*

"We moved a lot in those years. We lived with relatives a lot of the time. I'd often leave the kids alone when they were asleep. Or I'd leave them with my mom, knowing she'd pass out early. I was an absolutely terrible parent. I yelled at them a lot. I didn't want them. One time I wanted to punish Tom, so I moved out and left the kids with him."

When Cindy and her husband were twenty-three and twenty-four, respectively, they decided to go for alcoholism treatment. Cindy has no memory of why or how they decided to seek help. She's not even sure if it was a joint decision. She clearly remembers looking at herself in the mirror one day and seeing her mother.

"I have no memory of calling for help or where my husband fit in. We separated and got back together that first year, and we've both stayed sober. It has been six years now."

All during these years Cindy's father was continuing his inappropriate sexual behavior whenever he was around.

"My dad didn't stop touching me. He'd grab my rear or come up behind me and lean against me, putting his hands on my legs and rubbing them,

telling me how I was 'filling out.' I kept thinking, Fathers don't do this to their daughters, do they?''

Cindy was still so overcome with powerlessness around men that she clearly presented herself as a person who would not fight back or protest. She was a prime victim. And like most Adult Children, she still wanted her father's attention. She'd had so few healthy people in her life to offer a sense of normalcy, or self-respect, that many of her old patterns continued.

Then Cindy began to reject her husband whenever he tried to touch her.

"I was so scared of being touched by anyone. I'd freeze when my husband came near me. It wasn't just him, either. I couldn't even stand to have one of my women friends touch me. I was aware of how paralyzed I was. But I didn't know what was happening to me. I thought I liked to be around people, but here I was, trying to isolate myself. I couldn't believe this was happening to me. But no matter how much I isolated myself physically from other people, I still couldn't tell my dad to stop.''

Memories of incest first came to Cindy when she was sharing her Fifth Step of Alcoholics Anonymous. The heart of the AA program is found in the Twelve Steps (see appendix, page 555). In the Fourth Step one takes a searching and fearless moral inventory. The Fifth Step is sharing that inventory with another human being and your Higher Power. It was in this process that Cindy was confronted with more truth of her past.

"Finally I had to face the fact of the sexual abuse in my life. At first I told myself, 'Well, it wasn't so bad. This sort of thing happens in all families.' I thought it was normal. I had trouble even saying the words sexual abuse. I kept referring to it as 'this' or 'that.' Naming it made it more real, and I didn't want it to be real. I was afraid I wouldn't be able to handle going through the remembering, that it would be too much. But I was also so full of hurt and shame that I didn't want to admit it to anyone else.''

Cindy's recovery was stymied. She was clean and sober and proud of it. But she was also so flooded with self-hate, rage, and fear that she was dying inside. She struggled painfully for several months, but her attraction to recovery was the strongest pull. She began to attend an Adult Child therapy group.

In her ACOA group, Cindy found that other people were telling her over and over that what she had experienced was emotionally, physically, sexually, and spiritually abusive.

"I was in a horrible dilemma. The more I remembered, the more I tried to block what few memories I had. But the more I tried to forget, the more I would remember. My body would shake. I wanted to spend all my time in the shower. I felt so dirty, as if something or someone were on me and wouldn't get off. My paranoia about other people was completely out of control. I thought everybody was looking at me. I thought they all saw me as dirty. I knew I had to go back and try to work this out or I'd just end up using again and feeling totally crazy.

"In the end, I chose to live through it again. But this time I wasn't going to do it alone. I knew I had to tell my scary, shame-filled secret to someone."

It was this that finally led Cindy to ask for help. Someone suggested that she see a sex therapist.

"The therapist helped me separate my own stuff from what had gone on with my dad, my brothers, and the other men in my life. She taught me about my own body. I learned the difference between good touch and bad touch. She validated many of my fears and helped me understand that I'd had good reason to be afraid."

Through her work with the therapist and in ACOA, Cindy began to get in touch with some of the feelings that she had locked away.

"The abuse was probably the hardest, scariest issue I had to deal with. I prayed for strength all the time. I still do. Initially I was even angry that I had to see the therapist. I told myself that if I hadn't been abused as a kid, I wouldn't be in so much pain now. There were many times when I thought of giving up and putting it all in the back of my mind. I even thought of taking my life. Thank God I didn't."

Cindy's struggle is common to the recovery process. Many people who were sexually abused would like to take a big eraser and "make it all go away." That is the role alcohol, drugs, and promiscuous sexual behavior served for Cindy. The truth is, no matter how hard you try, it won't go away. Attempts to deny or forget just prolong the pain. As painful as facing the truth is, it is the only way out of the cycle of abuse and all the hurtful consequences that occurred with it. Truth is the only protection from denial and deception. It will mean freedom and choice. Cindy was willing to trust that.

"But in my heart of hearts I knew I couldn't forget anymore. I finally made the commitment to look at the abuse instead of denying it. It was reality. I couldn't pretend that being abused hadn't affected my adulthood. My marriage had been at risk many times. We would fight and argue. But instead of trying to work it out, I'd go find another man.

"That had always helped me forget my pain before, why not now? But I knew that running from reality was no longer an option.

"I have lived with fear all of my life. What I began to learn is that letting go of that fear required a deep sense of trust. It required surrendering to God, to my Higher Power. That was really hard. How do you trust something you've never seen or touched or felt, especially when everyone you have seen or touched or felt has damaged you?"

You learn to trust slowly. You learn to trust by allowing others to be a part of the process. Cindy's continuing recovery from her addictions is what helped her at this point. She used what she had learned in that recovery to empower herself to take further risks.

"The memories were actually physically painful. At times I thought I would die. I kept thinking about self-mutilation. I kept thinking about getting wasted on drugs and alcohol. Yet somehow I believed I could and would get through this. So I let myself be with the pain. I knew I had no control over this, but I also knew I wasn't alone—and it wasn't an earthly being. Whatever I'd glimpsed of a Higher Power in my work in AA was with me. I came through. I came through with a stronger connection to my Higher Power and to myself. I am no longer willing to believe that I am at fault, or bad."

One of the most difficult issues for Cindy was confronting the reality of her past and then confronting the people who had hurt her.

"I was afraid of confrontation. Confrontation meant you would get shamed or hit, or you'd run into denial. I was also afraid to confront the shame, guilt, anger, and sadness I had."

But it was so important to Cindy to find out what others knew that she tried talking to various members of her family. She asked her sisters if they remembered any abuse. They said that they did remember their father treating Cindy differently and making sexual remarks to her. But then they discounted that by saying, "That was just Dad. You know the way he is." Cindy didn't even get that much acknowledgment from her mother or brothers. And when she confronted the abusing brother, he told her that they hadn't done anything that all brothers and sisters didn't do. Only recently has one brother actually listened to her without discounting her perceptions.

Very often Adult Children and incest survivors receive no validation or support from family members. When they open the subject, they are often made to feel "wrong" or "bad" for saying such things.

Whether or not to confront family members is a decision all recovering incest survivors have to make. Confronting abusers or family members is not necessary for the healing of all survivors. It's an individual process and an individual decision.

What is important is knowing your motives. Many survivors want to discuss it with family members to gather facts from others. This was what motivated Cindy. You may want family members to validate your perceptions that these things occurred. You may want to break the silence. You may want others to know so they'll be more empathetic to who you are. You may want revenge. It's important to know your motives. If you know why you want to confront the family, you are able to look at your desire more realistically and as a result will be more likely to get your needs met.

Many incest survivors have confronted family members, shared with nonabusive family members, and felt good about the process. Others only feel greater rejection. In consideration of talking with family members, talk with others who've had similar experiences. Share your hopes and expectations, and strategize what you want to say. On the other hand, other incest survivors have chosen not to talk to family member(s) and have felt very satisfied with their ability to move on in recovery.

Cindy was still having problems confronting her father, though.

"My dad's behavior toward me hadn't stopped. Whenever he came around, he would talk about past affairs he'd had and how many times he could make women come, as if I was supposed to be impressed. I felt like throwing up on him. I was scared to be around my own father.

"My dad would still touch me and make gross, sick comments about me. I was trying really hard to stay with myself and not allow him to abuse me. But it's so scary and so hard."

Finally Cindy put a stop to the cycle of abuse. She decided that, for now, she wouldn't confront her father about what had happened in her childhood—but that she would stop his present abuse.

"I can finally say that my father no longer has control over me. I will not allow him to abuse me any longer. For the time being, I won't see him or talk to him.

"I feel like killing him, and I'm glad I'm angry. It's about time. I never thought it was okay for me to express my anger because if I did, I wouldn't be liked or people would leave me. But my friends have shown me that they won't leave me if I feel anger. I had to trust them and have faith that they would stay. I was scared to trust, but they have stayed.

"I now know that I no longer have to carry my father's pain. I'm done being 'loyal' to him—and loyal I was. I'm not responsible for his actions. I can be free of him. I can now work on being a mother to my own children and a wife to my husband.

"Today, I'm beginning to learn how to deal with my feelings of helplessness. I'm discovering that even if I can't change a situation, I do have options in the way I choose to respond to things. I do have power because I always have choices.

"When I think about how long I was abused, it makes me cry. I get very sad and scared. But I know I have the choice whether or not it continues. I thank God for my friends, my husband, and my children. But most of all, I thank God that I'm finally, finally able to love myself enough to say No!

"I am a miracle. And I thank God for the blessing of being allowed to see myself as a miracle."

JOSH
Age: 31
Partner Status: Divorced
Occupation: Physical therapist
Recovery Process: AA, six years
    sober; Adult Child therapy

After graduating from high school, Josh remained at home and attended nursing school. While he was in the nursing program, he was finally forced to confront his father's violence.

JOSH: "It was a subzero night in January. I had just started nursing school, and I was working at our local hospital. I'd just finished a forty-eight-hour shift. There was a blizzard, and I had an accident on the way home. I had to contact my father to get information about our insurance, which meant I had to call six or seven bars before I found him. He was furious over the phone, and I was scared to go home, but I was so exhausted I went home anyway.

"When I walked in, my father was standing in the kitchen, naked as usual, except he was holding a shotgun. I just froze, not knowing whether to run or to stand and face him. I stood there for what seemed like an hour. I knew he was drunk. Then he started yelling about how I'd always cost him money, how I'd ruined his life. He then picked up the shotgun and aimed it at me.

"I was afraid of dying, but I was tired, really tired. I turned my back on him, saying, 'If you shoot me, you're not going to get away with it.' I felt him scream, and then he began hitting me with the butt of the gun. Somehow I managed to get away and slept in the car."

The next day Josh fell asleep during a nursing exam. He realized that he was unable to function, so he went to talk to the director of the program. As first he was afraid to tell anybody the truth; he was afraid no one would believe him. However, once he did open up to the director, she took him to see the school counselor, who got him into a psychiatric hospital for three months.

"They diagnosed me as depressed with hysterical tendencies. I underwent hypnosis, along with sodium pentothal treatments. I attempted suicide again. I just wanted to be crazy and not have to go home. My parents never came to visit, just my girlfriend."

Josh was even willing to be crazy if that meant not having to go back home and keep living as he had been all of his life. He had no answers, no solutions. The system he was seeking help from kept enabling his belief that "he was the problem." Many do not escape being institutionalized repetitively, but fortunately Josh discovered that he was not crazy and that he found no value in being perceived as crazy. After three months he returned home. However, having to deal with his father sent him right back to using drugs.

"From the first word my father spoke to me when I got home, my own disease worsened. For the next seven years I drank and used as often as I could."

During this period, Josh married a woman who was also an Adult Child. Neither one was in recovery at that time, and within two years the marriage ended in divorce. By now Josh had left nursing school, but he was studying to be a physical therapist.

Soon he was in a relationship with a woman who had been court-ordered into treatment for her alcohol and drug abuse for traffic violations. In going to see a counselor with her—to help "fix" her—Josh was confronted with his usage. He openly admitted he was alcoholic. With that, he began to participate in Alcoholics Anonymous. It was as if he'd been ready and waiting, as if he'd just needed the correct opportunity. Unfortunately, after thirty days sober, he relapsed. And in that relapse he made his last suicide attempt.

Josh had used various means of attempting suicide over the years. One time he used pills; another time he tried to slash his wrist with a knife; this time he lay down in the middle of a major highway, hoping someone would run over him. Later he commented wryly, *"I wasn't even good at committing suicide!"*

While Josh was in a psychiatric hospital because of his last suicide attempt, a very astute nurse counselor suggested he seek co-dependency treatment.

"There was a therapist there, a dynamite lady, who taught me that I wasn't crazy, which was what I'd always assumed until then. She saw something in me that I wasn't able to see—an intuitive ability to help others who suffered the way I did. She told me: 'Josh, you're bright, and you give great feedback. But when are you going to be important enough to yourself to focus on you?' That statement changed my life. With the help of God, I didn't leave treatment."

After he was released from the hospital, Josh went back to Alcoholics Anonymous and also began attending Adult Children of Alcoholics self-help meetings. He is continuing in both programs.

"I had to do both programs at the same time because I was in so much pain. I had too much rage inside me to stay sober, so I had to let some of the rage go. This is what I was able to do with my Adult Child work. I also needed it to help me separate from my family. What I had to learn immediately was how to establish boundaries and how to take care of me. I couldn't have stayed sober without this."

The ability to set limits is vital to feeling good about oneself. Survivors and Adult Children are not skilled at defining their time, at protecting their bodies, or at putting themselves first. Amy, Cindy, and Josh all had to learn how to set limits and establish boundaries in order to recover. When they did begin to set limits with their family members, they were protecting themselves and freeing themselves at the same time. When we can protect ourselves from situations we don't want to be in, we experience confidence, power, and self-respect.

"With the help of my therapist, I have begun to change my old patterns of behavior and to stop being a victim. I got involved with a grief therapist. I had so many grief issues. I felt as if I'd been dead all of my life. I have had to grieve for the childhood I never had. I have had to do rage work around specific instances of sexual and physical abuse. I needed to learn healthy ways in which to physically respond to my abuse. I found I needed to scream, and I needed to hit—for that I have used battacas [heavily padded sticks] and pillows. Therapy gave me a safe and secure environment in which to do that.

"Allowing myself the rage was so scary. I always felt that if I got in touch with my rage, I'd be just like my father. This made me so fearful of my rage that I stayed a victim. By getting in touch with my rage I have been able to free my inner child. I have been able to let go of so much pain. I also found out I am not like my dad. I don't have to hurt myself or anyone else when I'm angry. Before, I couldn't get past the rage to feel anything else. But letting go of my rage has made it possible for me to get in touch with all my feelings. I can now separate anger out as its own feeling as well.

"Getting in touch with the rage was freeing and exhilarating, but it's only one chunk of my healing. Nevertheless, it's been a vital chunk, and it has made it possible for me to love myself."

Adult children and incest survivors have many times found it helpful to physically release their feelings of rage. In order to feel safe with the intensity of their feelings, this is best done with a therapist with whom you have a trusting relationship. Psychodramatic and Gestalt therapy techniques are more frequently used, where you confront an object or other person who symbolizes your parent(s) and speak that which has not been previously safe to say. With the use of pillows, battacas, possibly tennis rackets—any object that can be held but is nonhurtful—you can physically respond with your anger. Although not all incest survivors or Adult Children have found this necessary, many have found it very helpful. For Josh, it was very freeing.

It is easy to see the similarities between Josh's experiences and those of the two women. The effects of abuse are equally profound whether the victim is male or female. Yet, while they have much in common, it has been less acceptable culturally for men to show any feeling but anger. As a result, men express their pain differently from women. Very early on, male and female children are given messages about feelings that are specific to their gender. They learn that it's okay for girls to cry, as they are viewed as the weaker sex. However, boys cannot cry, but they may assert their anger. They are told that, aside from anger, feelings are weak, feelings are feminine, and it's not okay to be feminine.

Because of these cultural messages, male incest survivors spend a great deal of time trying to think their way out of feelings rather than feeling them. This is complicated further by being raised in a home that is both alcoholic and incestuous. It means that even greater pain will have to be discounted and repressed in order to survive.

Josh needed to get in touch with his rage, as did Amy and Cindy. But as a male, it is even more important that his rage not be a reenactment of the one feeling males are allowed. Michael Lew, author of *Victims No Longer,* says: "In their attempts to counteract feelings of vulnerability and impaired masculinity, adult male survivors can end up feeling that their only protection lies in intimidating the world with a theatrical display of anger."

Josh's work around anger was not about intimidation, because he was not protecting his vulnerability. Josh's anger was a form of indignation over the injustices he'd suffered. He was also able to feel his sadness and fear and his tremendous sense of loss. He is learning to get in touch with his entire range of feelings.

"My life is by no means perfect. I married another ACOA after I was two years sober, and that didn't work out, either. However, I have learned some valuable lessons. I realized that by choosing women who were nonrecovering ACOAs or addicts, I was still trying to fix my mom and bond with her. My mother has only gotten worse over the years, and it still hurts that I can't do anything about it. But today I know that I do have choices about how I live my life.

"I see my father about twice a year now. He's still drinking, but I no longer allow him to be a threat to my existence. Today, one of my brothers is six months sober, and my younger brother has been involved in Adult Child recovery for the last six months. I'm no longer the only one in my family in recovery.

"My life is fuller than it's ever been. The people I have in my life today are there because of my healthy choices, not because I was limited to the attitudes I grew up with. I now help other Adult Children learn to make their own choices. I help them understand and deal with the trauma of growing up with people who are addicted."

Amy, Cindy, and Josh would have faced the hardship of "double duty" simply by the fact that each had two alcoholic parents. But adding the incest complicated the issues exponentially. Their need to protect themselves has been so much greater that it has led to a severe splitting off from their emotional selves. Greater shame and self-blame leads to more severe depression, alcoholism, and drug abuse at a younger age. And this, in turn, leads to eating disorders, thoughts of suicide, and suicide attempts.

Yet all three are in recovery today. Cindy and Josh needed to become clean and sober first before it was safe to address these issues. Amy, on the other hand, had to begin acknowledging the incest and her rage about it before she could get sober. Once they were no longer medicated and anesthetized, all three discovered that their lives would be severely limited until they addressed both their Adult Child issues—and the incest. Because of their experiences in AA, they had begun to trust the process of talking.

Hopefully, the experiences of these people will help incest survivors who have not had any previous experience with self-help groups feel safer and more trusting about reaching out to a resource.

Recovery Considerations

The stories we've shared throughout this book, and particularly in this chapter, are testaments to the inner strength and survival capacities of children. Being incest survivors in chemically dependent families creates ''Double Duty/Dual Identities.'' For many this often means triple, even quadruple duty.

The trauma these people have experienced has been profound, and in recovery it is imperative that they address both issues. Which one should be addressed first is usually clear, because you identify first with either the incest or the alcoholism, and that dictates how you reach out for help.

Many Adult Children don't remember the incest until they begin their ACOA recovery. As you begin to let go of repressed thinking and controlled behaviors, you will begin to feel more and more. As you become more trusting of others, memories will often begin to surface.

That is what occurred for Cindy. She had been in recovery from her alcoholism a few years. She was feeling safe—not needing to protect herself as much—and suddenly the memory was there.

Other Adult Children seek counseling because they begin to experience flashbacks or a flood of memories of sexual abuse. Many people seek help not because they have identified either the family alcoholism or the incest, but because of depression, difficulties in relationships, or compulsive behaviors and addictions.

USING RESOURCES

In my experience, both Adult Child and incest survivor issues need to be and can be addressed simultaneously. Many Adult Children work on the incest with a therapist while also attending ACOA self-help groups. Or they attend Incest Survivors Anonymous and ACOA or a similar combination. Because not all ACOAs are incest survivors, if your recovery is primarily in ACOA groups, it is important for you to have an opportunity to meet in a setting where the focus is on incest.

It may be feasible and desirable to have both individual therapy and a group experience at the same time. Should you be too frightened to join any group—either a self-help group or a therapy group—you may want to begin your recovery with an individual counselor. It may be necessary for you to work one on one for a time before you feel ready for a group experience.

But be aware that group opportunities are there, both for therapy and for self-help, and that both are extremely valuable. Talking with others who have had the same experiences as you is extremely validating and supportive. You deserve that. Other group members will not reject you. They will understand, believe, and support you.

Above all, because life was so unsafe for so many years, your own personal sense of safety must be your first priority. There is no right way and wrong way here. Know that you are free to begin your recovery with the process that appeals to you most and feels the safest.

Adult Children and survivors also find comfort, direction, and hope in reading materials. There are many books on the healing of incest survivors. In fact, there are more books on this topic than on any other issue covered in this book (see bibliography, page 575).

The thoughts below may offer you some directions to consider in your recovery.

UNDOING DENIAL

Truth is the only protection from denial. It is denial that has kept us shamebound. It is truth that will lead us to recovery. This in turn creates, or maintains us in unhealthy relationships, compulsive behavior, and/or addictions. It is shame that keeps us immobilized and depressed. Although we were victimized as children, we do not deserve to continue to live our lives as victims. We are survivors. As traumatic as the experiences were—we survived.

It is important to allow yourself to remember the past so that you can separate yourself from the abuser and from the internalized shame. You will need to talk about the experiences so that you can put them into perspective. In your childhood you saw these events through the eyes of a vulnerable child. This child believed that you must have deserved what you got, that you were bad. As an adult it is safer to speak to the injustice and the unfairness and the terror that were a part of the experiences.

However, it is important to speak the truth so that you can receive validation for your experiences. The validation was not there when you were a child. You deserve to know that your perceptions were correct. You may not get this from family members, but it can come from others familiar with abuse issues.

Not talking about it is a form of minimizing and denying the experience. It is a way of continuing to negate and deny yourself. The truth is the only way out of the cycle of abuse. The opportunity for validation is only one of the reasons the group experience is so important in recovery.

As you begin to speak your own truths, you might also want to carry the following truths in your heart:

- It was not your fault.
- You are not bad.
- You need to break the silence.
- You must not do this alone.

ANGER AND RAGE

It is healthy and necessary for incest survivors to grieve for the losses of their childhood. There was so much fear, humiliation, hurt, sadness, and confusion, and all of that needs to be talked about. But, ultimately, you must address your anger and rage. Josh makes this point so well when he says that until he was able to speak about his rage, he couldn't let go of his victim role. His fear of becoming enraged and hurtful to others kept him immobilized.

It is understandable that Adult Children would feel tremendous power in their rage and be fearful of that power. Yet survivors may be equating abuse and power. From experience, survivors learned that to be powerful one must be angry and hurtful toward others. But you need not be hurtful with your rage. There are many ways to open up to all of your feelings without harming anyone else or yourself. And once you do, you will experience a freeing of your pain that allows you to create a healthy framework for expressing your internal power.

Anger is part of the healing process of all Adult Children. Victims and survivors are either totally detached from, extremely frightened of, or overwhelmed by this feeling. If you don't feel anger, ask yourself "Where did it go? Why isn't is safe?" Be open to the fact that it is there—it just may not be very visible. Often, people have to confront their rage before they can separate out anger and any other feelings. People who are abused—and who are unable to focus their rage at the abuser—take their rage elsewhere. It can become an addiction or show up as compulsive behavior such as workaholism, perfectionism, compulsive masturbation, eating disorders, critical self-talk, chronic illness, or self-mutilation. You do not deserve to be rageful with yourself. This rage turned inward is really personal violence. It is okay to be angry. It is not okay to be violent with oneself or with others.

Directing your rage—not necessarily literally—at the abuser(s) and those who didn't protect you is pivotal to recovery. That rage can be directed toward the perpetrator(s) either face to face or symbolically. Many survivors find that physical releases of anger are helpful, such as hitting inanimate objects with a battaca or tennis racket; throwing objects into a safe place; or yelling. Experiential forms of therapy such as bio-energetics, psychodrama, and Gestalt are often helpful. As rage is released, it becomes easier to identify many feelings. Rage has been the holding tank for fear, sadness, and pain. Recovery means learning to explore and accept the entire range of human feeling.

Both Adult Children and incest survivors learn early on to be internal controllers. And because they learn to control all their feelings and to dismiss all their needs so well, when they do begin to feel, they may also feel out of control.

Giving up internal control and feeling is contrary to what you've done for years in order to survive. Chances are, when we believe we're roaring, we're still only letting out a peep. To us, expressing any truth, any feeling, is so foreign that it is overwhelmingly frightening. Yet the more frightened you are of your rage, the greater safety you will feel in letting it out in a therapeutic context with the help of a professional who is familiar with Adult Children and incest survivors.

Remember, anger is a universal human experience. We all have it. Anger is a normal emotional response when someone hurts or wrongs you. It is not to be confused with blame. Blaming is anger that moves in circles, not directed out and released. Releasing our anger constructively allows us to work through the problem. Releasing anger gives us freedom. When anger is released in an honest, direct, constructive manner, it dissipates.

Recognizing anger also allows us to identify our needs. Anger is a natural response to exploitation, and it can be used as a cue for setting limits and boundaries. Anger is an important cue for self-care.

POWERLESSNESS

It is essential in recovery to recognize how little power you had as a child and to grieve over the trauma of being victimized. It is also vital to identify the ways you attempted to acquire power to overcome your terrible sense of loss. For some it was in fantasy, for others it was by hiding, for still others it was by eating or by starving.

An important aspect of recovery is to claim the power you do have today. You are no longer the child who was victimized. You are an adult who was once abused and once raised in an alcoholic family. You can go back and retrieve all the power you didn't have then. You do that by challenging the internalized messages that you learned to believe. You need to sit down and make a list of the messages you internalized about yourself—messages such as:

- You aren't worth anything.
- You'll never amount to anything.
- No one will ever believe you.
- You are stupid.
- You are bad.
- You aren't trustworthy.

Once you have made your list, you need to toss out those messages that you don't want to continue to incorporate into your life today and create new messages in their place. You can change these messages to:

- I am of value.
- I am important.
- I speak the truth.
- People will believe me.
- My perceptions are accurate.
- I am bright, capable, trustworthy.

Then you need to repeat those messages on a daily basis to yourself. Say them over and over until you feel them in your heart and believe them. Obviously, many feelings will arise as you do this. It's all part of the grief process. These are feelings that need to be identified and ac-knowledged. Just be patient—yet persistent.

Another way of reclaiming power is by establishing healthy boundaries. By setting limits and boundaries, you are protecting yourself. When we are taught to be the object of another person's prerogatives, to put another person's wants and desires first, we usually have to acknowledge the pain associated with having lived that way before we can set limits for ourselves. Along with that pain comes much sadness and much anger. Once the grief work has begun, it is easier to say: "I need. I want. I deserve." You will also find it easier to establish boundaries and limits in those areas where your needs and wants have to be protected and addressed.

By establishing boundaries and setting limits, the Adult Child survivor begins to use the words *No* and *Yes* with freedom. That also takes much work. It was not safe to say *No* as a child. Without the freedom to say *No, Yes* was said with tremendous fear and helplessness or out of a desperate need for approval and love.

Recovery means talking about the many times you couldn't say *No* but wanted to, and the anger and pain that goes with that. Recovery means seeing the ability to say *No* as a friend to protect you. It offers you choice. You have the power and right to say *No* and *Yes*. You will find that *Yes* is a gift that is offered freely rather than out of fear or the need for approval. Recognize that by saying *No*, you are actually saying *Yes* to yourself. Just as important, you also have the right not to say *Yes* or *No* until you know what it is that you want.

RECLAIMING RIGHTS

As children from troubled families, so many of our rights were neglected and/or taken away. It is important to go back and reclaim that which was rightfully ours in childhood. This is an aspect of reparenting that is vital in recovery. It is important that the following rights be integrated into your hearts and minds because of the incest you have experienced:

- You have the right to choose who can and who cannot touch you.
- You have the right to distinguish how you are touched and for how long. You have the right to determine what type of touch is accept-able to you.
- You have the right to say *No*.
- Not only are these your rights—they are rights you deserve.

TOLERANCE OF INAPPROPRIATE BEHAVIOR

Adult Children who are incest survivors lived for so many years with chemically induced abusive behavior that it began to seem normal to them. As a result, adult survivors are not skilled at recognizing people's intrusive, disrespectful, and/or abusive behavior.

A part of recovery is learning to identify the inappropriate behavior you experienced in the past in order to be free to identify it today. If you still minimize or deny the unacceptable behavior of the past, you won't have the skills to recognize it in the present. Learning to identify behavior that was inappropriate in the past, coupled with acknowledging and trusting your feelings, will make it much easier to recognize inappropriate behavior in the present. Add the belief that you deserve respect, and you can begin to set limits. Does this seem like an impossible task? No. It's very possible, and you can do it.

FORGIVENESS

As a group, Adult Children in general are desirous of understanding their parents' behavior. They are quick to bypass anger and jump into forgiveness. This has more to do with their fear of anger and need for approval than their desire to forgive.

Before forgiveness is truly possible, you must reclaim your emotional experience. By doing this, you also reclaim your power—without this, forgiveness will not occur.

Yet seeking to forgive your offender is not a necessary part of your recovery. Focus on your life—not what you believe you should or should not feel about the abuser. In your grief work, and in reclaiming your own life, you may come to find that you have less and less anger with the abuser. In time you may have only a distant sense of sadness, a remnant of anger. Clearly, an important goal in recovery is to have your anger with the offender no longer interfere with how you care about yourself or how you live your life. But it is unrealistic to expect yourself never to be angry again with the offender for the molestation.

Some people get confused about forgiveness, particularly when they realize that their parents were also abused as children. Although that information is helpful, and can put your family experiences into perspective, it does not erase the violations you experienced.

Remember, should you forgive, while you no longer blame the offender you do still hold the offender accountable for his or her actions. And you can and must continue to set limits when you are around that person. Forgiveness does not mean having a flash of insight and then resuming the old family roles.

Many people want to forgive themselves for things they did to others when they were children, often in response to having been hurt themselves. You may have physically hurt a smaller or younger child, or an animal. You may have molested a younger or smaller child, or, as Josh did, you may have initiated sex with other children. In the process of forgiving yourself, I hope that you will find compassion for your own vulnerability. Please try to remember that you were just a child. In *The Right to Innocence,* Beverly Engel reminds her readers that:

- You were a confused, disturbed child or adolescent acting out your pain.
- You were sexualized too early—long before you were emotionally and physically able to handle it.
- You had not yet developed a moral code, which is true of all children.
- You are different from the perpetrator because you are trying to change so you won't hurt anyone like that again.
- Just as you are not a bad person because of what someone else did to you, you are also not bad because of any sexual or cruel acts you committed as a child as a consequence of the abuse you sustained.

On the other hand, if you believe you were old enough—probably sixteen or older—to be held accountable for your actions, and if you believe you acted freely, knowingly, and of your own accord, you may be suffering from healthy guilt. You will then need to learn from your actions so you do not repeat them.

Ask yourself, "Why was this a mistake?" "What were some of the other consequences?"

Find a way to atone for what you have done. Be accountable for your actions.

Seeking to forgive oneself means developing an empathy for how vulnerable you were as a child. Remember that forgiveness is a cleansing of your pain. You were just a child with the resources of a child.

CHEMICAL DEPENDENCY

Because so many abuse survivors become chemically dependent—which is even more likely when they are Children of Alcoholics—you should be open to questioning your own chemical use. Before you can recover effectively from your Adult Child survivorship issues, you must address your own possible dependency. You cannot heal from childhood sexual abuse if you are addicted to alcohol or drugs.

If it is possible to reach out for help regarding your ACOA and survivorship issues, but not chemical dependency, then go ahead and begin where you can. Just be aware that, in time, you will need to look at the role alcohol and other drugs play in your life.

REPEATING THE ABUSE

Without recovery, victims of physical and sexual abuse may become either abusers themselves or silent partners to their children's abuse. Both alcoholism and abuse are generational. It's almost unheard of to find only one abuser and one victim in any abused family. But the chain can be broken when people take action not to repeat the pattern. If you recognize this behavior in yourself, or you are fearful of it occurring, reach out and ask for help now! You can and must stop any abuse. You do not have to abuse or be a silent partner to the abuse of your children. There are people who can and will help. While there are specific resources listed in the appendix (see page 571), help can also be found through your local crisis line, family service agencies, and rape crisis centers.

RELATIONSHIPS

Adult Children and incest survivors frequently have difficulty in relationships and understandably so. When one is Double Duty/Dual Identity, the reasons for this difficulty become even more complex.

Yet healthy relationships are possible. If you aren't in a relationship, you can learn a lot about intimacy in the context of a close friendship. Remember, as you recover specifically from ACOA/Incest issues, you are developing a more complete sense of yourself. And this is the basis of your strength in any relationship.

Work on knowing what you are feeling. You aren't going to be able to identify the relationship's needs if you don't know what your own feelings are. Being in a healthy relationship means acknowledging your own needs and feelings. It also means maintaining healthy personal boundaries so you can distinguish whose needs and feelings are whose and who is responsible for them.

Learning autonomy, knowing what you want, what you feel, what you need, and what you believe, allows you to develop as a unique entity, separate from others. Adult Children survivors are so often enmeshed with others that their personal self-worth is dependent upon making people feel good and important, on making other people happy, on seeing that other people's needs are met. You have to have a sense of yourself that is separate from others before you can have the healthy relationship you want.

In all relationships there is a need to learn healthy negotiation and conflict resolution. There was no model for this in the families of most COAs or incest survivors. Fear of anger and the need for approval are two Adult Child characteristics that clearly sabotage healthy negotiation and conflict resolution. You can only perceive options when you know your power. Conflict resolution is only possible when you have a healthy basis from which you can say *No* or *Yes* to your partner.

If you are in a relationship while you are working on these issues, this process will change and challenge your partnership. This can be very stressful. But if both of you are committed to growing, it can lead to greater health and happiness.

The courage it took to survive incest, and to survive incest in an alcoholic family, is cause for great celebration. Although recovery can seem an overwhelming task, when we are willing to allow others to walk through the process with us, we will see the darkness fade from our lives. We will find the freedom and happiness that we have always deserved, but that was postponed. May you find your happiness today.

I am no longer willing to believe that I am at fault or bad.
                                        —Adult Child Incest Survivor

Notes

1. *Los Angeles Times* survey, August 1985.
2. H. Giaretto, *Child Abuse and Neglect* 6:3 (1982).
3. D. Russell, *The Secret Trauma: Incest in the Lives of Girls and Women* (New York: Basic Books, 1986).

4. C. Black, S. Bucky, S. Padilla "The Interpersonal and Emotional Consequences of Being an Adult Child of an Alcoholic," *Journal of International Addictions* 21 (May 1986) 213–232.
5. J. Conte and D. Sexton, "Relationship of Adult Sexual Abuse Survivors to Adult Children of Alcoholics" (Accepted for publication in *Journal for Interpersonal Violence,* 1991).
6. S. M. Sgroi, *Handbook of Clinical Intervention in Child Sexual Abuse* (Lexington, Mass.: Lexington Books, 1982).

6

Eating Disorders

What I learned from growing up in an alcoholic family was that the world was a painful and scary place. Food became my means of escaping from those feelings.

—Adult Child

Compulsive overeating, bulimia, and anorexia are all aspects of the same disease—food dependency. Compulsion, obsession, and denial are the common denominators that weave through these dependencies.

Most people who are compulsive overeaters are not obese. They are much more likely to be chronically ten to twenty pounds overweight and preoccupied compulsively with food and body size. Compulsive overeaters react to sugars and starches in extreme ways. They experience mood changes ranging from euphoric highs to irritability, from feeling nurtured and comforted to being in a mental frenzy or stupor.

The most visible eating disorder is overeating that results in obesity. Although this chapter discusses the psychological factors that influence extreme overeating and create obesity, it must be remembered that under some circumstances, obesity can be caused by purely physiological conditions. There are rare metabolic exceptions and genetic considerations that create obesity. Nonetheless, whatever the reasons for obesity,

245

the psychological, social, and physical consequences are severe. It has been well established that obese people have shorter life spans due to strokes, heart attacks, and arteriosclerosis.

Bulimia is a second form of eating disorder. Bulimics overeat, typically in binges, and then they purge through laxative use, diuretic (water pills) abuse, or by forced vomiting and compulsive exercise. Bulimics, like most compulsive overeaters, tend to be within ten to twenty pounds of average weight. The binge and purge cycle of bulimia closely parallels the highs and crashes that drug addicts know so well. First comes the euphoric high of the binge, then comes the drastic expulsion of the food.

Anorexia is a third type of eating disorder. Anorexics, however, are obsessed with *not* eating. They may even have an unnatural fear of food. Anorexics starve themselves—a compulsion that is often reinforced by the biological euphoria produced by starvation.

Starving and bingeing/purging can produce serious medical problems ranging from dehydration and disturbances in the body's fluid and mineral balance to irreversible liver damage, diabetes, hypoglycemia, heart attacks, and kidney failure. In some cases, gorging and forced vomiting rupture the stomach or esophagus, causing infections and death.

Whatever the form of the disorder, eating takes on a compulsive quality. People feel driven to eat or to starve as though they had no choice. This compulsion effectively blocks awareness of their feelings and serves to distract them from anxiety and from unpleasant feelings and memories. When people are frightened of their feelings, or experience painful feelings, excessive food intake or extreme food deprivation helps them deny and repress the pain.

Overeaters also indulge in food when they're happy and joyful. Many overeat as a reward. Food can become the answer to any feeling.

People who feel poorly about themselves often use food for solace. Those with low self-esteem and a tendency to isolate themselves are much more likely to regard food as a friend. Food nurtures. Food anesthetizes.

People who are overburdened with shame, who have come to believe they are defective or bad, often find that compulsive overeating is the best way to assuage this pain. However, it can also be a form of self-punishment—a consciously abusive act. Overeating fuels the bulimic's sense of shame, while purging is sometimes an attempt to alleviate even greater shame. The anorexic may unconsciously be looking for a way to become invisible, to disappear.

Bulimics and anorexics often feel revulsion about their bodies and starve or purge themselves as punishment. This revulsion may be fed by a distorted perception of their bodies. They often see themselves as fat when they are quite thin or of average body weight. Overeaters may be repulsed by their bodies and overeat in response to their feelings of futility and powerlessness. Yet overeaters usually have distorted perceptions, too. Most often they believe they're smaller than they actually are, yet some see themselves as larger than they are. Early on, they all quit looking in the mirror. And they all tend to be disconnected from their bodies.

Both overeaters and undereaters have a great deal of difficulty verbalizing their internal experiences. This is because they're removed from both their feelings and their needs. They don't recognize the internal and external cues and signals that serve as indicators of their true needs.

People with eating disorders also display a significant amount of passive-aggressive behavior. They often appear compliant and passive on the outside while feeling and often denying their deep anger and resentment inside. They then act out that hostility against their own bodies.

These are people who struggle constantly with issues of powerlessness and control. Often they experience themselves as totally helpless in a very frightening world. The overeating may symbolize their feelings of being out of control. It certainly reinforces the powerlessness.

Bulimics and anorexics often have major issues around perfectionism. They have bought into the notion that if they can control their exterior, they can become more acceptable in their interior, where they often feel fear, hurt, loneliness, and shame. The control they experience with food may be the only control they feel they have in their lives.

In Western culture, food is largely associated with nurturance. Children are routinely given food to soothe or as a reward. We are programmed from a young age to use food to fill our emptiness. Children literally hunger for love and approval, and when that is missing in their lives, food often becomes an alternative.

Eating disorders are referred to as "diseases of isolation." Those with eating disorders tend to have spent a tremendous amount of time in isolation filled with loneliness. As children they often experienced being alone as being abandoned. They internalized this feeling of abandonment as proof that they were not of value. Food became a substitute for human interaction. When parents weren't available, food provided the solace. But the fact that the hurt feelings weren't assuaged went unnoticed. Additionally, much of the behavior that fed their disorder was secretive, which created even greater feelings of loneliness and shame.

Eating disorders, particularly obesity and anorexia, can also be a way of calling attention to oneself—a way of expressing anger and rage; a way of rebelling and acting out. Compulsive overeating is often a way of pushing people away. Especially when one has been sexually abused, being overweight may be an attempt to keep people away to prevent further abuse. For anorexics, starving is a way of attracting attention while still keeping people at a distance.

It is important to recognize that in every eating disorder, the relationship with food becomes addictive. And, as with any addiction, the relationship to the addiction becomes the major focus in the person's life. Food addiction is much like any other substance and process addiction. It moves through:

- Loss of control
- Denial
- Increased dependence
- Change in tolerance
- Impaired thinking
- Preoccupation with and the control of the addictive substance
- Manipulation of one's environment to obtain the desired effects
- Lying
- Obsession
- Guilt and remorse
- Physical deterioration

Adult Child Issues

Research has clearly demonstrated that Children of Alcoholics are more prone to become chemically dependent. However, only recently have we begun to recognize that other compulsive and addictive behaviors can also be attributed to being raised in an alcoholic family. One of the most common addiction/disorders in American society centers around eating.

Reports indicate that 15 to 20 percent of the general population of women report eating disorders. It is widely believed that the majority of people with eating disorders are women. Yet it is my belief that men with food addictions are only just now being recognized. A disproportionate number of men and women with eating disorders come from physically or sexually abusing homes. In a study by Drozd, 1986, 59 percent of female ACOAs reported currently or previously having an eating disorder, as compared with 19 percent of the control group.[1] It will be of value for the reader to see how, in other chapters, compulsive overeating, bulimia, or anorexia were responses to physical and sexual abuse.

Adult Children often routinely medicate the pain of their past and of their present with food, becoming overeaters in the process. They fluctuate between the need to be in total control of their food intake and feeling totally out of control. Their poor self-esteem, often coupled with self-hate, contributes to self-destructive behavior that manifests itself in overeating, bingeing, purging, and starving. Once they are into these distinctive patterns of self-abuse, they shroud themselves in shame, and their need to hide and keep secrets becomes even more pronounced.

The Adult Child characteristics that appear to be integral to those with eating addictions are:

- Control and powerlessness
- Perfectionism
- Repressed feelings—particularly anger and shame
- Shame
- Needs

Control and Powerlessness. Children need to experience a sense of physical and psychological safety in their lives. They need primary caretakers to set healthy limits, to provide nurturance and support, and they need to have expectations that are appropriate for their age and experience. When parental figures do not establish the appropriate parameters and levels of control that produce a sense of safety, children accurately feel profound loss and powerlessness. They often act out that powerlessness, or they seek ways of controlling their lives by any means necessary. COAs struggle with their powerlessness on an ongoing basis. For many Adult Children, the intake or lack of intake of food is the only place in which their power lies. They seek control by attempting to manipulate what they have the power to affect. By finding the areas they can control, bulimics and anorexics learn to exert control and literally hang on for dear life. Overeaters also overfuel their bodies in an attempt to feel that they have some say over what they do.

Perfectionism. COAs often seek perfectionism in an attempt to be in control and/or mask shame. Sometimes areas they can affect are so limited, their only control rests with their bodies. Their preoccupation with needing to look good is often an external way of protecting themselves and protecting their family. If they look good, they believe their problems and those of their families will remain hidden from others. No one will be able to see beyond the false exterior to the real chaos and sickness in their lives. Starving and purging are clearly actions in pursuit of perfection.

Feelings. COAs are people who live with chronic fear, loneliness, hurt, and disappointment. They experience resentment and anger. They live with embarrassment and guilt—often believing that there's something terribly wrong with them. Theirs becomes a life of shame. Food offers solace, and it also deadens the pain.

Shame. Adult Children were raised with physical and emotional abandonment. They did not get the approval, the attention, or the love they needed. Very early they came to believe there was something extremely defective inside them, that they could never be good enough. If there had also been physical or sexual abuse, they experienced being treated as objects, not as people. These were major acts of boundary violation. Food anesthetizes the pain of the growing-up years and fills the emptiness that comes with past and present shame. Anorexics or bulimics often seek to escape from their feelings of inadequacy by driving themselves to perfect their bodies by starving and purging. Overeaters seek to compensate for their early abandonment by nurturing themselves with food.

Needs. These dysfunctional families are alcohol- and drug-centered rather than child-centered. These children learn that adults are not going to be available to attend to their needs on a consistent basis. They also find out that they can't even meet their own needs because they are just children. As a result, they learn to repress and minimize their needs, often becoming so good at it that they cease to be able to recognize their own needs. This behavior often brings on depression—a valid response to years of not having their needs met. But their depression makes them even more socially and emotionally isolated. Compulsive eating is a way of attending to those unrecognized needs as well as a response to the depression that is fueled as a result of needs not being met.

Life Stories: Growing-Up Years

Why is it some children develop eating disorders, others become chemically dependent, and still others develop different compulsive disorders? That's difficult to answer. However, once you look at an individual's history, the reasons usually become more obvious.

Some eating disorders reflect physiological predispositions. Just as there may be a chemical tendency toward alcohol and other drug addictions, there may also be a predisposition toward obesity. With eating disorders, you will often see that the adult was a child who tended to be more socially and emotionally isolated.

In the following stories, you will see that food played a significant role from a very young age. Food was the mother's way of nurturing when she was bankrupt of other emotional resources. Dysfunctional parents often become preoccupied with food and body size and image in their need to control. For some, chronic childhood illnesses fed isolation, and food provided nurturance in times of stress.

The four Adult Children who are sharing their stories have had to struggle with eating disorders. Clearly, anorexia and bulimia are predominately female disorders. Males tend to fall into compulsive overeating that sometimes results in obesity. I've split the stories equally between men and women because as more men are entering Adult Child recovery, many of them are identifying compulsive overeating as a response to their Adult Child issues. These life stories illustrate how overeating, starving, and purging became responses to being raised in chemically dependent homes. Three of our life stories are about compulsive overeaters.

Skip was dangerously obese all through childhood—his top weight was 400 pounds. Yet for fifteen years now he has maintained an average weight of 170 pounds.

At the age of fourteen, Gloria came close to dying of anorexia. In her twenties she physically recovered to confront yet another level of recovery.

Felicia struggled with the meaning of food all during childhood, then became a compulsive overeater and finally bulimic. Gloria and Felicia reflect family histories of sexual abuse. Felicia and Skip are alcoholics.

Paul struggled with being "husky" as a child and twenty-five to fifty pounds overweight as an adult until he recovered in Overeaters Anonymous. The grandchild of an alcoholic, Paul was raised by two Adult Children. His story is amazingly representative because so many people with eating disorders come from third-generation alcoholic families. His parents' Adult Child issues played a strong role in the development of Paul's eating disorder.

SKIP
Age: 40
Mother: Co-dependent
Father: Alcoholic
Birth Order: Youngest of four
Raised: Indiana, Midwest
Socioeconomic Status: Middle class

SKIP: "My father drank alcoholically until I was five years old. Then he stopped and went to Alcoholics Anonymous for one year. After that, he was a dry drunk with no emotional recovery. Although I have very little memory of my life from the time I was three until I was nine, I do have a sense that his 'not drinking' was so fragile that none of us in the family could breathe for fear he'd start drinking again.

"He'd come home from work, get on the couch, eat dinner alone at the coffee table, nap, and then go to bed. I remember feeling fearful, as if I needed to keep a lid on myself in order to avoid contact with him."

Skip describes his father as being abstinent, but with no emotional recovery. That occurs for various reasons, but the most common is that the alcoholic doesn't stay involved in an active recovery program. This is what happened to Skip's father. He went to AA for one year and then "stayed in control." He controlled himself by not drinking, and he controlled his family with his silence.

The fact that Skip cannot remember events from the time he was three until he was nine implies that his experiences of that time were overwhelmingly frightening. Sometimes the traumatic events that damage a child's sense of security and self-worth are overt—such as physical abuse. But the trauma is not so blatant in Skip's situation. Although silence is not often regarded as a source of significant trauma in a child's life, Skip and his siblings were subjected to their father's punishing silence. He was not just a quiet man—he was blatantly rejecting. His menacing silence was emotional torture to all the family members. A child developing a sense of identity and self-worth raised in an emotionally cold family internalizes the feeling that he must have caused this coldness. There must be something deeply wrong with him, something that makes people not want to respond to him.

Skip's description of "keeping a lid on" himself is an accurate meta-phor for many children of troubled families. He needed to keep a lid on his feelings, on his emotional self. But, as a consequence, he couldn't keep a lid on the food. His need to control all his feeling manifested itself in his being controlling with food.

Skip's mother was a nurse. Since she worked the 11:00 P.M. to 7:00 A.M. shift, she had very little contact with Skip's father.

"I rarely saw them talk. Mother was nurturing and caring, but she also remained quiet and isolated. She worked very hard at her career, at home, and at church. I always knew she cared for me, loved me. But I also knew that she was controlled by Dad."

At dinnertime, Skip's dad was served his meal by his wife at the living room coffee table, in front of the television set. The four kids were served at the kitchen table.

"We sat down, ate, and left. Any talk was negative, derogatory, caustic. We hurled our hurt at each other."

Skip's mom didn't sit at the table, she just kept moving about, doing things. In time, three of the four children ate themselves into obesity. Skip's sister and one of his brothers were also over two hundred pounds by their late adolescence.

Skip's mother was a co-dependent. Her own sense of powerlessness had to be severe for her to keep silent about her children's obesity—as both a mother and a health professional.

Although Skip remembers his mother as warm and kind, he still felt a sense of emotional abandonment as she continued her downhill spiral into helplessness. Yet although Skip knew that something was wrong with his family, he was unable to identify it.

"My dad didn't talk to me at all, and my mother wouldn't acknowledge that there was anything wrong. But my life was filled with this engulfing terribleness—and I thought it was me."

Skip was screaming inside for someone to say something. This is the "Don't talk" rule taken literally.

"I wanted my father to tell me there was something wrong. I wanted him to tell me it was his fault. I wanted to hear it was not my fault. Later, as I got older I needed him to tell me he was proud of me. I didn't get any of those things.

"My home atmosphere was very frozen. I couldn't identify my feelings at that time, but I was constantly filled with the thought that whatever was wrong was my fault. I knew that we were all on our own in this family. My siblings and I were part of the family group, but each of us was alone."

Skip had trouble in school, beginning in the second grade when he developed a 20 percent hearing loss.

"School was a horror for me. It was only the occasional kind gesture from a teacher that would make me feel as if I could cope at all. When I developed my hearing problems, which were accompanied by severe headaches and infections, I discovered the pleasure of being home during the day, minus my father, and the peaceful solitude that brought. While my frequent absences also increased my sense of being out of place at school, what felt best to me was to be home during the day alone. It felt safe."

Even after his hearing problems were corrected, Skip continued to seek the safety of his solitude by feigning illness and staying home from school. This is when his eating began to take on emotional overtones.

"I would frequently order sweets from the milkman, and I continued in this pattern for years. Eating and television were my friends, and there was a woman on a local talk show who became my mother/mentor."

There was Skip, home alone watching television, finding comfort in his television friends, while the shows and commercials subtly, if not blatantly, reinforced the idea of food as a primary caretaker. Family shows such as *Leave It to Beaver, Ozzie and Harriet,* or, more recently, *The Brady Bunch,* demonstrating familial love, connectedness, and happy times with healthy eating—interspersed with "M'm-M'm good!" commercial invitations to eat—had to make Skip even hungrier.

Skip's solitude at home, coupled with his sense of differentness, kept him from making friends until high school. His relationships with his siblings were typical of an alcoholic family.

"My next oldest brother and I were close. I was less alone because of him. I do have a sense of his being on my side at times. My oldest brother was absent most of the time, mostly because he was very involved in sports. But I was also afraid of him because I didn't know him; he was a stranger to me.

"It was my sister, the oldest, who was my hero. She cleaned the house, made straight A's in school, and took care of me when I was

young. She was the one who really raised me. Most of the nurturing I experienced came from her.''

Skip weighed 225 pounds by the time he was ten, which made him physically very different from the other children. His physical size alone would have put a distance between him and others. But he was also a COA—and most of them, regardless of size, walk through childhood feeling different and separate from others.

Nevertheless, Skip began to look outside the family for support and companionship.

"There were many kids in my neighborhood, and they became important to me. I remember that I was always giving and doing for them, frequently buying them things and being a chameleon to their needs. This was where my main nurturing came from. Nurturing from taking care of others was a very early lesson for me.''

It is a common story to hear of fat children giving their peers money—buying them things—in hopes of securing friendships. There is such a stigma in our society associated with being fat that few children want to be friends with a fat child.

Yet all children need and want friends. A sense of belonging is vital to a child's self-esteem. Skip was caught in the middle of a dilemma. He was struggling with being in a dysfunctional family where he felt no sense of belonging and also with having no sense of belonging among his peers because he was a fat child. The need to buy friendships makes sense when one feels unworthy and inadequate.

However, Skip did have two close childhood friends. Because he was so fat at such a young age, the buddies he acquired early on became long-term friends—he was unable to make new ones as he got older. But, as friends sometimes do, in adolescence Skip lost one of them to new and different interests. And this loss was directly connected to his weight.

"In high school, when my first friend became interested in girls, I felt left out. I was fat. I knew I couldn't compete in that world.''

Already struggling with school—and life—Skip lost his one remaining friend to a fatal car accident when they were in high school.

"I was so unsupported and so unable to cope with my grief that I dropped out of school for a while. Ultimately it took me six years to finish high school. By this point I weighed four hundred pounds, which greatly added to my sense of inferiority.''

The death of a dear friend at any age is a major loss. But to lose one's only close friend as a teenager is even more difficult. There is the sadness, the anger, the loneliness, the sense of abandonment. But there are also the existential questions of life and death: "Is dying painful?" "What is death?" "How did my friend feel about me?" The level of pain is overwhelming, and a child has no way of knowing if it will ever end.

Skip had nowhere to take his pain, nowhere to find solace—except in food.

The compulsiveness of his eating may or may not have been conscious. Skip may have been so disconnected from his emotional self that the pain may not have even registered emotionally. Yet it is at this time that he lost all control of his eating.

When Skip describes his family, it is with an eerie calm. It's as if he slowly and quietly gained his four hundred pounds without anyone's noticing. Yet four hundred pounds is a violent attack against one's body. It's difficult to imagine that one could launch such an offensive with no one in the family paying him any attention.

Skip was aware of feeling unremitting self-hate.

"I would constantly tell myself I was 'no good'; that I was a terrible person."

Most of Skip's conscious self-hatred had to do with the family environment. He was totally detached from his body image.

"When I was very young I told myself that as long as I stayed under two hundred pounds I'd be okay. By sixth grade I had passed that. But I let it pass without much recognition. I would stand in the mirror and only see myself from the head up. I didn't see my lower body at all. I would get obsessed with my hair. I had to make sure my hair was perfect, that it was combed and sprayed. If my hair was okay, then I was okay."

By the time Skip was sixteen, his father had begun drinking again—beer on weekends. He continued this until a year before his death.

Slowly, Skip moved emotionally into adulthood—under a cloud of sadness, with an inner core of hate and fear toward his father. Food quieted the anger and comforted the sadness.

"I was aware of nothing but an intense, overwhelming sadness. I would feel very sad in response to television shows, movies, and the stories that I would read. I can remember sometimes locking myself in the bathroom with some sad story and sobbing.

"In addition to the sadness, I had a lot of anger. It was a conscious, internal hatred of my father that came through frequently. But basically, it was if I were in a functional coma all those years."

GLORIA
Age: 26
Mother: Co-dependent
Father: Pill-addicted
Birth order: Oldest of three
Raised: Northeastern city
Socioeconomic Status: Middle class

Gloria was blatantly affected by several generations of alcoholism in her family. This meant that her parents had unacknowledged Adult Child issues of their own, which may have led to her father's chemical dependency.

GLORIA: "Many of my memories of my maternal grandfather are of his being sloppily, happily drunk at our many family parties. As a kid I may not have been bothered by this, but as I grew older I was annoyed by his messy speech and slobbering kisses. My mother and grandmother both denied for years that he had any problem. The women in my family are supreme nurturers/victims/deniers/martyrs. The men are fostered, protected, and made into gods."

Gloria's paternal grandfather was also an alcoholic and very abusive. One of the still existing family secrets is that Gloria's father and his siblings were all chronically sexually abused by their father. Many times, as a young man, Gloria's father had had to knock out his father when he was on a drunken rampage. Out of the violence and pain of his own upbringing, Gloria's father developed a strong vision of what a family ought to be. In the end he became a controlling, tyrannical, pill-addicted autocrat.

"I didn't know that it was pills that were making my dad the way he was. I really never thought about why. I was just too scared. By the time I was born, my dad was already taking prescription medications. He kept the pills beside his bed in a drawer. Once, when I asked him about them, my mother clearly let me know I was not to tell my father that I knew about the pills. It was as if I was bad or wrong for seeing them. After

she told me not to tell my father, she told me harshly: 'Get out of this room.' I understood it was a subject that was never again to be spoken about.''

Gloria learned early in life that she should never do anything to disturb her father. Underneath his "master of control" demeanor, there was always the silent threat of violence.

"My mother taught me that, at all costs, I should never do anything to hurt my father or make him angry. I lived in constant fear of his awful silence that could, at the most unexpected moment, flare into red-faced rage. I have a mental image of myself in a crouch, like a dog that looks up pleadingly, hoping not to be beaten but expecting it, hoping to please the master but knowing it will never happen. The master will not, cannot, be pleased.''

Every person in this chapter has had to respond to issues of control by their parents. For Skip and Gloria, parental control is perpetrated on the family in silence. The father's extreme silence had the power to instill immobilizing fear into all of the other family members. The "Don't talk" rule was enforced through silence.

As with many COAs, Gloria's feelings toward her father were very conflicted. He often spent time with her and gave her treats. But he was also unpredictable in his behavior toward her.

"My early years were spent both adoring and dreading my father. When I was very young, before I reached puberty, we would spend a good deal of time together, taking long walks, digging for fossils, watching Godzilla and Dracula movies. My father was the 'good guy,' the one who bought me Twinkies and soda, the one who spent money.

"But I would also get these terrible insults from my father. They were always delivered with a laugh. He'd tell me I was fat, ugly, and stupid. He would tease me incessantly. If I cried, he'd laugh. If I got angry, he'd laugh. Finally I decided never to show my hurt again.''

When a parent is addicted to prescription pills, a child has greater confusion about their parents' usually hurtful and erratic moods and behaviors. Because children are less likely to relate the use of pills to their parents' behavior and the mood in the home, they are even more likely than most COAs to believe they are responsible for the hurtful feelings, that there must be something wrong with them. Shame begins early.

In these cases, the children often find the nonchemically dependent parent to be the "heavy." The chemically dependent parent may be easier to manipulate, may simply be absent, or at times may seem more fun or likable than the other parent.

"My mom was set up as the 'spoilsport,' the bad guy, the heavy. She was frugal—but I thought she was mean and stingy. She was careful about our eating well—but I thought her very disappointing as a mom. Other kids' mothers gave them sweets at lunch. I got an apple and maybe a plain oatmeal cookie."

It is possible that Gloria's mother's caution about food was her way of being the "good mother" or the "perfect mother." As her husband progressed in his illness, she had an even greater need to be "good" or "perfect." Her "goodness" was also a way of being in control. She demonstrated her "goodness" in other ways as well.

"To me, my mother appeared to be an extremely strong and overwhelmingly good person. I knew I could never be as unaffected, as noble, as unselfish, as she was. So I gave up my will to her. When we'd go clothes shopping, I'd let her choose my clothes. I would express no opinion at all, although I seldom liked the clothes she picked out."

Gloria eloquently describes what occurs for many COAs—they lose themselves in someone else. This is the beginning of her becoming invisible.

Gloria's best memories are with her brother Bobby, who is two years younger. Bobby was the funny, outgoing one. Although he had a violent temper, he usually kept it hidden. Most of the time he was affectionate and demonstrative. Gloria was quieter, less social, more reserved.

"Bobby and I played many imaginative games together with a whole troop of Christmas elves. We even took the trouble to divide the troop into two branches of the same family. It would take us hours to name the elves and then identify their family relationships. This was almost more important than starting the game. We shared a bedroom for many years, and we'd lie awake at night playing games and talking.

"One of my most poignant memories is of something that happened when we were both still in grade school. As we got ready for bed, Bobby wanted to kiss me good night. But I wouldn't let him; I refused to let him touch me. I had always hated being touched and to touch. But Bobby was always very affectionate, as was my mother. My mother was pleading with me to give Bobby a good-night kiss. Bobby was crying, saying that I didn't love him anymore.

"I lay on the bed, staring at the ceiling, 'knowing,' with the same

awful certainty that I would later feel about eating food, that I could not kiss him—that if I had to kiss him, I would die. I would somehow cease to be. I didn't cry; I didn't feel anything about Bobby's pain.''

Gloria had been able to let others know her physical boundaries non-verbally. But with Bobby she had to muster the strength to speak to her beloved brother. It is difficult to fully understand what touch meant to Gloria—but it clearly was frightening to her. She has no doubts about her love for this brother. For her to reject him in this manner meant this was her last stand of physically pushing people away.

Although Gloria has no memory of any sexual molestation, her father had been an incest victim—a fact that his wife wasn't aware of until twenty years after their marriage. Gloria described her father as very undemonstrative physically. He wouldn't let others touch him and wouldn't touch others.

"He refused kisses, he'd push you away, move his head; you couldn't touch him.''

It is possible that Gloria needed to define her physical space in a manner that couldn't include others. She was responding to her lack of psychological safety—a chronic fear of some unknown rage. Her father provided the modeling—no touching.

In school Gloria was one of the "smart ones." She had a few special friends whom she would play with, other girls who were also good students.

"Grammar school was largely an unpleasant experience for me. My good memories of that time have to do with after-school activities. My family lived in an apartment, but my friends all lived in houses. I loved going to their homes because there was a good deal of privacy and often a yard to play in.

"By seventh and eighth grades, there was a lot of drinking going on at parties. I was never a part of the 'tough' crowd. My friends and I were the ones most often tortured and teased by them. I never dated or drank. I wore glasses and braces and was very shy around boys. I spent my eight years at that school in fear—of both the students and the teachers.''

Although Gloria continued to excel academically in high school, her sense of being an outsider became even stronger.

Solitude was something that offered comfort to Gloria. But in this solitude she also discovered the isolation that would soon lead to her eating disorder.

"I spent a great deal of time alone. On Friday nights, my favorite thing to do was sit at my desk, writing page after page of stories about girls my own age going on dates or learning about the facts of life. I also read lots of poetry and wrote verses myself, all of which rhymed. It wasn't until I was in high school and discovered the Beatles' lyrics that I started to experiment with 'free verse' and began writing more imaginative, less narrative poetry.

"In many ways, books saved me. Books gave me a world more real to me than the one in which I lived. I chose books for the fantasy and the challenges they offered me. I wasn't just a bookworm; I was a book vulture."

Part of Gloria's fantasy life centered around her image of herself as a caretaker.

"I would create a scene and then enter it. Usually there would be one or two girls, a few years younger than me, girls I knew by sight at school. I would be the 'mother/guardian' of those girls, and they would always be weak or helpless in some way, either physically frail or in some sort of trouble. I would order their world, keep it in check, and protect them."

Her fantasy was soon to become real—although she was the one who would be physically frail and in trouble. Her "trouble" was the end result of her trying to protect herself, of putting her world in order, of holding everything in check.

"In my freshman year of high school I must have heard the inevitable talk about diets. Girls that age are obsessed with how their bodies look. On some level something must have clicked: 'Ah, yes! Diet yourself to nothing! Martyr yourself. Starve yourself for attention!'

"I have no memory of making a decision to diet. But the following summer, when I was working at a day camp for the mentally retarded, I began to control my eating. Soon I was eating very little.

"From September of that year to January of the next I went from 105 pounds to 74. I was so physically weak I couldn't walk to school. I had lost nearly all of my hair. I was in such pain from the strain on my muscles that my mother had to spend hours rubbing my back. That was the onset of my anorexia."

Gloria's story is typical of many people with eating disorders. They are very disconnected—not only from their bodies, but also from their feelings and from any insights. Gloria had very little control over her life;

her mother even picked out her clothes. She describes walking in her mother's saintly shadow as she is subjected to cruel teasing by her father. At home and at school, she always felt like an outsider. Self-starvation was a clear cry for help from a young girl who was dying on the inside.

PAUL
Age: 43
Mother: Adult Child
Father: Adult Child
Birth Order: Oldest of two
Raised: Midwest and California
Socioeconomic Status: Working
    class

Paul was born within a year of his parents' marriage. All the time he was growing up, he kept getting the message that, because of him, the family had been burdened with increased responsibility and financial problems. He always felt as though he had to make up for his early arrival.

At a very young age, Paul was expected to respond emotionally like an adult.

PAUL: *"I came into life immediately having to excuse my existence."*

In addition to obviously arriving earlier than planned, Paul was also a sick child. He had major health problems—rheumatic fever, pneumonia, chronic asthma.

"I was told that because of the medical costs, my dad had to work two jobs and limit his career goals and enjoyment of life. I remember my parents' joking about how I'd have to make a lot of money someday to pay them back for this sacrifice.

"From the beginning, I had the sense that I was the person responsible for all the family stress, and that I was obligated to repay this somehow. As an adolescent, my major career goal was to make enough money to buy my parents a house, even though I knew that would not set things right. There was nothing I could do to repay them for the pressure and stress that I had brought into their lives."

Both of Paul's parents were Adult Children, although neither became alcoholic. However, the family dynamics were no different from those of alcoholic parents. They simply continued to play out the dysfunctional scripts of their own childhoods. When you are an Adult Child, issues of control, inability to know what normal is, unhealthy boundaries and limit setting, need for approval, inability to make decisions, low self-worth, poor problem-solving skills, inability to listen, inability to play, and shame will gravely interfere with the ability to parent effectively. The inability to express feelings, issues of control, and unhealthy boundaries were all prevalent and hurtful to Paul.

"My dad's stepfather was an alcoholic. He was a harsh disciplinarian, uncaring, and mean. My father was always being blamed and always felt responsible as a child for everything that went wrong. He picked up that way of dealing with children and passed it on to my sister and me. I had this sense that I was obligated to him for the sacrifices he made for me. At the same time, I felt angry at not having had a choice. I relieved that guilt by overworking to try to deserve some good things."

Paul's mother's father was also an alcoholic.

"My mother grew up bringing buckets of beer home for her father and raising all of her siblings. My mom had learned to worry and avoid conflict. She also had chronic health problems, and she would attack me as being heartless and cold-hearted when she felt I wasn't empathetic enough about her problems."

Paul was confused early about boundary issues. He wasn't taught to have an appropriate sense of who was responsible for what. His parents were unrealistic in their emotional and social expectations of him. They held him responsible for their feelings and their adult problems.

"Everyone was worrying about someone else's feelings and discounting their own. My mother would feel sad and worry about something going on with me. Rather than see that as my mother's sadness and worry, my father wanted me to be different so she wouldn't feel sad or worry. No one wanted to take responsibility for their own problems—they always blamed someone else."

As Skip had done, Paul would come to find that chronic illness played a significant role in his eating patterns. Because of his illnesses, he was often encouraged to eat to regain his strength.

"When I was seven, my sister and I stayed with my mom's parents for a few weeks. When my parents came to pick us up, they were shocked—

*we had both gained considerable weight. My grandmother had given us
large dishes of ice cream at night to keep us from missing our parents
and also to reward us for being well behaved. At this point food had
become not only necessary for my health, but also a reward and a soothing substitute for emotions."*

Paul attended Catholic school until the fourth grade, when his family
moved from the Midwest to California.

*"The school was run by nuns, who were great at instilling guilt and
reinforcing the idea that children had to be responsible. We were even
taught to feel guilty for feeling shame! We had to bring money for orphans
and were told to pray at any free moment for the suffering souls. When
we were caught talking in line, we were told souls were suffering in
purgatory because we were not praying to get them out.*

*"I felt miserable about moving. And my parents only made things
worse by letting me know that they were leaving home, family, friends,
and jobs to go to California just because of me."*

Paul believed that his family moved to California because of his health.
This only added to his guilt. It also inappropriately gave the issues of his
health and food a lot of power.

A healthy family might also have made the same decision to move. But in
a healthy family the parents would have taken responsibility for the decision.
In Paul's family the adults were unable to do that. Instead they chose to hold
their young child responsible for whatever went wrong from then on.

Guilt was burned into Paul's chest—a guilt that he understood all too
clearly he'd never be able to get rid of. Like many COAs, he found that
no matter what he did it wasn't going to be sufficient. He would never
be able to be enough or do enough for his parents. In time food would
become the only thing that symbolically allowed him to feel "full," "substantial," "worthy," "enough."

When the family moved to California, Paul began to attend public
school.

*"Again I was the outsider, trying to figure things out, trying not to make
mistakes that would lead to embarrassment and family shame. I avoided
competition, except in math. I was really quick with flash cards, so I'd
compete in that area because I knew I could succeed. Sports competition
was out of the question because I was not good enough.*

*"When I was in fifth grade, I had whooping cough and was out of
school for several weeks. I remember coming home after my first day*

back and having a peanut-butter-and-jelly sandwich and a glass of choco-late milk to unwind from the stress of the day. That became a pattern, and I began to gain weight. When I got to the point where I needed 'husky boy' clothes, my mom began to express concern about my weight.''

Eating after school is common for most children, but Paul was aware that he was eating in response to stress. The other issue was that his mother was going to try to control this part of his life.

Paul learned quite young that he could use his frail health to avoid doing physical activities that his parents wanted him to do. While his poor health made guilt a major theme in his life, he found that food could be an answer to his confusion and pain. At times he was able to vent his anger by using his poor health to his advantage.

"When my parents wanted me to fish, play Little League, or go to a social function, I would get sick to avoid it. I was scared of social situations. I was afraid of how I was supposed to act. I was angry that I was to go to please them. I was angry that they were always trying to control me."

Paul said he also played jazz and rock music very loud to deal with his anger. What he understood clearly was that it couldn't be expressed directly.

Paul and his sister got along fairly well. There was some competition, because Paul easily got A's, while his sister had to work hard for her B's. But she was the one family member with whom he tended to have a healthy relationship.

"I felt relief that there was someone in the family who didn't want me to parent or take care of them. I would feel good about my achievements with her and not worry about having to discount them to avoid hurting her."

As in many alcoholic families, mealtimes were stressful. Children with eating disorders often describe the need to eat all they can as fast as they can—and to get away from the table. Anorexics describe feeling so tense at mealtimes that they could eat very little. They would pick at food, push it about their plate, but eat nothing. Some children, often overeaters, describe not having any specific dinnertime and feeding them-selves all evening long—potato chips, ice cream, macaroni and cheese, all starches and sugars.

"We generally ate our meals together, and they got pretty heated at times. To me, they were the great myth of what the family was supposed

to be but was not. Mom controlled conversations to avoid conflict be-
tween my dad and me, while we chafed at the bit to do battle and raced
to see who could eat the fastest. This became a habit for me—eating
quickly without savoring or absorbing the food."

Paul was socially isolated for the most part while growing up. Although
he usually had one close friend, that friend was often as lonely and isolated
as he. Together the two would create their own fantasy world in which
to play.

"My pattern was to find other outsiders and fuse with them. In some
way I would live vicariously through them, especially if they had more of
a social life. I would gain access to social events through their friend-
ship."

"In general, school was a place of stress. There were the straight-A
students, but I was always below them. Socially I felt out of it with most
groups. I felt I didn't like what other people did for fun. Having gone to
Catholic school, I was embarrassed by the open sexual behavior of the
other students, and I didn't feel comfortable at weekend drinking parties.
What I enjoyed doing, I did alone. I just felt strange and different."

Paul's illnesses kept him home a great deal, increasing his sense of
isolation.

"I never felt as if I fit in; I was always trying to adjust to getting back to
school. I got used to working at home alone on schoolwork and then
reading, or going off into fantasy, or watching television out of boredom.
I was creating my own way out."

Paul continued his pattern of isolating himself and eating. He would
gain weight and then go on a diet. His parents would comment on his
self-control, but then he would return to his old eating habits and the
weight would come back.

Paul had been six feet tall from the time he was a freshman in high
school. Being tall, he tended to look "big and husky," but not obese.
But food had become his major focal point, and he perceived himself as
"fat." However, pictures taken during his childhood show a youngster
perhaps ten to fifteen pounds overweight, and in high school, he was
about fifteen to twenty-five pounds overweight. But because of his parents' constant responses and comments, Paul perceived himself as fat
and that something was wrong with him because of his size.

From the second grade on, Paul had a distorted body image, much like

Felicia, whose story follows. He was overweight, and by high school he would be a compulsive overeater and would remain so. Although fifty pounds was the most weight he would gain, his whole life was preoccupied with food and body size.

Although Paul's parents may have been trying to be supportive by acknowledging his self-control, they quickly undermined this by being critical, emotionally distant, and blaming. Therefore he placed little value on receiving attention from them.

"Whenever the weight returned, it was back to dieting and feeling fat, disgusting, weak, unfit, undeserving, undesirable, and scared that I'd be fat forever, scared that I would gain more weight.

"My childhood was mostly about fear and shame. I was always so frightened of possible conflict. I also felt I was responsible for my parents' terrible inability to be happy."

Paul lived in fear of taking on more and more guilt. He was already carrying an enormous burden—the happiness of his entire family. This was exacerbated by the shame he felt around the role of food in his life. The burden became expressed in his body size.

FELICIA
Age: 41
Mother: Alcoholic
Father: Alcoholic
Additional Dynamic: Incest victim
Birth Order: Youngest of two
Raised: Texas
Socioeconomic Status: Upper
    middle class

Although both of Felicia's parents were alcoholic, she did not recognize that drinking was a problem. Because her family life had all the trappings of material success, she assumed her parents' focus on drinking was "normal."

FELICIA: "The days in our house focused on cocktail hour, which began promptly at five P.M. On weekends and holidays drinking began earlier, but 'never before noon.' The air was filled with tension at all times, but

I could never put my finger on what was wrong. I guessed it was some-
thing wrong with me."

Looking back now, Felicia is able to see that the family was clearly alcohol-centered. Her parents were constantly preoccupied with the anticipation of drinking or actual drinking. The message was clear—the day began at cocktail hour. The kids were regarded as a "duty." They were attended to physically and materially, but emotionally they were abandoned.

The alcoholism in Felicia's family was covert, as it is in the families of many Adult Children. Felicia is the type of Adult Child who often says, "It wasn't that bad." In her case, both of her alcoholic parents were in the early stages of chemical dependency. The term *covert alcoholism* is often used to imply that the consequences are less tangible. But Felicia was responding to the alcoholism long before the signs of chemical dependency became blatant.

It is my belief that alcoholism always affects children negatively, whether the parents are in the early, middle, or late stages of chemical dependency. It is often denial that reinforces one's perceptions of covert or overt alcoholism. Felicia would clearly suffer from her mother's Adult Child issues and her chemical dependency; from her father's chemical dependency; and from her maternal grandfather's sexual molestation of her.

There is no such thing as "It wasn't that bad." The hurt and loss in this family are tremendous. Felicia's denial allowed her to minimize the effects of being raised in her family. It allowed her to avoid the pain.

Felicia's mother also came from a family with two alcoholic parents. In addition, her father was physically and sexually abusive. Because her mother's alcoholism was not blatant, Felicia was responding as much to her mother's criticism and negativity—all unresolved Adult Child issues— as she was to her mother's drinking.

Felicia's mother became even more critical and negative after 5:00 P.M., something Felicia now realizes was a result of her drinking.

"My mom was a very angry, controlling person. This certainly began in
her childhood. And she did have reasons to be angry with my dad. He
was very passive and didn't listen to her. He also acted as if he didn't
need her, and all my mom wanted in her life was to feel needed. All I
wanted was to at least be heard. I never was."

This generational cycle repeats itself not just physically, but emotionally. Both Felicia and her mother would become alcoholic, both focused on food and body image, and both were starved for love and attention.

Felicia's father wasn't very accessible while she was growing up. Through some shrewd financial investments he started his own real estate business, which was very prosperous. His work consumed most of his time. Cocktail hour began as soon as he got home from work.

Felicia feels that the only things with which her father was able to connect, with any sort of intimacy, were alcohol and food. Her father was overweight, and Felicia's mother was always trying to control his food intake.

"Overeating was a way to be like Dad. He was always sneaking food, and my mother criticized him constantly for this. Then I stepped into his shoes. I had finally discovered a way to be like Dad and not like Mom; to connect with Dad and to disconnect and distance myself from Mom."

Felicia's eating patterns would come to be a struggle in response to control by her mother and abandonment by her father.

With hindsight, Felicia now sees that overeating, mimicking her father's behavior, was a way of bonding with him. Overeating was a wonderfully hostile response to her mother's controlling behavior. Eating, when her mother was trying to control Felicia's intake, was power.

Despite her father's unavailability, Felicia kept trying to get closer to him, to connect with him, but she didn't know how. She kept thinking that there was something wrong with her.

"I wanted to be like my dad. He seemed like a better choice than my mom. At least he was rational and funny. Mom was always so serious and so negative, judgmental, and critical. She was always trying to control Dad. I tried to protect him, but I failed. I tried real hard at everything, but I was never enough."

The notion of limited supply pervaded Felicia's family life.

"Was there enough vodka around for Dad's martinis? Enough bourbon for Mom? Enough money? Enough time for me? Enough love?"

Unfortunately there wasn't enough attention and demonstrated love for Felicia to feel good about herself, so food became her fix.

Felicia says repeatedly that she was never good enough. She was never good enough to get her mother's approval or her father's attention. In time she would find food to be the only solace for the emptiness in her life. She would also discover that she could never eat enough to fill herself up. Her need could only be filled by the overt love and attention of her parents.

Felicia's mother was a housewife. Felicia grew up with a sense that she was always in her mother's way. She also felt a constant sense of disapproval from her mother.

"I just wanted her attention, and she was always too busy! She had to get food ready.

"My mother was also a perfectionist. She was preoccupied with doing everything right. Nothing was ever good enough for her. I remember my mother coming into my room and pulling clothes out of my drawers and then telling me to clean up my room. I felt as if nothing were mine, that at any point I would be subjected to close scrutiny and made to feel inadequate."

Felicia was living in a family where she was emotionally abandoned. By age six this vulnerable, needy child was being periodically molested by her grandfather.

Felicia and her sister were sent to live with her mother's family—although her parents knew they were alcoholics—for some weeks when her father became seriously ill and needed to be hospitalized. During this visit her grandfather sexually molested her. For the next six years Felicia's grandfather would come to town one or two times a year. He would "help the family out" by taking Felicia places. He continued to molest her on these outings. Felicia remembers little of what happened when they were together, but she does remember the fear, shame, and humiliation she felt.

Eating disorders are not just a frequent response in Adult Children of Alcoholics, they are also common among survivors of sexual abuse. Food—compulsive overeating, bingeing, and starving—meets the same emotional needs when one is the child of both an alcoholic and sexually abusing family, and the likelihood of an eating disorder occurring in such a case is even more pronounced.

Felicia already understood that there was something wrong with her. She knew she seemed to be a constant problem to her parents—that, basically, they didn't want to hear from her. She couldn't go to her parents and tell them about the molestation; her parents had sent her to her grandfather's in the first place. Her grandfather was someone she was supposed to love. Felicia's response to the incest was to be compliant and to quickly pretend it didn't happen. She shut down emotionally: Don't think. Don't feel. Just eat.

It was shortly after this that Felicia began to love sugar.

Felicia's parents were very good about providing for her materially, and at the age of seven she turned to horseback riding as a way of winning attention and praise. She would compete in riding events, often for candy bar prizes. It was at this time that she began to get fat.

"I usually won the races I competed in, and I brought my trophies home— on my body. I got the praise I was hungry for, but I felt as if the hugs were for what I did, not who I was."

In addition to being an excellent horseback rider, Felicia was a very good student.

"Overall, school was always a positive experience for me. I did well, and my parents approved. We all had high expectations for me. I was a year younger than the other kids in my class, so socially I was immature. But my grades were good and seemed to be all that was important."

Felicia was learning that looking good and performing well was what her parents valued. The more she became conscious of that, the more she felt ignored and nonvalued. She was starving for love, but she felt as if she were simply a decoration for her parents. In her conflict to get love and approval, she would continue to perform, but she also sabotaged the "looking good" with overeating.

Felicia spent much of her time alone, riding. When she wasn't practicing for a competition, she would ride her horse out into the woods, then find a place to sit and read. She was most comfortable by herself. This was not a sign of self-acceptance, but one of isolation based in fear, a lack of acceptance, and shame.

In Felicia's family the alcoholism was more subtle because the trauma was not yet blatant. Nonetheless, she was experiencing abandonment on a chronic basis. Her emotional needs were being consistently ignored as a result of her parents' alcoholic personalities. Also, she was repeatedly molested by her "trusted" visiting grandfather during these years.

Although isolation had become a way of life for her, by the time she entered high school Felicia began to feel the pressure to be like the other kids. It was during her senior year in high school that drinking became a part of her social life. She and one of her friends would go out on a regular basis and "party."

"Alcohol and food was the glue that bound our friendship. She was my drinking buddy, and I was hers. By the time I began college, most of my friendships revolved around using alcohol and pot. I was too scared and

*too much in control to use LSD or other heavy drugs. Alcohol was 'okay.'
But I was not okay when using it. I began to be scared that I might have
a problem.''*

The Role of Food

Food often plays a very significant role in the lives of children from alcoholic families. It can offer solace to the child who is feeling hungry for
love or attention. It can be a friend for the child who feels isolated and
alone. A child who develops an eating disorder often substitutes food for
the intimacy that is lacking in the family.

However, when these children become overweight, they can find the
issues of growing up in an alcoholic family doubly difficult. Self-esteem
erodes even further, and self-loathing increases. The child feels the shame
twice over—both for the alcoholism in the family and for his or her "ugly"
body.

Overeating is another way of "stuffing" your feelings, something Children of Alcoholics learn to do at an early age. The child may wish to be
"invisible," but the overeating is also a cry for attention. As one Adult
Child puts it, "It's a way of killing yourself with food."

Anorexics may be trying to become less and less visible in order to
hide from the inner pain. They may be reacting to the lack of control in
their lives, and food intake becomes the one area in which they have
some power.

There is also the problem of never feeling as if you're good enough.
Becoming anorexic is often a striving after perfection—the perfect weight,
the ideal body image. Unfortunately, perception of one's body usually
becomes distorted.

The withholding of food may also be a form of punishing oneself for
being "bad." In fact, both overeating and starving can be forms of self-
punishment. Bulimics struggle between the two. They flip-flop between
being out of control in their use of food to comfort and punish and being
overly controlling in seeking perfection—the way they present themselves to the world.

In recovery, you have to be able to identify the role that food—or lack
of food—has played in your life.

Role of Food for Skip. In both childhood and adulthood, food was Skip's
best friend. Food was solace. It was nurturance. It helped to anesthetize
the pain. But it was also a source of added shame.

SKIP: *"People stared at me; I couldn't fit into chairs. The way I felt about my body, the way I felt about me, just increased my sense that something was wrong with me. I had absorbed all the uncomfortableness of my family in those four hundred pounds."*

Felicia says that *feeling* fat was a symbol of her shame. For Skip, *being* fat was the symbol of his shame. Here is a 225-pound ten-year-old boy; 400 pounds by his late teenage years. Skip is screaming for help! But his family is so frozen in silence, the only way he or his siblings can speak is through their overeating—and still they are ignored!

"Prior to my recovery, eating was always secretive. I would eat mainly at night, nonglorious food like peanut butter and bread, bacon and eggs. My secretiveness with food also extended to stealing food from friends' refrigerators, eating off other people's plates as I carried them from the table, eating things I rescued from kitchen trash bags.

"Privately I ate to fill myself and quiet my pain. Publicly I ate in a manner that would allow me to avoid attention from other people. I would eat moderate helpings, a salad, no dessert. I would be as invisible as possible. I felt so unworthy in my life that I had to counter any rightful healthy attention I could receive. Then, privately, I would counter that positive attention with negative feelings about what I was shoveling in my mouth.

"Even when I was an adult and rapidly losing my weight, my sneakiness continued. I would be at a dinner party and I'd find a reason to leave the table and sneak into the kitchen. I'd find a spoon, get to the freezer, find the ice cream, open it up, gulp down large tablespoons, put the lid back on, clean up the spoon, and wipe my hands because ice cream can often be messy. Then I'd calmly return to the dining area without the other guests being aware of my behavior.

"Throughout all this, I was constantly trying to lose weight. Every month I'd start a new diet; it would last from three days to two weeks. I was obsessed with this constant yo-yoing. It was a very effective tool for avoiding myself, which is what I had been trained to do."

Many people with eating disorders become as addicted to dieting as they are to eating. But the dieting is just another attempt at control— one that is usually doomed because the emotional component of the addiction is not being addressed.

Role of Food for Gloria. Gloria's eating disorder occurred so quickly that she has little memory of that time. Her inability to remember is part of being so removed from her feelings, as well as the disorientation and confusion that is created by starvation. In retrospect, with therapy she is aware of feeling that if she ate food, she would cease to be; food would suffocate her.

GLORIA: *"I never thought about food until the crisis was on me. I do know my mom was very careful about our eating. At school I was teased a lot about the strange foods in my lunch box. The other kids always had peanut-butter-and-jelly sandwiches on white bread. I had health foods and whole-wheat bread. I would get angry with my mother for being so different and making me feel so different.*

"Also, my dad and grandfather often told me I would get fat and never get a husband if I kept eating so much. I always liked food, but I didn't carry extra weight. All I knew was, I was doing something wrong."

Gloria was fighting for her life, but, ironically, in doing so she was also killing herself. She wouldn't eat because she was afraid that if she did, she wouldn't know herself. She had very little sense of her wants or her feelings—it wasn't safe to know them. Yet she literally hungered to find herself.

"It wasn't until I began to 'diet' that I began to obsess about being thin. It began by my eating very little, and by eating in a very ritualistic way. I would forbid myself all the foods I loved and would exercise compulsively."

At the onset of her anorexia, Gloria, who was five foot six inches, weighed 105 pounds. Within six months she was down to seventy-four pounds. She lost her body hair. She lost the fat pads on the bottoms of her feet. She was too weak to walk. She suffered from muscle pain. And she was so severely dehydrated that her skin became chapped and broken, resulting in scars. Gloria was in desperate need of help.

*R*ole of Food for Paul. Paul chronically felt left out, alone. As with Skip and Felicia, he never felt he was good enough. In addition, he felt totally responsible for his family's unhappiness. Finding no way to feel good about himself, he made food his best friend.

Compulsive overeaters develop a love-hate relationship with food, and a self-hate relationship lies in the nurturance and solace that food provides. It helps to take the eater's pain away. The hate relationship develops because the food becomes a source of shame. It represents a loss of control and powerlessness that feeds an already deep-seated shame.

PAUL: "Can a bowl of ice cream be your major sensual experience of the day? For me, ice cream became a tool for self-nurturing. Food was a comforting friend, a sexual friend, that deadened the feelings of stress, anxiety, worry, perfectionism, anger, shame, guilt, and embarrassment. I could relieve those tensions with soothing foods."

While Skip disassociated from his body, Paul was very focused on his body.

"As a child I was sick and weak and warned that I'd have a 'chicken chest' if I didn't learn to breathe better through my asthma attacks. When we got to California I remember feeling embarrassed about taking my shirt off or wearing shorts because of my pale skin and flabby upper body. Swimming lessons were painfully embarrassing and frightening.

"As I gained weight, much of it was in the thighs and buttocks, so buying pants became very traumatic. I always had to buy large-waisted ones with wide legs. And then I had to try them on to see if they were cut full enough. So now I was self-conscious about the lower part of my body, too. To top it off, I developed breasts because of the fat."

Every fat child has stories of shame about clothing. If shopping can be avoided, it will be. Clothing styles are a part of fitting in, an essential element in belonging. Fat children can't wear stylish clothes. Skip's mother bought his clothes at an outlet that sold uniforms.

For adolescent boys, competing in sports is almost a rite of passage. Any boy who dislikes athletics and is not very developed athletically struggles to some degree with his self-esteem and image. Being overweight creates even greater difficulty in this struggle.

"I felt physically incompetent in sports because of my weight. Early on I withdrew from competition, so I did not develop any skills. That gave me an ongoing self-definition of 'fat kid' in PE. It was also how the coaches and other kids saw me. Showering in the gym was horribly embarrassing."

Teens differ in the timing of their sexual development, but they all agonize to some degree over what is right for them. Feeling anxious, confused, and fearful is a natural part of the process. But the COA has an even greater struggle because of mixed messages regarding sexuality. Adding a distorted, negative body image to one's emerging sexual feelings creates even more confusion and fear.

PAUL:"Sexually, I felt unattractive. Food helped me over the lonely weekends, while simultaneously making me feel even more undesirable. I was an awkward loner who already felt self-conscious with girls. The weight just added to my negative self-image. My sexual fantasies focused on forcing girls to have sex. The idea of some girl wanting to be sexual with me never entered my mind.

"I'd practice playing basketball, volleyball, badminton, and tennis—but I practiced them alone, except for school PE classes. The one good thing was that I was tall. When I felt good, I would see myself as tall, thin, strong, and limber. But when I felt bad about myself, I'd see my body as fat, dumpy, and weak. The confusing part was that my head said I was fat whether I was or not.

"Growing up in my family gave me a painful and scary view of the world. Food became my only means of escape from the feelings that view produced."

Paul's food and COA issues are similar to Skip's and Gloria's. But Skip's compulsive eating resulted in obesity and Gloria's in anorexia. Paul was a compulsive overeater who internalized an image of being fat and not good enough that would become part of his yo-yo cycle of dieting.

*R*ole of Food for Felicia. Despite her mother's careful restriction of her diet, Felicia got very mixed messages about food. Still, her problems with food did get her attention—and that was the important thing.

FELICIA: "Food was love. Food was attention. Food was a way to connect with my dad and break away from and rebel against my mom. Food was the answer. Food was the solution. Food was also a friend.

"My mother controlled my food. My sister could eat cookies, peanut butter, and ice cream while I could not. She could have hamburgers and hot dogs. I got only the meat. At the time I couldn't feel anything, but I now know that I felt deprived, as though there was never enough of anything."

Felicia got the attention she wanted. But it was negative attention that sliced away at her self-esteem.

"The same mom who controlled my diet also fed me whenever I was sick, happy, proud, sad, angry, or even just uncomfortable. She'd always say, 'You must be hungry. You need to eat. With a full stomach, you'll feel better.' Eating, not eating, gaining weight, losing weight—anything and everything about food got me attention. With food I was the center of the universe. I got the attention I craved."

To be fed as a response to all one's needs, whether physical or emotional, makes it difficult for anyone to differentiate hunger from other bodily signals. Felicia was primed to see food as the answer to all of her unspoken needs.

The issue of control is major for all ACOAs. For Felicia, control and food were all bound up together.

"My childhood relationship with food was all about control. My mom controlled everything I put in my mouth, or at least she tried to. I didn't learn to control or manage my own food. All I learned was how to rebel, how to sneak, how to be dishonest with her and ultimately with myself. And I felt such shame, even then."

Felicia's shame reflects not only her perception of her body as "not right," but also her dishonesty and low sense of self-esteem. Not only does this create problems for Felicia around food, it also teaches her not to trust her own perceptions. She learns that she cannot trust others to meet her needs. To get what she wants, she has to manipulate and deceive.

Compared with Skip and Paul, Felicia was closest to an average body size. Although she felt fat, she was only somewhat overweight, not obese.

"In high school, I felt fat. I realize now that feeling fat was synonymous with feeling insecure and lousy about myself. Feeling fat had little to do with what I looked like or how much I weighed. Feeling fat was the symbol of my shame."

Food was also a solace for her shame and humiliation about the incest. Food was her friend at a time of much fear, shame, and loneliness.

Food played an early role in the dysfunction of these COAs. Although some people with a childhood eating disorder attend to it during their youth, for most, treatment and/or recovery doesn't occur until adulthood—if at all. When food addiction begins in adulthood rather than childhood, it usually fills the gap left by the cessation of another primary addiction, such as chemical dependency or workaholism.

Felicia found she needed to get sober first before she could deal with her issues around food. Skip recognized his chemical dependency only after recovery from his food addiction. Gloria recognized her food addiction at age fourteen—only to be confronted with the symptoms of yet another food addiction in her twenties. One addiction often masks another, and one addiction often replaces another. In these life stories, three of four people were adults before they could recognize and actively address their food addiction.

Life Stories: Adulthood and Recovery

SKIP
Age: 40
Compulsive overeater
Occupation: Psychotherapist
Recovery Process: Self-help,
    therapy

Skip continued to live at home after he graduated from high school.

SKIP: *"For the first few years after high school, I made no attempt to work. My parents silently accepted my being there. My brothers also stayed at home, but they both worked. Finally, when I was twenty-three or twenty-four, I ventured out and got a volunteer job as a teacher's aide. I didn't believe I was worthy of any pay."*

Food continued to be an answer for Skip. Very little changed in his life during these years, aside from increasing loneliness, sadness, and shame. Then, when Skip was twenty-five, his father had heart surgery and died of complications resulting from the operation.

"When my father died, I initially feigned remorse, but that lasted only a few moments. Then I felt an incredible sense of freedom, a glimmer that I was normal, I wasn't awful, that I had self-worth. I began to realize I had strength. Suddenly I felt important in my family. I planned the funeral. I settled the estate. I took care of the bank accounts. At my father's funeral, my uncle mentioned to my mother that she might need to make some provisions for me regarding my care. But now I was helping to take care of the family."

Skip's isolation and weight were so apparent that his uncle assumed he would need to be provided for financially. To the outsider Skip's inability to function was apparent. Yet until his father died, nothing was ever said. Skip's father had been given tremendous power by his family members. But the moment his father died, Skip immediately reclaimed his power.

Unless there is some type of outside intervention, it usually takes an event as powerful as the removal of the source to create change. Yet even then many people have such a deep-seated sense of helplessness that they may be immobilized and unable to respond as Skip did.

It was as if Skip could find no identity, no value in himself, as long as he felt his father's presence. His response was to numb all of his feelings, to kill himself slowly with food. The larger he became, the greater became his need to remain isolated; he had to respond not only to his family's dysfunction, but to the deep, internalized shame he experienced because of society's view of fat people.

"After my father died, it was as if his toxicity died, too. Somehow my inner child was reconnected with my Higher Power. I had the sense that I was no longer terrible. My father's constant silence had given me a clear-cut message—he hated me. I compounded that by eating and putting on weight in order to feel hateful.

"After his death, however, I began to realize that I didn't need food the way I had in the past. After seven months I had lost over one hundred pounds. Without my father's constant presence, I was able get a true sense of myself. For the first time I knew that my body wasn't representing to the world who I really was."

Skip got a job working at a children's home. Two of his co-workers, both male, offered him positive role models of unconditional acceptance. He continued to lose weight. After working there for four years, Skip left and took a part-time job working for a nationally based diet center. It was through this job that he saw the benefits of counseling.

"I got a lot of affirmation from my class there, but eventually I had to leave because I wasn't comfortable with their system any longer. I continued to work in the child-welfare field and began two years of Gestalt training. Through this, I went into therapy with one of the counselors from the training. I also heard about the Adult Child self-help program and began to attend meetings."

By this time Skip's weight had been drastically reduced. On the other hand, his drinking had increased. This is not a surprising progression. First of all, Skip is biologically at high risk because the sons of alcoholic fathers are more likely to become alcoholic than any other identifiable group of people. Second, without a recovery program for an eating disorder, people often replace one addiction with another. Skip was involved in a healing process, but it wasn't an active recovery program for his food addiction. By placing himself in a nontoxic environment, he was growing. He had healthy, caring people in his life. But he had not yet dealt actively with his shame. All the repressed feelings of his childhood were still there to haunt him.

"I was feeling better and beginning to succeed. But I was also beginning to drink. I was continuing a lifelong pattern of abusing myself and also sabotaging my career success. I even flirted with suicide on occasion by drinking and driving. Another time, I took both alcohol and pills, hoping to die but wanting it to be seen as an accident. I was going through a real inner struggle. Finally I crashed. It was then that I entered a treatment program for co-dependency and alcoholism."

A therapist at the treatment center identified the alcoholism, although Skip was initially very resistant to the label.

"I felt it meant that I wasn't in control, that there was one more thing I had to give up, that I was wrong, and, even worse, that I was like my dad. Yet the facts were there—I was clearly self-destructive in my drinking.

"The woman therapist who confronted me about my drinking also played a significant role in helping me struggle through my resistance. I knew something major was happening at this point because, for the first time in my life, I believed that people truly loved me for just being me. I was feeling unconditional love. In the beginning, I'm sure I continued my sobriety for her. This was not romantic love I was experiencing. It was the realization that another human being truly found value in me, and I didn't want to do anything to mess that up."

Six months after that Skip was sober, and after doing a great deal of work on his own, he began to attend AA meetings. Later on he also began attending Overeaters Anonymous meetings. In both cases he continued to feel out of place and very self-conscious.

"I didn't feel as if I was good enough to warrant the help of others."

Dealing with his food addiction proved much more difficult than dealing with his addiction to alcohol. Yet it was in OA that Skip felt an identification more quickly. After some time in this process, he started to attend ACOA meetings. All three groups continue to be a part of his recovery program.

Although self-help meetings have been integral in his recovery, Skip first accepted and surrendered to his dependency in an inpatient co-dependency program. Since then he has participated in psychotherapy and also in reconstruction therapy. The reconstruction workshops he refers to are usually a therapy environment in which a group of people work specifically on co-dependency issues. This is generally an intense therapy experience of working together daily over several days (often three to eight). Role playing and psychodramatic therapy techniques coupled with group process create an intensely cathartic experience that facilitates inner healing. It was there that Skip finally focused on his anger.

"Anger was the feeling that frightened me the most. My own anger was by far the most difficult and most important feeling I had to 'own' for my recovery. Owning my anger was the only way I could reclaim my childhood.

"Expressing anger was difficult for me because I'd learned very early that it wasn't safe to talk about anything. The rules in our house were: 'Don't talk. Don't lose control.' I had only heard my parents fight once, and then it was a very moderate argument. I didn't believe that I had the right to be angry. I wasn't worthy. I thought I had to settle for the little I had. In order to work through my anger, I had to reclaim my child from my dad.

"Today, recovery means taking care of my inner child. It means recognizing my many feelings and my needs and nourishing them with attention and respect—not with food. It means reintroducing little Skip to my mother, who has begun her own recovery process. Finally, I'm beginning to get the maternal nurturing I needed and deserved as a small child.

"Other Adult Child issues I've had to work on are control and powerlessness. Eating became the only way I could keep busy and avoid myself, since I thought I was so terrible. Nowadays, without my food dependency, I am not able to feel as bad. Without food, I am not overly controlling. I am learning to face the good things about myself rather than feeling self-hate. Without my food, I lose my main incentive to think strictly in terms of black and white. My life now has meaning beyond merely dieting and bingeing.

"I've managed to stay connected with my mother and my sister. My sister and I are still close, and she too has begun a recovery process.

"Today, I operate a great deal from feelings. I do what I want to do. I now understand that I am important, and that my own needs have to come first. My life is balanced between work, play, solitude, and friendships—my family of choice. In any twenty-four-hour period, I usually have

some contact with all those areas. If I miss any of those parts of my life, it tends to be play, but generally I have a balanced life.

"My body image is where my last real pieces of work have been focused. I feel great sadness for the stress I have put on my body. I also have a great regard for my body for 'staying with me' and helping me survive. My body and little Skip are very connected, and I find it very important to keep expressing my love and appreciation of them. I've even allowed myself to have some cosmetic surgery in the last few years. It's taken such a long time to give myself the attention I deserve. Every day now I'm grateful and happy for myself and my body in some way or another."

GLORIA
Age: 26
Compulsive eater, anorexic
Occupation: Copywriter
Recovery Process: Therapy

When Gloria was fourteen her anorexia was so completely out of control that many people openly confronted her parents, particularly her mother, about how sick Gloria looked. One day Gloria saw a television report about anorexia and identified herself. She then went to her mother, telling her what was wrong and asking for help. She asked her parents to put her in a treatment program.

GLORIA: "I remember becoming rapidly and horribly unhappy with my diseased life. I didn't understand what was happening to me or why. I wanted very badly to be well, and I was very upset with the whole thing. I also knew I couldn't do it on my own—I was way out of control. I knew that the only way I could get better was with the help of my family.

"I asked to be taken out of my home and put in a program run from a hospital. It took my family many visits to different doctors to find the therapist who really saved my life. Although this occurred before there was much public awareness of eating disorders, my parents did find a therapist who was an expert in the field."

In spite of their dysfunction, Gloria's parents ultimately had the ability to respond to the fact that their daughter was dying. Gloria said her mother had been angry with her for months for not eating, but that she'd seen Gloria as being willful. Yet pride, fear, and ignorance did not get in the way once they thought they had a diagnosis for what was wrong—anorexia.

Gloria continued to see her therapist regularly on an outpatient basis for the next two years, and she quickly responded to treatment.

"I immediately liked this therapist. I saw him two times weekly and then once a week for over two years. I was so sick that I missed school from December through March, but I felt hope. I was silent for a long time in my sessions. I didn't know what to say. I didn't know there was anything inside of me. But he talked to me, and I began to eat for him. He told me I had to."

Gloria's therapist was a wonderfully safe person for her. She remembers a trust exercise he once did in which he picked her up and set her down.

"I was willing to let him touch me. I let him pick me up. But all the while I knew he was going to drop me. I waited for him to drop me. And he didn't. I was astonished—he didn't drop me!"

Gloria was learning about safety, about trust. In many ways her therapist became a surrogate father. Within six months her physical state was stable. However, she has never regained all of her muscle strength, nor the fat pads on the soles of her feet. She can still see scars when her skin is cold and chapped. Her hair has never been as full as it was.

After completing high school, Gloria went on to college. At twenty-six she has spent nearly all of her adult life in college. For the past two years she has been a copywriter in an advertising agency.

Gloria was very young when she began her recovery. At the age of fourteen, however, she lacked the years and the emotional and mental resources to experience the emotional recovery she would later desire. Although the therapy during high school literally saved her life, she would need to address many more issues in her young adulthood.

"When I began college I was still thin, fearful of being fat, and had difficulty gaining weight. But in my junior year I was under so much stress that I began to overeat.

"Food was never an innocent pleasure for me. There was always the fear of overeating. And now that's just what I was doing. I clearly ate to punish myself. I wanted to punish myself for all the negative things I was feeling about myself—anger, hurt, pain. I would eat alone when no one

else was home. I'd take the phone off the hook. There was this ritualistic feel to it all. Now I was lord and could eat as if I were Henry the Eighth or an Amazon queen."

This compulsive binge eating was a signal to Gloria that her eating disorder wasn't over. As with any addiction, recovery was an ongoing process. Gloria would need to deal with her recovery issues on a continuing basis.

"I realized that I had to abandon the dreadful cycle of guilt and punishment: that I had to reject self-abuse. For me, part of this healing has meant strengthening my friendships with older women, working out my issues with the other women in my family, learning to love myself as a woman, and realizing my own strength. As both a Catholic and a recovering Adult Child, I still had vestiges of the saint syndrome: 'One must be all things to all people.' This was certainly reinforced by the role women played in my family."

Gloria needed to learn to love herself as a woman and to realize her own strengths. Eating disorders are often a feminist issue because many women in our society base their self-image on men's perceptions and value of them. At this time in our history, "Thin is in."

Culturally, women are defined and learn to define themselves by their body size and physical attractiveness. For many women, feeling fat is often equated with the belief that one is horrible and worthless. Although men can and do suffer from food addictions, they are not so quick to build their self-esteem solely on body size. They also create value around athletics, job status, and material possessions.

One of the main issues Gloria has had to deal with is her old need to feel "smaller" than a man, if only physically.

"While this is just an old habit for me, it is still hard to break. I feel at peace with myself, with my own intellectual and emotional powers now. But it's hard to get rid of the idea that the thinner one is, the lighter one feels, the faster one moves, and the more graceful one appears. When I'm involved with a man, I still eat less than I normally would, even though the man will usually say that I could stand to gain some weight.

"It annoys me that eating is still a 'problem' for me. However, I am much less hard on myself now than I've ever been. If I eat too much, instead of loathing myself and calling myself a stupid pig, I talk to myself in a soothing manner. I forgive myself and try to figure out why it happened."

Gloria's old sense that if she doesn't stay extremely thin she'll cease to be is becoming much weaker. It's an old habit, an outworn point of view, based on overemphasizing the superficial aspects of her self-image.

"Taking care of myself is a relatively new idea for me, and one that I am working on to make a healthy new habit. When I was young I used to test my endurance in lots of small ways. For example, I'd leave the car window wide open on a cold night and let the icy wind whip my face numb before I'd close it. Now I take along gloves in sixty-degree weather, just in case I get cold. Another way I take care of myself is to eat three meals a day instead of one.

"I'm working on a number of issues now:

- *Self-care—truly taking care of myself.*
- *Respect—having real regard for my own intelligent, heartfelt choices.*
- *Self-reliance—learning to believe in and rely upon myself.*
- *Trust—learning to trust my feelings and judgments and to trust other people.*

"Two years ago, at work, someone showed me the twelve questions that help someone know if he or she is an Adult Child. I immediately answered 'Yes' to all of them. I've always been looking for balance. 'All or nothing' behavior has been my norm. I've always had trouble with personal boundaries. And I've always been a sponge for the energies of others.

"So much of my life I had no sense of my own space. I was hardly in my own body. I had trouble keeping my own secrets. I would tell people my secrets to purchase intimacy. I've never been malicious—only pitiful. Being an amoeba describes me as well. I easily merge into others. Recently I've been learning to feel and be separate from others. Now I can set healthy boundaries.

"I'm also on much better terms with my issues of control and powerlessness. My entire life I've struggled with my feelings of powerlessness. Rigid control was my only answer. Today I speak my feelings—no more self-distrust. Today I have a sense of me. As I connect with others more and more, I'm finding my own strength. And I'm also finding strength through my love of nature and the arts."

Gloria had been starving for validation and attention, as is the case with so many other COAs. And, as with the others in this chapter, food was an attempt to meet those needs. For Gloria, depriving herself of food was a cry for help that symbolized her emotional starvation.

"I am seeking to find the strength to stand alone, but not be isolated; to know who I am separate from others. I'm learning self-respect and how to provide my own sustenance. In my next love relationship with a man, I hope not to be so pliable, so good, so forgiving, so ready to care at all costs. For years I could not be intimate. But lately I've been too ready— still moving from one extreme to the next, from a stone to a blade of grass.

"I'm continuing to work on acknowledging and showing my strengths, on admitting my full worth."

PAUL
Age: 43
Compulsive overeater
Occupation: College administrator
Recovery Process: OA, Al-Anon

Paul began attending junior college after he graduated from high school. During this period he became more and more aware and resentful that his father was trying to find his own identity and worth through possible accomplishments of Paul's. Paul deliberately chose a college path that was not as apt to lead to a high-paying career by majoring in sociology. Later, when he received his bachelor's degree and then his master's, he deliberately did not attend graduation ceremonies in order to deny his father the opportunity to gloat or take any credit for this achievement. Although Paul's anger may not have been readily apparent to him, it was close to the surface.

Up to this time Paul had been a social isolate. He usually had only one friend at a time. He tended to pick peers in crisis, focusing on their lives instead of his own. He continued this pattern when he became romantically involved, marrying a woman who was a practicing alcoholic. She also had three children and had just left a violent, battering, alcoholic man.

PAUL: *"I could protect her. It gave me something to focus on. It gave my life meaning. I was comfortable with the fear and the excitement of impending negativity. However, within months of our wedding her drinking was way out of control. I felt like a failure. At the time we married, I was at a low weight; but within months I started eating again."*

Paul's marriage was at least as chaotic as his family's home life had been. After their child was born, his wife began having extramarital affairs that he knew about.

"While we were married, I constantly grazed [nonstop picking and eating] *through the painful times of betrayal, feeling worse and worse about myself and the weight. Frequently the only pleasant times in our house were spent planning and preparing meals. But the meals themselves were battlegrounds. So at times I expressed my anger by withdrawing from food and meals. Other times I ate to stuff my anger.*

"The eating was also hidden. Besides grazing all day, I would stock up on soothing things for nighttime and eat alone while my wife was out."

Paul was beside himself. He lacked the skills and the self-worth to do anything but accept his lot. Again he was left feeling that, no matter what he did, it wasn't right. As always, food was his ally, literally his only friend.

Paul and his wife finally divorced—at her initiation and his compliance. He got a full-time job working for a food vending machine company. This was as suicidal a move as an alcoholic getting a job as a bartender.

"I was driving around with a whole truck full of chips, candy, and other junk food. My anger and resentment with work problems or my life came out in the truck. Now, instead of waking up from a daze in front of the refrigerator, I was waking up from a daze in the front seat of my truck, surrounded by candy wrappers."

In time, Paul's ex-wife became sober and suggested that he try going to Al-Anon.

"What made me take her suggestion was not so much her recovery in AA as my own pain, powerlessness, and feelings that I was going insane. I felt very little connection between what I did and what was happening in my life. I began to realize that being 'nice' would not bring people who cared about me into my life. But I didn't know that I had any other choice.

"What I learned through Al-Anon had to do with self-care. I discovered that I first had to be nice to myself before I could draw people to me who were kind."

Paul was in such pain, and so lonely and confused, that he was willing to listen to what others said—and it seemed okay. Within six months he began to confront his problem with food.

"I could no longer lose weight or control my eating. Twice a doctor had told me that I was in danger of bringing on diabetes because of my obe-

sity. He said I had to lose weight. I realized that I was killing myself with food, and I knew that that was insane.

"So with the three catalysts—Al-Anon, which encouraged my self-love enough to make my eating habits appear crazy; the vending route, where the food stealing and bingeing made me realize that I had lost control; and the visits to my doctor, who said clearly that my eating was killing me—I had to find help. I turned to another Twelve Step program: Overeaters Anonymous. This time, no authority figure sent me. I went on my own. It meant I had enough self-esteem to be able to love myself enough to do that."

Through Al-Anon and OA, Paul began to deal with both his overeating and his ACOA issues.

"The first issue in recovery for me was self-care. I gave myself acknowledgments for each step of progress I made—for being abstinent that day; for making it through the day with some sense of serenity. It became important to me to do kind things for myself: feeding myself an attractive meal, taking a long hot bath, walking in the rain or on the beach. It felt like letting the kid have a place to come out in safety. It also felt like letting the real adult come out in safety while parenting the child."

Paul also had to deal with the conflicting loyalty issues common to children growing up in dysfunctional families.

"The rule of not talking about 'negative' stuff outside the family made me feel as if I were being disloyal when I first entered OA. I stopped Al-Anon for six months, hoping I could do just one program at a time. But then I started feeling crazy about family and relationship issues again. So I concluded early on that, for proper self-care, I need both programs each week to remain stable. With them both, I can generally tell when I am hiding from life through work, sleep, or whatever.

"It's important for me to realize that my recovery must be my priority. I can no longer allow people-pleasing or parent-pleasing responses to bring me down enough to turn to food again. I need to act on my own behalf on the issues, whether or not my parents understand or support me."

Paul has found that self-care and self-acceptance mean learning to accept and love his own body, something he was never able to do before.

"The self-care stage involved a lot of body work so that I could learn to love myself with whatever body I had. I would stand naked in front of a mirror, saying that I loved my thighs and my butt, parts of my body I *had never liked because that was where I always gained the weight. I learned to take someone shopping with me so that I'd stop picking out clothes that were too big—I needed help to stop thinking of myself as fat. By including that person, I was also breaking the isolation and secrecy I'd grown up with. Women started noticing me and approaching me, and I began to think that I might be sexually attractive, which was very hard for me to accept at first. It was a completely new way of looking at myself."*

Another area Paul realized he needed to work on was honesty and forgiveness. He had spent years hiding his eating and feeling terrible about himself for it.

"I had to learn to avoid grazing while preparing and cleaning up after a meal. Initially I set a time limit on my meals to avoid overeating. Eventually I could become less strict with myself because the honesty and forgiveness had healed so much of my self-loathing.

"I know that when I start slipping back into my old patterns, I never 'get away with it.' Even if the weight doesn't shoot up right away, my sense of honesty is affected, and the emotional and spiritual parts of the disease kick in. That's when the old self-critical, condemning, perfectionist ACOA has to start getting honest again—but gently. At times I tell myself, 'I will not eat, no matter what.' At other times I need to quiet the critical part and say, 'My job is to love my Higher Power. To love Paul. All else is a gift.' "

The next issue Paul had to come to terms with was "normalcy."

"I'd always felt different from other people. I now realize that I have a disease that makes me different. By accepting the disease, I have actually learned how to be with people, how to express myself in groups more freely, how to initiate relationships and maintain intimacy. I no longer have to hide out to survive. Just because I can't eat like normal people doesn't mean I can't learn the social skills required to work, achieve, exercise, and love like other people.

"I've also learned to deal with the issue of making mistakes. I've learned to acknowledge my mistakes without condemning myself or having to beat myself. Before, when I made a mistake, I became the mistake, and I attacked myself or gave up in despair. I believed that if I couldn't do something perfectly, I wouldn't do it at all."

Adult Children often struggle with perfectionism. It's common to see them trying to do recovery perfectly and, when they realize that's not possible, castigating themselves and even giving up in futility.

"Now I see that I set too rigid a standard for myself. I'm just setting myself up to fail. If I think that I can control all of my food issues once and for all and never slip again or get sloppy about my eating habits, then I lose the part of the process that is mine—the footwork in the present."

Paul is recognizing the concept of "staying in the here and now" in recovery. He knows he has to take responsibility for himself in the present and not project into the future or obsess on the past.

Because recovery with food addiction cannot be the "all or nothing" approach that recovery from chemical dependency demands, the struggle over doing recovery "right" is even more difficult for people with an eating disorder. Once they learn that even if they're less than perfect, they're still okay, then they'll be able to live with less fear and a greater willingness to include others in their ongoing recovery.

"My current issue is trust. It's taken seven years in recovery to make it a focused process. I have to trust that I can have an answer that may not always work the way I want it to, but that this is all right. I have other options. I can ask for feedback from others. I can look for help from my Higher Power. The decision is still up to me. I can make a choice about abstinence and live with the outcome. And if it doesn't work, I can decide to change what I'm doing instead of giving up."

Both Al-Anon and OA have played an important part in Paul's recovery.

"I've not been able to do this with just one program. However, with two it's easier to find a balance with my shifting compulsions. Now I can maintain my recovery day to day, rather than switching to a new compulsion.

"As a child, my parents were unable to give me the love and support I needed. So I intellectualized and ate my feelings away. In recovery I have learned to value myself and my feelings. I've learned to choose people in my life who enjoy and love that balance.

"Now, instead of avoiding risk taking or doing whatever others tell me to do, I've learned to trust my decisions about my life and my judgment on how much risk taking is safe.

"Sometimes I have to pretend that everyone I love is dead in order to decide what is best for me or what I want. At other times I think of myself as my own child so I can balance my nurturing for myself with what I give to others. These trusting, loving skills show up in how I'm dealing with food, because food mirrors my feelings. This is one way my Higher Power helps me learn balance.

"The trust seems to lead to hope. While I don't know what is next in recovery, I trust my path and the Higher Power that is unrolling it before me. And I trust me."

FELICIA
Age: 41
Compulsive overeater, bulimic
Occupation: Account Executive
Recovery Process: AA, therapy

Felicia's eating patterns continued through college. Shortly after high school she went to business school and moved out of her parents' home.

FELICIA: *"My roommate—an anorexic nursing student—and I had an apartment. We ate toast with mounds of butter and cinnamon sugar, and then we'd starve ourselves. I'd binge and sneak peanut butter, ice cream, and cookies. I'd often steal food out of the refrigerator at night, hoping she wouldn't notice."*

Felicia's primary choice of binge food has always been ice cream and cookies—the foods her mother offered her sister but not her, and her father's favorite binge foods as well. Alcohol also became more and more important in Felicia's life. For her, drinking was synonymous with eating.

But drinking had brought a twist to Felicia's eating disorder. When she began to drink regularly, as a senior in high school, she also frequently became sick and would throw up. She quickly discovered that, after the initial distaste, she felt relieved.

"After I'd thrown up a few times, I found that if I drank enough, I could just get rid of it by vomiting. I'd just go do it and then use mouthwash— I learned early on how to keep my clothes clean during it. I'd discovered a new secret. It didn't take me long to realize that I didn't have to drink to throw up. Vomiting was also the answer to my chronic overeating. I could be totally out of control with eating, yet control my weight the entire time."

Although many compulsive overeaters have been secretly purging for generations, Felicia's purging took place before bulimia had the public recognition it has today.

Compulsive eaters experience powerlessness and a sense of being out of control, but purging restores some sense of control. Unfortunately this only helps to keep the eating disorder hidden and never dealt with. Not only is this psychologically dangerous, it can also be life-threatening if repeated vomiting ruptures the esophagus or the stomach and causes hemorrhaging.

Felicia saw herself as obese when in reality she was not. Most of the time she was generally twenty pounds heavier than the perceived norm. Occasionally this would climb to thirty to forty pounds over the norm. But whatever her weight might be, her relationship to food was always unhealthy. Her use of food had prevented her from learning a healthy way of expressing her feelings. In fact, it had created greater isolation and the need for secrecy in her life. It gave her a false sense of nurturance and satisfaction. And it fed her already existing shame. But when she became bulimic as well, she pushed all of these problems into overdrive.

This is when Felicia became engaged to Jack. She starved herself down to the thinnest she had ever been as an adult. And she moved back home for a month until they were married.

"I was a bundle of nerves while I was staying with my parents. By this point I was sneaking food, starving myself, drinking alcohol nightly, and doing something else I never told anyone about—wetting the bed. I was such a wreck that the doctor prescribed Valium. I was loaded when I got married, but I was thin."

In her marriage Felicia was seeking to fulfill the social aspirations of her socioeconomic background. She had found a well-educated husband; she worked and took night classes at a community college; she partied to show life was fun, and she became a mother.

Food was still the central dynamic in Felicia's life. However, after she got married, she and her husband also began a pattern of drinking every night. As is common with so many people with eating disorders, alcohol became addictive for Felicia as well.

"Food and wine were interchangeable for me. Instead of eating late at night, we'd have a few drinks. We got into gourmet cooking and wine tasting. Then I became pregnant, which was a great excuse to eat.

"I always felt fat and was always trying to lose weight. My husband didn't say much about it, but I knew he disapproved just by his looks. He would also buy me clothes that were too small. My mother had always

bought me clothes too big for me. No one ever bought clothes for the real me. They bought clothes for their fantasy of me.

"After the birth of our second child it took me a long time to lose the weight that I had gained. My husband backed off from me sexually. He said I was rigid, too uptight, not playful or sensuous.

"He plugged right into my fears that I wasn't enough as a woman, as a wife, as a sexual partner. What hurt the most was that part of me knew that he was right. In reaction, I did what I knew best when I hurt: I ate and I drank and I threw up. I ate and I drank and I threw up. I felt crazy and depressed. I began to realize that I'd lost any of the control over food or alcohol that I'd once had. That scared me.

"As our marriage fell apart, I was devastated. The model I'd learned from my parents was that you dealt with pain by using alcohol. I'd never felt this much pain before because I'd never been allowed to feel. Alcohol, at least temporarily, killed the pain. Alcohol became my friend. I was lonely and scared, and I couldn't turn to my family. They had always told me whenever I cried that I was being silly or shouldn't feel that way. And now my worst fear—that I wasn't really enough—had come true. My marriage was ending, and I felt like a failure."

Felicia and her husband separated. She went back to work part-time and finished her degree in business administration. But her patterns of binge drinking and binge eating also continued. The pressures of school, the divorce, and taking care of two small children made her let go of some of her perfectionism, but Felicia still felt that she just wasn't "enough," as if there weren't enough of her to go around. And, in reality, there wasn't. Felicia had become Superwoman. To nurture herself, she ate and drank, drank and ate.

For reasons she didn't understand, Felicia took a course on alcoholism, even though it wasn't a part of her requirements for school.

"In the class, we had to write about an addiction. I picked food. At this point I went to Overeaters Anonymous and lost fifteen pounds the first two months, but I was anxious and as close to going over the edge as I'd ever been. I was on overload, out of control. OA was working only in terms of weight loss. But once again someone else was controlling my food—my sponsor."

Felicia was using her sponsor the only way she knew. She perceived her sponsor as an authority figure, as the critical, judgmental mother with whom she'd been in a lifelong power struggle. A sponsor is a member of a Twelve Step program that you choose to be your mentor, guide, confidante. He or she is a person you share problems and successes with, who can offer feedback or guidance if you share honestly. Until Felicia dealt more fully with her underlying problems, specifically her anger toward her mother, she would continue to have difficulty using a sponsor. Her Adult Child issues were clearly interfering with her getting the most out of a self-help program.

Felicia was having problems letting go and accepting a Higher Power. Because she felt her drinking was "under control," she didn't tell her OA sponsor about it. She had allowed herself a glimpse of her eating addiction, but her denial was greater toward her alcoholism. Before long she found that she could not address her eating addiction without first addressing her alcoholism.

Interestingly, while Skip began to lose weight before discovering he had an alcohol problem, most food-addicted alcoholics need to stop their dependence upon alcohol and drugs before they can adequately address the eating disorder.

But Felicia's tolerance for alcohol dropped. What she was learning in her alcoholism class made her face up to what was happening in her own body.

"I had been able to write off or rationalize away all sorts of early- and middle-stage symptoms of my alcoholism. But a drop in tolerance meant my liver wasn't working.

"Then we had to write a paper on a female alcoholic and discuss our feelings. I was overwhelmed with feelings. The next thing I knew, I was in the kitchen with a carton of ice cream and a bottle of Kahlúa liqueur. I looked at them—the food and the alcohol—and I began to cry hysterically. I called a friend who'd been sober for nine months and asked her, 'How do you know if you're really an alcoholic?' I was at an AA meeting the next morning."

Although her recovery had begun, Felicia still had to deal with the old feelings that were a part of her ACOA upbringing.

"Taking on the label 'alcoholic' brought with it a lot of shame. I felt as if I'd failed once again. As I started to deal with how lonely I was and how empty I was, I was so overwhelmed with pain that I turned back to food.

"I had never lost the food obsession. I had never let go of my mother's critical messages about me and food. I had not surrendered. I had made people, not God, my Higher Power. I began to binge again.

"By the end of year one of sobriety in AA, I had come a long way. I

was less anxious, less critical of me and of others, more able to attend to my children, and doing better in school. However, my new drug of choice—actually an old one revived—was clearly sugar."

Felicia's weight had gone up to 180 pounds, and she turned to therapy in order to deal with the bingeing.

"In therapy I began to address my drive for perfection and my negativism. In AA I had included food as a part of my daily meditation, my daily writings, and of my daily inventory. My AA sponsor and I worked the steps for this food addiction. Yet I had never told anyone about the purging—which I continued to do."

People often find that they can attend several kinds of self-help meetings. In Felicia's case OA, AA, ACOA, and Al-Anon would all be appropriate. As many people do, she combined her food and alcohol addictions and attempted to work on both, predominantly in AA. Although this may work for some, it's most likely to be successful only when alcohol is the first drug to be abused. On the other hand, trying to work on both addictions at once can also feed one's denial—primarily the denial regarding food issues.

That is exactly what occurred for Felicia. She was now sober, she knew she had Adult Child issues, she felt a great deal of shame about her body and eating patterns—yet she was still hanging on to control. Not all the truth had been acknowledged or spoken. So, as much as she was making a stab at recovery for her eating disorder, Felicia was still trying to control her own program. She was discriminating what she would and would not be honest about rather than surrendering and being totally honest. She was still externally focused, hoping outside entities would provide control against her overeating.

"Aside from periodic OA meetings and using AA to attend to my eating disorder, I also sought out a nutritionist at times, and an exercise coach. But I remained inconsistent with healthy eating and exercising. I would still binge and purge (not yet telling anyone I did so), I still hated my body and was preoccupied with what others thought. I still felt I needed others to control my eating. Yet this still led to my rebelling when they or I put limits on me around food. I still felt defective, a failure. I still couldn't look in a mirror."

Felicia was a bright, successful career woman who had been in touch with all the appropriate resources for over five years—OA, therapy, and AA. But AA was the only consistent resource in her life. And not surprisingly, recovery from alcoholism was the area in her life where she was having continuous success. She was alcohol and drug free. She was more connected with healthy support people. Her self-esteem was growing, and she was experiencing some joy in her life.

Finally, after five years of sobriety, Felicia's denial cracked. Her controlling behavior, her manipulation of people, places, and things, were out of control. She began to have flashbacks about the childhood incest, and she knew she must seek therapy.

"When I began therapy, my analyst had me do some 'body' work. It meant first seeing my body. All of my life I had avoided mirrors. If I passed anything that showed a reflection, I'd be so anxious I'd nearly have a panic attack. My experience with incest had affected everything that had to do with my body and all that I had done to it. When I looked in a mirror I saw my grandfather."

In dealing with her shame and anger over the incest, Felicia uncovered a lot of rage. As she has grown more and more in touch with the rage, she has been able to release the blocked energy, to release the shame. The more she remembers, the more she is able to parent her inner child who never received the nurturing she needed and deserved.

But Felicia's anger, shame, and need for control—and her struggle with powerlessness—was not related to the sexual molestation alone. It was also connected with her parental relationship. Felicia found that she couldn't deal with one area without tapping into the other. She also discovered that, until then, she had been controlling her Adult Child therapy.

Once the incest was recognized, once Felicia began to release her feelings safely, her sense of shame lessened and she found greater self-acceptance. This empowered her to address other sources of anger and to see clearly how her anger had fueled her eating addiction.

"I knew I had to get angry, but I couldn't. I was bound to my powerlessness."

Felicia had taken a very depressive stance in life. She had used both food and alcohol to provide solace and to anesthetize the pain.

"I was angry at my mother for controlling me. I was angry at her criticism and her perfectionism that had so warped my values. I was angry at her for trying to make me a copy of her. Angry at her for treating me differently from my sister. Angry at her for not listening! Angry at her for not making me special! For not protecting me! For robbing me of self!"

Felicia's recovery is still ongoing. After grief work around the incest, her mother became her focus, because the loss in that relationship was more blatant than the loss of her father. It's easier to identify a loss when it's tangible: Mom did this! And she did that! The loss of her dad was more subtle because it came from what he didn't do.

As many ACOAs do, Felicia found it necessary to address only the issues that felt safe. Food had been the most blatant issue, so she began recovery in OA. But it was in AA that she really felt at home. Her alcohol issues were the safest place for surrender to the recovery process. But food, especially sugar, had been her best friend all her life. The deep and emotionally charged issues underlying her eating disorder would need time, patience, and courage to uncover. It took over five years of active recovery from alcoholism before the incest could and would present itself. And it was only after she began to address the incest that she was totally prepared to deal with her issues with food.

After a year of working with the incest experiences in therapy—with continuing involvement in AA—Felicia found that she could be much more consistent in abstaining from sugar. And after not purging for six months, she was finally able to talk openly about it.

"I am much more loving to myself around food now. I've really done some incredible work—with God's help—in learning to love at least most of my body. I am much less critical of myself than I used to be. Today, I can look in the mirror and enjoy it. I'm like my own teenaged daughter— forever looking in the mirror. My body now has sensations I've never felt before. I was always so busy controlling and discounting, I never even knew I was in pain because I could never feel. I missed over forty years of internal sensations. I was constantly focused on the external— the image, the goal, other people's approval and attention. Now I have my body back. I have me back."

At last Felicia could begin to recognize how much she had neglected her femininity.

"For the first time I have come to recognize that I had experienced masculine power as abusive. Today I'm reframing that to see the positive aspects of both masculine and feminine power. I see masculine power as competitiveness, as the ability to set limits, to focus on self as well as others, to get results. I see feminine power as softness, creativity, receptivity. I see it as beingness, as process. I want to have access to all sides of me. I particularly need to work on the feminine side—to be more in touch with my intuitions and internal signals. I want to trust me. Up

to now, food, alcohol, and my ever-vigilant control had squashed all of that.

"I had rejected and abused my physical being. Today I can look at myself and like what I see. I buy pretty clothes, softer clothes, clothes with color. I nurture my body with exercise, massage, and healthy food. With my friends in self-help groups, my sponsor, my therapist, my Higher Power, I believe for the first time in my life that not only will I be okay, I am okay just as I am."

Recovery Considerations

PRIMARY ADDICTION

Although Adult Child issues are clearly connected with eating addictions, the compulsive eating that results in obesity, bulimia, or anorexia needs to be accepted as a primary addiction. People with eating disorders need to become involved in a program specializing in eating addiction. It may be a self-help group of Overeaters Anonymous, a psychotherapist who specializes in eating addictions, or an outpatient or inpatient eating addiction program.

Eating disorders are abusive to the body, and it is helpful to begin with a total assessment of your health to determine a baseline against which you can measure your ongoing physical recovery. Therefore it is important that those with an eating addiction receive a physical examination by a specialist in eating disorders. It is necessary to discover whether there are any physiological causes for the obesity. Then the physical consequences of the addiction need to be diagnosed and treated. Once a commitment is made to follow through on such a program, it is possible to pursue Adult Child issues. I have not found it helpful to put a specific time frame around the period that people are in food addiction recovery before they begin Adult Child work. Once a commitment is made to an eating addiction program, I believe one should begin Adult Child work on the issues around one's relationship with food.

MULTIPLE ADDICTIONS

Addictive personalities often have more than one addiction. As you saw in this chapter, Felicia had an eating addiction and was also chemically dependent, Skip became alcoholic after he began recovery for his eating disorder. Many recovering alcoholics discover in sobriety that they are food-addicted. Food and alcohol often work in a close partnership—either they are abused simultaneously, or one is used to discourage overindulgence in the other.

It's easy to begin to feel overwhelmed when you have to respond to more than one active recovery program. The most important thing to understand up front is that having more than one addiction is quite normal for people with eating and chemical dependencies. Each one needs to be addressed as primary. Do not try to substitute one recovery program for another. The next thing on the agenda is to pay attention to how Adult Child issues contribute to the addiction and/or influence recovery.

It's very common to compare one's recovery rate from one addiction with one's recovery from another addiction. Because there are many similarities in the process of recovery, people often negate the differences. Personally, I would hesitate to say that recovery from one addiction may be easier than another. Recovery from any addiction is different from person to person—and it is always miraculous. Although much progress has been made with understanding alcoholism and drug dependency as diseases, the public still tends to perceive eating disorders as willful behavior. They are not. In addition, there is a significant difference between recovery from eating disorders and other addictions, particularly alcohol and drug addictions.

For chemically dependent people, abstinence from alcohol and mood-altering drugs is the core of recovery. But critical to the understanding of eating disorders is that those with food problems cannot abstain from eating. One must eat to live. This fact creates an incredible difference for the food-addictive person.

When people recover from chemical dependency they learn to live their life without using any alcohol or drugs to compensate for emotional states. On the other hand, the food-addicted person must learn to live by adjusting to degrees of use of the very thing they're addicted to—food. It's very difficult to regulate the intake of any addictive substance. Food addicts, whether anorexics, bulimics, or overeaters, must rethink what food means to them and then apply that understanding to their lives. They know that compulsive eating and compulsive starving causes them to think, feel, and act in a manner different from "normal," just as chemically dependent people know that drinking or drugging medicates and anesthetizes feelings. While chemically dependent people can stop all alcohol and drug usage, overeaters must deal with food several times a day. This is a difficult challenge, but recovery is possible, as demonstrated in the lives of these four people.

SHAME

People with eating disorders feel such incredible shame. Often the eating addiction see-saws between compensating for the shame and creating the shame. It can become a downward spiral. You must remember that there are deep-seated reasons for the disorder, and that there are people who will both understand this and be of help. You are not a bad person now, and you have never been a bad person. What you have been is scared, lonely, angry, powerless. One of the most important gifts you can give yourself is the opportunity to meet others who are recovering from eating addictions. They will understand and not judge. And they can offer direction and hope.

INCEST

If the need to control, starve, purge, or overeat is in any way connected with a response to incest or sexual molestation, the sexual abuse must be addressed specifically. Incest is prevalent in our society, and an eating disorder is a common response. Whatever the experience, believe me, you were not at fault, and you are not a bad person. You don't need to punish or purge yourself any longer.

FEELINGS

Those with eating addictions are extremely disconnected from their emotional selves. Most Adult Children struggle with learning to identify and express their feelings. They struggle with fears of what will occur should they show their feelings. But the emotional self of the person with an eating disorder is directly linked to this disorder.

In the process of recovery from food addiction, one must experience emotional recovery. Overeating, starving, and purging are defenses erected to protect one from further hurt and pain. Unfortunately, these defenses don't work. Using food to manage feelings may temporarily distort one's perception of the truth, but it cannot alter the truth. Feelings may be disguised, denied, and rationalized, but a painful feeling will not go away until it has run its natural course. Adult Children must talk about their fears of what will occur when they learn to identify their feelings and express them.

Anger is the feeling most repressed in eating addictions. In recovery it is vital to begin to understand that feelings are signals and cues. Feelings are there to help us, to befriend us—not to hurt us. Feelings will not make us go crazy. They can be particularly painful when they're stored away or denied for many years. But it is possible to walk through the pain.

Be open to the fact that you have many repressed feelings, and that you have legitimate things to be angry about. Anger is a natural reaction when one has been hurt. Personally, I don't think it is possible to be raised in a family affected by as much incredible loss as the ones we've been discussing and not be angry. Some Adult Children have more reasons to be angry than others, but all have some anger that needs to be acknowledged to allow for a more complete recovery.

You must face your anger about things that happened to you in the past. Acknowledging anger will not take away all of the hurt, but it does cleanse one's emotional wounds and initiate healing. Once you acknowledge your anger at the past, you will be able to experience the whole rich range of feelings in the present. The anger you might feel at the current experience will become clearer, not clouded by anger and issues from the past. Not being able to identify and display anger is the same as denying it.

As we address how our feelings are connected with food, we can begin to recover from the compulsive eating, the starving, and the purging.

CONTROL

For bulimics and anorexics, seeking control is the central issue. Obesity is more representative of being out of control. The Adult Child must develop healthy concepts about power and control. We often attempt to control people, places, and things—for example, through the image we present to others—or we control our bodies to mask shame or to compensate for incredible feelings of powerlessness. As adults there are choices available to us that we didn't have as children. Any sense of powerlessness we may feel now is often self-imposed.

It will be important to explore what control and power meant when we were children. Without that exploration, a key connection to what overeating, purging, or starving means to us now will be missed. Usually the grief work in that area is necessary. After that, putting the past behind us will be vital to recognizing and accepting where our power lies today.

ISOLATION

Those with eating addictions have often lived isolated from others. Do not isolate yourself during recovery. Isolation leads to loneliness, to controlling behavior, and to greater shame. You deserve better.

Because eating disorders are so much diseases of isolation and control, I believe that it is paramount that one begins the group process quickly in recovery. You are not the only person with this problem, and the faster you realize that, the faster your shame will lessen. A group experience can sound so frightening, but the sooner you try it the better. This is one case where I find that plunging in can be particularly useful. It can be of great help in learning to relinquish the tight control you've maintained over every aspect of your life.

PERFECTIONISM

There is no perfect recovery. People who are compulsive perfectionists were usually raised in families where parental figures had unrealistic expectations of them. As children they internalized those expectations, and today they continue to operate on unrealistic expectations.

When they were children, they needed to do things right—"right" meaning no mistakes—in order to lessen their fears of abandonment and to get approval. As adults these people continue to attempt to be perfect. This is often reflected in their image of the perfect body. They struggle with self-hate and disgust at not matching their perfect image. And they take it out on themselves in their overeating, anorexia, or bulimia. Until we can come to terms with our common humanity, it is likely that many of us will continue to overeat, starve, and purge.

In recovery, the source of this perfectionism needs to be dealt with so that you can come to terms with the fact that you are enough, that you are of value, that you are special, that you are important. We are all vulnerable. We all make mistakes. That's how we learn.

Today I don't eat compulsively, nor do I deprive myself. Most important, I am able to do that without living in fear of myself.
—Compulsive Overeater, Adult Child

Notes

1. L. Drozd, "A Sense of Self Model for the Treatment of (Female) Children of Alcoholics." (Ph.D. diss. California School of Professional Psychology, San Diego, 1986).

7

The Adult Child Who
Is Chemically Dependent

*My father died from his alcoholism. Today the difference between my
father and me is that he died from his and I do not have to die from
mine.*

—Adult Child

W hen you are raised in a chemically dependent home, alcohol and
drugs become a central fixture in your life. Alcoholism and other
addictions become a norm that is rarely, if ever, questioned.

Some COAs' earliest memories of play are creating their own bars and
playing "barmaid" or "bartender" or playing "spin me around so I can
be drunk, too." Alcohol has already become a tremendous force in their
lives. It has the power to make their lives miserable. It has the power to
render their parents out of control. These kids see their parents use
alcohol and other drugs to successfully escape their feelings, responsibilities, and pain. By the time children from alcoholic homes reach adolescence—and sometimes even before—they may begin to emulate their
alcoholic parents' behavior by turning to alcohol to erase their pain.

Alcohol and other drugs, such as marijuana, speed, cocaine, ice, crack,
Librium, or Valium, offer children an escape from a life full of powerlessness, loneliness, and fear; they medicate, they anesthetize. These mind-
changing chemicals offer children a way to feel connected with others. In
the Adult Child, they reduce the sense of isolation, offering a way of
fitting into the crowd. This is a powerful countereffect to the "alone in

the crowd'' syndrome so characteristic of children from alcoholic homes. Alcohol and drugs offer a way for COAs to have fun. They can give the user a sense of power. The alcohol/drug abuse may even be a child's way of relating to the alcoholic parent on the adult's own terms. Many Adult Children who became chemically dependent as youngsters say that their drinking and using gave them something in common with their parents for the first time.

Every child who was aware that alcohol was inflicting a terrible wound on the family has said, ''It will never happen to me!'' And meant it. They boast defiantly that they will make sure they don't end up as their ''old man'' did, or they make a powerful statement not to repeat what happened in their lives because of their mother's drinking. They believed that they would have the willpower, the self-control, and the knowledge to be different. They believe some miracle will free them from the gut-wrenching fear born out of their family experience.

The problem is, becoming chemically dependent has nothing to do with willpower, self-control, or knowledge. If it did, I believe that children from chemically dependent homes would be the least likely to become chemically addicted. Yet these addictions do repeat themselves within families.

This phenomenon becomes understandable when you observe the modeling these children have had for drinking and using chemicals. It is also obvious that alcohol and other drugs provide a relief and an escape from a very painful life. Moreover, there is evidence that strongly supports the physiological tendency toward chemical dependency when one is the Child of an Alcoholic.

Physiological Predisposition Toward Alcoholism

Children of Alcoholics are significantly more prone to chemical dependency than any other group of people. Research has shown that sons of alcoholics are fives times more likely to become chemically dependent and daughters of alcoholics are two times as likely to become chemically dependent than individuals not raised in alcoholic homes.[1] It is estimated that as many as 60 percent of the adults and 75 percent of the teenagers in chemical dependency treatment programs come from alcoholic homes.

More and more research is beginning to show that this greater likelihood of chemical dependency is due, in part, to genetic factors. Research comparing the incidence of alcoholism between twins such as the Veterans Administration study has supported a genetic predisposition to alcohol. In this research identical twins were not only more likely to share the disease of alcoholism than fraternal twins, they also manifested more organic symptoms of the disease, such as alcoholic cirrhosis and psychosis.[2]

Adoption research confirms this genetic predisposition as well. Sons of alcoholics were four times more likely to become alcoholic than sons of nonalcoholics, regardless of whether they were raised by their alcoholic biological parents or by nonalcoholic adoptive parents. Adopted sons of alcoholics reared by nondrinking parents were just as likely to become alcoholic as sons reared by alcoholic biological parents. By contrast, sons of nonalcoholic biological parents, adopted by alcoholic parents, did not become alcoholic at an unusually high rate. Adopted daughters with alcoholic biological mothers were three times more likely to become alcoholic than other women, even when reared from an early age by nondrinking parents.[3]

Metabolic research has revealed that Children of Alcoholics, ranging in age from eight to thirteen, had lower zinc levels than children of nonalcoholic parents.[4] This finding suggests that before any alcohol ingestion, Children of Alcoholics have the same zinc deficiency that manifests itself in the chronic adult alcoholic population. Zinc deficiency has been associated with cerebellar dysfunction, learning disabilities, and schizophrenia. These findings suggest that school-age children may already be physiologically prone to alcoholism, and they support other research pointing to abnormalities in alcohol metabolism in Adult Children of Alcoholics.[5]

Schukit's research indicates that it takes more alcohol for sons of alcoholics to become inebriated, but they have less ability to detect its effects than their peers, which sets them up for a higher level of intoxication before they identify being under the influence.[6]

In general, chemical dependency is linked directly to a physiological change in tolerance to alcohol or other drugs. It is accompanied by a psychological dependence characterized by personality changes, rationalization, denial, loss of control, and manipulation of the environment to make alcohol and drugs more accessible.

The progression is insidious. It demoralizes social interaction as well as physical and emotional well-being. It destroys the spirit. Once a person has crossed the line from social drinking to dependency, there is no going back. Recovery lies in breaking the pattern of denial and in seeking help that will support a life free from the ingestion of all mind-changing chemicals.

The Progression of Chemical Dependency

By the time Children of Alcoholics become adults, many already have several years of drinking and using behind them, and they have passed over the line into their own dependency. Others are only beginning to drink. Either way, a COA generally moves through the progression of chemical dependency much more quickly than the child of a nonalcoholic.

Children of Alcoholics may, in fact, find themselves in "middle stage" chemical dependency from the start. Others will start drinking in the early stage and gradually move through all the other stages of dependency. The younger a person is when they start drinking, the faster they will move through the stages. Females tend to progress through the stages of addiction more rapidly than males. A young female COA may never have a single day of "normal drinking." With all of these variables in play, the progression of the disease may be very rapid indeed.

The Dual Identity

When people are not only addicted, but have been raised in an alcoholic/addicted family, they have two identities. They are, first of all, chemically dependent; second, they are Adult Children of Alcoholics. Both issues will need to be addressed in their treatment and recovery.

Whether one issue needs to be addressed first or whether both need to be dealt with simultaneously depends on a variety of factors. Some chemically dependent people find that Adult Child issues affect the quality of their sobriety. Others discover that Adult Child issues set them up for relapse. Still others must address their Adult Child issues before they can recognize their own chemical dependency.

SOBRIETY FIRST

It is my professional opinion that if people are alcohol- or drug-addicted, they need to be clean and sober before they can adequately address Adult Child issues.

It is a monumental task simply learning how to get clean and sober and stay clean and sober. Historically, the Twelve Step self-help groups— which have had the most success in helping people accomplish that task— have found there is little room for ambiguity in the early months. I strongly agree. Generally speaking, I believe that abstinence needs to be in place before other issues in recovery can be addressed. Only after some sober time has been achieved do we have the opportunity and the resources to look at underlying problems.

In those first few months we've typically focused on how not to use or drink and how to allow others to become part of that process. We're learning how to listen to others who have gained abstinence and sobriety and how to follow their direction. We're busy putting the practical aspects of daily life back in order. This period of embryonic sobriety is not usually the best time for us to confront and challenge "family of origin" issues. Working on both issues simultaneously is too fragmenting. Very often we lose sight of the priority to not drink and use, and we will relapse.

Most individuals need to focus on recovery from addiction for as long as one to three years before they are emotionally, socially, and mentally prepared to begin another significant phase of the recovery process.

After at least three years of sobriety, there is usually little to prevent us from addressing the way Adult Child issues might be interfering in our lives.

Even when chemically dependent people make major changes in their lives and are grateful for their sobriety, they often find that the quality of their sobriety may be hampered by their Adult Child issues, even though they are working through a Twelve Step program. For example, addicted people are often accused of being on a "dry drunk." This is a phrase used to describe a chemically dependent person who is physically clean and sober but lacking an emotional recovery process. Although they abstain from alcohol and drugs, their negative attitudes and often their behavior have not changed. In actuality they are displaying Adult Child symptoms such as rigidity, an inability to trust, or the need to be in control.

Unfortunately, any combination of Adult Child traits may contribute to eating disorders or compulsive behaviors such as workaholism or compulsive spending. They may also lead to inappropriate sexual behavior, sexual addictions, or extramarital affairs. Any or all of these hamper the development of healthy personal relationships and increase the likelihood that they will be distant and possibly even abusive. Nonrecovering Adult Children are more likely to experience depression, feel loneliness, and possibly even have thoughts of suicide—or actually commit suicide. This is a rough way to live sober. People deserve more, and more is possible. Addressing both identities—alcoholic and Adult Child—is often the key to a sustained and happy recovery.

PREVENTING RELAPSE

Many addicted Adult Children need to address specific Adult Child issues as they are getting sober in order to prevent a relapse. Adult Child issues could interfere with their ability to get and to stay clean and sober.

Often these relapse-prone issues are shame-based. For example, incest survivors frequently need to do some initial work around the molestation to develop enough belief in their worth to get sober. Sometimes rage, which is often based on people's profound feelings of inadequacy, will interfere with the ability to listen and follow directions long enough to become or stay sober. Many chemically dependent people must have an opportunity to address their shame, grief, and loss before they have the strength even to believe that they deserve to be sober. Such people usually need to be guided by a helping professional who is a chemical dependency specialist, knowledgeable about addictions and Adult Child issues.

The following relapse markers should help determine which Adult Child issues may need to be addressed up front to aid one's efforts toward sobriety and to help prevent a relapse.

RELAPSE MARKERS

Rigidity, Inflexibility:
• Inability to accept direction.
• The need to be right.
• Only seeing options in an "all or nothing" perception.

Inability to Ask for Help:
• Being saddled with the inherent feeling that all tasks are your responsibility.
• No faith in others.
• Asking for assistance being perceived as a sign of weakness.
• Not asking for assistance out of fear.

Inability to Trust:
• Rigid self-reliance.
• Inability to let go.
• Inability to achieve closeness.

Desire for Excitement:
• Living life steeped in crisis.
• Without crisis, life is perceived as empty, boring.

Inability to Identify Needs:
- So busy responding to others' needs and wants, unable to focus on self.
- Low self-esteem, resulting in an inability to value and respond to personal needs.

Not Seeing a Crisis Until It Is a Problem:
- Inability to recognize cues and signal of a problem until it reaches crisis proportions.
- Denial, minimizing realities.

The Need to Look Good:
- By presenting one's physical self in a positive manner, one can hide the more vulnerable self.
- Distancing oneself from others to hide vulnerability.

Need to Be Perfect:
- A mask to cover shame.
- A way to look good.
- A manifestation of needing to be in control.

Control:
- The manipulation of people, places, and things in order to feel safe.
- The minimization and repression of feelings or withholding of feelings to feel safe.
- Compensation for feelings of inadequacy.

Shame:
- The belief that one is inadequate, defective, worthless.
- The belief that one is not capable, that one has inherent, irreparable faults.

Fixing Others:
- Focusing on others in an attempt to avoid focusing on self.
- Focusing on others to feel more powerful.

Inability to Identify Feelings:
- Not able to recognize feelings, therefore missing inner cues and signals to personal needs.
- Fear of losing control.
- Fear of exposing one's shame.

Enduring Intolerable Situations:
- Tolerating inappropriate situations; setting oneself up for victimization.

- Allowing others to be intrusive at one's expense.
- Being disrespectful of self.

Being Intrusive;
- Being disrespectful of others.
- Violating others' boundaries.

Wanting to Do Recovery by Oneself:
- Not being able to trust.
- Need to look good.
- Need to control.

All of the above issues have the ability to affect the quality of one's sobriety. In addition, not addressing them can prime a chemically dependent person for a relapse. In the past, when a recovering alcoholic demonstrated these markers, he or she used to be labeled as being on a dry drunk, when in fact such attitudes and behaviors may have resulted from being an Adult Child.

Adult Child Issues First

Many addicted people don't recognize the need to get sober until after they begin their Adult Child work. It is in addressing their Adult Child issues that they first begin to look at and identify their alcohol or drug addiction. For some people, it is simply safer to begin recovery with Adult Child issues; yet how much they do in recovery will be limited until they are clean and sober. Others simple cannot recognize their own addiction or believe in themselves enough to get help until they have lessened their denial and shame with Adult Child work.

Addicted people who begin ACOA recovery first may or may not find it necessary to postpone further Adult Child work to focus on their chemical dependency issues. If they are at a very early stage in their addiction, they may be able to work both programs simultaneously. However, if they are more middle- or late-stage addicted to alcohol or other drugs—particularly if inpatient treatment is necessary—then it is often helpful to delay involvement in an ACOA program and concentrate on a program of abstinence.

The key approach for the people attempting to work through both recoveries simultaneously is to allow themselves to develop the support of other recovering alcoholic/addicts. Such support is critical to recovery and abstinence. Interacting with clean and sober recovering alcoholic/addicts offers vital direction.

Life Stories: Growing-Up Years

The following are stories of five Adult Children who are chemically dependent. Their recovery period ranges from three to ten years of sobriety. If you identify with their addictive processes as you read their stories, be open to how alcohol and drugs may be influencing your life. See the appendixes, page 551, for further self-assessments. To have become chemically dependent is not a sign of weakness. It is not bad. It is simply a fact that warrants your immediate attention.

These five people will talk about their childhoods, the impact of alcohol on their lives, their recoveries, and how their Adult Child issues have come to play a significant role in their recovery processes. These stories may appear more dramatic than some of the others in this book since the consequences of being both an Adult Child and an alcoholic, a cocaine addict, a purging bulimic, or a sex addict are simply more blatant than with issues of perfectionism, loneliness, or never feeling good enough. Although these five people identify with the more hidden consequences, ultimately their addiction overrode their ability to hide or look good.

In addition, those of you who identified symbolically with life stories in other chapters may find that parts of your life story are in this chapter, too.

DENNIS
Age: 32
Mother: Alcoholic
Father: Alcoholic
Birth Order: Oldest of seven
    children
Raised: Northern California
Socioeconomic Status: Working
    Class

Dennis's recovery from Adult Child issues is one of the more common alcoholic stories. He had been sober many years before he began his Adult Child recovery. In fact, he became sober before there were Adult Child resources. Over the years of his long-term sobriety, Dennis had allowed himself to develop a level of honesty that has been difficult for many. Because of this painstaking honesty, Dennis was able to admit that he was still very lonely and frightened. He felt something was missing in his recovery and sought out an Adult Child recovery program.

Dennis grew up in a large alcoholic family. He was the oldest of seven, and he remembers his childhood as being filled with chaos. Both his parents are alcoholics, and his family has had a history of alcoholism and addictive/compulsive behavior. Dennis's grandmother died of alcoholism; his younger brother is a recovering alcoholic; his sister and another brother are both compulsive overeaters; another brother is both an overeater and a compulsive gambler; and his two remaining brothers are active alcoholics.

Dennis's father's drinking was always the primary issue in his family's relationship. Although his mother is also an alcoholic, Dennis's father was the more dominant figure in the household.

DENNIS: *"I can remember being Dad's favorite when I was really young, but about the time I was six or seven, that shifted. Suddenly Dad wasn't around anymore. He became a workaholic. When he was around, the only attention I got was negative. He was either telling us what to do or getting angry with us. He would become abusive and whip us with his belt. He was always sarcastic and would never give us a straight message. He seldom hugged us or showed any love."*

Dennis internalized the pain he felt over this lack of love and attention. He felt unhappy and abandoned; he wasn't able to express this verbally, although these feelings did play themselves out in his dreams.

"I had nightmares a lot. One dream I used to have was that I was looking for my mom in a department store. Finally I saw her driving down the road. She was gone. She had left me all alone. I still have this dream as an adult.

"I wet my bed until I was seven, and I used to suck my finger at night. I thought I was bad for doing these things. I remember waking up in the morning feeling, I'm bad."

Many young children wet the bed through their grade school years. While there are many theories about the cause of enuresis, pediatricians support the theory that stress is often the primary source of this behavior.

Dennis wasn't a bad child, but no one told him that. His thumb sucking and bed wetting were actually indicators of his need for greater nurturance and security.

Dennis remembers his family life being chaotic.

"There were lots of kids around, but none of us were very connected with each other. When I was younger no one ever stuck up for me. No one really ever paid attention to me. I could do what I wanted. My mom was always home. She always had dinner for us. It was just that I always felt lost in the house. She never seemed to have much time for us. In spite of this I never really thought about anything being wrong in our house."

Dennis was confused by the turmoil of living in a large family, and he was confused by the alcoholism. Neither he nor anyone else perceived alcoholism as a problem. The children grew up accepting chaos, unpredictability, mixed messages, and negativity as the norm.

Dennis went to Catholic school until he was in eighth grade, and for the most part he was a good student. His doing well in school was an effort to get approval and stay out of trouble. Yet he was not able to feel much personal satisfaction.

"I did well in school. I was an overachiever—I achieved for everyone else but me. I didn't do as well in sixth, seventh, and eighth grades because of peer pressure to be cool. But by ninth grade the pressure was more on me to succeed. I found out that if I did okay in school, I didn't get in as much trouble from my parents or teachers. I think in a way it was a matter of 'I'll be so good you'll be sorry for treating me poorly.'"

In spite of his determination to do well in school, most of Dennis's childhood and adolescence is foggy to him. This is because, after taking his first drink at thirteen, he fell into a pattern of heavy alcohol and drug usage.

LISA

Age: 42

Mother: Alcoholic

Father: Alcoholic; died when she
    was seven

Birth Order: Twin, one of four
    sisters

Raised: Wisconsin

Socioeconomic Status: Working
    Class

Lisa is similar to many Adult Children of Alcoholics in that the progression of her alcoholism moved quickly. Her drinking career spanned ten years, beginning in her late twenties. She got sober in her late thirties, and barely two years later a traumatic event led her to address Adult Child issues.

When Lisa was seven her father died in an airplane crash. Lisa's memories of her father are vague, but she does remember his drinking being a significant part of family life.

Lisa's mother was also alcoholic. Lisa said she didn't know alcohol was the cause of the problems in the home; she and her sisters thought her mother was just crazy. Excessive drinking was the norm. Lisa remembers her mother drinking and using tranquilizers on alternate days. She says yelling took place with the drinking, and nonverbal hostility emerged on the nondrinking days.

LISA: *"My mother and I were never close. After my father passed away, her drinking changed from going to the bar periodically to drinking in the daytime. I could depend on her to be drinking every day when I came home from school. She would usually start about three-thirty in the afternoon and drink until ten or eleven at night. It seemed as if I was always fixing her a drink, or my sisters and I would take turns fixing her a drink."*

Pouring drinks for a parent is often the only or the best way to have a relationship with the alcoholic parent. It may be the only time they approve of you—the only time they notice you without saying hurtful things. Often the only attention Lisa could get from her mother was inappropriate and embarrassing.

"Mom was always asking me to sing for her when her friends came to visit. She would call me into the kitchen and tell me to join in or sing a favorite song for her. I was embarrassed, but I still liked the attention I was getting from her, so I would do it. I knew this would please her, which is what I was always trying to do."

Pouring drinks was a way for Lisa to be noticed. Singing for her mother, in spite of the embarrassment, was another way. Wanting approval so much that you do things that are painful to you leads children to be hurt by others most of the time. Lisa was a prime candidate for victimization.

"I began to hate coming home from school because I knew it was always going to be the same old thing. My mother would single me out and yell at me. Then my sisters would tell me that I was just imagining that Mom

didn't like me, that I was being too sensitive and overreacting. I would believe them and just keep trying to please Mom. I always wondered what was wrong with me because nothing I did ever seemed to be okay to Mom.''

No matter what you do, it's never good enough. This devastating attitude makes children try to be perfect. As a result they fail or give up and never try. Either way they never experience accomplishment. The problem with seeking approval in an alcoholic family is that what works one moment won't work the next—this is the fundamental unpredictability associated with alcoholic behavior.

One of four girls, Lisa was a loner and very shy as a child. She did spend some time with her twin sister, Laney, who was more outgoing.

''I always wanted to be a part of everything Laney did. She was my best friend as well as my sister. I could always turn to her for help, protection, and advice. Sometimes I would have girlfriends, but never more than one at a time. I just preferred to be alone and on my own. I never felt close to my other two sisters. Laney got along with both of them. But if I tried to get close to them, I felt as if I didn't belong. I always felt like I did things wrong and they didn't like me. It was easier just to stay by myself.

''The only person who ever believed me was Laney. Mom was always depressed or had something wrong with her. And if I tried to talk about it to my sisters, they would agree that she was crazy. They said that that was just the way Mom was. That was all there was to it. We never made any connection between her behavior and her drinking.''

Lisa's close relationship with her twin is classic twin behavior. Twins often form a tight and very private bond that creates greater isolation from others. Compensating for the loneliness in a troubled family, that bond can become even tighter.

It's common for children not to recognize a parent's true condition—to believe the parent is crazy rather than alcoholic. They may not identify it because 1) they don't have enough information; 2) they don't see the kind of drunkenness that is so often associated with alcoholism; 3) they don't see the drinking; or 4) they would feel greater helplessness by believing Mom to be alcoholic rather than crazy.

Lisa never knew what to expect from her mother. Often her mother would abuse the children verbally, accusing them of things they hadn't done.

''My mother became belligerent when she drank. Sometimes Laney would take the blame for something I was supposed to have done, when neither of us was at fault. Mom would always find something to be angry about.

Laney could always talk her out of her anger, but if I tried to do this, it only made matters worse.

"Mom would never believe me, or she wouldn't listen. She would verbally harass me for days. Many times she would say, 'You hurt the ones you love the most.' She had me convinced that she loved me so much that that was why she was always punishing me. I would think, She really does love me. She doesn't hate me. I grew up feeling and believing I was the crazy one, the bad one. I was a loner who was confused and didn't trust myself or anyone else. My goal was to stay out of the house."

When she was a teenager, Lisa began dating a boy she felt really understood her and how she felt. The boy had a twin brother who began dating Laney. Things seemed to be going well until, at fifteen, Lisa became pregnant.

"Once again, my mother was angry with me. At least this time I felt she had a reason. I felt very guilty for getting pregnant. I went to a home for unwed mothers and had planned to give up my child for adoption. This plan soon changed, however. When my mother was drunk she begged me to keep my son. I remember telling her, 'For you I will, Mom.' Inside, I felt as if I really should give him up. I wanted him to have a proper home with two parents, but I felt guilty, so I brought him home."

Lisa's profound need to please, her need for her mother's approval, was so great that it prevented Lisa from making a decision out of choice. She made a decision out of the need to please her mother. In her need to get approval, Lisa had never learned to make decisions on her own.

"Once the baby was home with us, my mother started saying that I was too young to be a mother and she wasn't going to be responsible for raising another child. She said she had already done her share. I was working full-time and going to school, but I let her know she wouldn't be doing anything at all, that he was my son and my responsibility. I'd really started to hate her by that point. I let her know I would raise my son without her help or support. I felt betrayed, confused, hurt, and angry."

When Lisa was eighteen she and her baby's father got married. He had been in and out of jail before they married, and once they set up a home together, Lisa realized that he, too, was an alcoholic. The marriage lasted for ten years, during which time Lisa had two more sons and a daughter.

"I didn't have the foggiest idea how to be a mother or a wife. I'd had four children by the time I was twenty-three. I stayed in that marriage

until I couldn't stand it any longer. I thought I'd lose my mind before it was over. I left the marriage at age twenty-nine, again feeling very angry, hurt, and confused. I just kept asking myself what I'd done wrong.

"I always felt as if I must have done something wrong to keep the marriage from working. I wasn't drinking at the time, but I didn't know about AA or Al-Anon. I just knew that the marriage's failure must have been my fault in some way."

The script for Lisa was clear. She was always at fault. She must do better. Hurt, anger, and confusion followed her from her mother's home into the years of marriage. Lisa never had the ability to try life on her terms until age twenty-nine.

BOB
Age: 37
Mother: Co-dependent
Father: Alcoholic
Birth Order: Oldest of two
Raised: Northwest
Socioeconomic Status: Upper
    Middle Class

Bob's story depicts the life of an Adult Child who drank abnormally from the first day he began to drink. Although he became dependent on alcohol at a young age, Bob was nonetheless functional. He was able to earn a law degree and begin a successful practice before his disease overcame him.

When Bob was a child, alcoholic drinking was the norm. Alcohol was so central to his family, it infiltrated every aspect of his life, even his play time.

BOB: "I remember one time when I was a kid we had a washing machine delivered to the house, and my parents let me keep the large packing case to play with. I decided to make a bar out of it and put a board on the back of the box to hold the bottles I'd fished out of the garbage to serve my imaginary patrons. I was only about six or seven at the time.

"I knew that my father drank and that I didn't like it, but no one was there to tell me what alcoholism was. It was as if we were supposed to be a happy family, but there was always this unacknowledged problem—

his alcoholism. It was there, and I was, too, sort of like going to a picnic where it rained a lot.

"Financially we were okay. Emotionally, though, it was as if my father was frozen in a huge block of ice. I think he tried to be close to us when we were kids. He just wasn't very successful. He was always embarrassed by positive emotions unless he was drinking. I grew sick, however, of the emotions he expressed when he was drinking. They weren't real for me, somehow. I didn't believe them. I suppose I just grew to distrust anything that came out of his mouth while he was drinking."

Bob's father made an effort to spend time with Bob, but their times together were usually marred by his father's drinking behavior.

"I remember his being a Boy Scout leader and our going on camp outs and canoe trips, but it wasn't really 'good' time I spent with my father. Even though we were both there, he was always in charge. He couldn't listen to others. Life was his way. There was no flexibility. He was so rigid. There was no fun.

"We would go on trips as a family, but what I remember the most about them were bad incidents involving my father's drinking. His drinking would frighten me. I would hear him at night bouncing off the walls on the way to the bathroom. He was overweight and usually naked, and the whole thing was disgusting. Sometimes when he drank early he would fall asleep; then he would wake up and prowl the house in the middle of the night.

"Mostly I have this image of my dad sitting in front of the television, drinking. I never felt he had any interest in me.

"I felt lots of love during my childhood from my mom and relatives, but really very little from my father. I remember Dad's constant need to be supported, reassured, and told that he was a good father. He would elicit these responses by telling us that he was not appreciated, that nobody knew how hard it was for him, that nobody really appreciated him, and that all he was good for was money. All the while he was about as accessible as a prickly cactus. He wanted us close, but he dodged us when we approached. Emotionally, as far as my father's love was concerned, we were living on bread and water."

Bob did have some support from his mother and other family members. Even so, the support of others cannot completely compensate for the wounding of a child by the alcoholic parent.

"I felt as if my mother was very available to us when we were growing up. She didn't work outside the home, and I have a warm feeling about *her being there. To be sure, we never discussed Dad's drinking, but she was dependable, caring, and loving. I also had a very warm relationship with my maternal grandmother. Mom used to visit my grandparents for coffee almost every day, and I remember playing in their house, eating Grandma's cookies and cakes. Theirs was an open, loving family, and I loved to go there. I also had a special aunt and uncle who had no children of their own. They lived near us, and I often stopped to visit them on my way home from school."*

Bob said that high school was a slow start for him, but "a strong finish."

"I felt awkward, unattractive. There was the 'in group,' the athletes and the cheerleaders, and then there was the other group. I was in the other group. However, this was the academically superior group, and I got a lot of satisfaction from being a part of it. I had at least found something I could do well."

Bob also had a significant relationship during his teenage years. He said it was not a sexual relationship, but one that was important to him.

"She made me feel good—maybe just by paying attention to me. It gave me someone to talk to, though we didn't talk about family things. But I could talk about other things—like my classes, and what I wanted to do later." Bob went on to college, emotionally numb and without much thought about his growing-up years.

MARGARET
Age: 35
Mother: Alcoholic
Father: Alcoholic, sober her
    growing-up years
Birth Order: Youngest of four
Raised: Maryland
Socioeconomic Status: Working
    class

Margaret's story is an example of an alcoholic whose Adult Child issues interfere with her ability to do what she needs to do to maintain sobriety. She must work on her Adult Child issues to prevent relapse.

Although both her parents were alcoholics, Margaret's father became sober three years before she was born. Her father recently died at the age of eighty-nine. He was thirty-eight years sober in Alcoholics Anonymous. Margaret's mother began to drink when Margaret was three years old. Margaret is certain that her mother is an alcoholic. She remembers her drinking constantly, the slurring of words, the many fights between her parents. Basically she describes her mother as being "not available."

Margaret's dad was considerably older than her mom and was retired when Margaret was born. Her mother had been a maid in a hotel. Margaret remembers little of her childhood and describes her early years as vague.

"My childhood was slow, a nothingness. My mom was real unavailable, and Dad was only accessible after he came home from an AA meeting. That's when I could approach him with my homework and he would help me. He was always in a better mood then."

Margaret's association of her father's involvement in Alcoholics Anonymous was positive, as his return from meetings was a positive time. Yet Margaret was in an unusual position in that her father, who was actively involved in a recovery program for his alcoholism, was married to a practicing alcoholic. In spite of Margaret's father's recovery from addiction, Margaret's family was still a highly dysfunctional family unit.

What Margaret remembers most is the constant fighting between her parents and cruelty on the part of her brother and oldest sister. Margaret says that the kids basically raised themselves.

"My brother and my oldest sister were much older than I was. My youngest sister was only three years older, but we weren't close. My brother lived with us until he finished high school and joined the service. I used to dread it when he came home, and as a defense, I would always get sick. He used to tell me that I was always so bad. And he and my sister used to have to lock me in the closet.

"I remember having lots of nightmares as a child. I would dream that our house had been blown away in a blizzard. When I woke up from the dream, I would feel terribly blank and alone because no one ever even knew I was gone. I used to cry myself to sleep at night. I don't remember how old I was, or when I quit having the nightmares, or when I quit crying myself to sleep. It was probably the same time I decided I didn't care what happened in our family anymore, that I wasn't going to be affected or hurt by it ever again."

Margaret had abandonment dreams. Many Children of Alcoholics have nightmares. And even if they haven't experienced such dreams in childhood, many people will have them in their adulthood. Margaret's dreams were most frequently about being alone or being left alone. While abandonment is a major dream theme, powerlessness and scenes of being terrified are also common.

Margaret attended Catholic schools for twelve years. She had a boyfriend.

"Being Catholic, I expected to marry this boyfriend. After all, being sexual and being Catholic meant you would get married."

But then the boyfriend broke up with Margaret. She was devastated. It was at this time she began to drink and use drugs.

JOE
Age: 54
Mother: Co-dependent
Father: Alcoholic
Birth Order: Only child
Raised: South
Socioeconomic Status: Middle class

Joe's story reflects the life of a practicing chemically dependent person who begins his recovery by looking at Adult Child issues first. It was during his ACOA recovery process that Joe recognized that he was also chemically dependent.

Joe was raised with a violent and emotionally abusive alcoholic father and a mother who suffered from severe emotional problems.

JOE: *"I have a key word for my childhood: terror. I grew up terrified—of the violence, the yelling, the screaming, the rage, and the battling that went on in my home. My father was physically abusive to my mother and to me. He would also abuse me through silence. He would withdraw from me—abandon me by refusing to speak to me.*

"There was the terror of being isolated, abandoned, of being disliked, of being alone, of not being okay, of not being wanted, of being responsible for my parents' problems. Somehow I learned that if I could be perfect, there would be no problems in my home."

This need to be perfect, and his deep sense of isolation, overflowed into Joe's dealings with other children.

"Even in kindergarten, and all through grade school, I felt this separation; I felt that I'd never belonged, that I was always on the outside looking in. I never felt accepted. I always felt rejected."

The emotional chaos and lack of support and attention that Joe had to face at home left him without any clues about how the rest of the world interacted socially.

"I can remember never knowing how to do things. Never knowing how to act, never knowing where to stand, or what to say, or how to talk, or what to wear. I didn't know how to be popular, how to be sociable, how to get along with other people. I spent most of my childhood in isolation. I read a lot. I read whatever I could. I read alone. I read when I was around others. I was frightened, and reading offered me solace. I would also ride my bicycle. I would ride and ride and ride. I would ride anywhere and nowhere, just to be riding away from it all."

The one social outlet Joe had that was comforting was time spent with his cousins. Joe was an only child, and he had an aunt and uncle with five daughters. He would often ride his bicycle to their home.

"It felt good there. We played. Sometimes it got so busy with all of those kids that I would withdraw, but it was a way to be away from home and not alone. Besides, they did give me attention."

Being an only child made Joe's challenge even greater. Like many only children, he experienced even greater loneliness and isolation. Yet he could break through the isolation, and he found support through a more stable family. But having to return to his own family sabotaged his ability to reach out and find comfort and protection through others.

Joe also found solace playing Little League baseball.

"I played rather well. I was a natural hitter. My mom was supportive in that she arranged for me to have uniforms and the transportation to get to games, but my dad wasn't the least bit interested. When I moved into high school and then changed schools, I didn't play ball anymore. I was afraid of the new kids, it was a larger school, and there was no reinforcement from my parents or anyone to play."

Joe says that at an early age he adopted the attitude "Nothing ever works out anyway, so why try." This overwhelming sense of powerlessness is characteristic of many COAs. Joe's attitude pushed him into a

pattern of starting projects but never finishing them or following through—
such as with baseball, as a student, with careers, and even marriage.
This, too, is common for many COAs.

Joe describes himself as playing each of the roles one often finds in an
alcoholic family, which is typical of the only child.

*"I was the clown. I would cut up in school. I was more disruptive than
harmful. I was the irresponsible one. I had learned early on that I would
never be good enough, so I was a genuinely lazy kid. I wouldn't feed the
dog. I wouldn't rake the leaves. I wouldn't do the schoolwork, at least
until I was harassed. At home I always felt as if I were in the way, that
things were my fault. I always asked myself—and still do at times today—
'Why didn't my dad like me? What did I do wrong?' At school I was the
scapegoat, often the butt of heavy teasing and jokes."*

As an adult, when Joe was in college for the second time, he moved
into the super-responsible role, into workaholism, and into perfectionism.

*"I could play any role. And I played them one right after another, never
knowing who I was, and never being me."*

By the time Joe was a teenager, the insanity and abuse in his family
was completely out of control. In despair, Joe fantasized about suicide.
This is a common experience for many children in troubled families.

*"I didn't really know what was going on except that I knew the whole
thing was nuts and I hated it. My high school years were the worst of
all. My father's rage increased; my mother's hysteria increased. I hated
my father's drinking. I hated my mother's hysteria. I wanted out, and I
did a lot of fantasizing about that. If I died, how would they feel? I wanted
to die. I wanted to kill myself, but I never got up the courage to do it."*

Most children raised in chemically dependent families don't identify the
problems within the family as being alcohol- or drug-related. They, like
the people in this chapter, believe that they are the problem; or they
believe that one parent is bad or that money is the issue. The child is
usually convinced that the problem is whatever the parents are putting
the blame on or whatever excuses they are using to rationalize their
circumstances.

Those children who are able to understand that alcohol is a main contributor to the problem, or who see it as the key issue, often promise
themselves and others, "It will never happen to me! I will make sure I
don't drink like my dad. I will never treat my kids the way he treats us.
I will be home at night. I will play with my kids." They are so well

intentioned. Ask a young child who sees drinking as a problem in his home if he will drink when he becomes an adult, and he will tell you "No!"

Yet most begin to drink in their teenage years. They drink for the same reasons that their parents drink. They drink to be like their friends. They drink because it is supposed to be fun. They drink to escape, to relax, to deaden the pain. But they drink with the firm belief that they will never become like their parent(s). They rationalize that becoming chemically dependent is the result of no willpower and no self-control.

Whether or not they recognize the problems in their life to be alcohol-related, most Children of Alcoholics will drink or use other drugs. Despite their desire not to be like their parents, they often do repeat their family history.

The Role of Alcohol

The Role of Alcohol for Dennis. Dennis was a very young teenager when he discovered that drinking provided something he felt was missing in his life.

DENNIS: *"When I was thirteen, I took my first drink. It was at a cousin's wedding, and I wanted to be like the grown-ups. I hated the taste, but I kept on drinking. Then I felt the glow, and—it worked! At one point I hit one of my cousins and took a swing at my dad. He decked me, but I still thought I was having a great time.*

"Every time I drank after that, I would get sick as a dog. But I would swear on a stack of Bibles that I would still do it again. I got drunk because I had a hole in my gut so big, and when I drank that first time it got filled up. It was the solution. I filled up the hole with booze and then with drugs. It worked. That was all I knew. Nobody paid any attention to my drinking. They thought it was cute, or they didn't notice."

Dennis continued to drink more and more and then moved on to other drugs.

"There was only one reason that I ever ingested alcohol—that was to get blitheringly numb. That's what I wanted to be. My friends and I decided that alcohol was 'uncool'; it was something that our parents used. So we started taking other drugs. I eventually got into doing PCP, which could wipe out any type of feeling. I could decide what to feel. I felt relaxed, not so manic or intense.

"Even heroin addicts were afraid to take PCP in my dosages, and that

made me feel powerful. People saw me as crazy, but that was okay. Drugs helped me feel a part of my user friends. People used to laugh and call me 'Loadie' or 'Stoney.' I wanted to wear that name as a star on my lapel. I looked up to those people. They were fun, cool—especially cool— and I wanted to be like them and liked by them. So I smoked a lot of pot, did acid, speed, PCP, and cocaine.''

The Role of Alcohol for Lisa. Lisa did not drink or use drugs until her marriage ended when she was twenty-nine. She said she may have had one or two drinks in the course of a year, but she was not even a social drinker.

LISA: *"I was so repulsed by my husband's drinking, and I didn't want to become like my mother. It simply did not occur to me to drink. I didn't want anything to do with alcohol.''*

When Lisa's marriage ended, she had custody of all four children. She had a full-time job at a telephone company and soon became involved with a married man. She said that his being married was safe for her and prevented her from marrying again. It also kept her from feeling so weak and frightened that she'd be tempted to go back to her husband. She said she thought drinking was what single people did. She felt as if she'd been let out of prison, and it was her turn to live. That's when she began to drink.

"Alcohol helped me to cope. I just seemed to fit in better when I drank, and I could finally talk to people. It was fun and exciting to me in the beginning. It gave me courage. I wasn't afraid or shy anymore. My mom and I could even communicate a little. I thought that drinking was the thing to do. I just wanted to have fun.''

Within two years Lisa felt her life was "out of control." One son was getting loaded a lot, another one had told her he was having sexual problems, another son wanted to move back to his father's. She felt as if she were a failure. All of this was coinciding with her slide into alcoholism.

"I remember drinking at a bar after work one day and someone asking me if I was getting drunk. I said no, that I was just running and trying to cope. I had become the one thing I had never wanted to be—just like my mother! I was unpredictable, belligerent, and obnoxious. I had no fear. I would fight with whatever man or woman got in my way.''

Lisa was to drink alcoholically for the next eight years.

The Role of Alcohol for Bob.

BOB: *"By the time I reached the age when I first began experimenting with alcohol, around sixteen or so, I'd seen enough alcohol to float a small country. Everywhere I went my father drank. He loved to eat out, and he was always drinking in the restaurants. He drank in the bars, and I would have to go pick him up. He was forever late to family gatherings or school events because of his drinking. But my exposure to my father's excessive drinking made drinking seem normal to me."*

As it was for Dennis and Lisa, alcohol was an immediate answer for Bob. Alcohol was an answer to the problems and questions that were never safe to pose.

"By the time I was in college, I thought it was okay to have a drink every night before going to bed. I doubt that there was a night in the next fifteen years that I did not drink. It didn't strike me that no one else in the dorm had a drink every day. I didn't think it odd to take a bottle along on a trip just in case I couldn't get access to liquor. I didn't think it was odd to put liquor in a mouthwash bottle so no one would know what it was. I'd had a nodding acquaintance with alcohol at an early age, so it was easier to ignore the early-warning signs of my own alcoholism.

"I believe I drank in part to relax, to relieve pain, and to hide from alienation and vague feelings of anxiety. But the problem was bigger than that. I drank to get rid of, to hide, or to mask the way I felt. Looking back now, I know I drank to relieve myself of my Adult Child issues. I drank to feel better. I knew I was screwing up, but I didn't know what to do.

"I also used to drink because I felt guilty about drinking. Yet I couldn't stop. I felt so unhappy knowing I shouldn't be drinking, yet I couldn't not drink.

"In college I was a compulsive studier. I clearly had a problem with alcohol, but I managed to function well enough to graduate fifth in my law school class. It was very important for me to succeed and do well. I was always so terrified that I was flunking out. School was the only way I knew to prove that I was worthwhile. I was trying to prove to others, but even more so to myself, that I was okay. I did have fun at school, but mostly that involved drinking. In the end my drinking and the demands of law school took its toll. I wouldn't ever want to go through that again. I remember flying to see my girlfriend one weekend and hoping the plane would crash so that I could get out of this whole thing honorably."

Bob's drinking gave him something in common with his father and sometimes provided a bond between them that didn't exist in other ways. However, his father's drinking also created a desire in Bob to separate himself from his father's behavior.

"I probably felt closest to Dad when we were both drinking. The alcohol melted away both of our inhibitions, and in a way we could talk more easily then. But I had to catch Dad when he was in the convivial phase of his drinking, and that never lasted long."

Bob married in his last year of law school.

"Anna came from a loving family that drank normally. Things got better for a while. Being with Anna, I wasn't so lonely, I felt better about myself. I adopted her family and spent a lot of time with her father and brother. In essence I tried to substitute Anna's family for my own. I came to regard my family as a biological trap. At this time my work was going well, but soon my drinking became even worse.

"I really didn't have the ability to control it. I never wanted to drink in front of my wife, so I created a lot of projects that took me away from her. I used to go to the cellar a lot to work on things. It got so bad that I even started to urinate in jars downstairs so I wouldn't have to go upstairs for her to see me. I was also experiencing blackouts."

The Role of Alcohol for Margaret.

MARGARET: *"The first time I remember drinking was after school at a girlfriend's house. I wasn't drinking for any particular reason. It was what teenagers did. I wasn't a very happy child. I was pretty aimless. So, anyway, here I was. We were drinking screwdrivers; I don't remember how many, but I do remember walking home and noticing that my lip was numb. I thought it felt wonderful, and I wished that I could always feel that way."*

In addition to drinking, Margaret began to smoke marijuana.

"The first time I smoked pot, I thought, This is great stuff for me! My mind seemed to open up to new ideas, and I saw the world in a whole different light. It wasn't long before I was using pot almost every day, and then daily just to maintain. When I drank, it was for total oblivion. I also used relationships so I wouldn't have to feel lonely. I was very promiscuous."

After high school, Margaret took four years to complete two years of college. She was basically consumed with alcohol and drugs.

"I went to class and partied a lot. I took mescaline, blotter acid, psychedelics, speed, cocaine, alcohol, marijuana. For a while I did some small-time selling of marijuana. I took whatever a boyfriend or dealer friend would give me."

When she was twenty-five Margaret joined the Air Force, looking for some "orderly direction" in her life. She had always thought she would have her life together by the time she was twenty-one, but it took until she was twenty-five to wake up and realize she was not getting there. Yet she continued to drink and smoke pot on a daily basis. Her promiscuity interfered with her ability to get certain clearances. She dealt with that by marrying shortly out of basic training.

"I married a heavy drinker and knew it, but I thought we would quit together. Not long after we were married, I went for help on the pretense of my husband's needing the help."

The Role of Alcohol for Joe. By his later high school years, Joe was emotionally desperate. His use of alcohol was an immediate love affair.

JOE: *"During my senior year in high school I was invited to a fraternity rush party at a local college. It was there that I took my first real drink. It was beer, and I loved it. I was an alcoholic from the first swallow, a practicing alcoholic. I had been a time bomb waiting to explode. I got very drunk and blacked out. I carried on like a real idiot, from what people told me. I woke up the next morning with a bad hangover and no recollection of what had happened. What amazed me, though, was that I was sort of a hero with this group of fraternity people. I had immediately found a friend in alcohol. I had found a way to get through one more day without killing myself. I had found a way to be accepted. I had found a way to be a part of a group, to be popular. I had found something to fix me, something to fill up that horrible empty hole inside, something to make me feel adequate, okay, and able to cope."*

Joe spent his college years binge drinking every weekend.

"I never drank except with total insanity. I never drank for any purpose except to wreck my brain. I could never control my drinking."

Finally Joe's grades suffered from his drinking. During his junior year he dropped out to work in the oil fields. He finally went back to college to study engineering.

"I got serious about my studies and discovered my second real fix: ac-complishment, achievement, good grades. I was either obsessed with working or binge drinking. Because I would do it only twice a month or so, I still had the illusion that I was controlling my drinking, despite my bizarre, stupid, and life-threatening behavior when I was drunk."

Joe got married and continued to go to school to obtain his doctorate in order to teach at the university level.

"I was very much a workaholic. I had also become sexually obsessed, and I was a compulsive spender. I would always grab anything to fix me— my bachelor's degree, my master's, a Ph.D., a wife, a child, another child, a drink, a new car, something to buy, something to spend. I also became addicted to self-defeat, addicted to self-destructive behavior.

"I got a job teaching at a university. This whole time period was one of outrageous drinking and very egotistical, aggressive, and antisocial behavior. My lack of responsibility, my compulsive spending, and my drinking began to dominate my life. I became more and more confused and more and more terrified. My wife and I divorced after sixteen years of a marriage that had always been rocky. There was unhappiness from the start. She fit my pattern that 'no matter what I did it was never good enough,' and I was obsessive, compulsive, and addicted."

Joe said he didn't participate much at all in the raising of his children, who were eleven and thirteen when he left the family.

"I hardly realized I had children. I was totally preoccupied with myself. Although I did want to provide for my family, my life-style interfered with that.

"As each one of my fixes failed, I would look for another one. I became addicted to self-help books. I kept thinking that I would find the magic secret that would fix me, the thing that was going to make me okay. When I finally ran out of fixes, I hit bottom. No one would have guessed except a few of those closest to me that, despite my outward appearance, on the inside I was terrified, panic-stricken, and functioning at the edge of survival. I was lacking any sense of self-worth or self-esteem. Every-thing was disintegrating, everything."

Chemical dependency is said to be a cunning, baffling disease, and I believe this is true. One of the most confusing aspects of chemical de-pendency is how it varies in visibility.

Joe's addictions, although not so blatant to him, were obvious to those around him. Dennis was so lost in his chemicals, he had to have someone else—his father—intervene. Bob was disintegrating quietly, his disease apparent only to his wife.

It's unlikely that Margaret would have found anyone to help her address her issues because she surrounded herself with others similar to her. Yet instinctively, when she hit her own bottom, she knew there was help out there—even though she moved toward recovery by seeking it for her husband. Lisa's drinking was obvious to her and those around her, but it would take getting "sick and tired of being sick and tired" before she sought help.

Life Stories: Adulthood and Recovery

Recovery is the process that begins when the chemically dependent person begins to realize that alcohol and/or drugs is the source of the problems in his or her life. Along with this realization comes the insight that stopping alcohol or drug usage is not as simple as deciding to control it or willing it away—they are going to need help in order to stop. The hardest part is understanding that recovery means total abstinence from all mind-changing chemicals.

Some people seek help very willingly after a period of physical, mental, emotional, spiritual, and social devastation. Others seek help grudgingly, wanting it but preferring to control how they get and use the assistance offered. Still others seek help only to satisfy another person's desires.

When one is chemically dependent, that's the issue that's nearly always going to have to be addressed first. Yet the problem is more complex for people like Joe. He was a compulsive spender, sexually obsessive, and a workaholic in addition to being addicted to alcohol and other drugs. His family life had been severely affected by all of these issues. Where does such a person begin recovery? Unfortunately, many people begin with the money, sex, work, or family issues without identifying and focusing on the chemical addiction. Very often they spend years not finding answers. This is made more difficult by the fact that there is a tendency for addicted people and those around them to want to focus on anything but the addictions. Because it is such a primary addiction, alcoholism and/or drug abuse is the one issue dependent people will fight the hardest to maintain. The result is that they are never able to recover in the one area that offers them the greatest opportunity to recover in all the other areas of their lives.

We revisit Dennis, Lisa, Bob, Margaret, and Joe as they describe their recovery processes. They tell us what led them to recovery from their chemical dependency and how their Adult Child issues interface with recovery from this dependency.

DENNIS
Age: 32
Partner Status: Single
Occupation: Actor
Recovery Process: AA—twelve
    years sober, ACOA, therapy

Dennis got sober when he was twenty years old. Dennis's father had become sober the year before, and he was instrumental in bringing Dennis to Alcoholics Anonymous.

DENNIS: "I hated my dad when he first got sober. I resented him and resisted him. But my life was truly unmanageable. I hurt, and I didn't know how to take the pain away. Not even the drugs were doing it anymore. Finally my Dad intervened. All I'd ever wanted was for my dad to be there, and there he was. I didn't understand what he was saying, but I had no energy left to fight him. I was really screwed up."

Dennis's father played a strong father role for a person so newly sober. He saw his son's addiction and reached out to help. Those not familiar with alcoholism recovery might assume this is an obvious response. But Dennis's father had been alcoholic a long time. Many people who have only been sober a year are not yet able to influence their families. In fact, often out of guilt, they take a very passive role. Dennis was fortunate because his father was not willing to be passive.

"I went to my first AA meeting and did what they said. I didn't use, and I didn't drink. I don't remember much about those first few months, but I know I liked feeling part of a family."

Alcoholics Anonymous gave Dennis the sense of belonging he had yearned for as a child. It became a family unit for him. While that may sound understandable because he was only twenty, it is often just as true for the person who is older.

"AA parents me as my parents had not been able to. The slogans and the Twelve Steps offered me a path that made a lot of sense to me. I

had been raised Catholic, and I liked the spiritual part of the program. I was ready. So I spent the next ten years growing up.

"When I was thirty years old—and ten years sober—I found things still weren't as they seemed they should be. I was still frightened a lot. I felt lonely. I could never really put together an intimate relationship. I had this sense that I was doing what I was supposed to do, but that I wasn't able to decide what I wanted in life. I had heard about Adult Child self-help groups and decided to try one."

Dennis's Alcoholic/Addict and Adult Child Issues. Dennis had some very specific work he needed to do in ACOA about his anger at his dad. First of all, that anger was getting in the way of how he was relating to his father. Second, in some ways AA was becoming the symbol of how he felt about his father. Dennis needed to address the anger at his father in order not to push AA out of his life.

DENNIS: *"I loved my father so much when I was a kid, but socially and emotionally he abandoned me. I was never able to address that issue. One day, after I started going to ACOA meetings, I broke down and started accusing my father and calling him names. I did it again six months later. When I let him have it a third time, expressing the hurt I felt and crying and crying, my dad finally said my anger was okay, but in time I would need to realize that he had done the best he could.*

"That's when I came to the realization that these issues were my issues. I went to him and apologized for my behavior. He cried in my arms. It was so powerful. I felt such incredible love. It was a real catharsis to be able to confront him with my feelings, and I don't put the blame on him anymore."

For Dennis it was important to confront his father. He was also fortunate that his father was able to hear what he had to say. One day Dennis may also want to say some things to his mother or work on issues related to his mother.

"My mother is also in recovery—she got sober the same day I did. But I always related more to her co-dependency issues than to her alcoholism."

Like most Adult Children, Dennis has focused his internal work on the parent whose loss of relationship was more blatant. There is nothing wrong or hurtful in that, it's natural. Yet in time Adult Children are able to see that it is a family disease, and there are issues to be resolved around the nonalcoholic co-dependent parent. In Dennis's case the co-dependent parent is less visibly chemically dependent. Dennis not only found friends in AA, he clearly responded to the basics of the program: the Twelve Steps. (See Appendix, page 555.)

"The Twelve Steps are the meat and potatoes of both the AA and ACOA programs. But after ten years of being sober I found an identification in Adult Child self-help groups that has been vital to my recovery.

"In ACOA I have found a place to talk about my fears, sadness, and anger. Prior to ACOA I had not learned to deal with my feelings. I was still denying my feelings even after ten years of sobriety. Feelings left over from childhood were running rampant and intruding on my adult life. Denying my feelings was as self-destructive to my recovery as the denial of my alcoholism had been to my sobriety. I had become emotionally paralyzed."

Dennis had found that until he addressed the feelings he had repressed in his childhood, it would continue to be difficult for him to identify and express his present-day feelings. As a youngster he only knew how to medicate his feelings. Yet at thirty he still had not yet learned how to be safe with his feelings.

"In the program, dealing with the issue of God was helpful for me. God has the power to take away obsession. But I still needed to make that connection with all my obsessions—lust, caffeine, people, chaos, over-activity, negative and abusive people. I knew I needed to 'let go, and let God,' but I needed something more. In ACOA I was able to find that missing link.

"In ACOA, it felt safe to talk about your past. I heard others talk about their childhoods, and I identified with what they were saying. I'd not had the experience of talking honestly about my growing-up years before. Talking about the past takes the power out of childhood messages.

"I had internalized messages such as 'My needs are not important,' 'Boys don't cry,' and 'I have to do everything by myself.' In ACOA I learned where these beliefs had come from and had the opportunity to counter them. But first I had to recognize what they were. Identifying with other people has a tremendous value.

"By learning to understand my feelings, I've made tremendous gains in my ability to maintain relationships. When I came into ACOA I was clearly in a relationship crisis. I am now learning to share how I feel with other people. While I am in a relationship, I still find intimacy intimidat-

ing—but I'm working at being more responsive to my girlfriend's needs and not being so selfish and showing my emotions more. Today I am ready to make a commitment to the woman I have been in love with for the past four years.

"I'm also working at learning how to play. Up to now I've always needed to be accomplishing something—or acting as if I was. By knowing my feelings better, I'm more aware of my needs. I can relax more. I'm also able to be available to others because I don't spend so much energy protecting myself. That has helped me in my relationship with my dad.

"Through ACOA, I've been able to work out a lot of the stuff with my father. Today he's a doting grandfather. And he gives to both his kids and his grandchildren—he wants to make up for the time that we lost. We do things together. I can spend the whole day with him. I never could do that before."

Both the AA and ACOA programs are important to Dennis's recovery, and he recognizes that each program has something special to offer.

"I'm going to AA and using my sponsor. I go because my foundation is there, the basics are there. It's a stronger program in the Steps. I also attend one or two ACOA meetings a week and see a therapist with my partner so we can work on some of our relationship issues, such as communication.

"The first two and half years in ACOA I developed a better sense of my feelings. I can cry when I need to. But I still need to find a balance— sometimes I focus too much on feelings.

"I do relate to my AA program, and I believe that ACOA has enhanced my AA program. I've done a better inventory. I've worked the Steps harder. I learned a better God consciousness. I began to feel God, not just know about God. Since this time I have also found my faith in God through church to be a major support to me. I had been so angry with God as a child and have struggled, but today I have given my Higher Power my trust.

"I'm a stronger person. I can face life better. I can go the extra mile. I have a better capacity for closure.

"Recovery is a process. Much of this recovery has been difficult, but it is happening. It's a better way of life. I feel the comfort that comes from it. Today I can sit and be quiet. I'm less depressed, less angry— far less angry—and that makes me more loving."

LISA
Age: 42
Partner Status: Single, three living
    adult children
Occupation: Student
Recovery Process: AA—six years
    sober, ACOA, therapy

After eight years of drinking, Lisa hit her bottom. She called her brother-in-law, who was in AA, and went with him to her first meeting. What she remembers about that meeting was the laughter. She said she identified with the feelings and knew she could be helped. When she was close to a year sober, she relapsed and drank for another nine months. She says she wasn't convinced that she was alcoholic. However, after several months of drinking, lengthy blackouts began to convince her. She went back to the AA program.

LISA: *"In the first year of my sobriety, I never understood how being the Child of an Alcoholic had anything to do with my alcoholism. I was just trying to get sober and have some kind of consistency and order in my life. I just concentrated on the Twelve Steps and going to meetings. Finally I was able to laugh and to think clearly. But at the same time I was beginning to feel depressed, alone, and afraid again. I knew I had to keep trying in order to get my life together. Yet my whole life I had tried to be strong and never ask for help."*

It was best that Lisa's initial focus was on getting sober, for she would soon have to face two major traumas. In doing so, she found that she now had the skills to cope without drinking—in the past that would have been her first and only option.

The first trauma occurred when Lisa's sixteen-year-old son fatally overdosed. She was one year and twenty-nine days sober. This is when Lisa realized that she had more to deal with than the issue of her own sobriety.

"My world fell apart. I didn't drink over it, but I thought I was going to lose my mind."

In addition to dealing with the tragic loss of her son, Lisa became aware of another trauma in her life that she had suppressed until then. She had been an incest victim as a child.

After a relatively short time sober, Lisa began to have flashbacks of being sexually abused by her father. Then, after her father died, she was molested twice more by different men in her neighborhood. Awareness of this abuse is still something new for Lisa; and the new memories are still continuing to present themselves.

Alcohol was no longer an option for Lisa in dealing with the death of her son. She needed to openly grieve his tragic loss. But out of this depth of honesty she found the courage to face the sexual abuse—a secret that had remained hidden for years.

Lisa also had the strength to seek help in dealing with the loss of her son and the incest. She had learned in her first year of sobriety that it was okay to ask for help.

Lisa's Alcoholic and Adult Child Issues.

"I had not been aware of ACOA until very recently, and my sobriety and my recovery program have changed dramatically since the time of my son's death. I have learned that getting sober is not enough to have a meaningful life. I have had to deal with each and every issue of my childhood and rebuild a foundation for myself other than the one I was taught. The past four years of therapy, along with the ACOA program, have saved my life.

"In dealing with the incest issue, I have also begun to deal with my Adult Child issues, which I feel are directly related to my alcoholism. Everything I was taught when I was little I have repeated as an Adult Child. My drinking was no different. I drank to cope, to be a part of things, to fit in. As a child I wanted to be a part of my family, but my feelings were ignored. I was never heard and always felt afraid. When I drank I could talk, feel, and be heard. I would never have been able to communicate with people or deal with the stress otherwise. My mother drank to cope and to communicate. I did the same thing. I never realized how much I had become like her until I got sober.

"Through recovery, I can now say how I feel most of the time without being angry or afraid. I can feel what my feelings are instead of being numb. I know that my feelings are valid. I am able to make decisions for myself and feel good about those decisions most of the time. I no longer need someone else to tell me how I'm feeling.

"I am able to look inside of me and not be ashamed of who I am. I no longer feel the need to run away and hide from who I am. I am happy to say that I love me today for who I am and not for what I thought I was supposed to be. I have my own identity, and I am forever grateful for this. I can trust my own judgment and even trust a couple of other people in my life today.

"When I was little I was never able to think like a child. I always thought like an adult. The messages I received about love and friendship were that they were mixed with pain and masochism, confusion and betrayal. I had to relearn about love. I have had to redefine morals. I have had to redefine spiritual beliefs. I am learning about boundaries. I am learning about choices. I have learned I am not crazy. I know it is okay to feel, to cry, to be angry. I have learned I don't need to be abused to be loved. I have also learned that life can be fun."

Lisa has learned a lot in the past six years. At times people question how such a transformation is possible. The answer is that Lisa had direction and support—and she was willing to risk and willing to follow direction. She used several different tools, but they were compatible—therapy, Alcoholics Anonymous, and ACOA. Her therapist was also knowledgeable and respectful of the alcoholism recovery process.

By facing her own alcoholism and recognizing the Adult Child issues in her life, Lisa has been able to begin dealing with alcoholism as a family disease.

"My life is my own, and I am responsible for it. I can see the damage I have done with my own children. My two sons are both chemically dependent. My oldest, I feel, has a drinking problem. He doesn't think so. My youngest is addicted to marijuana and alcohol. My daughter just recently admitted that she is an alcoholic, although she is not ready to give up the bottle just yet.

"My mother has not been through a recovery process but today due to age and health problems is abstinent. While my mother has not changed significantly, because of my own recovery, I have come to forgive and to love her.

"By dealing with my own alcoholism and my ACOA issues, I have been able to share my experiences and discoveries with the other members of my family. My twin, Laney, and her daughters have begun to read some Adult Child literature. They are now willing to admit that there is a problem. Today it is my life's aim, and deepest hope, that the generations to come won't subscribe to not feeling, not talking, and not trusting."

"Knowing that I must be honest, and having a trust in God, has been my salvation. The Twelve Step program has allowed me to have a recovery."

It is a difficult challenge to get sober, to begin to address your own Adult Child/incest issues, to respond to the major trauma of losing a child, and then be open to looking at the next generation in your family. To keep these potentially overwhelming issues in perspective, one needs a solid foundation of recovery and the willingness to stay close to the program.

BOB
Age: 37
Partner Status: Married, two
    children
Occupation: Attorney
Recovery Process: Outpatient
    alcoholism treatment
    AA—three-and-a-half-years
    sober, Adult Child group therapy

Bob sought out Alcoholics Anonymous and periodically made attempts to be sober. Like many alcoholics, he attempted sobriety for several years before he was able to maintain it.

BOB: *"Prior to my being married, I had once walked myself into a central office of Alcoholics Anonymous and told this man there that there was something wrong with my drinking, that I didn't have the ability to stop. He offered to take me to a meeting. I went, and for a whole summer I didn't drink. But I quit going to meetings because I felt I was different from the other people there. In my own mind I wasn't ready to stop. I then continued to drink for another couple of years."*

Bob drank during social occasions, but his refuge was the cellar of his house. That was his private bar.

"A few times my wife had approached me while I was in the cellar. Pretty much aware of what I was doing, she told me she was concerned for me. She said that what I was doing was not normal and not healthy. One day she mentioned that she wanted me to go to the church to listen to a talk

about alcohol problems. That led to an assessment by an alcoholism counselor. Then I went back to AA, but I didn't like it.''

Bob himself had been periodically questioning his drinking. Otherwise he would not have so readily responded to his wife's confrontation. Yet being chemically dependent and a driven Adult Child, he would once again struggle against the help that was available.

"I developed a home group, but I wasn't ready or able to use it. I would not drink as long as it was a typical day, but I drank on the holidays and whenever I went to my parents'. I found plenty of reasons to make exceptions for being able to drink.

"I struggled with recovery for my alcoholism for some time. I knew something was wrong, but I didn't really know what to do about it. Although I was going to AA, in reality I was holding on by my fingertips. I started having a relapse every two months or so—not serious blowout drunks, but just drinking even though I knew it was part of my program not to drink.

"A friend of mine in AA had just completed an Adult Child course and thought I might be interested, so I signed up. I was searching for something, although at the time I didn't realize that what I was searching for was my own acceptance and surrender. Together with the other people in the Adult Child group, we agreed not to use mood-altering chemicals. No problem for me—I thought—I was in AA and a recovering alcoholic. It didn't take much, just a little truth, and I cried and cried. I was a little boy full of tears. I was getting a lot out of the program, but I wasn't sober. Finally my therapist convinced me to enroll in an outpatient program for my own alcoholism. This led me to the formal treatment that has made the difference for me.''

It is difficult to ascertain whether or not Bob was an alcoholic who simply had not surrendered, or if his Adult Child issues of feeling different, and anger at his father, were interfering with his ability to get sober. But it is more obvious that the initial grief he experienced in speaking about his Adult Child issues was connected with the surrender that facilitated his sobriety.

In alcoholism treatment he was advised not to focus on his dad's alcoholism, but rather on his own. At that time Bob's focus on his father was becoming a diversion from focusing on himself. The lessening of his grief was important Adult Child work, and it enhanced the beginning of his recovery. But now his continued focus on his father only served to keep his focus off taking responsibility for himself.

"I struggled for a good while with wanting to focus on my father. But I finally gave in because I was tired of fighting. I was simply exhausted. It was safer for me to deal with his alcoholism—less shameful, perhaps— than facing my own. The Adult Child issues were the magnet to treatment. But once there, they were an obstacle that had to be moved aside, to be returned to at a later date."

Bob's Alcoholic and Adult Child Issues. By recognizing the problems that he faced as an Adult Child, Bob found that he had to deal with the issues of control, trust, and risk taking as a part of his recovery.

"I'd always had a 'Don't take any risks—don't rock the boat' philosophy. Expect the worst, I thought, and be happy if something better happens. It was a pretty gloomy outlook on life, but I thought it reduced my chances of getting hurt. In recovery, I've had to learn to reach out to people, to take a few chances. I've had to risk disclosure so that I can clean house emotionally and let others come to know and love me. I feel that intimacy is worth having, but it requires taking risks.

"I have trouble trusting people. At the office I check the math of junior lawyers and recheck documents for the hearings that I do. At home I check to see if the doors are locked before I go to sleep, even if someone else tells me they've locked them. I find I'm getting better about these things. The whole treatment process for me involved letting someone else decide what might be better for me, learning to do what I was told, and trying to see if someone else's approach would work better."

Letting other people be a part of one's recovery process creates a lot of vulnerability. Disclosing to others, depending on others, is very frightening when one has never felt safe doing that. So often we don't even know how closed we are until we are given an opportunity to look at ourselves symbolically through a medium such as art therapy.

"I struggled to do this recovery business myself for several years before I underwent formal treatment. Even in recovery, when I drew pictures in art therapy, I drew only myself. I drew in no counselors, no helpers, no support group, even though I was in their midst and they had their arms outstretched to help me over the bumps."

Bob has had to work on his ACOA tendency to see things in extremes, with no middle ground.

"I often see things as black or white, all right or all wrong. I want to categorize a thing or a situation and then put it where it belongs, in this

slot or that one. I tend to do this rather quickly, often without giving the issue I'm classifying the time and attention it deserves. It's been hard learning that while some things are black and white, other things are gray.

"Long ago, because of my father's alcoholism, I categorized alcoholism as bad. In my childhood, certainly no good ever came from it for me, only problems. Now I understand that it is a disease, and good things can come from recovering from it.

"I've also had to realize that my recovery may be different from another person's. There are many roads that lead to recovery. It's not a cake recipe where there is precisely one cup of this and one cup of that. It's more like a stew where you start with what you have in the refrigerator. I've learned that my way isn't for everyone. Now I can share my thoughts about what has worked for me, but I'm not insulted if someone doesn't do it my way. Life and recovery are more multifaceted than that. I won't die if things aren't a certain way. I'm learning to loosen up, to let go of some of the rigidity and stiffness I learned as a child and still carry with me today. Those were, and still are, things that impede my recovery."

Bob is now able to identify and be a little humorous about how his perfectionism can interfere in the quality of his sobriety. Perfectionism is often a way for people to compensate for feeling defective, for feeling shame.

"I keep struggling with my tendency to work for a 'perfect recovery.' I get compulsive about it. I have a three-by-five card file box with the Twelve Steps on index cards, though to my credit I don't have much on the index cards. I have Twelve Step tapes that I listen to in my car on my way to business meetings.

"There's a risk that my perfectionism will spoil the pudding. I remember reading the inspirational goals of Twenty-Four Hours a Day [a meditation book familiar to recovering alcoholics] *and being frustrated that I had not achieved them yet. Finally I switched to a different book, but not until I threw the book against the bathroom wall."*

The insights Bob has gained through work on his Adult Child issues have had a strong impact on his recovery as an alcoholic. He has specifically looked at his need to look good, his control issues, his guilt and shame, and now his feelings about his father.

"My need for acceptance and reassurance and my general desire to 'look good' had made it difficult for me to be honest in recovery. I'm getting

over it, but it's still hard for me to say something if it might hurt someone, even if it needs to be said.

"I sometimes attempt to control people by trying to get them to do what I think they should. Although I'm getting better about it. Now I recognize when I do it. On at least two occasions in after care [post-treatment therapy], people have rejected my efforts. But we talked about it. And once I got over feeling rejected, I felt relieved and happy that I didn't have to be responsible for them.

"I'm a little too comfortable with guilt. I feel guilty about things I'm not responsible for. So now I'm making an effort not to be responsible for other people's recoveries and other problems over which I have no control.

"I was mortified when my wife told her parents about my problems and my alcoholism treatment. I felt they would see me as less than perfect. I was still trying to look good. They responded very appropriately and positively, though. I realize that I cannot talk myself out of their love for me."

It is very powerful for alcoholics feeling shame to discover that others truly care and love them. But in order for Bob to learn that, he first had to be honest with himself and others. While he was initially horrified that his wife was breaking family denial when she told her parents, this revelation led Bob to being able to accept their love.

"Embracing the disease concept of alcoholism helped me go a long way toward forgiving my father.

"Today I understand that my father is also an Adult Child who has the disease of alcoholism. Yet it still hurts me to watch all of that when I'm powerless to change it. I feel as if my father is a million miles away. He's like one of those stars whose light comes to Earth from millions of miles away. When it comes, it is faint. It has to be a clear night, and you have to wait an eternity for it to come. I try to break in there with hugs, tell him I love him. It feels good to me to try, and I do, but I feel frustrated by his lack of response. He doesn't want to be in the same room with me alone. Obviously my recovery threatens him, as does my mother's recovery in Al-Anon."

When an Adult Child is in recovery and the other family members are not, there will be distance in their relationships. It will be frustrating as well. Although Bob can have a relationship with his father, he will need to have fewer expectations, as his father is still alcohol-affected. If he can do this, it will result in less frustration. He's much more likely to have a closer relationship with his mother, as they have in common their mutual involvement in Twelve Step programs.

"Today, sober for a few years, now the only thing I miss about my drinking days is that when I drank with my father we had a bond."

Acknowledging that there was such a significant payoff in his drinking—it offered the only connection with his father—takes a lot of honesty. It's painful to admit that alcohol is the basis of an intimate relationship. Bob will need to own the sadness, and very likely the anger, that will come as a result of this awareness.

"I'm also angry and feel cheated that the disease has taken my father from me. But that's okay. It's okay to feel angry and hurt. I can't rewrite my childhood."

Bob is like the majority of addicted Adult Children; he is the product of second-, third-, and even fourth-generation alcohol/drug-affected thinking and parenting. He cannot rewrite his childhood, but his recovery has begun, and he can rewrite the script for his children.

"I can, however, make things a whole lot different for my children. And today many of my greatest joys are my playing—literally playing—with my children and their friends, and participating in their lives. We have wonderful family meals. Every Sunday we have people over, I cook, we share the food, the kids play. It's a harmony I really like.

"I think the shame I feel over my own alcoholism is a refinement and purification of the shame I felt as a child over my father's alcoholism. On an emotional level, I drank a liquor twice-brewed. To think that I would end up like my father, that my disease could do to my children what his disease did to me, was a prospect too horrible to comprehend. This was the raw meal of shame that I milled and baked into a fine pastry. You'd think this prospect would strengthen my denial. But I feel that the fear of ending up like Dad made it easier for me to admit that I was powerless and ready for a change. I saw the road I was walking down, and I was scared to death.

"It was difficult, though, recognizing what my father and I had in common. I tried hard not to do the things my father did, at least superficially. He drank in bars; I drank only at home. We were always waiting for him to come home; I always came home before I drank. He would cry for help; I would ask for none. Superficially we were different; but underneath we had the same disease.

"My recovery has taught me that I am not my father. I am different.

I am thirty-seven; he is sixty-two. I am recovering; he is not. He brought his family full term into their Adult Child issues; I am doing what I can to break the cycle for my family in my lifetime. Still, deep down, I think my shame for my own alcoholism is stronger because it is an extension of my shame for him.''

In recognizing the depth of shame, alcoholics and addicts such as Bob need to remember how important it is to work on recovery in both areas.

"I believe I have to work on my Adult Child issues for my recovery to progress. It's like I'm moving a heavy log. The whole thing is just too heavy to move all at once. To make progress, I have to lift one end up and move it forward, then pick up the other end and move it forward, and then just keep repeating the process.

"Today I recognize that feeling of joy, and I love it. It comes from loving people, and I have a hunch it comes from loving myself and seeing good in myself. It comes from realizing that it is okay to be an alcoholic, and it is wonderful to be a recovering alcoholic.''

MARGARET
Age: 35
Partner Status: Remarried, two
    children
Occupation: Office manager
Recovery Process: Outpatient and
    inpatient alcoholism treatment
    AA—six years sober, Al-Anon

Within a year of joining the service, Margaret went for help for her husband and his drinking problem. At this time she was also pregnant. Within a few more months she and her husband asked to leave the military, using medical leave as the reason. Margaret's husband simply wanted out, and she didn't know what else to do but follow, even though she says she loved the military. She liked the structure it gave her.

The treatment program asked her, as the spouse, to monitor her own drinking and limit it to no more than three drinks.

MARGARET: *"Now I was pregnant, and yet I clearly didn't want to re-spond to the three-drink limit. The counselor suggested I go to AA. I instantly thought, I can't go there, that's my Dad's program! I knew AA worked. I had watched it work for thirty-plus years. I wasn't ready.''*

Margaret gave birth to a baby girl and continued to drink and use. It became clear that she couldn't control her alcohol use. Margaret was exhausted with the emotional, mental, social, and physical chaos characteristic of what so many alcoholics experience prior to surrender. There was no spiritual struggle; she was spiritually bankrupt by then.

At the age of twenty-nine, Margaret decided to quit drinking. A week later she also stopped her drug use. She began going to AA. It was also shortly after that that she and her husband divorced.

"At first all I knew was that I was an alcoholic and that my father was an alcoholic. He had been sober in AA for thirty-eight years when he died, which was two months before I got sober. So, obviously, I was the child of an alcoholic. I did fine in AA for two years. I didn't have a compulsion, and the people all seemed to understand how I felt and what I was going through. I had found unconditional love and acceptance. But then I began wondering, 'Is this all there is?' ''

Margaret knew factually that she was a COA. While many people know that to be a fact about themselves, that does not mean they understand how they have been impacted by the family system.

Margaret then married a man she had met in AA, and they moved to a new town. Although she was looking forward to starting a new life, she found it difficult to connect with the people in her new AA meetings. At first she thought that it was just a result of the move and of being in a strange town. But then she began to realize that the problem ran deeper than that.

"I had difficulty sharing my gut feelings in meetings because I really didn't know what my gut feelings were. My sponsor didn't give up, though. She just kept at me, and little by little things began to come out— no real biggies, just little things that I didn't want to look at.

"We would talk about my 'sticking my head in the sand.' I remember as a young girl learning about how the ostrich would stick its head in the sand so the enemy would think that it was a bush. The ostrich wouldn't pull its head out until the enemy had gone away. I really thought that, like the ostrich, if I didn't see it, it wasn't there and couldn't hurt me.''

Margaret continued to avoid dealing with her problems until certain events made her confront her feelings.

"My husband, Larry, was going through a custody battle with his ex-wife for their son. I had my daughter from my earlier marriage, and finally his son also moved in with us. We decided that we needed more money, so I went to work full-time. I was offered a job in an alcoholism treatment center as the after care treatment secretary. Part of my job was to cover staffings, and I began hearing the staff talk about patients who hadn't dealt with certain issues. I realized that I hadn't dealt with these issues, either, in three years of sobriety."

At this time Margaret's daughter came down with a serious illness, which reinforced the point that counseling was something the whole family needed. Margaret continued to go to AA meetings, but she felt she wasn't getting what she needed out of them. She was finding it more and more difficult to cope with her feelings. She began thinking that Valium would make her feel better, but she knew that that was just another side of her addiction. Finally she sought help through her supervisor at work, who helped her check into a recovery center.

"My first night there, one of the leaders of the group asked me if I'd ever thought of myself as a Child of an Alcoholic. All I could do was cry. That's when I began to work on my co-dependency issues. I began attending Al-Anon meetings in addition to my AA meetings.

Margaret's Alcoholic and Adult Child Issues.

"I truly believe it is almost impossible to be happy, joyous, and free in sobriety if you don't work on your Adult Child issues. And even if you don't know that you have any, they still have a way of surfacing on their own. In AA I sometimes feel alone and different. I'm glad I've found Al-Anon. There are a lot of Adult Children there. I don't know if I could stay sober without both groups.

"I didn't start focusing on my ACOA issues until I was faced with drinking again. There was a co-dependency group available in that program. I never really knew that my co-dependency issues were getting in the way of my recovery until I was hospitalized. And then I did so only because at that point I had to face the fact that just not drinking or using was no longer enough."

Margaret realized that the behavior she had learned as a child in an alcoholic family was making her own recovery more difficult.

"Several things were getting in the way of my recovery. One was my ability to 'look good' and 'act good' even though I was in turmoil. I would

do this at work and at AA meetings. Even if I'm pouring my heart out to somebody, I still have a way of coming across as though I'm able to handle it all by myself.

"I've always had difficulty asking for help—on top of an ability to endure intolerable situations for a long time. I stick my head in the sand and keep thinking things will get better or that the problem will go away. I also have trouble identifying my own feelings and my own needs. I'd rather try to 'fix' other people so I don't have to look at myself and take responsibility for what's happening.

"I began reading Adult Child literature and was able to recognize that 1) I had difficulty asking for help; 2) I had difficulty identifying feelings; 3) I preferred to fix others while negating myself; and 4) my enduring intolerable situations had been learned in childhood.

"By recognizing these issues, I've been able to work on them, but it's still very difficult for me. If someone identifies my feelings for me, I can tell if that person's perception is right or not, but I still find it hard to express those feelings myself. I used to think that the only feelings a person had were happy, sad, glad, and afraid. When I saw a feelings list, I was amazed at how many different feelings there were. I had decided at a very young age that I wasn't ever going to let anyone hurt me again. The only way to do that was not to feel. It has been very hard to unlearn that behavior.

"I've also had a hard time with my need to fix other people. I didn't know you couldn't do that. I thought that if I concentrated on everyone else, I wouldn't have to look at myself. So I concentrated on what was wrong with my husband, my stepson, my work, and the world in general. Thank God for Al-Anon! I still try focusing on other people sometimes, but my Al-Anon meeting brings me right back where I need to be."

Another issue that Margaret had to come to terms with was her denial of her mother's alcoholism and the effect that had on her.

"One of the things I've had to face is the fact that my mother is also an alcoholic. I had always known that my father was, but I had never thought my mother had a drinking problem until I got sober. Even then I never thought her drinking affected me.

"Through my Al-Anon program, I began to explore the feelings I had about my mother's drinking. I realized that even now when she drinks, I get scared and confused. I feel lonely, just the way I did when I was a child. She was never there for me. She was never available to comfort me when I cried. She was never there to help me with my homework. I

worry about her health, but I know that I cannot control her drinking. I love her, but when she drinks, the alcohol comes through and I lose her."

Margaret is learning to express her own needs. As an Adult Child, this is something that has always been extremely difficult for her.

"Because as a child I often didn't know what my needs were, they didn't get met. Then I would become angry with other people for not making me feel better. Yet I couldn't tell them what my needs were. I'm now having to deal with the fear of saying those needs out loud. When I do take the risk, though, people often respond positively. Now I'm able to recognize when I'm sitting on my feelings."

AA and Al-Anon are both essential parts of Margaret's recovery.

"I don't feel I could stay sober by just going to AA meetings. I need help with my ACOA issues, or I'll deceive myself into thinking that if I just took this or that, I wouldn't have to feel that way anymore. My recovery has been a rocky path. I'm grateful for AA, Al-Anon, and the ACOA concepts. While my path is still bumpy, the healing has begun."

JOE
Age: 54
Partner Status: Single, two children
Occupation: Accident investigator
Recovery Process: AA—three years
    sober, ACOA, Course in Miracles

Joe began drinking in his college years. He was chronically addicted to alcohol, cocaine, and a multitude of other drugs. Not only was he chemically dependent, but his compulsive personality fed into workaholism, sex addiction, and overeating. In spite of how chronic his addictions were, Joe first found recovery in Adult Child self-help groups, and from there he found his way to Alcoholics Anonymous.

JOE: "I was bankrupt. I was worse than zero in every area of my life, working just enough to scrape by, when my daughter called me one day. She had shared many times how alike she thought we were, how we both felt alienated, how no one understood us, how we knew that we were okay somehow, deep inside, but that something was screwed up.

"That day she had been to counseling, and she said, 'I finally found out what our problem is.' Then she began to tell me about her counseling and the Adult Child Twelve Step program. She brought me the literature, and I identified with it immediately. I knew that I had found the answer. I'd always asked, 'What's the matter with me?' My first Adult Child self-help group meeting was like a white light experience. Through the ACOA literature and meetings I began to realize what was the matter with me. I had a feeling of intense gratitude, of finally knowing that I'd identified the problem, and that I'd found the solution."

Joe said it was in ACOA that he discovered he didn't want to drink anymore. He didn't believe he was alcoholic, but he began to attend AA meetings regularly to help him not drink.

"Finally, after going to AA meetings for three months, I had heard enough people talk about their lives that one night it hit me. I was one of them! I began to work the program, and I was very content for six months until I hit my sober bottom. I couldn't function sober. I couldn't face life without medication. But I also knew that was no longer an option, that it wouldn't work.

"One night driving home, I stopped at a red light. I was crying, and then I heard this little voice—my inner guide, my Higher Power—say, 'Joe, you can recover or die. You can work the Twelve Steps or die. Those are your only two choices.'

"I had reached that point, the real bottom. My only options were recover or die. I was out of bullshit. I was all out of delays and fixes. I had to work the Twelve Steps or die. And I knew that. I called people that night, and I got sponsors, and I began to work the Twelve Steps in both AA and ACOA.

"I am three years past that point now, and I've had some very rough times. It's a roller coaster, and I've hit some very hard bottoms. But now I'm seeing that they get farther and farther apart, and less and less intense."

Joe's Alcoholic/Addict and Adult Child Issues.

"I have needed both AA and ACOA programs in my life. My AA program has helped me to stay sober, to not drink and use. And it has also taught me a great deal about living life on life's terms.

"My ACOA program has really taught me to break out of the patterns

of my past. I've been astounded when I've identified these hurtful patterns—seeing how what happened then has affected what happens now. This has given me the courage to change these patterns: my compulsive spending; my overeating; my self-destructive, self-defeating, suicidal behavior; my sexual obsessions; my workaholism; my pursuit of esteem through accomplishments; and my terror of abandonment. So much of this has come from listening to other people and their stories. I share, and I listen. Other people have helped me tremendously.

"For the most part, I've lived alone during recovery. I had a relationship in which I chose a partner who wasn't able to be there for me emotionally. For the first time I was able to move out of the relationship without falling into a suicidal, life-threatening depression."

Recovery from Adult Child issues of abandonment becomes evident when we can feel the pain of loss but not toss out all that is positive in our lives because one aspect hurts.

"My depression is almost nonexistent today. And I've made major progress in all of my chemical and nonchemical addictions. I'm clean and sober chemically. Nonchemically I'm much better in my workaholism, my terror of abandonment, and my compulsive spending. I still isolate myself at times. But I'm getting to feel better around groups of people, even though I still feel awkward occasionally. I'm certainly not perfect. But I'm on the right path, and I feel that things are getting better every day."

As people recover from chemical dependency, they often uncover other addictive patterns. It is unrealistic to expect to resolve all of these issues quickly. Patience is a virtue that needs to be developed. One way to do it is to acknowledge the little steps we take in the process.

"Often I have to look back at what I was like a month ago or six months ago or two years ago to realize how far I've come. Today I want everyone to know that I am happy. When I was in denial, I never once dreamed that I could ever be happy. When I was drinking, I'd forsaken all hope of ever being happy. But today I am. I'm happy even when external circumstances are not good. Basically I'm happy if I work my program and use my tools.

"I've learned to be my own loving parent. One of the major things I learned in my ACOA program was to get off my own case, to stop beating myself up verbally, to stop second-guessing, criticizing, and fault finding. I've learned to stop telling myself that I'll never be good enough, never be right. I've learned to tell myself that I'm okay. I know I'm going to

make a lot of errors—errors are a part of being human. I've had a lot to learn about just giving myself a break.''

In his recovery Joe has learned a great deal about forgiveness and self-love.

"My feelings about my parents have roller-coastered in my recovery years from intense hatred to an intense compulsion to rescue them. My dad has recently died. I will probably always wonder what he thought of me. Prior to his death I used the detachment I learned about in Al-Anon. I learned how to be there for my parents without hurting myself. I have also forgiven and released, and I think our relationship today is as good as it will ever get, and that's okay.''

Joe has discovered what is essential to so many recovering alcoholics/addicts, a way to allow a Higher Power to be incorporated into his life.

"The bottom line of my recovery is the concept that only God fills up the empty hole inside. I've tried to use everything else to fill it up, but it was never enough. I kept wondering what was missing, what was wrong. All my chemical and nonchemical dependencies were symptoms of the one disorder—my separation from a Higher Power. I had the insane belief that I knew better than God how to create myself and how to run and manage my own life. Today I almost always find that if things aren't going well, it means I've been trying to run my own life again, that I've been trying to get my own agenda in, and that I haven't been asking to know God's will for my life.

"The Course in Miracles has been another significant factor in facilitating my spiritual path. Through prayer and meditation I've been able to hear this inner voice better and better, and I've learned to trust it even further, and to use it as a daily guide. It's very important for me to stay in the here and now, one day at a time, and not try to see how everything fits into a pattern or plan for ten years down the line.

"I'm very grateful to AA, ACOA, and the Course in Miracles for bringing me back to the concept of a Higher Power. I find the knowledge that I can turn my life over to God very comforting.''

Profiles for Recovery

In this chapter we have discussed the stories of five chemically dependent people who have chosen to explore their Adult Child issues. Each individual has traveled a unique path to the integration of a sobriety program with ACOA work.

Dennis, at the age of thirty-two, has been sober the longest—ten years—as he begins his Adult Child work. He could not have begun it much earlier, as the concept and resources for Adult Child recovery have only been available within the last ten years. Also, most people beginning their Adult Child work are in their thirties and forties. It often takes time in adult life for these issues to escalate to the level where an Adult Child feels it necessary to seek recovery resources. Although Dennis is young, the fact that he had been a part of a Twelve Step program facilitated his ability to recognize problems earlier than other Adult Children and to seek resources. However, he was well entrenched in his recovery from addiction when he began his Adult Child recovery.

Bob and Margaret are clear that their Adult Child issues interfered with their ability to use their AA recovery program. It was necessary for them to work on these issues to prevent relapse.

Although Bob was in a self-help program, he was not able to stay abstinent. His ACOA issues repeatedly interfered with his sobriety, and he would drink. But once he sought professional help for his Adult Child issues, his alcoholism was soon recognized as the immediate issue of importance. Bob entered an alcoholism treatment program, and his focus, in early sobriety, was directed at his primary goal of abstinence. But the key to understanding his addiction lay in finally dealing with childhood issues around his alcoholic family. Only after he had begun this work was he able to accept his own alcoholism and his need to achieve and maintain sobriety.

When Margaret was a few years sober, she began rationalizing the use of Valium as a response to her problems with daily living. However, before she started to use, she was directed to an ACOA program, and at last her day-to-day problems began to resolve themselves.

Lisa may have had more time before her Adult Child issues smacked into her recovery process, but grief at the death of her teenage son, when she was only a year sober, put her in touch with family-of-origin issues that could no longer be denied or ignored.

Joe is one of a small but growing percentage of people who seek help for ACOA issues first and in doing so recognize their own alcoholism and get help for it.

No matter which profile one identifies with, it is my strong belief that Adult Child issues will in time deeply affect the quality of a person's sobriety. Exploring one's double identity as an Adult Child and addict can be an extremely fruitful source for self-examination and long-term recovery.

ALCOHOL/ADDICT TEENAGERS AND COA RECOVERY

This chapter has been directed toward the Adult Child who is chemically dependent—not to the chemically dependent teenager. But it is my belief that these young people also have two identities. However, while I believe it is both possible and more appropriate for Adult Child alcoholics/addicts to separate their issues, I find neither to be true for the COA teenager. The older teens—seventeen-, eighteen-, nineteen-year olds—may be able to deal with these issues separately, particularly if they do not live at home. But while younger teens, and those at home, need first and foremost to understand the need for total abstinence, it is crucial for them to work on COA issues simultaneously. They need a place to share their feelings about their family life. They need adults outside the home to provide structure and places where they can be involved in age-appropriate activities. They need to learn the traditional Al-Anon principles of how to live in their families while also taking the best care of themselves.

RECOVERY RESOURCES

There is no one right way to receive help. There is no one way to experience recovery. However, given the nature of the disease of chemical dependency, I feel it becomes one's primary identity. Being an Adult Child, then, is one's secondary identity. It is my bias that one cannot fully address one's Adult Child issues if one is not clean and sober. Practicing chemically dependent people are not capable of being honest with themselves or anyone else. They think delusionally.

The most likely resources for recovery lie in two areas. First, the self-help groups: Alcoholics Anonymous, Cocaine Anonymous, Narcotics Anonymous. More people have received help through these Twelve Step programs than any other resource. Self-help groups are free of charge and widespread throughout the world. See the appendix, page 551, for additional information.

Second, there are the chemical dependency treatment programs. These are professionally staffed and structured programs that may be outpatient or inpatient. Although there are inpatient services that offer a detoxification program, usually both inpatient and outpatient services offer individual and group therapy resources. Available resources and costs vary. Local councils on alcoholism and information and referral sources are listed in the Yellow Pages under "Alcoholism Information and Treatment Centers."

People can and do recover through other resources as well—for example, through their church, spiritual therapy, and other kinds of self-help support groups. But for the majority of chemically dependent people, the answers tend to be found in the combination of Twelve Step self-help groups and professional treatment.

Resources for working on Adult Child issues include individual and group psychotherapy as well as such Twelve Step programs as the Adult Children of Alcoholics and Co-Dependency Anonymous self-help groups. Traditional Al-Anon meetings have always been and continue to be another resource for Adult Children. People who have Double Duty issues or are Dual Identity may find it safer to begin recovery with a helping professional. But even where this is true, it also helps to be open to the transition of using self-help groups as well.

SPECIAL CHALLENGE OF SUPPORT

One of the difficulties recovering alcoholics and addicts often encounter in pursuing their Adult Child work is a lack of support from other recovering alcoholic/addicts.

It is difficult for people who have found a path that has produced miracles in their lives to be open to another approach, particularly one that touches so closely on areas where they are extremely vulnerable. They are often critical of others as a defense. As chemically dependent parents, they are vulnerable about the way their addictions have affected their own children and, again as a defense against their own pain, are critical of others wanting to do Adult Child work.

When this occurs, it is important to remember that you are getting feedback from individual personalities within a recovery program. It is not the program itself that is being critical. Nowhere in the writings of Alcoholics Anonymous and Al-Anon does it say that one should continue to minimize, discount, or deny the pain of one's past. Above all, these are programs that recommend honesty as a basis for recovery; these are programs that teach self-responsibility.

Adult Child recovery means taking responsibility for oneself today as an adult. To do that, people have to explore their childhood years, speak the truth of their experiences, reframe hurtful internalized beliefs, and learn skills that they didn't have an opportunity to learn as children. Adult Child recovery is not meant to replace addiction recovery. It is meant to enhance every part of who one is.

Although people approach these issues from different directions, it is clear that when one is both an Adult Child and chemically dependent, one has two identities. The issues that affect both of these identities must be addressed if recovery is to be ongoing.

My recovery has taught me that I am not my father. I am different. I am thirty-seven; he is sixty-two. I am recovering; he is not. He brought his family full term into their Adult Child issues; I am doing what I can to break the cycle for my family in my lifetime.

—Adult Child, Recovering Alcoholic

Notes

1. C. Black, S. Bucky, S. Padilla, "The Interpersonal and Emotional Consequences of Being an Adult Child of an Alcoholic," *Journal of International Addictions* 21 (May 1986) 213–32.
2. A. Hrubec and G. S. Omenn, "Evidence of Genetic Predisposition to Alcoholic Cirrhosis and Psychosis: Twin Concordances for Alcoholism and Its Biological End Points by Zygosity Among Male Veterans," *Alcoholism: Clinical and Experimental Research* 5 (1981): 207–15.
3. M. Bohman, *Archives of General Psychiatry* 35 (1978): 269–76; M. Bohman et al., *Archives of General Psychiatry* 38 (1978): 965–69; D. W. Goodwin, *Archives of General Psychiatry* 34 (1985) 751–55.
4. J. C. Kern et al., *Journal of Psychiatric Treatment and Evaluation* 3 (1981): 169–73.
5. M. A. Schuckit and V. Rayses, *Science* 203 (1979): 54–55.
6. M. A. Schuckit, *Journal of Studies on Alcohol* 45 (1984): 334–38; *Archives of General Psychiatry* 41 (1984): 879–84.

8

Gay and Lesbian

Fear was what I knew growing up. I was afraid of coming home, being home, of leaving home, of being away from home. I didn't want to be whoever I was or wherever I was.

—A Gay ACOA

"Dual Identity," a special form of Double Duty, means experiencing two identities simultaneously. In this case it is being both an Adult Child and gay or lesbian as well. Dual Identity often magnifies one's Adult Child issues. Because so many people are fearful and prejudicial toward homosexuality, gays and lesbians often face a constant struggle to feel good about themselves. Experiencing the homophobia so prevalent in our society, whether covert or overt, becomes a way of life.

When still quite young, many gays and lesbians learn to both deny and hide important aspects of the self from themselves and others. This leads to confusion and difficulty in trusting their own feelings and perceptions. They may find it difficult to trust others and to live with others' judgment, rejections, or punishment. They learn that to survive—to avoid being verbally, emotionally, and possibly even physically abused—a part of them must remain invisible. This continual discounting of self makes it difficult for them to feel good about who they are. As a result they segregate or fragment parts of their selves and their lives. Unfortunately, this often results in isolation.

While homosexual children may have had to deny who they are in terms of their sexuality, children in the alcoholic family have had to deny their feelings and experiences of living in a deeply dysfunctional family. The tendency is to ignore one or the other of these issues, not recognizing how the combined dynamics of being both an Adult Child and homosexual reinforce each other. This chapter is about validating these experiences and how the dynamics of being lesbian or gay in an alcoholic family are profound examples of the Double Duty syndrome.

Growing up in an alcoholic family is difficult all by itself. Growing up gay or lesbian in an alcoholic home creates an environment in which children have an even greater need to defend and protect themselves from being hurt.

Although homosexuality and chemical dependency are different phenomena, COAs and gay and lesbian children often respond to their cumulative life stresses similarly. Loneliness, fear, isolation, denial, shame, being secretive, and not feeling good about oneself are already common issues for many gays and lesbians. Unless they were raised in an atmosphere that encourages them to develop high esteem, society's homophobia has made it necessary for gays and lesbians to adopt many Adult Child strategies. Both have to respond to an environment that does not feel safe: on the one hand the threat is posed by the community, on the other by the family. This leaves very little room to hide.

As young children they internalized terribly hurtful messages:

- You are different.
- You should be ashamed of what you do and therefore ashamed of who you are.
- It is not okay to be who you are.
- You can't trust your perceptions.
- You mustn't talk about what is occurring.

These unspoken messages create a life of guilt and shame—a life ruled by secrets and denial. With that denial comes incredible fear, loneliness, isolation, and self-loathing. Unfortunately, too often neither gays and lesbians nor COAs experience any sense of belonging. Yet the sense of belonging, of feeling connected with others, is vital to a child's development and sense of self-worth. Growing up, many gays and lesbians have a sense that they are different, and yet they wonder why.

Not every gay or lesbian will identify with these issues, nor has every gay or lesbian had these experiences, but these experiences are very common themes for the gay and lesbian Adult Child.

Life Stories: Growing-Up Years

The following life stories are from five gays and lesbians, ranging in age from twenty-eight to forty-two, who were raised in chemically dependent families. During adolescence, all but one recognized that their sexual orientation was different from that of their peers. But for all of them the struggle around "coming out" publicly as gay or lesbian was relatively brief. They all accepted their sexuality at a young age. Clearly, being children in alcoholic families was much more traumatic than being homosexual in a heterosexual society.

Although we will discuss a number of issues, we will explore in depth the intensified dynamics of secrets and denial, guilt and shame, coming out, and Adult Child recovery considerations.

Please keep in mind that although the following stories are about people raised in chemically dependent families, it is not my contention or theory that being raised in a dysfunctional family creates homosexuality. There are a multitude of theories regarding homosexuality, ranging from physiological to psychological frameworks. These are gay and lesbian children who happen to live in disturbed families. In a few of these stories you will see how a child may feel greater safety with the parent of one sex as opposed to another. And you'll be able to trace how such limited interactions may strongly influence later friendships and even shape the coming-out process. Nevertheless, being raised in an alcoholic/dysfunctional family is not cited as a cause of homosexuality.

ADRIENNE
Age: 33
Mother: Alcoholic
Father: Alcoholic
Stepfather: Alcoholic
Birth Order: Youngest of four
Raised: Midwest
Socioeconomic Status: Working
    class

Born into a family of two alcoholics, Adrienne was conceived as the result of one of her mother's extramarital affairs. She says that both her mother and her mother's husband were alcoholics for as long as she can remember, as were most of the people they associated with.

Adrienne's earliest memory was that of guilt.

ADRIENNE: *"I felt guilt for being alive. I was told that kids were to be seen and not heard, and I got the distinct impression that they were a hassle to have around. This, in addition to fear, shame, and isolation, dictated how I felt about myself as a child, as a young woman, and as a lesbian."*

When Adrienne was three her mother married Ed, her third husband. He was a violent, abusive man who constantly criticized and threatened Adrienne and her three older siblings.

"I would cower in bed listening to my parents fight and waiting for it to escalate into physical violence. At this point I would calmly walk out, sit down, and watch him.

"My mother told me that Ed would be less likely to hit her with me around—so I understood it was up to me to save her. When I was nine and doing 'guard duty' during one of these episodes, Ed put a gun to my head and threatened to kill me and my mother. I remember sitting there smirking, and thinking, F—— you.

"I hated my stepfather. My allegiance was to my mother, who I literally saw as my lifeline and comrade. Together, we would scheme how to deal with him, how to negotiate around his moods. I prided myself on being 'the best at handling him' of all the siblings and at being considered very grown-up for my age. I felt repeatedly devastated and betrayed when my mother would take him back after he'd beaten her or my brother. We owned two houses side by side—one supposedly for guests, but which was used more frequently as Ed's 'doghouse.' He had to stay there as punishment for beating up my mother or threatening us all. Whenever this happened, the local police would be called, and they would sit patiently in the driveway waiting for the whole thing to calm down."

Adrienne was caught in a web of confusion. She vacillated between feeling like her mother's confidante and protector and feeling abandoned. This is because, when Adrienne's stepfather wasn't available, her mother relied on Adrienne's strength and ability to cope. But when the stepfather was available, her mother relegated Adrienne to the role of neglected child.

"Growing up, I felt I was never quite good enough. But I also felt I should know how to do everything perfectly without any explanations. It

was unsafe to ask questions, since my stepfather might call me stupid or scoff at my not knowing. I learned to fake things quite early. I faked being courageous, tough, and self-sufficient when I was actually very needy and scared. I faked knowing how to do something when I was confused and frightened, so that my ignorance would not be revealed. I faked being together and unaffected by criticism and humiliating comments, when I was really emotionally devastated.''

"Never feeling good enough" is a common consequence of the stresses experienced by COAs, and Adrienne gained a lot of practice at this long before she would even know that her sexual identity would be added to the list of her inadequacies.

"School was always just sort of an okay place to be. I was an above average student as a way to get approval from teachers. I wanted to be liked. Fortunately, one teacher gave me a lot of encouragement with my writing, and that helped me aspire toward college.

"But I was most influenced by my family. My stepfather was extremely sexist and bigoted—a mean version of Archie Bunker. I got the message at an early age that it was bad to be female and therefore horrendous to be lesbian. He believed that women were stupid and inept, and in fact my mother seemed basically weak and powerless around him. She worked as an uncredited partner in their various businesses, smoothing over his rough relationships with people—but all he did was criticize her constantly. I got the idea that men were a hassle, like having another child to take care of. They had to be humored and manipulated.''

Adrienne's siblings were considerably older than she, a sister and brother fifteen and thirteen years older and another brother seven years older. Adrienne felt closest to the older brother. She describes him as the family hero and remembers looking to him as a father at times. She remembers him as the only gentle man in her life. But Adrienne did as so many COAs do—she sought refuge outside the home.

"I spent as much time as possible away from home. Happy childhood memories are mostly of times I spent at my grandmother's home or at the home of my baby-sitter, who was a grandmotherly sort of person. My own grandma moved away when I was six, but she returned when I was eleven. I always had this feeling that I didn't quite belong at home, that home wasn't safe. For most of my young adulthood I continued to act this out, not really settling into places where I supposedly lived, and letting myself be 'adopted' by established couples.

"When I got involved in my first major, healthy relationship four years

ago, I continued to sleep on friends' couches at least once a week during the first months of living with my lover because I simply didn't feel safe where I lived.

"As I became aware of my sexual and romantic feelings for women, it never occurred to me to consider telling anyone. At eleven I was crazy about my best friend, and my first crush was on my high school gym teacher. I was sure that I was the only one who was falling in love with and sexually fantasizing about her girlfriends.

"To figure out what was 'wrong' with me I read Everything You Always Wanted to Know About Sex, *which I read as saying basically that homosexuality is a sickness. I believed this and clung to the author's assertion that adolescents might have homosexual feelings until they turned fifteen or sixteen, after which they would (hopefully) become normal. I was crushed when I turned sixteen and was still sexually and emotionally attracted to my girlfriends, my brother's wife, and my teachers. I felt that my lesbianism was literally a curse, and I was later shocked to discover that some women actually chose to become lesbians."*

At such a young age, Adrienne internalized that she was wrong for loving girls. Already having learned that it wasn't safe to talk about her feelings and ask questions openly, she refused to squelch her feelings totally but secretly sought information through reading. However, she would find that the literature classified homosexuality as a sickness, a malady of the mind. Having received no validation for homosexuality as a natural way of being, wherein she could find acceptance for herself in the world, she secretly hoped her feelings would change.

At the time Adrienne graduated from high school she was actively involved in what she called "street fundamentalist Christianity." She was enrolled in a religious college, but her stepfather was not willing to financially support her there, so she enrolled in a state college. Over the next few years she struggled with her sexual identity, assuming that the right person could help her become straight. However, by the time Adrienne graduated from college she had come to accept her lesbianism.

JOHN
Age: 28
Mother: Co-dependent
Father: Alcoholic
Additional: Parents recovering
    today
Birth Order: Youngest of six
Raised: Southeast
Socioeconomic Status: Upper
    middle class

The youngest of five children, John grew up with a father who was an alcoholic and a mother who spent a good part of his youngest years in and out of hospitals. (Some of the hospitalizations were for medical reasons, others were stress-related.) John himself was often very sick as a child. He had an operation when he was six for an inherited upper-respiratory disease and several eye operations as well. John's father was a builder, his mother a housewife.

John's mother was hospitalized for the first time when he was four. He described those times as confusing and frightening.

JOHN: "We would get notes from her. But I was always protected from all information. No one would explain to me why she was in the hospital. I don't know if my brothers and sisters were kept as protected as I was. At some point I was told she had tumors in her head.

"What I remember so clearly about my younger years was that I used to lie down on the floor next to the vent that led to my parents' bathroom, and I would hear my mother crying all the time. She would go and hide in the bathroom and just sob for hours. This happened every night. Dad would be asleep on the couch, and Mom would have done all the dishes. Then she would go upstairs and cry. I would lie there, listening to her, because I knew it was as close as I could get to her. She would go to church all the time, and I could not imagine why this God she worshiped would put her through so much pain and agony."

During his growing-up years, John related much more to his siblings and his mother.

"My father was the provider. It was as if he was this person who was 'out there.' He was away from the house a lot. When he was home I

*remember most the unpredictability of his moods and how we were sup-
posed to behave. The message was loud and clear. We were responsible
for his moods. My strongest image of him was dozing on the couch. This
was also the time we would ask him for things. He would murmur 'Yes'
just to get us out of there. I don't remember ever connecting any of what
was occurring with alcohol and certainly not with alcoholism.''*

John's childhood relationships with his siblings were varied and typical
of both a large family and an alcoholic family. He describes his relationship
with his oldest brother as one of great rivalry and remembers they fought
a lot. He saw this brother as the family foot soldier, the little adult trying
to be in charge. John idolized his oldest sister and wanted to get close to
her, but it was as if she were always just out of reach. He saw her as
someone safe yet far away from him.

He remembers that he and his middle sister were particularly close.
She was his protector, his mediator, his mother, tucking him into bed
each night. He says he and his youngest sister would always plan things
to do together, but being close in age they were forever arguing.

John idolized his second oldest brother, Paul, who was also gay. During
his teens John made many attempts to reach out to Paul, sensing that
they might be able to talk about the sexual feelings John was having. But
Paul seemed scared and avoided talking with John. How much of the
"Don't talk" rule Paul was abiding by—due to the fear and shame of
being gay, or to the isolation of being in a chemically dependent home—
is difficult to say. Most likely both played a role.

John attempted to deal with the family dynamics by taking on various
roles at different times.

*"I played every role there is in the alcoholic family: I adjusted; I was a
placater; I was the responsible one; I was all of those things at different
times. I acted out as well.''*

John was aware of his sexual attraction by the time he was nine.

*"My first gay encounter was when I was in the fifth grade, and it contin-
ued with the same person until I was a junior in college. The 'Don't talk'
rule was firmly intact. We never discussed what we were doing. From
the beginning we used either alcohol or pot in order to be sexual. We
started by taking shots from his dad's liquor cabinet, and that would make
the sex okay. As the years of our interactions progressed, so did our use
of chemicals. My adolescence was made up of fear, secrecy, and repression. Alcohol and other drugs were clearly an answer for me.*

"My own addiction began when I was only twelve years old. Even when I was as young as six, I remember the buzz I would feel when I drank cough syrup. I used to love it! By the time I was twelve, alcohol had become a major form of escape."

John's own addiction precluded his having many clear memories of his family during his teenage years. In many ways he became a lost child, lost to alcohol, drugs, fear.

John's use of alcohol and drugs began at a young age, which is often true for COAs. Many begin to drink and use by the time they're eleven or twelve. John's use of pot and alcohol during sexual encounters is not unusual for either heterosexuals or homosexuals. In preadolescence and adolescence, sexual behavior is often synonymous with drinking and using.

John's fear of being caught and of making others ashamed of him were far more traumatic for him than his actual sexual behavior. Clearly, he was being raised in a family so shrouded in secrets that no matter what his sexual behavior might be, it would have been performed behind a veil of secrecy. The fact that his behavior was homosexual simply multiplied his fears. Alcohol and drugs would become a temporary answer to both his fear and his secretive behavior.

KIM
Age: 33
Mother: Chemically Dependent
Father: Co-dependent
Birth Order: Third of four children
Raised: West Coast
Socioeconomic Status: Upper
    middle class

Kim grew up with well-educated, liberal, professional parents. When she was three her mother was hospitalized for the first time with a "breakdown"—and this led to abuse of tranquilizers and alcohol.

Kim says she remembers being given a lot of attention in her first three years.

KIM: "And I spent the next twenty years trying to recapture that time. My mother was the type of person who drank in isolation. She would go to her bedroom and lock the door for hours—even days."

Kim also remembers that her mother had good times as well as bad. But Kim had a sister who was severely depressed.

"My mother saved her good times for my sister."

Kim spent her growing-up years by being the "junior mom" in the family.

"I was responsible and a hard worker. I got good grades in school and took care of my depressed sister. Through my adolescence I continued doing many mother-type things, also playing lots of sports—that was my relief. My oldest brother escaped early by getting the most healthy family time. Then he left for college. My next brother was an angry scapegoat, always in trouble and being punished; I was the family caretaker and responsible child. My sister internalized everything and became progressively more depressed. She committed suicide at eighteen.

"My focus of concern was the family. I was the only child who really named the elephant in the living room. I pointed out to my parents repeatedly and loudly that they had problems. Finally, one night at the dinner table when I was sixteen, I announced flat out that my mom had a drinking problem. It was denied. It was then I started trying to figure out how I could leave—and if that would be deserting my sister.

"I took my mother's inaccessibility very personally. I went around looking for nurturing, and got a lot of it from the mothers of my girlfriends, particularly my best friend's mother. Female teachers were also very important. My girlfriends were very important. What I felt as a teen was that if anything happened to any of my close friends, I would die. When my best friend would be gone for two weeks every year on a family vacation, I'd be almost nonfunctional with worry. She, and her family, were like emotional life rafts to me."

Kim's ability to depend on her friends for emotional support was one of her strengths. This response to her unhappy home life was not driven by her sexuality—it was the reaction of a young COA seeking friendship and validation.

Aside from "one moment" during her teens, Kim was not aware of feeling sexually attracted to women until she was in her twenties. The one moment took place one night when she was fifteen. A girlfriend was spending the night. While they were sleeping in separate beds in the middle of the night, their arms touched.

"It didn't feel sexual, but I knew there was something different. It was not just a casual touch. But I didn't spend any time thinking about it. I

had boyfriends. But although the time I spent with boyfriends was pleasant enough, looking back, I'm aware that it was as if I was waiting for something more. Boyfriends were just a ho-hum experience.''

Kim felt a strong bond with the women in her life but would come to experience great loss in her relationships with all three women in her immediate family.

"Through my youth, three females in my family were most important to me—my mother, my sister, and my aunt. But by my mid-teens, my mother's disease was progressing, my sister was going nuts, and my aunt had moved across the country.''

The loss Kim experienced in her relationships with significant males in her life was not as strong as the loss she felt with the three women. Kim never had the opportunity to develop a strong initial male bond.

"There were three men in my life at the same time, but for whatever reasons, they were not as important to me emotionally. I blamed my father for my mother's inaccessibility, because he was often the gatekeeper between her and myself. He was preoccupied with work, my mom, and their traveling. My parents had invested wisely and often traveled abroad. I remember clearly being told, 'We need some time away from you kids.' I idolized my oldest brother, but he wasn't around very much. And my parents set up my older brother and me as rivals. Although I was younger, they perceived me as the most capable and gave me more responsibility, which my brother greatly resented.''

DAVID
Age: 32
Mother: Co-dependent
Father: Alcoholic, violent
Birth Order: Youngest of three
Raised: Northwest
Socioeconomic Status: Working
    class

David grew up with an alcoholic father who was constantly depressed and suicidal. He describes his family life as a mixture of his father's violence and his mother's pleas for the violence to stop. The parents were so focused on each other that they basically neglected and ignored their three children.

DAVID: "They never had time for us. We were three little parents at a very young age. I liked playing house with my sister. At first glance my family looked very nonsexist, allowing their little boy to dress in girls' clothing and play 'housewife.' But in reality our parents had little interest in the differences among us. We were simply 'the children,' and as such we were kept sheltered as much as possible from the insanity that surrounded us. My mom would try to shelter us by redirecting Dad's attention away from us—keeping us on a separate floor from Dad or trying to calm him down in front of us. Or we were used in little ploys to keep my father from doing something crazy, like leaving my mother or killing himself. I do not remember one day when my father was not drunk.

"My house was predictably unpredictable. After a while, the nightmarishness became commonplace, and my father's self-involved, depressive, suicidal behavior was the expected norm. But I never got over the anxiety; neither did my brother and sister. We didn't talk about it much, though. I remember once declaring to them that I didn't believe in God, because He did not stop my daddy from drinking. The unfairness of the world hit me at a young age. I was angry—incredibly so."

David felt despised by his father. He felt he was never "good enough" for his father, that there was something wrong with him.

"We never talked. We never got along. As time went on, it didn't matter what my father wanted, and it didn't matter what I did—he was always dissatisfied. I felt singled out by him. It was not that he saw me as unique, but rather that somehow I touched a primitive sort of nerve in him, and he despised me.

"He would drink, and cry, and tell me that he loved me. But then he'd let the neighbor's kids ride the tractor on our farm—a pleasure that my younger brother and I were denied because we 'might get hurt.' Of course my sister wasn't allowed to do these things, either—she was a girl, and he didn't like girls much. Although a drunk, my father was an incredibly perceptive man. It may have been the part of me that was feminine rather than effeminate that he so disliked."

When David reached puberty he realized that he was "different" from his friends. He tried to alter his behavior in order to fit in.

"As I approached puberty, I awaited the time when, like my friends, I would start to look at girls' breasts and be interested enough to make

lewd bathroom comments. Instead, I learned to be quite a little actor. I would talk about the female physique with as much fervor as my friends, but I felt like a fake.

"I began to read books about sex. I was aware that I was attracted to some of the male teachers and to some of the boys in high school, and I was terrified. I began to feel the same sense of loss that I felt about my family. I had never experienced the kind of family that television depicted on My Three Sons *and* Father Knows Best. *Now I was cheated again because I saw my friends experiencing something I was not able to— adolescence."*

David desperately needed to feel validation for being who he was. He wasn't asking for a lot—simply to have a basic childhood need met. But by adolescence he knew this validation would never come from his father. Yet when the time came that he knew he should be able to get it from his friends, his lack of sexual interest in girls made him feel that his own body and heart had betrayed him. Once more he was to find that he was perceived as different in a way that was not acceptable.

"So I escaped into fantasy. I became obsessed with rock-and-roll singers and dreamed of living in faraway places. I drew, and I wrote poetry. And I denied every feeling.

"I also escaped into mystical books. The writings of Kahlil Gibran seemed to be a source of purity—they gave me a sense of peace. I was continually torn between my desire for security, sunlight, and joy—and the cloudlike darkness that overshadowed my home.

"Being gay, even though I was fighting it, was just one more struggle I had to go through. Once again I couldn't live normally. All I'd ever wanted was to live and feel normal. I wanted to have happy parents who were nice to each other and the kids. I wanted a father I could talk to. And now I didn't even feel a part of my friends. I couldn't join in the conversation because I wasn't interested in girls and I wasn't athletic.

"There was a double loss—the loss of family image and family life and the loss of friendships and peers. And then came a third major loss. Everything I was reading about gay men told me they were effeminate and listened to disco music. Once again I didn't fit in. I was a hiker and a gardener. I listened to Crosby, Stills, and Nash. I didn't even fit into what I thought the gay world was!"

JEAN
Age: 42
Mother: Co-dependent
Father: Alcoholic
Birth Order: Oldest of two
Raised: South
Socioeconomic Status: Middle class

Jean grew up with an alcoholic father whose rages made family life frightening and miserable. Jean's mother was very co-dependent and constantly catered to or excused her husband's behavior.

JEAN: *"Even before my father had begun to drink a lot, he was volatile and very angry. He had a raging temper, with no patience or tolerance for anything. He would misplace his tools and then blame my brother or me. He would yell if he got frustrated trying to do a project around the house. He would yell at my mother for forgetting to put milk on the table for his coffee, even though she waited on him hand and foot. He would yell about the neighbors, about his co-workers, or his boss—but he would never confront them directly. I was afraid of my dad. The drinking just made it worse. I would do anything to stay out of his way."*

By the time Jean was nine, her father's drinking had increased significantly. At the same time, her mother began to work outside the home.

"We never talked about what was really going on. We pretended that our family life was happy. But it was violent with a lot of yelling and drinking. We never knew when Dad would be home or how bad he would be when he arrived.

"I remember one Christmas Eve when we were getting ready to go to my grandmother's house to celebrate with the family. My father was raging drunk and threw all of my mother's clothes out the door into the snow. There was screaming and tears. But when we got to my grandmother's, Mother made excuses for my dad not being with us, saying he wasn't feeling well. And she reminded my brother and me not to tell what had really happened. Christmases were filled with fights and drinking. They were filled with fear and faking it—pretending that everything was wonderful. Faking it was the only way to survive."

Sadly, Jean's life was typical of many COAs, ridden with chronic fear. She was clearly afraid of her father's behavior whenever he was around and terrified of what he might do in the future. Jean's emotional survival was based on suppressing these fears and pretending that life was wonderful. That fear increased her need to deny. And before long she was going to have to learn that it was necessary to deny her "differentness" as well.

"I felt different in the first place because my dad yelled and got drunk and because I couldn't talk with anyone about it. But I also felt different because I was a tomboy and always wanted to do things that boys were allowed to do, like play baseball and football, climb trees, and play with trucks. I also felt different toward other girls. And I knew I felt different. I would feel protective, like I knew guys were supposed to feel about girls."

Jean's first crush was on a camp counselor when she was eight years old.

"She was not particularly attractive, but she was warm, gentle, and loving. I felt safe with her, and I felt strong with her. I could forget all the battles and the drunken rages of home when I was away in a safe place like camp."

Jean felt awkward about feeling attracted toward her female friends or teachers and kept her feelings secret from her friends. When she was sixteen she began dating boys.

"I was attractive and popular, so I dated frequently. I usually went out with two or three guys at the same time, never going steady with one particular boy. They were nice, boys my mother would approve of."

It was also at this time that her mother learned to drive, bought a car, and moved Jean and her brother out of the house.

"It was a secret move, while my dad was at work. My mother took only the bare essentials because she didn't want to leave my dad with nothing. We moved because my dad's drinking and raging were getting worse. We were gone for only a few months, but I remember this as a very calm and peaceful time.

"I had been my mother's confidante since I was twelve, and now I was my mother's counselor as well. I listened without sharing any of my own feelings. My role was to be there for my mother. It made me feel very adult. I loved it because it gave me a connection with my mother.

"But then my parents reconciled, and we moved back home. My dad learned to control his temper, and my mother learned how not to provoke a fight. We spent the next couple of years walking on eggshells.

"Although I still had this sense of being different, by the time I was in high school I was fitting in more. I was in the band, I was in honors classes, and I was college-directed. My mother's father wouldn't send her to college because he said it was no place for women. But my mother had always encouraged me to get a college education. Surprisingly, my father was also proud of my academic achievements and supported my going to college. I graduated from high school at seventeen and moved out of that environment when I entered college in the fall."

Irrespective of the fact that Adrienne, John, Kim, David, and Jean are gay and lesbian, they were children brought up in families affected by chaos, unpredictability, and unrealistic expectations on the part of the parents. They lived with chronic fear and loneliness. Adrienne had to respond to chronic physical abuse; John was a chronically ill child whose father was absent a lot and a nonentity when home and whose mother was so emotionally distraught that she required hospitalization. Both Kim and John describe their parents as extremely inaccessible, clearly due to the chemical dependency and co-dependency. David was extremely anxious from living with a very critical alcoholic father who fluctuated from suicidal depression to violence. Jean lived in chronic fear of the next argument or fight. Their struggle to feel "good enough," "adequate," and "of value," will be significant as a result of their being Adult Children.

These are people who deserve a path to recovery for the losses and traumas of their childhood. Acceptance of themselves, including their homosexuality, is much more likely when ACOA issues are addressed.

Special Issues for Gay and Lesbian ACOAs

SECRETS AND DENIAL

Gay and lesbian Adult Children have spent their lives keeping secrets. Like other children in alcoholic homes, they have had to keep the secret of the alcoholism. But on top of this, gays and lesbians are burdened with the secret of their own sexual identities, finding it necessary to keep secrets from a family that is already laden with secrets. This results in the "living the lie" syndrome, in which the children have to deny both what the family is and who they are. They become adroit actors, keeping up the illusion of a heterosexual self as well. These secrets accentuate the fear and shame of being discovered.

For Adrienne, keeping secrets was an accepted, seemingly necessary, and at times an even enjoyable part of everyday life in her family.

ADRIENNE: "When I was young I was puzzled by the thought that in court people were expected to 'tell the truth, the whole truth, and nothing but the truth' just because they had their hand on a Bible and were on a witness stand. It seemed ridiculous to think that someone would tell the truth when at best it would probably get them into trouble and at worst bring punishment and ridicule."

Adrienne remembers conspiring with her mother to keep secrets from her stepfather.

"I'd feel clever and passively victorious at 'putting one over' on him. When he called me stupid, in addition to feeling stupid and bad, I would also revel in the fact that I could successfully lie to and manipulate him. There was no positive payoff for being honest for honesty's sake, so I learned to omit information and to lie whenever it was necessary to protect myself. As a co-alcoholic, I also distorted and omitted information whenever I thought some-one 'couldn't handle' the real facts. I was also passive-aggressive and used sarcasm or the silent treatment to express anger.

"My friends were all ACOAs, so the violent, erratic behavior of male alcoholics seemed normal. I thought and acted as though people from nonalcoholic families were boring. I lied to myself, denying that my family was oppressive and abusive, that in fact I would have loved to trade in my family for an Ozzie and Harriet model."

It is very difficult for children raised in alcoholic families to say, "I hurt," "I'm sad," or "I'm afraid." But it is doubly difficult and unsafe for gay and lesbian COAs to say those things. Children who feel hopeless, who doubt that life could ever be different, tend to do what Adrienne did—they take pride in learning how to survive. For instance, Adrienne was proud of her ability to lie and manipulate. Such children feel strength in their anger, and they will scoff at what seems to them to be an impossible dream—a nonoppressive, nonabusive family.

The secret-keeping skills that Adrienne learned in her chemically dependent family made it easier for her to keep her sexual feelings a secret, too.

"When my lesbianism began to emerge at the age of nine, I kept these feelings a secret. They just confirmed my sense of being guilty, defective, not good enough."

Being raised in such an abusive family environment, Adrienne had already strongly internalized a sense of shame. She was also hearing clear messages that to be homosexual was bad. So when she became aware of her physical attraction to girls, this added a new burden of shame.

John said he learned to keep secrets at a very young age.

JOHN: *"It was easy to do because nobody wanted to talk about anything that was going on. I spent most of my childhood afraid.*

"I was fearful of being ostracized because I'd seen a neighbor do that to his gay son. I saw and heard teenagers pick on gay guys. As a little kid I was already being picked on for that. I was constantly afraid of being beaten up. Their verbal threats and name calling really terrified me.

"I never told anybody until I was seventeen that I was gay because I was scared to death. I was not only afraid that others would find out about my being gay, but I was afraid that my family would be criticized for my gayness.

"I also didn't want to add to the family pain. We already had so many problems. One of my sisters was abusing chemicals, two sisters had eating disorders, and one brother was openly gay. And, of course, there were my alcoholic parents. I was so afraid of being a negative reflection on my parents."

It is ironic that John was still trying to uphold the family "image" when it was already riddled with stigmatic addictions. John's reactions to his family's dysfunction reflects the incredible strength of his denial and the desire to be a caretaker.

John's need to cover up his true feelings, his true identity, led him to do various things to convince other people he was okay, which to John meant not being identified as gay.

"Anyone who has ever tried to hide a secret knows the games we play with ourselves and others in order not to be found out. Overtly we change our expressions, our manners. We become accustomed to delivering desired responses, signals, and messages. We alter our stories, abilities, and pronouns. This game of trickery requires constant attention and energy, and we end up living a chronic and painful lie."

The denial that goes into maintaining the false image of normality plays a big part in the life of an alcoholic family. Although members of the family are often silent about the secret of family alcoholism, it is nevertheless a secret they all maintain together. Yet being gay or lesbian is an individual secret that creates even more isolation for the homosexual COA.

This need to deny and the sense of faking it makes it very hard for gay and lesbian children to interact socially with other children their age. They often feel like outsiders when they're with peers—outsiders twice over, first because of the secrets of their home life and second because of their sexuality.

JEAN: "I felt different from the beginning. I always wanted to be a boy. Even when I was as old as fourteen or fifteen, I still wanted to do the things boys did. I didn't want to have to wear dresses—although I did, and people said I was pretty. I still felt different, even though most people thought I fit right in with our group in high school. I felt as though I was playing a role, faking it, being an actor.

"Faking it seems to be a good way to describe much of my growing up. I faked being a girl. I faked being a good student. I faked being comfortable around my classmates. One rule stood out: Never talk about what went on at home to the kids at school. This always made me feel as if they were better than I was."

KIM: "I learned how to keep major parts of my life secret from others— sometimes even secret from parts of myself. So it was easier to keep my lesbianism a secret from my family, until my recovery from my Adult Child issues made the pressure of the secret too heavy. So, breaking the secret of my sexual orientation with my parents two years ago seemed to me to be intertwined with what I learned as both an untreated ACOA (don't share) and a treated one (share and let go of the consequences). Actually, it has turned out pretty well."

Adult Children will often do anything to avoid further rejection. One of their major sources of self-protection is denial. They use denial to discount their homosexuality as well as the pain of the alcoholic or chemically dependent family. Denial coupled with secrecy adds fuel to this sense of shame and escalates the inner conflict.

SHAME AND GUILT

Shame is a very strong emotion in children. Shame is the belief that there is something inherently wrong with who we are. When we're shame ridden, we believe we're inadequate, different, or bad. Simply put, guilt is when you make a mistake; shame is when you believe you are the mistake.

Children in alcoholic families live lives of shame and fear. They're afraid that someone will find out what their family is really like. They're afraid people will see the violence, the ugliness, of their lives. They're afraid of feeling exposed and publicly shamed. Out of shame, they also take on the burden of feeling personally responsible for the family's disease.

Children in alcoholic families also experience a great deal of guilt—the feeling of regret or responsibility about something they have done or have not done. But much of their guilt is false guilt; it is a sense of responsibility for other people's feelings and actions. True guilt is the feeling of remorse for one's own feelings and behavior. It implies that one has developed a sense of responsibility for one's personal actions and feelings.

The alcoholic family's message is: "Don't talk about what's really happening. Don't talk about your feelings." But for the gay or lesbian child, there is an added message: "Hide your sexuality. You are not acceptable." It is very, very difficult for such children to feel good about who they are. In a society that largely condemns the expression of sexual feelings between people of the same sex, children who are gay or lesbian are made to feel ashamed and guilty for being who they are.

Adrienne describes feeling chronically guilty and shamed much of her childhood and until she was several years into recovery.

ADRIENNE: "Guilt is a still a knee-jerk reaction I have for many situations for which I am not responsible. I felt particularly guilty about having been born in the first place—especially when I found that I wasn't planned and was borderline illegitimate [the consequence of an extramarital affair]. I felt as though I'd wrecked my mother's life—that she could have had an easier life if I weren't around. My mother seemed to operate from guilt, and I learned it quite well. I felt guilty if I disappointed somebody, made them mad, or made waves of any kind.

"And I certainly felt shame about my sexual thoughts and attractions. My lesbianism felt like a curse. I was terrified—and I ate. As a child and teenager I was always about twenty pounds overweight. It was just enough so that I could be unattractive and guys wouldn't bother me much. It was a part of my way of dealing with my fears, my guilt, and my shame for being who I was."

JEAN: "The shame I experienced was first related to my family. I was ashamed of who we were and how we lived. The next piece of shame was related to my sexually addictive behavior in college, which was fueled by both my own homophobia and my alcoholism. My next wave of shame came after my college years when I got involved twice with married men. I felt shame because they were married and again because of the conflict of my feelings of attraction for women."

For Kim, as for Jean, there was greater shame in being part of a dysfunctional family than in being a lesbian.

KIM: *"Not being too aware of any lesbian feelings, there was no shame connected with my sexual identity. My shame—and I certainly felt shame—was based on Adult Child issues. I was most ashamed for having needs. My parents were away a lot, and I wanted them to be in my life more. Whether I felt this more than my siblings is hard for me to know, but I was clearly the only one who felt devastated when they were away.*

"My needs were normal childhood needs. I wanted my parents involved in my life. What I remember most is that somehow I was bad for wanting attention. I was bad for having needs. Somehow by age four I was supposed to be this totally autonomous creature. The words I felt about myself were 'dumb,' 'stupid,' and 'bad.' So I did the best I could to become that autonomous little person and not feel the pain associated with being abandoned."

Adrienne masks her shame with anger and compulsive eating. Jean masks her shame with sexually addictive behavior and alcohol. Kim finds a less blatant defense: she becomes invisible. David becomes isolated. And John discovers alcohol and drugs. These are ways that anyone affected by shame could respond.

Others respond with depression, or perfectionism, or by getting involved in hurtful and destructive relationships. Compulsive spending and workaholism are other possibilities. The ultimate act of shame may be suicide. In such cases a person may be feeling "I am worthless. I am hopeless. I do not deserve to live."

The responses to shame vary, but consequences of shame are the same whether or not one's shame emanates from childhood disruption or homophobia. However, gay and lesbian Adult Children bear the weight of Double Duty shame and feel it even more intensely.

DAVID: *"The strongest feelings I had as a child were guilt and shame, first because I was gay. I honestly think I would have traded anything to be heterosexual in my adolescence. Not that my fantasies weren't pleasant—they were natural and comfortable—but the aftermath was torture. The second reason for my guilt and shame was my family environment. I was afraid my friends would find out who I really was and they would abandon me."*

David describes his childhood as a cycle of fear, guilt, and shame; fear, guilt and shame; fear, guilt and shame.

DAVID: "I always felt wrong about everything. Certainly my parents always told me I was wrong about everything. So when I had these other emotions—love, attraction, and sexual feelings that seemed so natural— I was confused and immediately felt wrong. I felt shameful, and incredibly guilty. In essence, I equated good, happy feelings with being wrong. I can remember always being fearful of disapproval and rejection. By my teenage years I knew I wasn't going to get any approval from my parents, so my peers were my only chance. But once again I was different, and this was not acceptable. I had to disown myself to be accepted."

JOHN: "I had a terrible sense of fear when I was growing up. It was the basis for so many emotions, actions, and motivations. I was afraid of coming home, of leaving home, of being away from home, even of being at home. I didn't want to be wherever I was. I felt guilty about practically everything.

"I saw the pressure and the anxiety that was provoked when my brother and other gays I was aware of came out. No one seemed to understand homosexuality. Everyone seemed to want to change it, to control it. It was just crazy. And I was scared. I was fearful that I might be gay. And if somebody found out—that just fueled my sense of living in fear and the sense of shame that went along with it. I felt trapped, and I wanted to escape. I've always punished myself a lot. I think I did that with my own addiction. I put myself through hell—isolation, suicide attempts, self-hatred, shame, which led to outbursts of rage and resentment."

Both Adrienne and David had the experience of hearing clear messages about the evils of homosexuality.

ADRIENNE: "My negative feelings about being a lesbian were exacerbated by my stepfather's physical and verbal abuse not only of me, but also of my brother. Stan was seven years older and also gay. When I was eight I remember my stepfather getting drunk and chasing Stan around the house, threatening to kill him because he was 'a goddamn little faggot.' The message was loud and clear that being a homosexual could literally get you killed."

DAVID: "Once my sister used the word queer in the house. I do not know when the shouting, the banging, and the threatening stopped. I was no more than eight or nine at the time. The next morning, I asked what the word meant and why my father had gotten so upset over a word. My *mother told me that it meant 'men who play with each other.' I felt ashamed, and I declared to myself at that point that I was not 'one of them.' It was not what Daddy wanted.*

"When my father used the term homosexual, *or any variation of it, I was filled with shame and regret. The way he used that word forced me to stay in the closet. To prove him right would have meant an utter loss of self and independence. But I ended up losing my self anyway by staying in the closet."*

Any parental condemnation about a child's sexual orientation is usually exacerbated by society's taboos. The child hears from school, from peers, and from the media that homosexuality is bad and immoral. If the child has also grown up exposed to religious beliefs that condemn homosexuality, the part of the recovery process that asks one to accept the help of a Higher Power becomes very difficult.

DAVID: "My parents' religious fervor succeeded in making me a guilt-ridden young man. I would pray to God to take away the 'cross'—and it was not my father's alcoholism I meant. I think I would have traded anything to be heterosexual. I, too, became very religious and safely tucked myself away from facing my sexuality."

JOHN: "I felt as if the fighting in the family were all my fault, and that if I would just do what was right, then everything would be okay. In my strict Catholic upbringing, the concept of sin and punishment was so strong that I lived in fear and perpetual guilt because it wasn't possible to be the saintly child they described.

"The two most important areas of my life were my family, which was being torn apart by alcoholism, and the Church, where I felt only rigid condemnation. I was so confused about the Church. I can remember a particular Bible verse that says, 'If you are poor, I will feed you; if you are naked, I will clothe you.' Every time that was said I always pictured a naked man. I don't know what others pictured, but I knew that was wrong, and that I was wrong for thinking it. I finally had to give up on the Church because I felt so guilty. All I know is that sex, which began when I was very young, had to be secretive and hidden."

COMING OUT: OPENLY PROCLAIMING ONE'S SEXUAL IDENTITY

Spending one's childhood laden with fear, guilt, and shame makes one extremely vulnerable. Living with a sense of differentness that has been discounted, denied, and held secret would understandably confuse and overwhelm any young person. All children need to be able to feel safe speaking the truth. They need to be able to talk honestly about their feelings and perceptions. They need to be able to trust that others will listen. Ultimately, to feel good about themselves, they need to unload the secrets, to be honest about how they're living their lives.

An important part of the recovery process for Adult Children is to talk honestly about one's childhood and adult feelings and experiences. It means sharing the secrets that have been shrouded with shame for so long. But the homosexual Adult Child has two major secrets: chemical dependency in the family and his/her sexual identity. These Double Duty issues reinforce the difficulty of acknowledging either one. But recovery means learning self-love and self-acceptance, and that requires painstaking honesty, with oneself and with others.

Although people are slowly coming to accept the struggles involved in growing up in an alcoholic family, most of society is still ready to condemn homosexuality as wrong. The long-internalized shame often adds to the complexity of the coming-out process. While Adult Children have learned that the "Don't talk" rule no longer applies to the subject of alcoholism, gays and lesbians can still pay a big price for talking openly about their sexuality.

Adrienne's coming-out process began in college. But first she had to overcome her stereotypes of homosexuals as seedy lowlifes hanging out in bars. She had begun seeing a therapist in college, who told her to "get off the fence" and decide once and for all whether she was straight or lesbian.

ADRIENNE: *"After a torturous process, I decided to give up fighting my feelings for women and declare myself 'bisexual.' That was much easier to accept than simply being a lesbian. I starting hanging out in discos with gay men.*

"Then I met Rosa. Rosa was a gorgeous, feminine, happy Chicano lesbian who befriended me and introduced me to other lesbian women. Rosa defied my stereotype of lesbians as ugly, miserable, short-haired, lecherous alcoholics puking in bars. For the first time I was able to see that lesbians could be bright, productive people. I was thrilled to be able

to identify. I embraced this new community of friends, feeling that I had indeed come home.''

In her fourth year of college, Adrienne moved off campus and began to be actively involved in the gay community. She became a lesbian separatist. She had come out.

For the first time Adrienne had a sense of belonging. For the first time she was feeling accepted for who she was. In becoming a separatist she was fully embracing herself. However, she had not yet recognized some very important issues that would interfere with her ability to truly love herself.

"Although coming out seemed the answer to my problems, I had a long way to go. My co-alcoholism was in full swing, and my relationships were either fleeting sexual flings or unrequited love with my best friends. I had a terrible body image and was intermittently bulimic. All of my friends were from dysfunctional families, and none of us knew about the ACOA phenomenon."

Although Adrienne had come out as a lesbian, it would be a while before she began to address her Adult Child issues.

For Kim, the two were meshed.

KIM: *"My coming-out issues were intertwined with my co-dependency/ ACOA issues. Although I had begun my first lesbian relationship when I was twenty-one, neither I nor my lover had labeled ourselves lesbian. We were 'good friends' who slept together. Living in denial was natural for me—it was all part of living life on autopilot."*

Kim had been raised with a mentally ill sister whom she dearly loved and had always sought to protect. Kim's attachment to her sister was one of the most significant relationships in her life.

"My sister killed herself when I was in this lesbian relationship. I was devastated—totally overwhelmed emotionally. I went into a major numbing period for four years, putting most of my grief issues on hold, and certainly the lesbian issues. I was nonsexual for those four years."

Few ACOAs can grieve for such a loss because they never learned to feel the "lesser" feelings, let alone the deepest of all. The sadness, the powerlessness, the guilt, and the rage that Kim felt had no safe avenues for expression. Numbing herself totally was what she had to do simply to keep walking through life.

"I worked eighteen hours a day at meaningless jobs and eventually went to graduate school. It wasn't until 1983—four years after the death, five years into the relationship—that I began to think of myself as lesbian."

It is nearly impossible to address your sexual identity when you are in total denial. It is impossible to address your sexual identity when you are frightened of dealing with any aspect of your life.

KIM: *"Although when I was a teen I'd labeled my mother an alcoholic, somewhere along the way I got back into denial. There was a lot of stuff around protecting my parents after my sister's death, so I was in denial about everything—my mother's alcoholism, the reality that my sister had killed herself, and my own life-style.*

"As a result of being suicidally depressed, I sought therapy and was fortunate in finding a wonderful therapist. She guided me gently through the morass, and in time I came to terms with it all. I was able to grieve for my sister, myself, the end of the five-year relationship, and everything else that needed to be grieved for.

"Until I came out as an ACOA, I could not come out as a lesbian. I think my emotional connection with women is very much part of growing up with an alcoholic mother, so it makes sense to me that coming out meant breaking the silence about my family pain."

After a tumultuous struggle to come out as gay, David was quick to realize that his family issues were very significant in how he felt about himself.

David left home as soon as he was able to make it on his own. He graduated from high school at seventeen, but because he still needed to be the "good boy," he waited until he was given permission to leave at eighteen. He had become involved in a fundamentalist religious group, and once he was eighteen he moved into a religious community. He was there six months and then moved across the country to join another religious commune, where he lived for the next four years.

DAVID: *"I ran away as far as possible. I told myself that it was all over. I continued to deny my sexual feelings. I joined religious groups that treated sex with as much fear and loathing as I did. I thought I had safely tucked myself away from facing my sexuality, but the fantasies continued. And this led to even greater feelings of guilt."*

David says he spent those four years trying to quell all of his feelings, trying to believe that God had not made him gay. Any feelings he had became sublimated in the belief that he was a disciple of brotherly love.

At twenty-one, David left the religious community. He says he left without a lot of thought or insight—he simply knew that he was terribly unhappy. He next enrolled in a liberal but religious college, which led him gradually to release his extreme "all or nothing" thinking. It was at this college that he heard a professor speak of gays without negative judgment. This was a first. The professor first said that due to his religious beliefs he'd been against homosexuality. But then he'd had to confront the fact that two of his dearest friends were gay and that he loved them. Once the issue became personalized, he said he had to rethink theology. This was the beginning for David.

"It was my first experience with that kind of thinking. It was my first hint that it was okay to be gay."

David then transferred to a secular school. There he recognized many students who were gay. But he still wasn't ready to handle so much exposure, and he transferred to a Catholic college. Not until then did he learn that his dearest high school friend was also gay.

"The first person I had ever loved was to become the first person I would have a physical experience with. That was when I was finally able to face myself.

"I began therapy. I was discovering my true self. I began to experiment with the word gay and eventually to use it proudly to define an aspect of myself that had so profoundly influenced my life. Several years after that, I began to experiment with a new set of words: Adult Child of an Alcoholic. I soon learned that being raised in an alcoholic home was the cause of my frequent depressions and confusion. That, too, was a coming-out process."

Like many homosexual Adult Children, David came to feel proud to define himself as gay. But resolving his Adult Child issues was an ongoing struggle.

Jean did not begin her coming-out process until her early thirties. By then her active addiction to alcohol made it even more difficult.

When Jean graduated from high school, she decided to go to a women's college, hoping to find an atmosphere in which she could feel accepted for who she was.

JEAN: *"I liked the idea of all those women in one place, and I had great hopes of meeting others who were also interested in women. However, I did not meet any other lesbians, although I'm sure there must have* been some there who were in the closet. I had crushes on other women, but I pushed those feelings away and dated guys.

"I never felt as if I fit in with the other students, although I tried. A sexually addicted friend suggested that all I needed was to get 'screwed.' So I began to pursue a sexually active, promiscuous life-style for a few months, sleeping with some of the local college men.

"Finally, at twenty-three I experienced the thrill of sex with a woman. I will never forget the elation and the intensity of my feelings. But the liaison was very secret. We didn't even discuss it. We pretended that nothing was going on.

"I kept my sexual orientation very secret and continued to date men. My longest-term relationships were with married men. I even convinced myself that if I got married, my preference for women would go away. My drinking was also progressing strongly at this point.

"Through my twenties, I established and maintained several very close friendships with one or two women at a time. I felt attracted to them, but I vowed that I would never ruin the friendship by expressing my attraction. However, when I was thirty one of my women friends and I became lovers. We had been in a co-dependent relationship for three years, supporting each other's progressive alcohol abuse and exploring what it meant to be lesbian and scared in the Midwest in 1979. Alcoholism ultimately brought an end to our relationship.

"After another three-year relationship ended, I was tired of repeating the same patterns, and I thought that therapy might help. Had I known that the therapist was a recovering alcoholic who specialized in substance abuse, I think I would have tried to find another therapist. I wasn't about to give up my alcohol, nor was I willing to admit or accept the fact that I was an alcoholic. But she accepted my life-style and could understand my issues with lesbian relationships. That felt more important than the alcohol at the time."

Jean would need to get clean and sober before she could address her Adult Child issues and become self-accepting. Her therapist knew this, but she also understood that if she confronted Jean about her alcoholism before Jean had decided to trust her, Jean would run from therapy. It takes a finely skilled therapist to judge the timing correctly, but she did. The therapist's acceptance of Jean as a person was pivotal to Jean's remaining in therapy and to her ultimate acceptance of and surrender to her chemical dependency.

"Eventually, with my therapist's help, I was able to admit that I was not in control of my chemical use and abuse. I attended a Cocaine Anonymous *meeting and then went to my first AA meeting. I was terrified. I was sure all 'real' alcoholics would remind me of my father. But no one reminded me of my father. Everyone hugged me and accepted me, even though I was alcoholic and gay. This was when my real recovery began.''*

Jean had struggled to come out when she was actively addicted to alcohol. However, as a clean and sober person she can now continue her coming-out process without the other issues getting in the way. When you are addicted, your thinking is distorted, often delusional. You cannot make healthy decisions for yourself. Your choices are limited. People are just as (if not more) apt to respond to you in disgust, confusion, anger, or fear as an addicted person as they are to you as a homosexual.

John's coming-out process began in his teens, and it has been slow and gradual. It was important for him to come out to his parents. In his progressive coming out, John was more influenced by his parents' acceptance than were the other people in this chapter. After he had told his parents, he was better able to work through his own conflict about bisexuality and homosexuality. All this was made possible by the fact that John's parents had entered recovery during his teenage years and the family had become much more child-centered. Even though the children were older at that point, these circumstances probably greatly influenced John's need for his parents' acceptance.

JOHN: *"Growing up as a gay, alcoholic, addict, and Child of an Alcoholic, I felt as if my ticket were pretty full. At the age of twenty-one, when I was starting to get sober, I still had problems dealing with my sexuality. I was extremely homophobic, extremely paranoid. I felt isolated. I didn't want to hurt anybody. I felt that any expression of sexuality—my being me—would destroy the family and cause pain and shame and anger. I did everything to cover up. I dated women. I had dates for every event.''*

While John was in residential treatment for his addiction, his father came up for family day. This is when John told his father about his sexuality.

"I was so scared to tell him that I had three counselors in the room. I told my dad about me, how I felt, and what my fears were. My father told me that he had known about my sexuality for about three years. We sat and cried, and then we went for a walk, arm in arm, and it was really nice. After treatment we went home and told my mom. Actually I told her I was bisexual because I do enjoy women and enjoy being sexual with women.''

What John has described is a process for both individuals and families in active recovery where new and healthy rules are practiced. These are:

• Break the "Don't talk" rule. Speak the truth.
• Express your feelings.
• Offer and allow yourself to receive support.
• Take responsibility for yourself.

Over the next couple of years John came to accept that, as much as he enjoyed and was able to be intimate with women, his true sexual orientation was as a gay man.

"Living as a gay man, I know what it is to own an important part of myself that society condemns or ignores. It can be difficult enough dealing with your sexual orientation when you're growing up, but an alcoholic parent adds further complications and hardships. Today I like me. I know I am gay, not bisexual, and I have far less shame or fear of telling others of my homosexuality."

Gays and lesbians know very well that the coming-out process is on-going. Often one has to confront it on a daily basis. With each new person one meets, one must decide if owning one's sexual identity is relevant. Then one must decide whether or not to reveal it. Most gays and lesbians have developed a finely tuned internal radar mechanism that they perpetually scan, asking, "Is it safe to be me?" For those who have grown up in a chemically dependent family, the Adult Child issue of being hypervigilant refines this skill even further. Nevertheless, this is an incredible emotional burden, and it requires a lot of energy to maintain.

Unfortunately, there is an assumption that most people are heterosexual unless they say otherwise.

JOHN: "What is different about us is invisible. Because it is invisible, we're often subjected to cruel, hurtful statements from others who don't realize they're being insulting."

Gays and lesbians deserve to go through life with the dignity and respect due all human beings—regardless of sexual orientation.

Life Stories: Adulthood and Recovery

ADRIENNE
Age: 33
Partner Status: Relationship five
 years, parent of young child
Occupation: Music industry
Recovery Process: Al-Anon, ACOA,
 therapy

At age thirty-three, Adrienne has been in a relationship for five years now. She is also the parent of a two-year-old son. She has been actively working on her recovery process for six years.

Adrienne moved to New York from the Midwest to work in the women's music industry for a performer who was herself a recovering alcoholic.

ADRIENNE: She promptly Twelve-Stepped me into ACOA/Al-Anon. Beginning my recovery work was difficult. I was a total co-dependent and workaholic, throwing myself into managing other people's lives and careers for very low wages. It took six years and a combination of my recovery program, good therapy, and intuitive work to have what I enjoy today—an interesting and successful business as a talent agent, a happy and healthy five-year relationship with my lover, and our two-year-old son."

She described the process of recovery as gradual and at times painful.

"Ultimately, though, it has been very gratifying. While I can still put other people's needs first, it isn't an automatic response anymore. Under stress I occasionally worry about catastrophe ruining my life, but I don't assume it will. I have learned to express anger directly and set clear boundaries and limits around what I will and won't do. I have a sense of humor and perspective about myself and feel mostly amused, rather than controlled, by irrational thoughts or fears. I no longer gravitate toward active alcoholics, co-dependents, and addicts as friends and associates; instead I choose recovering addicts, alkies, and co-dependents.

"I used to worry that I would be poor all my life, since I believed I was too stupid to be successful in business. Today, by using my ACOA traits—being responsible, organized, self-sufficient, a good problem-

solver, guide, and manager of people's lives—I have a successful career.''

Adrienne says that the denial of her feelings, which she carried well into her late twenties, is gone now. She is no longer numb and defended. She no longer overeats to cover up loneliness, isolation, and fear.

Recently Adrienne has been doing another significant layer of recovery work.

"Lately I've begun to remember being violently sexually abused by my stepfather. This memory surprised me, but it makes sense, given some of the difficulties I have with being sexually present, a lingering feeling of unexplainable shame, and a basic distrust and fear.

"During the abuse he would tell me he would kill me if I told anyone. Although I know statistically that lesbian and straight women have experienced the same incidence of sexual abuse, I've had to confront on a gut level the stereotype that sexual abuse made me a lesbian. I used to think that there had to be more to my low self-esteem than simply being raised in an alcoholic family. Remembering the abuse provided the answer.''

While lesbian women do not appear to have a higher incidence of sexual abuse in their history, people who are sexually abused typically do have significant distrust of males (assuming the perpetrator was male). Yet there is no substantial increase of lesbians among survivors of sexual abuse. Adrienne is a lesbian who experienced childhood sexual abuse.

The ways in which her incest affects her sexually is in her sexual behavior, not in her sexual identity. The shame an incest survivor experiences most often does affect sexual behavior—such as the ability to be sexually present (to not disassociate from the body), to ask for what the person needs, and to set limits. Adrienne is correct in believing that there was more than alcoholism in the family to create low self-esteem; the incest was a major violation not only of her body, but of her spirit as well.

"I feel honored to be part of a community of people who have overcome emotional and sometimes physical traumas to lead enriched lives. I am grateful to have established a spiritual belief and practice that nourishes and sustains rather than oppresses me.

"Today I'm enjoying the precious experience of parenting. It has been quite a challenge, stimulating issues that I thought were resolved. There is nothing like having a bright, inquisitive, secure, demanding toddler around to push all one's buttons. I have gained an acute understanding

of how difficult it is to be a healthy parent when you are not using sub-stances, let alone if you are. I consider myself pretty aware—yet some-times my partner and I throw up our hands in exasperation or frustration. (The good part is we throw our hands in the air, not at him.)

"I've learned firsthand how vulnerable and dependent little kids are. And this has given me more compassion for how I must have felt. I've also enjoyed vicariously reliving part of my childhood by playing with him and loving and helping him in a way that I missed.

"I am happy and grateful to be a lesbian and to live my life as openly as I do. Today I feel blessed, no longer cursed. There is truly an element of magic in relating intimately to women—a core understanding and con-nection that arises from simply being female and together."

DAVID
Age: 32
Partner Status: Relationship four
    years
Occupation: Psychologist
Recovery Process: Therapy

Today, at thirty-two, David has been in a relationship for four years. He has also been in therapy and has been actively working on his ACOA issues.

Initially in the relationship, David found it difficult to deal with his fears of being abandoned, and he was frequently depressed. It took two to three years in therapy, and the patience and stability of his partner, for David to learn to trust.

DAVID: "I understood healthy relationships in my head, but my fear of being abandoned was so great that my emotions overrode my intellectual understanding. I knew these fears were from my childhood. It just took time to overcome them."

After David received his doctorate in clinical psychology, he and his partner moved to a small city, which they are currently enjoying. Moving to a new place often intensifies the issues of coming out.

"As a gay person, I am open and out about my sexuality. I have not come out at my job, but I don't intend to make it a secret. We have already

established relationships with other gay couples. I am a member of gay and lesbian organizations. I am on gay and lesbian mailing lists. I am comfortable with being gay, and I know I can live my life personally and professionally as a gay person. Yet I do not immediately tell people my sexual identity. I find that it is not always helpful. I've learned to discern the appropriate timing to tell people without having to deny me in the meantime.''

David is describing a recovery process of learning to listen to his own cues, to trust and value his perceptions. To do this, he has had to develop a sense of who he is and what he wants beyond simply reacting to the events of his life. In doing so he is establishing healthy boundaries for himself.

For the most part, David's pain about his family is gone. Today he has a relationship with both of his parents and all of his siblings. He describes himself as the thread that keeps the family together, the link between his parents and the other siblings. He says it is strange to go from feeling like the black sheep to being the favored child. He believes his parents are so relieved that he has left the "Jesus freak" world, and so proud of his being the first in his family to earn a Ph.D., that they are grateful for what he's doing for the family.

David laughingly says that his mom may be accepting his homosexuality because he hasn't "been stolen by another woman." He believes she always tried to counter the blatant rejection he received from his father as a child. However, possibly as a result of aging, David's father is reaching out more and indicating that he wants to have a relationship with David.

"I can now accept and love my father for who he is. Not that the memories will be forgotten, but I can own those feelings and accept them."

The AIDS issue has affected David's life significantly.

"AIDS is just one more thing that makes me think that life is so difficult. At times I have become very pessimistic and have reverted to my old coping mechanisms by ignoring the issue. I've tried not to talk about my friends who have died from AIDS. I don't hide the fact that I am gay, nor the fact that I am an ACOA. But I do find myself wanting to hide the pain I feel at the tremendous losses I've experienced as a result of the AIDS epidemic. I have to make an active effort to fight the denial.

"In my recovery in general, I am learning to be more assertive and not to overreact to things as much. I can now acknowledge the validity of my feelings. I'm able to own my rage, love, lust, fear, sadness, and

the myriad other human emotions that were blocked out for so many years.

"And yet when I have to deal with personal tragedies in my life, it's still easy to slip back into my old patterns of avoidance and pain. But my intellect and my new coping skills help me do what I need. I struggle against the old familiar response as I forge what I know is a much healthier one. I'm still struggling against 'all or nothing' thinking, and I need people to point that out to me. But I'm getting better. I'm less critical of myself, more aware of my own needs, and much more realistic about my expectations in my relationship.

"Today I have less and less need to define myself through awards and accomplishments. While they're nice, they don't make me a better person. Who I am as a person is what empowers me. And underneath everything, I now know I'm okay just the way I am.

"I'm not a victim any longer. I've learned to recognize my strength. I can affect situations and change how I react to them. I have choices. I feel empowered. All this is very different from my childhood.

"Today I feel a benevolent presence all around me. I really believe I am loved, that I am acceptable. I have gone through most of my life feeling unlovable. Today I trust I am worthy of love. Oh, I can be critical of myself, but I no longer feel worthless."

JEAN
Age: 42
Partner Status: Single
Occupation: Public relations
Recovery Process: AA, therapy

At forty-two Jean is enjoying a successful career as an advertising manager for a major corporation. She has a beautiful home and healthy, supportive friends. Although her parents consider her the "good child," she still struggles with her sense of not being good enough. But with the support of Alcoholics Anonymous and therapy, she is learning to accept herself as she is and to love herself.

JEAN: *"I've been sober for four years now. I've accepted my addictions, and I'm learning how to accept myself. I'm even learning to accept my feelings—at least some of the time. I like myself now. I'm no longer afraid that people will reject me because I am a lesbian. I'm no longer afraid that people will reject me because I'm an alcoholic. My recovery has offered me the opportunity to develop healthy friendships with both heterosexuals and homosexuals. But, even better, now I get most of my acceptance from within.*

"Accepting myself hasn't come easily. It's been painful, and I've been rebellious. I've denied and denied and denied—my addictions, my father's alcoholism, my mother's co-dependency, my fear, and my anger.

"However, when I began to participate in a healthy Adult Child therapy group, I learned that it was safe to gradually remove the wall that had kept me separate from myself and from others. I've discovered that the real pain is never as bad as the fear and anticipation of the pain.

"My parents and I remain both physically and emotionally distant. I have a role that I play with them. I am the successful daughter, I'm the good daughter. Not much has changed since I was a kid. I was always afraid that my mother wouldn't love me if she knew who I really was, and I always felt rejected by my alcoholic father. I have never directly told them what was really going on with me, and we still don't discuss my life-style. But what has changed, and what is most important, is that now I'm okay with this."

Jean is not presently in a relationship, but since she's been sober she's had two short relationships.

"At this moment I'm learning to be more honest with myself and my partners. At least now if I get into an unhealthy relationship, I have the sense to get out if it doesn't seem to be workable."

Jean recognizes that the most important thing she can do for herself is to come to terms with the pain she feels.

"To continue to grow, I know I will have to allow myself to be vulnerable. I cannot hold my pain inside any longer. If I don't allow myself to feel the pain, I will simply keep running from it and not dealing with it. So now I'm learning to walk through the pain a step at a time. The things that have been vital to my recovery are my Twelve Step programs, my therapy, a healthy network of friends, and my Higher Power. I have learned to listen to my Higher Power."

KIM
Age: 33
Partner Status: Relationship five
    years
Occupation: Administrator of
    nonprofit agency
Recovery Process: ACOA, Al-Anon,
    CODA, therapy

Kim has actively pursued her recovery in therapy and a Twelve Step program for over seven years. At thirty-three she now lives in northern California, where she is successful in her career as an administrator of a nonprofit helping agency. She is happy in her relationship of five years.

Kim had begun therapy for her depression and was being treated with antidepressants when she met the woman who was to become her next partner.

KIM: *"After the breakup of my first lesbian relationship, which had lasted five years, I soon met someone new. This woman was a recovering alcoholic who quickly directed me to Al-Anon, saying it would be helpful for us both since I was now the partner of a recovering alcoholic. It was there that I clearly began to identify my Adult Child issues, and this led me to Adult Child self-help and co-dependency groups and to therapy. All of them have been vital in helping me find the answers to my life.*

"I think, in some ways, that being lesbian has facilitated my recovery. I went to visit my parents recently—we live two hundred miles apart— and saw lots of relatives I hadn't seen in years. I was struck by something I saw more clearly than ever before—every single woman on my mother's side of the family, a four-generation span, has struggled with some kind of serious mood disorder, mostly severe depression. Upon my return home, I shared this insight with friends, and one of them asked me how I'd escaped. At first I said I hadn't, and I told her about my own severe depression and three years on antidepressants. But then I realized that I really had escaped. And I think being a lesbian had a great deal to do with it. Being surrounded by women helped me value and empower all that I am. Listening to feminist music and exploring a very different

culture aided me in rejecting dysfunctional family values and helped me develop new healthy values for myself—after I'd bottomed out.

"Life as a lesbian is for me clearly different from life as a heterosexual. I know that sounds very obvious. But it was a life-saving discovery for me. The times I have felt the craziest, the most suicidal, the most depressed, was when I could not see how I was different from my mother and sister. The only choices I thought I had then seemed to be either suicide or alcoholism. Affirming my lesbianism gave me more choices, more options, more of a chance for a positive outcome."

Kim says she believes she still carries some emotional burdens of the family that she might not if she weren't lesbian.

"My sister's suicide leaves me the only girl child in the family. Chances are I will never have a child, or if I do, it will create a complex family issue. I have some feelings of regret about that. Some grieving comes up periodically that is tied in with the ACOA 'responsible child' struggle that I'm still fighting.

"Along the same lines, I think about other things with sadness, like not having a more accepted kind of wedding or household. There's also something in there about wanting to show my parents that I'm normal, that I'm happy. That I did okay. I know they blame themselves for my sister's death—as I did for a long time—and I want to show them they did the best they could as parents. How they handle my lesbianism is an integral part of how they feel as parents, and for them that is negative. Part of the Adult Child issues I'm still working on is trying to protect my parents from me and themselves.

"So, where am I now? I'm very happy. I spent several years in therapy and have been in and around Twelve Step recovery programs for four years. My primary external compulsion has been workaholism, something that continues to surface every now and then. The only chemical I ever abused was nicotine, which I recently quit. I've been in a relationship almost five years now with the woman I intend to spend my life with. I have a good solid career.

"My parents and I are on good terms. My mother's chemical dependency is still a family secret. But I don't push it into the open like I used to, and she doesn't drink around me. My parents accept my life-style and even sent a birthday card to my lover this year. Happy endings are possible—for those who want them."

JOHN
Age: 28
Partner Status: Single
Occupation: Chemical dependency
   specialist
Additional: Parents in recovery
   today
Recovery Process: AA, therapy

Six years clean and sober, at twenty-eight John is a chemical dependency counselor in Colorado.

Five years ago John suffered a series of illnesses and lost a great deal of weight. He had chronic fatigue, swollen glands, and was experiencing wide mood swings. Finally he was diagnosed with ARC (AIDS-related complex).

JOHN: *"I felt as if I were dying. I had no control. So I placated and adjusted and took care of everyone else. I hid how I felt and what I thought. I hid my fears because I didn't want anyone to worry about me. I tried to take care of other people so that they would be okay with my illness.*

"I feared for my family. I was afraid that because I was gay, because I was an alcoholic, because I was an addict, and now because I had ARC, they would be hurt. I was afraid of what this might do to them, how they would be affected by this.

"When I found out, I called Mom and Dad and told them that I was very sick. They flew up to be with me and were very supportive. We all learned as much as we could about the disease. But I felt so much despair at the time that I was planning to kill myself. I had even made all the preparations for ending my life, but my mother kept calling me every day, asking me if I had seen a doctor.

"Finally I went to a doctor, who hooked me up with a therapist. With the therapist's help I worked through my suicidal feelings and set out to discover my own identity. I began to reevaluate, reframe, and relearn. I discovered how to get in touch with my inner child and the experiences of my childhood, and this helped clarify my needs today as an adult.

"The characteristics of being an Adult Child with ARC and an Adult Child who is gay are the same. The emotions are the same. ARC is simply

another set of circumstances in which I must be responsible for myself. For a while I was blaming God because He was putting me through yet another dark time. I almost totally lost any sense of Higher Power that I'd gotten from my Twelve Step program. I kept thinking, Why did God do this to me?

"As part of my ACOA recovery, I have to take responsibility for my health. There is no changing it. There is no denying it. It is real."

John has been able to look at his ARC as an opportunity to examine his life more deeply. But before he could do that, he responded very normally with denial, anger, blame, and depression. Ultimately he has come to acceptance. This is a process he may repeat several times. But John had some tools as a result of his participation in recovery from both his alcoholism and his ACOA issues that would help him to confront his illness and go on living his life, instead of seeing himself as dying.

Regardless of what is happening physically, there are still choices you can make about your life.

"Today I know that God is not punishing me by giving me this illness. It is not my fault. And the illness is not my identity. I am not a bad person because I have ARC. God and I are in this together, and He is still a power greater than anything I know. Most of the time I am grateful for what I am able to learn.

"Unfortunately there still has to be the secrecy. There are times when I cannot be open with people about what is going on with me.

"I used to share my pain with people in order to take theirs away. But I don't do that today. Their pain is theirs, and my pain is mine. Their pain is no greater than mine because they are experiencing it. I don't have to take it away. And I don't have to share my illness for pity. In fact, I don't share it with most people because I don't want it to be the focus of 'How are you?' "

As many Adult Children are doing today, John is learning to have healthy relationships.

"While I'm not in a primary relationship, I feel capable of being in a healthy relationship. In the past I experienced sex without much honesty or intimacy. Today I'm working on getting to know the other person and allowing the other person to get to know me. That doesn't happen in five minutes. I want the other person to be able to say he likes me, that he likes how I treat myself and him, that he is comfortable with my health issues. Honesty is vital, and practicing safe sex is automatic in my recovery."

Adult Children have spent years keeping perceptions and feelings a secret, guessing at what other people want, attempting to get approval, and communicating in a distorted manner. The result often produces both chaos and excitement. But maintaining this fever-pitch emotional environment also means maintaining dysfunctional ways of being.

"I still struggle with my need for chaos and excitement. But I am no longer isolated. I am no longer invisible to myself and others. I can look at myself in the mirror, I take care of myself. I've been working out, I eat properly, and I sleep well. I feel good about myself, my work, and my life.

"I've also been working on my own homophobia. I'm talking more openly about who I am. I'm tired of changing my pronouns and lowering my voice to sound more masculine to fit what people want. I want to be acknowledged, not discounted. I want the same respect that anyone else gets. If I'm in a restaurant with another man, I want to be acknowledged the same way a heterosexual couple would be. I want polite respect.

Today if someone asks me if I'm married, I say, 'No, I am gay.' I like that."

What John is describing is the Adult Child recovery process of learning to value oneself and to live one's life without chronic fear. Recovery is about healthy risk taking, and John is clearly taking those risks. Although he may be fearful initially, he is being more honest with himself and others, and this enhances his self-esteem.

"Now that I'm no longer in denial, I know that I have felt a great deal of pain in my life. But one of the reasons I know this is because I also feel so much love and pleasure. With this new understanding of myself, I feel so much room for growth, so much desire to be at peace with myself. I don't want to wait for death to bring me peace. I'm striving to find that peace today and every day of my life."

Recovery Considerations

Adrienne, John, Kim, David, and Jean were all raised in actively chemically dependent families. All but one recognized their sexual orientation in their preadolescent or adolescent years, adding to their sense of:

- Never being good enough
- Feeling different
- Feeling shame and guilt

Today all five proudly embrace their sexual identities. They recognize the impact of chemical dependency on their lives and have begun a process that not only facilitates the healing of childhood wounds, but offers them the respect they deserve as human beings regardless of their sexual orientation.

Because of the Double Duty—the synergistic effect of being gay or lesbian and an Adult Child—it may take a bit longer to feel safe enough to begin and maintain one's recovery work. It is important that gay and lesbian Adult Children be very caring and patient with themselves. While you have the same issues as heterosexual Adult Children, you may find the following considerations especially relevant to your recovery process.

SELF-ACCEPTANCE

All Adult Children must work on developing greater self-acceptance. This awakens as we begin to develop compassion and empathy for ourselves as children. Once we own the child within, the vulnerable, innocent child fully deserving of validation, it will be hard to see any of the ugliness or depravity that gays and lesbians often learn to associate with themselves. That sense of wrongness and shame has come from messages internalized from those who are themselves frightened and confused about sexuality. Just because they were taught that homosexuality is bad doesn't mean that it is bad. Sexual orientation is not bad; it just is.

Self-acceptance and self-love also mean addressing one's own homophobia. The messages gays and lesbians constantly hear are that homosexuals are sick, dirty, immoral, ugly. Having to contend with the pressures of external homophobia on a day-to-day basis is at best disheartening. But dealing with internalized homophobia is even more difficult and painful. Gays and lesbians often learn to accept homophobic values. They believe that because they are different, there is something wrong with them. This is demonstrated by David, who sought a counselor so he could become heterosexual; by Jean, who believed that her feelings were wrong; and by David, who prayed that he would change.

One significant aspect of recovery means addressing this internal homophobia, because it is impossible to experience recovery while rejecting oneself. Homosexual or not, if people are homophobic, their choices of responding to others and to life are limited and compromised.

ISOLATION

Because gay and lesbian Adult Children have lived so much of their lives "not talking" about the real issues, they are even more isolated, both emotionally and socially, than most ACOAs. They have less trust in the process of being open and honest about their feelings and perceptions. Even when they're highly motivated to be more honest with themselves and others, the layers of protection can only be lifted slowly.

It is common to find many gays and lesbians who do not appear to be socially isolated. However, their friendships will often be segmented. They will share certain parts of their lives, but not others, such as whom they live with, whom they love. Although this serves to protect, it can be very isolating emotionally. To avoid such a segmented life, many homosexuals become even more socially isolated, relating only to a very small number of people they can be open with. Isolation often becomes habitual, and many gays and lesbians learn to discount their loneliness by deluding themselves into thinking that isolation is "alone time." A certain amount of alone time is healthy, but it can easily become an unhappy escape.

Because of greater feelings of differentness, it is important to have the opportunity for validation of perceptions and experiences that often can only be affirmed by other gays and lesbians who are in recovery. It helps to lessen homophobia, both internal and external, and it offers one the opportunity to see homosexuals as bright, capable, insightful, and sensitive—and just as good at practicing self-care and having healthy relationships as heterosexuals.

Most homosexuals find that they benefit from both gay/lesbian and heterosexual support groups. These groups may be based in either traditional therapy or self-help. Gay and lesbian community organizations may be able to direct one to "recovering communities" and other social resources. It is important for anyone in recovery to understand that in life in general we cannot get all of our needs met by one person or in one place. The path to self-acceptance and recovery will involve a number of resources.

Reaching out, becoming less isolated, eases homophobia—it lessens fear, loneliness, and shame. It is the beginning of recovery.

REJECTION AND ABANDONMENT

As young children, ACOAs live with chronic fear of abandonment. As homosexuals in a heterosexual society, gays and lesbians are constantly being rejected for any and all aspects of who they are simply because of their sexual orientation. Being homosexual means living with a heightened likelihood of rejection and/or abandonment. Yet there are gays and lesbians willing to offer support, and there are growing numbers of heterosexuals who accept gay or lesbian individuals for who they are.

The Adult Child issue of ''not trusting'' can interfere with one's willingness to come out, when in fact the acceptance may be readily available. By addressing this issue directly, gay or lesbian Adult Children have a more realistic opportunity to assess the fears that relate to their homosexuality.

Adult Children are known for their hypervigilance. If they have experienced a lot of rejection in their lives, they will be hypervigilant about any future possibilities of rejection. Most gays and lesbians have had to learn how to defend themselves emotionally against possible rejection. But there's an added dynamic here. The Double Duty of being both homosexual and an Adult Child may prompt one to read rejection into an encounter when, in fact, it is not occurring. Because of this hypersensitivity, Adult Children tend to set others up, to test their loyalty. Therefore, they need to examine these feelings and discuss their fears. The truth is that sometimes rejection is occurring and other times it is not.

NEED FOR APPROVAL

A common characteristic of Adult Children is seeking approval. Being raised in a dysfunctional family denies them the validation and approval they need to develop an internal validation system or positive self-esteem. This is why they continue to seek approval from others as adults. Three cautions might be helpful here:

- *First,* it is possible that as a gay or lesbian, the need for approval is so great that one can be indiscriminate in disclosing their homosexuality and as a result set themselves up for being rejected or abandoned.
- *Second,* it is possible that this need for approval may prompt the gay or lesbian to pass as a heterosexual and develop only segmented relationships.

- *Third,* it is possible that out of fear or rejection, the gay or lesbian will build a defensive wall and reject opportunities in which others could offer approval and acceptance.

Recovery means learning how to become "self-approving." It means inviting healthy people into your life who will offer approving messages. What is hurtful is being dependent on others to make you feel good about yourself. As you seek friendships within both the healthy gay and lesbian community and the healthy heterosexual community, you will find others who will be approving.

Nevertheless, it is vital to keep working on your ability to affirm and empower yourself. Don't rely on any one person for all of your outside validation. It isn't fair to that person, nor is it fair to you. There are many others who can and will offer validation, and you will blossom even more as your network of healthy support grows.

DIFFERENTNESS

Heterosexual Adult Children in recovery often say they no longer have the sense of differentness or separateness from others that had so characterized their growing-up years. They claim that the "alone in the crowd" syndrome disappears.

As gays and lesbians move on in their recovery process, the sense of being separate and different also lessens. Yet their sexual orientation does make them members of a minority population. In that respect they will differ from other ACOAs.

However, one vital distinction is very important in recovery. In the past, being different was equated with shame. In recovery one discovers that being different does not mean one is bad. At this point one needs to become comfortable with one's differentness. In addition, the tendency for Adult Children to view the world with an "all or nothing" perspective can make them feel even more negative about being different. But once this view of the world begins to open up, it becomes easier and easier to see how similar they are to other people in spite of the differences. Homosexual or heterosexual, we all have the same needs and deserve the same as everyone else.

COMING OUT

Coming Out in General. Honesty is integral to Adult Child recovery. Recovery cannot work with selective honesty. Yet that doesn't mean we

have to share everything with everyone. Being honest means first learning to be honest with yourself. Then it means choosing environments that
feel safe so that you can be true to yourself. Part of the recovery process
is learning to discriminate whom we share information with and what is
appropriate to share.

You deserve to live life free of fear and free of shame. One way to do
that is to begin the coming-out process. On the one hand, honesty is not
necessarily easy. On the other, one pays a very high price—one's integrity—by continuing to be dishonest. Many gays and lesbians have come
to believe that being honest with oneself and the world is much easier
than remaining in the closet.

Living a closeted life means attending weddings, funerals, and family
occasions alone or inviting a member of the opposite sex to be with you
to keep up the pretense. It means lying about who you are when applying
for jobs or credit or buying a house. Blatantly lying throughout one's daily
life takes an incredible toll on one's self-esteem.

When one grows up with unpredictability, the ability to compartmentalize is often well developed. Although compartmentalizing one's life from
a fear of homophobia is sometimes necessary, it may also be an Adult
Child habit that may not be as necessary as we think.

Coming out often means being honest about the one aspect of who you
are that you've felt the greatest shame about and have fought the hardest
to keep secret. It is difficult to trust the value or the safety of the process
of coming out in a homophobic society. And as an Adult Child, you may
have even greater difficulty trusting or finding value in honesty.

However, some gay and lesbian Adult Children find that recovery begins by first addressing their sexuality. Typically, once the "rule of silence" has been broken in one area, it loosens up other areas and allows
one to discover new insights. Heterosexual Adult Children don't usually
begin their recovery by revealing their deepest secret. So if you begin
your recovery process by coming out, you need to acknowledge the courage that this process takes. Other Adult Children get to start with smaller
truths, and some gays and lesbians begin their recovery in a time frame
that allows them to come out gradually.

Although being gay or lesbian adds to the pain and struggle of being
an Adult Child, there are many ways in which dealing with one issue can
have a positive effect on dealing with the other.

David said that when he went into therapy for help with being gay or
to change his being gay—he wasn't sure which—it was the second time
he'd heard that it was "fine" to be gay. All he needed was to hear it
again, and he was willing to accept it. He said at that point he gave up

his struggle and began to come out. But he adds that the process of accepting who he was opened up Pandora's box. He had to face how he'd come to be so fearful of his feelings, how he'd come to hate himself, and how he'd come to feel so different.

David said he'd thought those issues were the result of being gay, and yet he knew his heterosexual brother had the same issues. Coming out as gay forced David to deal with being an Adult Child.

Jean said that once she had accepted herself as a lesbian, her ACOA issues of isolation and feeling different could be dealt with. She is also aware that recovery from her co-dependency issues will allow her to have healthy relationships.

This is not meant to imply that working on ACOA issues will automatically make being gay or lesbian more comfortable. Jean points out that while she can work on her fear of rejection and abandonment as an ACOA, she still has to confront the reality that being lesbian means she continues to risk a higher level of rejection and abandonment from others.

Many gays and lesbians reflect that the coming-out process is usually much more distressful at the beginning than it is over time. Remember, you're the one who decides whom it is safe to share this information with. You don't have to begin with the person whose approval is most important to you. You don't have to begin with the person who frightens you the most.

When heterosexual Adult Children begin their recovery process, they're usually doing it with strangers. They seek a counselor, a therapist, or a self-help group. Often they don't find support or validation from the members of their family of origin or even present-day family members. In addition, they have friends who care about them, but who don't really understand what they're going through. You may want to begin your coming-out process with a gay or a lesbian counselor or therapist who is sensitive to these issues or with a gay or lesbian social group or a self-help group.

While the decision to come out is often fraught with stress, many people experience relief and exhilaration as they come out. It relieves the hurtful energy that has burdened them for so long. When one can get beyond the societal fears and stigmas, being gay or lesbian becomes as normal to the homosexual as being heterosexual is to those who are straight. It is the homophobia, internal and external, that is so painful.

Choosing the right environment is important. Some areas of the country and some communities are generally more supportive, and others are more homophobic—especially rural areas or smaller cities. Gays and lesbians owe it to themselves to find places where it is safe to own who they are and where they can receive validation and support. Telephone hot lines and gay and lesbian resource centers in major cities can often offer suggestions.

Coming Out to the Family. In coming out to family members, Adult Children need to keep in mind that their family most likely has little or no history of positive affirmation of sexual behavior in general, let alone homosexuality. In dysfunctional families heterosexual sex, which is the perceived societal norm, is rarely talked about or portrayed positively. Consequently, when the subject of homosexuality arises, there is even less likelihood of a positive response.

If your family wasn't very accepting of you when they thought you were heterosexual, it will be all the more difficult for you to believe that they will be able to accept you as a gay or lesbian. But remember, the issue here isn't so much your sexual orientation as it is their inability to be accepting in general. Chemically dependent families are characteristically critical of and quick to blame others. These are families characterized by denial, not speaking the truth, minimizing, rationalizing. Family members are not used to speaking of sadness and fears about little everyday things and finding support.

Often the time one comes out to family members is the first time that any honesty has taken place in the group. One is telling a major secret with little or no practice to people with no history of favorable reactions to even little secrets. While there's no one right way to come out to one's family, this is the first time there has been any direct and honest communication. Remember that a negative response could result as much from the shock of honesty to the dysfunctional family system as from homophobia.

Some gays and lesbians decide not to formally come out to their parents or siblings, and this may be a healthy decision. For others, those who are socially isolated from parents and siblings by choice, the prospect of coming out with one's sexuality is an easy and healthy decision. Yet another choice is to be involved in the lives of parents and siblings and include one's partner in those relationships without ever stating the facts. Many gays and lesbians say they find acceptance from family members if the facts remain unspoken. Coming out and saying, "I am lesbian, gay," or, "I sleep with him or her" could set up the family to react in a way that would not allow the relationship to be as comfortable as it is.

As you experience Adult Child recovery, you become more aware of your needs, and you can identify your feelings. This means that you can establish healthier boundaries and find greater self-acceptance. When you no longer view life from an "all or nothing" perspective, you become more trusting of your perceptions, and you can ascertain a greater range of options. With recovery, the coming-out process is made easier, and the right path for you can evolve in a healthy way.

ACQUIRED IMMUNE DEFICIENCY SYNDROME—AIDS

While thousands have died from AIDS, many people are struggling through various stages of acceptance with their illness. Having a chronic and potentially fatal illness is a major issue in and of itself. Knowing that you will not be able to live your life to full term, that your life is being taken away before you have achieved what you have desired, is a stunning loss.

Much work has taken place around the issue of learning to accept such a prognosis. We know that the first reaction is denial. After that come four more stages: anger, bargaining, depression, and, finally, acceptance. If one is infected with HIV and is an unrecovered Adult Child, this process is all the more difficult. Adult Children may use the denial skills they developed in their dysfunctional families to get stuck in the denial stage and never find peace or acceptance. They may also become very self-destructive as a result of being overwhelmed with their feelings for the first time.

Other ACOA issues can seriously interfere with proper treatment. Having learned not to ask questions could severely limit medical options. The inability to ask for help could make the process more difficult physically and very lonely emotionally. Not having come to terms with parents or siblings could create a powerful emotional and/or financial burden. Not trusting one's perceptions could interfere with using important medical information to one's best advantage, and most important of all, it could deeply affect the choice of how to continue to live one's life.

Often the first time people take a long, hard look at their lives is when their health is seriously threatened. In recovery from ACOA issues or alcoholism, many people have been able to find gifts at a time when others perceive only painful loss. Regardless of what is happening physically, there are still choices you can make about your life. If you haven't begun a recovery process as an ACOA, or if you are chemically dependent, it's never too late to begin. *Do not wait.* Many benefits come with recovery that will allow you to make sense out of your illness and help you to take charge of your life at last.

To lose a friend, a significant other, or a life partner is tragic. To lose many friends in a relatively short time span can be overwhelming. Under such stress, many Adult Children resort to old defense mechanisms—

they shut down, numb out, and isolate themselves. To handle the grief, some of that is necessary. Even denial has its uses. But, ultimately, in order to cope in a healthy manner, you need to walk through the process of grief. To do that you must know and trust your feelings; and you must include others in your process. Without some Adult Child recovery it will be difficult to grieve the loss of friends and/or partners. Some people discover that this crisis may be the starting point of recovery from Adult Child issues.

Do not isolate yourself during this time. Reach out. Talk about your anger. But be aware that the anger is not about being homosexual—it is about the disease, about the AIDS virus taking loved ones away. Talk about your hurt, the gut-wrenching pain. Talk about your fears. Talk about the joys you have had with your friends and loved ones. Precious gifts can come out of the process of sharing honestly with a friend who is so ill—gifts for both of you.

RELATIONSHIPS

In many ways homosexual Adult Children aren't any different from heterosexual Adult Children when it comes to relationships. Most people who have been raised in troubled families have difficulty in relationships. They often engage in personal relationships that do not meet their needs, where communication is hurtful and distorted and everyone has different goals. At times they are in abusive, violent relationships.

Remember, Adult Children come from families where it has not been safe to talk openly and honestly. They haven't learned to trust; they often have not learned to negotiate or problem-solve. Many times they have not learned how to share. Some ACOAs have learned intrusiveness and disrespect of others' boundaries. Others have learned to tolerate inappropriate behavior and often find themselves victimized. This certainly does not lay the groundwork for a healthy relationship.

In relationships between unrecovered Adult Children, both partners often come from a shame-based background without the skills to create a healthy environment. There is also the added dynamic of living in a homophobic society that reinforces the conflict homosexual couples experience in trying to stay together and work out issues. It's hard enough for heterosexual couples to do this, but there are even fewer positive reinforcements or expectations for homosexual couples.

Nevertheless, tumultuous relationships among gays and lesbians do not have to be the norm. With recovery from Adult Child issues, you can invite healthier people into your life and come to have healthy expectations for relationships. There are gay and lesbian couples who have lived together for many years in highly successful relationships. Although they tend to be less visible to the younger population, they are there, and seeking them out as positive role models is always helpful.

Healthy Adult Children choose partners with whom they can enter into mutual agreements. They are respectful of their own boundaries—of what feels safe and good—and are equally respectful of others and their boundaries. This is true whatever the sexual orientation may be.

A significant and hurtful dynamic in a gay or lesbian relationship is the potential for invalidation when it's not safe to come out as a couple. The inability to feel safe in having your partner join you at a social event at work, with your family, or in the community can create a strain on the relationship. Even when partners attend social events together as a couple, it may not feel safe to openly touch in tenderness or support. You may have to lie when you introduce your partner. Going to social events as a couple is often a setup for rejection. And every time this occurs, you have to deal with the implicit message that a homosexual relationship is wrong. These circumstances often force gays and lesbians in relationships to participate in social events separately or not at all. Yet one of the joys of a relationship is sharing—both the good times and the hard times. A circumscribed life is frustrating. Homosexual ACOAs continually have to make compromises that heterosexual ACOAs do not have to make.

Because of this, homosexuals in a relationship need to work even harder at being available to one another as a support. Communication is even more necessary. Knowing what your feelings are and finding appropriate expression for them is vital. Problem-solving skills are another important requisite. Adult Child recovery offers gays and lesbians new skills that give them a greater range of choices in their lives.

You don't have to live a life plagued with always having to be socially separate from your partner. Today you can choose to spend time with those who will offer you and your partner support and validation and meet your interpersonal needs. There are other gays and lesbians and heterosexuals who will lovingly accept you for who you are. But before you allow such people in your life, you will usually have to confront your own internal homophobia first. Remember, the people we choose to be around reflect the person inside us.

CHEMICAL DEPENDENCY

We know now that Children of Alcoholics are more likely to become chemically dependent. Research indicates that daughters of chemically dependent families are two times more likely to become chemically dependent; sons are five times more likely to become chemically dependent. Research also suggests that a gay or lesbian person is two to three times more likely to become chemically dependent. Therefore being both an Adult Child and homosexual warrants special caution in regard to alcohol and other drug usage. Anyone wanting to assess his alcohol or drug usage should use the "Am I an Addict?" self-assessment test in the appendix (see page 564). This is an objective tool that can help you keep yourself honest and healthy.

Remember, chemical dependency is a primary illness. Until it is addressed, it will be difficult to work on Adult Child issues and even more difficult to work on gay or lesbian issues. But also remember, gay or straight, chemical dependency is treatable. Thousands of gays and lesbians are clean and sober today. They have dealt with all the fears about what it means to have a sober life. There are gay and lesbian self-help meetings of Alcoholics Anonymous, and there are gay- and lesbian-oriented treatment programs. It is also a fact that many gays and lesbians experience a wonderful recovery while attending mainstream Twelve-Step groups.

PUTTING FEAR AND SHAME BEHIND YOU

Nobody deserves to live with shame and fear because of growing up in an alcoholic family. Certainly no one deserves to live with shame because of a specific sexual orientation. Adult Child recovery means putting the fears and shame of your childhood behind you. It means challenging hurtful belief systems and learning healthier skills. It means valuing yourself, believing in yourself. Each of us is very special. Each of us deserves to believe that in our hearts. I believe that when gay and lesbian Adult Children address their issues, they experience greater opportunities to be true to themselves.

Today I believe I am acceptable.
Today I trust I am worthy of love.

—Lesbian Adult Child

9

People of Color

Black, Brown, Red, and Yellow people are not the problem. We may be people with problems, but we are not the problem. We are people with differences. We are people with a wealth of cultural and ethnic traditions, belief systems, values, customs, and coping styles.

—Adult Child

lcoholism is a nondiscriminatory disease that knows no ethnic, racial, or socioeconomic boundaries. Anyone who drinks can become
chemically dependent. But for many ethnic minorities, the abuse
of alcohol and other drugs is one way of coping with poverty, unemployment, and racism.

People who feel rejected and powerless in the face of cultural dominance often turn to alcohol and drugs to numb the pain. However, being
a person of color can by no means be equated with dysfunctional consequences. Ethnic cultures are rich in tradition, spirituality, and enduring
moral values. They place strong emphasis on the family, and they hold
children to be sacred. But alcohol and other drugs can destroy this rich-
ness. As readers move into this chapter, it is my hope that they will
acquire a better understanding of the experience sustained by a child of
color in an alcoholic family. *When I use the words minority or racial
minorities, I am referring to the nonwhite population, people of specific
racial groups. It is in no manner meant to imply "less than."*

Much of what is true about alcoholism and the dynamics of alcoholism in a white family holds true for the addicted racial minority family—for example, the signs and symptoms of the progression of the disease and the family rules of "Don't talk," "Don't feel," and "Don't trust." However, the fact that certain racial groups experience a disproportionate frequency of chemical dependency cannot be ignored. In these instances progression of the disease is often much swifter and much more likely to be fatal.

Although research varies about the prevalence of alcoholism among minority communities, it clearly points to severe health problems among various ethnic groups. Alcoholism is considered by many to be the number-one health problem in the black community. The black alcoholic is much more apt to die prematurely than the white alcoholic. Cirrhosis of the liver has caused approximately twice the number of deaths in the black community as in the white community—in all age groups. In some cities, cirrhosis rates among black males can be as much as ten times higher than those for their white counterparts.[1]

Of the ten leading causes of death in Native American communities from 1978 to 1980, alcohol abuse was implicated in four. These include accidents, cirrhosis of the liver, homicides, and suicides. Alcoholic cirrhosis caused the death of one in four Native American women; this rate is thirty-seven times higher than their white counterparts. And 25 percent of all Native American mothers who bear a child with fetal alcohol syndrome (FAS) give birth to another child similarly damaged. Unquestionably, substance abuse is the number-one health problem in these communities.[2]

Hispanics are said to be the second-largest minority in America, as well as the fastest-growing group. The people who are called "Hispanic," "Latino," or "Chicano" are a heterogeneous group whose origins are Mexican, Puerto Rican, Cuban, Central American, and South American, as well as other Spanish-speaking cultures. In addition, Hispanics are racially and ethnically diverse: they can be white, black, or Indian or any combination of these. Because the Hispanic population is so heterogeneous, it has been difficult to get a clear picture of the relationship between alcohol use and abuse and the attitudes of the Hispanic community.

Nevertheless, despite these diversities some clear patterns are beginning to emerge. A recent study of Hispanics in California revealed that they rank high on both ends of the drinking scale. In comparison with the general population, greater numbers of Hispanics either drink very little (or nothing at all) or they drink heavily. The variance is attributable mostly to the differences in drinking habits between Hispanic men and women.

Latino women, for example, are far more likely than their Anglo and black American counterparts to abstain from alcohol.[3]

A study of autopsy reports in Los Angeles revealed that 52 percent of all deaths among Mexican-American men were alcohol-related. The statistical percentages for white men were 24 percent, for black men 22 percent.[4]

Information about the substance abuse issues involving Asian/Pacific Americans has been sparse and inconclusive. One of the difficulties in ascertaining information and offering resources is that there are approximately twenty nationalities covered by the term *Asian American*. This group includes Chinese, Japanese, Hawaiians, Samoans, Koreans, Cambodians, Thais, Vietnamese, and Filipinos.

In the *Alcohol and Health* monograph on special populations (1981), researchers suggested that "the impression that Asian Americans do not consume as much alcohol as other Americans and Europeans is generally supported by research studies." The theories behind this are: 1) Orientals, especially Chinese Americans and Japanese Americans, on average metabolize alcohol up to 30 percent faster than Caucasians. As a result they develop a physiological aversion to alcohol. 2) Cultural taboos and community sanctions against excessive alcohol consumption are very strong.

Yet it has also been suggested that, as more and more Oriental families are "Westernized," or assimilated into American culture, there will be more separation from some familial traditions, and this may result in more drinking. At the same time it is important to recognize that young and Adult Children of Alcoholics do exist in this population, and they, too, have the right to treatment and recovery.

One of my major concerns in writing this chapter was not wanting to oversimplify the complexity of the issues confronting the troubled family of color. Adequately discussing the complex Double Duty/Dual Identity issues of various racial groups was a major challenge. Although our other life stories presented portray a wide range of socioeconomic levels, people of color are overrepresented among the unemployed, the undereducated, and those living below the poverty line.

While this chapter is not an extensive analysis of minorities, I hope that it will offer validation and insight to the experiences of Adult Children of color. It is also my intention to sensitize all of us to some of the added considerations involved in living and/or working with people of color.

In truth, each of these chapters deserves its own separate book and each racial group its own chapter within the book. In addition, each ethnic group also merits individual chapters written from a male and a female perspective. However, this book was not intended to present an in-depth exploration of multiracial issues, but rather concerns the overall phenomena of Double Duty/Dual Identity in the lives of Adult Children across the board.

Growing up in a chemically dependent family and being a person of color often involves much more than Double Duty when one considers generations of racism, poverty, learned helplessness, and despair. These are lives that seem to be challenged by "multiple duties." It is important to resist oversimplifying and negating the complexity involved in recovery for minorities, yet we have to begin somewhere.

The lives of the six Adult Children in this chapter—all people of color—express the special issues of Double Duty for minorities. Their sharing offers an opportunity for their special difficulties to be more clearly recognized, more deeply appreciated, and more widely addressed. While people are people, it is only by recognizing both our similarities and our differences that we have an opportunity for recovery.

Addiction has become a vicious cycle in minority communities. Children of color growing up in alcoholic families have had to defend themselves not only against external and internal prejudices, but also against familial alcoholism. For many this has also meant defending against alcoholism in the ethnic communities. The pressures faced by minority ACOAs certainly warrant recognition as Double Duty.

All Adult Children are similar in that they were raised in alcoholic families where they learned not to talk, not to trust, not to feel. This is doubly true for people of color growing up in dysfunctional families who also suffer from the dysfunction of a larger society—racism. Coping with the outside pressures of racism and the inside pressures of family alcoholism greatly magnifies the "Don't talk," "Don't trust," "Don't feel" dynamic. Very early these ACOAs learn the law of shame—the feeling of never, ever being good enough. Although the pain of childhood can come to an end for Adult Children in recovery, as people of color they have to respond to the pain of racial prejudice for a lifetime. Minority Adult Children in alcoholic families often perceive their own color and culture as a liability rather than learning how to build positively on their differences.

While survival roles and rules practiced by COAs are similar, there are also significant differences for minority children living with familial alcoholism. For example, racism and discrimination have played a major part in their generational history. Often acculturation issues must be considered. In addition, the roles of the extended family are prominent. These differences affect the outcome of the treatment process and recovery.

Many minorities can certainly identify with the Adult Child issue of feeling different. The color of their skin, their accents, and their culture set them apart from the white majority. And no matter how much minorities assimilate, even after education and integration they can never change the color of their skin. Many people of color learn at a very young age that their color is not okay. This swiftly becomes internalized as shame—the belief that they are somehow defective. They learn that they can't trust majority people, that they will never be accepted for who they are. The issues they confront as both Children of Alcoholics and children of a racial minority become doubly traumatizing.

Life Stories: Growing-Up Years

The life stories of each of these individuals could have appeared in other chapters—two have two chemically dependent parents, three are themselves chemically dependent, five of the six have experienced chronic physical abuse, and one experienced sexual abuse.

Although those Double Duty/Dual Identity issues are acknowledged, this chapter will focus on the dynamics of racial identity, the impact this has had on the lives of these people, and how the issues of differentness, discrimination, shame, denial, and secrecy magnify their Adult Child issues.

These stories are told by three women and three men between the ages of twenty-seven and fifty-six. There are two Native Americans, two Blacks, and two Hispanics. Both Native Americans lived a life of poverty on reservations; the Hispanic man lived a life of poverty, constantly moving between migrant worker communities. All three experienced chronic violence; two became chemically dependent. One Adult Child has a lower-middle-class Puerto Rican and Mexican background. The black male Adult Child grew up in a professional family. The black woman ACOA grew up in a working-class family in the sixties. There are no Asian American life stories, nor have we discussed acculturation issues that typify the great numbers of Hispanic and Asian families currently moving into the United States.

BONNIE
Age: 29
Ethnicity:
  Mother: Puerto Rican
  Father: Mexican
Father: Alcoholic
Mother: Co-dependent
Birth Order: Second oldest of six
Raised: Texas
Socioeconomic Status: Working
   class

Bonnie's mother met her father after coming to the United States and serving as a dietitian in the army. Bonnie's father had been in the U.S. Navy and was then in the civil service. As is common to many COAs, Bonnie's mother was also an Adult Child.

BONNIE: *"My mother's father would be loving one minute and an angry, violent man the next. Since he was a 'macho' man, it was accepted that he would drink with the men after work, and also that he would occasionally beat his wife or children if they 'needed' it. It was considered proper in their community for women and children to be very subservient and respectful of the adult men in their families, no matter how the men behaved.*

"My father was another macho man. My mother knew he drank when she met him. Even though she promised herself that she would never marry an alcoholic, she still married my father. His drinking was the cause of many fights and breakups between them."

Marrying a person who obviously has an alcohol problem is typical of someone who has a high tolerance for inappropriate behavior. Such expectations typify a person with low self-esteem, who doesn't expect better in life.

Drinking was considered appropriate for the men in Bonnie's neighborhood. It was a legitimized social activity, and there was a certain degree of peer pressure for the men to spend time together drinking at the local bar.

"After a hard day's work, it was expected that the men would meet at the local cantina to drink. It was the only time I knew of that Dad spent with his male peers. It was considered routine among the men of the community. In fact, if someone didn't show up at the cantina, the men would joke that his wife wore the pants in the family and wouldn't let her husband go drinking with the men. This was considered to be quite an insult.

"But my father was also a churchgoing man and was the treasurer of the St. Vincent de Paul Society. He was also a member of the school board and a supervisor at work. He was a well-respected man in the Mexican community."

That Bonnie's father could drink alcoholically while maintaining his status in his community shows how socializing in bars with his male friends was an expected community activity. Such collusion in society made it easy to rationalize his abnormal behavior. It also makes dissident family members feel guilty when they have negative or hurtful feelings since the rest of the community regards this person so highly. To speak up and say there was something wrong about your father's drinking would have been totally unacceptable. It is difficult to respond to a problem in a healthy way when doing so would be perceived as betraying your family.

Although Bonnie's father was alcoholic, he was still capable of functioning reasonably well in certain areas of his life. However, each year that alcoholics move through the progression of their disease, they become less functional. Children often remember the years of conflict when the alcoholic parent presented him- or herself to outsiders as okay, while behaving at home like someone overwhelmed with confusion and pain.

Bonnie's father's drinking became progressively worse as the children grew up. He spent less time with the family and more time out drinking with his friends. Bonnie says that she has good memories of her father being playful with the children when they were very young, but that over time he became erratic in his moods and behavior. Gradually he also became more demanding and abusive. He would come home later and later, at times passing out on the floor.

"When he'd come home, he'd eat and then go straight to bed, saying that he had to get up early. He always insisted that he didn't have a drinking problem since he took care of his family financially. But we never saw him during the week. He left before we woke up. When he came

home, he would eat his dinner alone—if he didn't pass out. He became a stranger to us. The only time we did hear him or see him was when he was fighting with Mom or yelling at us.''

By the time Bonnie was in junior high, her father had become physically abusive, particularly to his wife and an older sibling. On one occasion Bonnie's mother suffered a concussion from being hit; another time her father beat Bonnie's sister so severely that the family had to restrain him physically.

Bonnie's growing-up years were spent with other Hispanic families. She didn't give a lot of thought to being different from whites, but she did feel more comfortable with other Hispanics.

The family didn't have a lot of money, but the children were able to attend a private Catholic school from first through twelfth grades through after-school jobs and scholarships. Bonnie's parents valued education, and Bonnie was a good student. In high school she found she loved biology. She also belonged to the church choir and a Girl Scout troop.

"Prayer was always very important to me. When I was in eighth grade, God was my confidant. I had no one else I felt I could talk to. My life at that time was one big, long prayer. My father was drinking heavily and coming home later and later. My mom was becoming more and more haggard. She was very much the co-alcoholic spouse. She was constantly nagging and screaming at my father about his drinking. I kept my own problems to myself because there was no way my father would be of help, and I just didn't want to burden my mom—she had enough problems.''

Bonnie took on the role of the good kid, the responsible one—the hero.

"The youth choir and the Girl Scouts at church were my outlets. My father wanted to keep us all at home, away from 'outsiders.' But my mother fought to allow us these outside activities and encouraged them. She wanted us to learn to be independent, and I will always be grateful to her for that.''

Youth activities, such as Girl or Boy Scouts and choir, are wonderful resources for children, but even more so when one grows up in such a troubled family. These were opportunities for Bonnie to be free of fear in safe settings. There she could be a child, with no unrealistic expectations placed on her. Resources such as these give COAs the inner strength to continue their survivorship.

Bonnie was fortunate that her mother—as frightened as she must have been—insisted that she have these opportunities.

Because a greater percentage of racial minority groups live below the poverty line, COAs who are children of color often have fewer opportunities for such activities.

Bonnie also learned, as do so many COAs, that by helping other people she could avoid her own pain and be perceived as a good child.

"I never had problems making friends, but I tended to have one specific person I latched on to. Usually this person was extremely shy or unpopular and would always greatly appreciate my friendship. My friends were often people that I wanted to help change in some way. I think it was part of the co-dependent behavior that I learned growing up in my family."

Bonnie had four sisters and one brother. The sisters were very close, but as children they were unable to discuss their father's alcoholism. As Bonnie's father's drinking got worse, he gave the family less and less financial support, leaving Bonnie's mother to pay most of the bills. Bonnie's parents finally divorced when she was in high school.

"My mother was left with five kids to support. My father took my little brother to live with him. My mother let him because he said he would take it to court and fight her if she didn't. But my dad didn't act as though he liked my brother—I think he did this to punish my mother. She didn't know how to fight him, and she knew someone had to take care of my father. My brother was only in the fifth grade. To help pay the bills, the oldest kids took part-time jobs while going to school."

Alcoholism is often financially burdensome and draining of family resources, and this has grave consequences for children in low-income families. Childhood becomes shortened when money is a problem. Children often have to go out and get jobs to help support the family simply to survive. Often they spend a lot of time worrying about basic daily needs. Yet, like Bonnie, they have reasons to pride themselves on their survivorship—they are proud of being tough.

After high school, with the help of scholarships, Bonnie went on to college.

PAM
Age: 28
Ethnicity: Native American
Mother: Alcoholic
Father: Alcoholic
Birth Order: Oldest of three, plus
    four stepsiblings
Raised: On reservation, Washington
    State
Socioeconomic Status: Poor

Pam's mother was raised in a violent, alcoholic home. She married her first husband at age fourteen, and over the next eight years she had four children.

When Pam's mother married Pam's father at age twenty-two, she was running away from an alcoholic husband. At the time her kids were starving, and she turned them over to her parents. She had three more children with her second husband. Over the years, periodically, the older four children would come and live with Pam and her brother and sister.

Pam's life was characterized by overwhelming poverty. There was no running water in her house, and electricity was wired only in the bathroom. Her closest neighbors were relatives whom she would periodically seek out for comfort. Her memories of safety are of times she would stay at her grandmother's. But she doesn't remember feeling different or apart from others—most of the families she knew lived just like her family. Most of the people she knew were relatives—aunts, uncles, cousins. Violence and alcoholism were tolerated and accepted by almost all, allowing cousins and relatives to look beyond and still find a way to connect with each other.

Pam has fond memories of animals as friends. She describes being very imaginative as she and her brother and sister would play in the woods among rabbits, squirrels, birds, and deer.

In her early years, before her mother divorced him, her father was a mechanic and welder on the reservation. He was an alcoholic who might or might not drink on the weekdays. But Pam remembers that weekends were filled with her father's and mother's drinking. Her father would be gone for hours or come home drunk with drinking buddies. Her mother and father often got into fights and went their separate ways. Pam would wait for them to come home, anticipating their violence.

Nevertheless, Pam didn't see drinking as a problem—it was the accepted way of life. But she hated the violence.

PAM: "I was always so scared. Things were so out of control. I saw a lot of violence. The joke was: 'What is Indian love? Hickeys and black eyes.' It was accepted for women and wives to be beat up. I would try to stop my parents but couldn't."

This way of life only fed Pam's shame and her sense that she lacked value because she was a Native American woman. What a tragic lesson to learn, and at such a young age.

Survival in the face of extreme neglect and abuse is all Pam knew in her life. Typical of the oldest child in an alcoholic home, Pam became the responsible child. Although she tried to fulfill her role, it was unrealistic to expect a child to be able to handle such chaos.

"My parents used to leave on Fridays and not come home until a few days later.

"Once when I was about eight, my parents were gone, drunk somewhere, and there was this big bear on our back porch. We didn't have any locks on our doors, so I had to use knives to lock the doors. The bear was ripping everything apart. My brother and I unplugged the stove and pushed it up against the door. Then we went and got my dad's shotgun. I was going to shoot the bear, but I couldn't even lift up the gun. I was holding the front while my brother and sister held up the back end. For some reason I didn't shoot. But I remember having to do other things like that and not thinking anything about it.

"Another time when our parents were gone, there were thirteen kids at our house, five in diapers. I was in charge. My sister burned her leg on the exhaust of a motorcycle, and I sent my brother to get my aunt and uncle, who lived two miles away. They took care of us a lot by bringing us food and heating oil. Well, they came and we drove my sister to the hospital. But I got in trouble for getting my aunt and uncle involved and for not keeping my sister off the bike."

Generations of Pam's family had lived in a community that accepted alcoholism. Chemical dependency was so widespread on the reservation that it was natural for Pam and her siblings to be left to care for themselves. Moreover, there was little or no community response. While Pam speaks of her grandmother and her aunt and uncle as sources of comfort, they did not or could not respond in a manner that would prevent her from experiencing severe neglect and physical abuse.

"My dad used to beat my mom to a pulp. She threw things at him, too. It used to remind me of TV cartoons, the way she would slide across the room. Once she slid under the television, and it fell on her and I thought she was dead."

It is difficult to believe that children survive as well as they do under such catastrophic conditions. Pam had to develop an incredible ability to detach emotionally from the pain in her life. That ability would come to permeate all aspects of her life as a COA. She had to use all the denial she could muster to go to school, to play with her siblings, to go places with her father.

While Pam's struggle to survive was extreme, she still fought valiantly for what any young child longs for—to play with animals, friends, and siblings, to feel loved, and to belong.

"My dad was always nicer to me than he was to my mom. He favored me. He took me places. When he'd go drinking in town, he'd take me along. I spent a lot of time in the car while he was in bars. My dad never hit me, but my mom abused me a lot. She favored my sister. Mom would only slap her, but I got hit and kicked. I can remember her taking kitchen utensils and trying to stab me."

When Pam was ten her parents were in a serious automobile accident. Her mother was critically injured and was hospitalized for several months. As a result, the three children were sent to a mission boarding school, where they remained for the next year and a half.

"This was my first introduction to the reality of prejudice. I had never before given much thought to being Indian. Living at the mission was scary and lonely. We were bussed to a public school, where the non-Indians didn't like the Indians—and the Indians didn't like the non-Indians. I remember it being a very hostile place. The kids were always fighting, and the Indian students were always getting into trouble with the teachers.

"Prejudice was alive. It was hard for me, as I did not see our differences. I thought we all had a lot in common—both the Indians and the non-Indians. But the more I was exposed to the prejudice, the more I became proud of my Indianness. I became determined to learn all that I could about my heritage and to become an advocate for Indian people."

When Pam returned home she found that the drinking and fighting not only had not stopped, but in fact appeared to have escalated. Her parents soon divorced. Pam's mother moved to a different state, taking her three youngest children. Pam describes the next several years as the most traumatic and painful times in her life.

"I missed the reservation, my dad, and especially my gram—her warmth and her love and her humor. My mother's drinking increased, and she became even more abusive toward us kids. She remarried again, this time to an Indian man from one of the coastal tribes. He was not only alcoholic, but also addicted to drugs. After a year of their living together, my mother became pregnant.

"I remember crying about the pregnancy. I felt so guilty because some of my feelings were of not wanting this child. I knew that I would be the primary caretaker. I loved this baby, though. I sat up in the hospital for two days waiting for her arrival. I was even given the honor of naming her.

"My stepdad beat up my mom a lot. There was a time when he beat her up so bad and there was so much blood that I ran and got the butcher knife and told him I was going to kill him. I held him at bay with the knife while my brother ran and got the police.

"Through all of this I was the responsible child. I did what I could to hold things together, but mostly life was about trying to survive. School was relief for me. I loved school. It was a breath of fresh air. I liked the attention I got. I was encouraged and supported by my teachers. I enjoyed sports and was good at gymnastics. I was also good in drama and was encouraged to try and do something with my talents as an actress. I had been acting my whole life, so I should have been good.

"When I was sixteen, one night my mother came into my bedroom where I was sleeping and grabbed me by the hair. She dragged me down the hall and into the living room and began beating me. I ended up with a broken jaw and broken ribs. It was a terrible scene, with my stepfather quietly watching and my sisters screaming and crying. They sent me by bus to my father's without my having seen a doctor.

"Arriving at my father's was a major relief. His first words were 'I love you and this will never happen to you again.' I then went to the doctor. At that point all I felt was relief. I knew it was over for me—I would never again tolerate abuse.

"I only stayed at my dad's a few months. Living with my dad, his girlfriend, and her kids wasn't working out. There was a lot of jealousy. So I decided to move back to Washington and live with a man I knew.

My dad agreed under two conditions—one, that I would finish school or get my general education degree, and two, that I would not marry this person. I agreed.

"I didn't finish school, and we lived together approximately two years. He was fifteen years older than I—I was sixteen. It was a desperation relationship. He was my way out. He was a severe alcoholic. I was going to cure him and fix him and make him all better. He promised me he would never hit me. I had told him if he ever hit me, I would kill him."

Pam's bottom line, the key to her maintaining any internal strength, was vowing that she would never again be hit. Although she had a high tolerance for emotional abandonment, she was a master of survival.

Then came the final straw.

"One night we were at a party when the police came. They gave me the car keys and said my boyfriend wasn't to drive home. We were outside on the lawn, and my boyfriend was angry. He picked me up off my feet and threw me down. I had a beer bottle in my hand, and I cold-cocked him on his head and took off for home, running.

"I waited for him to come back, and when he did I freaked out. I tied him to the bed with a sheet. The bedroom had sliding glass doors with a wood stick in them, and I took the stick and beat him until he bled from one end of his body to the other. Then I stopped. I had everything packed, and I got on a train and went back to the reservation."

Pam had nowhere to go except where she'd come from. But she wasn't through fighting for herself. Children who have experienced that much abuse tend to become either ongoing victims or fighters.

"I was now almost eighteen, and I was determined to take control of my life. I didn't know what I'd do or how I'd do it, but I knew I would do it."

She did it the only way she knew, through another man.

"I went back to the reservation and lived with my grandmother. But the only way I knew how to live life was to be in a relationship. I had watched both my parents go from one mate to another. So I looked for a nice, gentle man who wouldn't hurt me. I didn't want someone who would abuse me. The bottom line was that I would not be hit.

"A year after I was back, I married a reservation cop. He wasn't Indian. I wanted someone who was educated, who had a steady job, and who didn't drink. I was nineteen, he was twenty-one, we married nine months after we first met. Although he was white, he'd been living on

the reservation, and he was proud of my being Indian. Nobody told me I had to love him.''

Although it might be easy for others to see that someone with such a history would have additional problems, Pam was developing a foundation that would be important for her future growth. She was seeking a non-traumatic, peaceful household. She had identified alcohol and violence as the sources of the problems in her life.

CHUQUE

Age: 38
Ethnicity: Hispanic
Mother: Alcoholic
Father: Alcoholic
Birth Order: Second oldest of six
Raised: Southwest
Socioeconomic Status: Poverty

Chuque spent most of his early growing-up years traveling with his family—migrant workers, all—from Arizona to California and back. He remembers his father being a violent alcoholic who divorced his mother when Chuque was six. He and his siblings remained with his mother, who was also alcoholic and who would go on to marry several more violent alcoholic men. Chuque doesn't remember much of his childhood—although the longer he is in recovery, the more he remembers. He describes his growing-up years as being surrounded by violence and heavy drinking.

CHUQUE: *"Violence and alcoholism were a way of life. The fighting while drunk was often referred to as 'having some good drunks'!*

"When I was in grade school my mom would repeatedly disappear for long periods of time. She was in a hospital as a result of beatings, but we were never told where she was. All we knew was that she'd disappeared again.

"My godfather would then take all of us children to his home. Although he was alcoholic, too, he was consistent. He was nurturing. He was my role model. I would go to sleep knowing he was in the house and wake up knowing he would still be there.

"When my mom returned we went back to her. Most of the time when I came home from school no one would be there—sometimes my mother

*would be there drunk. I never saw her getting drunk, I would only see
her after she had returned from the bar boisterously drunk.''*

While Chuque lived a life of violence, ''people pleasing'' and caretaking
became his major roles.

*''I always held my mom sacred. My job was to clean her up, take care
of her. I would see her get beat up by men, and I was powerless to stop
it. I only had the power to nurse her and clean her up.''*

Yet one cannot continuously perform these roles when one is surrounded by rage and violence. Chuque struggled to not respond to violence with violence. How do children emotionally survive the pain if they
don't fight back? They become severely immobilized and depressed, which
leads to greater victimization for themselves. Or they medicate.

*''By eighth grade I had seen so much rage and beating, I actually almost
killed a person with my hands. I vowed then never to hit anyone again. I
can remember all three of us boys being set up by my stepdad to fight
each other, and the one who cried would be whipped.''*

Chuque's parents worked in the fields, but the kids were sent to school.
Chuque started drinking and using when he was thirteen. He had been
introduced to pot by his uncle, who was a heroin addict. He quit school
early in high school.

*''There was no one encouraging me to stay in school. When I was fifteen
I moved out and was on my own. The street became my teacher. I was
angry when I left school. I was told my people were good with their hands
and that would be how I should make something out of my life.''*

When he quit school and hit the streets, Chuque became involved with
the Chicano/Mexicano human rights movement. This was the late sixties.
All the while he was continuing to drink and use heavily.

*''The movement gave me a sense of belonging. It offered me hopes,
dreams, aspirations. All of my people pleasing came out in the movement.
I would do anything I was directed to or asked for. I desperately wanted
the approval of these people.''*

WILLIAM
Age: 56
Ethnicity: African American
Father: Alcoholic
Mother: Adult Child
Birth Order: Oldest of four
Raised: Midwest
Socioeconomic Status: Middle class

William was raised in the Midwest, where his father was the first black male teacher in his area in the public school systems. Although both parents had teaching certificates, his mother did not teach because at that time it was not permissible for two blacks married to each other to teach in the same system at the same time.

In his early childhood, the neighborhood William was raised in was partially white and predominantly Jewish. But by the time he was seven it had become an all-black neighborhood. By second grade the classroom had only black children. And until his father came to the local junior high school, all the teachers were white.

William knows now that his father was alcoholic. But during his growing-up years he didn't think much about his father's drinking.

WILLIAM: *"My dad was gone most of the time. He had two jobs: he taught during the day and found extra jobs at night, such as being a groundskeeper at a park. He provided for us well. What I remember most is that he was a disciplinarian. It was always awkward for me because he was well liked and respected by others, but at home I didn't have much of a sense of him. He would be real quiet, didn't want much to do with us.*

"He wasn't mean, he'd just sit there quietly and drink. I can remember finding bottles he'd hidden. I wasn't sure why he was hiding them. But because he was hiding them I thought it had to be kept secret. He was the boss in the house, so I kept the secret. I thought that this was what all fathers did—they worked and drank."

Although William has very little sense of his father, he remembers his mother well.

"I picked up very early from my mother that I was not acceptable. I always felt judged by her—and judged as bad. She was very strong willed and ex-

tremely cutting with her tongue. I felt like the stereotypical stepchild. She distorted things so much that I always looked bad. Yet, like my father, she was a catalyst, the focal point of the neighborhood. She was a skilled manipulator—good at getting things done, and done her way."

William's next sibling was four years younger than he. He says that when the baby was born he really felt abandoned by his mother. The next two siblings were ten and twelve years younger than William. He didn't feel close to any of them. He describes spending most of his childhood out of the house because it didn't feel comfortable to be home.

"I ran around with the guys at school. With them I felt a part of things. I never felt my mother or father cared very much about what I did or whether or not I was home. They were mostly preoccupied with other things or the other kids. I tried to get my dad's approval through sports because he had been an all-American in track, but I was small and not that fast. By high school I'd given up trying.

"I fit all of the roles COAs adopt. In grade school I was a good student until the kids started teasing me about being teacher's pet, and I realized I wanted their approval more than my parents'. By junior high school I'd become the adjuster. I really wasn't invested in what was happening at home. In high school I did do some acting out, though most of it was kept under wraps. For a year I kept a stolen car. It took a lot of skill to have a stolen car and use it and not have your parents find out. But then again, they weren't paying much attention. (Ultimately, when the cops found out, they found out!)"

William's experience in an alcoholic family is different from those of the others in this chapter. His losses came more from what he didn't get and from what didn't get said rather than through blatant pain or trauma being inflicted. But there's a common thread.

William was emotionally abandoned by his parents because of his father's physical absence in the home and his preoccupation with drinking when he was home. The nonalcoholic parent was the one with the cutting tongue, the one from whom William felt the most direct pain. It was his mother he felt direct rejection from, the one from whom he internalized messages that he was unacceptable. But his father's lack of involvement was also a nonverbal message implying William's lack of importance. Although his father staunchly held down two jobs to support the family, William got little else emotionally from him.

William spent summers with his mother's parents in the northern part of the state, and he has good memories of those times. He remembers little of his grandfather.

"He drank and spent most of his time downstairs in the basement where he kept his bottle. He'd start his drinking early—in the morning. At night he'd be out gambling.

"Around the house he stayed out of the spotlight. Yet when my grandfather and my two uncles were together there would laughter, partying, and lots of drinking. I knew then that I wanted to be a part of them. They were my favorite relatives. When they were drinking they'd talk so freely, and that made me feel free. I felt accepted around them. It made me feel good."

William had his first drink at fifteen, but it made him deathly ill, and he didn't resume drinking with any regularity until he was out of high school. Yet when he reflects on his childhood, he remembers that it was the times associated with his relatives' drinking that made him feel the most accepted.

After high school William did what was expected of him and went to college. But he made poor grades and was put on probation. He switched to a smaller school, thinking that would be the answer to his poor grades. But he quickly found that he had little motivation for studying—he was enjoying his drinking a lot more. His next step was to join the Air Force. He spent three years in the service before being dishonorably discharged for bad conduct.

ETTA
Age: 42
Ethnicity: African American
Father: Alcoholic
Mother: Co-dependent
Birth Order: Youngest of four
    children
Raised: Urban, northeastern city
Socioeconomic Status: Working
    class

Etta was the youngest of four children born in a seven-year span. Her father was a factory worker and her mother a teacher's aide who often picked up additional jobs.

Etta's first memory is of violence.

ETTA: "I was four and I was in the kitchen. My father had a chair poised over my mother's head and she had a knife at his throat. She told me to run and get my grandmother (who lived nearby), and my dad told me if I moved, he'd kill her. All I could do was stand there and cry. I cried and cried and cried.

In Etta's family childhood meant endless arguing. Her parents argued continually about money, as Etta's father was also a compulsive gambler. They argued about her father's infidelity.

Like most of the other COAs in this chapter, Etta witnessed physical abuse. But in her family the children recognized it as wrong. They saw their dad as bad for being a violent person.

"One night when I was six years old, my father started to beat up my mom. My sister hollered out to all of us to jump Dad. We did. All four of us attacked him. We hit, slapped, kicked, yelled. Four little wild, uncontrollable energies attacking the big bad giant. He was drunk and couldn't control us. We had a heydey. It stopped the violence for that night."

Etta's relationship with her mother was that of a protector, perceiving her mother as a victim. She does credit her mother for fighting back during violence. Yet she can remember times of experiencing her mother's defeat.

"At times my mother would just sit there and weep. She would sit me on her lap while she cried, and then we'd both cry."

Etta was too young to understand her mother's words, too young to be a true confidante. But she internalized the incredible sadness and pain. Etta was a chronic bed wetter until third grade; she also had very bad asthma and several allergies. All of these are signs of internalizing the family dysfunction.

"Chaos and crisis reigned supreme in our household. I'd lock myself away in my room and hide to get away from all the yelling and screaming. Everybody fought—both parents and all the children. Then there was always the threat of the lights and gas being shut off due to lack of payment. But I was tough."

Etta says she was a serious little adult by the time she was three, which is reflected in childhood photos. The source of stability in Etta's life were her maternal grandparents. It was at their house that she felt safe.

"At my grandmother's we had predictable mealtimes and bedtimes. We went to church. People didn't yell. Sometimes we'd stay the entire summer, and we were often sent there when my father was on a binge."

In spite of the family drama, both of Etta's parents strongly valued education. One of Etta's pleasant childhood memories was of her father taking her to get her first library card. She remembers her father reading at home and telling her that she would need to work twice as hard to get ahead in the world because she was black and only one generation away from slavery.

Etta's parents divorced when she was thirteen, which only added reinforcement that she couldn't count on anybody for anything. Although she did continue to see her father, she felt she could only rely on herself.

In order not to go on the welfare rolls, Etta's mother had to work two and three jobs, leaving Etta to fend for herself. The stigma of being poor was so enmeshed with being black that, to Etta, education seemed the only way to avoid having to live a life of poverty and crisis.

It had been drilled into Etta that she had to be smart, that she had to have real accomplishments to get ahead. So school became a wonderful source of comfort and escape.

"I read a lot, and I wrote a lot of poetry and short stories. I won awards for writing."

Etta's family was Catholic, and she had always attended Catholic schools, where she was strongly rewarded for being so mature. By high school Etta belonged to lots of clubs and worked on the yearbook and the newspaper.

"I was always the last one to leave the school. I only left at six P.M. because the grounds were closed then. I always volunteered for things because I knew if I went home, nobody would be there. My brothers would be hanging out on the streets, and my mother would be gone to her second job."

Etta was a lone figure in her family—she and her siblings were each fighting for survival. Her oldest sister was "an abusive dictator," and her oldest brother kept having to protect Etta from her. While Etta and the oldest boy tended to be of a more sensitive temperament, her other brother was physically violent toward the other kids and himself. Etta remembers that *"he would often bang his head against the floor."*

Sibling violence is very common in families where children don't have the structure and parenting they need to learn how to problem-solve and express their feelings safely. It is also a common reaction for children who witness abuse and/or are the recipients of abuse. Etta's father was the model that validated the internal message, "It's okay to abuse others physically."

Some children will be abusive to themselves rather than hurt others. This reflects even greater social isolation. Head banging is not uncommon in children who want to escape their internal pain. Sometimes it reflects a child's attempt to drown out the pain.

While many COAs find an escape from their pain in alcohol and drugs, others find it elsewhere.

"In my adolescence I experimented with drugs briefly, but I found I had no tolerance for them. Instead I probably acted out my dysfunction more by working very hard at school and taking care of everyone but myself."

Etta's hard work was rewarded with a scholarship to a prestigious eastern college.

Special Issues for ACOAs of Color

DIFFERENCES—DISCRIMINATION

Children growing up in alcoholic families often feel like outsiders among their peers. They know that their home life is different from that of other families. Their mothers or their fathers are not like their friends' parents. The alcoholism keeps them isolated from their peers and from the community. They often walk through life feeling different from others but not knowing why. It adds up to feeling different in a vague but clearly negative way. The internalized message is: "I feel different. There is something wrong with me."

Growing up as a member of an ethnic minority adds immeasurably to the COA's feeling of isolation. Such children feel different because they are constantly told they are. They look around at the white majority, and they feel like outsiders. Their skin color is different. Their families tend not to have as much money as the white families they see. The role models they see on TV or in the movies are usually white and middle class. Minority children often feel locked out with no way to get in.

Five of the six people in this chapter grew up before there was any widespread use of minorities in advertisements or commercials or as tele-vision characters.

ETTA: "When a black person would appear on TV, we would run through the house screaming, 'There's a colored man on TV—hurry up or you'll miss him!' "

This was also a time when minorities were stereotyped as criminals, servants, or savages.

Much of what minorities had reflected back to them about their own ethnic groups was negative and often violent. When John Kennedy was assassinated, Etta was at a school that was three-quarters black.

"Racial tension at this time was so high that we were terrified. We were all saying that we hoped it was not a black man who had killed the pres-ident. We'd all seen pictures of Emmett Till hanging from a tree in Mis-sissippi for looking at a white woman, and we knew we'd all be severely punished if a black man had murdered the president. We were forever vulnerable because we were different—because we were black."

This deep sense of vulnerability and fear reflects the minority percep-tion of the world as a hostile place.

Children from alcoholic families already suffer from low self-esteem. They believe something is wrong with them, that they are not good enough. This is made doubly devastating by the ethnic stereotypes and rejection that minorities have to struggle against in a white-dominated society.

High school was where Bonnie first had to deal with how others treated her because of her ethnic background.

BONNIE: "It was at the private high school I attended where I first learned about being in a minority. The popular girls were all blond and blue-eyed. They went to lots of parties and had their own friends. My friends were all Mexican American. I always felt inferior among whites. But even among my friends there was a difference between the Mexican Americans who were of 'Spanish origin' and the 'wetbacks' or pachucos straight from Mexico."

Bonnie even lived with racism within her own family. Her father was extremely racist toward darker-skinned Mexican Americans. He pro-jected his shame onto others of his own heritage.

Bonnie's mother, on the other hand, was extremely proud of being Puerto Rican and imparted those feelings to her children. The dichotomy between one parent's pride and the other's shame created an even greater inner dissonance in Bonnie.

Not only do children learn about racial prejudice through the stories parents tell them, but their parents also teach them that they will be treated differently: "Don't expect to be treated the same as your white friends." Although minority children are warned of the probable experiences, they are given conflicting messages about how to handle it. Some are instructed to show white folks that they aren't inferior by being twice as good or encouraged to display abrasive attitudes toward whites. These messages create a lot of inner conflict because the children are also being encouraged to learn the ways of whites in order to succeed in life. Success is equated with emulating whites—implying inferiority for the person of color. The contrasting compensation among minority people is to praise the unique virtues and superiority of their own racial group and to ridicule the dullness and predictability of majority group members.

PAM: "The differentness I have felt even extends to my own family. I am light-complected and have green eyes, and this makes it difficult for them to accept me. Out of our entire family, neither my brother, my sister, nor I were enrolled into the tribe. They wouldn't accept my mother because she is not a qualified Indian. My mother needed to be one-quarter blood of the tribe we lived with. But she was a mixed blood of three other tribes, and so was my father. I was so angry. I was proud to be Indian. I wanted to be a part of my own people, and I couldn't even belong there. I never felt as though I fit in or was a part of anything."

By not being on the tribe rolls, Pam was also denied certain rights— hunting and fishing rights, land rights, and scholarships to school. She was angry and wrote letters, but it was clear that she was angry with the governmental organization, not the people of the reservation.

A sense of belonging is vital to a child's self-esteem. By not fitting into the Native American society with blood rights, Pam again internalized the feeling of not belonging. Fortunately her paternal grandmother had instilled a sense of pride in her for being Indian that would resurface in adulthood.

"I took pride listening to my grandmother's stories. Knowing our family history made me feel not quite so small and unimportant. I learned that family was bigger than just my parents and my brothers and sisters. I needed to be connected with something larger than our immediate alcoholism and violence. I had grown up thinking I was Indian. But I had been *too busy just trying to survive to really think about what it meant to be or not to be Indian.''*

Being light-complected made it difficult for Pam to be accepted among her people. And, unfortunately, she didn't have the social supports within her own family that would help her confront such intraracial issues.

CHUQUE: *"I was aware of the differences—the differences between white and Mexican neighborhoods. The authorities were white. I was aware of differences among Hispanics. The lighter skinned you were, the more likely you would be successful. The more I got involved in the movement, the angrier I became. I read about losing our land, our culture. I wanted to read about people who looked like me and spoke like me, people who offered me pride in my culture.''*

Yet Chuque says color became his flag of defiance. Unfortunately his anger became very self-destructive. At that time he did not have the internal strength to develop that pride and use it to his advantage. Chuque came from a family riddled by alcoholism and violence—and a community riddled by alcoholism and violence. For many COAs of color, or white, this violence is generational. But Chuque had also been generationally affected by the despair, powerlessness, and rage that comes from a life of poverty and oppression.

While the minority child encounters discrimination in the white community, this discrimination becomes internalized. It is only "safe" to act out within the ethnic community.

William felt his greatest sense of differentness within the black community itself.

"Sidity," which is slang for "stuck-up," refers to both light-complected blacks and children whose parents were professionals. William was caught between both categories—he was dark-complected, but the child of a professional.

WILLIAM: *"When your parents were educated and you had a bit more money, it seemed you became part of a clique. We all went to the same church—an Episcopal church. I thought its teachings were very rigid. I hated it. I envied my other friends who weren't in church.*

"Then there was this woman in the neighborhood who wanted to give us kids a greater sense of identity. She would organize trips to concerts and museums. Some parents were clearly teaching their kids they were better than other kids. Then you would see them leave the area and try to go to school in the white areas.

"While I was part of this group because my father was a teacher, I

never liked it. I always identified with the other kids, I wanted to be a part of them. It was also hard because, while I was a part of this group, we didn't have as much money as most of them had, and that would often be embarrassing."

William would use his "chameleon" skills to fit into both worlds. He would yell, "Sidity!" at the light-complected and upper-class kids and at the same time grudgingly be a part of that group.

Etta experienced feeling different from others because she had grown up in a violent alcoholic home and also because she was black. She knew that more violence was associated with the black community than the white community, and this sense of negative difference between blacks and whites was an unconscious source of shame.

ETTA: *"It had been drilled into me since I was young that we as blacks were to emulate whites in order to be accepted in this world. My parents were always comparing blacks and whites—all comparisons were framed around the white world. I interpreted this to mean that if I was good, I'd be perceived more like a white person, but if I acted bad, then I was black."*

Etta was given a scholarship in high school that enabled her to attend an all-girls' academy. It was here that her blackness really stood out.

"I felt like a toy—the 'other.' I was treated with condescension, fear, and fascination. On the one hand, at the academy I was the expert on being black—whether I wanted to be or not. But when I went into the village without my classmates, I was treated with suspicion and hostility."

Like many COAs, Etta was the hero child in her family. At this time in the late sixties, the historical events unfolding around her added pressure to her need to be the hero—she wanted to bring dignity and pride to her race. Although this desire was noble, Etta had no one with whom to talk about her role in the family, no one who understood her problems as the only black person in a formerly all-white school. There was no one available to help her recognize and cope with her feelings. So she continued her old pattern of emotional denial.

Often minority children learn the harsh lesson of prejudice from their parents' horror stories of discrimination.

ETTA: *"My father was in the service as a young man, but he would never discuss what it was like. I asked him about it once, but he told me that he couldn't talk about it because it was so painful.*

"He fought in Italy, and at that time although blacks and whites fought together, when they were off the battlefield, they were segregated. My father said they would gather all the black people together like cattle, take their weapons, and put barbed-wire fencing around them. They couldn't get passes to go to town like the white soldiers. Once one of my father's black friends sneaked into town and was shot and killed by one of the white American soldiers.

"My father had been in the automobile detail at the time, but he asked to be moved to the front line. He said he wanted to have a gun in his hands as much as possible because you couldn't trust anyone.

"I felt so bad for him as he told me this. He had tears in his eyes. He seemed ashamed. It was as if he had been stripped of his dignity and made to feel helpless. It was as if they had taken away his pride and he couldn't fight back. He was forced to accept being second class or nothing."

A child's response to this kind of story is strongly influenced by the parent's response and level of self-esteem. Etta's father was full of shame, despair, futility, and rage. Here he was, fighting for a country that constantly negated his being in humiliating ways. He had struggled with his rage at whites and the white system and at himself for his powerlessness. By the time he told Etta this story, all she heard was his powerlessness and shame, which by now were also exacerbated by his alcoholism.

SHAME

Discrimination within the minority community is a source of shame. The color of one's skin, the place of one's birth, or the financial status of one's family can make a major difference in the way the member of a minority is viewed within his or her own community. The shame that minorities have been made to feel about their heritage is often acted out within the ethnic community.

Although Bonnie's mother was proud of her Puerto Rican identity, Bonnie learned to be ashamed of her Mexican American heritage. Although her father was active within the Hispanic community, his own prejudice and self-loathing were very strong.

BONNIE: "It had been hammered into me by my father and friends that I should be ashamed of being Mexican American. My father seemed to despise his own ethnic origin. All this was very confusing to me.

"My father's prejudices became especially clear once we kids started dating. Since we lived in a Mexican American community, it was obvious that the boys we would meet would be of those origins. When we brought boys home to meet Mom, we were usually lucky enough not to meet up with Dad, since he was seldom home.

"However, if he was home, he would chase the wetbacks out of the house. He called them 'wetbacks' if they appeared Mexican to him. You can imagine how confusing this was to me. I knew that the term wetback was a derogatory one. But I also knew that my father was Mexican American, and that I was half Mexican American. My father would say 'wetback' or 'Mexican' with such venom in his voice that I didn't have to guess how low that person was in my father's eyes."

For Bonnie, as for other Adult Children of color, class differences created shame. She was fortunate to receive scholarships and work-study positions at a school that allowed her to attend a college preparatory Catholic school. But she stood out among the other students as a Mexican American who was poor. Her sense of isolation was made even worse because, while other kids had time to socialize at school, she had to work at part-time jobs to make ends meet.

Pam felt separate from others and ashamed of how she lived.

PAM: *"I was ashamed of being so poor. I was ashamed of the alcoholism, my parents' lack of involvement in my schooling, the yelling, and being embarrassed in front of friends. I tried to separate myself from it all. I wouldn't allow others to come to my home because I didn't want my friends to be exposed to my family. To my knowledge, none of my school friends were as poor or had such violent families.*

"I always felt like the fifth wheel at everything. I never felt good enough. Aside from how we lived, when we'd periodically move off the reservation I would be called a squaw. Yet on the reservation, because I was light-complected with green eyes and had such a mixture of various Indian bloods in me, I belonged nowhere."

Chuque was blatantly shamed when he was publicly swatted at school for speaking Spanish. He was forced to speak English.

CHUQUE: *"They said we talked like chickens, and then we would be punished for speaking our own language."*

Chuque remembers always feeling ashamed. He had no sense of identity or self-worth. His life was shrouded with the shame of poverty, violence, and color.

"Like most of my darker-skinned friends, I used to wash with Clorox in an attempt to lighten my skin, or I wore long-sleeved shirts to cover my skin. White was beautiful—not brown."

The shame that William felt seemed to come from his mother's disapproval and criticism. Then again, he went through a period where he had to deal with being called "Lips" by an older neighborhood boy.

WILLIAM: *"I thought I had big lips, although that isn't really so. But every time I heard him call me that, I felt less than."*

Despite her criticism, William's mother was a good role model for fighting for what one wanted.

"My mother was bold. She would go anywhere and do anything she wanted. From her I learned to say what I wanted and not to be passive. Unfortunately this tended to come out the most when I was drinking."

William doesn't remember feeling much shame, but he registers strongly with fear. Nevertheless, like many Adult Children, he isn't able to pinpoint specific things he was afraid of. He just remembers living in a constant state of fear.

"And when I drank, I felt relief. I had no fears. I felt good about myself from the first drink—even though I got sick."

William's drinking filled a void, a terrible emptiness familiar to many who become alcoholic and to many who were raised in alcoholic families.

ETTA: *"The different shades of brown skin can be a plus or minus in your life in both the white and black communities. I have never understood the white idea that all black people look alike. We come in all colors. There are many blacks who hate being 'high yellow' and being mistaken for white. It upsets their sense of personal identity as well as their sense of belonging to the black community. At the other end of the spectrum, the darker-skinned black people may be distrustful of fairer-skinned blacks, believing that they get preferential treatment."*

Etta speaks of the feelings of inadequacy that came with being a token brown-complexioned black in white schools.

"I felt I had to do whatever was asked of me in order to be accepted."

This is a message internalized by many COAs. But it is doubly reinforced when one is a black child trying to be valued. In addition, since Etta was raised in a transitional generation, she always felt as if she carried the burden of her race.

"I could never be myself. Any success was as tenuous as if I were walking on quicksand. I was forever wondering how others were interpreting the things I did and the way I acted. That was what it was like being black in a white world."

DENIAL AND SECRETS

The prejudice that minority children encounter sometimes makes them feel as if they have to deny who they are. This feeds into the denial syndrome that Children of Alcoholics have already learned to practice, and it sets up a conflict within the child for a sense of identity.

In order for children to feel good about themselves, they need to hear positive messages from their parents—and they need to hear them consistently. Never feeling good enough is a common experience for children from unhealthy families. When a child hears hostile messages about who they are—their ethnic group, their color, their family's language and way of doing things—from the outside world, they need strong, healthy parents to help them deal with this.

For Bonnie, these negative messages were particularly difficult to deal with because so many of the hostile racial messages originated from within her own family.

Bonnie learned to keep her Mexican ancestry a secret, although her mother had taught her to be proud of her Puerto Rican background. But her father's attitude toward his own Mexican identity and that of other Mexicans, coupled with the prejudice Bonnie encountered in the white community, taught her to try to hide who she really was.

BONNIE: "I would tell everyone with great pride that I was Puerto Rican and that my father came from Spain. I learned to speak English without the slightest hint of a Spanish accent. In fact, I was proud when people asked me if I came from New York because of my accent. Even to this day I find myself taking great pains to explain to people that I'm not Mexican, that I'm half Puerto Rican and half Mexican American. I would feel insulted when people asked me if I was Mexican, and I'd feel flattered if they asked me if I was Italian."

Denying who you are and keeping secrets is a part of the Adult Child's legacy. You are taught not to allow others to know the truth about yourself and your family.

PAM: *"The violence and alcoholism couldn't be kept a secret, but the 'Don't talk' rule was certainly intact. Don't talk meant you didn't try to find answers or ask why. Everybody knew what was happening, but you only reacted to it as you needed to. You were supposed to pretend everything was okay. You were supposed to pretend nothing was really happening. Somehow we were supposed to ignore the hurt and the pain. The violence was always minimized."*

Chuque's experience was similar to Pam's. He lived in a community that was so severely affected by poverty and alcoholism that many things couldn't be kept secret because they were acted out publicly. But even then, the "Don't talk" rule about the rage and violence still applied.

Chuque also had his own personal secrets, as many Adult Children and alcoholics do. They have learned to discount and minimize to such an extent that they don't even recognize the secrets they are keeping until a recovery process starts. They keep secret about incidents that caused resentment, and anger, and embarrassment. They hide their shame.

CHUQUE: *"My life became one big secret. I couldn't share anything with anyone. I trusted no one."*

Trust becomes even more difficult for minority ACOAs. Their lives lack predictability, safety, and honesty within the family; and for many they lack predictability, safety, and honesty outside of the family.

WILLIAM: *"I didn't know we had any secrets. We just didn't talk about anything. We didn't talk about my dad's, grandfather's, or uncles' drinking. We didn't talk about where I was when I was out. We lived in the same house, but there wasn't much closeness. I felt terribly confused because everyone really liked my mom and dad, but I felt separate from those feelings. We never sat down and did things together."*

ETTA: *"My mother didn't believe in other people knowing your business. We were never to make scenes in public. She drilled it into us that we were never to talk about my father's behavior to anyone, not even to our friends. So most of the time we kept our feelings bottled up inside. We were never to talk about the violence that went on our family. My grandparents, my aunt and uncle, and my cousins were never aware of the fighting. My father's drinking simply wasn't considered abnormal."*

While the "Don't talk" rule that Etta's mother is reinforcing is characteristic of chemical dependency, it is doubly reinforced in the minority family. There, the unspoken edict is: *"You don't tell people what's happening in our black family."*

Most ACOAs move into adulthood without much awareness that they were raised with alcoholism. People have stereotypes of alcoholics, and we usually manage to exclude our parents from those stereotypes. We may know our parents were drunk a lot. And perhaps they were violent. But if we bought into the 'Don't talk' rule, that reinforced not thinking about it as well. When we don't think about what's going on and only react as a way of surviving, then the family alcoholism does not get identified.

In addition to not talking and not thinking, many people of color growing up in an alcoholic home may not perceive drinking as a priority problem if the family has little financial stability. These families are focused on where the next job will come from, where they will be living, how to get the car running, whether there's enough money to take a child to the health clinic. Nevertheless, as complex as the issues are, if the alcoholism is not addressed, the problems will only become exacerbated.

Life Stories: Adulthood and Recovery

Up to now the Adult Child recovery movement has been composed primarily of white mainstream people. It doesn't have to stay that way. This movement is meant to be a recovery process for all Adult Children. Although differences among cultures need to be respected, each of us has something vital to learn from the other. We can all grow together.

It is always shocking for people to realize that children who grow up with adversity, such as alcoholism and violence, are able to be professionally successful, develop personal and intimate relationships, parent children effectively, and become an active, constructive part of their neighborhood and community. ACOAs are incredible survivors. Their strengths must not be denied; rather, they need to be acknowledged and supported.

How is it that some Adult Children have the capacity to reach out to others? As traumatic and painful as life can be for anyone in an alcoholic family—and particularly for those who are Double Duty/Dual Identity—survivorship usually means that, as children, they found a source of support that could be drawn on for strength. Some sought guidance, protection, and the opportunity to be a child from their extended families.

Others found that their strength was backed up by education. Still others drew strength from tradition and spiritual or ethnic values.

The following section brings you up to date on the adult lives of Bonnie, Pam, Chuque, William, and Etta. We have also included the story of Jesse Old Coat, another Native American. You will see that in spite of their strengths, their wounds began to fester. This led them to seek out resources to help them with their own addictions and Adult Child issues.

BONNIE
Age: 29
Ethnicity: Puerto Rican/Mexican
Partner Status: Married
Occupation: Physician
Recovery Process: Church, self-
   education

After high school, Bonnie was able to attend college on scholarships. During those years she made more white friends. As she met many other people on scholarships, she began to feel less inferior due to class differences. Once again she found she had a love for biology, although she was intimidated about her chances of succeeding in this field because she'd always been told that Mexican Americans did not perform well on tests. However, she met a male Hispanic counselor who encouraged her, and she grabbed on to his support. She also felt that any educational success she might have would be significant in building family pride. Hers was not an individual goal, but one that would feed her family's sense of identity and self-esteem. After graduating from college, Bonnie went on to medical school.

Even though her parents had divorced, Bonnie had occasional contact with her father.

BONNIE: "After I was accepted into medical school, I went to visit my father to tell him about it. I was so excited. I couldn't believe that I had actually been accepted into medical school! I expected pride, joy, admiration—all kinds of wonderful things from him.

"I will never forget his words to me: 'Chicago! Chicago is full of blacks! Well, just don't bring me back any little black monkeys.' To my father, a Mexican or 'wetback' was pretty low on his list, but a black was about as low as you could get. I didn't cry. I didn't get angry. I ignored the

comment and continued to talk about how exciting medical school was going to be.''

In a healthy family system, parents would be proud of a child's academic achievements. Becoming a physician is an esteemed ambition within all cultures in the United States. But two dynamics come into play here that will prevent Bonnie from receiving validation from her father or a sense of celebration for her accomplishment. First, he is alcoholic. He's led an alcohol-centered life. By this point he's been chronically alcoholic for many years. Before him stands a daughter he's barely even known, and she is reminding him of her accomplishment and fueling his guilt and shame about his way of life. Second, once again he is reminded of his lack of accomplishment due to the fact that so many avenues were closed to him because of his ethnic heritage. His racist remarks remind us of his anger and his shame.

Through reading and the psychiatric training she received, Bonnie has gotten in touch with some of the feelings she had stuffed as a child and a young adult.

"Now, years later, I feel the hurt, anger, sadness, and pity that I would not allow myself to feel as a child. It wasn't until I was seeing a therapist to deal with my fear of public speaking that I realized how deeply my father's reaction to my acceptance into medical school had affected me.

"The therapist asked me to draw the feeling I had in the pit of my stomach when I tried to speak before a group. When I showed her the fierce-looking drawing, she said, 'Why, this looks like a little black monkey.' I immediately burst into tears when she said it, but I have done well with public speaking ever since.''

This revelation was highly significant for Bonnie. It is a portion of grief work connected with her father's shame.

Even though Bonnie is about to graduate from medical school, she still struggles with low self-esteem and has had a hard time acknowledging her own accomplishments.

"At times I feel that I got into medical school only because I'm from a minority and am female. I got honors in certain courses, but I tend to think that was simply because my professors liked me, not because I deserved the acclaim. I still tend to minimize my accomplishments—it's something that I'm working on now in recovery.''

It is possible that Bonnie received scholarships and, at times, preferential treatment because she is a minority female. In the past several years Affirmative Action guidelines have helped establish more women and people of color in many jobs and schools that used to exclude them. But that does not mean Bonnie didn't deserve her admittance and wasn't capable. She earned the right of entry to medical school as much as any other qualified applicant. After acceptance she still had to perform to an acceptable standard to remain in medical school. It's sad that she still has to prove that she's "good enough" to gain her rightful place in society because she is a minority and a woman.

Many Adult Children feel like impostors. High-achieving ACOAs often feel fear riding close to their hearts. If they haven't begun to deal with their shame issues, it is often difficult for them to feel adequate or secure despite their obvious capabilities. There is often the lingering fear that what has been given so tentatively can always be taken away again. Believing that your color influenced your position certainly fuels an already existing impostor syndrome.

Recently, though, many people of color have accepted that their color may offer advantages and opportunities—and they don't question their capability. But Bonnie was raised to question herself every step of the way, and this has seriously affected her self-esteem.

Bonnie has found support in her recovery process both from her Higher Power and from her sisters.

"My faith in God has been a positive experience for me. I tend to want to solve everyone's problems, and when I start feeling weighed down, I realize that I'm trying to do it all alone again and that I don't have to. I can turn to God and let all my problems go. When I do, I really feel at peace.

"Another source of support has been my sisters. We each admit to worrying and praying for the others, and we keep in contact as often as we can, even though we live in different cities. The three oldest sisters, including me, can discuss our lives openly, and we talk about Dad's alcoholism."

However, not all of Bonnie's family members have been able to deal with the truth about their father.

"I recently tried to talk with my youngest sister about our father's drinking. She asked me, 'Exactly where do you draw the line between a drinker and an alcoholic? I'm not so sure Dad was an alcoholic!'

"After all we'd been through, I was shocked. All those times when Dad couldn't think, talk, or walk straight. All those times we found him passed out in the living room or bedroom. And the worst times—when

he beat on my mom or my oldest sister! I couldn't believe my little sister was saying that. But I've come to realize that my two youngest sisters and my brothers aren't yet able to talk about Dad's alcoholism as well as Mom and the oldest three. I'm still hoping that one day we will all be able to be open with each other."

After five years of courtship, Bonnie married a Mexican American man, and they are expecting their first child.

"I love my husband very much. He is my best friend. However, I knew when I married him that he was overweight, that he smoked pot as well as cigarettes, and that he drank. For the first three years we were married, I nagged him about his weight, drugs, smoking, and drinking, although his pot use was very infrequent and he only drank excessively when his family visited. He kept saying that because of my family history I was exaggerating his drinking. Maybe that's true. But I'm not so sure."

Bonnie was distraught to think she'd married someone similar to her father. It is very easy to say, "It will never happen to me," and yet repeat the pattern. It is likely that Bonnie saw only the differences between her husband and her father. Her husband may have a different style of drinking—personality often accounts for differences in drinking behavior.

Yet all alcoholism becomes similar as people move into the middle and late stages of the disease. It is possible that Bonnie's husband is in an earlier stage of alcoholism than her father was at the same age. Because we didn't know our parents at the age they met, we aren't as likely to recognize early-stage alcoholism in our partners.

Bonnie began to talk to her husband and to people at her church. At a church retreat she spoke of her fears to a priest who then introduced her to literature on alcoholism and Adult Children. This is when Bonnie's recovery began. Typically, people of color find their way to recovery more through their churches than whites do. With her priest's urging Bonnie has attended Adult Child workshops. In light of her recovery, Bonnie's husband has begun to examine his own history of being raised by an alcoholic relative, and he has cut back his drinking severely. Together they have seriously addressed how alcoholism has and can still affect them, and they are actively pursuing a new life.

"I'm trying to concentrate on the things I love about my husband. And I'm working on my own flaws—of which there are many. Our relationship is improving. I'm always so busy trying to be strong that I just don't give others enough credit. Too often I assume they're too weak or not up to

things, and that I have to be strong for them. I realize that many times I have mistakenly believed I was being 'Christian.' But what I've really been doing is taking the attitude of superiority and not giving the other person a chance.

"In working on my ACOA issues, I'm becoming more self-aware. I can still be compulsive, although it tends to come in spurts. I am a very infrequent drinker, although I did experiment with drinking and even tried pot when I was in my twenties. I think I just needed those props to fit in at the time. Now I don't take drugs of any kind, not even aspirin for a headache. I would rather get to the root of the problem than just treat the symptoms."

Bonnie's self-awareness is also leading her to deal with her low self-esteem, part of which stems from the shame she was made to feel growing up as a minority.

"One thing I still have a hard time with are my feelings about relationships with people I perceive to be my superiors—professors, my husband's boss, older physicians. My husband and I are being invited to more parties where I will encounter these people, and my feelings are very ambivalent. I want to go and have fun, but I hate going because I feel uncomfortable and inferior to the people there. I feel fine when I'm with my peers, but with 'superiors' my conversation is stilted and I try to leave as early as possible.

"I worry about this attitude because I feel as if I'm missing out on important things. I can't help but wonder if this has to do with the fact that my father instilled such a fear of authority—a fear of him—in me. We were never allowed to show anger toward him or question his authority. My mother has told me that, as a small child, I was very outgoing and vocal, but that as I grew older she saw me turn into a meek little mouse. That's something I have seen happen with many Latin American females."

Fear of authority figures is very common among Adult Children because authority figures, specifically parents, so often instilled fear, insecurity, and a sense of inadequacy when they were little. These feelings intensify in adulthood and are then projected onto other authority figures. Although Bonnie recognizes that her fear of authority is not rational, until she does further work on her issues with her father, this will continue to be a difficult area for her.

Bonnie is about to graduate from medical school and begin her residency.

"I'm becoming more aware of the pluses and minuses of being an Adult Child of an Alcoholic, and I am learning to break the cycle. I will soon be doing my residency in psychiatry and plan to do a fellowship in child psychiatry. I would love to be able to help other children break the cycle."

Although Bonnie's recovery is not based on a Twelve Step program, she has found resources through her church, through the literature, and with her husband to create her own meaningful recovery.

PAM
Age: 28
Ethnicity: Native American
Partner Status: Second marriage,
    four children
Occupation: Curriculum
    development specialist
Recovery Process: Native American
    spirituality

After the incident of beating up her alcoholic boyfriend, Pam went back to the reservation and lived with her grandmother. A year later she married a reservation policeman.

PAM: *"The tribal police officers only had jurisdiction over enrolled tribal members. My husband was a county police officer and had jurisdiction over everybody. The fact that I married a non-Indian wasn't accidental. I was looking for someone who was not going to hurt me. I was determined not to live with an alcoholic or an abuser ever again. At that time my association with being Indian meant living a life of violence. I was like both of my parents, I didn't know how not to be in a relationship. But I was determined to handle my marriage differently. This wasn't easy because I kept hearing comments that I was a 'cop lover' and that I thought I was too good to date my own people. This discrimination took a long time to die down."*

In the earlier section, Pam said Indian love meant hickeys and black eyes. She had no positive role models to reinforce any difference. She didn't know how to live on her own. She craved love but was still so focused on survival that she felt she would only be safe if she married a man who was not Indian.

"I was married to someone who was educated, had a steady job, and didn't drink. We had two kids, a dog, and a station wagon. I thought I'd done everything right.

"Then my husband and I moved to the western part of the state because he'd been transferred. We were good friends, but I finally realized that the love was not there for me. My marriage had been a time of healing, a time of transition, during which I learned to be honest about what I wanted and didn't want. I slowly came to see that what I had just wasn't enough. And after four years of marriage, I divorced him."

Often Adult Children purposely seek a safe person to be with in their first significant, committed relationship—"safe" meaning nonviolent and nonalcoholic. Unfortunately, some still pick alcoholics, but ones whose style of drinking is different from that of their parent(s); others, not understanding what it means to be chemically dependent, pick someone who doesn't drink but uses another drug. At times they pick what appears to be a nonviolent person only to witness the violence erupt quickly after the commitment is made. COAs have not had healthy models for relationships. They tend to choose people just as unskilled as they when they enter relationships.

Pam was fortunate that none of those surprises occurred. Nonetheless, she chose a man she would value but not come to love. She was only just beginning to learn about love, trust, friendship, and what she wanted out of life.

Pam was single and raising her two children when she met the man who would become her present husband.

"We met at work—both of us worked at an Indian treatment center. I was afraid of being in any relationship—much less one with an Indian. So we were friends for several months. But then we began to date, and finally we moved in with each other. He saw my internal struggle and knew that it was mine. He allowed me to be me and let me take my time."

Pam was not seeking or wanting a relationship when the man who became her second husband began to approach her. She resisted, and he waited patiently. He was able to see the positives in Pam that she was only beginning to discover. As she worked through her own problems, he did not take her struggle as a reflection on him. He loved her unconditionally and was willing to wait until they could meet on equal terms.

"Six years before, when I was working at the Indian Health Board, I had the opportunity to attend a conference where I heard a speaker talk about Adult Children of Alcoholics. I had heard of this before, but I hadn't identified myself as one. As I listened to this speaker, I began to cry. That was the first time. I've cried a lot since then. In the past it had taken a lot for me to cry. But now there was so much rage in me from my past that it was time to cry."

As a child raised in a violent home, anger and rage had been Pam's first feelings. She knew she was angry. But all healing really takes a giant step when the angry person can begin to cry.

Recovery includes tears over the old pain and present-day losses. Crying is the release of energy that has been used to maintain denial. The release of tears will allow Pam greater honesty with herself and others.

"So here I was struggling to find myself, and here was this patient, understanding, nonviolent Native American man. He had not been raised as I had—he'd grown up in the city, and his family was working middle class. He too had a deep sense of being separate from others, and, like me, he wanted more of his Native American heritage.

"It was important for me that my next husband be Native American. I didn't want to lose my culture and the heritage I wanted for my children—the bonding, the closeness. The basis of what life is all about."

In spite of the trauma Pam experienced growing up, she nonetheless was strongly connected with her Native American heritage. She was a part of something larger than herself, and she wanted to provide that meaning for her own children.

"Two years ago a small number of Indian people came together via the Indian Health Board to develop a Children of Alcoholics project. We began our work with a two-week training intensive that was very respectful of our native traditions and personally very healing. During the intensive I experienced anger, rage, hurt, guilt, shame—just to name a few. I could finally answer the question, 'What is wrong?' The pain of my childhood was alive inside me, slowly eating away my life without my even knowing. How could I parent my own children if I based my parenting on what I'd learned growing up? What could I do to break the cycle?

"A Native American spiritual leader was there to help us learn the forgotten ways of the old people and to help us understand what was happening.

"I felt so fragile, like a fine piece of china that would break at the slightest touch. But the support and bonding we had with each other was

tremendous. *After the training I felt like a feather. So much pain had been taken away, and there was so much to learn and so much healing to do. It was here that my ACOA understanding really occurred. This is where my active recovery began.*

"The group has continued to meet, and a lot of my Adult Child healing has taken place within this group. I continue to read and attend workshops. Today I am working a lot with the spiritual leaders in my tribe. I have found a balance in my life. I have no desire to run. I have stability in my life."

Pam has actively chosen to live her life differently from the way she was raised.

"I had never been a heavy drinker, although I did drink. But I had been raised around so much violence, I needed to be sober to protect myself."

Abstinence is a healthy policy for anyone, but particularly for any Child of an Alcoholic. In Pam's case, as the child of two alcoholic parents, she is genetically even more predispositioned toward alcoholism. Having two alcoholic parents is more common in the Native American culture than in the white culture.

"Today I don't feel the need to be physically violent. My way of dealing with an argument is to shut up, although I'm getting better about being able to talk things through. I can discipline my kids without being out of control. I am able to separate my feelings from theirs. And while I have to talk to myself when I get angry at them at times—I do not hit my kids."

Pam's caution about paying attention to how she disciplines her children is valid. Those who were abused as children are more prone to become abusers. In addition, Pam had experienced blatant physical abuse from her mother, which set up a script of female parent-to-child abuse. Pam has had a fear and hatred of violence for years. Although she places great value in nonviolence, she has had no models for nonviolent parenting. Her husband(s), friends, and her active spiritual and Native American recovery program are offering her new models, new alternatives, and new skills.

Today Pam is a curriculum development specialist.

"My work is predominantly related to education and mental health. I write stories for children, taking traditional legends and weaving into them information about childhood, alcoholism, and physical abuse. The stories are Native American–oriented, but they are relevant to all young children.

I am a certified community health worker, and I'm also finishing my bach-elor's degree in college.

"My husband and I are happily married, and we live near the reser-vation. We have had two more children after deciding that raising four children is right for us. My first husband celebrates holidays and partici-pates in celebrations with us.

"We often talk to our children about their history. My grandmother used to tell me about Indians and the 'Indian Indians.' She said that Indians are people who are Indian by blood but don't understand anything about their culture or heritage, but that the Indian Indian has a true spiritual balance. There is meaning to why we are here. The Indian Indian has an understanding of what Mother Earth has given us.

"Today my husband is learning and practicing traditional carving, and I am involved in traditional basket weaving. Our older children participate in this, although the younger children are still only able to watch. We participate in our tribal ceremonies and the Twanoh *dance. Even our two-year-old participates."*

Pam's Native American identity is central to her being. Working on her Adult Child issues has made it possible for her to feel pride in herself and her heritage.

"For me, it would be a false pride if I didn't have the ability to speak the truth about myself.

"The Creator has a wonderful way of working our lives."

CHUQUE
Age: 38
Ethnicity: Hispanic
Partner Status: Second marriage,
    three children
Occupation: Adolescent counselor
Recovery Process: AA, ACOA

Chuque married at twenty. By then alcohol and drugs were a primary part of his life. He lived with his first wife for six years, and they had two children who are now ten and thirteen.

Chuque describes the next fifteen years as promising himself, *"My children will never go through what I did,"* only to repeat a great deal of the family history.

CHUQUE: *"I married someone with whom I reran my parents' patterns—only I became my mom and she my dad. I was patient, she castigated, humiliated, and invalidated me. I was a raging alcoholic, angry with whites. I fought for whatever social movement gave me an identity at the time."*

Chuque took jobs where he was usually involved with helping people— as a caseworker or counselor in social agencies. But as his alcoholism progressed, he began to lose his career, his kids, his wife, and even the faith to believe that he deserved to live.

"I believed that I had failed at everything I had attempted to accomplish in life because I was a weak character, too gutless to change these things around me that I wore like a suit of armor.

"My need for excitement no longer worked for me. My defensiveness and anger no longer served their purpose. But I still had my drugs and booze to carry me through a few more tragedies.

"All of my relationships were built on foundations of resentment, rage, lust, and antagonism. I always feared abandonment, but I would promote it. Eventually I learned to beat others to the punch and reject them first.

"I came to hate all whites. The whiter you were, the more I hated your presence. I used drinking and drugging to give me motivation to lash out at all the whites I thought stood in my path.

"However, by 1983 I was emotionally and spiritually bankrupt. I was tired of politics, hatred, and negative thinking. In fact, I was tired of everything. I wanted to die. So I ran back to my family in Arizona. I ran away from the life I'd been leading to gain strength for my future."

Chuque returned to his family of origin, where drugs and alcohol were commonplace. He knew he was in trouble, but he didn't realize the primary problem was alcoholism. He'd returned to a family of enablers. Nevertheless, for the next three years he was able to hold down a job, even though he remained angry and indulged in a lot of self-pity. He was abusing alcohol and drugs daily—often with other members of his family.

But then Chuque began deteriorating physically, and this was noticed by his employer. He was losing track of time and reality; he was also experiencing major mood swings. Finally, he was referred to a therapist by his employer.

"My defeatism was strong. My denial was equally strong. I played games throughout several months of therapy. I didn't want the therapist to get close enough to take a good look inside this human garbage can."

Chuque's alcoholism was fairly classic. He continued to drink and use drugs, and he continued to deteriorate. However, somehow he managed to do what many alcoholics won't do. He stayed in therapy.

"Finally it got through to me that my life might be better if I didn't use or drink. Once I stopped, I quickly regained my health. I then found a job— even though I'd lost all my other jobs. But this job was in a Chicano organization. I worked with kids from the streets, and with their families and the courts. All through this my therapist was helping me regain my self-worth. And he coached me on how to handle my anger and depression.

"But then I began to drink and use again."

Chuque ultimately quit his job and moved back to southern California.

"A year after I was back, shortly after my son's eighth birthday, I asked my new employer for help. I had heard he was a recovering alcoholic."

Five months into his recovery, Chuque attended a conference for Adult Children for his work.

"I freaked. All of my resentment about my past, all my negative thinking and behavior, hit all at once. The rage of my past took over. I was a mess. I began to cry out of frustration and anger at myself personally for all the harm I had caused my children, my friends, my wife—and especially me. I was defeated. That's when I began my journey into ACOA and AA.

"When I first went to ACOA they told me I should go to AA and get sober and stay sober for a year. Then I could come back. I saw that as rejection. I was angry and frustrated. So I went to a Spanish-speaking AA meeting to see if they said the same things I'd heard in the English-speaking AA meetings. And they did.

"The following week I publicly admitted for the first time in my life that I was alcoholic. I turned myself in. I couldn't deal with the pain of my insanity any longer."

Chuque needed to address his alcoholism—to get and stay sober— before he would be able to deal with the other aspects of his life.

He is still sensitive to the injustices his people suffer, but he is learning that, rather than self-destructing in his rage, he has power in his life. His self-help program has taught him to recognize where he has the power to change things and where he does not and how to accept that. To his surprise, rather than feeling powerless, he feels strengthened for the first time in his life.

Church was important to Chuque when he was small.

"I was raised in an extremely God-fearing family. God was the entire answer for our woes in life, and we placed a lot of faith in Him."

In recovery Chuque has recaptured the meaning of faith again after many years of denying the existence of God in his life. He feels reconnected with his God. He also feels connected for the first time with sober members of his minority community.

"I learned very early as a child that 'truth' was a bad word in my environment. It was not valued. Lying became a defense mechanism for me. My journey to sobriety began when I told a roomful of alcoholics the truth about my powerlessness over alcohol."

Justice had always been important to Chuque, and he was motivated to struggle for the underdogs—especially Chicano Mexicanos.

"But social justice came last in my thinking when I hit bottom, because I became a revenge-filled person. In recovery I'm working hard not to confuse justice with personal anger. I strive for responsibility each day now.

"Recovery has been a roller-coaster ride of emotions—especially grief. But I don't feel alone any longer. Humor, honesty, creativity, and playfulness have become part of me again. I see myself as a builder once more, but this time I'm starting with myself first. Being generous and helping others has become my daily task, though it cost me a lot at first to admit I had been wrong and selfish. My self-respect is becoming stronger. I'm even letting go of my old inability to forgive because I was taken to task and challenged by people I had allowed myself to trust.

"I'm learning to deal with life in life's terms. I no longer stand rigid in defiance as I did when I felt beaten into submission by that world I fought in me and outside of me.

"At the age of thirty-eight, I have a lot to be grateful for. The path I have traveled to get where I am continues to teach me and help me move forward."

WILLIAM

Age: 56
Ethnicity: African-American
Partner Status: Remarried
Occupation: Behavioral therapist
Recovery Process: AA, ACOA

When William entered the Air Force they had just begun to integrate that service. There were only four blacks in his squadron. After basic training, he volunteered to go overseas.

WILLIAM: *"I felt like a hero in uniform. I volunteered for Korea but was sent to Japan. That was okay, I still felt I was serving my country. But before I went overseas I had to travel through the South, and I encountered something that I had not had to deal with before. I was told to go to the back of the bus. I couldn't eat at the counter in a restaurant. I was relegated with other blacks to a separate place to eat. I wondered who I was being sent to fight for. By now I was drinking a lot, and that compounded my rage. But rather than do anything constructive with my anger, I would say nothing about what bothered me and then break every rule in the book. I was finally kicked out of the service. I was court-martialed three times—one time for striking an officer and twice for insubordination."*

William said that at this time liquor was cheap and also that alcoholism was not yet being addressed in the military. Every time he was in trouble, alcohol was involved. In 1980 he repetitioned for an honorable discharge, on the grounds that alcoholism is a disease. His disease had been very blatant and should have been recognized and treated. He was given an honorable discharge.

After the service, William worked at a series of jobs, none of which lasted too long. His alcoholism interfered with every job and was clearly the cause of his terminations. A week before he was to graduate with a license in practical nursing, he was caught with liquor in his briefcase and kicked out of the program.

During that time William had met a nursing student and married her. They were married twelve years and had three children.

"It was a rough marriage. We fought all of the time—most of the fighting was drinking-related. I would stay away from home a lot when I was

drinking. My wife would accuse me of being with other women, but liquor was the other woman. We also fought about money. But the issue was really my drinking. We had many separations, and finally I left. I was close to the kids, but they suffered.''

Continuing to drink, William married another nurse. Two years later, when he was an orderly in a hospital, he was approached by a fellow employee about going to an Alcoholics Anonymous meeting.

"My new wife was bothered by my drinking, and when he told me about AA he also talked about Al-Anon. So I thought this would get her off my back, so I went to AA and my wife went to Al-Anon. At my first meeting I thought I was at a meeting of the Ku Klux Klan—people were all smiling and laughing, and I thought they were laughing at me.

"I didn't go back. But my wife kept going to Al-Anon. She learned about 'detachment,' and as a result she quit arguing with me when I was drinking, which was most of the time. That really confused me. I took it as a lack of love, and I moved out of the house. Now I could drink as I wanted, but soon I was in trouble at work because of my drinking. My employer asked me to go into therapy.''

William was fortunate because his therapists were very knowledgeable about alcoholism. They explained that he was alcoholic and that alcoholism was a disease. They also helped him realize that he didn't want to lose his wife. Although the therapists were confrontational with him, William felt that what they said made sense.

William had previously been to a psychiatrist who had only put him on an antidepressant, but he also had not been truthful with the psychiatrist about his drinking. This time he remained in therapy, was more honest, and got sober. After he had been sober fourteen months, he went back to AA and has continued his recovery there. Today he is fifteen years sober and still married to his second wife.

He asked his friend from work to be his AA sponsor and was given some good advice that he found particularly helpful.

"My sponsor told me that most of the people in AA would be white and many of them prejudiced. But he said that the prejudice was their issue, and that alcoholics could not afford to hang on to resentments and negative thinking or they'd start drinking again. I took that message to heart and developed the attitude that their resentment was their own and they could get drunk over it—but I wasn't going to.''

William's recovery from alcoholism and his wife's recovery from co-dependency were totally influenced by white therapists and other whites in recovery. He was initially approached by a white colleague, and his therapist(s) and AA sponsor were white.

"The therapist got my attention. I could relate to what he said. I never saw his color. Alcohol was what was central to my life, not color."

Although William needed to get sober before he could address his ACOA issues, he also became sober before the ACOA movement had begun. However, while he was studying to be an alcoholism counselor, he was fortunate to take a class at the beginning of the ACOA movement in 1980, where alcoholic families were described. He recognized his mother as an Adult Child and himself as the child of a passive alcoholic father. He also realized that both of his wives were Adult Children. He realized that as a child he had learned to ascribe to the rules: "Don't talk," "Don't feel," "Don't trust." He identified with all of the family roles. Most prominent was the sense that no matter what he did, he was never good enough.

William has continued his recovery in AA and ACOA self-help meetings.

"I needed both programs. The two approaches have meant a much more comprehensive recovery for me.

"Today I no longer have that hole deep inside me that needs filling. There is no emptiness in my life. It has been replaced by laughter and joy. It used to be that I couldn't tell the line between fear and excitement—I rode high on the chaos. But today I don't seek uproar. I know my feelings. I feel good about me. It got so I was always blaming others for my drinking, but now I take responsibility for me. What is so wonderful is that I share the ACOA programs with my wife and two of my children."

ETTA
Age: 42
Ethnicity: African American
Partner Status: Single
Occupation: Lawyer
Recovery Process: Spiritual
    Therapy, Twelve Step Program

Etta won a scholarship to a prestigious eastern college, where she was one of forty-two minority students.

ETTA: *"At this time I was extremely into black consciousness. I felt proud to be doing what I knew blacks were capable of. This was the first time blacks were being admitted to white colleges in great numbers. Unlike prep school, where I was the only black person, here I had a group of black people to relate to. The pressures of our differences were constantly in play because the white liberal world had suddenly discovered the Third World. I vividly remember student demonstrations about racism, Vietnam, and feminism. As minorities we were constantly on display, constantly under pressure to be different, yet the same. But we weren't the same. Our cultural schizophrenia was extreme.*

"My first boyfriend was a brilliant black scholar. He was also an alcoholic, which I didn't even notice. I was always at my best in extreme crisis management. Clifton risked his life and walked the edge in all kinds of ways. But he was an experienced tightrope walker, and even when he fell he managed to land on his feet. I lived through his drinking and infidelities, with my masterful co-dependency creating a shelter against the storm of his disease. We both finished school, but I went into a severe depression after I completed my thesis. I became extremely agoraphobic, although I had no idea what I was suffering from at the time. I only knew I was afraid of absolutely everything, and I couldn't leave the house."

Etta's depression is typical of so many hero Adult Children—and it came right on schedule. She had been the "responsible child" all of her life. Her identity was involved in performing, producing, and achieving. Without the opportunity to do that, she had no sense of her own worth. Her needs had been so negated in childhood that she didn't even know she had needs of her own. As a result she continued to negate her needs as an adult. Many Adult Children turn to compulsive behavior to mask their sense of unworthiness and inadequacy—some find alcohol and drugs, others experience depression.

Etta also experienced agoraphobia—the abnormal fear of open spaces. Agoraphobia is common among Adult Children. All their lives they have lived with fear. Finally, fear comes to the surface in a manner that interferes with their ability to function on a day-to-day basis. The agoraphobic is frightened of being swallowed up by anything and everything on the outside. This may not sound rational, but neither was the way Etta and others like her were raised.

"There was a major economic depression in the United States after Clifton and I graduated college. There were no jobs. We were broke, and our families had no money to help us. One day I just woke up and knew I couldn't live on the edge anymore. So I abandoned Clifton before he could abandon me. He was heading to medical school and planning on becoming a psychiatrist. I had been warned about how medical school wives get used up and thrown away. I knew I needed a radical change, so I left him."

This was Etta's first significant relationship—and it was full of warnings. But she had so little understanding of her own contribution to what had occurred between her and Clifton that she learned nothing to prevent further difficulties in future relationships.

Etta returned to her family and a stable black community, and in that safety she began to venture out again. She soon found a "good" job. For the next several years she found her sense of identity in her work. Then, too, work was much safer than men.

"My work life has always revolved around politics and communications. I started working for a law firm, editing lawyer's briefs. It was stressful, exciting work. Returning to my family was healing, especially because of my extended family, my grandparents. They provided an oasis of sanity in the sea of my own co-dependency and workaholism.

"However, by this point my siblings had begun to act out their ACOA problems. One of my brothers ultimately became addicted to sex and marijuana. The other brother has been extremely compulsive in his work and has had depressions so severe that he has twice attempted suicide with drugs. My sister has been treated as both a schizophrenic and a manic-depressive. She has been hospitalized numerous times and often medicated.

"But I just continued to accept all of the family drama and all of the pain and confusion. I just gutted it out no matter what was happening,

and 'saved' others whenever I could. I didn't know how I felt about anything. I could deny my feelings, stuff my needs, solve everyone else's problems, and look perfect even when I was dying inside. No one ever had a clue that daily life in my family and my community was so painfully dysfunctional. I lived the life of a Red Cross aide, racing from one life crisis to another. I was too busy rescuing others to even know that I had feelings and needs of my own."

The intensity of Etta's ongoing family dramas, and her role as hero child, made her determined to escape the family doom. And she did it in the most acceptable fashion—she went to law school and did brilliantly. After several years of firm work—and nearly burning out—she decided to teach law. In academe she often found herself the lone black woman in any department she was assigned to.

"Often I was in such extreme isolation that I felt my depression would never end. There was no black community at the prestigious universities where I worked. I felt such enormous internal pressure to live out the script of being one of the 'talented tenth' that I worked ten times as hard as any of my colleagues."

Etta managed to live her adult life in such an externally competent manner that few people suspected anything was wrong. She added one professional accomplishment to another. Compared with her siblings, her life was trouble free. She was self-sufficient, knew how to get things done. She kept so busy that those she considered to be close to her never once glimpsed the frightened, lonely child inside her.

"For years I worked at and maintained a long-distance relationship with a businessman who, though not alcoholic, had a deeply compulsive personality. We managed to love and torture each other for sixteen years. Today I often wonder how I could ever have endured a relationship with a man who was so emotionally unavailable. Lamar was the master of emotional abuse. He had developed the 'come here, come here, go away, go away' syndrome into an art form.

"My relationship with Lamar was such a contrast with the rest of my life. The violation that I experienced with him was so ridiculous. He would borrow money that he would never repay. He would routinely break promises. He would tell me I was his best friend and ask me for advice, and then withdraw and punish me when I gave it. He would accuse me of emasculating him, and when I suggested he see a therapist, he said that black people didn't go into therapy, that was 'white folks' bag.' "

So often others can't understand why a person stays in such a hurtful relationship. Yet any Adult Child understands it quite easily. Etta wanted a relationship. She had lived a life of loneliness. She had a high tolerance for abuse, which she had developed from childhood. The "Don't feel" rule made it very easy to maintain a relationship that didn't interfere with her work.

"It was when I hit bottom in this relationship that my recovery began. I made a novena to my patron saint, St. Martin de Porres, and prayed to find the key that would free me from a relationship that made me despise myself. It was as though every accomplishment I had ever achieved soured in the face of my obsession with a man who I realized could never love me in the way I needed to be loved.

"Every day of the novena I gained deeper and deeper insight into my problems with Lamar. On the ninth and last day, the message came: 'Release your addiction to this relationship. This relationship is your relationship to your father.'

"The message shocked me. Lamar wasn't alcoholic. At the time of this breakthrough I prayed and meditated and worked with Native American and African American spiritual practices. I worked on forgiveness and knowing that God makes a way where there is no way. I did a lot of reading on women's spirituality and joined a women's healing group. The support we gave one another was the first large-scale nurturing that I had ever received in my life."

Etta prided herself on her knowledge and achievements, but like so many Adult Children, she couldn't work hard enough to avoid the pain and vulnerability that begins to seep out in one's early and mid-thirties. When Etta's novena gave her a glimpse that she didn't deserve such a lonely relationship, she sought answers where she had found sources of strength before—in her religion and spiritual teachings. Although this was the beginning of her recovery, Etta was not yet familiar with Adult Child concepts, and she still had a lot of denial about her father's alcoholism.

"I was researching topics for a panel I was moderating on minorities and the law. In my research on community alcoholism, I stumbled on an ACOA checklist. I was dumbfounded. My whole life story was on that inventory. This was a major turning point in my life and the way I viewed reality. I finally had permission to turn in my hero child license."

Etta was ready to further her recovery. She quickly began to gather reading material about Adult Children. She sought out Twelve Step programs and conferences on these issues.

"There are days when the feelings that I have repressed come to the surface like a volcanic eruption. Learning to express my anger in appropriate ways has been really tough. Learning to say 'no' and making my own needs the priority has been my greatest challenge. But it has been so exciting to see that the world doesn't stop turning when I take care of myself first. People get on perfectly well and are most often far happier when I am not co-dependently managing their lives.

"I have had to deal with the depth of my sickness. I really knew I had been in denial when I finally remembered the time Lamar held a gun to my head in one of his fits. I don't remember feeling scared. I didn't feel anything. I never even told him that he would never do that again. I froze my emotions and just numbed out.

"Today that is changing. I don't want to be around abusive behavior. Today when I am dating, if I believe someone has an alcohol or drug problem, I don't hang around. I take care of me. They may be fascinating, talented people, but if they're addicted, I know I deserve better.

"Abandonment is still an issue I struggle with. Part of me is still terrified of being in an intimate relationship, of being vulnerable to rejection. I go through a lot of ambivalence about men. I still hear my mother's voice telling me, 'Never count on a black man for anything,' and I am trying to erase that tape."

Etta's recovery clearly portrays the process of recovery. Recovery is exhilarating, it's frightening, it's confusing—and, at times, it's exciting and fun.

"What is most significant for me is learning to ask for what I want and believing that my needs can be met. It is exciting to be myself—an outrageous, loving, dynamic black woman—no holds barred."

Etta has been able to incorporate her identity as a black woman into her recovery.

"Most of my close women friends are black ACOAs, and our recovery is even starting to be fun in places because we can make outrageous jokes about our co-dependency or compulsive overeating or addiction to excitement, and applaud each other's steps to serenity. We are a very spiritually based network—we share spiritual practices and support each other's mental health. We send each other books and cards. Many of us are single. Not by choice, but rather because so many of the men in our age group regard drinking, smoking, and polygamous relationships as part

of being a black man. However, when we reflect on the true difficulties of being a black man in the white world, we are learning to have more compassion for our menfolk. The tough part is not letting our compassion move us back into denial. There is real loneliness in having to limit relationships because you refuse to have your ACOA issues snowball one more time. But the sisterhood is powerful.

A Resurrection of Spirit

JESSE OLD COAT
Age: 45
Ethnicity: Native American, Cree
    tribe
Father: Alcoholic, Abusive
Mother: Co-dependent
Raised: Midwest
Birth Order: Youngest of two
Socioeconomic Status: Poverty
Partner Status: Married, four
    children
Occupation: Native American
    alcohol counselor
Recovery Process: Native American
    tradition, ACOA self-help

Jesse Old Coat's story is characterized by alcoholism, abuse, and neglect. His life has all the makings of the most extreme drunken Indian stereotype. But when we look beneath the surface what we really see is a young child whose spirit was ravaged yet who possessed the inner strength and guidance to fight his way back from despair to become a role model—not only to his own people, but to us all. I have chosen to present his story in a continuous format in order to maintain the spirit in which he speaks.

It is important to understand that any stereotypical elements in Jesse's story are the result of his being a member of a culture that has been robbed of its spirit; many Native Americans are so shame laden that they live lives of self-destruction. Jesse Old Coat's life offers us a moving testament to the power of resurrection and recovery within us all.

GROWING-UP YEARS

JESSE: "We had all the right things for an alcoholic family: deceit, violence, abandonment.

"When I was young I kept toys under my bed. When my dad would come home drunk, I'd hide under the bed where I couldn't be seen and play with my toys. I never thought about Christmas much. The first time my sister got a present was when she was eight. My mom was so excited to have something for her, she gave her the present two days early. When Christmas came around my sister still had nothing.

"I remember Mom crying by the stove because all she had to cook was corn meal for days in a row. My sister would take me to Grandma's because we would run out of food or coal.

"We didn't have time to think about what was right. The moment was all that mattered. The moment became our total existence. We were always going from yesterday to tomorrow. We never had any stable concept of rooting to things because we were always moving. We would just keep in the old path to stay alive.

"My dad was very violent. I remember seeing my dad beat my mother. There was always mud and blood on the floor. He beat me once with a boot so bad, my twelve-year-old sister grabbed a knife and jumped in between us. I was only six. It took a lot of courage for her to do that."

Jesse's major lifeline was his older sister. She was the one who fed him, clothed him, and protected him as much as she could.

Among many minority groups, the extended family serves as an integral part of life. However, because the Native American culture has such a high rate of alcoholism, extended families are often not the refuge one would hope for.

"I remember when we would all hold ceremonies, the tribal police would come and break things up. They would hit my grandma with sticks and chase her away. The women actually got raped by the police.

"My mom didn't say for my dad to beat her and rape her in front of the kids. It just happened. My mom didn't say, 'Let Jesse go over to Grandma's so this guy can molest him.' It just happened. I was only eight.

"My mother never hit me, but she abused me in other ways. Once an older teenager beat me up on the floor in our house right in front of her, and she just sat there drinking her coffee. I asked her why she didn't do anything, and she said, 'What am I going to do?' "

The powerlessness reflected in Jesse's mother's words is common to alcoholic families and generationally common to many people of color. The child who experiences this parental powerlessness feels emotionally and physically abandoned. This child has no physical protection and no psychological support.

Violence and sexual abuse are so interwoven into the alcoholic framework that it is difficult to separate them. The issues Jesse had to deal with as part of his healing reflect all of this. The higher percentage of physical and sexual child abuse on Native American communities reflects the chronic victimization and learned helplessness that dominates the lives of women and children in a male-dominated society. In such a setting violence is not to be questioned, and sexual abuse cannot be talked about.

Jesse had already suffered a great deal of trauma as a physically and sexually abused child in an alcoholic family, but the shame he experienced was constantly being reinforced by the larger society in which he lived.

"I went to Catholic schools. They were very vicious. There was a lot of shaming. The girls were shamed for starting their periods. And when the girls' breasts would grow, the teachers would wrap towels around them and shame them for it. People were degraded for natural things."

When drunkenness is a way of life, the alcoholic parent is totally incapable of seeing a child as a little person with all a child's needs for love, nurturance, and safety. Jesse was perceived as an object, without regard for his welfare and safety.

"I stopped going to school in the seventh grade because it interfered with my drinking. My dad used to get me drunk by the time I was six. He and my uncle thought it was funny to watch me fall around. I used to drink with my dad and my uncle. They were drunk all the time.

"My dad worked off and on. He would only work if my mom could work at the same place. We always lived on farms. We would move three times a year—from Montana to South Dakota to Washington State to Oregon and back to Montana. We were slaves to poor dirt farmers. If people didn't look down on us, I thought we were in the wrong place.

"We were always last. When I was in school Indians were always the last ones to be allowed to do anything. Even today I feel the most comfortable being last. I'm still the last one to get out of an elevator.

"My dad left when I was ten. We were in the car one day, and he pulled over to the side of the road and told me to get out. I didn't see him for many years after that. For the next few years my sister and I lived with my mom in a one-bedroom trailer house. Soon I was drinking

a lot and in trouble with the law because of truancy and burglaries. The turning point came when my sister left home to get married. She was six years older than I, and when that happened I felt totally abandoned and helpless. By the time I was sixteen the juvenile authorities had diagnosed me as a chronic alcoholic.''

In spite of his history Jesse joined the military when he was eighteen. But within two years he received a dishonorable discharge. He then began his wanderings to the Skid Row areas of cities up and down the West Coast. For many Native Americans who are alcoholic, life off the reservation means Skid Row.

''I was always the youngest drunk sitting in the middle of these old men on Skid Row. People would ask me what I was doing there. They expected an answer. I didn't know why I was there. If I could be in their fine house on the hill, I would be. I was just drinking my wine.''

During the next several years Jesse was sent to prison twice for crimes that were alcohol-related, all of which took place in bars. He also spent time in jail for public drunkenness. It was during one of his jail stays that he was introduced to Alcoholics Anonymous. Nevertheless, although he was told of such a program and became familiar with the Twelve Steps of AA, it would be years before he became sober.

RECOVERY FOR JESSE

''I got sober at thirty. I was in Portland, on Skid Row. I was bleeding in my sinuses from acute alcoholism and throwing up blood. I was taken to a hospital where the doctor said if I lived for three days, he would treat me. I started out on four tablespoons of warm Jell-O a day. It was good, like lemon in your coffee.

''I remember that I kept hearing a voice over and over in my mind. I saw this old man, saying, 'If you're tired of this life, there is somebody who cares.' When I got out of the hospital I automatically started walking toward Skid Row—and stopped.

''I began hitchhiking around the country, going to pow-wows, rodeos, ceremonies, celebrations. I started looking everywhere for this old man I had seen—or the someone he had promised would care. One day I was sitting beside the road, and all I had was a little bag with only a pair of socks and a candy bar in it. It was about three o'clock in the morning— and suddenly everything changed. Everything seemed different. The stars changed. The air changed. I cried until morning, sitting in the bushes. I

remembered what the old man said: 'Someone cares.' At that moment I realized it was me. I cared. If no one else in the world cared, Jesse Old Coat cared. That's what did it."

This moment of spiritual transformation came to Jesse in a manner that is common to his culture. As ravaged as he had been in his life, he was still able to connect with nature, still able to hear the voice of his Higher Power, the Great Spirit to be heard.

Jesse's sobriety was maintained through Native American traditions. He actively sought direction and guidance through tribal elders. Adult Children who practice traditional ceremonies often find that through the use of stories they can speak to the elders of their pain and hurt without experiencing blame or shame.

"I learned self-care through elders and sweat lodges. Elders are teachers of the past and of the future. Without the knowledge from the past there is no future. I followed the Twelve Steps of AA by using sweat lodges and Indian ceremonies."

Jesse supported himself with odd jobs in early sobriety. And he met Theresa, to whom he is married today. Theresa had a young son, and she and Jesse raised him together along with the three daughters they would have.

"I wanted to be well. To heal up, to have a life. I cared enough about myself now to make a new life. That's when I met Theresa, and together we never gave up on each other. Theresa had come from an abusive background herself, and we both had a lot of healing to do. But we pushed each other into a sound way of life. We did it for ourselves and for our kids. We never gave up."

After twelve years of sobriety, Jesse had already been an alcoholism counselor at a tribal center in Washington State for four years when he was given some reading material about Adult Children.

"I felt like someone had been following me around my whole life when I read about Adult Children of Alcoholics. Then I gave my wife the material, and together we related to it. In sweat lodges I began to remember everything I had been denying from my childhood.

"I would go into the sweat lodge all by myself every day until I began to understand myself. I found out I didn't like myself. I didn't like my mom, my sister, my dad. It was a difficult time for me. I wanted to die. I wanted to kill myself. This was after I had been sober for twelve and a half years.

"I took a total inventory. I did it every day after work until I knew who I was. I found out I wasn't responsible for any of those things in my childhood. What happened in my past should have nothing to do with how I treat my wife and kids now. I never beat my wife and kids, thank God. But when I was drinking I did. I'm just like everyone else. I hurt other people just like people in alcoholic families are being hurt today. It has been hard for me to learn to live with the fact that I am normal—a normal alcoholic; a normal Adult Child, with all the poisons and misconceptions, hassles and dirt that goes with it.

"I look back, and it seems as though everyone has to have something to work for, a campaign, a goal. Something to push for. There are two things in this society that prove my point. There is a great need for both women's protective services and children's protective services. Any time women and children need to be protected from the men, it means society is crumbling. The only way we can get out of this bind is to find out who we are individually. And stand up for that.

"All through my life I had a fear of abandonment. It comes from hearing as a child: 'Take him to Aunt Hilda's.' 'Take him to Grandma's.' Take him wherever, meaning: 'We don't want him.' This still causes problems between my wife and me. I still have that terror. I'm afraid that I will do something that will make her leave me—that I will cause my own abandonment.

"I became overbearing—an overbearing good guy. I was always asking her how she was, what she was thinking. I never left her to herself. She finally told me what I was doing. It took a lot of courage for her to tell me because she was afraid she would hurt me. She had learned in childhood that her duty was to please. And I was afraid she would leave me."

Recovery offers a parent an opportunity to raise children in a child-centered family as opposed to an alcohol-centered family. Jesse is not only grateful for his recovery, he is actively attempting to stop the generational cycle of physical, sexual, and alcohol abuse in his family.

"I remember taking my son downtown to show him where I used to drink. It was hard. I would take him to corners to show him where I was down on my knees begging people for quarters so I could buy another drink.

"I remember the tenth anniversary of the alcoholic center downtown. They had pictures of alcoholics up on the board, and there I was, lying on the sidewalk, drunk and dirty. There was big snot across my face, dirt on my eye. I tore it up. It scared me because it was just a breath

away. I take my son down there so he can talk to the drunks, so he can hear about all this from someone besides me.

"My son has never lived in an alcoholic family. I know he will pick up some of my Adult Child traits. But he won't have the pain that I carry. My son works in a peer helper program, and the other kids come to him and tell him what's going on in their lives. He came to me in tears one day and said that this girl he was working with lived in an alcoholic family and was talking about suicide. He didn't know what to say. We're working to fill the gap now so he does know what to say."

Today Jesse thoroughly celebrates his life with his wife and children. He is involved in school field trips and after-school activities. His children are involved in traditional ceremonies. His fears about his ability to parent are gone, and he cherishes the individuality of each of his four children.

"In my life, besides continuing to heal, I'm trying to set a pace for myself so that the young people can see me and what I do and won't be hurt by following my example. When I was young I used to sit in the taverns and be a tough guy. Now I'm down at the tribal center every day. I am either counseling, carving, attending weddings, funerals, potlucks, or pow-wows, or in the sweat lodge. If I'm not in my office, I'm carving a canoe or building a fire on the beach. People come around. It's my hope that if the young folks see that, they will know there is an alternative.

"We divide and categorize people in this world. We are not a Native American country now. But my being Indian is important to me. Yet it is only important to me. My being Indian doesn't necessarily do anything for someone else's life. The kind of person I am is what affects someone else's life. I have taken all of the anger, hate, and ugliness I grew up with and learned to be proud of who I am.

"I went home to South Dakota and asked the elders for a ceremony, and they brought out the sacred pipe. Every day they brought the pipe out. We have four colors that we use: red, yellow, black, and white. These are the colors of all the people of the world. There were red, yellow, black, and white people at the ceremonies. That was the only time I saw everyone equal. It was beautiful. I just cried to see that."

Jesse's recovery reflects the collective spirit that is common to Native Americans. His recovery began with his taking responsibility for himself—for the good and welfare of all. Such wisdom for a person who had been so victimized and so sick for the first thirty years of his life is incredibly inspiring.

Shame permeates and immobilizes an entire community when so many people live with chronic drunkenness in their immediate and extended families. Children such as Pam and Jesse Old Coat experienced their childhoods as a fight for survival of their spirit and physical being. At the same time Pam did have more stability in her life than Jesse. She had the strength of her grandmother and a bonding to her Native American family; there was slightly more money, and her father helped her feel some self-worth. By contrast, Jesse was abandoned to his own survivorship, and his body was more ravaged. Alcohol was his only model for living; it was the only answer possible to the devastation of his body and spirit.

While the two stories of Native Adult Children portray lives of poverty and extreme abuse, that is not the experience of all Indian Children of Alcoholics. Yet as extreme as many of these stories may seem throughout this book, they represent the lives of thousands of children of yesterday and, unfortunately, of today as well. Although other Indian Adult Children may not have had these extreme experiences, nevertheless the issues of differentness, shame, and denial—coupled with histories of oppression, poverty, and generational helplessness—are a part of their lives.

Every person in this book is a survivor and can take pride in that. I said earlier, there are reasons for how children who live with such adversity develop the strength to be the caring, capable people they are today. Children of color derive much of their strength from connectedness with an extended family. For the Native American it also comes from connectedness with the tribe. The extended family and a rich cultural history are often what keeps the inner child intact and the spirit of belief and self-worth alive.

The fact that Pam and Jesse both sought out traditional paths in their recovery is a testament to their cultural ancestry. They were both drawn back to something they had experienced as children that offered them inner peace and purpose in their being.

In the Native American culture, Indians see children as gifts of God. Traditional culture maintains an incredible respect for the child and for the elders. It is sometimes difficult for others to understand this when faced with the dysfunction and trauma that Pam and Jesse experienced as children. Yet these children never doubted their desire to be a part of their tribal culture once they were able to separate themselves from the active alcoholism in their lives.

Jesse goes in search of the person who cares because he has been told someone does care. Then he realizes he is the one who cares. Pam seeks out a nontraumatic environment by going back to her grandmother, the person who teaches her about Indian Indians. Tribal life is transmitted predominantly through storytelling. It is in these traditional stories that Native Americans learn they are part of a valued force larger than themselves. Something was instilled in Pam and Jesse very early on that gave them an inner strength and an inner guide.

However, for this strength and sense of value to be put to good purpose, the alcoholism must be addressed first. Until that happens it is likely that children such as Jesse will never have a sense of their worth and will not receive an education. These losses will fuel another generation of poverty, alcohol, and drug addiction.

Today, urban and reservation Native Americans are developing resources to respond to the dynamics portrayed here. Alcoholism needs to be addressed as the number-one health problem. Getting sober is a must. Developing programs for children to help them feel pride in who they are need to accompany this sobriety. The key will be in community change and in reestablishing and maintaining the traditions and values of the tribal cultures.

Differences between the various tribal cultures and differences between them and the white society do not have to result in conflicts. Differences can be as beautiful as the rich and colorful abundance of many kinds of flowers in one garden.

Recovery Considerations

One of the major problems in developing culturally specific resources has to do with the ethnic diversity among racial groups. Hispanics or Latinos in the United States come from several different Spanish-speaking cultures, Asian/Pacific Americans are equally as diverse in ethnicity and even more so with the greater language differences. The Federal Government recognizes approximately 305 different Native American tribes. Tribal populations range in size from fewer than 100 to more than 130,000. Each has a separate tribal government system and specific cultural traditions.

The likelihood of hearing information about resources and recovery from addictions is greatly restricted in traditional ethnic communities. It appears that the more mainstream minority people are, the greater the opportunity of hearing about recovery. However, the more isolated their life-styles, the more likely they are to continue living lives bounded by a lower education level, poverty, and unemployment. These are the circumstances that often feed addictions. Clearly this is a vicious cycle. The issues fuel addictions, but without sobriety one cannot effectively address those issues. Recovery programs, individual counseling, and long-term treatment centers are not often available to members of minorities who have limited means.

Yet the outlook is not as bleak as it sounds. The newly launched War on Drugs is beginning to direct societal resources into minority communities. As a result, the level of denial is decreasing, and more community-based resources are being developed. Traditionally there have been minority drug and alcoholism counselors in ethnic communities. One of the more visible changes is the increasing number of people of color in Adult Child recovery programs. Recent years have seen the development of Spanish-speaking or predominantly Hispanic, Black, and Native American Alcoholics Anonymous and Adult Child self-help groups. This is particularly true in urban areas.

One of the most encouraging models for recovering people of color is what is occurring in Native American communities. They have been the leaders in the ethnic recovery movement, actively working at developing sober communities. The Alkali Lake Band in Alkali Lake, British Columbia, says it has been successful in achieving 95 percent sobriety in their community.[5,6] This kind of success has come from Native Americans mobilizing within their own communities. While continuing to maintain the values and beliefs of their traditional cultures, they have also adapted the mainstream alcohol- and drug-treatment philosophies to create a workable model for Native American recovery programs.

The growing consciousness of the special needs of recovering minority people has resulted in the formation of the National Association of Native American Children of Alcoholics (NANACOA). The purpose of NANACOA is to facilitate positive change in individuals and communities to break the generational cycle of addiction among Native Americans. It is working to establish a national network and newsletter for Native American Children of Alcoholics and to develop educational and supportive information and training resources for Native American communities.

Responding to the specific needs of the African American community is the National Black Alcohol Council (NBAC) and the Institute on Black Chemical Abuse (IBCA). The NBAC's purpose is to increase the public's awareness about alcoholism among African Americans, to advocate culturally sensitive prevention and treatment services, and to offer community education and training.

The Institute on Black Chemical Abuse also offers culturally specific prevention, intervention, and treatment services for the population in its headquarter cities of Minneapolis and St. Paul, Minnesota. At the national level it offers workshops to educate community groups, consults with government agencies and private treatment providers, and collects and disseminates information and statistics about alcohol and drug use among African Americans. IBCA also prepares and distributes radio and television public service announcements and publishes booklets to educate those working with chemically dependent African Americans and their families.

The National Coalition of Hispanic Health and Human Services Organizations (COSSMHO) was developed in response to the needs of The Hispanic population and works in local communities developing model alcohol and drug prevention programs. It reaches out in a special way to eight- to twelve-years-old children and their families through school prevention curricula. The National Hispanic Family Against Drug Abuse (NHFADA) also works toward developing culturally appropriate prevention and treatment services relevant to the Hispanic community.

The National Asian Pacific Families Against Substance Abuse (NAPFASA) is a prevention and education group that is collecting and disseminating information on the nature and extent of alcoholic and other drug problems in Asian Pacific communities. It serves as a clearing house for Asian Pacific agencies and support programs that train chemical dependency professionals.

While these programs are in various stages of organizational development, their ability to respond to the needs of minority populations will be vital in breaking community denial, creating public awareness, and responding to the specific cultural biases and needs which are faced in their communities.

For Adult Child recovery, the most widely available resource has been the no-cost, Twelve Step self-help program. The leaderless group model, which is the basis for all Twelve Step programs, provides a nonhierarchal structure in which all are equal, and the cost-free format removes a significant barrier for those with limited financial resources.

Whether you are red, yellow, black, brown, or white, if you were raised in an alcoholic home, your Adult Child issues sabotage the quality of your life. Yet for a person of color, it is valuable first to acknowledge Double Duty/Dual Identity recovery. Just as physically disabled Adult Children must deal with visible disabilities that cannot be changed, Adult Children of color must also address how their indelible racial identity has affected and will continue to affect many aspects of their lives.

In order for Adult Children of color to move effectively through the recovery process and to benefit from recovery resources, there are several key issues that need to be considered in greater depth.

LOYALTY

For several years psychology has made it more acceptable for the white middle class to talk openly about trauma in their childhood. Yet the majority of Adult Children struggle to some degree with the issue of loyalty to their parents when they talk about the pain of their childhood. Although Adult Children experienced pain in their earlier lives, they often still love their parents. They most likely recognize that their parents never intended the harm but couldn't have done things any differently. The parents had diseases and were often raised in troubled families themselves. This issue of loyalty is, I believe, even stronger among multiracial groups. Culturally it is less acceptable to talk about family business outside of the family, and it certainly has not been as acceptable for people of color to speak about their parents in any manner that doesn't reflect utmost allegiance and loyalty. Talking about parents in any manner that would not hold them as reverent or sacred is perceived as betrayal. Again, these are people whose population and identity were historically subject to grievous attack; should they believe that they personally are doing anything to take away from the strength of their family, they will often retreat.

It is important to remember that talking about your childhood in Adult Child recovery was never meant to be a blaming process, nor does it need to become one. It is meant to be an opportunity to speak the truth about how you experienced your life. It is difficult to speak the truth about today if you continue to minimize and deny the first ten, fifteen, or twenty years of your life. Alcoholism and chemical dependency are not reflections of weakness on the part of your parent or your culture; if anything, they may be considered reflections of one's vulnerability as an individual.

Remember, although the concepts of Adult Child recovery were originally developed with a majority orientation, they were never meant to be the answer for all people. It is to be hoped that as people of color heal from Adult Child issues, they will create resources even more supportive of their heritage.

DIFFERENTNESS

When people of any sort walk into their first few recovery group meetings, they often feel overwhelmed and frightened. They usually have a need to defend themselves. They also tend to feel different from the others there and to question whether or not they belong.

When a person of color walks into such a meeting, all these feelings are intensified. The first thing they see is that they are visibly different from nearly everyone else there.

The color of their skin, their accent, and their culture may set them apart from the majority. No matter how much members of minorities assimilate—even after education and integration—they can never escape other people's responses to their ethnicity.

Remember also that all Adult Children have great difficulty trusting others. They have difficulty asking others for help. Few individuals find their comfort zone quickly when they first walk through those doors. It's very easy to attribute this discomfort to differences in color or class.

However, while it is important to recognize our differences, it is equally important not to get stuck in them. Sometimes what recovering people forget is that all of us are survivors. All of us are children raised in troubled families. And the reason we have all gathered together in these self-help groups is to recover from the trauma and pain of our childhoods and to begin to live healthy lives.

The differences discussed in this chapter were not meant to promote greater feelings of isolation. Rather, they were meant to sensitize you and others to the deeper issues of the Double Duty/Dual Identity experience by members of racial minorities.

As well, it's not necessarily accurate to say that people of color always find it easier to respond to their own group. Reverse racism and class differences may create antipathies between recovering people within the same minority group. The goal of recovery is not to limit any aspect of ourselves—and this includes limitations on the basis of color. I strongly believe that people of color cannot have the full recovery they deserve without addressing their cultural history.

TRUSTING PERCEPTIONS

All Adult Children have difficulty trusting their perceptions. As young people their perceptions were discounted and ignored. Many recovering ACOAs were told as children that what they saw or heard or felt wasn't true, was not accurate.

A typical response from a parent might have been: "Honey, you aren't really sad," "You have nothing to be frightened of," or "There's no reason to be angry!" This was usually followed by: "Stop it or else!" Some kids were told, "Mom really isn't drunk, she's depressed." Others were told, "Your father doesn't drink any more than anyone else in this family or neighborhood." As if that disqualified him from being alcoholic. It's highly possible in this environment that all his friends or family members may also be alcoholic. A child who has been physically abused may be told, "Your mom didn't really hit you. That doesn't hurt."

After years of hearing your own perceptions discounted, not trusting your feelings and reactions becomes a way of life. When the Adult Child is also a person of color, the confusion is compounded because you always wonder whether or not your color is influencing a situation. For example, say you go into a department store and the person who waits on you—in your perception—is angry and rude to you. As an Adult Child, you may first question what you did wrong—you assume you are at fault. Then you wonder whether this person is responding in this fashion because you are black, brown, male, female—or because he or she simply had a very bad day.

In recovery, all Adult Children need to look at how their perceptions have been discounted in the past and whether they're willing to trust their perceptions today. We all need to become self-validating. The more we can trust our own perceptions, the more we come to know ourselves and the better we are able to handle uncomfortable situations. The group process is of particular value in learning to share your perceptions with others.

DUAL CONSCIOUSNESS

In recovery, we explore not only how we see ourselves, but how we see ourselves in relation to others. In doing this we also explore how we believe we are seen by others. The following model was developed by Peter Bell, founder and former executive director for fifteen years of the Institute on Black Chemical Abuse.[7]

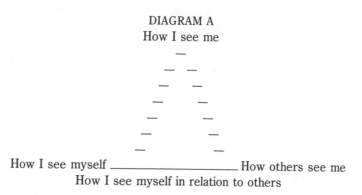

DIAGRAM A
How I see me

How I see myself _____ How others see me
How I see myself in relation to others

Bell says this model would work for all people if racism did not exist. However, in the United States today a person's identity is determined by more than just a simple interaction of "How I see myself," "How others see me," and "How I see myself in relation to others." The life of a person of color must also be explored against the backdrop of cultural schizophrenia.

Racial minority double consciousness is modeled as:

DIAGRAM B

How I see whites

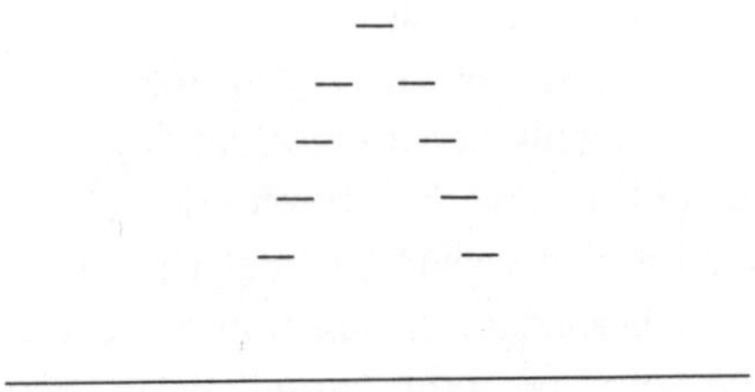

—
— —
— —
— —
— —

How I see myself in relation to whites	How whites see me

DIAGRAM C

How I see myself as a (Black, Latino, Asian, Native American) person

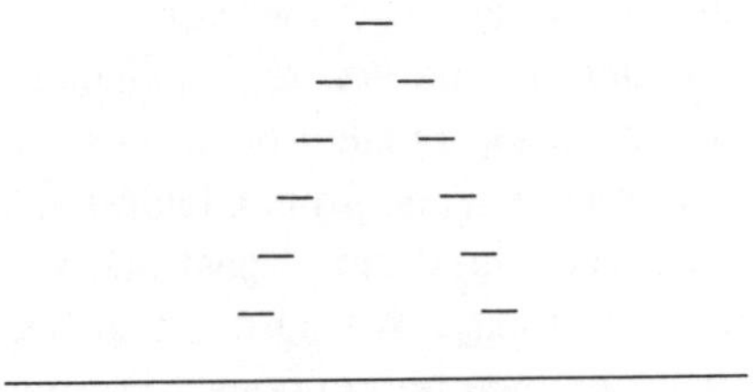

—
— —
— —
— —
— —

How I see myself in relation to other minorities	How others see me

In order to experience full recovery, minority ACOAs need to sort out the duality in which they have lived.

Although many people of color can and do work through these issues, when one is also an Adult Child, the old rules of not feeling and not thinking often take precedence and inhibit the sorting process. Moreover, many don't know what their needs are—or have learned not to ask questions even when they do. This also hinders the recovery process.

Above all, it is very difficult to deal fully with duality issues until ACOAs address their compulsive and/or addictive life-styles. At this point Adult Child recovery often makes it possible for people to explore what color has meant in their lives and, hopefully, to develop a greater sense of pride in who they are.

CULTURAL DIFFERENCES

Recovering Adult Children also need to address the differences in male/female roles in minority cultures.

In the Hispanic culture, for example, there is a strong sense of family pride and honor. There the wife and mother are often perceived as sacred, and the husband and father reflect the machismo view. Although the term is not clearly defined in many Hispanic or Latin cultures, in a traditional sense "machismo" was used to reflect strength, nobility, respect, and an honorable understanding between men and women. In practice this can be difficult for many Hispanic men; attempting to preserve their sense of dignity while struggling with language barriers, oppression, racism, and class differences can become so frustrating that they lash out at those they love. As a result, machismo has in recent years come to mean male dominance and heavy-handed authority.

All recovering Adult Children need to determine what their belief systems are concerning the roles of men and women in their culture. They need to examine whether or not their beliefs are helpful to them or hurtful. For example, take the word *machismo*. An Hispanic man has machismo. Does that mean he gets to be abusive with his strength? Does that mean it is all right for him to become addicted? Does it mean that he is supposed to give up his selfhood and become an enabler and a codependent? In a "macho" culture many practices that are hurtful to children have become an accepted way of life. Yet Hispanics have a great love for children. Machismo was never meant to hurt children. One can redefine the term in a way that is helpful to recovery.

Male and female roles in the African American community have been stigmatized by the myth of the black matriarchy. Black men are characterized as addicts, gamblers, and womanizers. Women are characterized as long-suffering, martyred superwomen whose only solace is their church. As Frances Brisbane and Maxine Womble say, "Although the woman is highly valued in black families, her importance is without an implied or expressed denial of male importance. Many times, and out of necessity, black men and women exchange sex role behavior and do whatever is necessary for 'family survival.' It is important for recovering black ACOAs not to buy into the myth of the matriarch because it disenfranchises men and distorts the role of women in a family system built on incredible survivorship."[8]

Without a clear understanding of the historical context, it is easy to misinterpret the continuing influences of the past on the lives of people of color. The African American population of the Americas came from Africans who were forcibly separated from their families and sold into slavery. On slave-holding plantations they attempted to re-create family systems, only to be brutally separated again and again by their owners. This disruption continued after emancipation, as blacks moved to the northern industrial cities. When faced with massive unemployment and discrimination, the black male was often forced to leave home to find any kind of work. If one overlooks this context, it is easy to buy into the stereotype of woman as saint and man as sinner.

It is vital that the survivorship skills of the African American be validated in the recovery process. This is a community that has survived incredible hardship and disruption through any means it could find. It should not have been seen as deviating from the white experience; rather, the variety, uniqueness, and complexity of black life must be acknowledged.

Among the Native American population, traditional male/female roles varied from tribe to tribe; some were strongly matriarchal, others patriarchal. Nevertheless, even where family systems were matriarchal, tribal councils and governing bodies were composed primarily of men. Today more women are beginning to take strong leadership roles in their tribes. Both male and female elders play a key role in the passing down of Indian culture and history.

Here, too, it is vitally important to understand the historical roots of alcoholism among Native Americans when doing recovery work. It is believed that the Native Americans had no previous history of drinking until alcohol was first brought to the Americas by European traders and explorers in the sixteenth century. Alcohol quickly became a medium of trade, and it was used to manipulate the Indians into giving up many of their valued treasures—most specifically their lands.

Although Native Americans were not immediately separated from family members as a result of these losses, they were separated from their land, usually through "removals" to more limited, less desirable lands often vast distances away. The tragedy was that their traditional home lands were an integral part of their identity as people. The earth was considered sacred and deeply linked to their religion and philosophy, as well as providing the economic base of their livelihood.

Many tribes fought bravely for their traditional way of life, but when the Indian Wars ended in the late 1870s, they became dependents of the Federal Government for all their needs. Only in the last decade or so has sovereignty been returned to many tribes.

Various policies of assimilation managed to destroy much of the remaining land base for most tribal people, and with this went their traditional belief systems, language, religion, and any sense of themselves as members of a unique, self-empowering, self-sustaining culture. What many Native Americans were left to face was racial prejudice, extreme poverty, helplessness, rage, and spiritual bankruptcy. Very often alcohol seemed the only escape.

This generationally enforced powerlessness has created a cultural self-hate unprecedented among any other minority group in this country. This is vastly more crippling to the human spirit than family dysfunction. Given this bleak picture, the strength and endurance of any traditional values and beliefs is miraculous. And this is why, today, Native Americans have such power to heal—both as individuals and as tribal communities.

RELIGIOUS AND SPIRITUAL PRACTICES

Religious and spiritual practices remembered from childhood are significant elements in the recovery of all Adult Children. However, for people of color involvement in church and spiritual practices tends to be deeply connected with a sense of identity and family heritage. Adult Children of color draw much of their strength from their unquestioning belief that something or somebody greater than they is watching over them. Because of this, these practices often become active resources in the healing process. These are more than traditional religious values; people of color have adapted the church and spiritual practices to fit the values of their own cultures. These adaptations are part of what has held their cultures together. One's involvement in what has been a source of internal strength and power needs to be supported in one's recovery.

When people speak from the heart, I believe healing occurs for all.
—Native American Adult Child

Notes

1. Analysis commissioned by the Task Force on Black and Minority Health, 1984-1985, Chapel Hill, N.C.: Duke University.
2. "Alcohol and Ethnic Minorities," Research report, *Alcohol and Health Report*, Vol. II, no. 2 (Winter, 1986-87).
3. *Ibid.*
4. *Ibid.*
5. *The Honor of All*, General Delivery, Alkali Lake, British Columbia, Videotape. (Presentation of the process in which the Alkali Lake Band community alcoholism was addressed.)
6. E. Furness, "Sobriety Movement Among the Shuswap Indians of Alkali Lake," (Ph.D. diss., University of British Columbia, Vancouver, B.C., 1987).
7. P. Bell and J. Evans, *Counseling the Black Client* (Center City, Minn.: Hazelden Publishing, 1981).
8. F. L. Brisbane and M. Womble, eds. *Treatment of Black Alcoholics, Alcoholism Treatment Quarterly* Series, vol. 2, nos. 3-4 (Binghampton, N.Y.: Howarth Press, 1985)

10

Physical Disability

I have probably become more accepting of my disability by working on ACOA issues. When you are learning to accept yourself, learning that you are okay, then you come to accept that all of you is okay.

—Adult Child

The majority of people in the world grow up able-bodied. That means their physical being develops, strengthens, and performs as it was designed to. While some people are grateful for this gift, most take it for granted or automatically assume they will be in good physical health. Yet many people are born with physical abnormalities that cause them to be disabled; some children are born with congenital illnesses, and some develop illnesses that create permanent disabilities. For others, accidents create lifelong disabilities. Many of the Vietnam veterans who have come home physically disabled and who are struggling to make sense out of their loss are also Adult Children.

In addition to identifiable physical disabilities, many children come into this world with learning disabilities. Sometimes these disorders are related to illnesses, sometimes not. Many children are developmentally disabled; they have a lower intelligence quotient and are less able to reason, conceptualize, and problem-solve. While they also merit our attention and concern, in this chapter we will address specifically the child whose disability is physical.

In play, most children walk, run, jump. They reach and grab. They look and listen. But some children cannot do these things. Yet, disabled or not, they too are curious, spontaneous, innocent, and desirous. They have all the emotional, mental, and social needs of other children.

Children who grow up with physical disabilities have to deal with their "differentness" as an ongoing part of their lives. They learn that they must approach the challenges of daily life differently from other people. They may need to ask for help where the able-bodied could be self-sufficient. They may need to allow for extra time to accommodate their disability. They have to cope with the looks and stares of others. And they have to respond to often ignorant, hurtful remarks about their disability. As they grow older they may experience social isolation or rejection by their peers, or their participation may be restricted. The physically disabled are also forced to deal with their own emotional reactions both to their disability and to how others treat them. That may mean responding to feelings of loneliness, fear, hurt, and frustration that emanate from situations and experiences able-bodied people don't encounter.

The healthier the family system in which physically disabled children are raised, the greater the likelihood that they will learn to accommodate to their physical limitations in a manner that allows them to live full and meaningful lives.

In a healthy family system, parents will offer support, validation, and help in solving the problems inherent in living with disabilities. Children with disabilities need parents who will facilitate their involvement in as many age-appropriate activities as possible. They need parents who will teach them appropriate ways of responding to the social hurts they will encounter because of their disabilities. Such parents allow their children to feel the grief associated with their differentness while at the same time fostering their emotional and social development through creative problem-solving. A healthy family learns to recognize the limits imposed by the disability but doesn't dwell on them.

Physical disabilities demand that families make adjustments. Even in healthier families, these adjustments create stress that can result in family problems. It takes the healthiest of families to create an atmosphere in which physically disabled children can feel good about themselves while maintaining a balanced life for all family members.

Children with disabilities are first confronted with their "differentness" when their disability begins to interfere with their social network. As long as they can participate with their siblings and play with friends, their differentness is not associated with shame, which is the belief that there is something wrong with them. Good examples of problem-solving would be the child with muscular dystrophy who is carried on his father's back to the lake as the other boys in the Boy Scout troop hike along, or the child with asthma who can spend the night at a friend's house because she brought her own pillow and bed linens.

When disabled children have healthy parenting, you see the family finding creative ways to mainstream them into the daily routine of family, school, and play. These children learn to feel good about themselves while accepting the limits of their disabilities and attending to their special needs.

Growing Up Disabled in the Chemically Dependent/Alcoholic Family

Many families are affected by chemical dependency, and within some of those families there will be children with physical disabilities. These children are being raised by parents who may not seek appropriate resources; who may not ask helpful questions; who are blaming toward the child; who have inappropriate expectations; and who negate the child's special needs.

Many variables will affect how a family responds to a disability: a key variable is the visibility of the disability—for instance, the response to cerebral palsy or blindness as opposed to asthma or a birth defect. The less blatant, the less visible, the disability, the more likely family members are to minimize the effects and the less likely they are to address the disability seriously. Because a disability such as asthma may be less visible doesn't mean it can't be deadly. Although a blatant disability such as the loss of a limb or a disease requiring a wheelchair forces those around the disabled person to acknowledge the disability, it often becomes the way they define that person. Unfortunately, that definition is often shrouded with fear and anxiety.

The progressive stage of the parents' chemical dependency and codependency behaviors also affects their ability to respond to the needs of a disabled child. In most chemically dependent families the responsibilities that should be assumed by the parents often shift to the children. The farther the parents have progressed in their dependency, the less likely it becomes that they will use appropriate community and medical resources—and the less likely it becomes that they will offer the support these children need to confront their emotional and social needs. The disabled child is left to be self-sufficient, and/or another sibling becomes their primary caretaker.

THE CARDINAL RULES OF THE DYSFUNCTIONAL FAMILY

Rule Number One: Don't Talk. In a healthy family one's disability is acknowledged. Everybody feels free to discuss it openly. However, family members don't focus on the disabled person to the exclusion of others, nor do they ignore special needs of the disabled person.

However, this is an alcoholic family; the "Don't talk" rule permeates all aspects of family life, including issues related to the disability. The "Don't talk" rule isn't necessarily literal—family members may periodically risk the truth. But people in alcoholic families generally discover that it isn't safe to be candid. They learn to minimize, discount, and rationalize, which in the end leads to not talking about the real issues.

The physically disabled child learns not to talk about the family alcoholism and not to talk about the disability. Both issues are treated as if they do not exist. The family system responds and revolves around the chemical dependency and the unhealthy rules that help to maintain it. Chemically dependent families are not child-centered families, and the problems of children are seldom the priority. In alcohol-centered families, the needs of the child are often negated.

Chemically dependent parents may use their children's disabilities as an excuse for their drinking and behavior: "I drink because of . . ." becomes one parent's convenient rationalization, while the other parent becomes depressed and isolated with a "Poor me, look at my child" attitude. The disability can also be used as a Ping-Pong ball between the parents. This makes it particularly difficult for disabled children to talk about themselves or the chemical dependency. Often there is so much chaos in the home because of the chemical dependency that the child's problems are easily ignored.

Rule Number Two: Don't Feel. The physically disabled child in a chemically dependent home also internalizes another cardinal rule of dysfunctional families—"Don't feel." Physically disabled children may feel a great deal of emotional pain because of their disability, but they have to suppress these feelings because of the alcoholic family dysfunction. They won't find the support they need to share feelings because of the dynamics of the chemically dependent family, in which they learn: "Don't feel, no one will be there for you."

Rule Number Three: Don't Trust. Physically disabled children typically need to rely on others more for help, but the message in the alcoholic family is that you can't trust people to be there for you. This sets up a drive for self-reliance that is all the more powerful for someone with a physical disability.

SURVIVAL ROLES

The disabled child in an alcoholic family is required to play the same roles as other children in alcoholic families—the responsible one, the adjuster, the placater, the one who acts out. But these roles are often more complicated and difficult because of the child's special physical needs.

The Acting Out child may be acting out not only the emotional pain associated with the family, but the emotional and physical pain associated with the disability. Disabled placaters may take to the role with an even greater vengeance to assure an even greater likelihood of getting positive attention from others. This may be their best way to secure friendships.

Some children have to totally deny their disability and not get their needs attended to at all because of the necessity of being the responsible child in the family. For others, the added sense of shame—feeling bad or inadequate—that comes with the disability may create in them an even greater need to become the adjusting child, the one who tries not to be noticed. The disability often accentuates each of these roles.

SHAME

Many Children of Alcoholics grow up believing that they are inadequate and inferior, that they aren't good enough, or that something is inherently wrong with them. This sense of shame is compounded for the physically disabled child. Because other people so often respond inappropriately to the physically disabled from fear or ignorance, these children grow up learning from others that there is something wrong with their differentness.

Both the alcoholism in the family and the physical impairment set these children apart from others, reinforcing their belief that they are not okay, that they are not acceptable. The shame and lack of opportunity to have adults intervene and help them learn how to cope with other people's thoughtless actions reinforces these children's fundamental lack of trust and restricts their desire to share with others even further.

GUILT

Physically disabled children often believe that they are adding to the family burden by being who they are, and this makes them feel guilty. Healthy parents can alleviate these feelings. But for the disabled COA, guilt often becomes an overwhelming self-loathing. Without the positive reinforcement of family members and friends, these children find self-acceptance very difficult.

UNREALISTIC EXPECTATIONS

So many Children of Alcoholics live with unrealistic expectations from their parents. This culminates in Adult Children who are high achievers, but who never feel that they are good enough. They hurry through life trying to do more and do better, ultimately becoming angry and depressed without understanding why. Or they do the opposite: at a young age they simply stop trying. Some ACOAs play the deadly game of both extremes and a seesaw of overachieving, and when success is in sight, self-loathing and a sense of unworthiness takes over; then they act out in some fashion that sabotages the effort. Just at the point of achieving the goal, these ACOAs stop trying, walk away, abandon the project or the relationship.

Disabled people in general often have to overcompensate for their disability. This means that disabled Adult Children have an even greater need to achieve, often trying to prove that they're okay through their accomplishments, but never coming to terms with the fact that their inner self has always been okay. Or they can adopt the attitude of some able-bodied Adult Children and simply give up—accepting helplessness and depriving themselves of the opportunity to have accomplishments that in fact are possible. But whether they overcompensate, give up, or ride the seesaw of both extremes, they have had additional reinforcement of their Double Duty. They are responding as both a Child of an Alcoholic and a physically disabled person. This sets them up for an even greater depth of helplessness or a more severe belief that they are not ''good enough'' despite their accomplishments.

Growing up with physical disabilities does not of itself create personal, emotional, and psychological problems. But growing up in a chemically dependent family does. Recovery for the disabled Adult Child means addressing both the physical disability and the Adult Child issue(s).

Life Stories: Growing-Up Years

In the following life stories, Christine, Liz, and Sarah have had to deal with blatant visible disabilities since birth or the toddler stage. Christine is a triple amputee. She is still unclear why she needed the amputations—alcoholic families leave many questions unanswered. Liz has cerebral palsy. Sarah is paralyzed on one side of her body.

Brian didn't discover that his physical disability had been caused by polio until he joined the Navy and they gave him a medical discharge. Michael was seventeen and about to graduate from high school when he was paralyzed in a motorcycle accident. This left him totally dependent on the people with whom he was already enraged.

There are many disabilities that do not get described in this chapter. The nature of a disability can affect certain Adult Child issues in specific ways. For example, hearing-impared children are certainly affected by the "Don't talk" rule. It sets them up for significantly more isolation than another disability might. Some children are disabled by progressive, often terminal illnesses such as muscular dystrophy. The nature of such a disease has a tremendous impact on children with progressive loss issues. Blind Adult Children might have even greater difficulty trusting their perceptions without sight.

It is my hope that readers will be able to gain enough insight into growing up with the dual dynamics of alcoholism and disabilities to apply the information and process to their own disabilities.

The issues of denial, feeling different, control, and powerlessness are common recurring issues in the lives of these five people and have played very significant roles throughout their lives. I believe we will cover the core issues of growing up disabled in an alcoholic family, and that this will validate readers' experiences and provide increased sensitivity to the Double Duty/Dual Identity issues in their lives.

CHRISTINE
Age: 36
Disability: Triple amputee
Mother: Co-dependent
Father: Alcoholic, compulsive
    gambler
Stepfather: Alcoholic, abuser
Birth Order: Oldest of two children
Raised: Midwest
Socioeconomic Status: Poor (until
    age 9); then working class

At six months of age Christine lost three of her limbs, both legs and an arm, as the result of an illness.

CHRISTINE: *"When I was about six months old, I became very ill for several days with a high fever and severe dehydration, which led to circulatory problems. Three of my limbs were amputated when gangrene set in: my left leg above the knee, my right leg below the knee, and my right arm below the elbow. My mother said they never attached a name to the illness. With two artificial legs, I began walking when I was about a year and a half old. That is how I walk today: on two prosthetic legs without other walking aids. I've never worn a prosthesis on my arm."*

When Christine was five her parents divorced. She spent her childhood going back and forth between two violent alcoholic homes.

"My father was a compulsive gambler and an alcoholic. After my parents divorced, my mother, my sister, and I stayed with her mother. My mother didn't remarry until I was about eight or nine, but my father remarried right away—an alcoholic with two children. Ellie, my stepmother, was ignorant and poorly educated, a coarse, vulgar woman who was abusive. Their marriage included a lot of violence. My visitation with my father was every Sunday.
    "When my mother did remarry, she also married an abusive alcoholic. She worked, and between her job and her preoccupation with her husband, my sister and I were left pretty much alone."

Despite her disability, Christine's role in the family was as the responsible caretaker. As the oldest child she was expected to do most of the house cleaning, to look after her younger sister, and to prepare many of the meals. Despite these responsibilities, the family seemed to completely ignore the fact that Christine had any special physical needs. Nevertheless they treated her differently because of her handicap.

"While there were chores that I was expected to do, there were other ways in which very little was expected of me. Because I was a girl, and because I was handicapped, I was never expected to do much with my life."

Christine and her sister were also subjected to physical abuse.

"Although I do remember being beaten by my mother a few times, most of the physical abuse in the house was directed at my sister. My stepfather beat my little sister often and was emotionally cruel to all of us.

"My father pitied me. I think that was what spared me most of the physical abuse my sister received. Both my stepparents targeted her for abuse. I felt guilty about escaping the beatings. Yet my sister, in her frustration, often hit me. We both engaged in bouts of hitting each other. All this abuse created a greater sense of isolation and a lot of self-hate."

Children who witness abuse are said to often be as traumatized as the child who is the direct recipient. They feel tremendous "survivor's guilt"—believing they are inadequate or wrong for not receiving a part of the abuse or not being able to protect their siblings.

With the psychological and physical abuse at home, Christine focused on achievement at school. When she was five she was sent to a school for handicapped children. In some ways the school was able to address her special needs, but the children were bused from all over the area, and she had a hard time making friends in her own neighborhood.

"At school I quickly learned that I was smart. I knew it, and the internal gratification sustained me, although there were few external rewards. My drive for academic achievement, and later for career achievement, was self-imposed.

"Rather than feeling proud, my mother felt threatened by any success I had. I don't remember ever hearing one supportive or encouraging word from my mother. I remember only criticism. My reaction was to withdraw. My father was proud of me, but he also pitied me. His pity was patronizing and served to separate me from the family and from other kids. Fortunately, I received some stroking in school because I was such a good student."

Christine was living with a major contradiction in her life. It had to lead to confusion. Although her family had low academic expectations of her, they obviously placed major expectations on her at home. As a young child on two prosthetic legs and without an arm, Christine was expected to be the responsible family caretaker.

Christine also spent much of her childhood going to doctors every few months to review her prosthetic needs.

"Periodically I would have to get new 'legs,' so I would have several sessions to get measured and fitted for a new prosthesis. I hated hospital visits because I was often put on display in front of many medical people in an amphitheater-type setting. Being shy, I was overwhelmed at such a loss of privacy. I felt ashamed of being handicapped, and it always seemed like a public humiliation.

"It was also an acknowledgment of my handicap, which was otherwise never acknowledged in my day-to-day family life. Going to the hospital, or being fitted for a prosthesis, were the only times my family's and my denial of my handicap was ever really challenged. Because of this, the hospital visits were always difficult for me."

The lack of acknowledgment of Christine's disability at home, contrasted with the blatant display of it in the hospital setting, is an example of the the "all or nothing" way of life so common in chemically dependent families.

When Christine was fifteen her mother and her first stepfather divorced. The following year her mother remarried.

"I had always been ashamed that my parents were divorced and that my mother had a different last name from mine. Her multiple marriages embarrassed me even more."

Clearly, Christine grew up in a chaotic, emotionally and physically threatening environment. As the Child of an Alcoholic, the need to reduce the trauma in her life prompted her to minimize the hardships caused by her physical disabilities. Children of Alcoholics learn at a young age to minimize, rationalize, and deny—all a part of survivorship. These skills are then transferred to other areas of one's life. For Christine, it was her disability.

BRIAN
Age: 53
Disability: Polio
Mother: Co-dependent
Father: Alcoholic
Birth Order: Oldest of four children
Raised: Upper New York State
Socioeconomic Status: Working
    class

Brian grew up in a large Irish family in the East. He was the first child to live after his mother's four miscarriages. When he was an infant, Brian contracted polio. As a result, one leg was severely atrophied and one of his feet deformed. He also developed a slight paralysis in the face. Brian's father was alcoholic, and so were his father's father and his uncles. Brian found his family and relatives frightening.

BRIAN: *"I was always frightened by my father's side of the family. There was always the threat of violence with them—not to me directly, but violence was the underlying tone for everything with them. Everybody was always angry. I don't believe I ever really knew my dad. He was always in trouble, drunk and fighting. My mother's father was always coming to bail Dad out of problems. My memories of childhood are of burning cars, family feuds, and fights. There was always a lot of confusion, a lot of uproar.*

"I always felt shame about my family, but I could never separate the shame I felt about the alcoholism from what was accepted growing up in an Irish family. I thought that drunkenness was a part of being Irish."

"My mother was never available to me. I remember her always being pregnant. She made the dinner, she did the laundry, but she never socialized with me. And I never felt connected with my brothers and sister because they were thirteen to eighteen years younger than I was. It was as if I came from a different world."

Brian felt that he never knew his father, and his mother was unavailable. They also sent him to live for extended periods of time with his mother's family. With that was added shame.

"I was my father's son. I was an extension of him. Therefore, I was responsible for the 'family shame.' "

He was sent to his grandparents because his parents were fighting, his mother was sick with repeated miscarriages, and there was little money to provide for him.

Although they were cold emotionally, Brian's mother's side of the family brought some stability into Brian's life. His mother's family was Irish Catholic, and the Church was a big part of their life. Brian spent a lot of time with members of the extended family who were not chemically dependent, although alcoholism was inherent in both sides of the family. The only overt affection that was ever displayed in the family was when someone was drunk. Brian says he always felt safer with his mother's side of the family, his more prudish, nonemotional aunt, uncle, and grandmother.

To escape the family chaos, Brian isolated himself, spending a lot of time reading. In addition, he spent quite a bit of time with a bachelor uncle who was also a loner.

"I would go places like the zoo, the botanical gardens, the movies— always by myself. I was alone. I didn't have a lot of friends because I was so scared of other people. I was ashamed of having them see my family."

Although the alcoholism was the greatest source of shame to Brian, his disability added to his sense of shame and differentness. Brian spent a lot of time trying to hide his deformities from others. While he was preoccupied with his disability, he says the family never, ever talked about it. They ignored it.

In a neighborhood where the emphasis was on being tough, Brian was a small child and, because of his disability, not very athletic. He attended Catholic schools for twelve years and was very bright. However, that trait wasn't particularly valued by his peers, so Brian tended to hide it.

"In school I quickly learned that I was smarter than most of the others. But it didn't help to be smart if you were small and not an athlete. Heaven help me for being smart. I tried to hide my brightness by not putting any effort into school. There were no rewards for looking smart."

While Brian's disability was less visible compared with others, he was engulfed with shame about it at a very young age. This shame was further exacerbated by the chaos in his family—his life was filled with fear and dread. He found little solace. It wasn't okay to be small. It wasn't okay to be smart. It wasn't okay to have a disability.

Brian lost what comfort his grandparents, aunt, and uncle provided when his family moved out of state during his high school years. By then he was working to support himself in various jobs, and he finished high school.

LIZ

Age: 31
Disability: Cerebral palsy
Mother: Alcoholic
Father: Co-dependent
Birth Order: Middle of three
    children
Raised: Mid-Atlantic urban
Socioeconomic Status: Middle class

Growing up in the mid-Atlantic region in an alcoholic family, Liz describes her mother as the alcoholic and her father as a very controlling co-dependent. Liz was born with cerebral palsy, which was discovered when she was a year old. As a result she has always had to deal with certain motor-coordination problems and has used crutches or braces to walk since she was three.

LIZ: *"My mother really couldn't give me much nurturing when I was growing up. She'd not learned any parenting skills because she was an Adult Child of an alcoholic mother herself. My grandmother was a very controlling person, too, and had never been available for her child. My mother didn't know how to be emotionally supportive."*

Liz's mother's drinking would become apparent as a problem during Liz's teenage years. Until that time Liz was more deeply affected by her mother's Adult Child issues. Her mother could have been in earlier-stage alcoholism when Liz was young; the symptoms would have been less noticeable. With the progressiveness of alcoholism, it is possible that Liz only noticed the symptoms as her mother moved into middle-stage chemical dependency. The other possibility would be that Liz's mother's onset occurred later, and because women experience a faster progression of the disease, the alcoholism truly didn't exist until Liz was in her adolescence.

Liz was close to her father while she was growing up. Her father would show his affection to her by teasing her which often resulted in making fun of her disability.

"Dad would play on my CP. I have a startle reflex—when I hear loud noises my body jumps involuntarily. Well, my dad would clap his hands to see me jump. While it sounds cruel, in many ways it was him in his joking manner. Pretty sick joke. I could see it as affection, but other times I would get angry and tell him, 'That's enough!' Supposedly it was his way of saying he cared, but he didn't really know how to show affection, and sometimes I didn't know if he really loved me or not."

Liz's father's behavior was obviously confusing. Liz had difficulty in developing any ability to trust her own perceptions. Under the guise of teasing, Liz's father hurt her in a demeaning manner. This behavior sets up a child to tolerate inappropriate behavior, which is an ACOA characteristic. The disabled child may have an even greater need to tolerate inappropriate behavior simply to get some degree of social attention.

"In my small neighborhood I experienced a lot of acceptance with kids of all different ages. The other kids let me play with them, and I got along with them pretty well. I had my own forms of hopscotch, kick the can, and dodgeball. But there were some things I couldn't do that the other kids could, and I would feel left out."

By the time Liz was thirteen, she was mainstreamed into regular school classes from special-education classes.

"Most of the kids in my new school were generally okay. Some kids were rude, but kids will be rude even if you're a little overweight. For the most part, I think the kids were pretty accepting."

Yet she says that when she began to experience insensitivity to her disability, she spoke up.

"Some people, particularly some teachers, didn't understand what my disability meant. When I was in high school we had a rule that you could only have three absences for the semester—and three tardies counted as one absence. Well, when the weather was bad, I would struggle by my locker, trying to get my boots off, and I'd be late for class. My tardies were adding up, and I was about to lose some English credits. I told my mom she would have to talk to the principal because I couldn't afford to

lose the credits. My mom did call, and the school agreed to allow me to keep the credits. Most of the time, though, my mom told me I needed to learn to fight my own battles.''

When Liz was younger and attended special-education classes, her friends would visit.

"My friends from special education would come spend the night at our home, and my mom would take care of them. But this was before her heavy drinking began.''

Her mother's drinking became much worse during Liz's teenage years. Liz said that at first her mother was only drinking at night, but then it progressed to drinking all of the time.

"There was always a drink fixed in every room. I was really scared.''

By the time Liz was seventeen, her mother's drinking was blatant.

Liz's role in the family was that of the "acting out" child. She was the one who tried to call attention to her mother's drinking.

"If I think something isn't right, I have to say something about it. My parents have always resented this about me, but I just can't stand phoniness. I never have, and I never will.''

Liz started to drink when she was seventeen.

"Some of the drinking was so I would be accepted socially. When school would get to be too much for me, I would party with my friends.

"When I was in college, my mother ended up in the hospital with meningitis and had to go through alcohol withdrawal. I thought she was going to die. I remember drinking for three days during that crisis.''

Liz is as prone as any COA to become alcoholic. Not only is there a greater tendency to be genetically predispositioned toward alcoholism, but alcohol often offers a COA a feeling of greater acceptance. Alcohol was also perceived by Liz as the answer to the pain. And Liz's cerebral palsy would also create feelings of being left out, creating another void alcohol could fill.

SARAH
Age: 31
Disability: Injury, paralysis
Mother: Alcoholic
Father: Alcoholic, abusive
Birth Order: Youngest of three
    children
Raised: South
Socioeconomic Status: Lower
    middle class

Sarah's father was drinking alcoholically before she was born. He traveled a lot as a result of his work, but whenever he was home he was angry and violent. Sarah was injured at birth. Forceps were used at the base of her neck during delivery, and this destroyed the nerves relating to motor control on the right side of her body. Because of these injuries, Sarah has always walked with a severe limp and has limited use of her right arm.

SARAH: *"My father was home only five times a year or so, and each time he was very destructive with physical violence and abuse. He would hit us whenever he got mad, especially my younger brother. My brother's way of dealing with that was to turn around and abuse me. I spent a lot of my childhood trying to prepare for my father to come home again or trying to settle down after he left. As a result, there just wasn't a lot of extra energy to spend on my handicap. Energy was spent on survival."*

Both Sarah and Christine learned to live with physical violence. Both women report that physical abuse was directed at another sibling, yet being physically disabled did not spare either of them from physical abuse. While there are very few ways any child can defend against physical abuse from an adult, a disabled child has even fewer options.

The fact that both Christine and Sarah said another sibling was usually singled out for the physical abuse may indicate that the adult abuser was attempting to exercise some control in an out-of-control situation. Yet no matter who is the direct recipient of the violence, even those children who witness violence are victims. Like Sarah and Christine, they experience fear, helplessness, guilt, and rage.

When parents are abusers in a family, very often siblings become abusers, too. Both Sarah and Christine felt guilty and sad about their siblings being abused, but both were also victims of sibling abuse.

Because Sarah's mother was chemically dependent, too, in some ways it was even more difficult on the family when Sarah's father was away.

"Life was probably more tense when Dad was away. No matter what we did, we never knew if it would be right or wrong because Mom was so unpredictable. She was always threatening us with what she'd tell Dad when he came home. Often she would even make things up. Things were really more clear when Dad was home. At least you knew what to expect."

Sarah's experience was similar to those of others raised in chemically dependent homes—her disability was ignored and minimized by her family members. Nor did her family help prepare her for other people's reactions to her disability, which was more visible because she wore braces.

"When I first started school, my disability became harder to handle because the other children would either tease me or baby me. When I asked my brothers what to do about this, they told me, 'Just kick them with those braces.' I remember trying that, but it reminded me so much of when my father came home that I never did it again."

When Sarah was twelve years old the family moved so that they could spend more time with her father, who was still traveling.

"Since my brothers are six and eight years older than I am, I was the only one in school at the time. This was the most difficult period I remember in my childhood—changing schools. No one was used to me in my new school, and I wasn't used to them. The kids ridiculed the way I talked, and they nicknamed me 'freak.' I didn't have a single friend in that school, mostly by my own choice.

"I was in a lot of emotional pain, but I never brought it up because my family loved living there so much. I never once mentioned how I was being treated. That was just a secret that I kept. I wasn't willing to risk my family's reaction—I was afraid that it would just be more ridicule."

It is easy to see the development of the powerlessness that Sarah began to experience at a very young age—the powerlessness and fear around what she experienced in anticipation of what would happen when her dad came home; the powerlessness and fear that came from living with a mother who was alcoholic, emotionally abusive, and unpredictable; and the powerlessness and fear she experienced as a result of other children's ridicule.

Special Issues for the Physically Disabled ACOA

DENIAL

Denial is about minimizing, rationalizing, discounting, ignoring, and hiding one's feelings and perceptions. As the six-year-old Child of an Alcoholic once said, "Denial is pretending things are different than they really are."

As children raised in alcoholic families, Christine, Brian, Liz, and Sarah all developed a strong denial system. It shielded them from the pain and confusion of real life in their disruptive families, and it fueled their ability to ignore the issues related to the disability.

The "Don't talk" rule in alcoholic families creates an atmosphere of denial—learning how not to live with the truth. These children learn to keep their mouths shut and pretend the problem doesn't exist. For the physically disabled child, the family code of denial usually extends to the child's disability—"If we ignore it, it will not exist." Although the family may respond or react to the child's special physical needs in some limited fashion, the child's emotional needs are usually patently ignored.

CHRISTINE: "My family never really talked about my handicap as a triple amputee, just as we never discussed the other problems in the house. It wasn't until I was in my twenties and in therapy that I began to recognize my handicap as a problem. I'd never talked to people about it. In fact, a big part of my mind had always denied its very existence. Because I could do just about everything, I believed I could hide my disability. A big part of me believed that if I didn't call attention to it, no one would notice— after all, my family didn't seem to notice.

"I remember sitting down to a meal once, and my younger sister said something about my disability. My stepfather hit her hard and said angrily, 'Don't ever talk about that again.' I remember feeling ashamed that there was something about me that was so terrible that no one could even talk about it. I also felt guilty that my sister had gotten hit because of me."

These children have to contend with the shame they feel about their disability and the shame they feel about their families. Even worse, they have to contend with that shame by themselves.

"I was ashamed of myself, ashamed that I was an amputee, ashamed that I didn't have a beautiful body, ashamed that I couldn't do everything other kids could do. I had very little self-esteem.

"The other shame I felt was about my family, especially my father's household. *My stepmother was always drunk and crude, and the whole atmosphere was crazy. I never wanted to take anyone there. And I probably felt that my parents were ashamed of my handicap. They may even have blamed my illness for their marital problems, although they had so many other problems in their relationship.''*

BRIAN: *''I couldn't separate the shame about my polio from the shame I felt about my family. I did try to hide it, though. I never wore shorts, and I would pad my shoes with sponges so that I could walk without a limp. At school, when I'd have to change in the locker room, I'd hide in a corner. For one thing, I didn't want people to see the blood that would be in my shoe because I'd been playing a sport that hurt my foot. If I pretended my disability wasn't there, if I ignored it and everybody else was willing to, then maybe it wasn't really there.*

''I spent a lot of time trying to make sure no one noticed my disability. I tried to keep things out of a physical context, usually by excluding myself. For a time, though, I did play basketball, and I loved it. But I could never turn to the right. One day the other players discovered that. From then on, once I got the ball, they would all scream and shout, 'Move him to the right!' I never played again. I realized that I couldn't be good at sports. I couldn't be included without feeling ashamed.''

These children believed that they must minimize their disability to make life easier. Their sense of shame imprisoned them in the ''Don't talk'' rule, and the ''Don't talk'' rule kept them securely locked in the shame. By the very act of denying their disability, they got denied.

When a family member has a physical disability, there is always a question about how much attention will be focused on it.

SARAH: *''I had worn braces when I was younger and had had two or three major surgeries on my legs, but my parents and my brothers never discussed it with me. I just thought that was the way it was supposed to be. I went to school like everyone else, played, and nothing was ever mentioned about my disability. I really didn't realize that I looked different to people. Looking back now, I can only guess that it was due to my parents' preoccupation with drinking and with each other. I was ignored, and my disability was ignored.''*

There are some positive aspects to not seeing the disability as the focus of a child's being. It is important for them to experience themselves as simply children, not as ''disabled children.'' Unfortunately, the alcoholic dynamic means most things are done in an ''all or nothing'' style.

Chemically dependent people either totally negate or totally obsess. There is no healthy balance. The "Don't talk" rule already exists in the alcoholic family. But in the Double Duty family, this dysfunctional dynamic is multiplied exponentially.

The "Don't talk" rule was particularly difficult for Liz, as it will be for some other ACOAs.

LIZ: *"I spoke out more than the other people in my family. Maybe it's because that's the only power I had—my mouth. I couldn't easily get up and walk away."*

Members of chemically dependent families have a lot of fear about addressing the alcoholism. Often the fear is connected to feelings of powerlessness and shame. Consequently the fear of addressing the alcoholism is easily extended to not talking about the disability. People fear talking about the disability because it taps into their core sense of powerlessness, disappointment, shame, or guilt. For denial to remain intact, no part of the truth can ever be consistently revealed.

SARAH: *"I now understand that my family didn't address my handicap for the same reason they didn't address the alcoholism or the abuse: It was just too fearful. In my family, if you acknowledged something, you had to 'fix' it. And I think they realized that they couldn't fix it. Also, life in my family was so out of control that they couldn't handle any more stress or concern, such as dealing with a physical handicap, so my handicap was ignored."*

Another aspect of the denial that takes place in chemically dependent homes is learning not to express feelings. For the parents it means ignoring the pain and fear that the children are experiencing. For physically disabled children, this denial includes ignoring the pain and fear they experience as a result of their disabilities. The pain may be physical, emotional, or both, but the family's response is to pretend it doesn't exist.

"Sometimes when I'd come home from school after the kids had been teasing me, my mother would notice that I was crying. She'd ask me why, and I'd tell her about the ridicule. But then she'd tell me not to cry because someday the others would be sorry, and that crying wouldn't help anyway."

While a person does not want to be defined by his or her disability, denying the disability to the extent this occurs in a chemically dependent family creates a severe diminishing of a child's legitimate emotional, social, and even physical needs. It firmly perpetuates a deep sense of shame that "there is something the matter with me for having or being something that cannot be talked about."

FEELING DIFFERENT

Feeling different from other people is something common to children who have grown up in alcoholic homes. The family secret of chemical dependency sets up isolation and a sense of shame. A physical disability simply adds to this sense of being different, of not being as good as other children. It makes one feel excluded, an outsider. Growing up in an alcoholic family and having a physical disability creates an even greater depth of dysfunction and isolation.

SARAH: "I was eleven years old before I realized that I walked differently from everyone else. One afternoon I was swimming at the country club. There was a boy there imitating people as they climbed onto the board, walked to the end, and jumped off. When he imitated me, I was mortified and looked over at my brother, who just looked away. I knew then that it was true. The incident was never mentioned between us, but I know that from that day I never felt the same again."

Brian had so accommodated to being a loner that he dismissed the loneliness that came with isolation. For him, this fear of ridicule and potential shame was of greater consequence than the loneliness.

BRIAN: "I felt so removed from my disability that in some ways I didn't feel different because of it. But then again, I never went to school dances because of my leg and foot, I never took my shoes off in the summertime, I never went to the beach. So I guess I did feel different. It was extremely isolating socially."

LIZ: "I don't remember my mom ever sitting down and explaining to me that I had cerebral palsy, but I knew I was different from the other kids. I knew it because I used crutches and braces and they didn't. It was also hard for me when my sister learned how to drive and started to go to school dances, things like that. I did learn how to drive, but my depth perception is so poor that I'm not about to risk anybody else's life or my own. In school I was socially integrated, but I wasn't asked to go to proms or on dates—it was frustrating and lonely."

Often children with physical disabilities attend special schools or special classes. While there are advantages to having a place to go to where the particular needs of physically disabled children are attended to, this segregation can add to the sense of isolation that such children—especially those from alcoholic families—already feel.

CHRISTINE: "When I was five, I started first grade in a school for handicapped children. Public education was not as accessible then. I attended that school from first grade until I graduated from high school. While the school was great in many ways, it was too small, too segregated, and too sheltered. It made it more difficult to make friends in my own neighborhood.

"My mother discouraged much contact with the neighbors. Inside the family, my sister and I were always fighting, so we were isolated from each other. It was the family dysfunction and compulsiveness that served to isolate me more than my handicap.

"Outside the family and school, my handicap set me apart more than my family's alcoholism. I looked different from other people, and I wasn't able to participate in everything. It was hard to feel that I belonged. People's stares were constant reminders that I was different. In school, my family's 'Don't talk' rule kept me from reaching out where there might have been some help and understanding."

Being treated as someone who is different makes the issue of trust extremely difficult for disabled ACOAs.

LIZ: "I have been patronized so many times in my life that when somebody shows me affection, I'm not sure what their motives are. My parents would have friends over and they would be drinking and they'd tell me how pretty I looked and stuff like that. I always wondered if they felt they had to say that because they were thinking, She might not ever have a man in her life to tell her she's beautiful.

"There are times when I felt really alone because I didn't get to do things that other people got to do. It wasn't that I couldn't do them; I just never got the chance. People don't interact with me because they're afraid.

"Recently a woman said to me, 'When I saw you walk, I was afraid to get to know you because I didn't know if you were going to die. I bet it's hard for people to get close to you.' I was really insulted by that because I feel I'm easy to get to know. It made me feel bad because it was just one more person telling me what her negative perceptions were.

"Unfortunately, there are a lot of ignorant people out there who won't even approach me. They don't know whether my disability is progressive; they don't know because they won't ask. So I have to pay the price of other people's ignorance."

The feeling of being different because of a disability feeds that same sense of isolation these children have because of their family's chemical dependency. This double duty makes it especially hard for them to develop a sense of belonging, to feel part of everything, all of which is essential to being able to feel good about themselves. Being different, and being treated as if that difference were unacceptable or frightening, contributes to feelings of low self-worth, inadequacy, and shame.

But being different doesn't mean one is wrong or bad. Being different can simply mean diversity.

CONTROL AND POWERLESSNESS

The issue of control is central to both the survival process of growing up in an alcoholic family and to one's recovery process as an Adult Child. To survive the chaos and unpredictability that permeates the chemically dependent family, young children learn to control as much as they can to bring stability into their lives. That control is often expressed externally through the manipulation of people, places, and things. Internally it means the diminishing of needs and feelings in order to feel safe. The child in the alcoholic family very quickly scrambles to a position of control or succumbs to a state of powerlessness—the flip side of being in control. Feeling not in control reduces many of these children to a state of overwhelming helplessness.

Many disabled children search for ways to feel a sense of power in their lives in order to overcome the powerlessness that is often part of their disability. That can certainly be a healthy response to their disability, but it also reinforces a highly controlling nature, and the issue of control becomes twofold.

CHRISTINE: *"The way I sought control was to be responsible. I took responsibility for most of the household chores—vacuuming, dusting, cooking, dishwashing, ironing. My responsible role was somewhat different, though. On the one hand, I wasn't always physically capable of assuming some duties. On the other hand, I had to be responsible for some things that other children didn't have to worry about, such as the care of artificial legs."*

BRIAN: *"When I was in the eighth grade, I worked as a golf caddy every weekend. I was a very small child, and this was a physically laborious job. I would work all day carrying two bags of golf clubs for eighteen holes. At the end of the day my leg would pain me so much that I could hardly walk, and the straps of the bag would rub the skin of my shoulders raw—but I simply considered that my badge of honor. I would give the money I earned to my grandmother, and she would use it to buy my food and clothes. I didn't feel bad about that. I felt that since I was compensating for my disability, it could be ignored. A brace on my leg would have been a sign of weakness. The message I got as a child was, 'No matter what the cost, you can't show weakness.'"*

Liz felt her powerlessness at times and looked to others to help her with the issue.

LIZ: *"Whenever I had problems, my mother would just cry and say, 'I don't know how to help you.' She would tell me that I needed to be strong, that I had to find a way to fight my own battles. I understood what my mom was trying to do, but I really was powerless in a lot of situations, and my life felt out of control. It was hard fighting all of my own battles."*

Although the message in a chemically dependent family is often "Fend for yourself," this is not always possible for children dealing with a physical disability. These children must rely upon others to help them in their daily routines even as they are faced with the unreliability of the people closest to them. They need to be independent of the family in order to survive emotionally, but often they're not able to be independent physically.

Sarah experienced the powerlessness to a greater degree than the others in this chapter. The dynamics of her life interfered with her finding the strength to seek control or feel any power.

SARAH: *"Control has always been a major issue for me—I felt so out of control and so victimized as a child. Because of the abuse, the alcoholism, and my disability, I felt there was nothing I had power over in my life. As a teenager I really felt victimized by my disabilities. A lot of that was self-pity. But I also learned that if you have a handicap, people seem to think less of you.*

"I victimized myself by limiting myself. I would say, 'People with disabilities can't . . .' I wanted to be an artist, but I wouldn't take any art classes. I thought people with disabilities couldn't produce art. I was so afraid to try things. My parents told me that no man would ever be interested in me, and that I would never be able to support myself. I really believed them. I was afraid I would have to stay with them forever."

Disabled persons have a healthy need to be independent. However, realistically, they also need to be able to rely on others to a greater degree than most people. Yet trusting others, relying on them, asking for help, is especially difficult for children in alcoholic families. They have learned that people are not to be counted on, that the only ones who are going to help them are themselves.

CHRISTINE: *"My determination to be independent seems to relate both to my family and my handicap. From as far back as I can remember, I knew I'd better take care of myself because no one else would. I've been told many times that I don't 'let' people help me or that I don't ask for help. It's true. When you grow up in an alcoholic family, not asking for help is a fact of life.*

"I had to take care of so much myself, cooking my own supper, taking care of the house, and so on. As far as my handicap was concerned, I was driven to be as capable and competent as possible to prove to everyone that I was a 'normal' person. I wanted to be treated like everyone else, and that meant being able to do as much as possible.

"From a practical standpoint, I try to control situations so that they are physically easier for me. I drive my own car so I can park in a convenient place. I arrange things in my kitchen so I can reach everything easily.

"While there's a practical basis for some of these things, I know now that as an Adult Child I've carried this farther than I needed. Over and above wanting to be competent, I have an overwhelming fear of being helpless. One of the things that helplessness means for me is dependence on my mother. And I have a terrible fear of that happening."

Feelings of powerlessness and the need to be in control will always be part of living with a physical disability. In recovery, those who are both Adult Children and disabled will find a fine balance between giving up the hurtful aspect of control and maintaining the realistic aspect they need to live with their disability. The healing of the ACOA issues of identifying and expressing feelings will be essential for them in responding to their sense of powerlessness.

Life Stories: Adulthood and Recovery

Each of these people has begun a recovery process. Christine had been in therapy to help her deal with her physical disability. She and Liz both found that ACOA, therapy, and self-help groups helped bring their healing full circle. Brian became alcoholic and needed to become sober before he was able to address his ACOA issues. Sarah began recovery as a result of co-workers doing an Al-Anon intervention with her.

CHRISTINE
Age: 36
Disability: Triple amputee
Partner Status: Single
Occupation: Marketing data
    processor
Recovery Process: Therapy

After high school Christine continued to live at home until she was twenty-three. During those years she received her college degree in elementary education. She graduated at a time teaching jobs were difficult to acquire, and after having to look at other career possibilities, she created a career for herself in business.

Although Christine saw herself remaining at home because of economics, in hindsight she believes she remained at home in part to offer protection to her sister. While COAs often can hardly wait to leave home, they often do remain in the home longer than other children for just the reasons Christine experienced: 1) to ease a difficult family financial situation due to alcoholism and 2) to offer protection to the other parent or siblings.

After her sister graduated from high school, and after working steadily for one and a half years, Christine moved out. It is probably not a coincidence that it was then that she began directly to seek help to deal with her disability.

CHRISTINE: *"I was in my mid-twenties before I began to deal with my handicap, but it was another ten years before I realized how dysfunctional my family was. Until then all my counseling work had focused on my handicap or crisis situations in relationships with men.*

"Finally a therapist I was seeing said, 'You're dealing with your handicap fairly well. It's your family that's the problem.' "

The therapist Christine has been seeing for the last three years is the one who helped her begin to deal with her Adult Child issues.

"Finding the right therapist was pivotal in my recovery. I had been in a few different counseling situations over a number of years before finding my present therapist. Each of those experiences was positive—they helped me through a crisis. But because of the complexity of my situation, a lot of important issues went unrecognized or unaddressed. I needed someone who not only had knowledge of dysfunctional families and the kinds of losses experienced by handicapped people—and the skills to handle those issues therapeutically—but also someone who would relate to me in an affectionate, nurturing, and very directive way. I am so thankful I found such a person. Even though I didn't consciously know what I was looking for, I think on some intuitive level I did.

"The vision of 'wholeness' that she has given me has filled me with a hope I've never felt before. This has been a major turning point in my life. Her steadfast reassurance that she would be my faithful guide out of the swamp of my depression kept me going through the hardest parts of the therapy."

Christine's desire for a spiritual meaning exemplifies recovery for so many Adult Children. In recovery, Adult Children often find that believing in something greater than themselves, in a loving Higher Power, brings their recovery full circle.

"What I assumed was a simple coincidence was that this therapist is a pastoral counselor. Of course it wasn't coincidental at all. For a long time, semiconsciously, I've been searching for a spiritual meaning to my suffering. The way I first related to religion was through that experience of suffering. Now, as I have grown in my recovery and in my spirituality, I have been able to glimpse true joy. I never believed there was such a thing as joy before; now I have experienced it. I believe that is what God wants for me. I haven't been able to achieve it all the way yet, but I'm getting there."

Christine has at times had to unravel her Double Duty issues from each other. For many people the issues are so meshed that simply acknowledging this entanglement, without seeking to separate each aspect, is all that can be expected.

"In thinking about the relationship between growing up disabled and growing up in an alcoholic family, I've realized that so many of the issues overlap, they're hard to untangle. I've seen how one situation so reinforces another that the feelings and behavior become that much stronger. Being in therapy has been a long process. It's only in the last three years

that I've realized that the separate problems were so close that they masked each other.''

A major problem that Christine and others who are disabled have to contend with is feeling okay about the person they are—regardless of their disability. Very often they did not receive the affirmation they deserved for their unique abilities and talents in coping with their handicap.

"In my family, my handicap was seen as either something to ignore or something to be ashamed of. My abilities and talents were not pointed out to me. I wasn't told that everyone has unique abilities and handicaps. The extra degree of effort I had to put into little things wasn't acknowledged or affirmed.

"Nobody told me or showed me how to handle the questions, comments, and stares I got from other people. I used to beat myself up for not being comfortable with children's questions and not knowing how to answer them. Then I realized that from my earliest years, I had watched my parents avoid strangers' curiosity. No one showed me how to be relaxed and open with other people. All I had learned was avoidance and fear. Now I can be very open with adults, and I'm learning to deal with children also.

"I realize that for Adult Children, choosing the people you want to surround yourself with is a big part of recovery. I believe this is even more important for handicapped people. We must seek out people who are going to be accepting, supportive, and encouraging: people who can help us see our potential. This certainly doesn't mean staying just within the handicapped community or the Adult Child community. It means allowing yourself to find people who are intelligent, open, loving, and interested in self-development. There are many such people in my life now.''

In her recovery Christine has come to recognize that there are many aspects to who she is: an Adult Child, a person with physical disabilities, a bright woman, a loving person, and a talented person. She does not have to limit her life to the old struggles of her childhood.

Christine has been actively working on developing friendships through group activities.

"Though many of my hobbies are solitary ones, such as reading and handicrafts—I've enjoyed needlecraft, cross-stitch, flower arranging—I also have a number of good close friends. In recent years I've become involved in a handicapped sports group, and I've learned downhill skiing. It's been exciting to excel in something that is physically demanding—

one that many able-bodied people can't do. It took a lot of work to sort out my feelings about my handicap before I was ready to join such a big group. But by being in it, I've been able to come a lot farther.

"A big part of recovery is learning about choice. I've discovered that everything I do or don't do is a choice, and that I always have options—many more options than I would have believed before. Hardest of all is learning that even my emotions involve choice. When that concept was new to me, I either resisted it or got down on myself for choosing 'wrong' or unhealthy emotions. Today I realize that I just need to learn how to respond differently. A lot of times just being aware that there are other possibilities helps me search for what they are."

Like most people with visible physical disabilities, Christine has had to struggle with personal relationships. But this is also a problem for many able-bodied Adult Children. By addressing her Adult Child issues as they relate to her disability, Christine will have many more healthy options.

"In my teens and even into my twenties, I thought no man would ever want me. Then I began realizing there might be one or two who might be 'open-minded,' but I'd still have to settle for whatever I could get. Between my handicap and my depression, I thought it would be hard for a man to love me. I didn't think I had much to offer. It didn't occur to me to ask what a man might have to offer me. This led to a couple of disastrous relationships.

"My romances with men have been few and far between, but they all definitely fit into the caretaker role. I seem to attract men who are in a great deal of pain. I did have one very good long-term relationship with a man who was very loving—but he was also very troubled. Ultimately he went back to his ex-wife.

"It was that boyfriend who told me that there was a big difference between depending on someone and being dependent, but it has taken me a number of years to understand what he meant. Now I know that it is not only okay, but it's healthy to be able to depend on someone. Choice is the key. It allows me to exercise my personal judgment about who to depend on and when, and I'm now learning the meaning of interdependence.

"I'm also learning that I have as many choices in a relationship as a man does. Now I'm able to figure out what I want in a man and make decisions based on those expectations.

"For the most part, there's been a steady improvement in the quality of my relationships. While there aren't many candidates in the wings, I'm becoming more selective about those who are. I'm also seeking ways to expand that available pool. The first step is realizing that fear might be limiting my possibilities. I am also realizing that I might have to make the first move with someone. Taking such risks certainly isn't something taught to handicapped women—or most female Adult Children, for that matter.

"Growing up, I got the message that handicapped people were not attractive potential mates. Certainly I was aware of my desire for a relationship and that this desire was normal, but I questioned how realistic that goal was because I obviously wasn't getting much practice with men. From my other handicapped friends I know I'm not unique. Generally it seems we have many fewer dates or relationships and tend to get married late, if at all.

"So now, in my thirties. I'm trying to learn how to initiate a dating relationship with a man. I didn't have a chance to do all the developmental stuff of learning how to build relationships in my teens. The stakes are a lot higher now. We're not teenagers anymore—we're complex adult men and women. I've generally had to deal with men a lot more experienced than me. The gap is closing now, but it was a big problem."

While Christine has dealt with many Adult Child issues, she continues to work with her perfectionism and fear of anger. Perfectionism is a response to her Double Duty, and the anger is related to having lived with violence.

"There were two strong reasons why I had to do everything fully and do it right. I had to try to please my mother and make everything 'all right,' and I had to overcome or hide my handicap to prove that I could do everything. I was always 'Little Miss Goody-Goody,' but my mother never seemed pleased. She was never satisfied, no matter how hard I tried.

"Even now I'm still trying hard to please other people. In dealing with my handicap, I've put a lot of effort into my walking, trying not to limp. Although I enjoy hearing people telling me they hadn't known about my legs, I've never felt that I walked well enough. However, in recent years I've become much less concerned with trying to walk perfectly. Accepting myself and my handicap has given me a lot of freedom.

"The feeling that is absolutely the hardest for me to acknowledge or express is anger. I understand now that it relates to the violence I witnessed growing up. I have a strong fear of anger, including my own. I know, at least intellectually, that this is partially responsible for my self-destructiveness, my depression, and my overeating. Although I still have a long way to go, I am learning the value of anger and am less afraid of it now."

"My life has taken on a whole new meaning by addressing the fact that I was raised in a chemically dependent family. I am in recovery and experiencing the rewards of the recovery process."

BRIAN
Age: 53
Disability: Polio
Partner Status: Married
Occupation: Professional marketing
    consultant
Recovery Process: Alcoholics
    Anonymous, various therapies

After high school Brian quickly left home and continued to work at various jobs, periodically attending college. At the age of twenty he signed up for the Navy.

Brian's polio was undetected when he entered the Navy. He quickly began to experience problems—pain and bleeding—with his foot. It was then one of the doctors diagnosed the childhood polio. Until then Brian's disability had never been addressed, diagnosed, acknowledged, or treated. It had simply been ignored. The diagnosis quickly developed into a medical discharge from the service.

Brian's reaction to the doctor's diagnosis was typical for someone growing up in an alcoholic family.

BRIAN: *"I didn't react to the news. I didn't have any feelings about it. I wasn't going to think about it."*

Following the steps of his family, Brian's alcoholism progressed quickly. He moved across country, had a wide array of jobs ranging from land surveyor, steel plant laborer, gas station attendant, and bartender, to purchasing agent. By age thirty he began to experience alcoholic delirium tremors. He would live several of these years on Skid Row in California beach cities. By age thirty-two he was having alcoholic convulsions. After several hospitalizations Brian became sober in a county alcoholism program, where he was introduced to Alcoholics Anonymous.

"By then I knew it was get sober or live my life in institutions. I made a conscious decision to try AA or give up on my life. I fell in love with

AA. It gave me my life—a path, a way to live. It gave me peers, provided parenting, offered me goals and a way to reach those goals.''

As with others in this book, Brian became sober before the ACOA concept was developed. He would be sober several years before he heard of the concept.

Today Brian has been sober sixteen years. In sobriety he has learned to be self-caring. He has developed friends and a career, and he married at six years' sobriety.

"I never knew I had any capability. It was in sobriety I learned I can do so many things I never previously knew. I can do certain physical things; I work out in a gym. I have a career. I am in a relationship. I can be a friend and have friends. I can also talk about having polio.''

He describes the process of working on his Adult Child issues as slow and indirect. He has read a lot and has attended workshops and periodi-cally been in therapy. His primary program of recovery is in Alcoholics Anonymous, and it is there that he has found answers to some of his Adult Child issues.

Brian's family never acknowledged the issue of his childhood polio. In fact, when Brian's wife brought up the subject with his mother this past year, his mother's reaction was, ''What polio?'' When Brian and his wife tried to discuss it with her, she acted as if she'd never known about it.

"I'd lived with being ignored for so long that I didn't see it as strange that no one in my family ever acknowledged my disability. It wasn't until I was in recovery and a recovering friend said that my parents' behavior was strange and neglectful that I ever thought anything about it.

"I still hide my leg from other people, and I still compensate for my foot. I have chronic pain in my leg, and I live with it on a daily basis. I still feel shame, as if there is something wrong with me personally for having a weak and deformed extremity. I've been working on my body image by working out. That has been helpful, but I also need to talk about what it has meant for me to have polio so I can recover from the emo-tional pain.''

Brian was not in a position to address his polio issues without address-ing being an Adult Child as well. The two were mixed, and some Adult Child recovery was important first. Like so many other COAs, Brian spent years medicating his feelings with alcohol—now he needs to be able to talk about them.

"As a kid I was hurt, confused, and angry, but I tried not to show those emotions. I learned not to let anybody see any weakness or vulnerability. I believed people would penalize you, that they would take advantage of you. This thought process can still affect my personal relationships, my work, and my ability to play. I'm still angry about my powerlessness and shame as a kid. I'd love to go back and kick the crap out of those big kids who used to beat me up as a child.

"As an adult I am working on it, though, and things are changing. I'm very competitive in all things. I love to play games, and I choose games I can win, such as shooting pool or playing cards. Today I understand that. Games are a way of getting revenge. I don't like that about myself, but I haven't been able to change it totally.

"Yet inside I'm a nice guy. I care for others. I can enjoy others. Obviously I'm still struggling with trust. I get confused when people like me."

Brian is clearly very angry. It's possible that because his disability was less visible, he was protected from having to confront it the way Liz, Sarah, and Christine had to. Being in control was a much stronger survival defense for him than the others, and because of this it's been more difficult for him to let go of that control in recovery. It's also possible that the issue of control is culturally more of a male problem. A male's identity is more bound to being physically strong and capable. Brian may have felt a greater threat to his self-esteem because of society's image of what men are supposed to be like.

"I still have a tendency to isolate myself. When I'm faced with a major problem, I cut myself off from other people and I don't want to talk about what's bothering me. My answer for almost any problem is to disregard the consequences and the pain and to handle it myself. If others attempt to interfere or to help, I tend to back away."

Brian is on the path to recovery at this time. He has gained significant insights into his life and behavior. Little by little he's beginning to take risks.

"Even today, with all of my understanding of ACOA issues, I'm still working at accepting myself and my disability. After all, knowledge without action doesn't lead to recovery.

"Sobriety, Alcoholics Anonymous, and my marriage are the true joys of my life. The AA program is pure and simple—I love it. I enjoy being married, and for the first time in my life I've allowed myself to love someone. Even more important, I've learned to trust someone. Because

I'm sober, I do have a program to work, and I have a support system to rely on. I believe that change is possible for me. Digging up the big old weeds is very difficult, but every time I do it, I get to plant new flowers."

LIZ
Age: 31
Disability: Cerebral Palsy
Partner Status: Single
Occupation: Counselor
Recovery Process: Al-Anon, ACOA
    self-help groups

Liz received her bachelor's degree in social work and health science, a double major. After graduating from college, she volunteered for four years in a crisis intervention organization and then also worked in a shelter for battered women and children. Liz is now thirty-one and presently not working.

Liz found that alcohol allowed her to feel more socially accepted and offered a way to lessen her inner pain. She drank in ways that were hurtful during her college years. But in her drinking she became out of control. She had episodes where she nearly choked to death on her own vomit, had to be taken home by others, experienced physical pain when drinking. After awakening from one of those times, she made a conscious decision to not drink again, and she has not. Liz was a survivor and wanted to be aware of her faculties, and she couldn't do that and drink.

Liz's recovery work began in Al-Anon after she graduated from college. After a difficult visit with her mother, she sought Al-Anon to help her confront her mother's alcoholism. After nearly a year and a half in Al-Anon, she was told of an Adult Child workshop. She went to a one-day workshop and found herself crying all through the day. But it took another nine months before she actively began Adult Child work. It took spending a week with a friend whom she found to be as critical as her father.

Liz: "I felt like once again I was a little child—so scared."

By this point Liz had spent enough time in recovery to realize that she needed healthier people in her life, and she became involved in Adult Child self-help groups. After two years of participating in Adult Child meetings, she regularly attends Al-Anon meetings, where she has been working on dealing with both her ACOA issues and how the challenges she faces with her disability are connected with those Adult Child issues. It is in Al-Anon that she can work with these issues one day at a time.

"Recovery work on my Adult Child issues has also helped me accept certain aspects of my disability. I've pretty much had to blend the two together, and I've figured out how to accept some things and take others in my stride. Rather than spending my Saturday nights in self-pity, crying because I can't get a ride, I rent a video and watch a comedy.

"I'm okay because I'm learning to accept myself totally. The disability does complicate the ACOA issues, but once you start working on one, it's going to begin to run into the other. Accepting yourself is accepting yourself."

In the past two years Liz has had three major crises and accidents related to her cerebral palsy that have kept her confined to her apartment. During this time she has had to confront major issues of loss. She lost her job when a financial grant ended—and the next day her father was murdered. Several months later she was in an accident and broke her leg.

In addition to these major issues, Liz is confronting an issue common to many women but made more complicated because of her disability. She has been addressing the problem of her "biological clock," recognizing that she will soon pass the safe childbearing age. Able-bodied people often assume a disabled person is incapable of childbearing and child rearing—but that is frequently not true. Liz would very much like to have the choice.

"I would like to be married and have children of my own, but my opportunities for meeting men are so limited. I am envious of my siblings' having children because it's not happening for me. I am fearful that the opportunity is slipping away.

"One of the hardest issues for me to deal with has always been the fear of abandonment. When my father died recently it made me realize how afraid I am of being left alone after my mother dies. I'm aware of how dependent I am on others, and I'm scared to be without my own family unit."

The more visible and obvious one's disability, the greater the likelihood that others will stay away. Many people are frightened and unwilling to become personally involved with someone with physical limitations. For these reasons the disabled person's family often takes on an even greater significance. The family may be a disabled person's strongest social and emotional support system. Obviously, if that family is still characterized by active chemical and co-dependency issues, it presents limitations to the recovering disabled Adult Child. If disabled Adult Children are dependent on their families—whether family members are actively using or recovering—they suffer from the realistic fears of being left alone as siblings create new family units and parents die.

Addressing abandonment issues, putting them into a realistic perspective, learning healthier problem-solving skills, perceiving greater options—these are the ACOA recovery skills disabled Adult Children need to develop.

Liz has found it vital to learn to trust others and to express her feelings. But her fears of how her body will react when she expresses her emotions make it very difficult for her to see her feelings as acceptable to other people.

"I would just like to hug the way other people do, but I am not physically balanced, so it's awkward. I really need to know the person so I can trust that the person is not going to get freaked out. I suppose I'm trying to protect myself and them at the same time. I want to be close to others— but talk about boundary issues! As Adult Children we have issues with trust, such as 'Don't touch me until I know I trust you.' That's a healthy motto. But for me it isn't just my ACOA stuff. My whole body reacts when I'm touched—I jump or lose my balance. Then I get embarrassed, and I giggle inappropriately.

"As much as I want to be touched, I find my lack of trust gets in the way. Sometimes when people in the program hug me, I feel they perceive me as a little girl, but they may just be hugging me as a friend. I don't think people are able to separate me from my disability, but this might be more my issue than theirs. Obviously recovery is ongoing."

Being able to rely on and trust others is an important issue for anyone—but it's even more important for a disabled person. Unfortunately, it's a skill one has a hard time developing in an alcoholic family.

Boundaries about touch need be respected by everyone; such boundaries vary according to need and trust. It may be more important for disabled persons to allow themselves to be tougher because they need to be carried, repositioned, or assisted with some responsibilities. Also, because of their need for greater medical attention, they often experience touch very differently from others.

But touch boundaries are often violated in alcoholic families. That was clear in Sarah's and Christine's situations. Children respond positively to an appropriately nurturing touch. However, many kids from dysfunctional families don't receive it. So when Liz questions touch, she does so out of an Adult Child perspective, while at the same time she must deal with how her body responds because of her cerebral palsy. This creates an even greater need to address what touch has meant to her and how she needs to project her boundary stance to others.

While Liz is confronted with major life issues, she is approaching her recovery a day at a time. She recognizes that as she is willing to take the time to identify her feelings and not just react immediately to situations, she is able to be more honest about her needs, particularly in relationships.

"The greatest aspect of recovery is to speak the truth. I need to be honest about my fears and my hopes."

SARAH
Age: 31
Disability: Paralysis
Partner Status: Married, one child
Occupation: Tax specialist
Recovery Process: Al-Anon

After graduating from high school, Sarah attended college. Today she is married and a new mother. Sarah's motherhood is quite significant since her own disability was a birth trauma caused by a forceps delivery.

It was while going to college that Sarah first confronted her co-dependency issues, but she did not enter into active recovery for another six years.

SARAH: *"One of the first issues I was hit with was whether or not it even mattered that I was in school. My mother had often told me that because of my disability I would probably never get a job and that I would have to be supported all of my life."*

Yet there was a strong survivorship mentality in Sarah, and she persevered. She did well in school and received a degree in business economics. But true to her mother's words, when she graduated she couldn't find a job in her field.

"I still thought of myself as unemployable, something I struggle with to this day. When I couldn't find a job, I found religion. In my opinion, religion saved me from active chemical dependency. The emotional pain was so great in college, and drugs were so readily available. But I found more relief in taking care of people than in taking drugs. Rescuing others became my disease. Religion and taking care of people went hand in hand in my mind.

"Having been sheltered and protected all my life, going to college was a major culture shock. Never having dated, never having had a boy express interest in me, I fell head over heels in love with a guy from my hometown. By the end of our relationship, I was trying to get 99 percent of my self-worth from him, and the other one percent from my brain."

The dynamic of getting one's self-worth through another person is common to many Adult Children. Children of Alcoholics grow up believing there is something wrong with them. As a result they often search for someone to be in a relationship with and attach their self-worth to the acknowledgment they receive—from this other person.

"I knew this guy couldn't handle being involved with a girl who wasn't a candidate for homecoming queen, but I kept on in a self-destructive pattern for six years. He never mentioned my handicap, but the clear message was that he couldn't be seen in public with me. That just reinforced my childhood experience of 'Don't ever talk about it.' It increased my sense that something was definitely wrong with me."

This relationship reinforced Sarah's shame, and it also gave her six more years of tolerating and accepting inappropriate behavior. This cycle feeds into a lowered sense of self-worth and greater victimization.

Shortly after that relationship ended, Sarah took a job where she sought to protect her vulnerability through rigid control.

"Power and control have always been major issues with me. As an adult I learned that I could gain power through controlling. I went from the extreme of feeling powerless to exercising excessive control in my life. And it was the issue of control that brought about the primary intervention with my ACOA issues.

"I was working for a man who was one year sober. He said that my attempt to control everything pushed people away. He said that he saw some family alcoholism issues with me and suggested that I meet with his sponsor, who was a helping professional in the addictions field. I met with the man, and my recovery began. They did an intervention on me,

clearly pointed out what they saw, told me where to find help, and sent me to Al-Anon. I went.

"One of the first things I learned was that if I wanted to get better, I was eventually going to have to look at all aspects of my life that caused pain—including my handicap. Today I'm comfortable with myself and the way I am, but the road has been rough. I've now been in recovery five years.

"When I came into the program at twenty-six, I had religion but no spirituality. I viewed my handicap as something God had 'gifted' me with, and I thought that I should be grateful. It wasn't until I'd been in recovery for two and a half years that I even began to address my handicap. My denial was good and strong, and I couldn't see the bigger picture. Before I entered recovery I thought that all of my problems came from growing up in an alcoholic home and from the abuse, both physical and mental, in my life."

Sarah's desire to get in touch with her feelings as a part of her recovery helped her deal with those parts of herself that she had to deny as a child.

"When I came into recovery I hadn't cried over my feelings for more than fifteen years. I'd been told that crying wouldn't change anything. But today I can get angry, feel sad, and cry over my feelings. It's not always comfortable for me, but I encourage myself by remembering that it is therapeutic. I no longer give my power away to other people as regularly as I once did.

"The man who helped me get into recovery eventually became my husband. He's taught me that while my body is different, it's nothing to be ashamed of, and other people can appreciate it.

"We recently had a baby. All of my ACOA issues came into play with my pregnancy. I worried about whether I would be a good enough mother. I tried to control all aspects of the pregnancy. I tried to do everything perfectly, to the point that it became both obnoxious and funny. Because I had been injured in the birth process, I had great fears that my child would be injured, too. Thanks to my recovery, I was able to address those fears with my doctor. He was great. He responded to my disability realistically and openly and to my anxieties about being a mother as well."

Recovery has enabled Sarah to deal with her fears and her anger. It is also allowing her to value her needs and to find her identity.

"Through recovery I have learned to be less manipulative with my handicap. I have learned to stand on my own two feet and become responsible.

It isn't easy at times, but it's now become the adventure I'd been told it would be early on in the recovery process. It truly is an adventure to see just how much I can uncover and to realize that 'it's just my cross to bear.'

"I can now see how my disability fed my inability to believe in myself, and that this causes me pain when I allow it. Having a disability can seem like a license to feel sorry for oneself. Others feel sorry for you, and at times it's easy to accept and take on that pity. Self-pity becomes convenient when you're scared.

"It's my lack of confidence that keeps me from leaving a safe and secure job doing tax work to pursue my dream of working with disabled people. I have an MBA, and I'm working on a degree in counseling. I would love to work with abused or disabled children, but my fear of rejection just keeps me stuck. But God is great, and He will bring me out in His own time.

"My story is just beginning. Dealing with the pain and grief involved in accepting a permanent handicap has been a very cleansing act for me. The biggest aid in my search for acceptance of my handicap has been the people in the program and the Twelve Steps. Without the Twelve Steps of recovery in my life, I would still be the frightened, shy, overweight lost child I was when I entered the program. The Twelve Steps have saved my life by bringing me from surrender to acceptance.

"By facing what I believe was the biggest obstacle in my recovery—my anger at my limitations—I have gained power over my insecurities, and my faith has grown. There's so much more I would like to understand about alcoholism and children and disabilities, but at least I now understand that I'm not less of a person because I'm disabled."

Disabled in Adulthood

Although these life stories reflect growing up with disabilities, this chapter didn't seem complete without acknowledging those who have become disabled in adulthood. Because of accidents and illnesses, great numbers of people become disabled in adult life. It is even possible that, with some physically disabled individuals, the anger and/or recklessness associated with being an Adult Child may have contributed to their accidents.

While children who have grown up in alcoholic families are survivors, they also have issues that create greater problems responding to their disabilities. For years they have been masters of the art of denial and minimizing. This denial is then applied to the reality of the physical trauma. These Adult Children are frightened of their feelings and often have difficulty expressing them. They are often unskilled in decision making and have little practice asking for input or for help. An Adult Child already feels different, alone. Then comes the overwhelming trauma of a physical disability.

MICHAEL
Age: 44
Mother: Co-dependent
Father: Alcoholic, abusive
Disability: Paralysis, at age 17
Birth Order: Middle of three
      children
Raised: Pacific Northwest
Partner Status: Single
Occupation: Financial manager
Recovery Process: Alcoholics
      Anonymous, therapy

Michael was paralyzed from the neck down in a motorcycle accident at seventeen. Today, twenty-seven years later, he has the regained use of his upper body and is able to walk with the use of canes.

Michael grew up with a physically abusive alcoholic father and a long-suffering, co-alcoholic mother. He was the middle of three children. Michael's role in the family was to be the "good child."

MICHAEL: *"The unspoken message I got from my mother was, 'I need you to be good. I need you to be good for my sake. If you are not good, if you are selfish, I will withdraw my love from you. If you are good, I will continue to love you and support you.'"*

Michael set about trying to please his mother, attempting to distance himself from his "dark side," the side he associated with his father. He was very active in church activities, and he excelled in school. But life at home was violent and miserable.

"My dad liked to hit us with his belt, especially on the backs of the thighs or hamstrings, and it left welts. I have a hard time remembering this now, although it was a very vivid part of my life then. I remember my brother and sister running from him. I remember the feeling of hopeless-

ness and helplessness of being able to outrun him easily, while knowing it was foolish to do so because it only made things worse."

Religion was a big part of Michael's childhood, and he attended Catholic schools for twelve years.

"I was a good little Catholic boy. I was ready to be compulsive, I was ready to find the structure that would tell me what to do and what not to do. My mother was saintlike in her religious devotion, and she certainly played the role of martyr. So I learned to be the good kid, blocking out this 'hole' that I perceived to be the darker side of myself, the side I identified with my father. I kept telling myself, 'Don't be angry, don't be selfish, don't be sexual.' I was an altar boy, and at one point I thought I wanted to become a priest."

Denial played a strong part in the way the family coped with the drinking and the violence.

"None of the stuff going on at home was ever talked about. To a certain extent we did acknowledge it among us kids, and even with Mom. Nobody really denied that Dad had a drinking problem. But at the same time nobody appreciated how much of a problem his alcoholism was. His father had been a violent, abusive drunk, and my mother told us that Dad wasn't as bad as he could have been, considering his background."

Michael's father's drinking grew progressively worse as Michael got older. Finally Michael had had enough.

"The physical abuse stopped when I was fifteen because I made it stop. One night when he was drunk and slapping my sister around, I threw my father out of the house. I humiliated him, and I humiliated myself in the process, but at least it stopped the abuse."

Michael began drinking about the same time.

"I know now that from the beginning I was drinking unusually—that is, I was drinking for effect. I was drinking more than my friends were, and I was the one who supplied the alcohol. I was trying to get them to drink as much as I did. It was always party time for me—at least for a couple of years."

The Accident. When he was seventeen, Michael broke his neck in a motorcycle accident.

"I was paralyzed from the neck down. I wound up in the hospital for a couple of months, strapped into a thing called a Foster frame—a sort of

rotisserie for human beings. I would lie on my back on this canvas, strapped tightly between iron rods, and every once in a while they would put a similar device over my face, bolt it down, and flip me over. This was so I wouldn't get bed sores. There I was, seventeen years old and suddenly paralyzed.

"I employed all the tools and tricks I already knew as a child in an alcoholic family to my sudden disability. What else was I going to use but denial, discounting, minimizing, rationalizing, and spinning fantasies?

"The doctors didn't know and couldn't say whether or not I would ever recover, or if I did, how much I'd be able to move. This was too much to take, so I didn't take it. I prayed, and I retreated into a fantasy of being able to run out of the hospital on my own two legs. I worked hard at not believing it. This couldn't be real. I retreated into denial."

Michael's parents came in shifts to visit him in the hospital. This added to Michael's sense of being responsible for what had happened, for adding an additional burden to the family.

"I felt incredibly guilty for what had happened. The thought of the expense to my family made me feel guilty beyond belief. The funny thing, though, is that my 'crisis' may have had a temporary stabilizing effect on the family. At least now there was something to galvanize our energies around. There was a crisis.

"I'm really good at crises—so is my family. Give us a car wreck, somebody getting hurt, a trip to the hospital, a suicide attempt, and we operate. Emotions go on hold very easily, and we function in crisis mode. It's very easy to do. It's like greased caretaking.

"My dad would come in the evening, and I would shut down emotionally. He'd sit there and read his paper for a while and then he'd get up and leave, which was okay with me. My mom would be there during the day, to feed me lunch and sometimes dinner. She was there to help me deny, to cope, to reinforce that this was not the way it was going to be, that I was going to recover and that's all there was to it, period."

While Michael was in the hospital he was receiving various drugs, such as Demerol, Valium, and Nembutal, which increased his depression.

The need to deny the seriousness of the situation and the isolation that surrounded Michael's family created another crisis over his ongoing care.

When a nun in the hospital talked with Michael's mother about his depression and suggested that they bring in a psychiatrist, Michael's mother didn't even discuss it with Michael, she simply vetoed the idea. When Michael's doctor wanted to send Michael to a hospital with a spinal injury rehabilitative unit, Michael, who was tired of being in the hospital, said he didn't want to go. Amazingly, his parents didn't intervene. They allowed him to go home instead. This example typifies the denial, isolation, shame, and inability to make decisions in the best interests of a child.

"Here were these people bonded together and all alone, and here I was, suddenly in the house and requiring total care. I know they were scared; they didn't know what to do with me. They didn't know how to move me. I had to be pulled up out of the bed and put into a wheelchair. It was all so disgusting and so horrible."

Control and Powerlessness. Like many Adult Children, Michael had struggled to find a semblance of control in a family that was out of control.

"I have experienced a need for control all my life. Now I was in a place and in a body where I had none at all. I couldn't take care of myself. I couldn't even move my bowels by myself—I was catheterized. It was all gone, it was all over. I was powerless and without control. I didn't want it to be and couldn't adjust to it."

Later, through the help of a physical therapist, Michael was able to move a bit at a time. Finally he was able to walk on his own using a cane. Because he'd had so many honors credits before the accident, he ended up graduating with his high school class.

Michael's parents divorced soon after he graduated from high school. And Michael began to abuse the medication available to him.

"As soon as I was independently mobile, I was down at the liquor store getting wine and mixing it with my pills."

Rage and Denial. Michael began college, but he kept himself shut off from other people. He was struggling through a period of self-loathing and anger. And he was also struggling with his powerlessness—the antithesis of control.

"I'm sure people were afraid to say hello to me, just from the way I looked and the vibes I was putting out. I was defensive and very, very angry. I hadn't adapted to being disabled. I didn't have a clue about what to do. I didn't want to be disabled.

"I was in physical therapy, and what I really needed to do to see how far I could recover was to work out. But I kept stopping exercise and starting it again. One of the things that contributed to my sporadic efforts was the fact that I was loaded all the time. I was taking at least thirty

milligrams of Valium a day and Nembutal every night to go to sleep. I had
a barbiturate hangover every day, and I was on pain medication all the
time.

"Working out was very hard for me emotionally. When I exercised, I
had to face exactly where I was physically—and it was never where I
wanted to be. I wanted to run down the beach again, to ride my cycle,
to dance—and I couldn't. The more I had to face myself physically, the
more I was aware of the sorrow, the regret, and the despair I felt, and
the more exhausted I would become, emotionally and spiritually. I had no
support at the time. All I had was my drugs, my alcoholism, my denial,
my rage, and a family that wanted me to get better. I was really alone,
and at this point I turned away from God.

"Much later, in recovery, I realized that I had fashioned my concept
of God the Father based on the only father I'd ever known, my own. I
was afraid, and no wonder—I had for a God a divine image of my own
father: withholding, angry, punitive, arbitrary. Someone whom I had failed
irrevocably and unforgivably, and who would make me pay. Even later
on, in the miracle of my sobriety and my recovery, I still expected to be
struck down at any moment.

"When I was injured, the loss was like dying without being dead. For
a long time I thought of myself as dead. I felt I'd lost what you lose when
you die: I lost my body, I lost myself, I lost my identity, I lost my abilities
in the world—the world of movement, of time and space, energy, muscle,
and blood. It was gone, and I was left suspended in a world where people
were still moving, were still doing, being, having. I was suspended in this
other place of unacceptable loss, and I was alone in it, and it was an
incredibly hard place to be."

Different and Ashamed. Michael spent the next three years dropping in
and out of college. His drinking became much worse, as did his feelings
of self-hatred.

"I felt guilty and worthy of condemnation, worthy of death. I was supposed to be dead. Somehow the accident was my fault. I felt as guilty as
if I'd planned it and carried it out on somebody else, as if I'd deliberately
crippled myself. And I felt I should be punished for it. I become more
and more suicidal, spiraling down more and more deeply with my drinking. Consciously I was resentful, I was isolated, alone, different. I was
feeling worse and worse all the time, becoming more and more of a drag
to be around, more and more depressed and interested only in drinking.

I became obsessed with suicide, obsessed with alcohol, and obsessed with drugs.''

ADULT RECOVERY

After two suicide attempts Michael ended up in a state mental hospital for a month, where he felt what it was like to be warehoused. While he didn't find a path to recovery, he nonetheless came away from the experience knowing suicide and hospitalizations as escapes were over for him. It took him a year and a half after that to get sober.

"I'd been asking for help for a long time. I'd started seeing therapists when I was twenty-two. But my alcoholism was not dealt with, my Adult Child identity was not dealt with, and I was not honest. There was hardly any way for these therapists to help me. I was hanging on to my own life the best way I knew how, trying to defend it.

"The therapist I had the last two years of my drinking allowed me to ventilate enough rage to stay alive, to not succeed in killing myself, until I got to the point where I hit bottom, made the right call.

"I went through a thirty-day treatment program to stop drinking. I stayed in it only because I knew if I drank again, I was going to die, and in spite of everything I was terrified of dying. I was finally ready to admit that I had never wanted to die at all. All I wanted to do was be alive, be a part of, be a human among other humans. And I knew that I absolutely lacked the power to do that. But I wanted to live so badly that I hung in there in the program.

"The treatment program pointed me in the direction of AA, so when I got out of the hospital, I began going to AA meetings. I was twenty-five years old. I went to meetings for three months before the message of total abstinence from all mind-affecting chemicals got through to me and I began to kick the drugs. I found a sponsor who introduced me to sobriety, to the Twelve Steps of AA, to recovery from my alcoholism and recovery from the personality that had developed in my alcoholic household.

"My father died of lung cancer one week after I got out the hospital treatment program. It took me a long time—ten years, really—before I could acknowledge my feelings about my father. It was the same with my feelings about my mother. Dad had always been the black knight, and Mom was the white princess. But I finally figured out that it wasn't just my father who wanted me to be an extension of him to fulfill his uncon-

scious needs. The same was true of Mom. She just went about it a little differently.

"The lesson that I learned early on was that you take care of people, and that you are good if you take care of them. You're worthy of approval, you're worthy of acceptance, you're worthy of love. If you don't take care of others, you're selfish, you're not okay, you're excluded, and that's it, over, good-bye.

"My parents didn't even know how to take care of themselves, so they certainly couldn't teach it to us. I never learned how to take care of myself. I never learned how to recognize that I had any needs of my own."

As Michael became sober, he began to address his disability and what it meant to him.

"Once I was clean and sober, suddenly the fog of drugs and alcohol lifted. Within my first year of sobriety, the pain for which I'd been taking all that medication ended.

"I had a wild time getting off the drugs. I stumbled around, went through all sorts of contortions physically. It was crazy. My sponsor worked on my sense of humor and got me to lighten up about it a bit. I found acceptance in Alcoholics Anonymous. In fact, I found people who accepted me more than I accepted myself. I found sobriety and a path toward recovery, and I started to use it.

"The Twelve Steps led me to experience a relationship with a Higher Power that was different from the neurotic relationship I'd had with God the Father. I began to experience being a part of my own universe, and I'm very grateful for that. It's the reason I survived. The strength to remain sober, the strength to pursue my own recovery, has come from some sort of connection with that thing within.

"For a long time, clean and sober, I did not deal with my body, with my disability. As a matter of fact, I dealt with it as little as possible. I was aiming at having another experience. Part of this was denial and disassociation; part of this was positive.

"The thing I was looking for was to identify with other people, to find the way I was similar to them and not the way in which I was different. I'd always felt different from, set apart from, inferior to, and less than others. Being disabled seemed to give me evidence that this was indeed the case: I was different from other people. I was isolated from them. No one understood my experience; no one possibly could. The evidence told me that I was different, different, different.

"This perception was piled on top of the feelings that I carried directly *from my alcoholic household. I had a sense of secrecy and shame about my real life, about my family. The result was a feeling of separation from, an inferiority to, other kids and other people and to the world in general. The disability made that sense even heavier.*

"Part of what happened for me early in AA was that I discovered how much I was like other people—not unlike them. I was just like other people. I was okay. I was the same. I was as good as. I was as worthy. The easing up of the burden of low self-esteem, the easing up of the secrecy and the shame, was very supportive. But even more important was finding out that other people have parents they were ashamed of, too—that other people also shared the shame, the guilt, for not loving their own parents.

"It's very important to know these things about other people. It's very important to break down the walls—not just the walls between other people and me, but the walls between me and me. In the early years of sobriety there was this process of identifying with and becoming a part of."

Later in sobriety Michael began to use therapy as a part of his program, as an adjunct to the inventory process. With the help of his therapist he began to get in touch with his body, to work with it, and to be patient and caring with himself. Part of the therapy involved body movement in order to express his emotions, thoughts, and feelings. It involved using exercises to ground himself physically and emotionally and to get in touch with his feelings about himself.

"This may not seem like a big deal to anyone who doesn't have a problem with his body, but to me it was incredibly painful to have to stand and look at myself in a mirror, feeling acutely the pain of loss that I had been trying to avoid feeling for so many years.

"Finally I began to experience that pain, and to get in touch with the fact that my body might be a source of some good feelings, too. This was very important to me, and it has carried over into the life I'm living now."

MICHAEL TODAY

Michael is now forty-four. When he'd been clean and sober five years, he went back to college to pursue a career in banking and finance, the field in which he now works. Michael still struggles with how difficult it is for him to be disabled, how difficult it is for him to feel out of control at times, and how hard it is to ask for help.

"On the one hand I don't like being disabled. It's a hard thing to experience, and it doesn't stop, it never stops. Being disabled is like a bad dream sometimes, a dream from which you never wake up. It just goes on and on. That's one truth, and I don't like it.

"On the other hand, I've gained enough acceptance and understanding to know this: I am who I am because of what has happened to me throughout my entire life. And I like who I am—I wouldn't trade it. In the beginning of my recovery, I would have traded places, traded lives, identities, with almost anyone else. Today I would trade with no one.

"If I were given the choice at this moment, certainly I would trade partial disability for 100 percent physical ability. But that doesn't seem to be an option. My disability is part of my path in this life, part of my experience, it has contributed to my being who I am.

"I worked so hard for so long at rejecting who I am, at convincing myself, 'This isn't me.' Today I believe that in an ultimate sense, this is true: I am not my body. But very, very important for my recovery has been the knowledge and acceptance that, on this level, I am my body, my body is me. Ram Dass said, 'Honor this incarnation.' I couldn't do that before. Now I can, at least a great deal of the time.

"Here's a tough one to accept: Suffering has value. Because of all of my suffering—as the Child of an Alcoholic, as a physically abused child, as an alcoholic and addict, and as a disabled adult—I have sensitivities, sensibilities, and compassion that I would not otherwise have had. These are valuable to me. Couldn't I have gained them some other way? This is a moot question, and one I'm convinced only distracts me from the here and now, from doing what's in front of me, and from dealing with reality. God/the universe/the Higher Power is certainly not afraid of suffering and is quite willing to use it as part of the means of getting Its job with us done. Part of the work I've had to do to recover has been to expand my own concepts of spirituality, or spiritual reality, to expand my acceptance to include this."

Recovery Considerations

Whether a person grows up with a physical disability or becomes disabled in adulthood, there are issues of loss. There is loss for what will never be and loss for what was. Yet even with disabilities, so many people have been able to find gifts with their struggle to live in the able-bodied world. Nevertheless, if you are an Adult Child, recovery from ACOA issues is the prerequisite to discovering even greater choices and freedom.

Adult Children have learned how to minimize, rationalize, and discount. Recovery means breaking that cycle. It requires acknowledgment of your total being—physical, emotional, mental, and spiritual. It means coming to love and accept yourself. For people with physical disabilities, that means openly addressing these disabilities. It means being able to love yourself for who you are—and that includes disabilities.

So often a physical handicap is either totally ignored and becomes internalized as a shameful part of oneself, or it becomes the total focus of one's identity. If the disability is very visible and affects every movement of one's body, then initially it is a primary focus of your own and others' attention.

But a disability does not have to be the essence of one's identity. As one learns to live with the physical handicap, it slowly ceases to be one's first preoccupation. It is true that it will no longer be the focus for your friends, family, or co-workers. Although certain factors, such as family and physical disability, influence one's life, you are who you are—a person who feels, hopes, dreams, and has abilities. To have the recovery you deserve, you should not reject or ignore your physical being any more than you should reject your abilities. But neither can you reject or ignore the influence of chemical dependency in the family.

It is my hope that people who have begun the process of Adult Child recovery will be able to address any physical disability and how it has influenced their life. It is also my hope that those who are most identified with their physical disability will be open to addressing their being Adult Children. Hopefully, the life stories these five people have shared will offer you some validation for your own experiences. But remember, it is necessary for the disabled Adult Child to go back and talk very specifically about how the following ACOA issues became a part of this response to disability.

ISOLATION AND DIFFERENTNESS

Adult children are often socially isolated. They suffer from the "alone in the crowd" syndrome. However, physically disabled children feel even greater social isolation. When they're with others, they experience the "alone in the crowd" syndrome as a result of their physical differentness.

Social awkwardness also reinforces social isolation. But this is apt to be just as much an Adult Child issue as one related to the disability.

It is very important for Adult Children who have always felt different to see how much they have in common with other Adult Children. This can be done in group therapy or in self-help groups with other Adult

Children. Discovering that you're not so unique often begins with reading the literature about growing up in alcoholic families. The more that disabled people can put themselves in settings with other Adult Children, the less they will experience a sense of differentness. Often there is a tendency to set oneself up for separateness and isolation by wanting to focus on the differences. But the way out of this isolation is to identify what you have in common with other Adult Children.

However, at the same time be cautious about ignoring where the differences lie. Some people use this process to bolster denial and the minimizing of their disabilities. Recognizing that issues don't have to be all or nothing—learning to find a balance—is part of recovery.

FEELINGS

In recovery, Adult Children with disabilities are often quick to speak about the gifts that are part of being disabled, such as resiliency, self-reliance, sensitivity to others, and taking risks. Such skills are strengths that should not be negated. They are valid. They don't have to be given up.

Many Adult Children think recovery is about understanding. But understanding is simply one aspect of recovery. Grieving for one's losses is also an important aspect of recovery. Without the grief work, I find that Adult Children cannot address their current emotional experiences. Grief work is about speaking to the fear, the sadness, the loneliness, and all of the feelings associated with loss. Identifying and expressing one's feelings is not self-pity. Only if one gets stuck in these feelings does this become a blaming or self-pitying process.

Expressing one's feelings is yet another part of the process. It is not the whole process—but it serves a vital purpose. Learning to identify and express feelings can often be difficult for Adult Children. In recovery you will have to address the feelings you've had about your disability and how it has affected your life. But it's only safe to do this when you feel safe with feelings. You may feel a tremendous sense of loss—loss of acceptance by others, loss of a normal childhood, loss of opportunities. You may feel sadness, fear, loneliness, anger, guilt, and other feelings related to your disability. At some point in the recovery process, feelings need to be acknowledged. If you've focused a great deal on one particular feeling, such as Brian's anger about his disability, you might want to try looking at the other feelings you might have been ignoring. You don't need to focus on the feelings you know well. Try focusing on those you've been hiding from.

For people who know anger, often fear, sadness, and loneliness are the most frightening feelings. For people who know sadness, often it is anger they are most removed from. Feelings range from joy, excitement, and love to pain, disappointment, anger, fear, terror, hate, and rage.

SELF-RELIANCE

Many Adult Children struggle with having become rigidly self-reliant. They get to the point where they don't even realize where or how other people can be included. This comes from a lack of trust in other people's availability and capacities. We didn't experience others being there for us as children. If you were physically disabled, you may have had to develop even greater resiliency and self-reliance because your needs were greater.

Recovery begins when you can recognize when it is important to be self-reliant and when it is healthier, more fun, and possibly easier to include other people. It means a willingness to question whether your self-reliance may actually be an ACOA issue of "not trusting." If that's true, know that you're not alone. Many recovering Adult Children will be able to identify with you.

ASKING FOR HELP

Children of Alcoholics learn that it is not safe to ask for help. They find people either don't respond or they respond inappropriately. As a result, they learn both greater self-reliance and not to see opportunities where others could offer assistance. To be disabled and not have people offer or respond to your need for help reinforces self-reliance. Often the disabled person only asks for help when it is absolutely necessary. Even then it is often a guilt-ridden request. Most Adult Children need to learn to ask for assistance.

Again, the issue is balance, not extremes. In recovery we are seeking interdependence. There are many life situations in which you have no control, times when you have to depend on someone else. On the other hand, there are many situations where you will be in complete control and rule the world. Most of the time there is a blend of both—an interdependence in which you take responsibility for yourself but are also open to other people's ideas and help. Not asking for assistance often leads to isolation.

CONTROL AND POWERLESSNESS

Adult Children have many struggles with the issues of control and powerlessness. As children we attempted to control people, places, and things to bring about greater order and predictability in our lives. We controlled our emotions and dismissed our needs, all to create some internal sense of order. But we were fighting something we were powerless to affect. As we realized this, some of us stopped fighting and became overwhelmed by our powerlessness. Add physical disability, and the issues can easily become compounded.

The Adult Child whose disability comes in adulthood struggles with control and powerlessness differently from those disabled from childhood. Should this disability occur suddenly (which it usually does in adulthood) to an Adult Child who has sought control in order to feel safe, there can be a shocking contrast between the present powerlessness and the control previously acquired through survivorship skills. Control is usually experienced as an "all or nothing" issue. Being in control means being safe; loss of control means being in danger and powerless to respond. The more severe the disability, the greater the overwhelming sense of powerlessness. This can easily lead to severe depression and possibly even suicidal thoughts or rage.

For recovery you need to explore what control and powerlessness has meant in your life. You might want to try to finish the following sentence-writing exercises:

- Losing control in my life meant _____ . Repeat that line five times and see what you say.
- Being powerless has meant _____ . Repeat that line five times.

There may be many intense feelings associated with these issues, but getting in touch with them is a vital step in recovery. Able-bodied or not, coming to accept what we have the power to affect and what we cannot is the key to co-dependency recovery.

NEUTRALIZING EFFECT

Some Adult Children with disabilities may find that what is typical for many ACOAs may not be typical for them because of their disability. They may find that having to live with the disability counteracts certain Adult Child issues. For example, some disabled people do not have difficulty asking for help. But others, like most Adult Children, struggle with the issue. Because disabled ACOAs may have felt forced to rely on others, they may have been able to counteract the rigid "Don't trust" rule in the alcoholic family. Responding to the disability may also have taught them greater flexibility and creativity.

RELATIONSHIPS

Very often disabled Adult Children feel so poorly about themselves that they will tolerate inappropriate behavior from others and even allow themselves to be victimized in relationships. That is common to the able-bodied as well. But some people with disabilities have fewer choices regarding friends or lovers. Their disability may limit the number of people with whom they come in contact.

Although the process may be difficult at time, recovery from Adult Child issues will increase your sense of self-worth and confidence, and this in turn will help you invite healthier people into your life. You have to learn to be honest with yourself and to like yourself before you can experience friendships and intimate relationships where another person will be able to both respect you for being you regardless of your disability and have a healthy respect for any limitations that are a part of that disability.

EXPECTATIONS

Adult Children learn early and learn well that no matter what they do it is never good enough. Many attempt to achieve by always striving to be good enough; others give up. This problem is compounded for the disabled child. What makes things more difficult is that disabled children are clearly given the message that they will never be able to do what others can. However, in response to this challenge, many disabled people have stretched their abilities to do exactly what they and others did not think was possible.

I believe the disabled person needs to take on such challenges. But you also need to recognize that not every challenge has to be conquered—it is an individual choice. Don't let the ACOA issue of always having to prove yourself to yourself and others exacerbate this issue. You are good enough just as you are.

Asking a physically disabled ACOA to look at both identities can be very frightening; so often only one aspect of identity has been acknowledged. Yet when both areas are explored and acknowledged, there is a freedom that allows one to live with far fewer fears and much greater love and self-acceptance. Personally, given the inner strength I see in ACOAs and people with physical disabilities, I am reminded that people such as Franklin Delano Roosevelt sat in a wheelchair afflicted by polio in his presidency. Helen Keller, blind and deaf, was an extremely famous author and lecturer. Beethoven, Child of an Alcoholic, became hearing-impaired at age twenty-one and would write his more famous symphonies, such as the *Eroica,* after the loss of much of his hearing. Present-day Jim Abbott pitches American League baseball with one hand—due to birth impairment. Author Ron Kovic, who wrote the book on which the Academy Award–winning film *Born on the Fourth of July* was based, is paraplegic because of injuries sustained in the Vietnam War, yet he is a tireless advocate for veterans' rights. People who are able-bodied have much to learn from people with disabilities. The same strength it took to respond to living with a physical disability in an alcoholic home can now give you the courage to move through your Adult Child issues and into recovery.

My spirit is on the way to being whole, whether or not my body ever catches up.

—Physically Disabled Adult Child

11

Moving On in Recovery

I wrote *Double Duty* out of my conviction that no one should have to go through life with the shame that is created in dysfunctional families. It is my belief that once we are able to understand the dynamics of our Adult Child issues, we can truly begin to work through them. In the life stories you have just read, you've seen how people have chosen various means of working through their issues. It is possible for each and every one of us to have recovery. We no longer have to live our lives based in fear.

The process of recovery allows us to put the negative influences of our past behind us and take responsibility for how we live our life today. It is a process that takes time, patience, and persistence. To put our past behind us, we must come out of denial and begin to speak the truth about our life experiences. We can no longer minimize, rationalize, or discount what really happened to us. We must own our experiences.

The Stages and Steps of Recovery

People tend to move through five distinct stages in the process of Adult Child recovery. The stages presented are a synthesis from the works of Julie Bowden and Herb Gravitz, authors of *Guide to Recovery.*

FIRST STAGE: SURVIVORSHIP

We begin by knowing that we can and will survive. While Adult Children deserve to feel good about their survivorship, they also deserve more in life.

SECOND STAGE: EMERGENT AWARENESS

This is where we recognize that there was something wrong in our childhood and we no longer deny it. We are free to acknowledge our experience and its effects on us. This is often an exhilarating stage—a time in which we feel a sense of direction and hope.

THIRD STAGE: ADDRESSING CORE ISSUES

Once Adult Children have accepted the influence of the past on their lives, they are ready to confront the core issues that have plagued them as adults. It is in this stage that the Adult Child is most apt to need the assistance of others to work through such issues as control; identifying and expressing feelings; needs; limit setting and establishing boundaries; and self-validation. Throughout the entire process the Adult Child is working on trust and shame.

FOURTH STAGE: TRANSFORMATION

This is a time of personal change, of putting into effect the things we've been learning, of risking new behaviors. Transformation leads to internal integration. The work on previous stages has helped us to trust our internal wisdom, and we are now in the process of discarding hurtful beliefs and replacing them with beliefs that nurture loving self-acceptance and self-care.

FIFTH STAGE: GENESIS

Although this is different for each person, Genesis generally involves a new openness to the spiritual aspects of life. This is when we begin to participate in the creation of our own world—not grandiosely, but realistically. Genesis marks the true beginning of our lives as expressed through our unique relationship to the rest of the universe.

As part of the process of working through these recovery stages, I have identified four steps that need to be repeated, often more than once, with each and every issue one is addressing. The four steps are:

- Explore the past
- Connect the past with the present
- Challenge the belief messages
- Learn new skills

EXPLORE THE PAST

Much of the initial process of recovery involves talking about the past. Many people find this both exciting and scary, but the purpose of talking about the past is to put it behind us. This is not meant to be a blaming process; it is the process of speaking your own emotional truth. You talk about the past to undo denial.

This is very important because it is often the first time in our lives that we have been able to talk openly about our experiences. Talking without fear of being rejected or punished allows us to release deep feelings that we have kept inside and that remain hurtful to us. When we do this with others who are participating in the same process, we receive validation for ourselves when we were young.

Most Adult Children have a skewed sense of what "normal" is. Only by talking about our experiences can we put them in a context that helps us recognize our needs and learn how to set appropriate limits and boundaries. More important, we are able to discard the messages that we aren't good enough or that we are inadequate. We begin to feel that we are of real value.

The grieving process is the most emotionally painful part of recovery. It can take months. At times Adult Children have been criticized for focusing on the past too much or for "staying in the problem," as opposed to searching for a solution. However, at this point we are in the process of owning our childhood experiences, and this takes a great deal of time. We don't remember everything all at one time, nor do all of our feelings come to the surface at once.

Adult Children need to own their fears, sadness, hurt, and anger. You don't necessarily want to do that with your parents, but you will want to do it with a counselor, other recovering Adult Children, or a trusted friend. We need to feel safe to be able to trust and to share our vulnerabilities. That can take time.

When we are exploring the past we are doing our "grief work," we are speaking of the losses in our lives. Because the pain of these losses has not been acknowledged or validated, taking the time to grieve for ourselves is important. Left unexamined, these feelings of loss grow into emotional time bombs that can become extremely hurtful if they have no appropriate avenues for expression. We act them out in depression, addictions, compulsive behaviors, hurtful relationships, difficulties with parenting, and so on. It is important that one ultimately moves beyond this first step. If not, you will become stuck in the process and it will become a blaming process, not a grief process.

CONNECT THE PAST WITH THE PRESENT

Another important step in recovery is that of connecting our past with our present. Here, the process focuses on insights. This is where we need to ask ourselves, "How does the past connect with who I am today?" Then we follow this with more and more specific questions.

"How does the fact that I spent so much time in isolation and in a fantasy world as a child affect me today?"

"How does the fact that I was so fearful of making a mistake in my childhood affect me today in my work?"

"How does the fact that I lived with so much fear as a child affect me in personal relationships today?"

We need to ask how our many feelings and behaviors in childhood and adolescence affect who we are today in all the many aspects of our lives, our self-esteem, our work, and our relationships. This allows us to focus more on the present.

CHALLENGE THE BELIEF MESSAGES

Early in the process of exploring the past, we also begin to challenge the childhood beliefs we internalized from our parents. These are beliefs that we heard verbally or experienced behaviorally. Often the messages we internalized were parental "shoulds". "You shouldn't trust others." "You shouldn't be angry." "You shouldn't cry." So we need to go back and identify those internalized messages or life scripts. We need to ask ourselves whether those messages are helpful or hurtful, positive or negative. We need to question whether or nor we want to continue to take these internalized messages with us throughout our adulthood.

Helpful messages would be:

All people deserve respect.
People are trustworthy.
You are of value.
It's okay to say No.

Hurtful messages we often heard were:

You can't trust anybody.
No one's going to be there for you.
You can't do anything about it, so don't bother.
Your needs are not important.

It's okay to keep the helpful messages. By acknowledging the ones we're going to keep, we take present-day ownership of them. They no longer belong just to our parents, they are ours as well.

The hurtful messages need to be discarded. This is often done in a symbolic form. For each message tossed out, you will need to create a new helpful one in its place. This is active recovery—you are taking responsibility for how you live your life.

LEARN NEW SKILLS

As we're reading, listening, and sharing, we're also taking another step. We're learning new skills. Much of recovery involves learning the skills we didn't get the chance to acquire in childhood. These are often such basics as:

Identifying feelings
Expressing feelings
Asking for help
Recognizing options
Problem-solving
Negotiating
Setting limits
Saying No
Saying Yes
Drawing attention to yourself in a positive way
Playing
Relaxing
Listening
Making a decision

Once we learn to use these skills, we're ready to live our lives differently. Now we have choices that haven't been there up to now.

With the healing that results from these four steps, Adult Children will free themselves from viewing life through the lens of addiction. Recovery leads to establishing a balance in life. While life will always pose certain restrictions and problems, the Adult Child now has a range of skills and the awareness of self to cope with and respond to the imperfections that come with life. Recovering does not mean you will never feel pain again, it doesn't guarantee good decisions nor prevent relationship break-ups. It won't necessarily give you the material things you desire. It will offer you an emotional freedom from the past, so that the past no longer dictates your self-worth and esteem. It will give you options; it empowers; it brings you into the "here and now."

In order to take these four steps, we need a continuous flow of information and support. Until the last few years we haven't had the information necessary even to understand what has been going on in our lives.

Recovery Literature

By reading books that support recovery, by attending lectures and workshops, and by becoming part of self-help groups or being in therapy, we can develop the language we need to begin talking about our experiences. We are people who spent our childhood years in sick families where people did not speak the truth and did not acknowledge what was occurring around them. We have so rigidly adhered to the "Don't talk," "Don't feel," "Don't think," "Don't ask questions" rules that, as adults, we really don't have the words or the understanding we need to describe our own experiences of the past or the present. Many Adult Children cannot discern one feeling from another. In addition, we often lack the ability to distinguish the normal from the abnormal.

Reading is often a good place to begin. It is a wonderful adjunct to both therapy and self-help recovery. It will familiarize you with the language that has become common to the recovery movement. More importantly, it will offer you a better understanding of what has happened in your life. Reading will allow your frozen feelings to thaw, and you will begin to realize that you don't have to continue your life with fear, shame, or other hurtful behaviors. Reading will show you that there is a path, a direction, out of the maze. It will help you realize that you are not alone.

As you read, you will begin to see yourself, and you will be amazed.

It's as if the author had been raised in your home or had been living side by side with you in your adult life. Nearly every other Adult Child has felt as you have felt: guilty, ashamed, frightened, alone, sad, so unique. Reading helps to lessen that.

But be open to going beyond self-learning and insight. Allowing yourself access to others in recovery is wonderfully validating. It is also freeing to share your issues in the safety of rooms where so many others will identify with you.

Self-Help Groups

In general, self-help groups have been extremely valuable to thousands of people with various maladies. Adult Children have found support, validation, and direction in recovery through Al-Anon, Adult Children of Alcoholics, and Co-Dependents Anonymous. Although most Adult Children who mention participating in self-help groups are usually referring to the Twelve Step process, as you read this book you will see that others found self-help groups in different ways.

In coming together with other Adult Children in self-help groups, you will learn more about what all Adult Children have in common. Participants talk about their struggles and successes while developing problem-solving skills. They also find comfort in the fact that they are not unique, not alone in their problems. Most often the participants come to regard the group as a healthy extended family.

Whatever path you choose, remember, it is important to give self-help groups a fair chance before you say, "That's not for me." Try out different meetings. In Twelve Step meetings the group will often recommend that the newcomer try at least six meetings before making a decision about further participation.

It is common for Adult Children to want to work out problems on their own, to keep their feelings stuffed and controlled. We learned to master that approach a long time ago. But now we need to recognize that our old ways aren't working for us any longer. We need to keep an open mind. The simple act of sharing with another person who has had similar feelings and has encountered similar situations brings us out of denial and isolation. This kind of sharing also offers us a greater awareness of ourselves and a feeling of greater connectedness with others. Often a group experience allows us to accomplish together what we cannot do alone. This is true of both self-help and therapy groups.

Therapy

There are many different types of therapy. Many Adult Children have already spent considerable time in therapy long before they discovered they were ACOAs. It is important to choose a path of recovery that feels safe to you. If you have found therapy to be valuable in the past, then it is likely to be even more helpful now that you are exploring this new information. It is possible that if you seek a therapist who gives credence to Adult Child issues, your experience will be much richer and more beneficial.

The types of therapy available differ, depending on whether the therapists work with people individually or in groups. Some therapies focus on the here and now, dealing with a specific problem; others are more process-oriented. Some are conducted for a specific period of time with all participants having the same goals; others are more long term, with or without a closing date. Here, the participants all have similar backgrounds and similar goals, yet work on issues specific to themselves.

Should you want to talk to someone about the fact that you are an Adult Child, and discuss specific issues, I recommend that you begin in one of two places. First, ask other Adult Children you know if they are in therapy and whom they see. Ask them what they are getting out of therapy. What do they like and what do they not like about this specific therapist and the process? Acquire the names of two or three therapists and make an appointment with each one for an exploratory session. This is your time to ask the therapist questions, to decide if this is the right person to guide and support you in your recovery process. Some people can make this evaluation in a short telephone conversation; others require a face-to-face interview. The important thing is to find a therapist who feels right for you and then to allow yourself to make a commitment to the therapeutic process.

The second way to get a therapist is by calling an information and referral service knowledgeable about chemical dependency resources. This is most often the local council on alcoholism and a chemical dependency treatment program.

Crucial to your recovery is that your counselor or therapist understand the process of chemical dependency and Adult Child issues. In the exploratory sessions you can ask if they have done any reading in these areas. Have they taken specific training in this field? If the therapist discounts or minimizes addiction or ACOA issues, consider moving on to someone willing to address such issues in your therapy. You do not need to be with a therapist who works only with Adult Children. However, you do need someone sensitive to what being an ACOA means, someone knowledgeable about the dynamics of being raised in a chemically dependent home and the effects these have on your adult life.

Pacing Yourself

Although the timing of the issues to be addressed in the process of recovery may be different for the Dual Identity Adult Child who has a primary addiction, the process is similar.

Because of the intensification of effects experienced by those who are DD/DI, it is important that you not judge the pace at which you respond to a recovery program or compare your recovery rate with other people's. Often, the beginning weeks and months of recovery are the most difficult for DD/DI Adult Children because of their greater fear of giving up control and of trusting, along with their experiencing greater denial and, certainly, greater shame. Although you will walk through the same process as others, you may need to take more time to do so. All recovery is taken in steps, not leaps and bounds. But sometimes the DD/DI person may need to take baby steps.

In addition, you will also need to address the dynamics of the added trauma in your life—physical abuse and/or sexual abuse; being an only child; or having two chemically dependent parents. And you will need to address any identity issues—being gay, lesbian, physically disabled, or a person of color. After recognizing the similarities among Adult Children and addressing the issues common to all, DD/DI ACOAs will need to retrace their steps: explore the past, connect with the present, and challenge the shoulds as they relate to their DD/DI. These first three stages tend to take a longer period of time, but once they've been explored, "learning new skills" comes as readily to the DD/DI as to any Adult Child.

While I've said it many times in *Double Duty,* I would like to offer this advice one more time. If you don't feel safe in a group process, you may find that individual therapy offers you an added safety net. For those who participate in Twelve Step programs, the concept of individual sponsorship is highly beneficial. While there are many rewards in the group experience, if you don't feel comfortable with it, simply allow your self-awareness to direct you to what is most appropriate for fulfilling your present needs. Your recovery deserves to be safe. Be patient with yourself.

Resistances

The two greatest resistances to recovery are first, wanting the process to be pain free, and second, wanting to do it all by ourselves.

Adult Children often want recovery, but they'd like it without the pain. That's understandable. It's not been safe previously to feel; we feel out of control and bad for being emotional. And should we begin to get in touch with our feelings, we often feel years and years of pain, which seems overwhelming. But we *must walk through the pain* in order to put it behind us. Today we have the inner strength and can do it! As vulnerable as we feel, nothing bad has to happen to us. And that is certainly true when we allow others to be a part of our process—which puts us in contact with the second resistance—wanting to do recovery in isolation.

When we are frightened, we can easily fall back into our old pattern of solitary self-reliance. Now is the time to remind ourselves of the price we pay for isolation. It is my belief that, even if we could do recovery by ourselves, we deserve so much more. For far too long we have lived in isolation—if not social, then certainly emotional isolation. We deserve to give ourselves the rich experience of allowing others to be a part of our process. There are thousands of Adult Children in recovery today who would be willing to offer you support through both self-help and therapy groups. There are increasing numbers of educators, counselors, and therapists who are skilled in walking Adult Children through recovery. Other people can help make recovery a much easier and, very often, a much safer process.

A Word of Caution

Adult Children have a tendency to want to make decisions when they are in the midst of their feelings: "I feel sad, therefore I must ____." "I am angry, therefore I will ____." While feelings are cues and signals about our needs, it is important to not make any major life changes in early recovery.

At that point it is easy to find fault with much of how we live our lives. We tell ourselves: "I never would have chosen this partner ten years ago if I hadn't been so sick, so I must get out of this relationship." "My job is as sick as the family I was raised in. I want to change careers." "I need to be that child I was never allowed to be, so I'm going to walk away from my marriage and children and recapture my childhood."

Although your relationship and your job may have problems, or you

want to go back to your childhood, making abrupt decisions in early recovery rarely leads to the dream scenario you have hoped for. Early
recovery may bring many feelings and insights, but you haven't yet integrated the new skills that will enable you to live your life differently.
When we make a change just "to make changes," we often end up re-
creating a situation identical with the one we are escaping. Even more
important, there is a tendency in early recovery to project feelings from
our childhood onto present-day situations.

With time, such projections lessen, and what seemed so bad is not
nearly the crisis it first appeared to be. As you develop new skills, you
will have the opportunity to act differently in your current relationships,
at work, and with friends. At this later stage the decisions you make will
be based more on choice. You may still choose to make certain changes,
but they will be based more on your present-day perspective, more on
the strong foundation of your ongoing recovery.

Love and Loyalty

While we can get very excited about recovery, telling the truth about
our past often makes us feel disloyal to our family. After all, we love our
parents. This is when we need to remember that being in recovery
doesn't mean we don't love our parents. Most of us do. Often we have
loved them against all odds, and that is why our hurts are so deep.

In recovery we aren't betraying those parts of our parents that truly
loved us. Healthy parents love their children and want them to live free,
happy lives. They don't want us to carry pain, fear, anguish, or loneliness
with us. They want us to feel good about who we are. At this point in
recovery the most important disloyalty to guard against is disloyalty to
ourselves for not allowing ourselves a new way of life.

If your parents have continued to deteriorate in their disease, your
new behavior will alter the nature of your relationship. Even if your parents have experienced recovery, your relationship may still need to be
redefined. That can hurt. But whether or not your parents are in recovery, *you* can have recovery. And you can maintain a relationship with
them if you choose. This relationship will have limitations—but the old
relationship had limitations, too.

You may be wondering how many of your feelings and perceptions, if
any, you might be able to share with your parents. Personally, I would
not recommend that you share much of your experience with your parents in the early months of recovery. After that, what you share, how

much you share, with whom and when, are important questions that need a great deal of thought. Generally speaking, we don't want to keep recovery a secret. At the same time, if our parents have remained sick, they will most likely respond hurtfully to any information we give them.

If you are thinking of talking directly to your parents about your recovery, consider approaching each parent separately. Then ask yourself: "What do I want to tell him (her)?" "Why do I want to say this?" "Will it help me if I say it?" "Am I saying it to hurt them?" "What do I hope will happen?" "How realistic are my expectations?" It is important to think ahead about what it is you want to disclose. "Living our recovery" as we relate to our parents is an even greater goal than sharing all of our feelings and thoughts with them.

The Reward for Going Deeper

So many feelings will awaken as you read this book and reflect on your own experiences. Please let me remind you again that, when you have bottled up your feelings for so long, it is easy to feel that you are losing control when they begin to well up. In the beginning we can feel overwhelmed by our emotions. Sometimes we don't even know what they are or why we are having them. Don't be critical of yourself at this time. The fact that you are feeling is significant. Adult Children frequently have many feelings at one time. Often you may not know the exact source of the feeling as you experience it. Sometimes we only know what we feel after the fact. But if you keep talking, in time the source will connect with the feeling. Practice identifying your feelings and gradually experiment with telling someone about them.

As you move through recovery, ask yourself periodically which feelings are the easiest for you to show people and which are more difficult. What fears have you about showing the more difficult feelings? If you are frightened of showing your anger or sadness, ask yourself what you fear will happen if you show that feeling. Tell someone about the fears. Are your fears based on your present experience, or are they from your childhood? So often we have fears left over from long-ago experiences, but until we question them we don't realize it. Now ask yourself what you need to do to be able to express those feelings. Then give it a try.

The recovery process is often described as peeling an onion—below one layer there is another and then another. Looking at DD/DI issues brings us one layer closer to the core. When you work intensely on a particular area, there may be a deep pain associated with certain feelings for a period of time. Then there will be periods where your recovery enjoys smooth sailing. But again, unexpectedly, you will find yourself confronting another serious and painful issue. Remember: you haven't done anything wrong, you just couldn't have reached this layer of recovery before you addressed the other layers. Sometimes the reward for going deeper is going deeper. With each layer of recovery you are a step closer to resolving old issues and letting go of the past.

Strategies to Help with the Pitfalls

We all have particular pitfalls in recovery, but they aren't necessarily unique to us. There are clues common to many of us that can be used as signals to warn ourselves that we are slipping back into old behaviors or attitudes. It will be helpful for you to identify yours and know what you need to do when you recognize them.

Take a minute right now to finish the following sentence in at least four different ways.

"I know I'm in trouble when I _____."
"I know I'm in trouble when I _____."
"I know I'm in trouble when I _____."
"I know I'm in trouble when I _____."

So often I've heard people say, "I know I am in trouble when . . .

I isolate myself."
I minimize my feelings."
I start critical self-talk again."
I get overinvolved in such areas as work or fixing others."
I feel inadequate or inferior."
I don't want to trust anybody."

We can begin to avoid these potholes if we know what to look for. But we also need to plan out what we're going to do if we find ourselves there. So take your specific pitfalls and develop a strategy plan for each one.

Isolate. Have a list of phone numbers of people to call. Tell them of my behavior. Identify my most recent feelings or talk about what was occurring at the time I began to separate from my feelings.

Minimizing Feelings. What am I really feeling? What message am I sending myself right now that is making me stuff this feeling? I'm going to challenge that message because I know it's an old message from the past. What is it I've been learning lately about healthy feelings?

Critical self-talk. Stop!! Quit projecting. Recognize that I'm into "all or nothing" thinking again. What is it I'm feeling right this minute? Keep telling myself, "It's okay to make a mistake."

Overinvolvement. What am I avoiding? What am I running away from? Whose approval am I seeking?

Feeling Inadequate. I'm going to make an effort to spend time with recovering friends. I'm going to pay attention to my daily victories. I'll praise myself for them. I'll give myself healthy rewards.

Not Trusting Anybody. I recognize that the issue is "all or nothing." Whom do I trust now? What is it I trust about that person? What little things do I trust with other people?

Now you will have a list of warning signs and a set of new behaviors that you can act on to counteract those old attitudes and messages. Planning ahead makes it easier for you to respond in a healthy manner when the time comes. And those times will come. We are human. Many of us are recovering from terrifying childhoods. All of us are recovering from close to twenty years, if not more, of hurtful messages and coping skills that no longer work for us.

Recovery is a step-by-step process. It is hard work. It is exciting work. It can be emotionally painful at times. It can be confusing at times. But, ultimately, recovery is validating and extremely rewarding.

The *Next* Step

As recovering Adult Children, one of the things we learn about ourselves is that we are people of courage and strength. When we were children we had the courage and strength to endure. However we responded to the pain in our lives, it was our way of surviving. We found our lifelines and used them well.

But today, in recovery, we find that we often need to give up those defenses. This can be very difficult—for they have been our major form of protection. Yet, one by one, we find we have the courage to do just that. It is not possible to read Double Duty/Dual Identity life stories and not see the magnitude of pain induced without also recognizing the inner strength that guides us to seek out and travel the path to recovery that helps us to overcome the pain.

Recovery comes for the Double Duty/Dual Identity person as we embrace all of our being.

Our body.

Our culture.

Our vulnerability.

Our strengths—which we developed in response to the multiple issues we had to deal with in our lives.

While the following manifesto has relevance for us all, I created it for, dedicate and offer it to those who have struggled so long and so bravely with Double Duties and Dual Identities.

Double Duty/Dual Identity Manifesto

- I take responsibililty for how I live my life. I no longer walk through life hiding behind masks for self protection.
- I no longer live a life based on fear and shame.
- I reject messages of shame, whether they come from others or through my own critical self-talk. I create affirming messages of love and empowerment.
- I am willing to ask for help. I am willing and able to include others in my process.
- I no longer accept a life of loneliness. Now I feel secure when I am alone, and comfort when I am with others.
- I am of value, and this remains true no matter what mistakes I might make.
- I trust in myself, and I trust in others.
- I no longer live in fear of being abandoned. I trust in my own value even when I feel the most vulnerable.
- I identify and establish healthy boundaries so I will not be violated, emotionally or physically. I am learning the skills I need to set the limits that maintain those boundaries.
- I identify and seek recovery from my compulsions, addictions, and self-defeating behaviors.
- I recognize I have choices and am willing to act on those choices. At the same time, I also recognize where my power lies.
- I take pride in my heritage. I acknowledge and embrace the healthy aspects of my culture.
- I no longer deny and reject parts of my physical being. I accept my body and find the strengths in my disabilities.
- I deserve to live a life unencumbered by sexual stigmas.
- I recognize and honor what is unique about myself and my personal history. I affirm the positives in my differences.
- I speak my truth.
- I recognize and celebrate my strengths.
- I believe in my right to happiness, dignity, and respect.
- I love and accept all of my self.

Appendixes

Anonymous Fellowship Acronyms

Common Acronyms of Twelve-Step Anonymous Fellowships Referred to within *Double Duty*.

AA	Alcoholics Anonymous
ACA	Adult Children of Alcoholics
ACOA	Adult Children of Alcoholics
CODA	Co-Dependents Anonymous
CA	Cocaine Anonymous
GA	Gamblers Anonymous
ISA	Incest Survivors Anonymous
NA	Narcotics Anonymous
OA	Overeaters Anonymous

Serenity Prayer

God grant me the serenity
to accept the things I cannot change
The courage to change the things I can
And the wisdom to know the difference

Appendix 1
The Twelve Steps of Alcoholics Anonymous

1. We admitted we were powerless over alcohol—that our lives had become unmanageable.
2. Came to believe that a Power greater than ourselves could restore us to sanity.
3. Made a decision to turn our will and our lives over to the care of God *as we understood Him.*
4. Made a searching and fearless moral inventory of ourselves.
5. Admitted to God, to ourselves, and to another human being the exact nature of our wrongs.
6. Were entirely ready to have God remove all these defects of character.
7. Humbly asked Him to remove our shortcomings.
8. Made a list of all persons we had harmed, and became willing to make amends to them all.
9. Made direct amends to such people wherever possible, except when to do so would injure them or others.
10. Continued to take personal inventory and when we were wrong promptly admitted it.
11. Sought through prayer and meditation to improve our conscious contact with God *as we understood Him,* praying only for knowledge of His will for us and the power to carry that out.
12. Having had a spiritual awakening as the result of these Steps, we tried to carry this message to alcoholics, and to practice these principles in all our affairs.

The Twelve Steps reprinted with permission of Alcoholics Anonymous World Services, Inc.

Appendix 2
The Twelve Traditions of Alcoholics Anonymous

1. Our common welfare should come first; personal recovery depends upon AA unity.
2. For our group purpose there is but one ultimate authority—a loving God as He may express Himself in our group conscience. Our leaders are but trusted servants; they do not govern.
3. The only requirement for AA membership is a desire to stop drinking.
4. Each group should be autonomous except in matters affecting other groups or AA as a whole.
5. Each group has but one primary purpose—to carry its message to the alcoholic who still suffers.

6. An AA group ought never endorse, finance, or lend the AA name to any related facility or outside enterprise, lest problems of money, property, and prestige divert us from our primary purpose.

7. Every AA group ought to be fully self-supporting, declining outside contributions.

8. Alcoholics Anonymous should remain forever nonprofessional, but our service centers may employ special workers.

9. AA, as such, ought never be organized; but we may create service boards or committees directly responsible to those they serve.

10. Alcoholics Anonymous has no opinion on outside issues; hence the AA name ought never be drawn into public controversy.

11. Our public relations policy is based on attraction rather than promotion; we need always maintain personal anonymity at the level of press, radio and films.

12. Anonymity is the spiritual foundation of all our Traditions, ever reminding us to place principles before personalities.

The Twelve Traditions reprinted with permission of Alcoholics Anonymous World Services, Inc.

Appendix 3
Symptoms of Alcoholism

1. PREOCCUPATION   YES   NO
   A. Do you ever look forward to the end of a day's work so that you   ____ ____
      can have a couple of drinks and relax?
   B. Do you sometimes look forward to the end of the week so that you   ____ ____
      can have some fun drinking?
   C. Does the thought of drinking sometimes enter your mind when you   ____ ____
      should be thinking of something else?
   D. Do you sometimes feel the need to have a drink at a particular   ____ ____
      time of the day?

2. GULPING DRINKS
   A. Do you usually order a double or like to have your first two or   ____ ____
      three drinks quickly?
   B. Do you sometimes have a couple of drinks before going to a party   ____ ____
      or out to dinner?

3. INCREASED TOLERANCE
   A. Do you find that you can often drink more than others and not   ____ ____
      show it too much?
   B. Has anyone ever commented on your ability to hold your liquor?   ____ ____
   C. Have you ever wondered about your increased capacity to drink   ____ ____
      and perhaps felt somewhat proud of it?

4. USE OF ALCOHOL AS A MEDICINE
   A. Do you ever drink to calm your nerves or reduce tension?   ____ ____

B. Do you find it difficult to enjoy a party or dance if there is nothing   ____ ____
to drink?

C. Do you ever use alcohol as a nightcap to help you get to sleep at   ____ ____
night?

D. Do you ever use alcohol to relieve physical discomfort?   ____ ____

5. DRINKING ALONE

A. Do you ever stop in a bar and have a couple of drinks by your-   ____ ____
self?

B. Do you sometimes drink at home alone or when no one else is   ____ ____
drinking?

6. BLACKOUT

A. In the morning after an evening of drinking, have you ever had the   ____ ____
experience of not being able to remember everything that hap-
pened on the night before?

B. Have you ever had difficulty recalling how you got home after a   ____ ____
night's drinking?

7. SECLUDED BOTTLE

A. Do you sometimes hide a bottle in the house in the event you may   ____ ____
need a drink sometime?

B. Do you ever keep a bottle in the trunk of your car just in case you   ____ ____
may need a drink?

8. NONPREMEDITATED DRINKING

A. Do you ever stop in to have two or three drinks and have several   ____ ____
more than you planned?

B. Do you ever find yourself stopping in for a drink when you planned   ____ ____
to go straight home or someplace else?

C. Are you sometimes one of the last ones to leave a bar or a drinking   ____ ____
party when you had planned to go home earlier in the evening?

D. Do you sometimes drink more than you think you should?   ____ ____

E. Is your drinking sometimes different from what you would like it   ____ ____
to be?

9. MORNING TREMORS

A. Have you ever had the shakes or tremors of the hands after a night   ____ ____
of drinking?

10. MORNING DRINK

A. Have you ever taken a drink in the morning to help you over a   ____ ____
hangover?

How many of these questions did you answer Yes?   ____

No one can settle for you the question of whether or not you are an alcoholic. If you answered even one question Yes, you will want to watch yourself. If you answered three or more Yes, of if you can notice a drift in the affirmative, you have a definite reason to worry.

Source: Women's Alcoholism Center, San Francisco, California.

Appendix 4
The Twelve Steps of Al-Anon

1. We admitted we were powerless over alcohol—that our lives had become unmanageable.
2. Came to believe that a Power greater than ourselves could restore us to sanity.
3. Made a decision to turn our will and our lives over to the care of God as we understood Him.
4. Made a searching and fearless moral inventory of ourselves.
5. Admitted to God, to ourselves, and to another human being the exact nature of our wrongs.
6. Were entirely ready to have God remove all these defects of character.
7. Humbly asked Him to remove our shortcomings.
8. Made a list of all persons we had harmed, and became willing to make amends to them all.
9. Made direct amends to such people wherever possible, except when to do so would injure them or others.
10. Continued to take personal inventory and when we were wrong promptly admitted it.
11. Sought through prayer and meditation to improve our conscious contact with God as we understood Him, praying only for knowledge of His will for us and the power to carry that out.
12. Having had a spiritual awakening as the result of these steps, we tried to carry this message to others, and to practice these principles in all our affairs.

Appendix 5
The Twelve Traditions of Al-Anon

1. Our common welfare should come first; personal recovery for the greatest number depends upon unity.
2. For our group purpose there is but one authority—a loving God as He may express Himself in our group conscience. Our leaders are but trusted servants; they do not govern.
3. The relatives of alcoholics, when gathered together for mutual aid, may call themselves an Al-Anon Family Group, provided that, as a group, they have no other affiliation. The only requirement for membership is that there be a problem of alcoholism in a relative or friend.
4. Each group should be autonomous, except in matters affecting another group or Al-Anon or AA as a whole.
5. Each Al-Anon Family Group has but one purpose: to help the families of alcoholics. We do this by practicing the Twelve Steps of AA ourselves, by encouraging and understanding our alcoholic relatives, and by welcoming and giving comfort to families of alcoholics.
6. Our Al-Anon Family Groups ought never endorse, finance or lend our name to any

outside enterprise, lest problems of money, property and prestige divert us from our primary spiritual aim. Although a separate entity, we should always cooperate with Alcoholics Anonymous.

7. Every group ought to be fully self-supporting, declining outside contributions.
8. Al-Anon Twelve-Step work should remain forever nonprofessional, but our service centers may employ special workers.
9. Our groups, as such, ought never be organized; but we may create service boards or committees responsible to those they serve.
10. The Al-Anon Family Groups have no opinion on outside issues; hence our name ought never be drawn into public controversy.
11. Our public relations policy is based on attraction rather than promotion; we need always maintain personal anonymity at the level of press, radio, TV and films. We need guard with special care the anonymity of all AA members. Anonymity is the spiritual foundation of all our Traditions, thus reminding us to place principles above personalities.

Appendix 6
Do You Have the Disease of Alcoholism?

Alcoholism strikes one out of every ten people who drink. Not everyone has the physiological makeup to become alcoholic, but anyone who drinks could be at risk. Alcoholism doesn't discriminate. It afflicts people of all ethnic backgrounds, professions, and economic levels. It is not known precisely what causes this disease, but drinking is clearly a prerequisite. Therefore everyone who drinks should periodically evaluate their drinking patterns and behavior. Here is a self-test to help you review the role alcohol plays in your life. These questions incorporate many of the common symptoms of alcoholism. This test is intended to help you determine if you or someone you know needs to find out more about alcoholism; it is not intended to be used to establish the diagnosis of alcholism.

	YES	NO
1. Do you ever drink heavily when you are disappointed, under pressure or have had a quarrel with someone?	___	___
2. Can you handle more alcohol now than when you first started to drink?	___	___
3. Have you ever been unable to remember part of the previous evening, even though your friends say you didn't pass out?	___	___
4. When drinking with other people, do you try to have a few extra drinks when others won't know about it?	___	___
5. Do you sometimes feel uncomfortable if alcohol is not available?	___	___
6. Are you in more of a hurry to get your first drink of the day than you used to be?	___	___
7. Do you sometimes feel a little guilty about your drinking?	___	___
8. Has a family member or close friend ever expressed concern or complained about your drinking?	___	___
9. Have you been having more memory "blackouts" recently?	___	___

10. Do you often want to continue drinking after your friends say they have had enough? ___ ___

11. Do you usually have a reason for the occasions when you drink heavily? ___ ___

12. When you are sober, do you often regret things you have done or said while you were drinking? ___ ___

13. Have you ever switched brands or drinks following different plans to control your drinking? ___ ___

14. Have you sometimes failed to keep the promises you have made to yourself about controlling or cutting down on your drinking? ___ ___

15. Have you ever had a DWI (driving while intoxicated) or DUI (driving under the influence of alcohol) violation, or any other legal problem related to your drinking? ___ ___

16. Do you try to avoid family or close friends while you are drinking? ___ ___

17. Are you having more financial, work, school and/or family problems as a result of your drinking? ___ ___

18. Has your physician ever advised you to cut down on your drinking? ___ ___

19. Do more eat very little or irregularly during the periods when you are drinking? ___ ___

20. Do you sometimes have the "shakes" in the morning and find that it helps to have a "little" drink, tranquilizer or medication of some kind? ___ ___

21. Have you recently noticed that you cannot drink as much as you once did? ___ ___

22. Do you sometimes stay drunk for several days at a time? ___ ___

23. After periods of drinking do you sometimes see or hear things that aren't there? ___ ___

24. Have you ever gone to anyone for help about your drinking? ___ ___

25. Do you ever feel depressed or anxious before, during or after periods of heavy drinking? ___ ___

26. Have any of your blood relatives ever had a problem with alcohol? ___ ___

Any "Yes" answer indicates a probable symptom of alcoholism. "Yes" answers to several of the questions indicate the following stages of alcoholism:

Questions 1 to 8: Early stage.
Questions 9 to 21: Middle stage.
Questions 22 to 26: Beginning of final stage.

Appendix 7
Are You a Compulsive Gambler?

Only you can decide. In short, compulsive gamblers are those whose gambling has caused continuing problems in any facet of their lives. The following questions may be of help to you.

	YES	NO

1. Do you ever lose time from work because of gambling? ____ ____
2. Has gambling ever made your home life unhappy? ____ ____
3. Has gambling ever affected your reputation? ____ ____
4. Have you ever felt remorse after gambling? ____ ____
5. Do you ever gamble to get money to pay debts or otherwise solve financial difficulties? ____ ____
6. Does gambling cause a decrease in your ambition or efficiency? ____ ____
7. After losing, do you feel you must return as soon as possible and win back your losses? ____ ____
8. After winning, do you have a strong urge to return as soon as possible and win more? ____ ____
9. Do you often gamble until your last dollar is gone? ____ ____
10. Do you ever borrow to finance your gambling? ____ ____
11. Have you ever sold anything to finance gambling? ____ ____
12. Are you reluctant to use "gambling money" for normal expenditures? ____ ____
13. Does gambling make you careless of the welfare of your family? ____ ____
14. Have you ever gambled longer than you had planned? ____ ____
15. Have you ever gambled to escape worry or trouble? ____ ____
16. Have you ever committed, or considered committing, an illegal act to finance gambling? ____ ____
17. Does gambling cause you to have difficulty sleeping? ____ ____
18. Do arguments, disappointments, or frustrations create within you an urge to gamble? ____ ____
19. Do you ever have an urge to celebrate any good fortune by a few hours of gambling? ____ ____
20. Have you ever considered self-destruction as a result of gambling? ____ ____

Most compulsive gamblers will answer "Yes" to at least seven of these questions.

Reprinted from Gamblers Anonymous *Combined Pamphlet* by permission of Gamblers Anonymous.

Appendix 8
Are You Addicted to Work?

Read the 25 statements below and decide how much each one pertains to you. Using the rating scale of 1 (never true), 2 (seldom true), 3 (often true), and 4 (always true), put the number that best fits you in the blank beside each statement. Once you have responded to all 25 statements, add up the numbers in the blanks for your total score.

____ 1. I prefer to do most things myself rather than ask for help.
____ 2. I get very impatient when I have to wait for someone else or when something takes too long, such as long, slow-moving lines.
____ 3. I seem to be in a hurry and racing against the clock.
____ 4. I get irritated when I am interrupted while I am in the middle of something.
____ 5. I stay busy and keep many "irons in the fire."

_____ 6. I find myself doing two or three things at one time, such as eating lunch and writing a memo, while talking on the telephone.

_____ 7. I overly commit myself by biting off more than I can chew.

_____ 8. I feel guilty when I am not working on something.

_____ 9. It is important that I see the concrete results of what I do.

_____ 10. I am more interested in the final result of my work than in the process.

_____ 11. Things just never seem to move fast enough or get done fast enough for me.

_____ 12. I lose my temper when things don't go my way or work out to suit me.

_____ 13. I ask the same question over again, without realizing it, after I've already been given the answer once.

_____ 14. I spend a lot of time mentally planning and thinking about future events while tuning out the here and now.

_____ 15. I find myself continuing to work after my coworkers have called it quits.

_____ 16. I get angry when people don't meet my standards of perfection.

_____ 17. I get upset when I am in situations where I cannot be in control.

_____ 18. I tend to put myself under pressure with self-imposed deadlines when I work.

_____ 19. It is hard for me to relax when I'm not working.

_____ 20. I spend more time working than on socializing with friends, on hobbies, or on leisure activities.

_____ 21. I dive into projects to get a head start before all phases have been finalized.

_____ 22. I get upset with myself for making even the smallest mistake.

_____ 23. I put more thought, time, and energy into my work than I do into my relationships with my spouse (or lover) and family.

_____ 24. I forget, ignore, or minimize birthdays, reunions, anniversaries, or holidays.

_____ 25. I make important decisions before I have all the facts and have a chance to think them through thoroughly.

_____ = Total

SCORING: *A total score of 25 to 54 points means you are not work addicted; 55 to 69 points means you are mildly work addicted; 70 to 100 points means you are highly work addicted.*

Adapted from Work Addiction: Hidden Legacies of Adult Children *by Bryan E. Robinson (Health Communications) 1989.*

Appendix 9
Are You Co-Dependent?

This checklist, created by Co-Dependents Anonymous (CoDA), can help you determine whether or not you're co-dependent. Mark the items that apply to you "always," "usually," "sometimes," or "never." If you see a pattern emerging from your answers and if you're concerned about the health of your relationships, you can find help and understanding at CoDA meetings.

CONTROL PATTERNS

_____ I must be "needed" in order to have a relationship with others.

_____ I value others' approval of my thinking, feelings, and behaviors over my own.

_____ I agree with others so they will like me.

_____ I focus my attention on protecting others.

_____ I believe most other people are incapable of taking care of themselves.

_____ I keep score of "good deeds and favors," becoming very hurt when they are not repaid.

_____ I am very skilled at guessing how other people are feeling.

_____ I can anticipate others' needs and desires, meeting them before they are asked to be met.

_____ I become resentful when others will not let me help them.

_____ I am calm and efficient in other people's crisis situations.

_____ I feel good about myself only when I am helping others.

_____ I freely offer others advice and directions without being asked.

_____ I put aside my own interests and concerns in order to do what others want.

_____ I ask for help and nurturing only when I am ill, and then reluctantly.

_____ I cannot tolerate seeing others in pain.

_____ I lavish gifts and favors on those I care about.

_____ I use sex to gain approval and acceptance.

_____ I attempt to convince others of how they "truly" think and "should" feel.

_____ I perceive myself as completely unselfish and dedicated to the well-being of others.

COMPLIANCE PATTERNS

_____ I assume responsibility for others' feelings and behaviors.

_____ I feel guilty about others' feelings and behaviors.

_____ I have difficulty identifying what I am feeling.

_____ I have difficulty expressing feelings.

_____ I am afraid of my anger, yet sometimes erupt in a rage.

_____ I worry how others may respond to my feelings, opinions, and behavior.

_____ I have difficulty making decisions.

_____ I am afraid of being hurt and/or rejected by others.

_____ I minimize, alter, or deny how I truly feel.

_____ I am very sensitive to how others are feeling and feel the same.

_____ I am afraid to express differing opinions or feelings.

_____ I value others' opinions and feelings more than my own.

_____ I put other people's needs and desires before mine.

_____ I am embarrassed to receive recognition and praise, or gifts.

_____ I judge everything I think, say, or do harshly, as never "good enough."

_____ I am perfectionistic.

_____ I am extremely loyal, remaining in harmful situations too long.

_____ I do not ask others to meet my needs or desires.

_____ I do not perceive myself as a lovable and worthwhile person.

_____ I compromise my own values and integrity to avoid rejection or others' anger.

Reprinted with permission of Co-Dependents Anonymous from the pamphlet What is Co-Dependency?

Appendix 10
Am I an Addict?

The following questions were written by recovering addicts in Narcotics Anonymous. If you have doubts about whether or not you're an addict, take a few moments to read the questions below and answer them as honestly as you can.

	YES	NO
1. Do you ever use alone?		
2. Have you ever substituted one drug for another, thinking that one particular drug was the problem?		
3. Have you ever manipulated or lied to a doctor to obtain prescription drugs?		
4. Have you ever stolen drugs or stolen to obtain drugs?		
5. Do you regularly use a drug when you wake up or when you go to bed?		
6. Have you ever taken one drug to overcome the effects of another?		
7. Do you avoid people or places that do not approve of your using drugs?		
8. Have you ever used a drug without knowing what it was or what it would do to you?		
9. Has your job or school performance ever suffered from the effects of your drug use?		
10. Have you ever been arrested as a result of using drugs?		
11. Have you ever lied about what or how much you use?		
12. Do you put the purchase of drugs ahead of your financial responsibilities?		
13. Have you ever tried to stop or control your using?		
14. Have you ever been in a jail, hospital, or drug rehabilitation center because of your using?		
15. Does using interfere with your sleeping or eating?		
16. Does the thought of running out of drugs terrify you?		
17. Do you feel it is impossible for you to live without drugs?		
18. Do you ever question your own sanity?		
19. Is your drug use making life at home unhappy?		
20. Have you ever thought you couldn't fit in or have a good time without using drugs?		
21. Have you ever felt defensive, guilty, or ashamed about your using?		
22. Do you think a lot about drugs?		
23. Have you had irrational or indefinable fears?		
24. Has using affected your sexual relationships?		
25. Have you ever taken drugs you didn't prefer?		
26. Have you ever used drugs because of emotional pain or stress?		
27. Have you ever overdosed on any drugs?		
28. Do you continue to use despite negative consequences?		
29. Do you think you might have a drug problem?		

"Am I an addict?" This is a question only you can answer. We found that we all answered different numbers of these questions "Yes." The actual number of "Yes" responses wasn't as important as how we felt inside and how addiction had affected our lives.

If you are an addict you must first admit that you have a problem with drugs before any progress can be made toward recovery. These questions, when honestly approached, may help to show you how using drugs has made your life unmanageable.

Reprinted from Am I an Addict?, *revised, copyright © 1986, World Service Office, Inc. Reprinted by permission of World Service Office, Inc. All rights reserved.*

Appendix 11
Are You Addicted to Prescription Drugs?

Because we tend to think of prescribed pills as medicine rather than as drugs, it can be difficult to identify an addiction to therapeutic tranquilizers or painkillers. Here are some questions to help you determine whether or not you may have a problem.

	YES	NO
1. Have you used tranquilizers or sleeping pills every day for longer than four months?	___	___
2. Have you used prescription painkillers every day for longer than six months to alleviate chronic pain? (Chronic pain is ongoing pain such as back pain or migraine headaches. It is pain that cannot be treated surgically and that does not result from a disease such as cancer.)	___	___
3. Do you need more pills than before to get the same effect?	___	___
4. Have you ever tried to cut down on your use of tranquilizers or painkillers?	___	___
5. Has your social, work, school, or family life been negatively affected by your use of prescription pills?	___	___
6. Has a close friend or family member ever expressed concern about your use of pills?	___	___
7. Have you ever manipulated a doctor to get prescription drugs?	___	___
8. Do you feel you cannot live without pills?	___	___

If you answered "Yes" to any of these questions you may be addicted. It's unsafe to try to give up tranquilizers or painkillers on your own or to attempt to quit cold turkey. If you are concerned about your use of prescriptions pills, consult a chemical dependency treatment center or a doctor you trust for help.

Appendix 12
Relationship Addiction

	YES	NO
1. Typically, you come from a dysfunctional home in which your emotional needs were not met.	___	___
2. Having received little real nurturing yourself, you try to fill this unmet need vicariously by becoming a care-giver, especially to men who appear, in some way, needy.	___	___

3. Because you were never able to change your parent(s) into the warm,   ____ ____
   loving caretaker(s) you longed for, you respond deeply to the familiar
   type of emotionally unavailable man whom you can again try to change,
   through your love.
4. Terrified of abandonment, you will do anything to keep a relationship   ____ ____
   from dissolving.
5. Almost nothing is too much trouble, takes too much time, or is too   ____ ____
   expensive if it will "help" the man you are involved with.
6. Accustomed to lack of love in personal relationships, you are willing   ____ ____
   to wait, hope, and try harder to please.
7. You are willing to take far more than 50 percent of the responsibility,   ____ ____
   guilt, and blame in any relationship.
8. Your self-esteem is critically low, and deep inside you do not believe   ____ ____
   you deserve to be happy. Rather, you believe you must earn the right
   to enjoy life.
9. You have a desperate need to control your men and your relationships,   ____ ____
   having experienced little security in childhood. You mask your efforts
   to control people and situations as "being helpful."
10. In a relationship, you are much more in touch with your dream of how   ____ ____
    it could be than with the reality of your situation.
11. You are addicted to men and to emotional pain.   ____ ____
12. You may be predisposed emotionally and often biochemically to becom-   ____ ____
    ing addicted to drugs, alcohol, and/or certain foods, particularly sugary
    ones.
13. By being drawn to people with problems that need fixing, or by being   ____ ____
    enmeshed in situations that are chaotic, uncertain, and emotionally
    painful, you avoid focusing on your responsibility to yourself.
14. You may have a tendency toward episodes of depression, which you   ____ ____
    try to forestall through the excitement provided by an unstable rela-
    tionship.
15. You are not attracted to men who are kind, stable, reliable, and inter-   ____ ____
    ested in you. You find such "nice" men boring.

Source: Robin Norwood, Women Who Love Too Much *(Los Angeles: Tarcher, 1985), 10–11. Reprinted with permission.*

Appendix 13
Sexual Addiction

                                                                                  YES   NO
1. Have you ever thought you needed help for your sexual thinking or   ____ ____
   behavior?
2. That you'd be better off if you didn't keep "giving in"?   ____ ____
3. That sex or stimuli are controlling you?   ____ ____
4. Have you ever tried to stop or limit doing what you felt was wrong in   ____ ____
   your sexual behavior?

5. Do you resort to sex to escape, relieve anxiety, or because you can't cope? ____ ____
6. Do you feel guilt, remorse, or depression afterward? ____ ____
7. Has your pursuit of sex become more compulsive? ____ ____
8. Does it interfere with relations with your spouse? ____ ____
9. Do you have to resort to images or memories during sex? ____ ____
10. Does an irresistible impulse arise when the other party makes the overtures or sex is offered? ____ ____
11. Do you keep going from one "relationship" or lover to another? ____ ____
12. Do you feel the "right relationship" would help you stop lusting, masturbating, or being so promiscuous? ____ ____
13. Do you have a destructive need—a desperate sexual or emotional need—for someone? ____ ____
14. Does pursuit of sex make you careless for yourself or the welfare of your family or others? ____ ____
15. Has your effectiveness or concentration decreased as sex has become more compulsive? ____ ____
16. Do you lose time from work for it? ____ ____
17. Do you turn to a lower environment when pursuing sex? ____ ____
18. Do you want to get away from the sex partner as soon as possible after the act? ____ ____
19. Although your spouse is sexually compatible, do you still masturbate or have sex with others? ____ ____
20. Have you ever been arrested for a sex-related offense? ____ ____

Source: Sexaholics Anonymous. Copyright © 1985 by SA Literature. Reprinted by permission.

Appendix 14
Are You a Food Addict?

	YES	NO
1. Are you intensely afraid of becoming fat?	____	____
2. Do you feel fat even when others say you are thin or emaciated?	____	____
3. Do you like to shop for food and cook for others but prefer not to eat the meals you make?	____	____
4. Do you have eating rituals (for example, cutting food into tiny bites, eating only certain foods in a certain order at a particular time of day)?	____	____
5. Have you lost 25 percent of your minimum body weight through diets and fasts?	____	____
6. When you feel hungry, do you usually refrain from eating?	____	____
7. If you are a female of childbearing age, have you stopped having menstrual periods?	____	____
8. Do you often experience cold hands and feet, dry skin, or cracked fingernails?	____	____
9. Do you have a covering of fuzzy hair over your body?	____	____
10. Do you often feel depressed, guilty, angry, or inadequate?	____	____

11. When people express concern about your low weight, do you deny _____ _____
that anything is wrong?
12. Do you often exercise strenuously or for long periods of time even _____ _____
when you feel tired or sick?
13. Have you ever eaten a large amount of food and then fasted, forced _____ _____
yourself to vomit, or used laxatives to purge yourself?
14. Are you frequently on a rigid diet? _____ _____
15. Do you regularly experience stomachaches or constipation? _____ _____
16. Do you eat large quantities of food in a short period of time, usually _____ _____
high-calorie, simple-carbohydrate foods that can be easily ingested (for
example, bread, pasta, cake, cookies, ice cream, or mashed potatoes)?
17. Do you eat in secret, hide food, or lie about your eating? _____ _____
18. Have you ever stolen food or money to buy food so that you could _____ _____
start or continue a binge?
19. Do you feel guilt and remorse about your eating behavior? _____ _____
20. Do you start eating even when you are not hungry? _____ _____
21. Is it hard for you to stop eating even when you want to? _____ _____
22. Do you eat to escape problems, to relax, or to have fun? _____ _____
23. After finishing a meal, do you worry about making it to the next meal _____ _____
without getting hungry in between?
24. Have others expressed concern about your obsession with food? _____ _____
25. Do you worry that your eating behavior is abnormal? _____ _____
26. Do you fall asleep after eating? _____ _____
27. Do you regularly fast, use laxatives or diet pills, induce vomiting, or _____ _____
exercise excessively to avoid gaining weight?
28. Does your weight fluctuate 10 pounds or more from alternate bingeing _____ _____
and purging?
29. Are your neck glands swollen? _____ _____
30. Do you have scars on the back of your hands from forced vomiting? _____ _____

SCORING: *Five or more "Yes" answers within any of the following three groups of questions strongly suggest the presence of an eating disorder: questions 1–15, anorexia nervosa; questions 14–26, binge eating; questions 12–30, bulimia*

Appendix 15
The Original Laundry List—
Adult Children of Alcoholics

THE PROBLEM

The Characteristics we seem to have in common due to our being brought up in an alcoholic household:
A. We became isolated and afraid of people and authority figures.
B. We became approval seekers and lost our identity in the process.

C. We are frightened by angry people and any personal criticism.
D. We either become alcoholics, marry them, or both, or find another compulsive personality such as a workaholic to fulfill our sick abandonment needs.
E. We live life from the viewpoint of victims and are attracted by that weakness in our love and friendship relationships.
F. We have an overdeveloped sense of responsibility and it is easier for us to be concerned with others rather than ourselves; this enables us not to look too closely at our own faults, etc.
G. We get guilt feelings when we stand up for ourselves instead of giving in to others.
H. We became addicted to excitement.
I. We confuse love and pity and tend to "love" people we can "pity" and "rescue."
J. We have stuffed our feelings from our traumatic childhoods and have lost the ability to feel or express our feelings because it hurts so much. (Denial)
K. We judge ourselves harshly and have a very low sense of self-esteem.
L. We are dependent personalities who are terrified of abandonment and will do anything to hold on to a relationship in order not to experience painful abandonment feelings that we received from living with sick people who were never there emotionally for us.
M. Alcoholism is a family disease and we became para-alcoholics and took on the characteristics of that disease even though we did not pick up the drink.
N. Para-alcoholics are reactors rather than actors.

THE SOLUTION

By attending Adult Children of Alcoholics meetings on a regualr basis, we learn that we can live our lives in a more meaningful manner; we learn to change our attitudes and old patterns of behavior and habits; to find serenity, even happiness.

A. Alcoholism is a *three-fold disease*: mental, physical, and spiritual; our parents were victims of this disease, which either ends in death or insanity. This is the beginning of the gift of forgiveness.
B. We learn to put the focus on ourselves and to be good to ourselves.
C. We learn to detach with love; tough love.
D. We use the slogans: LET GO, LET GOD; EASY DOES IT; ONE DAY AT A TIME, etc.
E. We learn to feel our feelings, to accept and express them, and to build our self-esteem.
F. Through working the steps, we learn to accept the disease and to realize that our lives have become unmanageable and that we are powerless over the disease and the alcoholic. As we become willing to admit our defects and our sick thinking, we are able to change our attitudes and our reactions into actions. By working the program daily, admitting that we are powerless; we come to believe eventually in the spirituality of the program—that there is a solution other than ourselves, the group, a Higher Power, God as we understand Him, Her or It. By sharing our experiences, relating to others, welcoming newcomers, serving our groups, we build our self-esteem.
G. We learn to love ourselves and in this way we are able to love others in a healthier way.

H. We use telephone therapy with program people who understand us.

I. The serenity prayer is our major prayer.

Appendix 16
Al-Anon: Is It for You?

Millions of people are affected by the excessive drinking of someone close. The following twenty questions are designed to help you decide whether or not you need Al-Anon.

	YES	NO
1. Do you worry about how much someone else drinks?	___	___
2. Do you have money problems because of someone else's drinking?	___	___
3. Do you tell lies to cover up for someone else's drinking?	___	___
4. Do you feel that drinking is more important to your loved one than you are?	___	___
5. Do you think that the drinker's behavior is caused by his or her companions?	___	___
6. Are mealtimes frequently delayed because of the drinker?	___	___
7. Do you make threats, such as, "If you don't stop drinking, I'll leave you"?	___	___
8. When you kiss the drinker hello, do you secretly try to smell his or her breath?	___	___
9. Are you afraid to upset someone for fear it will set off a drinking bout?	___	___
10. Have you been hurt or embarrassed by a drinker's behavior?	___	___
11. Does it seem as if every holiday is spoiled because of drinking?	___	___
12. Have you considered calling the police because of drinking?	___	___
13. Do you find yourself searching for hidden liquor?	___	___
14. Do you feel that if the drinker loved you, he or she would stop drinking to please you?	___	___
15. Have you refused social invitations out of fear or anxiety?	___	___
16. Do you sometimes feel guilty when you think of the lengths you have gone to control the drinker?	___	___
17. Do you think that if the drinker stopped drinking, your other problems would be solved?	___	___
18. Do you ever threaten to hurt yourself to scare the drinker into saying "I'm sorry," or "I love you"?	___	___
19. Do you ever treat people (children, employees, parents, coworkers, etc.) unjustly because you are angry at someone else for drinking too much?	___	___
20. Do you feel there is no one who understands your problems?	___	___

If you have answered "Yes" to three or more of these questions, Al-Anon or Alateen may help.

Appendix 17
Professional Resources

Anorexia Nervosa and Related Eating Disorders (ANRED)
P.O. Box 5102
Eugene, Oregon 97405
(503)344-1144

Cocaine Hotline (800)662-HELP

Children of Alcoholics Foundation (CAF)
200 Park Avenue, 31st Floor
New York, NY 10166
(212)351-2680

Institute on Black Chemical Abuse (IBCA)
2614 Nicollet Avenue South
Minneapolis, MN 55408
(612)871-7878

National Asian Pacific Families Against Substance Abuse (NAPAFASA)
6303 Friendship Court
Bethesda, MD 20817
(301)530-0945

National Association of Anorexia Nervosa and Associated Disorders (ANAD)
P.O. Box 7
Highland Park, IL 60611
(708)831-3438

National Association of Children of Alcoholics (NACOA)
31582 Coast Highway
Suite B
South Laguna Beach, CA 92677
(714)499-3889

National Association of Lesbian and Gay Alcoholism Professionals (NALGAP)
204 West 20th Street
New York, NY 10011
(212)713-5074

National Black Alcoholism Council (NBAC)
417 South Dearborn Street, Suite 1000
Chicago, IL 60605
(312)663-5780

National Coalition Against Domestic Violence
1500 Massachusetts Avenue, NW, Suite 35
Washington, DC 20005
(202)638-6388

National Coalition of Hispanic Health and Human Services Organization (COSSMHO)
1030 15th Street NW, St. 1053
Washington, DC 20005
(202)371-2100

National Hispanic Family Against Drug Abuse (NHFADA)
1511 K Street, Suite 1029
Washington, DC 20005
(202)393-5136

Native American Association for Children of Alcoholics (NANACOA)
P.O. Box 18736
Seattle, WA 98118

Parents United
AMACU Coordinator
P.O. Box 952
San Jose, CA 95108
(408)453-7611, ext. 150
Treatment oriented

Phobia Society of America
133 Rollins Avenue, Suite 4B
Rockville, MD 20852
(301)231-9350

Victims of Incest Can Emerge Survivors in Action (VOICES)
Voices in Action, Inc.
P.O. Box 148309
Chicago, Il 60614
(312)327-1500

Appendix 18
Self-Help Groups Based on the
Twelve Step Program of AA

ACOA Intergroup of Greater
  New York, Inc.
P.O. Box 363
Murray Hill Station
New York, NY 10016-0363
(212)582-0840

Adult Children of Alcoholics (ACA)
2225 Sepulveda Blvd., #200
Torrance, CA 90505
(213)534-1815

Al-Anon Family Groups
P.O. Box 862
Midtown Station
New York, NY 10018-0862
(212)302-7240

Alateen
Al-Anon Family Groups
P.O. Box 862
Midtown Station
New York, NY 10018-0862
(212)302-7240

Alcoholics Anonymous (AA)
Box 459
Grand Central Station
New York, NY 10163
(212)686-1100

Anorexics / Bulimics Anonymous (ABA)
P.O. Box 112214
San Diego, CA 92111
(619)273-3108

Batterers Anonymous (BA)
BA Press
1269 NE Street
San Bernandino, CA 92405
(714)884-6809

Cocaine Anonymous (CA)
6125 Washington Blvd., Suite 202
Los Angeles, CA 90230
(213)559-5833

Co-Dependents Anonymous (CODA)
P.O. Box 5508
Glendale, AZ 85312-5508
(602)979-1751

Gamblers Anonymous (GA)
National Service Office
P.O. Box 17173
Los Angeles, CA 90017
(213)386-8789

Incest Survivors Anonymous (ISA)
P.O. Box 5613
Long Beach, CA 90805-0613
(213)428-5599

Narcotics Anonymous (NA)
World Services Office
16155 Wyandotte Street
Van Nuys, CA 91406
(818)780-3951

Overeaters Anonymous (OA)
World Services Office
4025 Spencer Street, Suite 203
Torrance, CA 90503
(213)542-8363

Parents Anonymous (PA)
6733 South Sepulveda Blvd.
Los Angeles, CA 90045
(213)410-9732
(800)421-0353

Sex Addicts Anonymous (SAA)
Box 3038
Minneapolis, MN 55403
(612)339-0217

Sexaholics Anonymous (SA)
P.O. Box 300
Simi Valley, CA 93062
(805)584-3235

Sex and Love Addicts Anonymous (SLAA)
(The Augustine Fellowship)
P.O. Box 119
New Town Branch
Boston, MA 02258
(617)332-1845

Survivors of Incest Anonymous (SIA)
P.O. Box 21817
Baltimore, MD 21222
(301) 282-3400

Women for Sobriety
Box 618
Quakertown, PA 18951
(215)536-8026

Bibliography

ONLY CHILDREN

Sifford, Daniel. *The Only Child: Being One, Loving One, Understanding One, Raising One.* New York: Putnam, 1989.

EATING DISORDERS

Hampshire, Elizabeth. *Freedom from Food.* Park Ridge, Ill.: Parkside Publishers, 1987.

Hollis, Judi. *Fat Is a Family Affair.* New York: Harper & Row, 1988.

Orbach, Susie. *Fat Is a Feminist Issue: The Anti-Diet Guide to Permanent Weight Loss.* New York: Berkley Publishing Group, 1987.

Roth, Geneen. *Breaking Free From Compulsive Eating.* New York: New American Library, 1985.

——. *Feeding the Hungry Heart.* New York: New American Library, 1982.

——. *Why Weight? A guide to Ending Compulsive Eating.* New York: New American Library, 1989.

SEXUAL ABUSE

Bass, Ellen, and Laura Davis. *The Courage to Heal: A Guide for Women Survivors of Child Sexual Abuse.* New York: Harper & Row, 1988.

Blume, E. Sue. *Secret Survivors: Uncovering Incest and Its Aftereffects in Women.* New York: John Wiley & Sons, 1990.

Davis, Laura. *The Courage to Heal Workbook.* New York: Harper & Row, 1988.

Engel, Beverly. *The Right to Innocence.* New York: Fawcett, 1989.

Gil, Eliana. *Outgrowing the Pain.* New York: Dell, 1988.

Lew, Michael. *Victims No Longer.* New York: Harper & Row, 1990.

SEXUAL ADDICTION

Carnes, Patrick. *Out of the Shadows.* Irvine, Calif.: CompCare Publishers, 1985.

Schneider, Jennifer P. *Back From Betrayal: Recovering From His Affairs.* New York: Ballantine, 1990.

ADULT CHILDREN AND CO-DEPENDENTS

Ackerman, Robert. *Growing in the Shadow.* Deerfield Beach, Fla.: Health Communications, Inc., 1986.

——. *Let Go & Grow: Recovery for Adult Children.* Deerfield Beach, Fla.: Health Communications, Inc., 1987.

——. *Same House, Different Home.* Deerfield Beach, Fla.: Health Communications, Inc., 1987.

Beattie, Melody. *Beyond Codependency: And Getting Better All the Time.* Center City, Minn.: Hazelden Publishing, 1989.

——. *Codependent No More: How to Stop Controlling and Start Caring for Yourself.* New York: Harper & Row, 1988.

Black, Claudia. *"It Will Never Happen to Me."* New York: Ballantine Books, 1987.

——. *"My Dad Loves Me, My Dad Has a Disease."* Denver, Colo.: MAC Pub., 1979.

——. *Repeat After Me.* Denver, Colo.: MAC Pub., 1985.

Bradshaw, John. *Bradshaw on the Family: A Revolutionary Way of Self-Discovery.* Deerfield Beach, Fla.: Health Communications, Inc., 1988.

——. *Homecoming: Reclaiming and Championing Your Inner Child.* New York: Bantam, 1990.

Cermak, Timmen L. *Time to Heal: The Road to Recovery for Adult Children of Alcoholics.* Los Angeles: Jeremy P. Tarcher, Inc., 1988.

Fossum, Merle A., and Marilyn J. Mason. *Facing Shame: Families in Recovery.* New York: W. W. Norton & Co., 1986.

Gravitz, Herbert L., and Julie D. Bowden. *Guide to Recovery: A Book for Adult Children of Alcoholics.* Holmes Beach, Fla.: Learning Publications, Inc., 1986.

Greenleaf, Jael. *Co-Alcoholic, Para-Alcoholic: Who's Who and What's the Difference.* Denver, Colo.: MAC Pub., 1987.

Halvorson, Ronald S., and Valerie B. Deilgat, eds., with "Friends in Recovery" staff. *Twelve Steps—A Way Out: A Working Guide for Adult Children of Alcoholics and Other Dysfunctional Families.* San Diego, Calif.: Recovery Publications, 1987.

Kritsberg, Wayne. *The ACOA Syndrome.* Deerfield Beach, Fla.: Health Communications, Inc., 1985.

Middelton-Moz, Jane, and Lorie Dwinell. *After the Tears.* Deerfield Beach, Fla.: Health Communications, Inc., 1986.

Norwood, Robin. *Women Who Love Too Much.* New York: Pocket Books, 1986.

O'Gorman, Patricia, and Phil Oliver Diaz. *Self-Parenting.* Deerfield Beach, Fla.: Health Communications, Inc., 1988.

Robinson, Bryan E. *Working with Children of Alcoholics.* Lexington, Mass.: Lexington Books, 1989.

Sanford, Linda. *Strong at the Broken Places.* New York: Random House, 1990.

Smith, Ann. *Grandchildren of Alcoholics.* Deerfield Beach, Fla.: Health Communications, Inc., 1988.

Striano, Judi. *How to Find a Good Psychotherapist: A Consumer Guide.* Santa Barbara, Calif.: Professional Press, 1987.

Subby, Robert. *Lost in the Shuffle*. Deerfield Beach, Fla.: Health Communications, Inc., 1987.

Wegscheider-Cruse, Sharon. *Choicemaking*. Deerfield Beach, Fla.: Health Communications, Inc., 1985.

Whitfield, Charles L. *Healing the Child Within*. Deerfield Beach, Fla.: Health Communications, Inc., 1987.

Woititz, Janet G. *Adult Children of Alcoholics*. Deerfield Beach, Florida: Health Communications, Inc., 1983.

——. *Healing Your Sexual Self*. Deerfield Beach, Fla.: Health Communications, Inc., 1989.

——. *Struggle for Intimacy*. Deerfield Beach, Fla.: Health Communications, Inc., 1985.

RELATIONSHIPS

Covington, Stephanie, and Liana Beckett. *Leaving the Enchanted Forest*. New York: Harper & Row, 1988.

Cruse, Joe. *Painful Affairs*. Deerfield Beach, Fla.: Health Communications, Inc., 1988.

Lerner, Harriet G. *Dance of Anger: A Woman's Guide to Changing the Patterns of Intimate Relationships*. New York: Harper & Row, 1986.

Wegscheider-Cruse, Sharon. *Coupleship: How to Have a Relationship*. Deerfield Beach, Fla.: Health Communications, Inc., 1988.

INSPIRATIONAL

Black, Claudia. *"It's Never Too Late to Have a Happy Childhood."* New York: Ballantine Books, 1989.

Lerner, Rokelle. *Daily Affirmations*. Deerfield Beach, Fla.: Health Communications, Inc., 1985.

Somers, Suzanne. *Keeping Secrets*. New York: Warner Books, 1988.

Wegscheider-Cruse, Sharon. *Miracle of Recovery*. Deerfield Beach, Fla.: Health Communications, Inc., 1989.

Index